MARIANNE MOORE

A LITERARY LIFE

Also by Charles Molesworth

Gary Snyder's Vision:
Poetry and the Real Work—1983

The Ironist Saved from Drowning:
The Fiction of Donald Barthelme—1982

The Fierce Embrace: A Study in
Contemporary American Poetry—1979

Poetry

Words to That Effect—1981

Common Elegies—1977

MARIANNE MOORE

A LITERARY
LIFE

Charles Molesworth

ATHENEUM

New York

1990

Grateful acknowledgment is made for permission to quote from the following:

From *The Complete Poems of Marianne Moore*: "Logic and 'The Magic Flute'," "O to Be a Dragon," "I May, I Might, I Must," "Values in Use," "Hometown Piece for Mssrs. Alston and Reese," "In the Public Garden," "Leonardo da Vinci's," "The Camperdown Elm," and "The Magician's Retreat." Copyright © 1956, 1957, 1959, 1967, 1970 by Marianne Moore. "Leonardo da Vinci's," "The Camperdown Elm," and "The Magician's Retreat" were originally published in *The New Yorker*. Reprinted by permission of Viking Penguin, a division of Penguin Books USA, Inc.

Selected passages and quotations from *The Complete Prose of Marianne Moore* edited by Patricia C. Willis. Copyright © 1959, 1960, 1961, 1962, 1963, 1964, 1965, 1986 by Clive E. Driver, Literary Executor of the Estate of Marianne C. Moore. Copyright 1941, 1942, 1944, 1946, 1948, © 1955, 1958, 1959, 1960, 1961, 1962, 1963, 1964, 1965, 1966, 1967, 1968 by Marianne Moore. Reprinted by permission of Viking Penguin, a division of Penguin Books USA, Inc.

All photos courtesy The Rosenbach Museum & Library, Philadelphia.

This book is
for Helen and James

leaving its wasp-nest flaws
of white on white, and close-

laid Ionic chiton-folds
like the lines in the mane of
a Parthenon horse . . .

CONTENTS

PREFACE

In undertaking to write this book, the first full-length critical biography of Marianne Moore, I have enjoyed considerable help and support. The staff at the Rosenbach Museum and Library of Philadephia was unstinting in its assistance and unfailing in its good humor. Patricia Willis, of the Beinecke Library at Yale University, was curator of the Moore archive at the Rosenbach, and proved to be invaluable to me, as she has to every scholar and critic who has worked on Marianne Moore. Her successor, Eileen Cahill, was also patient and generous. Ellen Dunlap, the director of the Library, offered wise counsel. All in all, they made my experience of extended labor with archival material not only pleasant but stimulating.

My thinking about Moore's work and sensibility was shaped in important ways by what amounts to a whole new generation of Moore scholars. Several among these were especially important for me, either by their discussions of specific points, their supplying items of information, or by sharing their sense of one or another aspect of Moore's accomplishment. I would like to single out Jeanne Heuving, Chrisanne Miller, Celeste Goodridge, John Slatin, and Linda Leavell. A talk on one of Moore's poems by Hugh Kenner was especially timely and illuminating. For an understanding of modernism's intellectual landscape and artistic values I am indebted to Charles Altieri.

Several libraries also provided needed assistance, and I would like to thank the staffs at the Rosenthal Library of Queens College, the library at Lafayette College, at Dickinson College, the Berg Collection of the New York Public Library, the Beinecke Manuscript Collection, and the Cumberland Historical Society of Carlisle, Pennsylvania. Cindy Urban, of Sterret's Gap, Pennsylvania, was most welcoming and helpful, providing me with valuable information even as she was busy with the pleasures of her son's high school graduation. Andreas Brown of the Gotham Book Mart was also helpful with information about Moore's literary estate. An interview with Ethel Taylor was especially illuminating. Sarah Moore talked to me for three hours about her aunt.

A number of agencies also provided financial help in the form of grants and released time. The PSC/CUNY Summer Stipend, awarded by the Research Foundation, enabled me to spend time in Philadelphia. President Shirley Kenny, of Queens College, instituted the President's Award, consisting of a very generous amount of released time; her selection of me for such an award in the spring of 1988 enabled me to finish this book, and is sincerely appreciated. The travel fund of the Smith Chair at Lafayette College also proved to be helpful in several ways. I am especially indebted to David Johnson, who not only administered this fund, but, as chairman of the English Department at Lafayette, proved himself the most enlightened of administrators and a most supportive friend. Without his help in several areas this book would not have been written with the same pleasure. Indeed, I would like to thank all of my colleagues in the English Department at Lafayette for their friendly support and interest in this project. Several colleagues in the English Department at Queens College also lent support and insight: Bill Wilson, Joseph McElroy, Marie Ponsot, Malcolm Goldstein, and Bill Kelly were especially helpful.

The seminar in biography at New York University, graciously run by Aileen Ward, gave me stimulating ideas on a number of occasions. Fred Kaplan's advice about a number of matters was both thoughtful and effective. My ongoing conversation with Roberto Picciotto about several aspects of this book has had formative effect.

INTRODUCTION

In 1942, as the war in Europe was still being fought, Marianne Moore was asked to name the ten books she felt were most influential on her work. The request came from her friend Frances Steloff, at the Gotham Book Mart in New York City, and was to be used as part of a catalogue featuring new books. Moore responded with the following list:

1. Enid Bagnold: *Alice, Thomas and Jane*
2. *The Book of Job:* Notes by R. G. Moulton
3. E. E. Cummings: *Eimi*
4. Raymond L. Ditmars: *Confessions of a Scientist*
5. *The Faber Book of Modern Verse,* ed. Michael Roberts
6. Henry James: *The Prefaces,* ed. R. P. Blackmur
7. Bliss Perry: *And Gladly Teach*
8. George Saintsbury: *The English Novel*
9. Edith Sitwell: *Street Songs*
10. D. B. Updike: *Notes on the Merrymount Press*

This list, with its alphabetical order reflecting Moore's background as a librarian and her eye for detail, can be read as a self-portrait in books. Perhaps most important are the several entries that indicate her commitment to modernist aesthetics: the James *Prefaces,* the Roberts anthology, the Cummings, and the Sitwell. In fact, some poets might not list a book that critics would see as "too close" to the author's style, but

Moore's affinity with Sitwell's syllabic verse was not something that made her nervous. Almost twenty years later she would memorialize Sitwell by saying that "she gave me immense pleasure, intensifying my interest in rhythm, and has also encouraged me in my rhythmic eccentricities." Moore always praised generously and acknowledged all debts and friendship, both literary and personal. When she first published her work in national magazines, it was perceived as verse that relied on an arcane vocabulary, as did that of Sitwell, and its non-traditional forms were exaggerated by typographical devices, though not as radical as those of Cummings. It was called the "new poetry," and it baffled some people then as it still does today.

But while the list is modernist in its interest in writers who exhibited innovative and "eccentric" techniques, such as Sitwell and Cummings, it contains traditional titles as well. Such a combination is crucial to an understanding of Moore's literary sensibility. Saintsbury, for example, was a critic who represented the last twilight of the Victorian ideal of the man of letters; his aesthetic approach was based on a subjective, appreciative approach to literature that would be one of the main targets of modernist polemic. Yet Moore, who grew up as an avid reader of Dickens, Trollope, and all the nineteenth-century English novelists, admired Saintsbury and the traditional literary values he championed. She herself would often speak out for the necessity to make use of the past, and to acknowledge that all literature drew on problems and possibilities of expression that had been previously explored. Her admiration for Saintsbury was so strong that it led to a personal friendship with him that Moore greatly enjoyed, fed as it was by her devout Anglophilism.

The book by Bliss Perry, ex-editor of *The Atlantic Monthly* and a professor at Princeton and Harvard, was a modest and urbane autobiography, and one Moore referred to often in the 1940's. It showed her that literature could instruct an audience and transmit cultural and spiritual values as part of a lifetime occupation. Characteristically American in his trust in education as a force of civilization, Perry's concerns attracted Moore because her college education was one of the transforming experiences of her life. There was even a time in the 1940's when she toyed with the idea of writing an appreciation of college education in America. And, as always, her family context played a role: her mother was a high school English teacher, her brother

Warner became the head of the school system in American Samoa, and she herself taught at the Indian School in Carlisle, Pennsylvania. Perry and Saintsbury stood for the value of ethical content in literature, and insisted that culture was more than the exploration of attitudes or psychic states for their own sake, even if such exploration was what radical modernism espoused. At times her ethical values could make Moore seem rather like a reluctant modernist.

But the books by Ditmars and the Updike illumine her commitment to a sensibility that was at once modernist and individualistic. She always praised the work of natural scientists like Ditmars, seeing in their regimen of attentive observation and accurate description a major source for her own aesthetic. Often her poems reflect a desire for scientific objectivity, where the claims of ego and the imprecisions of subjectivity are disciplined by rigorous observation. Ditmars was a herpetologist who served as the Curator of Mammals and Reptiles at the Bronx Zoo, and Moore had reviewed his book, *Strange Animals I Have Known,* ten years earlier. She often spoke in praise of animals for their lack of self-consciousness, and when she wrote about them in her poetry she often selected ones that were quite rare, far from domestication. Such animals are interpretable as versions of herself, of course, seeking a thoroughly natural self-possession, yet remote, sometimes nocturnally reclusive, as if the romantic artist were redrawn in the lineaments of natural history.

D. B. Updike was a printer and book designer. His memoir tells of how he grew up fatherless but discovered his vocation "by pure accident" and applied to it a key, simple principle: "style does not depend on decoration but on simplicity and proportion." He was deeply influenced in his love of reading by his mother, "a woman of remarkable intellectual powers," and was an Episcopalian by inclination and background. For a while he worked as a librarian, and then in the publishing field. In all these points, Moore could readily identify with him quite precisely. But, just as important, Moore loved fine books, and would later become friendly with several bibliophiles. She often rewrote her poems in ways that refined their visual shape on the page. Her love of simplicity and proportion, however, frequently generated a tension with her need to be precise in detail and complete in all her references. She once said that she wanted to be as clear as her natural reticence would allow. Objective observation and romantic self-possession; simple proportions and precise details—these combinations created the source of much that is dramatic in Moore's poetry. From the instinctive expressiveness of Ditmars' animals to the well-shaped human artifact of Updike's printing, Moore would constantly mediate the realms of nature and culture, using them for and against each other in a dialogue of refinement and complexity.

Perhaps the most unexpected title on the list is that by Enid Bagnold. A book now largely forgotten, it is not even mentioned by Bagnold in her *Autobiography*. Moore wrote her good friend Hildegarde Watson in the spring of 1936 that she had found the book on her nieces' bookshelf, while visiting with her brother and his family in Norfolk, Virginia. *Alice and Thomas and Jane* (1930) was a children's book, drawn largely from stories Bagnold made up to amuse her own children. The children in the book get involved in various adventures, like being stowed away on an airplane, all without supervision and passing largely unnoticed through the adult world. There is, however, great ingenuity and wonderful bonding exhibited by all the children. The book probably reminded Moore of her own childhood, and especially the strong family bonds formed among her, her mother, and brother. As a child, Moore enjoyed the Rollo books, which featured travel to foreign lands, and the insouciant adventures of the animals in *Wind in the Willows*. She was never afraid to mention and recommend such books, even in a list of serious works. Bagnold herself would have been known to Moore because of her striking public career. She is now best remembered for the success of two works, *National Velvet* (1935) and *The Chalk Garden* (1956).

Coincidentally Bagnold, nearly Moore's exact contemporary, resembled the American poet somewhat in that she had, in a way, two careers: the first was spent circulating in bohemian art circles as a sort of culture journalist (actually a gossip columnist) for a London publication called *Modern Society*. Walter Sickert drew her portrait and Gaudier-Brzeska molded it; H. G. Wells tried unsuccessfully to seduce her, and Frank Harris succeeded. Later her circumstances changed considerably when she married Sir Roderick Jones, the head of the Reuters news agency, and hobnobbed with members of wealthy society. Her life epitomized in many ways that peculiarly modern mix of the egotism of artistic ambition and the vanity of upper-class leisure. One way to measure this may be to mention that her autobiography gives a detailed account of her facelift operation. Such personal vanity and revelation would be forever impossible for Moore. But still there were parallels. Moore first became known as an innovative poet in the bohemian circles of Greenwich Village in the 1920's. Then, beginning in the early 1950's, she became increasingly identified as an author whose picture would appear in *Life* magazine, and whose essays would eventually be published in *Harper's Bazaar* and *Vogue.* Though Moore was in many ways reclusive and discreet, in the last three decades of her life, bedecked with every important national accolade, she was celebrated by the elite of New York City's cultural and social worlds. This was another paradox in her experience: her sophistication, gained from being widely knowledgeable in her reading and highly cultured in her tastes, was at odds with a longing to be natural in her self-expression and reticent in her personal behavior. Indeed, one of the major themes of her later poetry, written by and large after she had become a public figure, was the need to avoid egotism and self-promotion.

The Book of Job, among other things a great drama of self-discipline, inspired Moore from an early age. But she had cause to list it in 1942, for her mother, with whom she lived all her life, was especially fond of it. Mrs. Moore grew increasingly ill in the middle 1940's, and her afflictions, like Job's, were borne as a demonstration of her faith. She was a very strong personality, a woman who faced and conquered many obstacles in raising her children and making her way in the world. Some of Moore's friends found her puritanical to a fault; others praised her sense of humor and style. She was the single most important person in Moore's life, not excepting her brother Warner, who was also very important to her. Together, the three of them approached the Christian faith as a lesson in strength vindicated through trials and temptation. For them, Old Testament figures like Job and Jonah, another key figure for Moore, would always illustrate the necessity for strong bonds of faith that were more important than outward ceremony or public recognition. When Moore's poetry received important public acceptance and national awards in the early 1950's, Warner told his sister that this was the vindication of their mother's dedication to them. Such ties of love reach beyond most human understanding, certainly beyond ordinary affection, though they would be proven in the most daily circumstances. At least in her family circle, Moore often conceived of the work of a literary career as a spiritual quest. But as this list of ten books indicates, it was a quest that had many horizons and many way stations.

Despite having a good deal of personal piety, Moore wrote no ostensibly religious poetry; in fact, relatively few explicit religious references occur in her poems. In 1950, she said cryptically that "self-evidently, imposed piety results in the opposite." For her poetry, the interaction between the realms of nature and culture serves as the great dramatic subject. This interaction is the ground for the crucially human experience of making choices. The realm of nature supports animals who operate without self-consciousness; the realm of culture features individuals hampered by an excess of that quality. To be human was, for Moore, to be involved in a world of choice. Making choices, however, was stringently circumscribed by natural instincts or overly complicated by cultural considerations. One of her finest poems, "Critics and Connoisseurs," deals with this dilemma, as do many of her other poems, major and minor.

The poem opens by plunging us into a crucial distinction in the world of culture. But artistic taste is quickly juxtaposed to simple observation. We move from culture to nature, as Moore's genius for the telling example and the striking metaphor leads her into a gallimaufry of animal and human efforts:

> There is a great amount of poetry in unconscious
> fastidiousness. Certain Ming
> products, imperial floor-coverings of coach-
> wheel yellow, are well enough in their way but I have seen
> > > something
> that I like better—a
> > mere childish attempt to make an imperfectly bal-
> > > lasted animal stand up,
> > similar determination to make a pup
> > > eat his meat from the plate.

Part of the modernist flavor of the poem comes from its daring to mix objects of high culture, like Ming crafts, with the mundane phenomena usually excluded from art altogether, like a pup eating from its plate. But this mixture, once disturbingly unusual and now more easily accepted by readers, illustrates how choice, even between different forms of fastidiousness, conscious or unconscious, permeates our experience.

Later in the poem we see, improbably, a consciously fastidious swan that "reconnoitered like a battle- / ship" and a "fastidious ant carrying a stick north, south, east, west." Both are seen in a series of transformations through figurative language that renders them both human and non-human, agents of nature and of culture. The observing poet presents them in rich detail, as if enjoying description for its own sake, like a student of Fabre, the great French naturalist whose spirit is close to that of Moore. But the objective description contains several implicit judgments and choices about the relations that make up and sustain our world; we know this in part because the poem is laden with words that refer to intention and purpose as well as event and action. And the many diverse actions of the poem seem part of some overall pattern, some deeply structured field of forces that operate in ways both obvious and hidden.

But like the poet she is, Moore is called inevitably to some summary judgment of her experience. We know that the swan, who "dominated the stream in an attitude / of self-defense," was a part of her richly rewarding trip to England in 1911. We don't know indisputably about whom she is talking in the poem when she says, "I have seen this swan and / I have seen you." It is perhaps her mother, though the tone of testamentary assertiveness is striking, especially when we remember that it is followed by the claim that "I have seen ambition without / understanding in a variety of forms." Is this sternly moralistic, or self-perplexed? Is the understanding lacking in the ambitious or in the observer? The poem ineluctably raises questions of moral value and human worth; we even begin to feel she might be trying to teach us something.

But Moore's modernist spirit asserts (or reasserts) itself, as she ends not with a claim but with a rhetorical question. She was later to say she liked poems that ended with a sort of quiet resolution rather than a stirring climax. Here, though, it is hard to parse the thrust of the question, hard to measure just what sort of balance pan is being used, and by whom. Critics have read the tone of this ending with considerable variance, some seeing it as derogating those with blind ambition, others seeing something like gentle satire mocking the futility of the overly fastidious. I would propose a different reading, one that hears a quiet, almost silent joy in the ability to claim the satisfaction of completing any action, even the most mundane. The ending, in my view, owes much to William Carlos Williams' red wheelbarrow, that symbol of the transcendently mundane, and by extension to American pragmatism—especially if we hear the right tone in the word "experience." But this version contains no final truth. To pick up the conclusion just after the ant has begun to circle back on itself:

> Then abandoning the stick as
> useless and overtaxing its
> jaws with a particle of whitewash—pill-like but
> heavy, it again went through the same course of procedure.
>   What is
>   there in being able
>   to say that one has dominated the stream in an attitude
>   of self-defense;
>   in proving that one has had the experience
>   of carrying a stick?

To my mind the word "proving" is crucial. To have had an experience does not, perhaps, portend much. But being able to prove that one has had the experience is, I think, to be able to move from the realm of nature to the realm of culture, just as being able "to say" that one has dominated is more significant than the ability to dominate. But the ambiguity of the rhetorical question suggests that for Moore saying and proving are inextricably bound up with "having" an experience in the first place. Speech and proof, however, are not enough to make us fully human; in fact, they can be empty of importance or misleading in their significance. As she says in one version of her famous poem called "Poetry," when poems "become so derivative as to become unintelligible, / the same thing may be said for all of us, that we / do not admire what / we cannot understand." And when Moore sent a copy of this poem to William Carlos Williams, in May, 1916, he wrote back to tell her "you are about the only one who sees any use in using his brain."

People often read Moore as a poet of beautiful surfaces, or gorgeous description, or fondly rendered but baroque detail. Just as often she is approached as an innovator, someone concerned to find new ways of formulating her eccentric views; this can be a way of deflecting attention from what she says. Her latter-day image presents her as a benevolent grandmother, a female bystander who will occasionally chide the world for its way of doing things, but who is there to reassure us about our fundamental goodness. I think it is possible to see her differently, to see her as a fully self-conscious artist involved in defining her individual vision against a subtle understanding of the world's complexities. But these complexities can be rendered, not into simplicities, but into humanly projected patterns that can please and instruct. "As if, as if, it is all ifs; we are at / much unease." This complaint is from "Elephants," one of her best poems, about one of her favorite subjects, but its tone of plaintiveness also contains more than a hint of affirmation. The "as if" is the "as if" of metaphoric language, art's way of rendering order, even if only momentarily and in the realm of the imaginary. But it is also the "as if" of virtual identity: Moore says that the human order can take on different roles for its members, that if we often weary of the weight of selfhood, we can also delight in its plasticity. She points to the range of our possibilities in "The Pangolin": "Bedizened or stark/ naked, man, the self, the being we call human . . ." It is we who call it human, this being of ours, this thing, this experience, that classifies us even as we name it.

It will not do to replace with something like tough-mindedness the picture of Moore's obscurity or eccentricity or what she called, in a different context but with a hint of playful self-description, her "Moorish gorgeousness." She is simple and complex, direct and subtle; her tone often blends the natural and the highly cultivated. Better if her readers try to maintain more than a single perspective. Moore, clearly one of the most well-read and intelligent writers of her generation, not excepting Ezra Pound and T. S. Eliot, never flaunted her learning. In an essay published in 1957, called "Subject, Predicate, Object," she spoke of the influence her mother had on her by awakening in her a strong curiosity in things like history. But she went on: "Curiosity; and books. I think books are chiefly responsible for my doggedly self-determined efforts to write; books and verisimilitude; I like to describe things." This is very revealing, because Moore is first and last a literary poet; her intelligence and experience are bound up with reading, in a way outmoded among many people today. She read voraciously, habitually, one is tempted to say indiscriminately and addictively, from The Book of Job to Enid Bagnold. It was at times as if she had rediscovered the medieval sense of "authority," that special sense of wisdom as originating with those who have lived before us and put their knowledge into some written form. Balancing this, with a paradoxical tension, was Moore's desire for verisimilitude, an accuracy that can be achieved only by closing up the handbooks and field guides and seeing for oneself.

In 1966, Elizabeth Bishop, one of the poets to whom Moore was closest, gave an interview that records a strong impression she had formed. While living in Key West, Florida, Bishop had become friends with philosopher John Dewey. Dewey had certain qualities that reminded Bishop of Moore, qualities that are often cited as being central to American poetry:

> Even at the age of eighty-five he missed no detail. He and Marianne Moore are the only people I have ever known who would talk to everyone, on all social levels, without the slightest change in their manner of speaking. I think this shows something important about Dewey and Marianne Moore—they have the kind of instinctive respect for other people which we all wish we could have but can only aspire to. No matter how foolish your question, he would always give you a complete and tactful answer. He loved little things, small plants and weeds and animals, and of course he was very generous in dealing with people.

Readers of American poetry may glimpse behind this description the shadow of another person: Walt Whitman. The emphasis on individualism, on democratic impulses, on the eye for detail, all these qualities are associated with our poetry from the beginning. But I have taken the connection between Dewey and Moore a bit further. It is Dewey's interest in "experience," developed in his early work in the 1920's and a constant focus throughout his career, that I think also connects the philosopher and the poet. In fact, I would suggest one of the best glosses on Moore's poetry is the third chapter in Dewey's *Art As Experience,* called "Having an Experience." For Dewey experience did not mean something crudely empirical, or, even less, something subject only to positivistic science. Moreover, aesthetic experience was a consummatory stage in our common, symbolically mediated, and environmentally integrated awareness as human beings. Moore read Dewey, especially in the 1920's, but I do not claim that she based her aesthetics exclusively or even centrally on his work. Yet her constant preoccupation with certain themes and images is very close in spirit to pragmatism, or "instrumentalism" as Dewey called his philosophy, at once the most widely influential and most widely misunderstood of American formulations.

Moore's use of armor as a central metaphor has focused much of the critical discussion about her work and her personality. In the common view, her armoring is fundamentally protective, the method that a defensive, even frightened, ego has of preserving itself from the grinding surfaces and conflicts of the environment, social as well as natural. Nothing, in my view, could be more misleading than this half-truth. Moore uses the imagery of armor, it is true, but it often signifies her desire to enter the world, to participate in its glories and horrors without losing her ability to make observations. In one of the first pieces of prose she published about her own approach to poetry, Moore said this in 1925:

> . . . a suit of armor is impressively poetic. The movable plates suggest the wearer; one is reminded of the armadillo and recalls the beauty of the ancient testudo. The idea of conflict, however, counteracts that of romance, and the subject is abandoned. However, the image lingers. Presently one encounters the iguana and is startled by the paradox of its docility in conjunction with its horrific aspect. The concept has been revived—of an armor in which beauty outweighs the thought of painful self-protectiveness. The emended theme compels development.

At first the image successfully combines the natural grace of the armadillo and the cultural artifact of the testudo, the large shield behind which the soldiers advanced during a siege in ancient Roman warfare. But the lure of romance, suggested by the medieval associations of armor, and conveying a world of wish-fulfillment and fantasy, cannot displace the association with conflict and even bloodshed. Poetry cannot be successfully imagined as a form of conflict, yet the image lingers until it turns into another, equally paradoxical. The iguana, docile and horrific, possesses enough aesthetic appeal to cancel, or at least "outweigh," the negative aspects. Beauty turns into force and conflict, only to be redrawn as startling docility. Art can be armored; one can cast experience into fixed poetic forms that manage not only to "suggest the wearer," but to be beautiful as well.

It is beauty that Moore created, but it was a beauty built on intelligence and a highly individual self-expression. As much as she chose to reveal and express, she also valued reticence and privacy. A psychological, even a psychoanalytic, biography of Moore might prove valuable, but I have chosen to limit my interpretations of her character by relying more on literary than on psychological questions. Hence most of my evidence focuses on the external facts of Moore's life. In part this is because I was not allowed to quote from the unpublished correspondence of Moore and her immediate family. I have, however, read all of the correspondence between Moore and her mother and brother, as well as that between Moore and the better known of her literary friends. The archive of her correspondence, notebooks, and other literary and personal material now housed at the Rosenbach Museum and Library in Philadelphia is one of the largest of any American writer. I hope scholars in the future will be given full access to it, and that the more valuable parts of it be published as soon as possible.

Moore was throughout her life intensely interested in authorship; she once remarked that she enjoyed reading about the lives of those who wrote books, and her criticism of others is often centered on the writer's intentions. What follows is an account of Moore's distinctive self as it developed with and through a lifetime of innovative expression; "the rhythm is the person," as she put it in 1938. What virtually every reader of Moore agrees on is that her poems are unlike those by other poets. She would have been pleased, even flattered by such a consensus, but only if such distinctiveness was credited to her art, not her person. Moore never, as far as I can tell, had an affair or a lover. Yet, paradoxically, Kenneth Burke called her one of the most sexual women he ever met. He meant, I think, that she was fully aware of all the dimensions of experience, physical and mental. As he put it, she knew about the twists and turns. What follows is an account of her experience, and at least a partial explanation of the paradox.

MARIANNE MOORE

A LITERARY LIFE

Chapter 1

FROM THE MANSE
TO METZGER

I. "The Wren's Nest"

Marianne Craig Moore was born on November 15, 1887, in the manse of her maternal grandfather, John Riddle Warner, then the pastor of the Presbyterian church in Kirkwood, Missouri. Only several months earlier, her mother, Mary Warner Moore, had separated from her husband, John, and arrived in Kirkwood, a relatively new and prosperous suburb of St. Louis. She came with her first child, Warner, then little more than a year old. When Mary Warner, as she was known by many of her relatives, left her husband, Marianne was not yet born. Marianne was never to see her father, since no reconciliation between her parents ever occurred. John Moore had become mentally unstable as a result of his loss of fortune in a scheme to build a smokeless furnace. He was to play no active role in the family thereafter, and Mary Warner refused all help from the Moore family. For the first seven years of her life Marianne was to live peacefully, very spoiled by her mother, as she later described it. Apparently she never sought to discover the fate of her father, though subsequently other family members found out that he recovered and became an employee of the asylum in Massachusetts where he was sent in 1887. Scattered contemporary references in letters to and from Mrs. Moore indicate that his breakdown had been accompanied by much weeping and recourse to frequent quoting from the Bible.

The manse of Reverend John Riddle Warner was a white building

1

with a porch, built for him by the congregation, and eventually surrounded by five smaller buildings. Mary Warner and her two small children cared for the pastor, who had been widowed many years previously, in 1863. Reverend Warner's wife was Jennie Craig, and it was her maiden name that became Marianne's middle name. After graduating with a Doctor of Divinity degree from The Western University of Pennyslvania, Reverend Warner had settled in the Cumberland Valley, near Gettysburg. It was here he met and married his wife, and where his family, with Mary Warner as a small infant, lived through the battle of Gettysburg in July, 1863. The pastor and his beloved wife tended to Confederate soldiers after the vicious fighting. But Jennie Craig Warner was to die only a few months after the battle, apparently from typhoid fever contracted in her work as a nurse for the wounded.

President Lincoln's famous address commemorating the struggle and its heroic fallen was only the first "Gettysburg address": Reverend Warner also gave a sermon on this famous and decisive battle. Apparently his had more immediate effect than did Lincoln's, for he was asked to give it over and over at churches throughout the East and Midwest. One of the congregations that heard it was so impressed by it that it called him to be its pastor. This was in 1866; he accepted and moved to Kirkwood in the fall. His small parsonage stood beside an oak grove in which the church was situated. The porches of the manse were covered with coral honeysuckle, as Mary Warner Moore described it. Mrs. Moore's devotion to her father was intense, and it culminated when she collected her father's sermons and wrote a prefatory biographical sketch to them. These were published in an edition that Mrs. Moore subsidized at some considerable expense, and with full hagiographical rhetoric and pious quotation, in Philadelphia, by J. B. Lippincott in 1895.

Reverend Warner had lived as a widow for several decades, until his death in 1893, having claimed that he would not consider remarrying unless he found another Jennie Craig. His refusal to remarry may have been an influence in his daughter's resolve to continue the raising of her children alone, even though she was not yet thirty years old when she was separated from her husband. Mary Warner and her two children were with Reverend Warner for the last seven years of his life, along with Mrs. Eyster, his widowed sister-in-law. Mrs. Eyster called the parsonage "The Wren's Nest," and the children must have taken pride in their grandfather and the honor in which his parishioners held him. Mary Warner Moore's rhetoric rises to an unusual pitch when she describes how the Reverend treated the children:

> Tiny feet now often pattered by the study door, offering to "Grandpa" the first temptation he had known for years, to neglect work for play; and little hearts were open to the sweet teaching of good and holy things, that was his to give even while he played with them. Thus they in his daily walk and conversation learned Jesus, and were to him a joy that was without alloy. "His walk and conversation!" Diamonds in the dew of summer and in the frosts of winter are not more radiant, yet not more intangible, than the beauty, the beneficence, of that daily walk and conversation.

This spiritual tone was natural to Mrs. Moore, and clearly she saw herself completing the role she had erected for her father as spiritual leader and yet an intimate friend to her children. Her son was to be especially devoted to the image of his grandfather, and Marianne could not have wholly escaped the influence of this sort of piety.

The Kirkwood parish must have prospered, for there was a new brick parsonage built before Reverend Warner died. The suburb's fate was tied to that of nearby St. Louis just west of the city, where many people were moving to escape the fumes and bad sewers. It was in the big city that another preacher had a famous poet in the family—St. Louis was where T. S. Eliot's grandfather, a Unitarian, watched over his parish. Many years later, after the two poets had become mutual admirers, Mrs. Moore told Marianne how the Reverend Warner would describe Reverend William Greenleaf Eliot and his son Henry Ware Eliot. According to this account, Eliot's father, Henry Ware, always wore black, had a face that resembled that of a terrier, and was constantly lost in thought. The description is in general accord with that of others, and since Mrs. Moore told this story before Eliot had become famous enough to have his background researched and exposed, her memory must have been accurate. It is indeed a remarkable circumstance that two of America's best known modern poets should have been raised within miles of one another, though perhaps less remarkable that they would have shared similar religious and social backgrounds.

The Moore children were educated in a Christian way, though in 1892, when Marianne was only five years old, her mother was to complain that she was not an especially adept pupil. She also described her daughter as having a funny mixture of dignity and impatience. It was an acute observation, and its echoes can be heard later throughout Marianne's life. That same year, however, during his twenty-fifth anniversary celebration at Kirkwood, the Reverend spoke of his time with the children as the happiest six years of his life. He planned to take them to the Chicago Exposition in 1893, but apparently his health prevented it. The children were allowed to look at picture books of birds if they ever got bored or rambunctious in the parlor, and "The Wren's Nest" was frequently serenaded by birds. Marianne's love of animals may have begun this early; she was even given a pet alligator. There were numerous kittens, and Marianne later recalled roses and clematis along the fence, and a tub of spatterdock by the back door. And when Warner broke his arm in the spring of 1892, Marianne was a great help, even tying his shoelaces for him. Many decades later the two would reminisce about how they lay awake at night telling stories; when one would finish, the other would take up with another episode. The two were apparently to live their entire lives without a serious quarrel, and Marianne never indicated anything but the deepest love and respect for her brother.

But soon there occurred the loss of another male authority figure, and this time it was Marianne's grandfather, whom she had come to know well. Mrs. Moore again raises her rhetoric, and records what is Marianne's first published utterance:

> Hand in hand, with one or both of them, had he approached the mercy-seat twice daily, and a natural sequence was it that those who had there knelt with him should now "lean hard" upon that Best Friend to whom he had gone, and that the little Marianne, born in his house and the apple of his eye, should pray, "Dear Lord, make our grandpa thy dearest angel. Do not let him stay sorry for us, but let him behold thy face, so that he shall be satisfied with thy likeness; and make him go up and down from heaven to earth, like those angels Jacob saw upon the ladder."

An unexpected beginning, perhaps, for a writer who was to become one of the major modernist poets. But there is something other than irony in the fact that these words of Marianne are indeed recorded, or even "written," by her mother, who was to be the poet's constant companion and friend for the next fifty years, and, according to Marianne, one of her major literary influences as well.

Near the end of her memoir of the Reverend, Mrs. Moore records a dream Warner had had of his grandfather. He saw his grandfather not as a preacher but as a king, in "a long white robe, with fringes of beautiful pink that flew all the time." As the kingly figure reached out his hand to the young dreamer, a bird flew to it, and the man fed the bird, who then flew off and returned with his mate, and both of them began singing to the figure crowned with diamonds. These two birds could easily represent Warner and his sister, of course, for Warner was to be constantly protective of her, in a way that often involved leading her to certain positions and attitudes. But whatever the symbolism, Reverend Warner was to exercise a lasting influence over the three Moores, who now were faced with a search for a new home. Mrs. Moore was always to call her son Warner, after her father, instead of John, her husband's name. But of course Warner wasn't anywhere near old enough to care for the family. So Mrs. Moore took her children to live with their uncle Henry, outside Pittsburgh. But within the space of two years, this uncle died. Once again Mrs. Moore faced the prospect of finding and organizing a home for herself and her two young children. And for the third time within the first decade of her life, Marianne had suffered the loss of a male authority figure.

Just after Reverend Warner died, Mrs. Moore had spent some time at the seashore in Massachusetts, near Gloucester, perhaps a place she had come to know when she had lived in Newton with her husband. Her later move to the Pittsburgh area came about because she was reluctant to return to Kirkwood, partly out of her fear that the Moore family would still attempt a reconciliation or offer help that she was unwilling to accept. The Moores were a family prominent as riverboat captains, and they lived in Portsmouth, Ohio, several hundred miles from Kirkwood. In 1894 Mary Warner was corresponding with Uncle Henry, who was managing a land company in Aspinwall, Pennsylvania, and he was urging her to revise her memoir of Reverend Warner, a task that she worked at diligently. Months later, residing briefly with Uncle Henry in Ben Avon, near Pittsburgh, she had a sizable income from her father's estate of $2400, derived in part from rent on the house in Kirkwood, a mortgage property in Pueblo, Colorado, and another in Pittsburgh. She was far from destitute, but her world could hardly have been promising or completely secure. Uncle Henry had died in September, 1895, and yet she sent the children back to school that fall, despite the "extravagance." Mrs. Moore would never relent in her commitment to education and culture, and she often felt that overcoming financial difficulties was more or less a natural part of such a commitment.

Within a year of Uncle Henry's death, Mrs. Moore had settled in Carlisle, Pennsylvania, and had begun teaching at the Metzger Institute. An unsubstantiated account said that there were members of the Craig family living near Carlisle, at a place called Welsh Springs. Years later, Mrs. Moore was to tell one of her daughter's college teachers that the family had come to Carlisle to be near people she knew; perhaps this referred to people who had some link with her father's church in Kirkwood. Whatever drew her to Carlisle, she was to live there for the next twenty years, establishing a network of friends, largely through her association with the Presbyterian church next to the Metzger Institute. This was the Second Presbyterian Church, and Mrs. Moore joined it rather than the First Presbyterian, which was closer to the center of town. The Second Presbyterian Church had split off from the First Presbyterian more than half a century earlier, in a doctrinal dispute. Many of the more prominent families in Carlisle had joined the Second Presbyterian, and the church began to flourish, especially under one of its pastors named Dr. George Norcross. It was Norcross who was pastor when the Moores arrived in Carlisle, and his character contributed greatly to their allegiance to the Second Presbyterian.

Warner was to go to high school at Dickinson, the prep school that was associated with the local college, while Marianne attended Metzger, a high school for young women. Many decades later, however, in yet another version of the story, Marianne wrote a letter to her cousin that said the family chose Carlisle because that was where Dickinson College was located, and she and Warner could both attend it, since it was one of the few coeducational colleges in the area. Undoubtedly, the idea of educating her children to the college level, and even beyond, was in keeping with Mrs. Moore's views. Though it is hard to be certain just why the Moores settled in Carlisle, they seemed to be happy there and may have retrospectively formulated several reasons for choosing it. Mrs. Moore was herself a graduate of a small college, but there is little reason to think that she had planned on a teaching career for herself. By the time her children were in college, however, she was increasingly exhausted by her duties as a teacher, and eager to give up the daily routine.

It is a striking tribute to her strong will, however, that Mrs. Moore shunned help from her husband's family and went off without much direct aid from her own relatives. To face the world on modest means, to secure a job, and to raise two children, eventually sending one to Yale and the other to Bryn Mawr, would have tested a woman even in a more socially accepting world than that of nineteenth-century small-town America. Mrs. Moore not only faced the world, she prevailed. Doubtlessly she would credit her religious faith for providing her strength of character, for she often talked about religion in a context of personal discipline and fortitude. Her letters to her relatives during the last 1890's, however, tell of her doubts and fears. In October, 1895, she told her cousin Mary Shoemaker that she more and more felt unable to take up anything that would put her in the public eye. Eight months later she wrote of her suspicion of society, apparently out of her self-doubt, but also because of its vanities. She was to pass on some of this defensiveness—this attitude that the world is a place where people are worn down, exposed, and broken by the press of events and responsibilities—to her daughter. Herself a graduate of Mary Academy and a doted-upon only child, Mary Warner Moore had an education that placed her in the upper percentile in matters of self-expression and cultivation. She was always conscious of culture, and not exclusively of a Christian sort. For example, she used to read Hawthorne's tales to the neighborhood children on picnics. Certainly she exposed her children, extensively and intensively, to secular literature. Her devotion as a minister's daughter might have led her to consider a narrowly reclusive life, but it was not what she finally fashioned for herself and her family.

In March, 1895, during her stay with Uncle Henry, she wrote out, in a letter to a relative, two of Marianne's poems. The young poet was not yet eight years old, and she was rhyming nicely: "The shadows now they slowly fall: making the earth a great dark ball." And another: "Pussy in the cradle lies—and sweetly dreams of gnats and flies." These two poems, written down without line breaks, precede by several months what had previously been regarded as Marianne's first poem. This more widely known effort was a Christmas poem, especially notable in the light of her later interest in gifts and tokens. It reads like this:

> Dear St. Nicklus:
> This Christmas morn
> you do adorn
> Bring Warner a horn
> And me a doll
> That is all.

A horn, maybe Warner's gift, survives in the family archive, but there is no record of the doll. The poem is illustrated, by the way, with a horn and a doll, both suitably labeled. The mother took great delight in her children, educating them seriously, and reporting to her cousins how they progressed. Despite several subsequent protestations by Marianne that she developed her desire to be a writer only much later, these early efforts, in addition to her Bryn Mawr output, clearly show she was engaged in literary expression from a very early age.

The Moore family regularly attended the Presbyterian church and came to be very close not only to the pastor, Reverend George Norcross, but all of his family. When, shortly after her arrival, Mrs. Moore began teaching at Metzger Institute, her daily duties brought her into close contact with all the Norcrosses. The Institute had been founded in honor of his wife with a bequest of $1000 from George Metzger, a non-communicant of the church who owned a pew there.

It was George Norcross who dominated life in the church and at the school. His was to be the longest pastorate in the history of the church, extending for forty years from 1869 until 1909. Norcross, an imposing figure, very probably reminded all the Moores of the Reverend Warner. He had graduated as a Doctor of Divinity from Princeton Theological Seminary, and had come to Carlisle from Galesburg, Illinois. The Carlisle church called him in part because of a recommendation of a Galesburg man who had moved to Carlisle and become the editor of the *Sentinel,* the town newspaper. The Second Presbyterian Church had split from the First Presbyterian because of a schism in 1832, when the pastor of the Second published an unorthodox book called *The Spiritual Life; or Regeneration.* The schism was healed in 1891, when both pastors were on vacation, as one local account put it. But the Second Presbyterian Church flourished under Norcross, building not only a new manse in the late 1860's, but also a new church building.

The Reverend Norcross was, besides being an important member of the community, a very learned man. On December 28, 1898, for example, he delivered an address to the American Historical Association, of which he was a member, entitled, "Erasmus, Prince of the Humanists." Published in the Association's journal, the address expressed the liberalism in matters of religion that would be typical of all the Moores, especially Marianne. In 1896, Norcross also gave a talk to the Scotch Irish Congress meeting in Harrisburg, Pennsylvania, on the history of the Scotch Irish Presbyterians in the Cumberland Valley. Such an interest in history, as well as in the fortunes of ethnic and national groups, would be something that Marianne shared, and it became the focus of some of her important poems as well.

George Norcross had married a second time after his first wife died early. His second wife was Mrs. Louise Jackson Gale, herself a widow of a professor at Knox College. The Norcross family included five children: four daughters and a boy who died at the age of seven. The third of these daughters was Mary Jackson Norcross, born on March 5, 1875. Mrs. Louise Norcross had a brother, Reverend Sheldon Jackson, who became the focus of Marianne's poem, "Rigorists." Mary Norcross, of an age between Mrs. Moore and Marianne, was to become a close family friend and one of Marianne's role models during the years in Carlisle. Marianne later acknowledged the influence the Norcross family had on her. The Norcross family was everything that Mary Warner Moore would have remembered from her childhood; the Norcrosses influenced her and Marianne as they envisioned a life of service in the manse after Warner became a minister. The ability of the entire Norcross family to combine religious rectitude with a sophisticated level of social and intellectual life was reflected in the Moores' aspirations and self-image throughout their lives.

It was also through the Norcrosses that Richard Pratt, who had fought with Custer, was able to raise funds and backing for his setting up an Indian School in Carlisle. The school was begun on the outskirts of Carlisle in 1879, the pupils being housed in Army barracks that had stood there previously. Several Indians were converted, and at least one was baptized into the Second Presbyterian Church by Reverend Norcross. It was the Indian School, of course, where Marianne taught for a few years after her graduation from college. The interweaving of

church work and institutionalized education, both at Metzger Institute
and the Indian School, was to dominate the early years of Marianne's
development.

By 1899, Marianne and her brother were cooking the home meals as
their mother worked hard at her teaching post. In April of that year,
Marianne noticed some monkeys at the zoo being protected by their
mother, and a snake that had shed its skin. In August, Metzger offered
Marianne free tuition, and she began her high school studies in an
organized curriculum. The neighbors in Carlisle included the Benét
family, with the children, Stephen Vincent, William Rose, and Laura.
The two boys were to become famous poets. Stephen's *John Brown's
Body* would become one of the rare "best sellers" in American poetry,
and William would serve as the editor of *Saturday Review*. Marianne was
to be close to Laura off and on: during the period after Marianne's
graduation from Bryn Mawr, for example, Laura was one of the few
people to whom she was showing her poems. Laura's memoir of these
early years contains two views of Marianne, both brief but tantalizing:

> Diagonally across to the left from Ammah's house in Carlisle lived Mari-
> anne Moore with her mother and her brother, Warner. She was a quiet
> child—very much of a "clam," I thought. She was not writing poetry yet,
> to my knowledge, but was very clever with her hands, doing tatting and
> embroidery. She loved cats, of which the Moores had a number. "I was
> sitting," I once heard her say, "one day on the porch with the elder
> kittens."

Marianne may well have been writing poetry by this time. But her
arch—and probably mocking—use of the word "elder" may have come
from her religious environment. T. S. Eliot was to remark forty years
later that Marianne's vocabulary had been drawn from the experience
of an American college education. This was evident even before she
went to Bryn Mawr. In terms of lexical range, Marianne was to be a
most distinctive poet.

The second view of Marianne shows her in a family context:

> I was delighted to see Elinor Hays again. One day she brought us an
> invitation from Mrs. Moore. Marianne Moore, her brother, and her
> mother were storybook people to us and we were thrilled. Honey's tact
> was remarkable, as she knew Auntie had a great fear of water, be it
> ocean, bay, or creek. "Mrs. Moore is taking her children for a picnic on
> the creek, Miss Rose. She and Warner will do the rowing; she has

invited me and hopes you will let Laura and Willie come too. She will provide the supper. They are not going far," quoted Honey. . . .

Years later, when Marianne and I had become real friends, I remember being asked to breakfast in their garden. When I arrived, I saw a neat little pot hung over a small fire and in it was a breakfast egg for me, as my hostess did not care for eggs. Mrs. Moore went busily in and out of the kitchen, making the coffee and bringing out the rest of the breakfast. Presently she called to her daughter, "Are you watching Laura's egg?"

Marianne replied in doleful tones, "It's been in and out so many times I don't know what it's like now."

It is hard to tell how many "years later" this egg incident took place, but certainly Marianne's exasperation sounds more like that of a teenager. It is one of the first suggestions that Marianne was not always meek and submissive where her mother's diligence was concerned. In many small ways, the clash between her dignity and her impatience was beginning to show.

The round of daily activity in Carlisle was filled with frequent social visits. It was in many ways a picturesque small-town American life, complete with Sunday School, a modest downtown shopping area served by trolley lines, and broad tree-lined streets on which stood wood-frame houses with large porches. The surrounding area was rich Pennsylvania farmland, and the poet's sense of nature as a place where human cultivation is highly visible—something evident later in "The Farm Show," the published excerpt of her novel—goes back to these Carlisle days. There was, to be sure, a cultural life as well. Not only the Benéts contributed to this; George Plank was a noteworthy local artist who, many years later, illustrated one of Marianne's books. The Moores apparently drew heavily on the resources of the local library. Philadelphia was nearby for shopping and concerts, both easily reached by the suburban rail system that would later serve Marianne so well as a college student at nearby Bryn Mawr. In the winter of 1904, she could report to her brother about a lecture she heard on the Russian czar, and a few months later about one on the North Pole. In the age before television and radio, the lecture circuits that served small towns in America were important sources of information and cultural attitudes; when Marianne moved to Brooklyn in 1930, she would continue enjoying this form of education, chiefly at the Brooklyn Institute of Arts and Letters.

Marianne spoke many years later of how she was reading with college in mind by the time she was sixteen. There was ample time for recreation as well, and Marianne and Warner socialized often as avid doubles partners at the local tennis courts; it was a game she continued to play with gusto when she was past fifty years old. In later years, she spoke about Carlisle with great fondness, never losing her genuine appreciation for the sense of local culture and community pride that she had first experienced there. For all of her considerable sophistication in cultural matters, Marianne began her entry into adulthood in a small American town, in some ways not much bigger than a village.

At the turn of the century, America was enjoying considerable prosperity, though the concentrations of wealth and population that were to define the industrial world of the twentieth century had at the same time created social problems of enormous proportions. The progressivism of the coming decades, however, in which Presidents Roosevelt, Taft, and then Wilson would slowly lay down the earliest foundations of the welfare state, had not yet dealt with the questions of child labor, the oligarchic control of wealth, subsistence wages, and unsafe working conditions. The citizens of Carlisle could hardly have dreamed of such a world where a modern, urbanized country of mass populations would be the norm. But before Marianne would move permanently to New York City, the new capital of the American Century, almost two decades later, there would be more than a hundred American towns with a population in excess of 100,000. Carlisle's population, however, would not reach 20,000 in the next seventy years.

Much of the art and culture that Marianne experienced in her teenage years was produced by and for a public concentrated in numbers that had been unheard of a century earlier. Yet the environment of her daily life in these formative years in Carlisle was that of a culture sustained by a smaller and slower scale of human activity. The values that held the Moores together as a family were, of course, not originally designed to adapt to an urban or progressive life; such values were in many ways part of a profoundly conservative outlook. Paradoxically, their family correspondence, and the tone and texture of their daily activities, suggest a cultured intelligence that would surely serve them more than adequately in the social world of a metropolis. The disjunction, if not the tension, between small-town lives and metropolitan views would work itself into Moore's poetry in many subtle ways.

Carlisle itself was a mixture of the time scales of rural and urban life. Because it was a college town as well as the county seat, Carlisle was not at all a "sleepy" little town. The town had many historical associations, having sent a delegation from its First Presbyterian Church to the Continental Congress. When George Washington visited his troops there during the Whiskey Rebellion, he attended services at the same church. Earlier still, the town had played a major role in the Indian Wars. But the town partook of the overall industrial and commercial growth of Cumberland County and the state of Pennsylvania only in the latter days of the nineteenth century. The state itself was the origin of much of the industry of nineteenth-century America, containing oil, coal, and steel as well as a highly developed rail and canal system. By 1895, the first trolley line began operation in Carlisle. This line would eventually offer not only in-town service, but connecting service with nearby towns and other rail systems. It was possible to use this line to travel not only to Philadelphia but also New York. In their travels, the Moores used these rail lines as well as the sea ferries that connected eastern coastal cities.

The trolley line helped take Carlisle out of the horse-and-buggy era, giving the town at least the first glimmers of the new structures of modernity. The local newspaper, the *Evening Sentinel,* covered the story with considerable fanfare. At first the scale of the line was modest, with four tracks, running north and south as well as east and west. The main north-south line ran along Hanover Street. The Moores lived at 343 North Hanover, north of the High Street. North Hanover was a broad, tree-lined avenue with large wood-frame houses set along each side. Most of the commercial district was strung along High Street; at the corner of High and North Hanover stood the county courthouse with its colonnaded cupola. At first, the trolley ran north out to a place called Diffley's Point, beyond the Moores' house. Then the line was extended all the way to the Indian School, whose students laid the final stretch of rail. Marianne would have been able to take this line directly to her teaching job at the school, which began shortly after her graduation from college in 1909. By the early 1910's, the trolley cars ran every fifteen minutes.

It was not only the convenience for shopping and local travel that made the trolley line flourish. Eventually, people in Carlisle went back to walking short distances rather than pay the minimal fare. So the trolley developers bought land nearby to build what were known as "trolley parks." Large tracts much like our contemporary state and county parks, with their well-landscaped ponds, rivers, and walking trails, these parks were the site of weekend excursions and picnics. The trolley company would offer special fares and service, often including late-evening service, in order to provide a bucolic outing for their customers. The Carlisle line served several such parks, chief among them Mt. Holly. Such places were clearly an attempt by the developers of the industrial world to serve the nostalgic desires of a population in a rapidly changing era. Cumberland County and Carlisle, after all, took their names from the Lake Country of northwest England that borders Scotland. This Pennsylvania landscape in some ways resembles that of the English countryside, and the Moores, all avidly Anglophilic, almost certainly appreciated the correspondence.

The coming of the trolley also made it possible for Carlisle residents to visit large-city department stores, such as Wanamaker's and Strawbridge and Clothier's in Philadelphia. Marianne seemed to prefer the former. She may have had her first acquaintance with these mercantile institutions through the large advertisements that ran in local newspapers, including the *Evening Sentinel.* Her hometown paper also ran a column called "Daily Fashion Hints," which featured line drawings of models arrayed with the latest "look." Marianne was an early and avid reader of advertising. She took great delight in the play with words that advertising was beginning to employ; she would later use such language in her own poetry. Beyond her lexical interest in such displays, Marianne was also stimulated to pay attention to her own appearance. Her concern with clothing began early, and though she would write an essay on the subject for *Women's Wear Daily* in her seventies, she had thought about it from at least her adolescence. The trolley, the newspaper advertisement, the department store were all inventions of the age that resulted in a modern, urbanized existence. As a poet, Marianne seemed to welcome such forms of modernity; unlike others writers, such as D. H. Lawrence, say, or, to some extent, Frost, she was never to lament at any length the onset of modernization as an insidious corruption of spiritual values. Later, in the 1930's, when she does complain of what she sees as a weakening of public morality, she doesn't link it with urbanity as such. And in the late 1910's and 1920's, when her poems take a satiric turn, the object of her scorn is likely to be a spiritual attitude, usually one associated with excessive self-regard.

II. Being raised "by hand"

The Moores seemed happily settled in the town of Carlisle. They would often eat in the dining hall at Metzger and would occasionally stay for dinner with the Norcrosses in their manse. Since the Norcrosses were well established in the social circles of Carlisle, Marianne and her mother were introduced to many people. In April, 1901, the Moores and the Norcrosses traveled to Atlantic City together. Earlier, Mrs. Moore had taken her children to the nation's capital and explained to them the wonders of the Library of Congress; years later, in 1914, Marianne would go there to see the recently published avant-garde magazine, *Blast.* Mrs. Moore wrote her cousin of having to undergo an operation in 1901 to remove an unspecified lump. Marianne helped her mother through the convalescence after the operation, and tried, with mixed success, to sell her own drawings of animals and landscapes at a local fair. Later that year, Mrs. Moore and Marianne visited Maine, which was to become a favorite vacation spot of theirs in coming years. In November, Marianne wrote a letter that is apparently the earliest surviving document in her hand. In it she tells a joke: if a man ate his mother-in-law, he'd be a "gladiator." Such puns became a staple in the letters Marianne and Warner were to exchange well after she graduated from college. Her impressively wide lexical range, one of the chief features of her poetry, was always addressed nimbly, and she practiced not only precise and exotic word choices, but also plain and even broadly comic ones as well.

In June, 1902, Mrs. Moore took Marianne to Washington, D.C., for medical treatment. The problems appeared not to be serious, and it was not unusual for people to travel such a distance to see a doctor. Mrs. Moore, in fact, frequented an osteopath, a Dr. Krohn, who later treated Marianne for an earache and back trouble. When a bill was introduced into the Pennsylvania legislature to ban osteopathy, Mrs. Moore lobbied her local representative diligently. The next month Mrs. Moore noticed in a Portsmouth, Ohio, paper the obituary of Captain Moore, a riverboat pilot, who was her father-in-law. She worried that the Moore family might try again to contact her to suggest some reconciliation. It was quite clear by this time that Mrs. Moore was intent on maintaining her independence. Such a trait would be passed on to her daughter, but with considerable ambiguity.

Marianne remembered later that in her high school years at Metzger Institute her favorite teacher was a woman who taught German and drawing. This latter subject became one of Marianne's lifetime avocations: she used her skills in the biology classes she attended in college, and was sketching flowers as late as the 1950's. This love of drawing was clearly related to her personal aesthetic, which relied so heavily on descriptive accuracy. This activity was supported by the theories of Ruskin, who made a deep impression on both Marianne and her mother. Singing lessons were also part of her high school years: her mother wanted her to take them not because she had a good voice, but because she didn't. Mrs. Moore felt her daughter should have a wide range of aesthetic experience and appreciation, even if she couldn't attain mastery in every respect. And there was also the intense and rapt reading, including many novels and all of Dickens, as well as Jacob Abbott's "Rollo" series of children's travel and adventure books, which Marianne received for good attendance at her singing lessons. These latter books may well have made for Marianne an unconscious connection between travel to new and exciting countries with the exercise of one's artistic talents.

Mrs. Moore's work as a high school teacher of English should not be overlooked when it comes to sorting out the early and lasting influences on Marianne as a writer. Mrs. Moore took her work very seriously; when the children were both in college she wrote them about various Shakespeare plays, and frequently gave them tips on composition and corrected their spelling. Since the position at Metzger gave Mrs. Moore the chance to establish herself socially in Carlisle, as well as solve the economic problems she faced after her father's death, she probably had much of her own identity invested in her role as a teacher. All three of the Moores taught at one time or another during their lives, and all three placed considerable emphasis on the values as well as the prestige associated with such work.

A more specific influence that Mrs. Moore passed on to her daughter were the views about literature she employed to instruct her students at Metzger. Her textbooks, written by F. V. N. Painter, were the *History of English Literature*, published in 1899, and *Introduction to American*

Literature, published in 1897. The first of these opens with an introduction that isolates race, epoch, and surroundings as the three chief
forces in shaping the national character and national literature of the
English people. Mrs. Moore underlines these three terms, though there
is no way of knowing if she recognized their indebtedness to the critical
theories of Hippolyte Taine, the nineteenth-century French critic
whose writings were very widely taught. His history of English literature
had been translated into English in 1886. In Taine the terms were
"race, moment, and milieu," and they were part of the movement of
Romantic nationalism that flourished in the last century through the
expression of the idea that a people's essential spirit is registered in its
language, more specifically in its written literature.

On page 13 of the Painter volume on English literature appeared a
passage that Mrs. Moore underlined and then copied out on the inside
front cover of the book. Presumably she agreed with Painter that such
lines accurately conveyed the spirit of the English people:

> Laughing at storms and ship wrecks, these sea-kings sang: "The blast of
> the tempest aids our oars; the bellowing of heaven, the howling of the
> thunder hurts us not; the hurricane is our servant, and drives us whither
> we wish to go."

It was by this sort of moral uplift that literature gained approval by many
people in an America that was concerned with genteel values. For Mrs.
Moore, such sentiments would have a personal resonance, given the life
trials she had recently passed through and, in some measure, still faced.

Also written inside the front cover of the textbook is the name of a
single author: "George Edward Bateman Saintsbury, Born October 23,
1845, Southampton, England." Marianne would eventually come to
meet this author and accord him a respect and friendship that might
very well have had its sources in her mother's respect for literary authorities. Saintsbury was a critic and literary historian whose reputation
is now considerably dimmer than it was during his lifetime, when he
had come to epitomize the Victorian value of high seriousness. Obviously, Mrs. Moore supplemented her sense of literary expression as
rooted in national "genius" with an appreciation of individual writers;
she pasted into her text small photographs of several authors. Taine
could well have been the influence behind this, too, for in his *History
of English Literature* he argued that "you study the document only in

order to know the man." Painter ended his survey of English literature with Ruskin, who was also to be an important influence on Marianne. The American survey ended with Oliver Wendell Holmes, but there was no representation by Melville, Thoreau, or Dickinson, the last two of whom were eventually to become important writers for her.

Marianne spoke of herself as spoiled by all the attention she received as a child, and said that she was raised "by hand." Yet the fact that she attended school where her mother taught may have had some negative consequences as well. Possibly she was expected to be better behaved than the other young women and perhaps expected not to call attention to her performance. It is only speculation, but her lifelong habit of being self-conscious about her social presentation might be traced back in part to this situation. For her part, Mrs. Moore was a lively teacher, one who attracted attention to her views and methods. The following account, drawn from the minutes of the faculty meetings at Metzger in the spring of 1904 (when Marianne would have been a junior in high school), gives some indication of Mrs. Moore's classroom approach:

> Mrs. Moore gave a very graphic account of the powers of imagination developed by some members of her class—which development went so far as to represent the Puritan forefathers as playing cards and indulging in dancing after a good dinner of turkey and mince pie. She also amused us very much by giving her method of healing the wounded self pride of a young lady who had excited the smiles of her class by her recitation or non-recitation in history. This method did not meet with the approbation of members of the faculty who felt its effects in subsequent recitations but the laugh we had repaid us for any extra trouble entailed. Other matters were taken up but the above was the chief feature of the meeting.

Years later, Marianne was to try teaching young adults and to feel that she was not really qualified for it. Perhaps her mother's apparent ability in this area generated standards that were hard to equal.

Warner also had some occasion to develop his expressive skills. He was the editor of his high school newspaper and was intensely committed to participating in athletics. His newspaper experience apparently impressed his sister and mother: Years later when the two women sailed to England, they published a daily newspaper on board the ship and mailed it to Warner to keep him abreast of their activities. This was a version of the family newspaper, called "The File," which was generally written by Marianne and filled with multiple puns and allegories based on animals and pet nicknames; its covert personal meanings are virtually impossible to decode. Later still, Warner was to spend some of his time editing and publishing a newspaper on board his ship in the United States Navy, filled largely with news and spiritual advice for the sailors.

By 1904, Mrs. Moore was already preparing Marianne's application for Bryn Mawr. Marianne was scheduled to take preliminary entrance exams in June, 1905. These exams were especially strenuous and Marianne required considerable tutoring, most of it at the hands of Mary Norcross, herself a Bryn Mawr graduate. Laura Benét, in the meantime, had been accepted at Vassar. The choice of a college was important, of course, and Warner was already busy preparing to go to Yale, where he was to be a classmate of William Rose Benét. Warner was keen at this time to be an engineer, and many of his subsequent summer jobs were taken with this in mind. Eventually he was to abandon engineering, his father's occupation, in favor of the ministry, his maternal grandfather's calling. As was the case with his name, his fate was to be determined more by maternal than by paternal influences.

By the late summer of 1904, Warner was already living in New Haven while his mother and sister vacationed, with Mary Norcross, at Monhegan Island, off the coast of Maine, having traveled out by steamship from Boothbay Harbor. Mrs. Moore wrote Warner that she and Mary Norcross were contemplating buying land there to build a summer home. This, of course, was the first real separation among the three members of an extraordinarily close-knit family. Mrs. Moore undoubtedly was aided in being resigned to the separation because Warner was engaged in furthering his education. But her hold over him and her desire to influence him in every important aspect of life did not at all abate. When he complained of her attention, she responded by saying that she didn't want to make him an automaton, but rather to adjust his "pitch" so that he could play out his own fate in a melodious way.

The correspondence between Mrs. Moore and her son over the next decade or so, until his marriage in 1918, reveals a great deal about her character and beliefs and reflects directly the sort of environment in which Marianne grew up. Mrs. Moore was a constant source of advice to Warner, and if he ever chafed at its amount and details he never said so in his letters home. Few if any of Mrs. Moore's instructional letters failed to include some humorous observation and some gossip about family friends and the local scene. These additions to the instructions lightened the tone of the correspondence, whether or not Mrs. Moore consciously meant to do so. But the instruction was unflagging, in matters social and spiritual; indeed these two realms often coincided. On September 6, 1904, for example, Mrs. Moore spoke of how difficult it is to be instructed by so low a teacher as money. Yet, she goes on to say, if we can achieve independence then we can later put aside the occasion of our moral ascent. No neater sublimation of the economic motive could be found, and the imagery of ascension has a nicely dual reference to both spiritual and economic matters. The prosperity and progressivism of the social world, however, was never to be a complete substitute for spiritual discipline.

Mrs. Moore worked long and hard at developing Warner's aesthetic sense as well as his moral responsibility. Evidently he was not so avid a reader as his sister, for one cannot imagine Marianne, even as a teenager, needing any more encouragement to read, widely and demandingly. One book Mrs. Moore pressed on him at this time was Ruskin's *Sesame and Lilies,* and it is easy to see this sort of work by a Victorian sage as epitomizing the work of a worldly writer in producing religious thought, as she put it. In fact, Mrs. Moore would even recommend reading such a book on the Sabbath, a day on which she refrained from most worldly activity. She also sent Warner a short essay of her own devising on "The Merchant of Venice" shortly after he left for college, perhaps a result of her teaching this play in her English classes at Metzger. But her attempts at uplift were more than balanced by a fretful concern for the details of daily life. Not only does she write to Yale to select Warner's courses for him, but a number of letters are exchanged during his first months at Yale in which the main subject is the size and nature of his bed. This subject is examined and re-examined, and even put in the context of his drawing of the floor plan of his room. Mrs. Moore is worried lest a too short bed cramp Warner and make him stunted. She supplemented this early advice with later notes on exactly how to make up his bed.

This might all be taken for the mere nervous concern of any hardworking mother to make sure her son does well in what was, after all, a very challenging undertaking in a context in which she herself had had no direct experience. But intermixed with this spiritual uplift and attention to mundane detail is a constant guidance in matters of personal behavior. She had warned him, in the summer before college, not to adopt a pose of high self-regard. In the same letter in which she tells him how to make his bed, she suggests that his behavior with young women amounted to secrecy, bordering on deception. (In 1915, Warner was to name as his main character flaw a disposition not to tell the whole truth.) Later, near Christmas time, she says she doesn't want him to be one of those who makes girls pay attention to him. As time went on, Warner's relations with his female companions were to become more and more a matter of grave concern for Mrs. Moore. When he eventually decided to marry some years later, after having broken off two or three near engagements, he did so with what seemed like unexpected quickness.

His mother even provided Warner with a model letter, in October of his first year, when, dissatisfied with his correspondence, she felt he needed to be told how to answer her queries and how best to relate his situation. He promised to improve. Surely some of this is the approach of the English teacher run somewhat beyond its regular course. On the other hand, her religious scruples prevented her from writing or mailing letters on Sunday, for she didn't like the idea of making postal employees work on the Sabbath. For Mrs. Moore, proper expression and proper forms, however, were often at least as important as proper beliefs and inner values. Writing was something that could be effectively modeled, and it was also something that could involve someone too much in earthly concerns. These ideas were seriously at work in the Moore household, and they had an effect on Marianne.

At the same time that Mrs. Moore was being exceptionally protective of Warner—and, presumably, Marianne as well—she was letting Warner slowly assume the role of advisor and protector for the family. She was, after all, a minister's daughter. Later, when Warner joined the ministry, she was apparently willing and even eager to return to a life of service in the manse. But after Warner had entered college, she began to keep him informed of many family matters, especially financial ones. She is quick to tell him, for example, in the spring of 1905, that there are new tax assessments against the Kirkwood house to cover the installation of electric lights and sewers, so she cannot afford to sell the house at this time. She also had to dip into her savings in order to pay the bills for Yale. When she would receive a letter from a Pittsburgh bank acting as trust for her rental property, she would send it on to Warner, though often making economic use of the blank side of the page for news of her own. This was a habit Marianne would pick up from her mother, both of whom were disposed to cover every available inch of their writing paper. Warner, on the other hand, was much less thrifty and less articulate, for he wrote with a large looping hand and conveyed considerably fewer details in his correspondence. Marianne must have indirectly learned about financial management as a result of this; when they eventually moved to New York, it was she who tended to the accounts for her mother and herself.

One special way Mrs. Moore had of showing her love for her children was to encourage and enter into their playful and very complex use of pet names. Eventually these names would be more or less stabilized. But first, they were often shifted from one family member to another, which makes reading the correspondence, for an outsider, somewhat tricky. Furthermore, names might spring up on a certain occasion, provoked by reading or some shared incident. The names in this context might stick for a while, or even be used in combination with others, most often other animals. Hence, Marianne might become "Fangs" (this from the dog in *Ivanhoe*) and Warner would be called "Dogs," or even "Two Dogs," when he apparently exhibited a double dose of the behavior that first earned him the name. Warner described his first Princeton-Yale game, a contest that he followed all his life, as a battle between "gators" and "turtles." He then makes himself into "turtle" or "biter" and Marianne into "gator."

Such play with pet names has a clearly innocent aspect, but the Moores used them for several purposes. The names are often of animals with a ferocious aspect, used here to express some passing frustration, rivalry, or enmity. Warner especially makes use of this, as he begins letters expressing frustration or disappointment by exaggerating the name and the animal's behavior, which in turn allows him to "condemn" it in playfully overblown terms. But there is one letter, written by Warner to Marianne on her seventeenth birthday, that uses the names in a small homespun mythology. Warner describes Marianne's birth as a "gator egg," which he, Warner, takes into his mouth and carries out of the marsh and back to his house, where he watches it hatch from the sun's heat. He signs this letter *"Biter, Great Turtle, Terror of Gator."* Obviously this "fable" of Oedipal power shows how Warner was concerned about supplying for his sister the salvation and protection needed by infant creatures, but also in effect to play the role of Marianne's father.

This playfulness extends to other nicknames as well. In the spring of 1905, with Warner more and more settled at Yale, and Marianne looking forward to her own entrance into college the next fall, the two begin to correspond more and more. Usually Mrs. Moore would write to Warner, and then Marianne would append a postscript of her own, usually no more than a sentence or two. But eventually she began to write at somewhat greater length. These early glimpses of her sensibility are revealing. Much of the writing is humorous, as in the sharing of jokes and corny puns. She even writes a February letter in mock Shakespearean dialogue about eating a mince pie. She tells Warner news as well, of Metzger Institute's acquisition of an alligator for the science laboratory and how the failure to get it to eat has made her most uncomfortable. She mentions how she has used the word "drool" in conversation, and Warner teases her about this; later she is to be lectured at Bryn Mawr against the use of slang by young ladies. She has stayed busy for the last few months with her painting lessons, and sends her brother a drawing of her favorite brush. Many of her letters include small drawings and illustrations, and years later she tells a friend that her first plan was to have been an artist. She warns Warner not to let his move into Pierson Hall, where many wealthy boys reside, inflame his desire for things he can't have.

But a series of exchanges in the spring of 1905 is especially interesting for the light it sheds on Marianne's relationship with Warner and their family life together. In the context of their use of pet names, Marianne begins to call herself Warner's brother. She signs her portion of some of the letters "brother," and sometimes "bro," and Warner jokingly insists on the longer form. This sort of teasing could have come from Warner's being in an all-male environment. But within a few months the motif is picked up by Mrs. Moore as well, who begins to refer to her daughter as "Uncle." She writes to tell Warner that when she really wants to irritate Marianne she switches from "Uncle" and addresses her as "Aunt Fangs," implying that Marianne preferred the male name. Marianne also responds by threatening to write a book called *The Tale of the Tyrant Fawn*, a reference to Mrs. Moore. In a sense this is a continuation, or variation, on Warner's little myth about his having fathered Marianne, but it also shows how willing the Moores were to try out roles with one another, roles that could not be played out anywhere but in the family circle. Underneath it is the "problem" of Marianne's gender, for while Warner has a clear sense of his eventual role in the world (he has already announced his desire to be an engineer and build bridges), she does not. At this point, her role is to be a member of the family, differently educated from the way men are educated and defined by their powers and their roles. Later, as a college senior approaching graduation, she would still have no clear sense of what her worldly position might be: drawn to publishing, advised against teaching, urged to seek secretarial work. But the almost incredibly fierce bonding that the three Moores had undergone since 1887 was to be playfully explored by this game of shifting family relationships. Such playing and shifting are very likely roots of Marianne's wonderfully complex sense of metaphor and lexical inventiveness.

In the summer of 1905, Marianne wrote of a dream she had to Warner, who was then working on a construction crew near the Maryland-West Virginia border. She and a friend were sitting down on the grass after a game of tennis. Warner was with them, but went off to get something over the knoll where the girls were sitting. As he returned, the girl friend looked up, saw him above them, and remarked to Marianne, "My, Warner's as straight as a ramrod, isn't he!" Apparently Mrs. Moore's concern that her son might too often adopt the mighty aspect seems to have had sufficient cause. Warner was a tall man, and he was always very protective of Marianne. But Mrs. Moore also once mentioned to a relative how Marianne would not exactly lie, but would shade the truth in order to protect her brother from any disciplining from their teachers. It is not surprising that Marianne would attach to her brother some of the awe a young person would reserve for a paternal figure. He was, after all, the man in the house, and he had been encouraged by his mother to think of himself as special, to be self-disciplined and outwardly flawless. Marianne must have learned that such values were of great importance; but they were, at the same time, meant and not meant for her to emulate. She was the minister's granddaughter, and she was to become the minister's sister. One way to imagine such a role might be to see it as requiring outward propriety without necessarily having obviously active strength of one's own. One image for such a set of virtues is armor.

Eventually, Marianne had to tell Warner that Metzger's alligator had been chloroformed: This happened in March, 1905, the same month her application for Bryn Mawr was sent in. In the meantime, Warner had begun to tutor a young pupil in New Haven, and Marianne was excited that he was earning some extra money for himself. Mrs. Moore informed Warner she had heard a great religious revival was going on in Wales, and she asked for news of William Benét so she might pass it along. Warner expressed concern that he had been dropped from the crew, but he took up track instead. For the next few years, he would spend a great amount of space in his letters relating the results of his track endeavors, sometimes describing races in detail and always reporting on the final standings. Marianne, in the meantime, had not only begun to be very conscious of fashion and dress, but to write about it to her brother. She met a Miss Brent from Bryn Mawr, probably as part of an application interview, since the college under its new president, M. Carey Thomas, was socially as well as intellectually selective. She told Warner that Miss Brent was loudly, but correctly, dressed, and that she was most impressed. A few months later, she excitedly described for her brother the hat she wore to tea at a Carlisle neighbor's house. She indulged her love of tokens and talismans by wearing a Bryn Mawr class ring, probably borrowed from Mary Norcross, while she took the entrance examinations the first week of June. The family letters, written by both Mrs. Moore and Marianne to Warner, and then responded to by Warner to both of them, were lively events, very frequent, written to Mrs. Moore's suggested schedule, and never allowed to displace Warner's energies from his schoolwork.

One animal that especially attracted Marianne from an early age, and which she associated with Warner, was the basilisk. She obviously discovered this animal through her extensive reading and seems to have taken a great liking to it. She begins to sign her letters with this name, and Warner addresses the portion of the letters addressed to her with the exclamation, "Great basilisks!" They discuss the spelling of the word and eventually form a club devoted to the exotic animal. Almost three decades later Marianne was to publish "The Plumet Basilisk," one of her more complex poems, which deals with several species of lizards, one of which bears the name basilisk. The creature of the title is noted for diving into rivers and streams, and his disappearing act has a dramatic conclusion: "the shattering splash . . . marks his temporary loss."

This is an armored animal, described at one point as living in a cocoon, its name deriving from the Greek word for crown or prince. To Marianne's mind, the plumet basilisk might well have been a fabulous version of the pet alligator she had back in Kirkwood, while living in "The Wren's Nest." And she had only recently been called upon to report on the death of Metzger's alligator. These alligators were the first in a long line of animals with exotic characteristics—armored, saurian, nocturnal, fabled—and some of them rare to the point of extinction, that would become for Marianne the focus of her descriptive powers as well as her metaphoric transformations. The basilisk had the advantageous double nature of being a member of a real species and the subject of mythic and sacred totemic power. Such a sacred and elusive animal would appeal to Marianne the poet, just as it appealed to the young woman on the verge of leaving her family's protection to imitate, if not exactly follow, her brother's recent passage into the larger world.

Chapter 2

35 PEMBROKE EAST:
THE BRYN MAWR YEARS

I. "In time of expressionary need"

When Marianne began to think about entering Bryn Mawr for the fall
term of 1905, she did so in a context of literary ambition. In December,
1904, she excitedly wrote to Warner, then a freshman at Yale, that she
had received three issues of the college literary magazine, *Tipyn O'Bob*.
For the next six years or so, this magazine was to be her main access to
print, and she devoted a great deal of her energy at Bryn Mawr to
writing and publishing both fiction and poetry for it. She was also very
excited to report to her brother that Henry James had been the commencement speaker at the college that spring; she had been told this by
Mary Norcross. A year later she was to begin reading James's *The
American Scene*, which was then being serialized in the *American Review*. Her summer reading prior to starting her freshman year included
Hugo's *Les Misérables*, Goldsmith's "She Stoops to Conquer," and
Balzac's *Magic Skin*. A great many of Moore's letters home talk about
her writing and her appearances in "Typ," as she came affectionately to
refer to the magazine. These letters reflect many of the themes that were
to be central to the poems and short stories she wrote as a college
student, themes involving ambition, artistic solitude, and the pressures
of finding a vocation worthy of her idealistic values.

In the simplest terms, Bryn Mawr was much more than a college for
Moore, and the institution meant a great deal to Moore even before she
entered it in the fall of 1906. For one thing it was the alma mater of

Mary Norcross, class of 1899, Marianne's neighbor and close friend. It was largely through knowing and respecting the Norcross family, two of whose daughters graduated from Bryn Mawr, that Marianne chose that college over the closer and less rigorous Dickinson College. Mary Norcross, in her thirties when Marianne began college, had two sisters who attended Bryn Mawr: Elizabeth, class of 1897, and Louise, class of 1900. It was Mary Norcross who tutored Moore and helped her gain admittance there, and to whom Moore wrote of her early homesickness, what looks in retrospect like a traumatic experience in her freshman year. Bryn Mawr was clearly Marianne's entrance into adult life. More important it was the place where one of the poet's earliest close friends had been formed and educated. It was also the place where family honor was to be exhibited and vindicated, just as surely as it was done by Moore's brother Warner at Yale.

Mary Norcross, familiar with and deeply loved by all three Moores, was nicknamed "Beaver," an apparent reference to her skill and trade as a weaver, but also perhaps to her diligence and artistic discipline. Mary was to remain an artist all her life, devoted to the aesthetic views of William Morris and the Arts and Crafts Movement then flourishing in America. Also committed to social justice, she was active in the suffragist movement and later in life worked as an educator of the underprivileged. She also served as the secretary for the missionary club associated with her father's church. In short, she combined a life of service with high intelligence and artistic talent. The playful animal nickname shows how Mary had fully entered into the innermost circle of the Moore family and how clearly she was on very intimate terms with both Marianne and her mother.

Mary Norcross was to exercise her commitment to the Arts and Crafts Movement by building a house in Sterrett's Gap, elevation 680 feet, just ten miles outside Carlisle. But this house was not just an artistic undertaking. One year after Mary graduated from college, she suffered a serious mental breakdown. It was from spending time at Sterrett's Gap recuperating from this illness that Mary conceived of the plan to build her own house. She bought 300 acres on a carefully chosen spot with magnificent views, and over the next several years spent many hours at work on this project. The land included a spring and a lovely mixed hardwood forest, from which Mary selected many of the woods used in the construction. She chose the materials herself (the house's main living room is built of a beautiful chestnut), and even supervised and helped the local people with the masonry work. If her first attempt at some innovation failed, she would tear it out and start over again. While the building was being worked on, and after it was finished, Marianne and her mother spent time there, always referring to it as "The Mountain." Mary herself called it "Deepwoods." Many years later, Mary's sister, in writing to the then-owner of the house, would describe it as Mary's life's work. It clearly began as a form of self-cure and it became a way Mary had of setting herself in the world, independent, somewhat removed, and constantly revising. The house and Mary's role in it may well have been a model for Marianne's sense of her place in the world, and how to deal with its adversities. And the trauma that occasioned the beginning of the house may have made Mary especially sensitive to Marianne's early difficulties at Bryn Mawr.

Mary Norcross obviously figured prominently in Marianne's personal development during her college years, as reflected in her letters home and the early stories she published in the "Typ." But it was not only the personal example of Mary Norcross that Moore had in mind as she wrote her fiction. Bryn Mawr was the place where she first received recognition as a writer. It was also where her social sense was first fully developed, in terms of her knowledge of a larger world of other people, as well as herself as an agent among other agents. Partly because her mother had prepared her by instilling high ideals and diligent work habits, as well as providing her with a sophisticated cultural background, and partly because of the kind of college Bryn Mawr was—or was intent on becoming—Moore's four years as a college student were of crucial importance. They affected her sense of artistic form and even her sense of language, especially the scope and texture of her lexical range. It might almost be said that Moore's poetry began at Bryn Mawr, to the extent to which it is the poetry of an educated woman who is extraordinarily sensitive to the history and social connotations of words. It is also at Bryn Mawr that Moore published short stories that show how her sense of social presence and values was bound up with the ability to perceive, in almost Jamesian fashion, the nuances of social intercourse and to regard them as perhaps the truest measure of character.

All of this is not to suggest that Moore was unrelievedly serious for four years. On a great many occasions she is able to write home about moments of great exhilaration, both of a social and an intellectual sort, and to tell of many parties, plays, concerts, lectures, pageants, and sports activities that often made it seem as if her schedule were pushed far beyond the breaking point, even for a young woman of energy and spirit. Many decades later, Marianne was to reminisce about her life at this period and recall her first sight at Bryn Mawr: the girls returning from field-hockey practice, all sweaty and with their hair disheveled. There were frequent visits home, a visit from Warner who came down from Yale, a trip to the nation's capital, and, near the end of her stay at Bryn Mawr, an especially memorable weekend in New York City. Moore also spent time exploring various religious services—the Quaker influence at Bryn Mawr evidently allowed or even encouraged such "sampling"—and she often described her reaction to various liturgical styles. And though she was treated by a chiropractor at one point for what appeared to be a possible case of scoliosis, or curvature of the spine, she stayed generally healthy throughout the four years and is even described after one physical exam as having above-average lung capacity. She took very intense delight, for example, in the field-hockey uniform that Warner sent her in November, 1905, on her eighteenth birthday.

Her letters home, after the shaky start of her freshman year, reflect an ever increasing sense of social self-possession. Her circle of friends, though it changed from time to time, was broad and interesting. Moore also spent a great deal of time shopping in Philadelphia, and her mother not only had her laundry sent back to Carlisle, but also worked hard on making many of her daughter's dresses. Often these were made from sketches Moore sent home of dresses she saw her classmates wearing or those in department-store windows. Style—in dress, religion, writing, and social behavior—was a constant preoccupation. At one point, Moore spends parts of several letters discussing and illustrating her "new" signature. This involved making a small loop in the downward "v" of the initial letter of both her first and last names. It is also during this period that she first sees, admires, and purchases a black tricorn hat, an article that was eventually to become her trademark. She was to become a poet of tokens and emblems and rare objects.

Her mind was always drawn to particulars; she apparently saw in them something like a compact version of otherwise inexplicable values and meanings. The college was a place where social distinctions mattered a great deal, and Marianne was introduced through her classmates to a realm of considerable wealth and culture, one where the rituals of living with others were highly codified and subject to the approval of a group of peers. The protective family circle of Carlisle, in addition to the close supervision at Metzger, was at once a good preparation for this new world, but also was to be set beside it in a critical way. Marianne was eventually to become relaxed and accepted in the social spheres at Bryn Mawr, and some of her longest friendships were to be formed there. Most important of all, however, was her discovery of the very idea of friendship; many of her stories are concerned with the details of a friend's moods and the difficulties in keeping such intimate relationships in good order.

At first, however, Moore was very unhappy at Bryn Mawr, and it might have seemed to her that her first semester would be her last. An acute case of homesickness came over her. Such homesickness would not be surprising, considering the tightness of the family circle created by her mother's fierce devotion and highly devoted sense of responsibility. But it was more than this, for the letters home in the first few months speak of a trauma that involved a genuine physical illness. Marianne had started the term by writing frequently to both her mother and Mary Norcross, but she discussed this condition first with Mary Norcross. After only a few weeks, by October 6, she is complaining to Mary that she can't eat and will probably have to take to bed. She says she never feels sorry for herself or abused, but speaks of a feeling of being drawn down by insuperable forces. Also she tells "Beaver" at one point that she feels her problem is deep-seated, though easy to conceal and control. Possibly Mary sensed something was seriously wrong and went to Mrs. Moore with the problem; in any case, Marianne and her mother were eventually able to deal with it. But Mrs. Moore reasserted her control, and correspondence between Marianne and Beaver apparently ceased. Mary Norcross might well have played a role as a mother figure to Marianne, but such a possibility was limited by the presence of Mrs. Moore, who, for neither the first nor the last time, asserted her sense of protection over and responsibility for her daughter.

The problem was clearly more than an ordinary schoolgirl's case of nerves. As Marianne describes the situation, she felt threatened with a dissolution of self, which could well have been the result of seeing herself as academically inadequate, or more probably as socially so.

Despite the rigorous tutoring of Mary Norcross to help her pass the entrance requirements, and despite her mother's constant social pressure, she was simply a college freshman overwhelmed with an unfamiliar world. In the fall of 1908, when Marianne was a senior, a local family from Carlisle sent their daughter, Elsie Johnston, to Bryn Mawr. Mrs. Johnston, the girl's mother, wrote to Marianne to thank her for watching over Elsie. By this time, of course, Moore was a self-confident upperclasswoman, and could easily act the role of protector. Mrs. Johnston does mention, however, that Elsie reported the "hazing" was not too bad. Such hazing, which may have entailed little physical strain but considerable emotional pressure, would likely have been a part of Marianne's first semester, too. Though Moore was very well accustomed to the teasing and playful hostility of her mother and brother, she may have misconstrued the tone of her classmates' initiation rites. Always very pacific in her temperament, she was often very shy in her first meeting with people. This shyness often led her to act with something like a ritualistic decorum, and while such a personality trait is usually developed before a person is of college age, the experience of her first year away from home may have left an indelible mark.

Six decades after her freshman year, Moore was to write a poem in honor of Katharine McBride, then the president of Bryn Mawr College. The poem includes these lines:

> Students—foster-plants of scholarship—
> at the beginning of the year,
> bewildered by anxiety and opportunity
> in the vibrant dried-leaf-tinctured autumn air,
> pause and capitulate, compelled to ponder
> intimations of divinity—

The clever phrase here, "foster-plants of scholarship," alludes to the students' displacement of their parentage, their substitution of one nurturing family circle for another. But the lines also show how the experience generates considerable anxiety as well as opportunity. The phrase "intimations of divinity" recalls the title of Wordsworth's great ode, "Intimations of Immortality," and adds to Moore's poem a further concern with the subject of personal growth and individuation. The poem will end with the lines that praise President McBride for "her exceptional unpresidential constant: / a liking for people as they are." It is hard not to hear in this poem a record of Moore's half-buried memory of the traumatic experience of her first term away from home, as well as a covert criticism of M. Carey Thomas' perhaps too-presidential constant of demanding more and yet more of her students, rather than accepting them as they are. "The free believe in Destiny, not Fate," says another line of the poem; in such a boldly axiomatic claim, Moore registers her struggle with the power and disruptiveness involved in personal growth.

The incident of her homesickness could very well account in part for Moore's need to be "armored" against the pressures of daily life, especially if those pressures involved self-generated standards of achievement and duty. The incident also shows how Mrs. Moore was to exercise a vigilant watch over her daughter, and how she was to become ever more unstinting in the great concern she had developed as her children's sole parent. But it appears that Mrs. Moore never considered withdrawing Marianne from Bryn Mawr; she was encouraging but adamant in her advice to her daughter to persevere through discipline and self-control. By counseling her in everything from what schedule she should adopt in writing letters (Mrs. Moore suggested Marianne follow her practice of not writing letters on the Sabbath, for example), to how she should store her summer hat, Marianne's mother treated her almost like a project in the formation of a vigilant will. In one of the family letters, sent in a "circle" from Mother to Warner to Marianne and back to Mother, Mrs. Moore reminded both children that the three of them were like a chosen people. This letter, dated October 19, 1905, must have reached Marianne in the midst of her homesickness. It contained a long sketch of the history of Puritanism and ended by urging the children to bear their burden directly.

What is most surprising about the incident is how thoroughly Moore seems to have recovered. Warner's visit to the Bryn Mawr campus a few days before Christmas may have helped, and was perhaps arranged to reassure Marianne. In one letter home in the middle of December, she says she wants to do nothing but write and write letters home, though she has nothing to say. This indicates a lingering homesickness, of course, but it also shows how writing itself has to become in part an outlet for her anxieties, a theme she mentions several times in the next four years. By March, 1906, the early spring of her freshman year, she is able to write with aplomb about such people as George Bernard Shaw, then a figure of great controversy and advanced ideas, referring to him as an ordinary man who coarsely desired to startle people, this in reference to her recent reading of *Man and Superman*. Such *sang froid* from a college freshman is rather startling, even in someone with Moore's highly developed literary sensibility. Part of this may well have been due to her desire to assure those who had any doubts about the propriety of her literary ambitions that she was quite capable of making mature judgments. And part of it is due to her high spirits and lovely sense of mockery, for she was often able gently to satirize all forms of literary and cultural pretensions, even her own. Such high standards regarding the expression of any belief, spiritual or artistic, were to become a constant part of her self-image. It is also true that she would glean from Shaw a great many of her advanced social attitudes over the next four years. This shows how she was able to draw on authority figures without succumbing to undue or stiffening respect for them.

In her second freshman term, Moore was able to get caught up in the energy of intellectual and social growth at Bryn Mawr. But still all was not smooth. She was criticized in January by one of her teachers for submitting a paper that was a network of quotations. This is especially striking in light of her later use of quotations as one of her chief stylistic markers. She remarked to her mother that when looking over the quotations some charmed her so much that she felt the paper could survive on quotations alone. It was also during this term that she found an Episcopal service little more than nature worship, and she was not at all surprised that people were converted at a revivalist meeting she attended (though apparently she herself resisted). Her religious feelings were always to be found somewhere between unbridled enthusiasm and a distrust of pantheistic vagueness. Her love of animals was already quite evident, and she enthusiastically sent home a picture of a John Gilpin horse she had found. Slowly but surely her sense of her own tastes and judgments was asserting itself, and the undertow of the first weeks away from home was losing its threatening force. During the May Day festivities at the end of her freshman year, Marianne appeared in fancy medieval costume, complete with lace and puffed sleeves, playing her part in a pageant that included maypole and Morris dances as well as dramatic performances. This celebration occurred only once every four years at Bryn Mawr, so Marianne was able to end her first year of college on a very distinctive note.

During the summer months of 1906, Marianne traveled to Silver Bay overlooking Lake George, New York, to attend a Bible school, which was really more of a conference center than a school. This was probably arranged through the Norcrosses and the ministry in Carlisle. Young women from a number of colleges, such as Vassar, also attended. In subsequent summers she attended other Bible camps, while Warner often pursued summer jobs, such as one working on a bridge with a construction crew outside Atlantic City. In the summer of 1907, he worked on a farm in Greencastle, Pennsylvania, while Marianne again attended a Bible school. Marianne, however, spent only six weeks or so at these camps and devoted some of her remaining free time in the summer to writing stories and poems. Warner's jobs often lasted throughout the summer, and then Marianne and Mrs. Moore would spend time with Mary Norcross at the Mountain House.

By the fall term of 1906, at the beginning of her sophomore year, Moore's sense of herself as a writer was to be largely shaped by her commitment to *Tipyn O'Bob*. (The title, by the way, means "a little bit of everyone," reflecting the Welsh origins of many of the communities in that part of Pennsylvania.) In the first week of October, she contemplated taking a part-time job at the college library to help with her tuition, but her mother strongly objected. This was probably a result of the freshman year incident, which Mrs. Moore would naturally attribute to overwork. Instead, Marianne took on the job of delivering copies of "Typ" in return for a free subscription. In January, 1907, she published her first story in the magazine, a brief effort called "Yorrocks." In writing home to report the news, she was rather blasé about it. Marianne also begins a pattern here where she complains about the self-consciousness that affects her writing. At this same time she turned over to the editor her second effort, called "A Bit of Tapestry." She was upset that the editor wanted her to change the ending so as to make it a love story, something she reluctantly consented to do. Presumably, since the published story ends with a happy resolution, her first impulse was to have the lovers in the story not be united. The story's theme of misunderstanding between friends or intimates and their consequent separation was to become an important one for her in the next few years.

In the middle of November she told her mother about a story in progress, which she proposes to call "The Man and the Minstrel." The characters' names, Angealetto and Vasco, are in keeping with the world of medieval romance she creates in her other stories of this time. However, this story doesn't survive, at least not in the form she describes it, though it may have been radically changed into "Yorrocks" or even "A Bit of Tapestry." What is striking is that it was to contain an incident in which a brother and sister have a scrap on a sailing ship off Monhegan. None of her other college stories have a brother and sister in them; in fact, all the blood relationships in the stories are just outside the nuclear family: uncles, nephews, and so on. The scrap between siblings could have been based on autobiographical incident, but the fact that many of the subsequent stories deal with various kinds of friction between intimates suggests how Marianne was exploring the whole area of the finicky balance of affections between adolescents who share their secret desires with one another.

Marianne published three stories in "Typ" during her sophomore year: the two mentioned above and "The Discouraged Poet," whose very title indicates how the theme of identification as an artist had become important to her. The story especially reveals a young writer's self-consciousness, for in it an aspiring poet decides to give up his art, and his wise mentor is able to deceive him into continuing it while creating the impression that it is the young poet's own decision. The task of writing, especially if conceived as a vocation, represented for Marianne the challenge of self-presentation, which entailed using the language of others while trying to define her own style. The threats to the young artist were essentially two: she might lose herself in her own concerns, or she would lack the maturity to say anything meaningful. It is also during her spring term as a sophomore that she suggests she will write an essay called "The Futility of Introspection." She mentions in December that the meter of Browning's long poems is disturbingly in her head. In April, she hears a lecture on Whitman's prosody. These concerns with rhythm and meter would resurface repeatedly throughout her life. She also writes home that she has adopted a theory that it always pays to be comfortably and fashionably dressed. The presentation of material was a key to its inner value.

Also during her sophomore year Marianne was to switch allegiances from a classmate named Margaret (Margie) to Peggy James, the daughter of William and the niece of the novelist. Margie, the classmate about whom Moore talked most frequently in the first term of her sophomore year, was an editor of the "Typ" and the person who first requested that Moore submit work for the magazine. (Marianne never reports her last name in her letters home, so an absolutely positive identification is not possible. It may be that this friend was Margaret Ayer [Barnes], who was an editor at the magazine and a member of the class of 1907. Many years later she had some success as a novelist, having resumed writing during a period of convalescence after an accident.) This young woman represented someone who had the maturity—or at least the appearance of maturity—for which Moore hungered. Margie may also have been someone who reminded Marianne of Mary Norcross, an artist and a maturer person with a clear sense of her own purposes in life. It was her close involvement with Margie that for a while raised for Moore many of the interconnected issues of friendship, sensitivity, and social acceptance. Several of her other friends objected to Margie, perhaps because they were jealous of her hold over Moore, or because she was reserved and distant at times. By the spring of 1907, Moore writes home to say she is giving Margie up, but not until after several months of irresolution and self-questioning had been occasioned by this friendship. In this letter she also talks of the attention that her publications in "Typ" have begun to bring her, though, again in good Puritan fashion, she calls such fame a delusion. At the same time she laments that the stories have not provoked a response from the people she most admires. At this period, writing is for Moore a means of social acceptance as well as a release for what she was to call "expressionary need."

Margie had been a friend largely through association with the "Typ" where she had been one of the controlling influences. Clearly, Marianne respected Margie's artistic opinions, and perhaps her talent as a writer as well. However, as Moore told her mother, Margie was difficult to get along with socially, being moody and changeable. From several letters home it became clear to Mrs. Moore that her daughter was too much under the influence of this older classmate. But despite the counsel of her mother, Marianne was increasingly affected with her affection for Margie, and this despite Margie's apparently being less than popular with her peers. No doubt some of the anxiety of the freshman year was still unresolved, and Marianne grew more and more enraptured with Margie as a role model while simultaneously more frustrated by her as a friend. In April, when Marianne was elected to the editorial board of

"Typ" and Margie was no longer associated with it, Marianne wrote home that she had apparently taken Margie's spot. Indeed, it is possible to speculate that Margie might have graduated in 1907. In any case, this incident epitomizes the psychological identification and displacement that accompanies maturation, but in Marianne's case the fact the friend was a writer and isolated from her peers is clearly significant. In retrospect it is clear that taking Margie's place on the editorial board of "Typ" was a sort of emotional displacement of the problems of friendship by the duties of writing. In her remaining years at Bryn Mawr, Moore's friendships and artistic development are constantly interwoven.

The winter of 1906–7 saw Moore writing home, in something like good Puritan fashion, to say that rebellion and despair are harder for her to control than her ambition. The rebellion and despair were probably in large measure the result of the extremely heavy academic load she was trying to master, for she seems to have been largely enthusiastic about her social burdens, despite their growing pressures. Her literary ambition was beginning to grow, however. In March, 1907, one of her teachers remarked of her two published stories that they reminded her of Rossetti. The compliment was immediately qualified, however, as the teacher added that Rossetti did not "think his poems." This remark recalls Matthew Arnold's suggestion that the Romantics would have been better poets if they had known more. For Moore poetry was to be, if anything, an act of intelligence, a way of situating the mind in the world, whether this involved emotion or erudition or ironic evasiveness. Responding to her teacher's reaction in a letter home, Marianne says she'd been working very hard on her stories as far as their ideas went and furthermore that she'd had to appeal to the Dean to defer writing a paper because of her workload. In the meantime, Moore says that good writing depends on simple, sensitive depiction of small things, this after reading Stevenson's *Treasure Island.* Her stories, as we will see, are much closer to Rossetti than to Stevenson, but still the remark shows how early on Moore was attracted to an aesthetic of accuracy and "small things."

A week after her election to "Typ" at the beginning of April, 1907, Moore referred to Peggy James as one of her new and favorite friends. Many letters during her sophomore and junior years mention Peggy, though the relationship, like the one with Margie, clearly had its ups and downs. There is a long period, late in her junior year, when Moore doesn't mention Peggy at all. Peggy's appearance on the scene shortly after the exit of Margie suggests that Moore needed a close soulmate to whom she could talk freely of matters artistic and literary. Moore told her mother that what she liked about Peggy was her ability to be at ease with literature, and to say things like, "Yes, I care for Hamlet a great deal." It was the sort of remark she and Warner might refer to as "droll" and is evidence of an attitude that clearly overlaps an important part of Marianne's own sensibility.

In June, 1907, between their sophomore and junior years, Peggy sent Moore some of her poems. Moore had asked to see them earlier, but Peggy was sending them now only on the understanding that they not be shown to anyone. Peggy was very emotional, and cried each time the school year ended at Bryn Mawr. But this particular summer she was reading Emerson's *Essays*, and, judging from the one poem that survives, may well have focused on the philosopher's reflections on "Friendship." The poem, sent from the James's home in Chocorua, New Hampshire, begins with a fairly standard description of nature:

> The hills wave on in undulating line
> Smiling and green and pleasant to the eye
> The faint autumnal breezes sway the pine
> And fleecy clouds are clustered in the sky.

After seven more stanzas, in which despair and melancholy begin to dominate, the poem manages an upbeat ending. With an unnamed companion standing with her, the speaker can attest that she "feels no more dismayed." In the letter that accompanied this poem, Peggy told Marianne, "I love you very much you know." A few weeks later another letter says that now she is feeling much better and her plans include reading a lot of philosophy this summer.

The next summer Peggy was able to send a very different sort of letter, but one that probably made a considerable impression on Marianne. Writing on her uncle's embossed stationery, headed "Lamb House, Rye, Sussex," Peggy told of her adventures in London with her father and his brother, Henry. She begins by thanking Marianne for the gift of a handmade handkerchief, an example of Marianne's own skill. She then goes on to relate how, after a four-day stay in Rye, "we struck London again, and Harry joined in." The group, which included Peg-

gy's parents, went to see "Cyrano de Bergerac," with the famous Co-
quelin in the starring role. After the performance, Uncle Henry,
according to Peggy, "said cooly 'it's too melodramatic, isn't it?' " This
remark enraged Peggy, who had been deeply moved by the experience
of the play, and she was only able with great restraint to keep her
temper. She was obviously as independent in her opinions, especially
considering her elders, as was Marianne. In the same London stay, she
also mentioned having lunch with a long-haired artist, who, it turns
out, was none other than Roger Fry, the famous critic and expounder
of Post-impressionism in England. Peggy was also "devouring" Meredith, so apparently her tastes were still more attuned to the late Victorian writers than the early modernists.

Peggy James is also the likely model, in part, for the female artist in
"Wisdom and Virtue," a story that Moore published in her senior year
and that she described as containing many "Peggyisms." The story
concerns a young woman's difficulty in making choices about her vocation, and so can easily be based on Marianne herself. Later in life
Moore developed and maintained friendships with a circle of women,
chief among them Hildegarde Watson, the wife of one of the editors of
The Dial, and Louise Crane, a wealthy heiress to a papermaking fortune, who was to become one of the executors of the Moore estate.
These women provided Moore with access to a very advantageous social
world, one that she might not otherwise have enjoyed. For a writer like
Moore, who in very important ways equated social style and artistic
sensitivity, these early and late sets of relationships were of great importance and benefit. For that matter, when Moore first established for
herself a public role as a writer of importance in the late 1930's, she did
so in large part through the honors and esteem bestowed on her by Bryn
Mawr.

Somewhat ironically, it is in the spring of 1907 that Moore, then an
upper sophomore, was advised by her teachers at Bryn Mawr not to be
an English major. This advice was based largely on her performance in
English classes as a writer of essays. It was felt, she wrote to her mother,
that her written assignments weren't composed enough. This meant
that her thinking was not as logical as her teachers demanded, and that
she was already showing signs of the use of something like metonymic
development—the movement from part to part by associative logic,

rather than the overall shaping of an argument by some explicitly coherent plan—that was to characterize the structure of her best poems. The advice bothered Moore, but she was for the first time being too dutiful and respecting of authority to set herself explicitly against her teachers. Part of her strategy in this matter was to present her writing, to herself and to her mother, as something "adjunct" to the more serious, but as yet unspecified, business of her life. In this regard, she turned eventually to a major in history and politics, though in the past she has mistakenly been described as having majored in biology. Her English teachers, especially a Miss Donnelly, turned out not to be her favorites, and she came to confide and trust in Mr. de Laguna, who taught philosophy and government courses. An exception to this was her teacher in "Imitative Prose," Miss King, who was to strengthen Moore's sense of the importance of inherited forms and styles of writing. King's course was built on a close examination of the devices of such prose stylists as Sir Thomas Browne, Francis Bacon, and Samuel Johnson. In her final year she proclaims Miss King the best teacher she's had, and she was often to cite such seventeenth-century prose writers as Bacon and Browne as major influences on her own style.

At the start of her junior year, comfortably settled into her room at 35 Pembroke East, Moore had become fully acclimated to Bryn Mawr, and she was about to expand her sense of herself and her vocation in important ways. She published two poems and four stories in "Typ" that year, her largest output of any college year. During the summer of 1907, Warner had argued, somewhat chauvinistically, that Bryn Mawr was not really providing a good education, comparing it to a technical college. But Moore's reading and the range of her cultural experience in her final two years at Bryn Mawr give the lie to such a claim. One chief item in this expanded range was Ibsen, especially "The Doll's House," which Marianne saw performed and recommended warmly to her mother. The didactic role of the artist, a role epitomized by the sense of social reform in Ibsen, enters more and more into her discussion of art at this time.

Of course, the feminist themes of Ibsen also figured largely in her admiration for this artist. However, she also continued to approach art from an aesthetic point of view, at one time writing to her mother about the importance of being disinterested and removed from personal desire in one's writing. The two strands of modernist literature—the aesthetic and the moral—were both very present to Moore's imagination, and she felt the attraction of both in defining her own artistic identity.

Moore heard a lecture by the social reformer Jane Addams of Hull House at the end of her sophomore year. She pronounced it wonderful, and discussed suffragism with her teacher Miss Donnelly during the following fall, but she was also continuing to write her stories. Mrs. Moore was perhaps her daughter's severest critic, then and throughout her life, and not only in a literary sense, as she was also constantly advising her daughter not to run after Margie and such friends as Peggy James. The extreme temperamental cautiousness of her mother in such matters was something that Moore at once struggled against and internalized.

But the fall term of her junior year was to conclude for Moore with a real triumph, the appearance of her story, "Pym," in the January, 1908 issue of "Typ." She described this as the best thing she had yet written, and though her writing would cause her considerable self-doubt along the way, she was very elated over this particular work. She borrowed a phrase from Henry James to describe her latest effort: "a generation of nervous moods." In November, while working on "Pym," she said that she wanted to stir things up both morally and intellectually and yet retain the sound of a sage and a conservative. She wasn't at all sure how she could manage this, however. At this time she was doing editorial work by reading other people's work for "Typ" and her letters home are filled with words (mostly expletives and filler) that are frequently crossed out, all clear signs that she has become extremely self-conscious about questions of style and precision.

In December, 1907, she visited Washington, D.C., and there met Warner. The trip was an important part of her effort to further her education in terms of both social awareness and artistic excellence. She attended the opening of the U. S. Senate (perhaps as part of her interest in her new major, politics), where she saw several senators she recognized. She also observed Teddy Roosevelt attending church and ebulliently expressed a wish to have him come and give the commencement address at Bryn Mawr. She also paid a visit to the Corcoran Gallery, where she saw work by John Singer Sargent, William Chase, and Childe Hassam. Two months later, she mentions a long walk she has taken with Peggy James and their discussion about plans to visit art galleries in New York City. Her horizons were surely expanding, and in ways that were definitely aesthetic as well as social.

After the beginning of the new year, 1908, Marianne began corresponding with a young woman named Marcet Haldeman, later Haldeman-Julius. Marcet had recently been a Bryn Mawr student who left the college abruptly for reasons that are not clear—possibly over the prospect of family moves. She returned to her home in Cedarcliff, Illinois, and within three months had moved to Kansas City. In any case, Marcet had already formed a close friendship with Marianne and maintained it through correspondence for the next eighteen months or so. Her letters afford a rare opportunity to hear how Marianne's classmates discussed their friendships and daily activities. The first letter from Marcet (those from Marianne referred to by Marcet are not available and perhaps do not survive) says that she will keep Marianne's letters and destroy those of Peggy, presumably Peggy James. The letter is filled with gossip, much of it innocent, though some of it about heartfelt reactions to slights and backbiting, and some of it expressive of tender and intimate feelings. Marcet praises Marianne's red hair and advises her to take up only with friends who prove true. She sends thanks for a valentine poem Marianne had written her, in which she is called a "fairy." Frances (possibly Frances Browne, who was to be a longtime friend of Marianne's) is criticized, and then the criticism is apologized for, perhaps because Marianne took exception to it. She asks Marianne to send her her latest story, presumably "Pym," published a few months previous, in the January, 1908 issue of "Typ."

Marcet also refers briefly to Margaret, apparently knowing of Marianne's loyalties, recently divided between Margaret and Peggy. She urges Marianne to be spontaneous and free, suggesting that she has heard Marianne's complaints about her own self-doubt. Her language is especially juvenile and romantic as she says Marianne is a poet who should "fling the purple vine about you in mad triumph." She reads aloud to her mother and four friends Marianne's recently published story, "The Boy and the Churl." Taking a bank job in Girard, Kansas, Marcet had plans to attend drama school, but by the summer of 1908 she was traveling in Italy. From there she brought back a reproduction of Botticelli's "Primavera," and sent it to Marianne, saying it resembled her. By the fall she is enrolled in the Sargent Dramatic Academy in New York City, eager to know all the gossip, and remarking on "The

Heart of a Blue Stocking," Miss Donnelly's article in the October, 1908 *Atlantic*. In January, 1909, she writes of having seen Isadora Duncan and a production of Wagner. She also insists Marianne spend part of a day with her when she comes to visit Hilda Sprague-Smith in the city. In May, she writes to excuse her lapse in correspondence, and then the letters cease with a July note congratulating Marianne on her graduation.

Read in the context of Marianne's letters to her mother, the letters of Marcet tell an intriguing story. In many ways they look back to Marianne's sophomore year when her anxiety over social and personal relations was still considerable. The letters show a social circle that is unstable and shifting, where confidences and sensitivities are exposed and yet frequently withdrawn. The main problem seems to be everyone's self-doubt. This self-doubt can be resolved, or at least manageably addressed, by resort to the world of poetry, since poems are both very intimate and testamentary. But Marianne's sense of her public identification as a poet is growing quickly at this time, as attested by the stories such as "Pym." While much self-doubt and ambiguity remain to be resolved, Marianne in her junior year is able to express to her mother, and also to authority figures at Bryn Mawr, a surer self-possession than she was able to exhibit to Marcet before her withdrawal in the winter of 1908. More important, however, may be how Marcet's letters reveal a relationship tied up with artistic expression. The story or the valentine poem becomes a token of one's friendship, a proof of sensitivity and a demonstration that one is willing to share, to open out that tender and guarded feeling. When Moore turns in her later life to a poetry of occasion, it must be read as also a poetry of friendship, an aesthetic of gift-giving, in which the token is at once an impersonal object and a deeply expressive gesture.

Later, during the spring term of 1908, an important incident occurred that shows a great deal about how Moore's sense of herself has grown and begun to stabilize. The president of the college, M. Carey Thomas, read one of Moore's poems, published in the "Typ," to the assembly at Chapel. This was either "To My Cup-bearer" or "The Sentimentalist," both of which appeared in the April, 1908 issue. We are not told precisely what the president made of the poem. But Moore does record that Thomas also mentioned one of the stories that had appeared in the same issue, "Philip the Sober." This story, according to

Thomas, was the sort of thing that made outsiders laugh at the college. She was probably referring to the story's archaic language and medieval setting. But what is interesting is Moore's reaction. She writes home to tell her mother that she is undaunted by such criticism; indeed, that she plans with feminine perversity to continue her writing with increased dedication. Some of this zeal may well have been inspired by her reading of Ibsen and her increasing attention to the issue of suffragism. Moore was able in this instance, moreover, to withstand the criticism of a feminist and an authority figure and to do so with an attitude that might well include an ironic sense of self-defense—what she calls her "feminine perversity." It may also be noteworthy to point out that a week after the president's mention of the story, Moore spent an afternoon in a cemetery near the college reading Milton. However Moore may have felt about the use of intelligence in poetry, she was quite prepared to investigate its emotional and atmospheric elements as well.

M. Carey Thomas was an influence upon Marianne through more than this one episode. If there was one authority figure who would rival Mrs. Moore, it was Thomas, whose influence extended into every corner of life at Bryn Mawr while Marianne was a student there. Though founded only in 1885, Bryn Mawr was to be moved sharply away from a school modeled on a religious seminary and toward the kind of secular institution that would compare favorably with long-established and male-dominated colleges. Thomas, only the college's second president, assumed a role in this transformation that is impossible to overestimate: she was at once typical of the large change in women's higher education and a distinctive spokesperson for its excellence. It was her plan, for example, to have the entrance examinations be as demanding as those of any other college. She even insisted that there be no Phi Beta Kappa chapter at the college, for she felt all of the students should strive equally for academic excellence. Often domineering, she more than once was involved in disputes with her faculty; once she was described in a Philadelphia newspaper as a "deceiving tyrant." Her unconventional nature, fostered in large measure by her Quaker background, was manifest in many ways. She invited her intimate friend Mary Garret to live with her in her residence on the college campus, for example, but she also hired single men to teach at Bryn Mawr, despite dire warnings about the possible consequences.

Thomas was an active presence in the school not only because of its small size, but because of her familiarity with all aspects of college life, having been its former dean. She frequently addressed the women students on all manner of subjects, from the use of slang in daily conversation to the most exalted sense of social obligations and personal character. By the end of her service as president, in 1922, she was taking to the Chapel's pulpit three times a week, speaking about travel on Mondays, books on Wednesdays, and politics on Fridays. She saw to it that the college offered a Ph.D. program in social work, and her founding in 1921 of a Summer School for Women in Industry was a striking educational innovation.

Herself a graduate of Cornell, with a higher degree from a European university (she became, in 1882, the first woman to be awarded a doctorate, *summa cum laude,* by the University of Zurich), Thomas was a strict taskmistress. She once made a tour of women's colleges and discovered to her horror that many of the female instructors had themselves never taken a college course. Determined not to let such slack standards prevail at Bryn Mawr, she was in many ways chiefly responsible for the heavy workload, intellectual rigor, and high sense of self-confidence imposed on Moore and her classmates. For example, Thomas had written in the February, 1908 issue of the *Journal of the Association of Collegiate Alumnae* that educators must "make it possible for the few women of creative and constitutive genius born in any generation to join the few men of genius in their generation in the service of their common race." The word "service" was not only a key term for Quakers, but one that entered into the vocabulary for higher education generally during this period. Of course, for Marianne it would also have echoes of life in the manse, where it applied to the role of women who aided a minister in his pastoral duties. In the same year, Thomas had become the first president of the College Equal Suffrage League, and she told Moore that she couldn't accept the idea of President Eliot of Harvard coming to talk at Bryn Mawr, considering how reactionary his views on women's education were. In this regard, she was in the vanguard of higher education for women in America.

But there were other features to Thomas's character and career that would have affected Moore. The college's emphasis on science and the need to take courses in sequence—as contrasted with the free elective system introduced at Harvard by Charles Eliot Norton—were a legacy of the Germanic style of instruction that Thomas herself had mastered in her postgraduate work. Thomas was also a secular person, even in some ways a worldly one, and she shocked her students when she announced from the pulpit that the happiest moment in her life was when she no longer believed in hellfire. Thomas could combine secular education and high moral probity in ways that startled some and impressed everyone. Bryn Mawr's influence on Marianne was considerable, and much of its impact can be traced more or less directly to the character of Thomas.

Perhaps more important, Thomas was capable of suppressing her own delight in art and matters of culture in favor of diligence and discipline. Always very widely read, she had written her thesis on *Sir Gawayne and the Green Knight*, but afterwards gave up any deep study of literature in favor of administration and educational reform. This attitude was perhaps what lay behind her "attack" on Marianne's story. Again, the emphasis on "service" as an ideal of social and personal value would not be especially conducive to the self-involvement of the artist. To the extent that Moore was still self-doubting about her artistic worth and commitment, Thomas's strictures may have set up a counterbalancing inner echo of resistance.

Many years later, in 1948, Moore was to review a book by Edith Finch called *Carey Thomas of Bryn Mawr*. The review is typical of Moore's prose, relying heavily on quotation, abrupt conjunctions and transitions, and a combination of elliptical and brusque tones. Nowhere does Moore mention Thomas's relation with Mary Garrett or her troubles with the faculty, but she does, however, stress Thomas's virtues to the point of exaggeration, even as she calls Edith Finch a "Vermeer of circumstance and idiosyncrasy." The review is a dynamically balanced model of tact and praise, and includes this paragraph:

> This account of frustration upon frustration and crusade after crusade to free the mind from legal and other barriers, extends in significance far beyond Quakerism, family, and period. Sobered by obstruction, with forces knit by the injustices of convention, Carey Thomas avowed what in life she contradicted: "Secrecy and guile are the only refuge of a down-trodden sex." The victim of gossip because she had discussed a scholastic matter with a German student on what her landlady termed "the betrothal sofa," she thence behaved as she had in the Cornell "elegant garden of young men," "not only with decorum but marked decorum" and said years after, "Bryn Mawr need not be the less guarded because it is good."

This writing owes a great deal to the tradition of hagiography, or saints' lives, where inner resolve not only overcomes all outward circumstance but the central character overleaps the standards of its society even while correcting its injustices ("not only with decorum but marked decorum"). But what also emerges is the theme of armoring ("need not be less guarded") and the trial by "obstruction," both themes Moore would have associated with her own memories of Bryn Mawr.

Many of Moore's classmates had highly developed senses of literary style, and the writing of stories and poems for *Tipyn O'Bob* was something that was approached seriously by a number of Moore's friends. A classmate, Margaret Morison, sent Moore a copy of a story called "The Spanish Jade," by Maurice Hewlett. The story appeared in the September, 1906 issue of *Harper's*, and Moore received it during the Thanksgiving break in 1907. What is striking about the story, which is otherwise a fairly typical romantic adventure story complete with an exotic setting, is how knowingly Morison has annotated it. For one sentence, which reads "God had been good, and the sword-flower a proof of that," she adds the marginal comment: "forced." In other places she pencils in comments such as "like Kipling but good" and "Meredith." In the margin next to the phrase "Esteban showed his fine teeth," she underlines the last two words and writes "typical villain." This sort of story, considering its atmospheric locale, is at least partially a model for the stories Moore published in *Tipyn O'Bob*. But the marginalia show that Moore and at least some of her classmates were reading contemporary fiction and using the principles of critical appraisal they had learned from their classes to assess such work. The literature of the classroom and the literature of the larger world outside Bryn Mawr were part of a common enterprise. And the issues of typicality and verisimilitude—issues that were to be a large part of Marianne's engagement with prose fiction, and her long debate with "realism"—were raised very early in her career as a writer.

During the spring term of her junior year, Moore began to write home about her sense of her own writing in ways that are partly defensive, partly assertive. Her indecision about writing as a vocation must have been affected not only by being identified as a writer by none other than the college's president, but also by the continuing skepticism of her mother. In her second year she had told her mother that she would let her read everything she wrote, but that she wouldn't write as well if she had her mother in mind. This tension, created by Marianne's having her mother as her "first" reader and most severe critic, would continue for many decades. Marianne obviously internalized her mother's very high standards, which alone would help account for her later habit of constantly revising her poems. But such internalization also accounts for the fact that the very vocation of writing is something that Moore is never completely at ease with. One letter, dated April 5, 1908, shows her in a moment of typical self-analysis, as she debated whether she could be a writer at all and avoid the pitfalls of egocentricity. She also muses on whether to follow the ethical concerns of Ibsen or the aesthetic path of Keats. What such concern shows, among other things, is how Moore already conceived of writing as a selection of one pure stylistic or moral alternative among others. Yet whatever one's stylistic choice, to be a writer meant inescapably to be an "egoist." This attitude marks Moore's writing throughout her life, for she may well be the modernist who most questions the value and effectiveness of an assertive artistic ego.

The spring term of her junior year was also one of considerable growth for Marianne, beyond the episode with Carey Thomas and the publication of "Pym." In February she wrote home to explain to her mother that distance and dissociation had become part of her aesthetic theory. In the same month she tells of how writing stories could leave her emotionally tangled and shrewish. This was also the time—in the first week of April—when she first decided to buy a black three-cornered hat. This particular tricorne, or one like it, was to become an indelible part of her public image many years later, but her concern with fashion was something that developed very consistently throughout her college years. Her mother, for her part, wrote back to give Marianne a detailed set of instructions on how to fold her napkin, how to eat rolls, and when to stand up and how; these things, Mrs. Moore urged, should become second nature to her. Marianne responded in part by praising Peggy James for being erratic, claiming that such people are most original and assuring her mother that she is at her best with Peggy.

Marianne also distinguished between bad poetry and bad prose, saying that since poetry is unconscious, one feels more foolish in writing it badly. She recognizes that poetry is a more sensitive production, but she also describes how a poem comes to her spontaneously, without any apparent emotional occasion. A few years later she would treat poetry more as an "objective" form of utterance, as if avoiding the most subjective dimensions of the lyric mode. In April she read Ibsen's *Pillars of Society* and, speaking of the ending of "The Doll's House," said it would be too frightening to any man of spirit. A few days later she told Warner that she was keen to have their mother read Ibsen. This is also the term when she first read William James's *Will to Believe,* and considered taking a course in pragmatism the following fall. Her interest in American philosophers had clearly been awakened. (She eventually took, however, a one-hour "elective" in biology, apparently in order to complete requirements for graduation.)

Moore also wrote home near the end of May about a classmate's mother who had a friend who was looking for poetry for the *Literary Digest,* a very traditional outlet. Mrs. Moore took up the hint and said she would submit some of Marianne's poems, probably retyping them for her at the Metzger Institute. Marianne had by this time become friendly with two English instructors, Miss Donnelly and Miss Fullerton, who apparently resided together. Marianne enjoyed tea with them and described their clothes in great detail. Miss Donnelly had recently published an article on finery for *The Atlantic Monthly,* which Marianne read without saying much about it to her mother. Since it is Miss Donnelly who suggested that she not major in English, Marianne's attitude toward these two women was somewhat ambiguous. One classmate writes her to say that if she is ever depressed by Miss Donnelly's criticism, she should recite to herself the uplifting poem by Arthur Hugh Clough, "Say Not the Struggle Nought Availeth." By the fall of her senior year she refers to Miss Donnelly as an artistic fake. There are strong hints in later correspondence that when she returned to Bryn Mawr, Marianne did not especially seek out these instructors at first, and in fact derived some ironic satisfaction from their acknowledgment of her achievements.

Donnelly's *Atlantic Monthly* essay, called "A Complaint on the Decay of Finery," reveals how much part of the world of Bryn Mawr was built upon a sensibility that many people now recall as the antithesis of the modern. The essay is clearly in the belletristic tradition, rife with allusions to other authors and cultural landmarks, and careful to build its argument on an appeal to sentiment rather than objective evidence. The argument itself centers on a lament that the fashion standards and variety of dress in previous ages have gone into decline: "Today finery

has become a thing for fashion-mongers to parley and trade with."
Donnelly attributes this decline not only to what she calls "the Convenient and the Correct," but also, implicitly, to the way the world of
commercial values has replaced transcendent aspirations. She further
suggests that "the hope of all finery is in art," for here the painter and
the author are able to record and pay proper homage to the dress of their
period. Donnelly concludes by claiming that the hope of art itself is in
"a good dressing." By this she means that it is important for the modern
artist to again take up finery as a subject, in fact "above all for the
student of manners to find in present-day fashion his great theme."
Joined in Donnelly's sensibility, art and fashion can even be read as
metaphors for one another, in large measure because they both rest on
a combination of contemplative self-refinement and escapist fantasy.

Though Marianne would eventually replace much of Donnelly's aesthetic nostalgia and belletristic sensibility for herself with a scientific
objectivity, the conclusion of this essay might well have struck her
forcefully. In later poems such as "Those Various Scalpels," "People's
Surroundings," and "New York," Marianne would turn to fashion and
dress as important focal points of her themes. Even later, she would
write directly about fashion and be a frequent contributor to women's
magazines in the last three decades of her life. Throughout her life,
especially with close female friends, fashion and propriety in clothing
would be sources of constant and deep concern for her. The sensibility
that Donnelly's essay reflects is also in some ways an important element
behind the short stories that Marianne was writing at Bryn Mawr. One
important equation survives from this sensibility to lend its strength to
her later poetry: the study of manners (and, by extension, morality) is
always to be linked to the surface appearances of cultural artifacts and
activities.

Moore's junior year ended with a commencement address that included the definition that "culture is the opposite of the obvious." The
speaker went on to suggest that the aesthetic man is always able to draw
two meanings from the plain facts. Presumably, the meanings included
the common sense or objective assessment, and the less explicit resonances and undercurrents in the situation. Such a formulation was
bound to appeal to the poet and fiction writer who was struggling with
the demands that self-reflection and self-awareness would make on an
impressionable young woman intent on achieving social mastery and

ease. The interrelationship between culture and nature is one of Moore's major themes—if not the most central of all the concerns in her poetry. The admixture of social experience, aesthetic forms, and personal expression that occupied so much of her imagination, and even her doubts, can best be seen as contributing to this central concern. By starting out in a close family circle that prized literature and self-expression through language, and by continuing in a somewhat closed society of privileged women in her college years, Moore was able to concentrate her energies on sharpening her ability to make distinctions, to appreciate ambiguity, and to prize a surety of style. Her love of animals and her occupation with the precise description of nature were ways of counterbalancing this engagement in the world of cultural codes and social structures. Moore was to remain a curious student throughout her life, and the object of her study was often the way culture and nature are interdependent forces, forces whose dynamic equilibrium did much to make up the very essence of being human.

As she approached her final year in college, Moore must have had the sort of apprehensions that confront every would-be graduate: what will happen to me when I finish? Will the final year be a true culmination? Where can the time have flown? The idea of Bryn Mawr as a special and protected place was reinforced by many details, as well as by the governing idea of education as something that demanded and deserved quiet concentration. Yet the larger world outside was always present. One rather stunning example of this was brought home to Moore by a long letter she received from a classmate who had graduated in the class of 1908, one year ahead of Moore. Caroline McCook does not seem to have written Moore prior to the summer of 1908, nor does her name figure largely in Moore's letters home. Perhaps a friendship flowered between them during Caroline's last year at Bryn Mawr. In any case, Caroline wrote Moore a long letter in June that she marked "Strictly Private." The letter began by telling of her visit to Princeton after her own commencement, where she met the head of the English Department, Willard Van Dyke, and his son, Henry. She had set a poem of Henry Van Dyke to music and performed it for him, at which point he was moved nearly to tears and offered her another poem. The incident is also marked by a very literate level of conversation, and may very well have been written specifically to impress Marianne with its many literary overtones. But more is to follow.

Caroline immediately went off to Europe for what amounts to a continental tour. While in London she saw Peggy James in the lobby at the performance of "Cyrano," a chance meeting she reported with great gusto. However, Peggy did not mention this incident to Moore, indicating that she was perhaps jealous, or she may have felt Caroline was too flighty to deserve comment. In any case, on the ship home, Caroline met a particularly handsome young man whom many of the other passengers had remarked on, and who had made his disdain for most young ladies very clear. It turned out that he was the nephew of none other than J. P. Morgan, then perhaps the richest man in America. A whirlwind courtship ensued, Caroline was proposed to and accepted, and by October of that year, the two were married. Caroline told Moore that her husband is also possessed of a fine literary skill, but that his letters and verses to her are too personal to quote. Needless to say, this incident was the cause of considerable gossip at Bryn Mawr, something of which Caroline was very aware. What was also striking is how Caroline importuned Moore to send her details about not only this gossip, but news of other classmates and teachers as well. Nearly a year later, Caroline wrote from Rome, reflecting on how self-centered life at Bryn Mawr was, and also how "grand" the wide world outside could be.

Marrying such a wealthy man might very well help any young woman find the world a grand place. Since Moore's letters to Caroline have not survived, it can only be a matter of speculation what her reaction to such a turn of events would have been. One might easily suspect some sense of irony mixed with a sense of bewilderment. Surely Moore would have appreciated the fact that in the space of one summer two of her classmates had written to her about the time they spent with the leading American novelist and the nephew of a multimillionaire. The roads that would eventually lead away from Bryn Mawr did not necessarily continue along a cloistered path. When Marianne had the opportunity to take a trip to New York City during her senior year, it made concrete a sense that the larger dimensions of the world were capable of being directly explored. Not everything need be learned from books, nor do the ideas and themes of literature present only escapist fantasies. Bryn Mawr, for all its distance from the worlds of commerce and strife, could still in some ways be an adequate testing ground.

In her senior year, Moore spent a lot of time reading French authors, continuing to develop her attitudes toward suffragism, and increasingly having her writing discussed by her teachers and classmates. She also discusses contemporary politics with Mr. de Laguna, and, surprised to hear he is voting for Bryan, counters that she prefers Taft, whom she praises as being free of self-interest. She would continue throughout her life to apply moral categories to her candidates for political office. Bryan, of course, represented the more progressive tendencies in American politics, though Taft had enjoyed the support of the liberal wing of the Republican party prior to his election. Both men were perceived as continuing the slowly developing middle course of Teddy Roosevelt, who in the preceding eight years as president had affirmed the rights of the larger public against the interests of both big business and labor. As it turned out, Taft was to alienate the liberal wing of his party and to lose the presidency to Wilson four years later, in 1912. This mistrust of "self-interest" formed the basis for Moore's praise of Herbert Hoover in later years, after her political judgments had become more explicitly conservative. Speculation could lead to a connection between the disinterestedness of the artist and the same quality she praised in the politician, but there are also other factors that contribute to Moore's later Republican loyalties, not the least being Warner's influence. But as with Thomas's reaction to her poem, Moore is able to proceed with zeal in the face of a contrary opinion voiced by someone in authority.

Continuing to have her experience of writing inflame her passions, Moore nevertheless vows in November to put aside concern for writerly emoluments and resign from the "Typ." But in the same letter she tells her mother of her plans to take the "Imitative Writing" course from Miss King, which was to introduce her in depth to the masters of English prose and heavily influence her aesthetic criteria. G. G. King was a friend of Gertrude Stein and she might have introduced some of her friend's writings to her students, though Stein had not yet formulated the highly experimental style that would make her a famous modernist. The class play, concerned with the "woman's question," was performed in the fall term of Marianne's senior year, with Peggy James playing the male lead. Just before the Christmas break, President Thomas gave Marianne passing marks for an oral exam in sight translation. In the same letter reporting this good news, she tells her mother that Mr. de Laguna has become her favorite teacher. In the next term, as graduation began to draw near, she also worried about what sort of job she might apply for. In February, for example, Mrs. Walker, a guidance counselor at Bryn Mawr, advised her that she didn't think she would like teaching and that she should pursue work as a secretary or in publishing. Moore herself admitted that her French and German weren't good enough to qualify her to teach, and that her command of languages was generally weak. The questions about employment after graduation would not be satisfactorily resolved until she arrived in New York City almost a decade later, and only then because of the circumstance of Warner's assignment at the Brooklyn Navy Yard.

During the term break of her senior year, even as her larger career concerns remained unresolved, Marianne had one of her most important experiences, especially in the light of later events in her life. This was a dazzling visit to New York City. Most critics have thought that her first visit to the city where she was to live for five decades took place in 1915, a visit often called the "Sojourn in the Whale," from a phrase Marianne used to refer to it. But this 1915 trip, important though it was, was preceded by one that lasted several days during the last week of January, 1909. This visit came about when Marianne accepted an invitation to stay with a classmate from Bryn Mawr, Hilda Sprague-Smith, whose wealthy parents lived on West 68th Street at the time. In two long letters to her mother (the first is 24 sheets long, written on both sides), dated February 2 and 4, Marianne gives abundant detail of all her activities during what was an extremely crowded trip. She begins by describing the mud and dirt of the unpaved streets and the bedlam created by the cabmen at the wharf. Central Park was lovely, covered all in snow. Her room at the home of the Sprague-Smiths' was elegant, with volumes of Kipling and James Russell Lowell on the shelves; this so impressed Marianne that she sketched the bindings and described their colors. The wealth was, by most measures, quite ostentatious. Hilda showed her father a check she had just received from her preferred stock certificates. The living room was adorned with two La-Farges and three Whistlers. Mr. Sprague-Smith taught modern languages at Columbia University, but he presumably had what was tactfully called "independent means." However, he was politically liberal, having founded and run a "People's Institute" that he described as a free league for working classes. Clearly an educated man, he spoke of values that had increasingly been identified as "progressive" and that reflected the major social reforms of the era. He asked Marianne if she were a socialist; she said she was, but not a Marxian. Sprague-Smith allowed as to how there was a good deal of socialism among artists; he opined that artists were bohemian and hence really proletariat. Marianne wrote to her mother that she heartily agreed. She told her host that all the Bryn Mawr girls were socialist in that they wanted clean politics, that she would have voted for Taft, and that she is really a gradualist. She then described for her mother the play they attended their first evening in the city, J. M. Barrie's "What Every Woman Knows." Marianne copied out from memory what amounts to virtually an entire scene of dialogue, with much detail about the actors and the scenery.

In her second letter, she continues her detailed descriptions. She visited the Tiffany studios and also saw St. Gaudens' statue of "Victory Leading General Sherman" at the southeast corner of Central Park. She attended a suffragist meeting with Mr. Sprague-Smith (and presumably Hilda, who, however, figures very little in the account of things). The meeting, sponsored by Sprague-Smith's "People's Institute," was attended by many notables from both the world of society and labor unions. John Dewey was there, as was Mrs. Stanton Blatch, the daughter of Elizabeth Cady Stanton, and Anne Morgan, the daughter of J. P. Morgan. The meeting took place in the great hall of Cooper Union in lower Manhattan. The main speaker was Prof. Charles Zeublin, introduced by Mr. Sprague-Smith. Professor Zeublin brought up few arguments that were new to Marianne, but instead played with words, saying that if politics weren't clean enough for women, then politics was treasonous. The newspaper account of the speech recorded one of his main points: "Suffrage is not a question of superiority or the lack of it; it is a question of personality, and that of the woman is as sacred as that of the man." Marianne also pointed out to her mother that English women were agitating successfully and had recently been granted the vote in municipal elections. The next evening Marianne attended a concert by Paderewski and described his playing in glowing and extended terms. All in all, this trip was the sort of exposure to metropolitan culture that a young woman from Carlisle, Pennsylvania, would hardly dare dream of.

Marianne told her mother that Bryn Mawr had recently been given a large gift for its endowment and that the faculty could now be much better paid. The connection between wealth and her own educational opportunities at Bryn Mawr could hardly have been more forcibly drawn. For much of her adult life Moore was beholden to wealthy people, from Bryher to Louise Crane, both heiresses to considerable fortunes, whose support for cultural enterprises was unstinting. In some ways many of Moore's references to culture have about them a very free and easy air. Consider, for just one example, the opening of her first poem in *Complete Poems:* "Dürer would have seen a reason for living / in a town like this. . . ." The meticulousness of Dürer as an observer of nature is part of the point of the rather casual tone here, as is its easy regulation in the service of his naturalism. But the world of early sixteenth-century German engravings is far removed from the small-town American scene she is describing. Yet these cultural points can be easily coordinated by anyone with the artistic and cultural literacy afforded by higher education. This education, in turn, rests upon a free and easy access to wealth that operates practically, in the manner of faculty salaries, and more "regally," in that it makes the private collection of such artistic masterpieces relatively unremarkable. Marianne closed the second letter to her mother by recalling how she read Browning's "Byron de Nos Jours" from a bound volume in Hilda's room, again drawing the binding's design for her mother. The focus of Browning's poem is the ironic perspective engendered by keeping alive a radical artistic and social vision in a later, less "romantic" age. It is conceivable that Marianne was alert to many of its ironies.

But what was perhaps the most abiding interest in Moore's senior year—outside of her concerns about graduation and its aftermath—was her growing curiosity about the relationship between the social and aesthetic realms, especially between socialism and art. Several factors contributed to this. Foremost was the constant discussion of the issues of suffragism and the "woman's question" on the Bryn Mawr campus. There was also the deepening involvement with Mr. de Laguna and his political concerns. Equally influential were such authors as Ibsen and Shaw, who were challenging the notion that the aesthetic realm automatically meant a form of escapism. There was also President Thomas's emphasis on the notion of "service." While Thomas was an elitist, and indeed even kept statistics on the ancestries of all her freshmen at Bryn Mawr (a result of eugenic views fairly widespread at the time), she still believed in political activism. But concern with evolution was a part of many people's progressive attitudes. In March of her senior year, for example, Moore attended a lecture by Professor Woodbridge of Columbia University, entitled "Consciousness and Evolution." The Arts and Crafts Movement, of which Mary Norcross was an adherent, was of course indebted not only to Ruskin but to William Morris, the English socialist, poet, and aesthetic theorist. All in all, Moore was part of an intellectual context that was sustained in large measure by a commitment to investigating the social role and responsibility of the modern artist. These concerns were immediately focused in the winter of 1909 when Moore read an article by Walter Crane in the January, 1892 issue of *The Atlantic Monthly* on why socialism appeals to artists. At the same time she was looking into an essay by a writer named Hobson, on "Ruskin as a Social Reformer." Four bound volumes of the *International Socialist Review* were also part of her research, presumably for Mr. de Laguna's course in General Philosophy. She heard a lecture on Nietzsche's *Thus Spoke Zarathustra* during the first week of April, bringing her exposure to the latest currents in intellectual discourse to a fitting culmination. The questions surrounding the possibility of a transcending social vision occupied much of Marianne's study as she approached graduation.

Moore was anything but conservative when it came to the "woman's question." In February, during her last term at Bryn Mawr, she wrote home at length to defend a radical position in an argument with her classmates about suffragism and women's rights generally. Women should have equal pay with men, especially if they have to raise children as well, she had insisted. The influence of Ibsen, and several suffragette speakers who had visited the Bryn Mawr campus, was making itself felt. Moore also wrote home about such visiting lecturers, a Miss Shaw among others, and told of suffragist meetings in Chapel. Miss Shaw spoke on February 13, her topic being "The Modern Democratic Ideal." Marianne reacted with deep feeling to this talk, saying that no one hearing it could fight against suffragism. The issues were not always treated with absolute seriousness, though, for she also mentions a suffragist "farce" staged by the students during a class picnic in the spring of 1907. As a freshman, Moore had complained about some anti-Semitic remarks her classmates were making, and now her social attitudes continued to develop along liberal lines. Not only did she speak against "class feeling," but she was deliberate in her defense of poor women, for example, in this same conversation about equal pay. Her stand against Bryan and in favor of Taft, when discussing the matter with Mr. de Laguna, shows that she was not consistently partisan in her politics, but she was more and more interested in such questions.

Meanwhile, she could report home about several triumphs in regard to her writing and publication. By March she is able to say that a Miss Crandall praises her poetry, but that as far as that goes she is quite spoiled on the subject, so Miss Crandall's approbation meant little to her. On May 25, 1907, back in her sophomore year, she had attended a performance of Shakespeare's "The Tempest" by the Ben Greet Players, an established repertory group, and was fascinated by the dramatic imagery of Caliban and the powerful transformation the actor was able to effect. She described the actor's voice in striking terms as being crowlike. She also remarked on Trinculo's line about Caliban: "A fish, or a man?" After gestating for two years, her poem, "Ennui," with the lines about the creature interchangeably man and fish, appeared in the March, 1909 "Typ":

> He often expressed
> A curious wish,
> To be interchangeably
> Man and fish;
> To nibble the bait
> Off the hook,
> Said he,
> And then slip away
> Like a ghost
> In the sea.

After this little poem was written, one of the faculty, a Mr. Sanders, told her the lines were "dithyramb glyconic." But this remark was quite unlike that of President Thomas's comments on "Philip the Sober." After discussing the poem with her, Sanders discussed it the next day in one of his classes, according to a friend of Marianne's who was there. He also told Marianne that he had brought the poem up with Miss Crandall, but had given up trying to explain it. Marianne feebly offered her own explanation, but then excused herself for writing things without any ideas in them. She may have been harking back to the teacher who compared her stories to Rossetti's, but then had said that Rossetti didn't "think" his poems. But, in a letter home dated March 15, 1909, she also says she had pleaded the privilege of her youth, and that if she waited for clear thought, she would lack incentive to write and would end up being too predictable. Here the lyric impulse is negotiating with the need for structure. A month earlier she had said her poems were sporadic, and she was amused when people praised them and treated them as if they were any normal sort of artistic achievement. The poem was from the unconscious in a way her prose was not, and the routine or drill needed to polish prose is replaced by a rhythm that is "caught" in her head without her even knowing what it's called.

What Mr. Sanders may not have seen is how the poem expressed Moore's divided state and her sense of an unstable self-image that wanted to flee into another dimension altogether. What is also apparent is that the image of escape is proceeded by an adroit move in which she is able to possess what one realm has offered her while not succumbing to the lure. Sanders was bold enough to rewrite the poem's last four lines to make them metrically smooth. His version read:

> "He'd nibble the bait
> like any man,
> And then take a weed
> and be fish again"—

In this version the mature professor, perhaps unwittingly, writes of a possible "sea change" that doesn't really occur, as the fish is content to consume weeds and be a fish. In the young woman's version the mythological creature negotiates both realms, human and ichthyic, though she needs a ghostly transformation to do so. Moore's poem, "The Plumet Basilisk," contained the lines about the man and fish when she published it over two decades later. This later poem would also end with an image of an undetectable disappearance.) At this same time she is also able to boldly tell her mother that what she calls "critical poetry" is the sort that has the strongest appeal to her since it is both impersonal and unforced. "Critical poetry" is presumably poetry with a satiric edge and that avoids effusive sentiment, just the sort of poetry that is to make up much of her first volume, in 1921.

When she apologized to Mr. Sanders that the poem "Ennui" had no idea in it, she may well have meant it didn't have the sort of direct or clearly implicit moral or thematic "statement" often demanded of poetry by those trained in late Victorian reading habits. In fact, she had first described "Ennui" to her mother as a verse of not very high character. For a college student who had not yet traveled widely and whose family background was somewhat tempered by religious morals, Moore was quite sophisticated about what sort of poetry she was writing, and she was also surprisingly able to judge it with abstract standards. Moreover, since the episode with President Thomas and "Philip the Sober," Marianne had gained considerably in her sense of herself as a writer. Now she was not only able to discuss one of her efforts with an authority figure, but was able to provide, at least to her current satisfaction, an explanation of the poem's origins and nature. On March 16, she included in a letter home another poem, "Rhyme on a Jelly Fish," about a creature from another realm. This is similar to "Ennui," but told more from the point of view of an outside, impersonal observer, one who watches as the jellyfish grows cloudy and floats away. It is not so much that these two poems, and others she was to write over the next decade or so, show that Marianne wanted to escape from moral concerns, as that she was intrigued by the lines of separation between realms. The reader is able to see these realms as, by turns, the realms of morality, aesthetics, or even politics.

But Moore's self-doubt could be not only the subject of her art but could sometimes even be directed against her writing. When in May of her senior year she was correcting proofs for "Wisdom and Virtue," the last story she was to publish in "Typ," she identified one of the characters, Uncle Duckworth, as the Mr. Sanders who had commented on her poem. The main character in this story is a female artist; this is perhaps the result of Moore's immersion in the arguments of suffragism. The main character at one point observes of her Uncle Duckworth that "emphasis was [not] placed on female professionalism." This story shows how the main character is intent on resisting her uncle's conservative social views and his attitude toward art. In fact, she has her female artist-character act quite like a slippery fish escaping to another realm instead of answering her uncle on his own terms. She wrote home the first week of May about an editor named Mr. Alexander, at the Ladies' Home Journal, with whom she had an interview, who gave her a long and salutary and galling speech on the fruitlessness of writing poetry; she told him that she wrote it as most people did, for the incidental gratification. Such a defensive dismissal of her motives for writing was something Moore would use later in life, even as she struggled with the gender-determined social role for a poet.

Only a few months short of graduation, Moore had another one of those horizon-expanding experiences, and this one seems to have come about in large measure by accident. While out walking one day she met a young woman she referred to as "Miss Haviland." This young woman, it turned out, had an uncle named Paul Haviland, who, she informed Moore, occupied a studio on Fifth Avenue near 33rd Street with a Mr. Alfred Stieglitz. This, of course, was the famous "251" Gallery, for many years a bastion of artistic modernism in New York, and one of the places Moore made a point of visiting during her second trip to the city in December, 1915. Miss Haviland took Moore back to her house and showed her photographs by her uncle. These were for Moore more striking than any paintings she had seen, and she told her mother that she was taken by storm when viewing them. The sharp-eyed, anti-sentimental aesthetic of Haviland would be just the thing to reinforce Moore's commitment to what she had earlier called "critical poetry." Coincidentally, Moore had recently taken out a book on color theory from the Bryn Mawr library, and she discussed the subject with Miss Haviland. Poems like "The Fish" and "In the Days of Prismatic Color" might well be traced back to this experience. Later, in the summer of 1910, Moore would write often about visual "scenes" in a way that suggested she had absorbed the retinal rigor of modern photography and painting.

The meeting with Miss Haviland was fortuitous, but it helped confirm Moore's dedication to the visual arts. Georgianna King may also have contributed to this feeling, because she was conversant with many of the latest developments in modern painting. And names such as Roger Fry, given her by Peggy James, would have led Moore's insatiable interests along the path of innovative movements such as Post-impressionism. Years later, Moore would even tell Ezra Pound that she thought painters were more genuinely experimental than the poets she knew. If her exposure to issues arising from suffragism and the progressive socialism of artists was part of Moore's entry into the ethical domain of the modernist sensibility, surely her exposure to visual artists such as Stieglitz and Haviland contributed to her fascination with aesthetic experience. Bryn Mawr was the place where both of these aspects of modern life were first presented to Moore and where she learned to treat them both with serious discrimination.

II. In earnest of merits

Like many artists before her, at some point Moore began to think of herself as a writer in a way that fully defined her nature. No longer would she write merely to express some momentary or unsettling feeling, but she would "make" literary works of art. Such an important shift occurred gradually, though it had clear markers. That Moore was thinking seriously about a career in the arts is supported by her attempts to get her poems published in national magazines during her college years. As early as the spring term of her junior year, as mentioned earlier, Moore was approached by a classmate whose mother felt Moore's poems should be submitted to the *Literary Digest*. This was indeed a national magazine, though of a decidedly unexperimental sort; it published an attack on the "new poetry" not many years later, just as Moore was breaking into *Poetry* and *The Egoist*. In the third week of April of her senior year, Moore asked her mother for help in copying out two poems for submission to *The Atlantic Monthly*. This, of course, was a much more prestigious outlet, and it shows that Moore was undaunted by her rejection by the *Literary Digest*, or at least that she realized the two magazines represented very different sorts of audiences. In the same letter in which she tells of the advice not to be an English major, in the spring of her sophomore year, Moore had presented the possibility of her artistic success in deflationary terms. Considering that many of her early reviewers, and many later readers as well, found her poetry dense and overly learned, this evaluation evidences a striking amount of self-knowledge. But still Moore could submit her work to such different places as *The Atlantic* and the *Literary Digest*, and this shows how her self-image was subject to constant fluctuation. What distinguishes Moore at this point from many other sensitive young adults is that her fluctuations seem to oscillate across extremes of both knowledge and doubt. Her grasp of modernist irony has very personal origins. But she also records, without comment, that *The Atlantic* sent the poems back the first week of May.

During her final term at college, Moore investigated several job possibilities, such as the interview with the *Ladies' Home Journal* mentioned earlier. She also was told by a classmate of a possible project helping a doctor in Baltimore write a book; another friend wrote to art school for her, but apparently nothing came of this. Evidently, the art school existed as a real possibility; years later Moore would tell people her first ambition was to have been a visual artist. The school involved was the Lyme School of Art in Connecticut, where one of her classmates studied. Moore was sent the brochure in the months immediately after her graduation, and several classmates asked her in letters that summer if her plans for being an artist were being fulfilled. But, though Moore continued to do pencil sketches and watercolors into her sixties, she was unable to pursue this particular avocation for the moment. Within a few years, however, some of her artwork would win modest prizes at the county fair in Carlisle.

She took a long walk with Peggy James on May 9, and sadly reported that her friend's scope of interests and concerns had narrowed. The dynamics of friendship were now involved with the phenomenon of people facing, or at least desiring, different social and vocational values. There was also the larger world to consider, something many of the young women often joked about uneasily, knowing all too well the special—and brief—status they enjoyed as college students. Near the end of May, Moore commented that philosophy, though abstract and infinite, was very much to her liking; this perhaps in part the continuing influence of Mr. de Laguna's teaching. She tells Warner that she still can't type well, and that she has many poems she wants to write and won't be ready to take a job until December, several months after graduation. On the list of books she wants as graduation presents she includes Whistler's *The Gentle Art of Making Enemies*, Pater, Sappho (translated by Wharton), a biography of St. Gaudens, and Xenophon. The young writer was clearly preparing to refine her sensibility further, as usual with a range of books from a wide spectrum of historical and aesthetic points of view.

Moore's poetry written during the Bryn Mawr years includes the eight poems she published in its literary magazine, as well as a few she copied out in her letters to her mother. Perhaps most striking of these published efforts are "Ennui," discussed earlier; a single quatrain called "Progress," which is reprinted under the title "I May, I Might, I Must," in the *Collected Poems;* and "To a Screen Maker." "Progress" is a poem about determination and self-definition. It may be the most well-mannered poem of rebellious feeling that Moore ever wrote, though its subtle metrics, with their accent on the consequentiality of "then" and the assertiveness of "I," suggest that Moore had many ways of saying daring things:

> If you will tell me why the fen
> appears impassable, I then
> will tell you why I think that I
> can get across it if I try.

This poem was not reprinted in book form for many years, until *O to Be a Dragon,* and again in the *Complete Poems.* The tenacity that it expresses is thus quirkily revealed in its publication history, with its "interlude" of almost five decades. The skill of "To a Screen Maker" is rather of a different order. Moore's first imagist-like poem, it was to be quoted, in a different version, by the then preeminent Imagist poet H.D., writing of Moore's poetry in an essay published in *The Egoist* in August, 1916. It shows Moore's early interest in objets d'art and the interplay between culture and nature that was to become her most enduring subject. The screen, of "weather-beaten laurel," the poet's wood, includes four carved figures: a dragon, a tree, a face, and a bower, complete with "a pointed passion flower / Hanging high." (In the version H.D. quotes Moore adds "a sea / Uniform like Tapestry," an early instance of Moore's penchant to see natural phenomena under the aegis of a cultural object.) Emblems of guarded security and "rustic" isolation, these figures suggest an artistic will both in their being carved and in their self-containment.

Another similar effort was an unpublished poem, quoted by Moore in one of her letters home, that offers gratitude to a classmate who has given her a yellow rose. This poem has several resonances. Not only does it inaugurate Moore's poetic concern with gifts and tokens, but it looks ahead to a painting of a yellow rose by E. E. Cummings, a painting Moore kept over her desk for decades. Such connections and associations between objects or events separated by long periods of time are typical of Moore's method of composition; they suggest in some sense that, for her, poetry writing was the creation, or perhaps the recirculation, of tokens of affection. There is also a poem from June,

1907, called "The Beginning of Discontent," that utilizes the idea of a token. Margaret Morison, one of her classmates, sent Moore a letter that month thanking Moore for a pin she had designed and given to Morison, who was also an editor on the *Tipyn O'Bob*. In this story the token marks one's own endurance, and by implication expresses self-doubt:

> "You know,"
> said I
> impressions grow
> and do not fade.
> And though it crumbles,
> that cornflower,
> the one who marked my
> place there, so,
> Has not forgotten me
> I know."

This poem, with its play between lasting impressions and fading mementos, suggests that Moore is troubled by friendships, especially as they are built on an uneasy mix between stability and change. At the same time the poem's counter-movement toward self-assurance shows how even with the slightest effort Moore was capable of creating resonance. But at Bryn Mawr it was in the world of fiction that Moore was to reveal her feelings most fully.

Moore's early stories form a remarkably integrated set of fictions, with a consistent genotype story and several recurring themes and moods. All in all, the stories grapple with and express Moore's early understanding of her art and her poetic vocation. Indeed, a great many of the situations and themes of the stories deal directly with artists and the convoluted decisions leading to an artistic vocation; those that do not treat this material deal instead with situations that can easily be read as allegories of such preoccupation. From the start of her college career Moore involved herself self-consciously with the nexus of forces made up of artistic ambition, moral duty, social decorum, and personal worth. These stories are clearly the work of a college student, albeit a very intelligent one, but they are also the work of someone who became, within a decade of graduation from Bryn Mawr, a daring and innovative modernist poet. In many ways remarkably pre-modernist, this body of fiction explores the world of a self-reflective artist faced with either the discomfiting interconnection of the aesthetic and the moral, or the agonized displacement of the one by the other.

Moore was to become a remarkably consistent artist, working with diligence on a body of writing that was to be much more intensive than extensive. She was also a thoroughly literary poet, for she had absorbed a great many influences and dealt with several "traditional" models even as she created her distinctively experimental verse. Her early fiction shows her at work on a tightly drawn set of themes and subjects that are at once borrowed from fin-de-siècle literary styles and yet made over into something very personal. There are many echoes of the aestheticism of the 1890's, but the stories are much more than faint echoes of stylistic masters. For example, all eight stories have a main character who is explicitly in the throes of indecision. Four of the eight have artists as characters, while six stories have a moment when the main character takes a long solitary walk. Seven of the stories have, as an important plot device, a visit by a single individual to another, solitary character. Three of the stories have an uncle and a nephew or niece, while another two have a guardian and his or her ward as characters. In no story does any relation drawn from the nuclear family appear: no father, mother, or siblings. The absence of the nuclear family may have been Moore's way of allowing her characters a fuller chance of self-development, but it may also have served as the source of the anxiety that many of her characters feel. In every story there is an emphasis on the environment as an expression of a character's life decision, and many have reference to the "woods" or a romanticized view of nature— the setting, often, for those solitary walks.

The immediate background of the stories, when seen in the light of such a survey, is obviously Bryn Mawr itself. Also woven into the stories was the atmosphere of the college itself, steeped as it was in Anglophilism and medieval motifs, as the mottoes carved on the college passageways and over the mantels in the main dining hall. The English flavor of the college was dependent on architecture and was to be reinforced by Moore's love of English literature from periods as different as the immediate past and the seventeenth century. Several of the stories are set in England, though Moore had not yet visited that country (this was to occur in 1911). The mottoes were to play an important role in Moore's imagination, and returning to Bryn Mawr years later she was to recall the powerful effect they had on her. One was the motto of the Earl of Pembroke, after whom Moore's dormitory building was named; translated freely it says, "That I may serve." It clearly embodied the notion that Carey Thomas addressed as "service," and also echoed the term used for life in the manse. Contributing as well to this sensibility were the gothic style of architecture and, perhaps most important of all, the generally monastic attitude toward higher education so strongly fostered by the president of the college.

In the four decades between 1870 and 1910, the percentage of all college students in America who were women virtually doubled, from twenty-one percent to just under forty percent. But despite this tremendous proportional increase, college-educated women still comprised less than four percent of the women of Moore's age in 1909. Moore was thus part of a large social movement in one sense, but she still had to count herself as a member of an elite part of society. Moore's early fiction reflects this combination: a background of large social change and a foreground occupied with developing a highly special distinction and motivation for herself. The flavor of Bryn Mawr was enhanced by the easy availability of a landscape that was made for long walks and solitary musings, a feature Moore often mentioned directly and indirectly in her letters home. There were also long walks taken with special friends, when questions of social standing or personal ambition could be explored in depth. It is no surprise, considering her environment as a student, that Moore's fiction would contain castles, servants, a constant preoccupation with transcendent values, and an otherworldly sense of adolescent self-reflectiveness. The conflict between the imaginative world of aesthetic release and the pressing world of moral duty was implicit in everyday life for Marianne at Bryn Mawr.

But these early stories are intriguing not simply because they reflect her environment. A careful reading also reveals how patterned and even compulsive are Moore's concerns as well as her artistic habits. For example, each of the first four stories seems to be rewritten in another, later story so as to provide a different resolution. "The Discouraged Poet" is rewritten as "A Pilgrim," as the young wandering poet of the first story leaves his guardian, but chooses to remain with the paternal figure in the second version. In "Pym" the artist in his bohemian situation appears to return to the support of his uncle, whereas in "Wisdom and Virtue" the female artist decides to continue on her independent course. In "A Bit of Tapestry" (which, as we saw, the editor of the "Typ" induced Moore to change) the man clearly accepts the woman he wants to marry, but only after she appears to reject him. Then in "Philip the Sober" the prince at first rejects the countess, but accepts her once she has revealed to him the nature of his own indecisiveness. In "Yorrocks" the irritation that exists between the two characters results in a separation, while in "The Boy and the Churl" the abrasiveness is resolved. It is this clear patterning of conflicts and resolutions that contributes to the feeling of the remarkable consistency of the "world" of Moore's stories. When we add to this set of four pairings the further realization that the stories have overlapping themes, such as the question of artistic or marital commitment and the indecisiveness attendant upon both, we can see that all the stories are virtual versions of one another.

Granted this integration of theme, motif, and atmosphere, the genotypical "story behind the stories," contains a number of clues to the inner recesses of Moore's preoccupations and anxieties. The genotype is formed by any number of forces, one of which is the daily condition of Moore as she traveled fairly frequently back and forth between Carlisle and Bryn Mawr, as well as the many visits classmates paid one another, often under circumstances much more formal than those in today's colleges. These exchanged visits often were fairly elaborate, complete with written invitations, dressing up, and the serving of teas and assorted savories. It was during such visits that Moore developed her social skills, and no doubt came to invest in such skills a lifelong sense of importance and value. Her sense of her own individuality had already been keenly developed by her mother's attitude toward propriety and the constant awareness of her own social background: at once the child of a professional class and yet without any sure sense of economic stability. Such concerns, while not directly addressed by the stories, are everywhere present in them, like a bass note that contributes much to the continuance of the complex counterpoint of awareness.

The genotype might be expressed in this way: An isolated artistic character is visited by (or visits) someone who represents a challenge to the artist's vocation, but this challenge only objectifies the artist's own misgivings, and the visit prompts the artist to reconsider the nature of his or her commitment. The artist decides to create or leave behind or display some token of that commitment as an "earnest" of the meritorious achievement that he or she eventually hopes to produce. "Earnest" is used in the legal sense of something given to bind a bargain and to serve as a sign of what will eventually be produced or delivered. It is rather like a simulacrum of a work of art, an effigy of the symbolic meanings that will follow. The misgivings of the artist are expressed through a series of personal irritations, irritations that center on small points of personal contact, misunderstanding, and sensitivity. The world of the stories closely echoes the world described in Marcet Haldeman's letters to Marianne. The genotype is thus entwined with the question of the relationship between art and life, more specifically the problem as it was posed by the aestheticism of the late 1890's: one must choose perfection of the life or of the work.

Yeats and Whistler, that other great aesthete, stand behind these stories. Moore directly refers to "the land of heart's desire" in "A Pilgrim," and to the "gentle art of making enemies" in "Yorrocks." What Yeats and Whistler represented to Moore in the first decade of the new century was not only the severity of artistic discipline and the rejection of all that is merely conventional in art, but also the challenge of replacing the traditional moral and social ethos with aesthetic values. Another obvious model at this time was Henry James, especially for his stories focused on artists, such as "The Real Thing" (1892) and "The Lesson of the Master " (1892). Here the argument of replacing spiritual and moral values by a commitment to artistic discipline is given one of its strongest formulations. Surely Moore felt drawn to such a substitution but just as surely she remained wary of its consequences: the beginning of a conflict that was to stay with her for the next half century or more. In Moore there is a distinctive struggle between traditional moral and spiritual values on the one hand, and the replacement of those means of cultural continuity with a self-justifying, self-conscious, yet skeptical, attitude toward the claims of art to be autonomous.

Though she never announces it directly as such, the theme of all the stories that deal with artists or vocational choices is that the full and unfettered recognition of the desires of the individual is a necessary but not a sufficient part of becoming modern. In an undated letter, Margaret Morison wrote to Moore to give her a reference to an essay by William James called "The Powers of Men," published in *American* magazine in October, 1907. This is a popular account of an essay James published months earlier in the *Philosophical Review*. Morison tells Moore, "I should think [it] would be interesting to you since your subject is Individualism." Obviously this is a reference to some paper or longer project that Moore was working on (this suggests the letter may have been sent in the summer before her senior year), and one that she discussed with her friends. Moore had earlier read James's *Will to Believe* and had hoped to take a course in pragmatism in her senior year. Morison goes on to synopsize the article in this way: James argues that most people fail to realize the full potential of their character; this is obvious when it is considered how their powers increase in emergency situations. Concern for the autonomy of the individual, as well as an ironic sense of the negative results that can stem from such an egocentric focus, would remain one of Moore's chief preoccupations throughout her life. Her own sense of her powers in college was full of conflict about just how much "self-realization" was necessary for any truly cultured individual, and how easily such powers could be swallowed up by egocentric concerns.

In "Wisdom and Virtue," the last story to be published in *Tipyn O'Bob*, Moore has her female character say, "Angels are not happier than men because they are better than men, but because they don't investigate each other's spheres." Here, the very tones recall those of a typical Henry James character, while the message obviously looks ahead to Moore's concern with artistic autonomy and the need for "armor." And in "Pym" Moore presents the point most explicitly and in tones that are both arch and potentially self-mocking. The narrator, named Alexander (alluding to the youthful conqueror of worlds), says, "It is all in the copy-books that a man may lay down his life for his individualism. I begin to be convinced." Moore ironically points out that such a claim for individual autonomy is universally recorded, and in unextraordinary contexts; this suggests the sort of wry deflating humor with which the poet was to test so many received opinions. We must also ask how aware the character is of the Christlike echoes of the formulation, and if he is being deliberately blasphemous. Likewise, the archness of the second line may very well recall the famous Yeatsian opening line, "I will arise and go now, and go to Innisfree," though Moore may be undercutting the self-assurance and imperiousness in the Irish poet's formulation. In any case, the content of her character's claim about copy-books and individualism combines in its content and its tonal qualification the core of her ambivalence about this very modern concern.

This leads to a story that merits special consideration in the light of the genotype. "Pym" is the most interesting and accomplished of Moore's early stories, and, as mentioned earlier, she saw it as a "generation of nervous moods." It originally bore the title "Reflections of a Literary Man," and in small scope it reiterates the form of those many stories about the achievement of autonomy through the discovery of one's artistic vocation. One of its main characters is drawn from life: the uncle was based on Professor Sanders. The central theme is of an older person's difficulty in trying to comprehend someone's hidden motives and sensitivity. Written in the form of five diary entries covering a three-week period, the story tells of Alexander Pym's attempts to prove himself as a writer. The other two characters are Alexander's uncle Stanford and a friend named Cob. The uncle clearly represents social propriety, whereas Cob stands for the artistic audience and approval that Alexander desperately seeks. Uncle Stanford wants the narrator to return to respectability and take up law; by story's end, the young man, in the best tradition of Jamesian ambiguity, takes up a pen and begins to write to "Dear Uncle—." This could be the acquiescence of a typical adolescent rebel, or it could be the first truly autonomous act the artist undertakes. (In June, 1909, Margaret Morison, after reading "Wisdom and Virtue," wrote to say that she "loved the description of the apartment . . . but I didn't get much out of the conversation." It was not the last time Moore's use of ambiguity would be frustrating to her audience.)

In "Pym," Moore's portrait of the artist as a young man nevertheless strikes a note that is rather tame and unmessy, since the only dramatic incident occurs when Alexander visits Cob, and, quite without provocation, destroys the manuscript he had brought along to show his friend. Immediately after this act of self-destructiveness, Alexander complains about loneliness and the strain of analytic work. Reflecting further, he says that he had been too bullheaded at the start of his writing career and will now "consecrate" himself to toil. What Alexander seems to have resolved, assuming he has not yet decided to study law, is, at the very least, to give over his writing "experiment" for the time being in favor of more worldly experience. "Nothing done for effect is worth the cost," he says in the closing lines of the story, and we can hear in this axiom Moore's mistrust of the elevation of style over content. The story conveys a considerable frustration in the face of a literary calling and can even be read as a plea for a utilitarian resolution.

Of course Pym's melodramatic destruction of his manuscript during the visit to Cob might well be ironic, since it is something done "for effect." This destruction can also be seen as the withdrawal of the token that Pym offers the world as his sign of merit. But it is a very equivocal token, for as he himself says, "Manuscript and hesitations seek the flames together." When he later decides to abandon his current lodgings, all he plans to take with him are a rug with a snail-shell design (symbolizing his self-sufficiency, perhaps) and a portrait, "of the unknown lady in the green dress." These two possessions are his tokens, respectively, of independence and transcendent commitment. But since he argues that his "love of the material" interferes with his newfound dedication, they in fact become tokens of his disdain for the material world of things. Here Moore could easily be again employing irony, just as Joyce did when he had his rebellious and self-sufficient artist, Stephen Daedalus, end his book with his mother packing his clothes for him. Moore shows us that Pym is still divided in his attitude toward life and his own commitments; he uses physical objects as tokens to convey his non-attachment to the physical, and says of his physical surroundings, "They are not an everlasting test of one's bigness." As measures of Pym's character both the tokens of the manuscript as well as the rug and portrait equivocate about what he is willing to give, and to give up, in his quest for life's meaning. The story could easily be read as implying that Pym will maintain, albeit subversively, his commitment to a non-utilitarian set of values.

The narrator's "mess," however, might be summed up as the mess of self-consciousness and an ambiguous sense of self-worth. Here Moore resembles other artists, such as Eliot and Yeats, who found in their quest for honest subjectivity and firm purpose a consciousness that brought about a paradoxical weakening of the self. At one point in the story, Pym has these circular reflections:

> I come to the conclusion that I talk about myself unduly. I don't as a general thing approve of putting checks on spontaneity. One's conversational and more practical abilities suffer somehow, through a straining to appear judicial and mature. One gets to the point where coercion is

indispensable to accomplishment. It is advisable, however, for the young
at all costs to avoid in the presence of the old and critical the appearance
of being effervescent.

It is hard not to read this passage as an "in" joke addressed by Moore to
her classmates, a way of advising them how to behave toward others,
but perhaps especially toward her. She was quite conscious about her
intention to put recognizable traits from her friends into her stories. In
any case, it clearly shows the strain of social intercourse as it was carried
on at Bryn Mawr among women whose awareness was constantly being
drawn to standards of behavior and sensibility. Whatever Moore wanted
to affirm by way of her own spontaneity, she quite obviously felt that
the way she was perceived by others made up a real and inescapable part
of maturity. Style, in short, was the question as much as it was the
answer, to both artistic and personal quandaries.

Besides Moore's equivocating mistrust of artistic poses and stylistic
display, "Pym" also shows us a glance at Moore's developing poetic. She
has Alexander formulate his sense of writing and its purposes and methods, against the pressure of both Uncle Stanford and Cob. He tells his
uncle that "there are times when I should give anything on earth to
have writing a matter of indifference to me." But he quickly recovers his
sense of purpose and continues, with a "modestly askance" look, saying
that "it is undeniably convenient, in time of expressionary need, to be
able to say things to the point." He adds that he likes "the thing for
the element of personal adventure in it." Many of Moore's later formulations about her poetic, from the early essay, "The Accented Syllable" (1916) to the later formulations of "Idiosyncrasy and Technique"
(1956), can be read as expanded versions of this double sense of expressionary need and personal adventure. Art, in this context, is best
understood as something impersonally pursued, yet at the same time it
is the fullest expression of one's personality. The real tension between
these two models was not something Moore could resolve easily. Behind this formulation of the tension is heard an analog of the Romantic
paradox stated by Coleridge when he defined art as rooted in "the desire
for spontaneity and the need for order." Moore became a post-Romantic
poet in her acceptance of the value of impersonality, but she was far
from being an unexpressive poet.

In 1943, Moore, continuing to explore questions she first took up as
a college student, published in *The Nation* what is perhaps her most

directly moral poem, "In Distrust of Merits." The theme of the poem is that one's merits are only as good as one's deeds, and any promise or verbal commitment to virtue must be redeemed by what she calls "action or beauty." Two phrases from this poem summarize the fictional experiments of Moore's Bryn Mawr years. First, she says "the blessed deeds bless / the halo." Reading such a line in a thoroughgoing modernist fashion, one could paraphrase it as a version of the clarion call of existentialism: existence precedes essence, no sign or token of value automatically bestows value. Second, "We are / not competent to / make our vows." Here Moore's irony comes fully into play, because she has, only one sentence earlier, made a promise. If we aren't competent to make our vows, surely no one can make them for us. No one can speak for us in our most important commitments, and yet we cannot speak competently for ourselves. The early stories teach us that we offer tokens of our selves, essentially in earnest of the merits we would attain, because in part, as Kierkegaard said, we are not able to measure our own moral worth. Only others can do that for us. Of course, in the early stories the experience of this moral and psychological paradox was not built on the same depth of experience as was the poem written in the midst of World War II, when Moore was past her fifty-fifth year. But even in the voice of the twenty-year-old college student, keen to please her superiors and vindicate her own individual worth, the dominant tone is one of self-reflexive irony. That self-reflexive irony is, of course, one of the main elements in the modernist vision, but for Moore it was also one of the more important legacies of her years at Bryn Mawr.

Chapter 3

HOME AT CARLISLE: 343 NORTH HANOVER STREET

I. "I am hopping slowly . . . from my perch"

After graduation from Bryn Mawr in 1909, Moore's life was poised between several possibilities for a career, or at least a "position" in the world, and a quietly settled home life. Warner had, of course, graduated a year earlier from Yale, had decided to enter clerical life, and was soon to enroll in Princeton Theological Seminary. Slowly Mary Warner Moore would adjust her sights and begin to conceive of a life of service in the manse for herself and her daughter. But in the meantime Moore faced the same sort of limbo that had affected Mary Norcross a decade earlier. In terms of the secular and modern world, what was she suited for by her education at Bryn Mawr? Was there anything she could do in Carlisle that would count as fully exercising her abilities? And if not Carlisle, where might she go? The years immediately after college were an odd time for Moore, since in many ways she returned to the formidable bonds of family, but she surely felt the loss of the social world of college, a world she had finally mastered after some difficulty. There was her writing to consider, and also her ideals of service, which might be put to the test in a teaching job. But both these possibilities were far from sure since she would still have much to do to prove herself in either area. She remained preoccupied by her poetry throughout this period, but she was still unable to find a place for herself where the writer's vocation could flourish.

Following the advice of a counselor at Bryn Mawr, she enrolled in courses at Carlisle Commercial College, courses that included short-hand and typing. Moore probably decided to do this while still at college, for she signed the entry register at the Commercial College on June 7, 1909. This period of instruction helped prepare her for her eventual employment at the Carlisle Indian School, and later at the Hudson Park Branch Library in New York City. But the courses were far from congenial for Moore, though she worked at them diligently. In the spring of 1910, she remarked to Warner that if her shorthand speed reached 120 words per minute she would pounce on a job. But the sort of job she envisioned, where secretarial skills of a high order would be necessary, never materialized. Instead, in terms of any gainful employ-ment, she seemed to have followed the path of circumstance more than of ambition. However, the path of writing was becoming clearer and clearer in her mind, and the seven years or so she spent in Carlisle after graduation and before her move to New York City were occupied with a growing interest in, and devotion to, poetry.

Warner had continued on his way after college by taking a teaching job at the Pingry School for boys in Elizabeth, New Jersey. During the next few years he was to be romantically attracted to several young women—quite seriously in two or three cases. The family correspon-dence shows as one of its main concerns the question of Warner's future, in terms of a profession and a wife. This focus may be somewhat exaggerated due to the fact that for several periods (in the fall of 1911, for example) there are few letters if any from Moore and her mother to Warner, though all of his to them do survive. Apparently Warner lost the letters sent to him, as he was moving fairly frequently in this period, and so the story has to be inferred from what his responses contain. Warner was not nearly as detailed in his letters as his mother, but he does refer at least briefly to the news from home. His letters reveal a young man, who eventually decides to become a minister, entering upon a social world of wealth and position, and seeing himself in increasingly self-assured terms. But the passage into full independence for Warner, while clearly more successful at this time than that of his sister, still takes place under the watchful eye of Mrs. Moore. Such independence may have been a source of value and self-worth for both Warner and his sister, but it was not to be granted without a struggle.

He spent some time with his sister vacationing in the summer of

1909 at Mackinac Island, returning home through Pittsburgh, where they visited relatives. Moore, for her part, had written her brother earlier in the summer about the new poems she was eager to submit to magazines. Throughout the next two years or so, she occasionally mentions her poetry to Warner, and almost always with some reference to its commercial possibility. She may well have meant to explain to him and to their mother that poetry was not a completely "otherworldly" activity. She may also have placed some of her own faith in herself as poet by using the notion of selling her poems. It was also perhaps a way that Moore had of managing her image as a poet in the modern world, free of the deeply subjective and theatrical dimension of creativity that was a hallmark of the Romantic era. In any case, she was writing often, and submitted poems frequently to many magazines all along the spectrum of commercial success, including the *Smart Set,* edited by H. L. Mencken; *McClure's, The Atlantic Monthly,* and *The Century.* She never published in any of these magazines. Her main outlet for her work for the next five years was *The Lantern,* the Bryn Mawr publication that succeeded *Tipyn O'Bob.* She published sixteen poems in this magazine before she settled in New York. Before her breakthrough with appearances in *The Egoist* and *Poetry* in the spring of 1915, this was the only place where her poems were published.

In the fall of 1909, Moore consulted a horoscope and jokingly wrote to her brother that the needle pointed to "Warrior" and that she was getting fixed up with a smart little breastplate and a jointed tail protector. The image of self-protectiveness could be playfully tossed about, but it only partially concealed both her resolution and her frustration. Warner in the meantime had become attracted to a young woman named Helen, and it was to be the most protracted and painful of his relationships prior to his marriage. In October his mother wrote him a long letter full of advice that included an admonition not to let Helen master him and not to let his own attitudes show so plainly. This exceptionally fine tuning of one's social and personal manner is something that Mrs. Moore was concerned about throughout Warner's education and entry into society. It is safe to assume that such detailed attention to the adjustment of social tone and attitude was extended to her daughter as well. What is important here is not just the sense of self-protection that is being striven for, but also the complex sense of balance. It was just such a sensibility that Moore herself had labored to develop at Bryn Mawr. The armor imagery and its attendant themes in her poetry must be seen as not just a defense but also a means to attain an active control over the world.

Though Moore was to enter her twenties in these years, her letters to her brother contain much that is childishly playful: the puns, corny jokes, and use of pet animal names continue unabatedly. Mrs. Moore continues to watch over her son, even to the point of advising him not to wear a frock coat to church but to be sure and wear nice gloves. Warner writes his sister a birthday letter in 1909 that contains five dollars and that offers the observation that her whiskers are as stiff as those of basilisks. He also relays the axiom that people no longer ask where you graduated from but what you can do. The ideology of the self-made man takes shape, even as he remarks that Helen's family is planning a trip to Iowa in their private railroad car. In December he gets a letter of introduction from Henry Sloane Coffin of the Madison Avenue Presbyterian Church to a Reverend Francis Brown of 700 Park Avenue. Within two months he announces that he plans to begin his preparation for the ministry by attending the Princeton Theological Seminary, starting in the fall of 1910. In the meantime his affections have shifted from Helen to a young woman named Louise. But the relationship with Helen is not yet complete.

Moore wrote to tell her brother that she should be practicing her shorthand, but instead she has chosen to reread her poems. She also sent him what is apparently her first typed letter, dated January 13, 1910, though for much of her life she remains a correspondent who prefers to write her letters by hand. She tells him a week later that her flageolet has been neglected, apparently referring to her verse writing; the image of the flageolet, a small flutelike instrument, reappears in "The Jerboa," a poem she would publish in 1932. Her poetry is filled with such references, which look at first to be fanciful metaphors, but frequently have a very personal resonance as well. Throughout her life as a writer, Moore was a recycler of images and references from many years previous; she also established something like a private set of references with her brother that became important coded elements in her poems. These coded images constitute a private allegory and spring from that strong distinctive sense of family bonding the Moores shared. When Warner reacts to his sister's poetry, it is almost always as a highly privileged reader.

Warner continued to have a great many social engagements, almost all of them with people of wealth and social standing. Moore tells him that she has recently seen a production of a play at the Indian School in Carlisle. Within eight months she will be teaching there. She was busy that spring reading stories to the children at the Carlisle Public Library, thereby beginning the work that she would later pursue in New York. But at the moment, in the summer of 1910, the big change in her life was her decision to take a position at the Melvil Dewey Camp at Lake Placid, New York.

The camp had been set up by Melvil Dewey as a commercial vacation spot and also as headquarters for Dewey's many "reform" activities. Melvil (né Melville) Dewey was a social reformer of the type well known in the later nineteenth and early twentieth centuries in America. At Columbia, for example, where he had started the first school of library science in 1888, women were admitted, much to the chagrin of many at the time. He was perhaps best known as the man who promoted a system of simplified spelling and the decimal classification system still in use in many libraries throughout the country. He represented a way for Moore to gain useful employment and still feel she was performing an important social service.

Perhaps Moore heard of the position at the camp through her work at the library in Carlisle, or even through the Commercial College. In either case, she went up on August 1, 1910, to take a job at a salary of $50 per month. Her main task was doing proofreading for the many publications Dewey sponsored and wrote, as well as taking dictation from Dewey himself. Dewey's school was to represent a mixture of bucolic retirement and the ethos of modernization, and so was similar to Moore's recent experiences at Bryn Mawr and in Carlisle. The camp's setting was idyllic, and Moore spent a great deal of time there taking walks in the forest and sleeping out on the porch of the main dormitory. She described Dewey to her mother as an enemy of cant and a strong individual; it was a liberating experience to be in his presence. He also taught her to answer letters by typing the carbon of the response onto the back of the original letter, a practice Moore adopted for the remainder of her life.

But it was not just as a commercial venture that this job offered new horizons. Evidently Moore had a number of suitors from among the young men who worked at the camp or who vacationed there. By the middle of August, she writes Warner that she has seven suitors, all dandies. But by September she tells him that she uses the word suitor loosely, since she appears not to take any of the young men seriously. Complicating the situation was the fact that a Mrs. Heston was keen to try her hand at matchmaking, but she complained that there was no more odious institution in modern society than a matchmaker. This is one of the last references, negative as it is, in Moore's correspondence with her brother over her entertaining the idea of matrimony for herself. At the same time, her plans for staying at Lake Placid were uncertain. In late August she asked her mother to send up her winter coat, implying that she meant to stay for several months at least. But a week later she says she's coming home the first week in October, as the camp has fallen on hard times financially and is cutting back on the staff. By October 13, she is en route home to Carlisle, and stops off in Albany to see Cousin Mary Shoemaker, from the Craig branch of the family.

But before Moore left Lake Placid, she had achieved at least some modest sense of herself in the larger world. Even on the train up to the camp she was writing home descriptions that owed something to the spirit of the photographs she was shown by Miss Haviland before she left Bryn Mawr. Looking out the window of the train, she saw a little boy in a blue suit leading a white dog up a lavender hill, and she said that this was surely modern art. In the same letter she describes how all along the way the trunks of pine trees were strewn in the ravines like a box of matches dropped in a darning basket. These observations and images are poised between the picturesque late Victorian aesthetic she was clearly beholden to in her Bryn Mawr stories and the emerging Imagist aesthetic only then beginning to appear in various publications. The use of sharp rather than vaporous detail, the emphasis on aesthetic distance as opposed to sentiment or even presumed empathy, and the notion of juxtaposed details and perspectives would begin to show up in her own poetry very shortly. One good example of the new style is "A Talisman," which she published less than eighteen months later, in the spring 1912 issue of *The Lantern*:

I.

Upon a splintered mast
Torn from the ship, and cast
Near her hull,

II.

A stumbling shepherd found,
Embedded in the ground,
A sea gull

III.

Of lapis lazuli;
A scarab of the sea,
With wings spread,

IV.

Curling its coral feet,
Parting its beak to greet,
Men long dead.

This transforms the things of nature into the things of artifice and culture, as do many of Moore's poems, and here it is done craftily with the break between the second and third stanza, which makes the bird over into a talisman almost "invisibly," as it were. The poem is without any of the late Victorian "emotional slither" that Ezra Pound was to condemn so forcibly, and yet its attitude toward death is essentially an aestheticizing one, in the tradition that stretches back to Keats at least. The Swinburnian influence that Moore described herself as being under at Bryn Mawr was giving way to a more modernist use of imagery and emotion.

Lake Placid was also a time of solitude for Moore, and she spent hours taking long walks, just as she had done at Bryn Mawr. On one of these she walked twelve miles, and visited John Brown's grave. On another she met by accident a man named Gilbert Hursh, as she spelled his name, of the *New York Globe,* and they discussed journalism, which had once been one of her possible career choices. Another accident afforded her an opportunity: apparently a cat was killed at the camp, and Moore decided to dissect it. Her training in the biology laboratory at Bryn Mawr stood her in good stead, for she accomplished the operation and reported it in detail to her mother. This shows that her love of animals was not a weakhearted one that would preclude scientific experiment, but was rather tied to her sense of curiosity and her desire to know about structure and complex form in the service of simple

expressive movement and gesture. When it came to the animal king-
dom, she was much more a natural historian than a sentimental sym-
bolizer.

On her twenty-third birthday she announced to Warner her plans
to travel the following summer to England with her mother. She confessed that she was concerned about where she might live. The question of where to live is increasingly tied up with Warner's vocation;
she would be content to live apart for three years while he attends the
seminary at Princeton. But it is clear that they wish to rejoin as a
family after this. He invites them to move to Union, New Jersey, for
the period of his continued schooling, and, somewhat surprisingly,
Moore indicates she has no desire to settle in New York City. Warner
is still resolving to break off relations with Helen, and begins to voice
the sort of "muscular Christianity" that will increasingly dominate his
spiritual vocabulary in the coming years. He speaks of his own stub-
born ferocity, and the images of warfare recur often when he discusses
spiritual struggle.

Near the end of 1910, Moore complains to Warner that she enjoys
rallies and "fests" but that she is hampered by what people think of her
and what she thinks of them. She knows her worries are needless, but
she cannot shake them; the social concerns from Bryn Mawr are still
with her. By January she has received her diploma from the Carlisle
Commercial College, though she has no immediate prospect of employment. Warner has received an invitation to Helen's wedding,
which he sends on to Mrs. Moore after drawing a sketch of a thumbed
nose next to the bride's name; Mrs. Moore chided him about this
offense against taste. The winter brought news from Charles Erdman of
Princeton Theological Seminary welcoming Warner into next fall's
class. Marianne complains that she has not yet impressed the world
with an abundance of verse; while her state may be somewhat passive,
her language describing it has some of the muscular tone of her brother's
self-image. In March she tells her brother that it is time to hop from her
perch and make something of herself. She is trying to make her poetry
less and less sentimental, and in the spring of 1910 publishes a short
poem called "My senses do not deceive me," and in the spring of the
following year one called "Things are what they seem." But she continues to be preoccupied with her own vulnerability as a writer and

concerned about criticism from an unappreciative world. The balance
and the armor are not yet fully "made."

Three poems by Moore in a sense grow out of these concerns as well
as out of one another, for they are early examples of her habit of
rewriting poems, sometimes so thoroughly as to create what must be
regarded as a completely new poem. The three related poems are entitled "My Lantern," "Elfride, Making Epigrams," and "To be Liked by
You Would Be a Calamity." The first was published in *The Lantern* in
1910, the second was scheduled to appear in *The Lantern* but apparently
never did; the third was published in 1916, in a magazine called *Chimaera*, edited by William Benét. Each poem is about the need for
self-protection and the threat of misunderstanding, of being transformed
or "mistranslated" into someone else's system. Here is the first version:

> The banners unfurled by the warden
> Float
> Up high in the air and sink down; the
> Moat
> Is black as a plume on a casque; my
> Light
> Like a patch of high light on a flask, makes
> Night
> A gibbering goblin that bars the way—
> So noisy, familiar, and safe by day.

The protective moat anticipates the nest that Moore wants unequivocally to leave, while her light is presumably her poetic vision, like the
glint on a sealed container that succeeds in illuminating little beyond
her awareness that the familiar light of day is far away. In one of her
own copies of this poem she had written two alternate titles, "A Preciosity" and "The Fearful Critic," as well as an alternate last line about
grinding bones for bread, which becomes the ending of the second
poem.

The second poem takes up the imagery of the banners and the light
on the flask, to retell rather dramatically the story of two characters
from Hardy's novel *A Pair of Blue Eyes*, who are literary rivals of a sort,
the one having negatively reviewed the other's novel. The subject of
the poem is a woman writer named Elfride:

> Devices as slender as pennons float
> Up high in the air and sink down; the moat
>   Encases her head like a casque;
>   Her light
>   Sorties, like high lights on a flask,
>   Requite
> Men with torrents of toads from lips of lead
> And then grind up her bones to make their bread.

The imagery here of casques and flasks, of promisingly high thoughts and threateningly low results, dramatizes a situation similar to that of "My Lantern," but if anything the medieval images make the emotions less clear. That Elfride has written a medieval novel may be what had drawn Moore to her in the first place, but the emotional energy of the poem is concealed behind a highly literary allusiveness. It is difficult to tell clearly if the solitary female figure has triumphed over the assaultive men, or if her victory is restricted to a purely imaginative realm.

By the time she comes to write the third poem, Moore drops the medieval imagery and the archaic diction in favor of more direct speech, but she also uses a Latinate vocabulary that courts a certain archness of tone and gesture. She has also moved from a poetry of images to one of discourse, and this will be important for her development in the next several years. One thing that marks the first book of poems that Moore publishes is a discursive structure in her lyrics: her poems often have an argument to make, a strong stance built out of a mixture of values and emotions that the speaker is sometimes more intent on defending than she is on expounding or clarifying. The link with the second version of the poem is made with the opening phrase, which is taken from the narrator in Hardy's novel as he summarizes Elfride's encounter with her unsympathetic critic:

> "Attack is more piquant than concord," but when
>   You tell me frankly that you would like to feel
>   My flesh beneath your feet,
>   I'm all abroad; I can but put my weapon up, and
>   Bow you out.

Gesticulation, it is half the language—
   Let unsheathed gesticulation be the steel
      Your courtesy must meet,
         Since to your hearing words are mute which to my senses
         Are a shout.

This is a bold poem in which the poet tells her critic how she is to be understood. What is more, she instructs him on the very nature of language itself, telling him that strong gesticulation is only part of what words are capable of, and that she has some other kind of register, some more subtly tuned sensibility than what he is used to. She is not about to offer her "flesh" for him to trample on. Read in the light of the two preceding poems, she has turned her defensiveness about her "light" into a very self-assertive and self-defining surety. The successive "versions" of this poem reveal a poet who sees expression as a form of combat, so that the element of self-protectiveness that she requires is more than a layer added to the self. It is, instead, a crucial element of that self and a way of assuring that expression and selfhood are possible. In the first "version" of the poem there is only one person; in the second, other people are referred to; in the third, other people are actually addressed. Again, armor can be regarded as essentially defensive, but it also allows its wearer to enter the fray in the first place; there is more than one kind of steel.

By the spring of 1911, Moore and her mother were completing their plans to go to England, their first time abroad and a trip that Warner was encouraging. Moore went to Baltimore for some unspecified medical treatment, and while there visited the Walters Arts Gallery, continuing her interest in contemporary painting, and the Johns Hopkins Hospital. She also spent some time watching local baseball games and sporting events in Carlisle. She told Warner of her excitement over the sports jargon, citing such examples as "swinging like a beer-sign," and "the old gum glove." She went as far as Easton, Pennsylvania, to watch a track meet between the Carlisle Indian School and Lafayette College. By May she had embarked on her first trip to England, a country she loved for its literature, and some of whose authors—not only Bacon, Johnson, and Blake, but also Saintsbury, George Moore, and Edith Sitwell—were to be important influences on her aesthetic.

On the last day of May she was reading to children on board the ship, the *Friesland*, which sailed from Philadelphia, while her mother complained about the idle talk of her fellow passengers. For both of them the trip had an educational and cultural purpose. They were to spend much time in galleries and museums in both England and France, equipped with Baedekers, those handsome nineteenth-century guides to travel that contained much information of the sort Moore doted on. On board ship they produced a mock daily newspaper, complete with columns, headlines, and lots of word play and pet names, which they included in their daily letters to Warner. They arrived in Liverpool on June 7, and the letters to Warner that follow are filled with enthusiasm and colorful, tumbling detail. From Chester they write about the picturesque countryside: "You see cows standing around pools of water and hear birds singing just the way you do in 'tales' of Old England and billions of hedges." Their aesthetic senses were highly exercised and every historical site, it seemed, was on their itinerary, just as Warner was always on their minds: "We heard an anthem at the [Chester] Cathedral at Vesper service that was better than any opera I have ever heard, and I made a drawing. There will certainly be a hallelujah when we go round these places with old Bullifant ears 'en croupe.' "

They spent several days in the Lake Country, and near the end of June were in Scotland. The rather bizarre musical stones in the Keswick Museum drew their attention. They visited Grasmere, where Dorothy and Wordsworth had returned after their travels to Germany, and saw Dove Cottage as well, which may well have reminded them of "The Wren's Nest" in Kirkwood, with its white walls, flowers, and "clipped fancy shrubs just like a Pennocks bouquet," referring to a well-known Philadelphia florist. In Glasgow, Moore purchased some writing paper, a constant preoccupation with her, and was reading some books she had bought on the local birds. They went south toward London. The first week of July they reached Oxford, after visiting Warwick Castle and the town "about the size of Carlisle." In this beautiful university town they saw Reynolds' portrait of Dr. Johnson as well as the author's teapot and desk. It was behind Magdalen College, in the Isis, that she saw swans feeding, the same ones that she put into one of her best known poems, "Critics and Connoisseurs." In the portrait gallery at the Bodleian Library she saw a trencher plate from Sir Francis Drake's *Golden Hind* and copied out one of the mottoes engraved on it. She turned this into a poem that she published as "Councell to a Bachelor" in a 1913 issue of *The Lantern*, and later in a 1915 issue of *Poetry*:

> If thou bee younge
> Then marie not yett.
> If thou be old,
> Then no wyfe gett,
> For young men's wyves
> Will not bee taught,
> And old men's wyves
> Bee good for naught.

The medieval language and the use of an axiomatic or motto form would have appealed to Moore, and it is hard to overlook the fact that this reflection on the difficulty of balancing one's life situation might have had a special edge for her. Vacationing among the multitudes of evidence of human will and purpose, success and failure, the poet must have been aware of her own project and its current state of development.

Moore's first line to Warner from the capital was, "Having once seen London you will live in a blaze of glory all your life." She may well have been remembering Dr. Johnson's remark that when one is tired of London, one is tired of life. They stayed at 22 Upper Bedford Place, in Bloomsbury, near the British Museum, today the locale for many bed-and-breakfast hotels. The two travelers took several day trips from London, where they spent almost a month, seeing Hampton Court Palace and Windsor, as well as many sights in the capital itself. Carlyle's house in Chelsea and the Tate Gallery, with its Rossettis, Whistlers, Burne-Joneses, were evident highlights, but they also admired the fashionable crowds strolling around Piccadilly. Moore considered Dr. Johnson's unfinished pew in St. Clement Danes Church a "great desecration." She copied a scene from an Etruscan vase in the British Museum as well as an Assyrian leopard that she described as having "pig eyes." There was also the eccentric Soane Museum in Lincolns Inn Fields, where she saw an alabaster coffin of Seti I that a teacher had praised, and Hogarth's series, "The Rake's Progress," a favorite of hers. Moore also found time to go to Vigo Street, where she went into Elkin Mathews' Bookshop and purchased two volumes of poetry, *Personae* and *Exultations*, by Ezra Pound, which had been published by Mathews only two years before. She had probably read or heard about Pound, recently "exiled" from his home in Philadelphia to London, by way of local gossip or perhaps some literary journalist covering this increasingly public figure.

By August 6, after trips to Salisbury and Canterbury, the Moores were on their way to Paris. Moore was charmed by the city, but her mother was not so impressed. She was a demanding traveler, and felt " 'doing' a city was as objectionable as 'saying' your prayers." Reflection was part of travel, and she wrote to her son, after seeing the Elgin Marbles, that warring and fighting were repellant to her, and that she'd rather give up what she had than scratch and fight for it. But still she realized that she, more than anyone, spoke of beating down the enemies within. Her daughter thought the Louvre contained many "rotten Rubens," but she delighted in the Dürers. They made a rendezvous with some Carlisle friends, Mary and Louisa Knox, and a friend of theirs. Moore found the Victor Hugo house, in the Place des Vosges, a "most spine quaking museum," obviously impressed by all the trappings of the man-of-letters as national hero. In Paris they did a lot of shopping for gifts for people back home, as well as things for themselves, "très bon marché," as Moore justified it to Warner. On August 19 they set sail for America.

The trip was in many ways a whirlwind experience, but in other ways a very rich and thoughtful one. For the young poet it may very well have seemed her version of the continental tour that was an important culminating event in the education of young Englishmen in the preceding centuries. Moore and her mother were Anglophiles and they went to England with a very positive set of expectations. By any measure these expectations seem to have been fulfilled. Moore wrote several poems, "Critics and Connoisseurs" chief among them, that incorporated either small details or substantial elements from the trip. Years later Moore was to be invited to go and live in England, or at least somewhere in Europe, by Bryher and H.D., but she rejected this offer, probably because Mrs. Moore was not willing to emigrate. But Moore's exposure to England and Paris was in some ways like the émigré experience that figured so largely in American culture in the 1920's, since it gave her a wider understanding of culture and the respectable position of the artist in a nation's life.

However, there is another part of her experience that was rather unlike that of the émigré writers. Moore loved English culture because it had an active relationship with the past, and her special modernism has a historical consciousness that is unique. In this she is much more like Eliot, with his use of Dante and Baudelaire, say, than she is like William Carlos Williams with his emphasis on the indigenous American spirit. Eliot's cultural borrowings, however, are part of the Latin legacy of European civilization, where Moore's tend to be focused on Anglo-Saxon, and Anglo-Irish, culture. (She described herself in a letter she wrote to Ezra Pound in 1919 as "Irish by descent, possibly Scotch also, but purely Celtic.") In the next decade she would write a number of poems about writers, and a large proportion of these poems are about figures—Shaw, Yeats, George Moore, Blake, Spenser—from the Anglo-Saxon and Celtic traditions. This is not to say that she never wrote about artists outside this tradition, or that her art is ethnocentric, since she also wrote about Dürer, Tagore, and Chinese art. But these questions of cultural diversity and distinctiveness will become a part of the background of her poetry, especially when she moves to New York.

Once she was back in Carlisle in the fall of 1911, she began teaching at the Indian School. This part of her life has been noticed before, largely because of the circumstances that led her to know the famous athlete Jim Thorpe, who was a student at the school. Of course Thorpe was to become a world-renowned figure in the Olympics of 1912, and while Moore loved athletics, it is fairly clear that she didn't particularly notice Thorpe in a personal way. Subsequently, when interviewed on the matter, she always spoke highly of him, but she offered little of the sort of telling detail that would have come from a close relationship. Of pressing importance to Moore at the time were the conditions of the job itself. The Indian School was quite large, enrolling several hundred students of Indian ancestry. It was part of a national system to educate this oppressed group. The level of education, however, seems to have been rudimentary, and the wages and working conditions were not at all of a high order. The atmosphere was dominated by the fact that it was part of a large governmental bureaucracy. Moore felt herself to be overworked there, and she did not seem to have had many of the sort of inspiring experiences usually associated with an enthusiastic young teacher.

By January, 1912, Moses Friedman, the superintendent at the Indian School, wrote to Warner to reassure him about his sister. Friedman had taken over as superintendent of the school from its founder, Mr. Pratt, who had relied on Reverend Norcross to help start the school. From Warner's letters to Friedman, it is clear that he did not have an especially close relationship with him. Obviously Warner had become concerned about his sister's wages or workload, or both, and had written to Friedman to express his opinion. A letter home a week later indicates that Warner feels she should stop working at the school. By February, Moore is experiencing some eye trouble, possibly related to the strain of the job, and she tells her brother that she may work at Metzger the following fall. Many of Moore's letters to her brother from this period are missing, so it is not possible to reconstruct what happened in detail, but Warner's letters home make it clear that the situation was fretful. Moore took a short leave of absence from the school in June, 1912, and extended it for three days while she visited a friend in Virginia. In July she reported to Warner that she had had some poems rejected, and continued to complain about the conditions at the school.

All this time Warner's social life was progressing very nicely. He had already begun to think about reuniting the family once his studies were complete and he took on a parish somewhere. Indeed, this is to be one of the main themes in discussions among the three of them over the next few years. Occasionally he wrote home on Yale Club stationery, picked up from the New York club where he dined with various ministers and other friends. His expectations about the family's living together may well have been heightened because of his sister's unhappy job situation. He writes with a homiletic rhetoric in April, 1912, that the family would be united in a minister's house for the first time since 1895. He receives word from his sister of Jim Thorpe's success in Sweden when she describes him as "the first all-round world athlete." She tells him that she makes a neighbor, Mr. Collins, gape at her "murmurings of socialism and woman suffrage." At this time she is reading Shaw's An Unsocial Socialist and busy writing her poems.

If Warner's prospects were bright while his sister's were considerably less so, their mother was busy in the spring of 1912 with an adventure of her own. The property in Pueblo, Colorado, that was part of the estate Reverend Warner had left her, was occupied by a man who fell behind in his rent and tax payments. The letters from the trust manager grew more worried. Mrs. Moore decided that she would have to visit the property in person. This would be a long and difficult trip, and a delicate situation for a fifty-year-old widow to undertake by herself. Nevertheless she went out by train in July and found herself in a lawyer's office in the then rather small town of Pueblo. A meeting was arranged with the tenant's lawyer and a payment schedule agreed on. Throughout the meeting Mrs. Moore was exceptionally firm and knowledgeable; she told her daughter, with distinct self-satisfaction, of how she had operated in a man's domain, and done so openly and successfully. Mrs. Moore wrote home on July 25, passing along praise from the trust manager for her handling of the situation, that she felt it demeaning to beg—even to the Lord in prayer—and she would hardly consent to doing it to a man. Clearly her religious sense had borrowed from, or lent something to, Warner's muscular Christianity.

What adds even more interest to this story is her daughter's part in it. While her mother was away, Moore wrote to her nearly every day. These letters are striking because they exactly mimic the style and content of Mrs. Moore's own letters to Warner. The daughter takes over the mother's role as house manager, informant, and social observer, down to the smallest details. So successful were these letters that Mrs. Moore wrote to her daughter that she didn't need to write poetry when she could write such letters. It is hard to determine whether she knew how negative this might sound to the struggling poet her daughter now was. Moore and her mother were actively thinking about suffragism and women's issues at this time (even Warner told of taking the suffragists' side in a conversation with ladies at dinner one night); their attitude toward the economic and political freedom of women was quite strong. Yet Mrs. Moore praises her daughter most highly by seeing her in a domestic situation, rising above, as it were, "mere" poetical aspirations.

Mrs. Moore was becoming more confident about the family's financial situation. In July, 1912, she told Warner they needn't worry about money now that the Pueblo situation was regularized, and she even said that another trip to Europe the following summer was possible. Warner often traveled to New York from the Princeton Theological Seminary, preaching as a substitute at various churches. Moore was now a "regular" at her teaching job, apparently somewhat more resigned to the situation. She even took a trip to Washington, D.C., to get licensed as a civil servant, which was required for employees at the Indian School. The talk in the family circle was about the near future and the possi-

bility of their living together. In October, Warner reassured them both
that any thought he might have of marriage had to take this fact into
consideration: any potential wife he might select would have to accept
their situation. There developed at this time between Mrs. Moore and
her son the habit of discussing religious issues more fully in their correspondence. For example, in November, Warner tells his mother that
he is planning a sermon about the proof of divinity from the Bible; she
responds by quoting Dr. Norcross, whose last sermon contained the
statement that "the strongest proof there is of God, is man's consciousness of him." This Emersonian notion would appeal to Mrs. Moore and
to Warner, who were less interested in the doctrinal than the devotional aspects of their religion. It might be more accurate to say that
they discussed the doctrinal aspects only to the extent that they affected
and heightened the devotional ones. Their devotion, on the other
hand, did not extend to any prolonged periods of retreat or contemplation, but seems instead to have been very involved with being in the
world in forceful and effective ways. Marianne, it should be said, never
ostensibly entered these discussions, and she seems to have been less
overtly devout in her attitudes. If she admired Warner's muscular Christianity, she did so quietly and from a distance.

In 1913 she published two short poems (a third, the "Councell to a
Bachelor," being the only other to appear that year); both of them deal
at least obliquely with religious subjects. The first, "Things Are What
They Seem," tries to accept the "given" world as the only one. Its
brevity conceals what may well have been a genuine struggle in Moore's
thought at this time:

> The clouds between
> Perforce must mean
> Dissension.
>
> The broken crock's
> Condition mocks
> Prevention.

This is one of Moore's most Dickinson-like poems, with its rather
intricate rhymes in a short space, and its use of a gnomic air and the
domestic imagery of the broken crock. The dissension could refer to her
current interest in suffragism, in which case the second stanza could be

a warning against the limits of tepid reformism. But the tone of the two word choices "Perforce" and "mocks" indicates that the poem was composed under considerable pressure.

The second poem is more accepting; it is called "The Beast of Burden":

> I think the scourge was made for men
> That they have the power to rise again.
>
> Because when scourged such beasts as I
> Have no alternative. We die.
>
> At death, we lose, man gains a soul.
> We forfeit, he attains the goal.

Here the main echoes are perhaps of George Herbert and the lesser seventeenth-century devotional poets. The idea of using the beast's rather than the man's perspective makes it more dramatic, of course, but perhaps Moore was struggling with herself in terms of the balance between "burden" and "dissension."

Moore continued to think of herself as a poet in important ways, despite a lack of public recognition. In 1911 she published no poems, and she was to publish none in 1914 either. These two 1913 publications, along with "A Talisman" and the archaic "Leaves of a Magazine" of 1912, are then the only guide to what she was thinking poetically. In 1915, of course, she was to appear not only in *Poetry* and *The Egoist,* but to publish a total of twenty poems, a very large number for her. Some of these were written before 1915, of course, but her duties in her first months at the Indian School may well have kept her from producing the kind of finished work that appeared later. She told Warner in February, 1913, that, on a trip to Washington, D.C., she had studied the Woman Suffrage program, and was planning to march with the authors and artists. The march was a large one, intended to impress the newly inaugurated administration of Woodrow Wilson. Moore's wanting to march in it is important, of course, as is her wanting to do so with other authors, since this clearly shows her self-identification at the time. In fact, writing and suffragism will come to occupy a large portion of her energies within the next few years.

But Warner advised her not to. In a letter of March 2, he suggested to her that such an action would not do her any good with the people back in Carlisle, especially those at the Indian School. A few days later he confirmed he was glad she had decided to heed his advice and not join the march (her letter to him is missing, unfortunately). It's hard to know how much of Warner's concern was due to an accurate sense of the reaction of, say, the superintendent at the school. Some of his feeling, obviously, must have been due to his own increasingly advantaged social position. Whatever the mix, he acted quickly and with effect. The incident shows Warner's own political opinions were on the way to turning more conservative, a trend that would only accelerate in the coming decades. It also reveals how Warner was taking on some of his mother's role in shaping his sister's character; earlier he had referred to her as "our Basilisk." Moore's reciprocal devotion to her brother, intense and lifelong, was that of a loving sister, but it had a childlike component to it as well.

Moore was becoming aware, during these Carlisle years, of a wider world, if only vicariously. A friend and neighbor, Mary Lamberton, had gone to New York City to investigate the death of women workers in the fire at the Shirtwaist Factory, and she reported to Moore of the many reforms then under way. Warner was also expanding his experience by taking a job with a minister in Langdon, North Dakota. He was there for the whole of the summer of 1913, from early May until September. He learned to drive a car, and described in bristling detail how he helped in an appendectomy on a teenage boy, performed without any anesthetic. The local girls were quite taken with him, and his self-assurance gained noticeably when he discovered that he could talk and preach better than the man he went to assist. He frequently made spiritual judgments about the people he met there and he never failed to take note of their social standing and manners as well. His sermon was praised by the minister as the finest one ever preached in the local church. His description of himself, in a letter dated May 21, is perhaps the highest expression of his muscular Christianity, as he describes himself as rock-ribbed and soldierlike, willing to demonstrate how manly a Christian can be. He was twenty-seven years old that summer.

In July he reassured his sister that even if her poems were rejected by *Book News* she shouldn't stop trying. Mrs. Moore was considering quitting her job at Metzger, and Warner advised her to do so. Mrs. Rose had brought to the house some of William Rose Benét's poems, published in *The Century* and the *Outlook,* and Mrs. Moore pronounced them admirable. Again, we have no record as to what her daughter may have thought of this judgment. Moore had heard about an account of crossing the Atlantic, written by Dreiser, and she rushed out to buy the magazine. In late September, Warner received an offer of a position in Scranton, for $1080 per year and the use of the manse, but he rejected it. In October he ran into Helen, his love of a few years back, but he proudly reported that he had the advantage of her; his letters brim with confidence. Another offer was made, this time for a church in Baltimore, and Warner traveled to the lovely little town of Havre de Grace, on the Maryland shore, to preach. He attended dinner parties frequently, and was usually active socially when he traveled; presumably these various trips were all in order for him and the different parishioners to get to know one another. In November he sent his sister a box of candy for her twenty-sixth birthday, and she responded with a very playful letter. In a moment of weariness she referred to her students as sluggards and gnats.

Near Thanksgiving Moore confessed to her brother that she had worked very hard on a poem and would be most disappointed not to see it published. At the same time she is reading *Life of the Spider* by Fabré, the great French naturalist, a book very close to the spirit of her poetry, with its intense descriptive energies of closely observed phenomena. Mrs. Moore reports about her housework and gardening, and how much better she feels now that she isn't teaching at Metzger. Mary Norcross has gone to the Suffrage Convention in Washington, D.C., and Laura Benét has had a poem accepted by *The Century*. Moore says she admires "The Three Ships" by Alfred Noyes, and plans to have her students at the Indian School memorize it for Christmas. She mentions a rejection slip from *Harper's* and has a bookplate designed for herself. Two weeks before Christmas she tells Warner that her poetry writing is ignored by her mother. As the year draws to a close she has to cancel her order for the bookplate, and Warner tells them that he plans to rise to the top of his calling and that he values his mother's advice very much. The family correspondence is at this time very relaxed, chatty, playful.

Warner and Moore were both to find 1914 an eventful year. He was to graduate from the seminary and be ordained as a Presbyterian minister, and she was to receive notice that her poems had been accepted for publication by *Poetry* in Chicago. But the year began with two problems: Warner had accepted a position in Baltimore for after graduation, and he was reluctant to tell his mother about it, perhaps because it did not allow for the family to be reunited. Moore's troubles at the

Indian School grew worse, and again Warner felt the need to intervene. Apparently the superintendent, Mr. Friedman, was concerned about socialists; Moore had to reassure him that she supported the present administration. But the trouble didn't stop there, for her students had been circulating a petition for signatures. They evidently complained of treatment or conditions at the school, and again Moore had to speak up and deny Friedman's allegations that she was behind the petition. By late January, Friedman had written directly to Warner, presumably in response to a letter from him. In February, Mrs. Moore complained that Moore took her teaching duties too seriously.

Then a series of public events served to complicate the situation. An article in the local paper reported that a teacher at the school had struck a female student. In March troubles increased when an administrator faced jail; this was an outcome of an embezzlement charge brought against school officials. There are a few times in subsequent months when the news was positive; for example, in May someone praised Moore for the good she was able to bring to the school, and Mrs. Moore passed this compliment on to Warner. But all the indications are that teaching at the school was far from a satisfactory situation for Moore, though Warner insisted she stay on for a year or two, as her salary was necessary for the family's security. Presumably the job was to be kept only until Warner could begin a ministry somewhere; again, the dutiful daughter and sister was playing her part in the family. But she was a long way from the "liberalizing" atmosphere of Dewey's camp at Lake Placid. Moore's political conservatism in later life may also have had some roots in this situation, for when she faced the authority figures at the school she did so with a tempered attitude, which was in considerable measure the result of Warner's guidance. Her brother would continue to exercise great influence on her views, especially those that concerned the affairs of the world.

II. "One need not know the way, to be arriving"

At the same time, and one is tempted to say as a reaction to these concerns of public deportment, Moore talked more and more often about her poems. She was busy submitting them to all sorts of places:

The Masses, under Floyd Dell's editorship, *Poetry and Drama, Smart Set,* and *The Atlantic.* She became more vocal about the editors who rejected her, and complained to Warner about their incomprehension. In March, 1914, she told her brother that she was writing a poem as an indirect attack on her detractors. Several of her poems continue to treat this subject, most notably "To a Steam Roller." Some of these poems are especially abstruse, as if her anger could never be unequivocally stated. But her poetry in this period—through about 1916—is also frequently epideictic, that is, a poetry of praise. She writes poems about Yeats, Shaw, Gordon Craig, George Moore, and Blake, all of which praise a quality of mind and a sensibility. At the same time there are poems that satirize incomprehension, usually of an aesthetic sort. This praise and blame culminates a few years later in "Critics and Connoisseurs," a poem that treats of the problem with considerable ambiguity and complexity. One of the important features of modernism is that it often creates an art about art, its conditions of possibility, and its special role in the world. Moore is centrally in the modernist tradition by writing often about how art offers a special understanding of the world, but one that is not always easily appreciated.

These poems are also about a personal struggle: her attempt to create for herself a working mode of self-expression so that her mind can find a way to take part in the world while not being lost in its welter. The last half of her poem on Gordon Craig, which appeared in *The Egoist* in April, 1915, reads:

> The most propulsive thing you say,
> Is that one need not know the way,
>   To be arriving. That forward smacks of prospect.
>
> Undoubtedly you overbear,
> But one must do that to come where
>   There is a space, a fit gymnasium for action.

This poem itself echoes many of the assumptions of American pragmatism as well as the modernist concern with process instead of product. It also exhibits that prize modernist trait of questioning one's own position when it says "Undoubtedly you overbear." The trust in process in this poem is balanced by the other poem that appeared in the same issue of *The Egoist,* "To the Soul of 'Progress,' " which opens with a negative image:

You use your mind
Like a mill stone to grind
   Chaff.

You polish it
And with your warped wit
   Laugh

At your torso,
Prostrate where the crow—
   Falls

On such kind hearts
As its God imparts . . .

The whole poem is an antiwar poem and an attack on those who would justify it by arguing for an abstract, deterministic notion of progress. People who use crows for divination or their minds only to process information will always be the enemy of Moore's way of thinking. Critics have observed that many of the poems of praise are addressed to specific individuals, often male, and the poems of blame are addressed to anonymous figures. In any case, these poems form a large set of reflections on the role of the mind in the world.

During the middle 1910's, poetry for the average American reader was still a matter of lovely descriptions of "soft" moods and a recital of approved moral axioms. Once again Moore complained to Warner in March, 1912, that *The Atlantic*, which was never to accept any of her poems, could not appreciate things that were new. In the same month William Rose Benét's portrait was hanging in the window at Brentano's in Philadelphia. She wrote to her brother that Benét was thought to be a founder of a new school of poetry, but added somewhat fliply that she couldn't afford to worry about such things. The insouciance of this remark was typical of her attitude, at least when talking to her brother. We know she must have had faith in her own aesthetic judgment, because not only does she say so in her poems, but she continued along the innovative paths she had only recently begun to explore. But she probably had moments of doubt as well. The months of late 1913 and early 1914 were filled with preparations for what would become her distinctive stylistic innovations. These poems were to be written in spite of the lack of an audience rather than as an expression of typical emotions.

A visit from Laura Benét in June, 1914, is the occasion for several harangues about poetry; Laura had earned $75 in the last year through publishing poems. Laura was probably the only "working" poet with whom Moore discussed poetry prior to her exposure to New York's literary world. Moore never gave any indication that Laura could comprehend what she was doing with her innovative poems, but it is nevertheless characteristic of Moore that she never wavered in her personal loyalty to her. A few letters from Laura to Moore survive from this period, though none from Moore to her. Apparently they were sending poems back and forth while Laura was living in Annapolis. They traded information about outlets as well, and Moore sent Laura the address of an English publisher that was sponsoring a competition for a book of poetry. Many of Laura's letters are rather frivolous, filled with details of flirting with various young men and the sort of idle talk of a young woman of leisure. To her credit, Laura, in an undated letter, asked Moore for candid criticism of the poem she'd sent her; one can only guess whether Moore supplied it. There is a scrapbook that Moore kept that contains a copy, from an unidentified source, of a poem by Laura Benét, one that has been reprinted from a journal called *The Delineator*. From other pieces in the scrapbook it is possible to date the poem, or at least its reprinting, tentatively as around late 1913. The poem is a typical example of the picturesque verse of the time; it resembles, in its scenic structure and its atmospheric coloring, nothing so much as a nineteenth-century painting of a genre scene. Titled "The Shoemaker," it begins with these lines:

> He might unravel a tale of woe,
>> Of nights when the winds are all awake
> And whirling wraiths of the winter snow
>> His crazy chimney rock and shake.
> And he sits by a guttering taper's light
>> Mending old shoes till the dead of night.

The poem ends with the phrase, "The quaint, old, tolerant shoemaker!" It is easy to see this poem as exemplifying all the features of late Victorian poetry that Pound castigated with the phrase "emotional slither." The poet speaks from a vantage point outside and above the world of the laboring shoemaker and rather imperiously imputes to him such qualities as tolerance in a barely disguised attempt to offer such virtues to the audience's commendation. The effect is one of moral smugness, with its edges softened by the use of sentimental "word painting." (One of Pound's injunctions was "Don't be 'viewy.' ") Moore's poems of this period reject most if not all of these features by several strategies: by addressing the person who is the subject of the poem as "you," she avoids the sense of turning the person into an object in a settled lesson on shared morality, and she eliminates easy "scenic" descriptions, using instead elliptical details and metaphoric contextualizing to convey the poem's "information." Moore was personally very close to at least one source of the kind of poetry she felt compelled to reject.

Laura, during the spring of 1914, singled out for praise two of Moore's poems, which she refers to as "Compensation" and "Heredity," but no poems, published or unpublished, survive under these titles. Laura was to remain friendly, though never very close, with Moore for several decades, so their artistic disagreements were not allowed to disrupt their relationship. The correspondence of the Moore family creates the impression that Moore may have realized that Laura's lack of talent or ambition would prevent her from ever becoming as famous a poet as her two brothers. But the sort of poetry that the Benéts wrote and published served Moore as something like a negative model. It was on July 6, 1914, however, that Moore received notice from Harriet Monroe that *Poetry*, a relatively new but important journal, would publish four of her poems, though they did not appear until the May, 1915 issue, almost a year later. So Moore eventually approached Laura with some armor of her own.

Several months later, Moore was typing up a manuscript of a book-length collection of poems to submit to a competition sponsored by the *Poetry Review*, as she explained to Warner on February 7, 1915. There survives a letter that refers directly to this manuscript. Dated September 30, 1915, it is addressed to Erskine MacDonald at Malory House in London; it mentions that previously, on February 20, 1915, Moore had sent MacDonald sixty-four poems for inclusion in a series of modern poets. The letter asks that the manuscript be withdrawn. (On October 27, 1915, she tells Warner that the manuscript was rejected because MacDonald found the poems not musical enough—not at all surprising in the light of his Georgian tastes. MacDonald himself had published a book of verse entitled *In Arcady, and Other Poems.*) Several things are revealed by this brief letter. First, Moore had amassed a considerable body of work if she was able to fulfill the quota of sixty-four poems. Second, her surprise several years later when H.D. and Bryher edited and published her first full-length book of poems couldn't have been so total as she sometimes suggested it was, since she had already attempted book publication by herself. Third, a pattern of dignity and impatience was evident in her self-image as a poet, since she could have the presence to submit a manuscript and also the self-reserve to ask for it to be returned. Assuming the manuscript contained poems from the Bryn Mawr years, and further assuming that some of the included poems were eventually destroyed, it can be gathered that Moore was actively at work in the 1910's writing and revising on a scale rarely if ever duplicated later in her career. From 1910, after Bryn Mawr, until 1917, before moving to New York, Moore published fifty-one poems, an average of over six poems a year. Over Moore's whole career of 63 years (from 1906 to 1969), she published just over 190 poems in magazines, an average of slightly more than three poems a year. In no subsequent year does she publish more than she did in 1916, though presumably some of these poems were written early enough to be a part of the 1915 manuscript. Of the fifty-one poems published between Bryn Mawr and New York, thirty-six were never collected into a book. The thirty-six uncollected poems from this period form what is virtually a hidden corpus of Moore's writing.

In addition to these published poems that Moore chose never to reprint, there is also a body of unpublished poems that exist in manuscript versions in the Rosenbach Museum. These unpublished poems total at least seventy-four lyrics, and would thus considerably increase the size of Moore's corpus. Of the seventy-four about half, or thirty-five, are from the Carlisle period. These are identifiable as such because the typed versions have Moore's Carlisle address in the upper left-hand corner. There are two poems from Chatham, New Jersey, three poems with her St. Luke's Place address, and seven with the Brooklyn address. Of the remaining thirty or so poems without addresses, most can be dated from internal evidence and through correlation with correspondence; many of these are from Moore's later years, after 1945 or so. But the Carlisle poems have another feature that sheds light on their place in Moore's image of herself. More than half of these unpublished poems, totaling nineteen in all, have "U.S.A." added as a fourth line to the Carlisle address. These nineteen poems probably formed part of the manuscript Moore submitted to MacDonald in London, for typing the fourth line would suggest they were being mailed overseas.

It is hard to characterize these poems as a single set of statements, and hard to discuss them in detail unless and until they are published. Still, some general observations about them can be made. Many of them carry in their sometimes lengthy titles a mark of the occasion of their composition. Many are addressed to a second person (six of them have titles beginning "To . . ."); this "you" is treated often as an equal, and less frequently is either criticized or praised. Many of them are written in rhyme, with regular stanzaic divisions; couplets and tercets are used as frequently as quatrains, and occasionally a longer stanza, of say seven or eight lines, with a more elaborate rhyme scheme, will make up an entire poem. These are often cryptic poems, sometimes trapped in references to literary or cultural moments or artifacts. The most frequent subjects and themes are the eternal qualities of art and the perception of a moral quality to be cherished in a moment of aesthetic insight. Moore's lexical range here is quite broad, the tone frequently light and playful, and the artistic control often evident. Though they tend to be short poems, the associative linking of the longer poems of later years can occasionally be glimpsed, though it is also clear that her great powers of innovative structuring and complex argument are not yet fully developed.

Most striking, however, is how the poems differ from the standards of Georgian verse that were then most dominant in London literary circles. Nowhere do we see the pastoralized nature of Georgian poetry, or its mellifluous rhyming, or its rather predictable vocabulary. Georgian poetry was in some respects a return to Augustan or eighteenth-century models, and it sought both to avoid the air of decadence exemplified by Wilde and others and to dampen that late Romantic urgency that animated D. H. Lawrence's poems. Lawrence was included in some Georgian anthologies, largely because of his pastoralism, but Georgian taste can perhaps best be represented to American audiences by the early Robert Frost. However, rarely would a Georgian poet make use, as Moore did, of a second person addressee or of a mocking, even taunting tone. Indeed, this taunting tone in Moore is most closely paralleled by the early socially satiric poems of Pound.

The Georgian poets saw themselves as innovative, matching the change in monarchs, from Edward VII and all he symbolized about exhausted Victorianism, to George V and the possibilities of a more energized culture. As such, the Georgians were not resolutely anti-modern, though they may appear that way today viewed back through the lenses of Pound and Eliot. Moore was later to become an admirer of Frost, but this first of her book-length manuscripts was in many ways closer not only to the Pound of the early social "portraits," but to the aestheticism of Eliot. Her concerns are much more focused on a realm of culture and social values than are the Georgians, who are in many respects poets of nature. Moore used the rhyme and stanza structures that would make her appear traditional, at least to a casual observer, while using tonalities and word choices that often had a very untraditional turn to them.

In the early months of 1912, Mrs. Moore had written to Warner to caution him about criticizing his sister too sharply. The letter uses a pet name and speaks in terms of intimacy. At this time Warner was criticizing Moore's poetry, by saying that it lacked focus. She took the criticism gratefully and called it absolutely to the point. In March, Moore gave Mary Norcross a copy of Max Eastman's *Enjoyment of Poetry* for her birthday. She was also occupied with trying to write a poem about war for a contest. (Several of her early poems have an antiwar theme, but it is impossible to determine which one might have been submitted for a contest.) Moore happily informed her brother that Floyd Dell, at *The Masses*, had included a note when he returned her poems. A few months later, when she tells Warner of the acceptance by *Poetry*, she is very calm about it, though she does ask him to send her some special stationery on which she can send them her "author's notes." From a later reference it is fairly clear that at the time of the acceptance she had not seen a copy of *Poetry*; apparently she had only gotten the address from some other publication, or perhaps a guide for aspiring writers. All this suggests that she had some sense of how innovative her poetry was in relation to what was accepted by the average reader. Certainly she became increasingly aware of its experimental aspect as she became well known and her poetry was to become the subject of critical focus, sometimes of a harsh and uncomprehending sort. But the question of an audience was to be a constant, although implicit, concern for many years.

Warner in the meantime was preparing for his ordination. His mother wrote him a very pious letter about it in May, praying that her son would conquer his temptations and that her daughter would buckle on her armor and enter the fight gallantly. In the closing phrase we learn that for Mrs. Moore the image of armor was a symbol of active self-definition rather than a merely passive form of self-protection. Mrs. Moore also began her reading, or perhaps rereading, of *Wind in the Willows* at this time; she explained to Warner how she and his sister meant to apply the names to each other. In Kenneth Grahame's classic, first published in 1908, the character called Rat was a writer of verses, so obviously that name would go to Moore. In addition, Rat was a daydreaming type, but very meek and playful in his own way. Mole is introduced at the start of the book as a sedentary homemaker, so that name was assigned to Mrs. Moore. Mole was also capable of being "impatient and contemptuous," too, attributes that Mrs. Moore would display on more than one occasion. Badger was a character with high standing and dignity in the animals' world, whose "unseen presence was felt by everybody about the place," and so Warner was given his name. But Badger was also a solitary creature who seldom ventured into society, though his advice on worldly matters was considered very valuable.

The enthusiastic use of the names from this children's book at just this time in the experience of the Moore family suggests that there are other reasons than simple delight that animated their interest. Both Warner and his sister had been out of college for five years or so, and Warner was moving closer and closer to an important change of status as he prepared to enter the ministry. Moore herself was obviously growing more and more excited by the elements of a new literary sensibility that she was seeing all around her, and that she was developing in her own way with her poems about critics and audiences, as well as the poems about role models such as Shaw and Gordon Craig. Mrs. Moore was obviously watchfully concerned about these stages in both her children, and she was probably equally concerned about her own situation. She knew that she might well be called to serve Warner in his new pastoral appointment within a matter of a few years, and she knew that her daughter was not going to teach at the Indian School indefinitely, and that she must have some prospect for herself, assuming that she would not join her mother in "service" in the manse where Warner would eventually reside. The world of Rat, Mole, and Badger must have seemed tempting in its innocence and stability to all three of the Moores, for it harkened back to those values that had strongly bonded the family over the preceding twenty years.

The two languages of Mrs. Moore—the language of Christian warfare and salvation and the language of childhood innocence—were alternatives to the matter-of-fact and businesslike language of moral watchfulness and social propriety. But all the languages were integrated in the hoped-for attainment of her children's success. Later that year, in October, the house in Carlisle had a fire, apparently not too serious, and a week later Mrs. Moore wrote to Warner in tones of sentimental reassurance, pleading for their happiness and joy together to continue. Warner, for his part, wrote home near Christmas to confess that he recognized his main character flaw as his disposition not to tell the whole truth. This flaw would come into play later when his marriage caught Mrs. Moore by surprise.

But perhaps Mrs. Moore was aware, even as she wrote, of her daughter's expanding horizon and her son's possible separation from the family in the near future. Moore would visit the library at Bryn Mawr and read the latest magazines in the late fall of 1914. Her Carlisle neighbor, George Plank, was beginning to make a mark for himself as an artist: he had designed a cover for *Vogue*, one that Moore would refer to years later as one of the finest she had ever seen. Moore mentions two such covers, one that appeared on the December 1, 1913 issue, and the other on April 15, 1915. The first shows a woman sporting a fur collar and fur trimming on her sleeves and hem. She is carrying an umbrella with a duck handle as holly leaves fall from the sky. In the distant background is a single cabin, snow-covered, and a few trees. The latter portrait is more striking and more modern in feeling. It shows a full-length profile of a woman clad in an extraordinary costume, a dress with multicolored streamers reaching to the floor. The background is a wall covering with a block print. Indebted in many ways to Whistler's full-length portraits of women, the picture is nevertheless quite original. In some ways it may even have suggested the model of Moore's complex poem, "Those Various Scalpels," though this poem, resonant as it is, very likely had more than one source. Surely both pictures appealed to Moore's sense of fashion, and since she recalled them so vividly many years later, they may have appealed to her self-image as well.

Throughout her years in Carlisle, Moore was an avid reader of many periodicals, and she kept scrapbooks that contained clippings of stories that caught her interest. She also included items that concerned her family, such as an account of a sermon on Jacob that Warner gave in January, 1914, at the First Presbyterian Church in Carlisle, and an account of his ordination at the Second Presbyterian Church, on May 15, 1914, with Reverend Norcross, then pastor emeritus, giving the ordination prayer. She possibly included items that showed her own activities as an author—though here a certain amount of speculation is involved. On one page of the scrapbook appear two clippings from a Carlisle paper, pasted side by side; the one on the right is dated May 19, 1913. The two concern, respectively, an exhibit of George Plank's artwork and two related lectures, and a meeting of suffragists addressing the issue of the legal status of women. Both of these items may have been written by Moore, but since they are unsigned, it is impossible to say this definitively. However, there are letters from this period in which Mrs. Moore tells Warner that she has taken Moore's "notices" to the paper. And Moore herself later told an interviewer that she published, anonymously, items about suffragism in the local papers. The item on suffragism is rather unremarkable in its content, written in a bland journalistic style.

But the piece on Plank's art is rather different. The headline reads "Large Crowd Hears Art and Music at Mbetzger[sic]." On May 26, presumably in 1913, the citizens of Carlisle, according to the account, were treated to two lectures, one entitled "The Mission of Music," by Cornelia Thompson, and the other called "The Joy of Art," by Winifred Woods, who is also mentioned as the organizer of the event. These lectures were held in conjunction with an exhibit of drawings by George Plank, and it is these works that the bulk of the article describes. One sentence is especially striking: "The partially symbolic character of the drawings, highlighted by a drollery of suggestion in the detail, compels attention." The choice of the word "drollery," the syntax of the sentence, and the thought itself, all suggest Moore's authorship. The article goes on to point out the repetition of pearls as a motif in the drawings, five impressions of Isadora Duncan, and a drawing entitled "Life's Inspiration," illustrating a poem by Louis Untermeyer. Though the evidence is circumstantial, if the pieces were written by Moore, they show she was busy trying to establish some credentials for herself as a journalist, an occupation she pursued off and on from her senior year in college until at least 1916. The article on Plank also suggests that their relationship was very friendly, and his art may have exercised more influence on her than previously supposed.

Many of the articles in Moore's scrapbooks were originally published in the *Literary Digest*, a publication that mixed feature stories and journalism about all the arts. One article concerned the set designs and costumes of Leon Bakst. Moore had developed an interest in stage design and followed the career of Gordon Craig closely; this may have gone back to her experiences at Bryn Mawr with May Day ceremonies and seeing the traveling productions of the Ben Greet players. But the article on Bakst speaks of the artist's attempt "to stimulate the imagination and the sense through color as the composer does through sound." Such an interest in synesthesia was a legacy both of Romanticism, where Keats uses it frequently, and French symbolism. The article, however, also contains a picture of a costumed woman, with a caption that reads, "Is this costume a poem?" Again, Moore may have had this in mind as she came to write "Those Various Scalpels," a poem that describes a woman bedecked in an elaborate costume that is brightly colored. It begins with these lines:

> those
> various sounds consistently indistinct, like intermingled echoes
>   struck from thin glasses successively at random—
>   the inflection disguised: your hair, the tails of two
>   fighting-cocks head to head in stone—

The article ends with the claim that Bakst's fullness of color "makes the Whistlerian idea hopelessly empty and inadequate." This refers to Whistler's tendency to limit his palate, even as he invoked synesthesia, as in his famous "symphony" paintings. Moore was probably engaged by this set of ideas and the implicit dispute it contained as she was struggling to define her own aesthetic standards. How colorful should art be, how aggressively should it range through its own materials? "Those Various Scalpels" ends with the enigmatic rhetorical question, "But why dissect destiny with instruments / more highly specialized than components of destiny itself?" This suggests that Moore may be telling herself that an overly refined art will fail to register the main outlines of her experience and hence lose its force in its details.

In the same scrapbook there is an article from the *Spectator*, dated

May 10, 1913, reviewing the famous book on Cubism by the French critics Albert Gleizes and Jean Metzinger. In this review it is asserted that "Decorum demands a certain degree of dimness." Such an aesthetic principle could hardly be applied without exception, but Moore probably pondered its relation to her own poetry. A few years later she will write "In the Days of Prismatic Color," which speculates on the quality of art before the fall from the Garden of Eden. The poem has as one of its main thematic points a sentence that argues a cryptic point: "Principally throat, sophistication is as / it al- // ways has been—at the antipodes from the init- / ial great truths." There was also an article from the *Literary Digest*, dated the same as the Bakst, that discussed the work of Fabre, the great French entomologist, whose work was based on an unswerving dedication to the closest observation and the most minute details. Moore told Warner in a letter that she had been reading his book, *The Life of the Spider*, during the Thanksgiving period of 1913. Whether sophistication lay in the dimming of details or in their heightened depiction was an artistic issue that engaged Moore throughout her life as a writer, for paradoxically she prized both what she termed "naturalistic" expression and scientific accuracy.

In early 1915, Moore wrote to *The Masses* to request the latest three issues. Another Carlisle neighbor, a Miss Hench, brought news of a magazine called *New Numbers*, and Moore excitedly sent off for a copy of an issue. She excitedly reported to Warner that the poets in the magazine were "wild," and she was at the same time expectantly watching for the issue of *Poetry* to appear with her poems in it. In March, 1915, when visiting Washington, D.C., she managed to see a copy of *Blast*, then newly published by Wyndham Lewis and Pound. Excited about its brash energy, she copied out some passages from it to "regale" Warner with. There is in the Moore archive an unpublished poem of ten lines from the Carlisle years, entitled "Ezra Pound," that ends with the line "Bless Blast!" She also noted down the addresses of several poetry magazines, such as *The Little Review*, all of which she expected to "buy" her, as she put it. And a week earlier she had responded to a request from *The Lantern* for some of her poems by gathering together a group and then removing the few she thought were the best. Her sights were changing.

But so, too, was the world of the little magazines, in London especially, but also in America, where Moore was soon to begin making a name for herself. Almost three decades later, in November, 1943, she would write to George Plank and recall a special alignment of perspectives, as she described the green trees she passed when she entered the church in Carlisle on Pomfret Street and looked across to the Plank house. There, she thought, were stored the issues of the magazines Plank would lend her, and this loan would be an important part of her entry into the world of modernist aesthetics. Moore mentioned "reviews," which could well have been included in magazines such as *The Egoist,* and she also mentioned *Blast* by name. Moore's recollective combination of a pastoral, a religious, and an avant-garde atmosphere in thinking about this episode is suggestive of how these orders were to mingle in her life in the coming years. The passage also suggests that very likely it was Plank who introduced Moore to Wyndham Lewis's literary and typographically radical journal, perhaps before her visits to Washington and the Library of Congress. Since Moore doesn't supply a specific date, but since she clearly idealizes the event, this bold loan by Plank was surely another formative influence on her artistic tastes in Carlisle. In October, 1914, she wrote her brother that she has had a letter from Plank, whom she called "Lizards Beetle Coat" (perhaps because of his dapper wardrobe and interest in fashion) and that Plank had been visiting with the other beetlewings in London, namely Yeats, Ezra Pound, and others. This was one of Moore's first references to Pound in her correspondence. Plank's role as a conduit of the new sensibility is thus hard to overstate.

Meanwhile, in London, Ezra Pound was busy extending his influence into several places. It was through his efforts that Richard Aldington, then married to Pound's ex-fiancée H.D., became poetry editor of *The Egoist.* This magazine began its life as a feminist journal, called the *Freewoman,* and then, after a short hiatus, *The New Freewoman,* beginning in the spring of 1913. At the beginning of 1914 it changed its name, at Pound's urging, to *The Egoist,* in part as a reflection of the philosophy of Max Stirner, a follower of Nietzsche who stressed the value-making power of a strong ego. Pound's own ego was also busy manifesting itself as the "foreign editor" of *Poetry* (Chicago), where Moore was to have four poems published in the May, 1915 issue. Additionally, Pound was publishing critical essays frequently, using a variety of pseudonyms, in *The Egoist,* and generally setting himself up as the chief arbiter of taste for modernism. He was one of the first to notice

Moore's unique talent, and was later—in the closing months of 1918—
to begin a correspondence with her. For her part, she became one of
Pound's staunchest defenders throughout his controversial career; however, she never condoned his vicious anti-Semitism, and was extremely
adroit in showing him the foolish limits of his attitudes toward women.
He might have learned as much from her as she learned from him.

A long letter written after she got back from the Library of Congress
shows a lot about her reading and the development of her faith in her
own poetry. She took out Yeats's *The Cutting of an Agate* and *Ideas of
Good and Evil,* which she described as being worth their weight in gold.
She was also very enthusiastic about Robert Frost's *North of Boston,*
then recently published. Looking at Amy Lowell's earlier poetry, she
found it very spotty and remarked this was encouraging, as more recent
work had shown that Lowell had changed a lot. She regarded Max
Eastman's poems as virtually worthless, showing she had little taste at
the time for directly social poetry. Pound's *Spirit of Romance* impressed
her, though she said it lacked the pyrotechnics of *Blast.* Her reading at
this time clearly had a contemporary slant to it, a rather aggressive one
in fact, much more so than in previous years.

On February 24, 1915, Moore mailed her brother a long and curious
letter in which she reflects on the war then being fought throughout
Europe. She had come to the conclusion that she would reduce her
opposition to the war, because war, she argued, affects only physical
life. This sentiment comes to full expression decades later in the poem
"In Distrust of Merits," where she says that "there never was a war that
was / not inward." This is also one of the main ideas behind her conservative turn during the Depression years, when she felt that people
were too concerned with material goods. She even complained a few
weeks later that books from America didn't get circulated in England
because England objected to America's non-participation in the war.
At this time American intellectuals were engaged in a deep and divisive
debate about this issue of non-participation. Randolph Bourne, writing
in *The Seven Arts* and *The New Republic,* was one of the chief spokesmen
for the pacifist point of view, while John Dewey eventually became one
of the major voices in favor of entering the war. Moore never entered
this debate directly, but her ideas about war were obviously to be
important for her overall view of human morality, which enters her
poems more explicitly after World War II.

On March 15, 1915, she communicated to Warner her excitement about *The Egoist*'s decision to publish three of her poems. Though their authors were not paid, she was so happy with the prospect that she said she would be willing to pay them for the delight of it. Richard Aldington had recently taken over from T. S. Eliot as poetry editor. Aldington was younger than Moore and H.D., but he was possessed of great literary ambition. Trained as a classicist, Aldington had met Pound shortly after he became involved with H.D., and Pound would often instruct them both in the rigors of the modernist poetic. In May, 1915, an issue of *The Egoist* appeared that was called a "Special Imagist Number." Edited by Aldington, it included not only Moore's poems, but the work of F. S. Flint, Amy Lowell, D. H. Lawrence, John Gould Fletcher, and H.D. Also included were essays on the new poetic theory, written by Aldington (on Pound), Fletcher (on Amy Lowell), Flint, and Harold Monro. Though his memoir, written much later, says nothing of Moore, Aldington was the first critic to mention her in print: in an article discussing Imagism published in 1915 in *Bruno's Weekly*, a small publication that circulated among the writing community in Greenwich Village. Moore herself was to publish a number of poems in this journal, put out by a colorful character and culture publicist from what everyone in the Village referred to as "Bruno's garret." Aldington called her work "promising," and may have based this opinion only on the two poems he accepted and the ones he saw in *Poetry* that same year. Partly because of the kind of poetry she wrote at this time, but also partly because she was championed by Aldington and associated in some ways with H.D. and Pound, Moore was to be thought of as an Imagist poet for many years. It was not a label she was comfortable with—indeed she would probably have rejected all labels at this time— and it is easy now to see that her poetry offers much more thematic argument than is generally allowed to Imagists.

Warner in the meantime heard his sister complain about her mother, who was refusing to buy an automobile and being generally unsympathetic to other people's points of view. Moore suggested her mother might need some time away from the manse of the Norcrosses' church. Reverend Norcross had died the first week of March and perhaps Mrs. Moore was trying too hard to be helpful. She had also recently been putting pressure on Warner to behave in a more friendly way to a young woman of whom she obviously approved, Alice McKenzie, who went by the nickname "Ben." Moore herself tried to arrange a rendezvous between Ben and Warner in Washington, D.C., but it did not work out. Warner was busy working at a church in Baltimore, assisting a Dr. Barr, and continuing his social life, meeting, among others, a young woman named Miss White. Within a year he was to begin military service at the Norfolk Navy Yard in Virginia. At first he joined the militia in a reserve capacity; he eventually received a Navy commission in 1917. By then, of course, President Wilson's attempts to maintain an armed neutrality in the World War had broken down and the country had entered what at first seemed a European conflict. But in the first week of October, 1915, Warner could write to reassure his family that their family bonds were stronger than ever.

Mrs. Moore wrote late in March to tell Warner that his sister was busy writing poetry, and that this reduced the mother to the role of poetaster, a role she did not seem to relish. Mrs. Rose reported that William had told her an English paper had mentioned Moore as an "imagist" and he would advise her not to be too closely influenced by the Imagists. Moore responded by saying that it wasn't possible to meet his views and please herself, and that she had gotten the Imagist anthology from the library. Moore was clearly the sort of person who wanted to know what others thought of themselves, and how they arranged the labels they used to come to terms with the world. Ironically Moore was proposed by Aldington for inclusion in the 1916 Imagist anthology edited by Amy Lowell. Lowell was disposed against adding new poets, and John Gould Fletcher, then a close advisor, cared little for Moore's work, so she was excluded. Though the Imagist movement was to be for many readers and critics the focus for modern poetry for the next several years, it was probably best for her that Moore's poetic identity was not inextricably tied up with it.

Meanwhile, *The Lantern* had accepted three more poems, and she sent more work to *The Egoist*, which accepted a total of five poems before the end of 1915. These publications pleased Moore a great deal, and though they were not the sort of prestigious magazines such as *The Atlantic Monthly*, they gave her an identity as a published poet. Her mother seems to have been intent on not praising this new identity, though she may have been playfully exaggerating her cool or disinterested reaction to Warner. In the meantime, *Poetry* sent her proofs in March, saying they would publish the five poems under the general title

"Pouters and Fantails." These are terms used to describe pigeons, and they may suggest the various quick-witted forms of display that the poems embody. Moore's public identity as a poet was taking shape.

The five poems published in *Poetry* were an odd assortment, especially considering they represent the first appearance in a major American magazine of one of the country's important modernist poets. As a group, they are decidedly less experimental than the poems of Moore that appeared in *The Egoist.* Two of the poems are on explicitly religious subjects: "That Harp You Play So Well," a poem about David the psalmist that is built around the acknowledgment that "Grief's lustiness / Must cure that harp's distress," and "Appellate Jurisdiction," which asks if God will redeem the speaker, a "castaway." These two poems owe much to George Herbert and almost nothing to Rimbaud or Pound. Two of the other poems are more secular: "Counseil to a Bachelor" is a versification in a single quatrain of a motto on a plate Moore had seen in the Bodleian Library in 1911; and "To an Intra-Mural Rat" is an intricately rhymed six-line portrait. This latter was not exactly like the sharply observed animal poems for which she was eventually to become so well-known, but is rather a coded poem, probably about herself (recall that her nickname was "Rat"), and her fascination with quick-wittedness. It shares a great deal in the spirit of the two poems she would later publish in *Bruno's Weekly* in October, 1916. The teasing ambiguity of the poem comes from its unnamed addressee: the poem can be read as being Moore's observations about her mother, or as the poet's using her mother to make observations about her (the poet's) own nature.

> You make me think of many men
> Once met, to be forgot again;
>   Or merely resurrected
> In a parenthesis of wit,
> That found them hastening through it
>   Too brisk to be inspected.

Moore's lifelong enjoyment of repartee with her mother included both childish word-play and the coining of serious axioms. In this brief poem the playfulness has an edge of animosity, if we choose to hear it: "Once met, to be forgot again." In any case, the close identification of the two women in their verbal habits may lie at the center of the poem; inside the walls of 343 North Hanover they shared a common nature.

The fifth poem is called "A Wizard in Words" (though the title is changed to "Reticence and Volubility" in Moore's first book, after which she never reprinted it). It is a gnomic two-voice dialogue about how one's values and perceptions change after death. Though religious in some sense, it also has a secular edge to it. It is the sort of poem one might expect from a young poet who has reflected on the question of spiritual discipline, but without being able to arrive at any clearly shaped attitude toward such a portentous subject. Moore's version of the problem has a wizard and a student, obviously representing two different generations and two different outlooks, in this brief exchange:

> "When I am dead,"
> The wizard said,
> "I'll look upon the narrow way
> And this Dante,
>   And know that he was right
>   And he'll delight
>   In my remorse,
>   Of course."
> "When I am dead,"
> The student said,
>   "I shall have grown so tolerant,
>   I'll find I can't
>   Laugh at your sorry plight
>   Or take delight
>   In your chagrin,
>   Merlin."

There are several ironies here: the student can be seen as wiser than the wizard, or, on the other hand, as simply more jaded. The wizard knows his life hasn't been sufficiently disciplined to satisfy the rigors of Dante's religious vision, but he apparently cannot change his course. The student outdoes the wizard in seeing through a superficial attitude to a firmer truth, but in doing so is hardly a satisfactory model for others, given the ambiguity of the phrase "grown so tolerant." There is also the question of who is voluble, and who is reticent. Each speaker has the same number of lines in the poem, so the terms must apply to their attitudes rather than to the actual amount of talk they utter or hold back. At the very least, the poem reveals that Moore has been able to see both attitudes and their dialectical relation with one another. Throughout the Bryn Mawr years, especially as her stories recorded, and even well into the 1920's, Moore will return again and again to the relationship between the often ineffective wisdom of age and the cynical knowingness of youth. In one sense, this is a version of the argument between the young writer and the older but uncomprehending critic. Eight years later, she will write in "Novices" of the irony of authors "acquiring at thirty what at sixty they will be trying to forget." As in so many Moore poems, the real problem is the difficulty in defining our values and qualities with any lasting precision, while recognizing that being human demands an attempt at some permanent assessment of our worth.

In the beginning of July, 1915, Warner seriously contemplated proposing marriage to the young woman from Baltimore, Miss White. Mrs. Moore sent him a long letter of advice. It counseled control and said serious people, as she put it, would always prefer this to falling in love. But what was more chilling was that Mrs. Moore also made one of her very rare allusions to Warner's father. She suggested that Miss White should be apprised of the past, hinting that the mental instability might run in the family and this was a shadow that would haunt one's life. She also insisted that Miss White, or any prospective wife, be made to understand that Warner's vocation as a minister came before all else. Warner went off to boot camp the next week, and before long was serving as a quartermaster in the navy militia. He expressed the hope that the sticking point with Miss White, presumably the fact of his father's illness, would not be serious. Within three months, however, Miss White rejected Warner's proposal, but not before several more letters of advice were sent by Mrs. Moore. It is hard to know if Mrs. Moore brought up her husband's "mental difficulty"—something she obviously tried hard to expunge from the family's consciousness—because of a genuine concern, or because she sensed Warner was serious about Miss White and this was the only way for her to control or slow down events.

Moore at this time had developed not only her literary identity, but was very involved in worldly matters, chiefly her suffragist activities. Her mother was involved as well, and, influenced by Mary Norcross,

both began to work with an organization, the Women Suffrage Party of
Pennsylvania, and its Committee to Organize Cumberland County.
Mrs. George Hays, a Carlisle friend, was also active, and she and Moore
would attend meetings and pass out leaflets together. In July, Mrs.
Moore attended a meeting at a neighbor's, a Mrs. Biddle's, where she
said Mary Norcross would get mud thrown on her effort, and that she,
Mrs. Moore, turned the mud each time in a decent way—without
"re-turning" it—but she was glad when the meeting was over. Two days
later she had to answer another neighbor, a Mrs. Eccles, who tried to
convert her to anti-suffragism. To this she responded that both sides of
the struggle meant nothing unless a person's whole soul were given to
Christ. Mrs. Moore's commitment to suffragism would not likely have
had a basis separate from her religious background, though she was an
independent woman with strong and educated views.

In national terms the suffrage movement was gaining considerable
strength and attention. In the Carlisle *Evening Sentinel* for September
24, 1915, for example, a long article reported on the rallies to support
the Susan B. Anthony amendment, as it was called, for women's right
to vote. The first rally was scheduled for San Francisco in September;
the second for Washington, D.C., in December. Locally, the women of
Pennsylvania were also continuing to make their political desires manifest. On September 2, 1915, again according to the *Evening Sentinel,*
40,000 people had attended a Grangers' Picnic in Carlisle to support
the causes of prohibition and suffragism. Near the end of September,
Moore and her mother distributed suffrage pamphlets at a fair and
Moore even stood on a chair to reattach a banner that had fallen
down. Moore did so much talking that a friend suggested she "go on the
stump," and she observed that everyone was respectful, and every man
but three said he would vote for suffrage that coming November. On
the first of October, a "Woman's Liberty Bell" arrived in Carlisle, and
the *Sentinel* urged "all organizations of this town—men's and women's"
to meet the bell and escort it through town. Moore and her mother
both went to the courthouse and there joined in the crowd that greeted
the bell's arrival. This device was part of the extensive national effort
to gain support for the suffragist amendment. On the same day, Moore
wrote to Warner on stationery carrying the letterhead of the Committee to Organize Cumberland County. She mentioned a prayer meeting
for suffragettes near the end of October, where the preacher had said he

wouldn't pray for the Republican party, but he would do so for the oppressed. Moore's suffragism was encouraged at Bryn Mawr, and for her it was presumably tied up with questions of "service" and the sense that women were capable and deserving of the full burden, as well as the privileges, of citizenship. For Mrs. Moore, suffragism seems chiefly to have been an adjunct to her Christian sense of the worth of any individual who had the character and strength of purpose to be self-disciplined. For her daughter, suffragism meant at the very least the need for a woman to define her own worth rather than accept or accede to the value system of someone else. Such a desire for independence was a critical part of Moore's poetic struggle at this time, as her poems continued to explore the many issues that lay beneath the structures of tradition and self-expression.

III. "The Sojourn in the Whale"

The fall of 1915 saw another important development in Moore's literary life: her friendship with H.D. was established. Hilda Doolittle, as she was called before Pound's renaming of her as an Imagist poet, was a resident of Philadelphia when Moore was in Carlisle attending Metzger Institute. In 1911, a few years after her brief try at college, she emigrated to England and lived there and in Europe for the rest of her life. In many ways she stood as a clear opposite to Moore: she was the daughter of a professor of astronomy at the University of Pennsylvania, who represented a very strong presence in her life, and she lived a life of bohemian wandering and sexual unorthodoxy. Her poetry was heavily indebted to Greek myth and archetypal symbols, which were markedly different from the precisely observed details favored by Moore. H.D. had been a classmate of Moore's at Bryn Mawr in the academic year 1905–6, and when her husband, Richard Aldington, accepted Moore's poems for The Egoist, H.D. wrote to ask if she were the same person she remembered seeing at a pageant in a green dress. At first H.D.'s letters were cautious, but also full of praise. She spoke of her own book of poems, recently published, as very uneven; she also described Moore as an anachronism. She urged Moore to write "untouched and uninfluenced by what goes on about you." This was good advice in many ways, though perhaps redundant in Moore's case, but it also showed how the leading modernist poet of inwardness would view Moore. Ten years later, when reviewing H.D.'s *Collected Poems* in the August, 1925 issue of *The Dial,* Moore could identify the precarious balance of inner and outer energies in H.D.'s work:

> We have in these poems an external world of commanding beauty—the erect, the fluent, the unaccountably brilliant. Also, we have that inner world of interacting reason and unreason in which are comprehended, the rigor, the succinctness of hazardous emotion.

This perceptive formulation must have pleased H.D., and though Moore was comprehending and positive, her own poetic always differed markedly from H.D.'s. Moore, of course, wanted to engage the world, at least to come to terms with its habits of mind and its tangled orders of nature and culture. She was enthusiastic about H.D.'s response to her work, even if H.D. could end an early letter with the claim that "life is very very hopeless," though she also asked forgiveness for the remark. What united the two women, however, was that they both recognized that "hazardous emotion" demanded rigorous and succinct expression.

Mrs. Moore excitedly wrote to Warner about H.D.'s "remarkable appreciation" for Moore's work; she further reported that Aldington wanted Moore to work on some Latin and Greek verse translations for him, and that H.D. had invited her to come and be with them in England, even though "in America they would be called poor." She also relayed the opinion that Aldington thought Moore's work was the best being done in America, this being even stronger than what he was to express in *Bruno's Weekly.* In late September, Moore was to read his remarks in the July issue of Bruno's publication, which she called "Greenwich Village." Aldington and H.D. had recently been caught between Pound's ego and the organizing energies of Amy Lowell, who was taking over the Imagist movement by democratizing the selection of poems, allowing each contributor to select his or her own work for the yearly anthologies.

Aldington was a writer who immersed himself in the literary life, and though he claimed not to like literary parties, he knew everyone. He was to write a novel about the war, *Death of a Hero,* that became a best seller. Filled with a hatred of provincialism and British snobbery, he was committed to liberal tolerance, and later staunchly defended the work of D. H. Lawrence. His memoir, *Life for Life's Sake,* is especially touching when he reminisces about the lost world of pre-1914 England. In some ways, he was a paler version of the late nineteenth-century man of letters, someone who instead turned to modernism where his many different talents as novelist, poet, editor, translator, and discoverer of new talent never quite came together in a coherent career. Aldington was only twenty years old when, according to his account, he, H.D., and Pound formulated the principles of Imagism at a London tea shop. The work of publicizing the new poetry was becoming more widespread and more heated. At the end of the first week of September, Moore "accelerated all [her] motions" as a result of H.D.'s letter. Mrs. Moore mentioned that her daughter was writing diligently on her reply to these new English admirers. Moore had found a supportive audience after all, and it was to be of a very special sort.

The fall of 1915 was filled with letters and encouragement from H.D. and Aldington, and many suffragist meetings, and it also included one of the most stirring of all Moore's experiences. From the last week in November until the ninth of December, Moore visited New York City and had her first introduction to the writing community in Greenwich Village. She referred to this trip, in describing it to Warner, as her "Sojourn in the Whale." The biblical story of Jonah in the whale was an episode in which the reluctant prophet tries to avoid his fate, but God intervenes so that he might eventually perform his duties. Moore meant the biblical allusion partly in jest, of course, but it had a revealing aspect as well. What emerges from the allusion, and from the trip as well, is a divided sense about what Moore's mission was. She was to use allusions to Jonah's story throughout her life, and—along with Job—this prophet was to have a special significance for her.

In October, Moore met, through Mary Norcross, a Mrs. Hale, the well-traveled daughter-in-law of Senator Hale of New York. Moore described her as an old Viking type with hair like corn silk, and distaffs on either side of her hair. On October 21, 1915, she had come to Carlisle to give a speech on suffragism, and she and Moore went for a ride together, during which Moore asked about the English artistic set, as Mrs. Moore described it to Warner. Mrs. Hale said, among other things, that Gordon Craig was repulsive and clammy as a person. She also talked about her unfinished novel, which Mrs. Moore found rather undignified. At one point, Mrs. Hale suggested to Moore that she should get out of Carlisle which was no more than a dead suburb, though Moore quickly added to Warner that the remark had been made in good humor.

But there was yet another connection between visitors to Carlisle and the larger literary world beyond. Moore had recently been spending time with Miss Rhodes, who had friends and "contacts" in New York City. Miss Rhodes, whom Moore never referred to by her first name, was a rather tall woman with gray hair and a lovely black velvet hat with gray silk bows. She had come to Carlisle in October to visit Mrs. Glass, the married sister of George Plank, and she knew the Aldingtons in London, where she had recently visited. She brought with her a lot of gossip about London literary life; not only did she know George Plank, but she also had met the people at *The Egoist*. Miss Rhodes was a basket maker, and a devotee of the Arts and Crafts Movement, then flourishing under the inspiration of William Morris. It was probably through this artistic commitment that Miss Rhodes had come to know Mary Norcross, and she even encouraged Moore to start an Arts and Crafts chapter in Carlisle. In October, Miss Rhodes's gossip was balanced by Moore's own reactions to things. Moore, for example, had taken a dislike to Dora Marsden, one of the backers of *The Egoist*, and she had discovered that Yeats had been busying himself about spiritualism to the exclusion of everything else. But in the same month, Moore could write to her brother that Miss Rhodes had told her all about her confederates (Moore's fellow writers) in response to questions about a dozen or so "brother rats." Moore learned, for example, that Henry James was writing a novel superintended by George Moore. Miss Rhodes was also invited to supper at the Moore house, and Moore showed her her poems, though again Mrs. Moore felt this was not in good taste. Mrs. Moore quipped that her daughter would give them nothing for a month, but instead they would be nourished by a sonnet, warmed by free verse, or sheltered by a ditty. Moore's writing was obviously stirred by hearing such reports of the literary world, and her brother remarked that the hobnobbings were very entertaining. Obviously Moore's interest was more than random; she already saw herself as a member of a group, even as she used variations on her pet name to describe her interests and activities.

Moore had recently gotten hold of the last Imagist anthology, and read Pound's article on Vorticism in the *Fortnightly*, though she had had to search hard to obtain it. Also, William Benét wrote Moore in the middle of November to say that he had especially liked her "To a Steam Roller" in *The Egoist*. Two weeks previously she had seen an article in the Philadelphia *Bulletin* by Gilbert Hursh, the young journalist she had met at Lake Placid. Three weeks earlier, on October 3, Alfred Kreymborg, editor at a magazine called *Others*, had accepted five poems in a letter to which he added a postscript describing her work as "an amazing output and absolutely original." This was the same man who had just the Sunday before written a piece for the Philadelphia *Bulletin* on Duchamp's "Nude Descending a Staircase," one of the most notorious works exhibited at the Armory Show in New York in 1913. Joseph Kerfoot, writing cultural criticism in *Life* magazine that September, said that "the new poetry was revolutionary and you might not like it, but it was worth the price of a Wednesday matinee to find out"; one of the magazines Kerfoot singled out was Alfred Kreymborg's *Others*. On October 30, she had received a letter from Devereux Josephs asking her for poems for a magazine he was starting, to be called *Contemporary Verse*. And while *The New Republic* and the *Yale Review* were rejecting her poems, the number and variety of places she submitted to was expanding.

Her reading at this point is especially revealing. Besides the Carlisle library, Moore would borrow books from the Harrisburg library when she went to visit friends there or to attend suffragist meetings. In the space of a few months in the fall of 1915, just as her poems were being accepted, and her knowledge of the literary worlds of London and New York was expanding, Moore read a number of autobiographies and memoirs. At least four of these are mentioned in her letters to Warner, and they are all by artists. They were Conrad's *A Personal Record*, *The Autobiography of Benvenuto Cellini*, Ford Madox Hueffer's *Memories and Reminiscences*, and George Moore's *Hail and Farewell*. All of these books dealt in one way or another with the world of the artist, and the ways in which one can enter such a world and come to be a part of it. She read all of the books very avidly. Conrad's book, she told Warner, was a real treat. Her mother, on the other hand, was so impressed with the Cellini, which, along with the Hueffer, she and Moore read aloud to one another, that she told Warner she wanted to buy an inexpensive edition of it.

Within the space of a few months, it seems, Moore's cultural and artistic life—both as a reader and as a writer of poetry—took on greatly expanded energy and purpose. Most important, Kreymborg had invited her to come and visit him in New York. Mrs. Moore had deduced from Kreymborg's acceptance letter that he was insufferable. Furthermore, she had raised very high standards to judge her daughter's poetry. In a letter of October 3, Moore told Warner that she felt she had enough poems for a collection. But, she added, their mother advised against it, for she felt her style was too ephemeral, and needed to be changed. It's hard to know what Mrs. Moore meant by a change in style; she may well have felt that Moore was being too "modern" with her hard images and ironic attitudes. Moore, however, was confident, and even though she had recently requested the manuscript she'd sent to MacDonald be returned, a book was a definite prospect in her mind.

There must have been some tension between Moore and her mother about all this, but Moore did quip that she hoped to see Gilbert Hursh in New York and even suggested he was one of Mole's "insufferables." She seems to have accepted the connection between artistic creativity and a bohemian or unorthodox manner. On October 7, she visited some rather pious family friends in Mercersburg, and told Warner that if she had her writing pad and her avant-garde magazines with her, she would stir things up. On November 2, Mrs. Moore observed to Warner that it was the nineteenth anniversary of their move to Carlisle. Eight days later, Moore took Kreymborg's essays out of the local library, though later she described them to Warner as not especially useful. There is more than a trace of willfulness in Moore's attitude, capable as she was of defending her poetic interests against her mother's suspicious or dismissive judgments. This willfulness was later to be seen as a sure sign of strength by her artistic contemporaries. One of those who was most impressed with her was Alfred Kreymborg.

Kreymborg was born in 1883, the son of a German immigrant who ran a cigar store in New York City. He left high school after two years, got a job, and found his way to a studio on 14th Street. There he moved into the rapidly growing bohemian circles of Greenwich Village. Guido Bruno published a small book of his "neo-realist" stories, and since one of them dealt with a prostitute, he was hauled into court by Anthony Comstock and his Society for the Prevention of Vice. In 1908 he had started a magazine called *The American Quarterly*, which failed after six months. It was to be the first of several such ventures. In this magazine he published Joyce Kilmer, the poet who wrote the sort of sentimental, genteel verse that appealed to a large audience. Kreymborg accompanied Kilmer to a meeting of the Poetry Society, but when he wrote a satire about the meeting, he lost Kilmer's friendship forever. Kreymborg was ingratiating and ambitious, and was soon to be swept along on the tides of modernism, becoming more successful as its spokesman than one of its exemplars. By 1908, Kreymborg had heard of neither Frost nor Sandburg, then not at all widely published. But he did meet Marsden Hartley who introduced him to many artists, including John Marin, Arthur Dove, Paul Strand, and especially Alfred Stieglitz. Another friend, John Cournos, gave him the name of Ezra Pound; Pound was to use Kreymborg's latest magazine, the *Glebe*, to bring out the first *Imagiste* anthology. *Glebe* was backed by Charles and Albert Boni, owners of an important bookshop and a publishing house. A later magazine, called *Others* ("The old expressions are with us always, and there are always others," was the motto that inspired it), was financed by the wealthy patron Walter Arensberg. Kreymborg, with his enthusiasm, his social connections, and his avant-garde disposition, was in many ways a perfect interlocutor for Moore in the world of New York letters.

The immediate occasion for the trip to New York City was not Kreymborg's invitation, but an offer from another source. Two family friends, the Cowdreys, had invited both Moore and her mother to accompany them to New York City, where they were to have a vacation stay at the YWCA. Mrs. Moore declined for herself, but wrote Warner that she would be happy to see Moore go; she could occupy herself exploring the activities in which she was currently so involved. In the meantime, Mrs. Moore would arrange to have the interior of the house painted, which was something that Moore herself would just as soon not be present for. Additionally, Mrs. Moore would only be exhausted by the trip, and their funds were a bit tight as well. However, her mother was able to order Moore a new coat from a Boston manufacturer just for the event. It was black with blue and green stripes, and had leather buttons the size of buckeyes. And so, with a suitable chaperone and a suitable outfit for the beginning of the trip, Moore, having collected many addresses, set out for New York, the place she was later to describe as a "savage's romance." She left in what Mrs. Moore described as gay spirits.

When she got to New York City, Moore stayed at the YWCA at 135 East 52nd Street. At first she attended some lectures at the "Y," one on

Isaiah and another on public speaking. She then called on Laura Benét, who was living in the city at the time, and went with her to visit her brother, William Rose, who was working at *The Century*. She realized that they had very little in common aesthetically, though they were able to agree to disagree. But a watershed had been passed and another link with Carlisle was strained. In the lobby of the Varick House, where she had gone to stay after leaving the "Y," she was saying good-bye to Laura when Kreymborg arrived. He was accosted by Laura and asked his opinion of her brother's poetry. Politely, he ducked the question. But Moore described her as pressing on, asking what Kreymborg thought of Louis Untermeyer's work. Here he could be more outspoken, and said that he found little merit in it. Moore then left with Kreymborg to have dinner with him and his wife, at their modest apartment at 29 Bank Street. She wrote to her mother that he was gentle and full of fun, with no bohemian exaggerations. At the time he was 32 years old, though he told Moore he was only 28; his wife shyly said that she was four years younger.

Many of Moore's introductions were to come through Kreymborg. It had been two years earlier, in the winter of 1913–14, that he had turned over a special issue of his magazine *Glebe* to Ezra Pound, who used it to edit the first volume of imagist poetry, called *Des Imagistes* after the French symbolist tradition to which it owed a great deal. Kreymborg himself was just then publishing his first collection of poems, *Mushrooms*. Largely in free verse, these poems showed little of the precision of phrase or lexical inventiveness of Moore, but they did have the right "modern" attitude. In "A Sword," for example, the new bohemian spirit is tricked out in a figure of speech that is not quite as striking as it means to be:

> Love is a sword,
> a million-bladed sword
> slashing the petty pates
> and sticking the smug
> stomachs of the past
> till the pink blood dribble,
> and with a roar of ribald song,
> flaunting the laughing boyish present
> against the stare and whisper
> of the doddering future!

Kreymborg was trying to do something very like what Pound was engaged in, for by putting himself in touch with many people he hoped to interpret and control the new movements in the arts. He and his wife took Moore to "291," the gallery on Fifth Avenue run by Alfred Stieglitz, where they met, among many others, the Zorachs.

She went a second time by herself to see "291"; she may well have still had the address in her notebook from when she had met Paul Haviland's niece at Bryn Mawr six years earlier. At "291" she saw the very latest in American and European art, as the internationalism in modernist culture was boldly on display. The exhibit mounted at the time was of work by a German architect named Blumner. She saw a Marsden Hartley hung next to Picabia, and some Picassos as well. In the back room of the gallery, she saw work by Man Ray, Marin, and Pendergast. She was also especially struck by a Steichen photograph of Gordon Craig. Stieglitz was his authoritative self, and she discussed with him several recent articles from his journal *Camera Work*, which was revolutionizing the art of photography in America. She found Stieglitz's photographs to be the most beautiful things she had ever seen, and described the man himself as "droll"—a very high compliment. Like so many others of the time, she fell under his considerable social charms, telling her mother that he was everything ideal, sane and modest, imperturbable and kind.

At "291" she also met Joseph Kerfoot, whose recent article in *Life* was one of the first notices about the "new poetry" to appear in a national magazine. She discussed with Kerfoot, and quoted from, several of the latest articles about contemporary writing in the journals and magazines. She also noticed that his shoes were not polished. Kerfoot and Stieglitz listened as she said that she was haunted by certain pictures, and they suggested that haunting was often a quality of bad art. She countered by saying she meant "haunting" to suggest the feature of a work that made you want to know what its sources were; at this the two men agreed that such a quality was indeed desirable. The conversation turned to the reviews by Francis Hackett, then a regular contributor for the *New Republic,* and Kerfoot agreed with Moore that he was a good critic. As she left, Kerfoot said that he hoped they would meet again soon.

With Laura Benét, Moore visited Bruno's garret, located over a drugstore on Washington Square in Greenwich Village. There, they saw one of this eccentric's dramatic productions, a vaudeville puppet show. She described Bruno as tall and pallid, with straight colorless hair, and he wore a black-and-white checkered serge suit. He gave her a copy of several pamphlets that he had published, as well as Kreymborg's *Mushrooms;* this rather innocent volume was soon to be the focus of some unkind parodies in the press. Kreymborg himself was between magazines, having published *Glebe* in 1913–14, and having just founded *Others,* which was to appear from 1915 to 1919. This ambitious young poet earnestly set himself up as Moore's advisor. He warned her against Amy Lowell and the Poetry Society, and opined that Pound's work had "fallen short." He also introduced her to the world of literary feuds, for he had had a recent falling out with Aldington. Moore, in a moment of what may have been true naïveté, offered to intercede and patch things up. Since she knew Aldington only through correspondence, and only for the briefest period, it is hard to tell if this offer was made out of a desire to impress or please Kreymborg, or because she felt such matters were easily resolved. Meanwhile, Mrs. Moore was writing to Warner that she looked very gravely, not to say sternly, at some of the experiences that had been so eagerly embraced by her daughter.

What might these people Moore met during her "sojourn in the whale" have made of this educated, highly articulate, culturally knowledgeable poet? To Kreymborg, she was "an astonishing person with Titian hair, a brilliant complexion and a mellifluous flow of polysyllables which held every man in awe. Marianne Moore talked as she wrote and wrote as she talked, and the consummate ease of the performance either way reminded one of the rapids of an intelligent stream." Surely it was a rare event to have a person arrive in the cultural and artistic capital with so much learning, sensitivity, and apparent poise. Though the magnet of artistic freedom and experimentation was to draw many of America's major writers from small towns throughout the country into New York—and Greenwich Village in particular—during the first three decades of the century, Moore's arrival challenges this almost mythic pattern. She had, it would seem, as much or even more to offer the metropolis than to take from it. Yet she seems in part to have wanted to be taken as another person who comes from the province to the capital in order to complete and vindicate her art. For example, she allowed Kreymborg to think that this was her very first visit to New York. Yet we know that her visit with Hilda Sprague-Smith six years before had exposed her to a good deal of the world of cosmopolitan culture. Throughout her life Moore was to downplay her skill and her role in the development of modern poetry, as in the famous interview where she said she only called her pieces poems because she didn't know what other category to put them in. This modesty was deeply ingrained in her temperament and by her mother's influence.

One way to glimpse Moore's state of mind at this point might be to look briefly at the two short poems she published together in *Bruno's Weekly* (October, 1916). They were not collected by Moore in any book, and they recall the tonal ambiguity and personal coding of "To an Intra-Mural Rat," published earlier in *Poetry*. Again, bearing in mind her nickname "Rat," they show a playful self-image that still has a serious side to it:

TWO THINGS BY MARIANNE MOORE

Holes Bored in a Workbag by the Scissors

A neat, round hole in the bank of the creek
  Means a rat;
    That is to say, craft, industry, resourcefulness:
      While
These indicate the unfortunate, meek
  Habitat
    Of surgery thrust home to fabricate useless
      Voids.

Apropos of Mice

Come in, Rat, and eat with me,
One must occasionally—
  If one would rate the rat at his true worth—
  Practice catholicity;

Cheeseparings and porkrind
Stock my house—good of their kind
  But were they not, you would oblige me? Is
  Plenty, multiplicity?

The first poem contrasts purposive labor with an activity that produces "useless voids." The animal outside the home manages to have virtues that the domestic image lacks; if Moore the serious poet is the "rat" of the first stanza, then the holes bored by scissors might be the result of needling critics who ask useless questions about an aesthetic they cannot understand. But the second stanza could also show Moore herself dreaming about a purposeless activity that produces only a void, thereby creating a "shadow" image of the poet as playful dreamer. The second poem might well be about Moore and her mother. Sharing a home means sharing one's sustenance; the poet may be suggesting that her mother's nourishment must be not only plentiful but various, or the "rat" will not be correctly valued. Rats are indiscriminate feeders, and by taking up everything thrown at them they make their "true worth" visible. In one letter to Warner, Mrs. Moore calls her daughter's poems "porkrinds," a covert reference that adds another dimension to the poem.

Even to one ignorant of Moore's nickname, the two poems express the importance of social bearing and the contrastive weight of differing moral virtues. Slight and playful as they are, the poems register a genuine tension about the importance of "style," since in them style is more than mere expressiveness. Style is the measure of character. But read as coded poems about the poet herself, these two short lyrics are concerned with self-definition and self-acceptance. And, of course, the second poem makes one of those distinctive redefinitions that characterize Moore's work at its most challenging. Multiplicity seems often to be required for plenty, even in some cases to be a synonym for it. But Moore focuses on the crucial differences between the two concepts, which can be both empirical and moral. One does not need multiplicity to have, and, more important, to appreciate, plenty. True plenty, Moore suggests, comes from otherness freely offered, and not from a mere variety of choices. The surest measure of self-definition comes when one is able to make such distinctions.

As the new year of 1916 began, Moore was back in Carlisle and interested in pursuing some career. The visit to New York likely increased her self-confidence, since she saw that she could converse on an equal footing with people who were shaping modernist culture. Not surprisingly, her thoughts turned again to the possibility of earning her way as a writer. She applied for a job at the *Ledger*, a Philadelphia newspaper, and she left off some of her reviews with her application. It is hard to know now which reviews these might have been, but it is clear that Moore's acute sense of literary values was developed through critical writing even before her days at *The Dial*. But the *Ledger* rejected her application, and for the time being she was without any prospects. In February she was to begin work for several months as a secretary for a wealthy lady, a Mrs. Gilbert, but this could not have paid very much. William Benét, in the meantime, was writing to her to get information about Richard Aldington and to ask her to comment on a few contemporary poems that he was planning to discuss in a lecture. A month later he took three of Moore's poems for his magazine *Chimaera*, but sent back some others with a note confessing frankly that he didn't understand them. The gap between genteel verse and the new modernist poetry was getting wider. In May, Warner proudly reported that a woman he met at the church in Baltimore had seen her poems in *Contemporary Verse*. So her public identity as a poet and writer continued to take shape.

The spring of 1916 was to bring about a very important change in Moore's circumstances. Warner was receiving numerous offers from churches in need of pastors. In April he mentioned a church in Chatham, New Jersey, was especially interested in him. On the first of May, five members of this congregation interviewed Warner and offered him $1200 per year and the use of the manse. By the end of the month he received the official form of the Presbyterian Church, the "Call for a Pastor," with the salary set at $1500 per year. He quickly told Moore and their mother that they would all be together again and move as a family to Chatham in August. Clearly it would be a major step for all of them, with an immediate and long-term effect on Moore herself. Immediately it meant that Moore would have less need for a career of her own, for now she would have a social role, at least in her family's eyes. On the other hand, it had the long-term effect of bringing the poet closer to New York City. When Warner married, and was later assigned as a Navy chaplain to the Brooklyn Navy Yard, it would be convenient for Moore and her mother to move to New York City. But if Warner had taken an appointment at a church farther west, this would have been less likely. So in a way Moore's career was being paradoxically shaped by Warner's decision, since she was to be placed in a position where she could be more intensively a member of her family and at the same time closer to the world of letters and modern art.

Back in February, however, Mrs. Moore wrote to Warner describing her daughter in very revealing terms. The picture given of Moore must be taken as accurate, but also as partial; it reveals as much about Mrs. Moore's plans for her daughter as it does about the increasingly self-assured woman who was at this time continuing to armor herself for a life of writing. Many women, more than men, need to be loved, Mrs. Moore wrote, but her daughter is different; not only does she apparently not need such supportive love, she is also unlike other women in not being content to settle for a weak spouse just in order to achieve it. If this is true of Moore, then obviously she would be better suited to service in the manse than to a place at the center of a family of her own.

In April, Warner wrote home about an incident on board his ship; apparently as part of a bit of horseplay, he engaged a Navy lieutenant in a wrestling match in front of the other members of the crew. Warner won the match and wrote about it proudly. Less than six weeks later he told Moore and his mother that they had a fight ahead of them—this in reference to the war itself but also to the work ahead of them at Chatham—and that they must keep watch together. His muscular Christianity often supplied him with a great many of his figures of speech, and he was confirmed in his ideology by the military life in which he was increasingly engaged. In many ways, the picture Mrs. Moore and Warner had of the poet in their midst was shaped by their own attitudes toward strength and self-sufficiency. Moore herself was shaped by these attitudes, and over the next several decades she is often to have recourse to a language about herself that equates humility with strength. For her, strength was a crucial virtue, though in women it often took forms that could be baffling or even self-contradictory.

In July, 1916, Warner finally broke off his relationship with Mary White, and he was spending time aboard the USS Alabama, sailing to Block Island and Newport. In August the Moores would be occupied with details about the move to Chatham. Because they were all to start living together again in September, there are few letters for the remainder of 1916, and none at all for 1917. The details of the Moores' daily life in Chatham are scant, and, as it turned out, their time there would be brief, since Warner would soon combine a naval career with his duties as a preacher. The only family correspondence for 1917 is a letter from Uncle Dudley, in late November, congratulating Warner on a wonderful event that will nevertheless pain his mother and sister. This is probably a reference to Warner's taking a commission in the Navy, for by the opening months of 1918 he is first stationed in Norfolk and then later aboard the USS Rhode Island at the Boston Navy Yard. In March, 1918, Warner first mentions Constance Eustis, whom he had met the previous summer while visiting Monhegan Island in Maine. By the end of the month he mentions the apartment he has found for his mother and sister. For several months Moore and her mother stayed at 39 Charlton Street—they took up residence at 14 St. Luke's Place in August—and they made a brief visit to the Norcrosses back in Carlisle in May. Warner says that he will answer to the pet name "Badger" if his sister wants him to, but to his mother "Mole," he will always be "Toad." And he advises Moore not to take a job doing office work.

In June, Warner writes openly of his engagement to Miss Eustis and laments his failure to provide for a continuation of the family life he had promised his mother. He says somewhat sheepishly in firmly stating the situation that he has no real defense to offer. With the impending marriage, and the recent departure from Chatham, all had suddenly changed. Apparently, from later references, Warner's appointment at Chatham did not work out particularly well; the indications are that the parishioners were not satisfied with his oratorical skills. The Navy commission must surely have appealed to Warner, however, as more than a weak substitute, for he was very happy in his new environment in the military service. And the courtship with Constance had proceeded rather quickly. In the letter of June 17 to his mother he signs his name "Warner" instead of any of his usual pet names. The tone of this letter is very self-assured, and he has made his commitment to Constance in an especially forthright, even slightly challenging way. By July the plans for the wedding are well under way. Mrs. Moore writes Warner a letter in the middle of July that doesn't mention the wedding at all, but does ask Warner to remain always conscious of his appearance.

At first the wedding was set for August 22, but because of the pressures of Warner's Navy obligations, it was moved up to July 29. The ceremony took place at Constance's family home, 1985 Sedgwick Avenue, in the Bronx. Marianne and her mother both attended. There followed a week later a letter from his ship telling of conditions on board and mentioning his sermon. This letter doesn't mention his new wife; it is clearly meant to reassure his mother that he is his familiar self. A week later, however, he writes his mother that she should call him "Warner" if it comes more naturally; presumably the pet names are no longer appropriate. Warner is about to draw a different family circle for himself.

The experience of her brother's wedding must have been complex for Moore. Surely she saw at first hand what his leaving their family circle did to his mother, and if she had any predilections to leave, she may well have reconsidered them. She was now in New York and the excitement of the metropolis was not to be lost on her, though her own immediate prospects, especially by way of a career, were highly uncertain. There was also the problem of coming to know Constance; in the next few years there would be serious strains between Moore and her mother and Warner's new wife. Most important, she must have seen that Warner's ability to move out of one family and begin another had been achieved at a certain cost, and only by his assertiveness was he able to carry through with it. This may well have reaffirmed any doubts Moore had about her own resolve or deliberation. While her self-assurance as an artist had recently received affirmation on several fronts, her personal resoluteness may not have been equally strengthened. Nevertheless, she was now to become a citizen of New York, Greenwich Village, and the republic of letters. She would now come to a new level of the "accessibility to experience."

Chapter 4

NEW YORK CITY:
14 ST. LUKE'S PLACE

I. "The little quiet part of it"

So much of the fate of Moore as a writer is tied up with her presence in New York City in the decade of the 1920's that it seems to be a destined conjunction. Yet the events that led her to Greenwich Village, the heart of the heart of modernism, were in large measure contingent. Once she arrived, Moore made the city her own in a complex way. She was often a poet of locales, as her poems about Brooklyn, Mt. Rainier, and Virginia attest. New York City, however, was to be both a locale and a state of mind for her. The ways she was able to mediate her relationship with both these aspects of the metropolis say a great deal about her poetry. She arrived in the city to live on a permanent basis near her thirty-first birthday, and many of her poetic themes and subjects were already evident. But there was much more to come.

In the first letter that Moore wrote to her brother from St. Luke's Place, dated July 18, 1918, she mentioned that she and her mother had visited the Metropolitan Museum, and there saw the marvelous collection of medieval armor. Moore ironically juxtaposed the expansive society of the modern city with an ancient mode of personal enclosure. This paradox will be felt throughout the next decade of Moore's life. As her family life in some way narrows, her artistic horizons grow dramatically. One important new factor in her artistic sense is provided by a letter from Ezra Pound, dated December 16, 1918, in which he asserts his strong and positive opinions about her work and tries to influence her in explicit terms. But she responds at some length in a letter of January 9, 1919, that reveals her sense of her self, her art, and her relationship to the current literary scene. She is apparently happy with her recent move, and combines an image of seclusion with one of expansion when she says, "I like New York, the little quiet part of it in which my mother and I live. I like to see the tops of the masts from our door and to go to the wharf and look at the craft on the river."

The new environment of the city would be reflected very soon in Moore's poetry, for example in "Museums," a poem that was unfinished and unpublished, and "Dock Rats," which was to appear in her first book of poems. The first of these contained lines that claim that "one goes to a museum to refresh one's mind with the / appearance of what one has always valued." The other poem recorded the sea's challenging expansiveness and the dock's signals, "shrill, questioning, peremptory, diverse," and yet offered the reassuring opinion that "shipping is the/ most congenial thing in the world." In many ways these two poems show Moore exposed to a much wider world while yet maintaining many of the habits and values she had when she arrived in New York. As her life unfolds in the next decade or so it does so in large part by revolving around two poles: one of fixity and containment, represented by her job at the Hudson Park branch of the public library and the apartment she shared with her mother; and the other an ever widening world of literary parties and friends, chiefly centered at The Dial. She was to find both arenas mostly congenial and comfortable, but the strategies for mediating between them were not altogether free of tension.

When the move to New York was first made, Moore suffered a rather severe illness. Her mother wrote about it several times in the winter of 1918 to Warner, then stationed in Norfolk, Virginia, describing Moore's pale complexion and the difficulty she had in breathing. Recalling from her Bryn Mawr days her above-average lung capacity, asthma and tuberculosis can perhaps be ruled out and the problem ascribed to a simple virus. This was the time of the great flu epidemic that claimed a million lives after the war, however, and there was genuine cause for concern. There is also the possibility that the cumulative effect of the move to new quarters, the congestion of the Village, and the emotional strain of her brother's departure all took their toll. Warner and his mother continued to discuss his marriage and its circumstances. He claimed that Mrs. Moore objected to his marrying Constance because she felt he had broken a promise to another woman, probably "Ben." Mrs. Moore wondered if the tension were not the result of Constance's assumption that monetary support for Warner's mother and sister would be burdensome.

Despite such potential misunderstandings and recriminations, however, the original family ties were to reassert themselves. Warner wrote from Williamsburg, Virginia, to say a church there was so very English that they were sure to love it (indeed, fifteen years later, a family visit to Norfolk is the occasion for some of Moore's best poems). Mrs. Moore described one of the parks in Greenwich Village as reminding her of London. Mrs. Moore is concerned about money, nevertheless, and tells Warner that she and Moore will try to live within the income provided by the estate left by the Reverend Warner. Much of Mrs. Moore's time during the first few months is spent in her doing missionary work and arranging their new apartment. Warner, only two months before the war ends, tells the sailors aboard his ship that the war was a personal war and had to be won in a personal way. Such a remark will be echoed decades later in one of Moore's most famous poems, "In Distrust of Merits."

In the opening months of 1919, after the war ended, Warner did a tour of duty overseas, aboard the USS Rhode Island. Moore began a heavy round of socializing. On February 2, for example, she attended a party given in honor of Eunice Tietjens, one of the editors of *Poetry*. The same day Mrs. Moore wrote Warner to relate how Moore had been spoiled to death at an *Others* party given in honor of Harriet Monroe, and that Kreymborg had stepped forward to introduce Moore to Miss Monroe. Monroe told a story of how Pound had described Moore as "the '*enfant terrible*' of all New York." Monroe, not to be outdone by Pound's asseverations, had answered; "Yes, and Pound wanted all of them to imitate her and that was impossible." Pound had already, according to Moore, badgered Monroe to take Moore's poems. Since Pound was steadily increasing his reputation as an arbiter of taste, such commitment on his part would at the very least call considerable attention to the newcomer. Three years later Monroe ran "A Symposium on Marianne Monroe" in the pages of *Poetry*, which contained some harsh criticism, but even at this earlier time it was apparent that the quality and reception of her work were to be contested.

The literary scene in Greenwich Village at this time was well on its way to achieving the sort of mythological status it was to enjoy for decades afterwards. Moore's part in this scene was unique and directly reflective of her personality and many of the thematic paradoxes of her poetry. One of the other women active at the time was Lola Ridge, with whom Moore was to become quite friendly, despite Ridge's considerably more liberal social attitudes. Ridge for a time was one of the editors of *Broom* and also a poet, and later worked at *The Dial.* On April 10, 1919, Moore related to Warner the details of a party at Ridge's apartment on East 15th Street, filled with the usual crowd but somehow more lively than usual. Moore wondered how they could get any work done considering their nocturnal habits, and she reassured her brother that she left by 11 o'clock. What seems to be the main difference in this party from Moore's point of view was the presence of older people. This is consistent with Moore's seriousness about literary matters and suggests that she did not view her work, as many of her contemporaries did, as a struggle between generations. Moore had already taken on the voice of an experienced partygoer by this time. Furthermore, she speaks of a "principle" in describing her sense of scheduling her own work, rather than a more neutral word such as scheme or routine.

On several occasions Mrs. Moore writes to Warner about parties that Moore has described, and the differing perspectives are illuminating. Again, it is possible that both mother and daughter are playfully exaggerating their attitudes to the social whirl of the *literati,* knowing that Warner would be amused by the ironic distance between them. But the differing versions nevertheless represent two quite distinct points of view. If Moore had internalized some of her mother's strictness, it does not seem that the mother shared very easily in her daughter's occasions for stimulation. Describing Ridge's party, for example, Mrs. Moore said the preceding night's party was very entertaining for her daughter, but that she, the mother, had gone to a prayer meeting, and, upon her return, spent the next hours making cranberry sauce in anticipation of Warner's visit, and also making sure her kitchen was neat and clean.

These domestic details, of course, set off Moore's daily life rather markedly from that of the prototypical Greenwich Village writer. The Village had recently become the center of a bohemian mix of low rents, artistic experiment, and political agitation. The mix of political and artistic forces of the early years of the century's first decade had culminated in the famous salon of Mabel Dodge and all of the colorful anarchy that went with it. Bill Haywood, John Reed, and many others of a radical political inclination had already achieved something like legendary status. There was also the famous hangout known as "Polly's," a restaurant run by Polly Halliday, and the famous Liberal Club on MacDougal Street, run by Henrietta Rodman, which had moved to downtown quarters in 1913. Many people were united in their liberal and radical social views, and their hatred of Comstockery, that quite strong vestige of American puritanical morality. It was the Comstock Committee that had taken Alfred Kreymborg to court on charges of obscenity for his story about a prostitute. After the war there were also the Palmer raids, one of the more virulent forms of anti-Communist anxiety, as well as crucial strikes in industries such as coal and steel. Early in the period, from near the turn of the century until just after the war, the concerns were often predominantly political and social, though after the war they became more social and artistic. The prototypical artist was in either case not usually seen as a homebody.

Indeed, at the time Moore first arrived in St. Luke's Place, that prototype was being embodied and polished by Edna St. Vincent Millay. She was a poet who might instructively serve as Moore's exact opposite. Millay won a national contest in 1912 with her poem "Renascence." Her arrival in New York five years later to become an actress at the Provincetown Theatre was utterly different from Moore's. The aspiring actress had achieved notoriety when, in 1917, her graduation from Vassar was prohibited, but eventually allowed, because of an infraction of the college's rules. She and her two younger sisters, both strikingly attractive, were the talk of every male in the Village, if common gossip is to be credited. Eventually, through her sentimental and rather wan poetry, plus her bohemian reputation and a well-publicized trip to Europe, Millay became identified in America's popular imagination as the very essence of the free-living, free-loving poet. Moore never mentioned Millay in print throughout this period, and this seems much more a judgment than an oversight. Whatever Millay represented to outside observers, she did not suggest herself to Moore as a model of the serious artist.

Mrs. Moore for her part was still trying to adjust to Warner's failure to bring the family together "in service," for now there would be no pastorate, at least no manse for her and her daughter. In April, 1919, she writes her son to remind him of the necessity for discipline, and tells him how, as a boy, he vowed always to take the harder course on principle. "Muscular Christianity" would mean something different to Warner, however. Moore says little of these matters in the letters to her brother, but it is hard not to conclude that she must have turned a reflective eye on her own career at this time. Around this time Mrs. Moore suggested to Warner that she and her daughter might go to live in England. This seems a remark based more on sentiment than any actual calculation, for a few years later Mrs. Moore will refuse Bryher's offer to have them do just that, with her support. Warner in the meantime was celebrating the birth of his first child, a daughter, and enjoying greatly the work in the Navy and everything about it; he had already decided he would make a career of it. He was teaching English and civics to "Filapenos," as he spelled it, and says that when they pledge allegiance to the United States, it reminds him of swearing allegiance to Christ.

Mrs. Moore continued to regale Warner with the details of Moore's social life, adding that they were important to her and that such gatherings as the party for *Others* were the only things that occasioned real spontaneity in her. At such parties it had become quite common for people to read their poems aloud and criticize them. Through such social activities Moore established herself as one of the wittiest and most dedicated of the new poets. It was at such a party that she was to meet Scofield Thayer, who suggested she send the poem she had just read to *The Dial*. She said she had already sent it and it had been rejected; he urged her to resubmit, and it was published as her first contribution to the magazine that was to be crucial in establishing her reputation. For the next three decades, her network was to be almost as private as Millay's was public.

During the first few years in New York, Moore's attention seemed much more focused on literary affairs than on anything else. On April 23, in the same letter in which Mrs. Moore remarked on her daughter's spontaneous delight in literary affairs, she told Warner that his sister had recently confessed to having a very dim religious faith. At the same time Mrs. Moore knew her daughter had had a very stimulating set of experiences the past twelve months or so, but that she had remained impassive about them, so the mother had not said anything about it. Here we see the other side of the intimacy of the nuclear family, for in

Moore's reticence to express her feelings, and in her mother's concealing her awareness of this refusal, something like a Jamesian drama is
played out. Tacit knowledge and emotional reticence become the key
elements in the relationship between equals and intimates. Also, we
can see that Mrs. Moore implicitly connected her daughter's artistic
activities with a dimness of religious faith, as if echoing Matthew Arnold's prediction that in the modern world poetry would take over the
function of religion. One of the continuing struggles between Moore
and her mother in the next three decades would involve the problem of
how literature might be defined as serving spiritual needs.

In the late spring of 1919, Moore attended the reunion marking the
tenth anniversary of her graduation from Bryn Mawr. Moore had asked
for and been given some Blake reproductions, for her graduation from
Bryn Mawr, and she kept these framed above her desk for all her life.
Now she was distressed to see that some Blake paintings were removed
from their honored place in one of the college's buildings, having been
replaced by what she considered a worthless painting presented by Miss
Garrett, whom she described as "Miss Thomas's great friend." She also
complained about the college's decorative style, and seem generally to
have voiced her opinions strongly. A meeting with Miss Donnelly must
have had some satisfaction, for her old teacher remarked on recently
seeing one of Moore's poems in an anthology; this was probably the
Others anthology for 1917. One of these poems was "Sojourn in the
Whale," about a country for which she felt a special attachment and
identification:

Trying to open locked doors with a sword, threading
    the points of needles, planting shade trees
    upside down; swallowed by the opaqueness of one whom the
seas love better than they love you, Ireland—
you have lived and lived on every kind of shortage.
    You have been compelled by hags to spin
    gold thread from straw and have heard men say:
    "There is a feminine temperament in direct contrast to ours,

    which makes her do these things. Circumscribed by a
    heritage of blindness and native
    incompetence, she will become wise and will be forced to give in.
Compelled by experience, she will turn back;

water seeks its own level":
   and you have smiled. "Water in motion is far
   from level." You have seen it, when obstacles happened to bar
the path, rise automatically.

We know from the earlier letters of Moore's about her second visit to
New York City that the image of a sojourn in the whale had great
resonance for her. Among other things, it conveyed the ability to
persist against adversity, to have a period of confusion become in fact
a trial and thus a new opportunity; in short, it was an image of revelation through darkness. Such adversity can be instructive for an individual or for a country. Here she uses the image to describe the
country of her foreparents, but also allegorically to suggest a self-
portrait. The feminine temperament and the ability, even the urgency,
to rise automatically against obstacles were—if not patently part of
Moore's character at this time—at least values that she aspired to in
finding her place in the world. This poem was written at least two years
before the Bryn Mawr visit, occasioned in part by the Easter Rebellion in Dublin and the ensuing civil strife, but she tells Warner that
it is one of the two poems she chose to read aloud during the reunion.
Its imagery of water rising against an obstacle contrasts sharply with
Yeats' famous image of the patriot's heart turned to stone, in his
"Easter, 1916."

In the same letter that Mrs. Moore describes the Bryn Mawr reunion
to Warner, she tells him she is glad Moore has returned to her "boyhood" interests. Warner's response also refers to his sister's "boyhood."
In some sense they were both trying to keep Moore in an infantile or at
least adolescent state. By returning to the sort of play with gender (in
their nicknames, for example, Moore is often called by a male name)
they were evading the issue of Moore's womanhood, and setting aside
questions about her career and her place in the world.

The captain of Warner's ship knew someone at *The New York
Times*, a Mr. Adler, and Warner arranged for his sister to meet this
man in an attempt to secure a position for herself as a reviewer. During the first week of September, Moore visited the newspaper, and
eventually submitted a trial review, of a book called *Old and New
Masters in Literature*, by Robert Lynd. It is a rather stiff effort, the sort
of thing one might expect from a beginner who was trying too hard to

cover all points. Nothing further came of this effort. In the first week of October, she told Warner she didn't fit in with the idea of a daily publication; editors at such places were not interested in fine distinctions and meditative depth, two important features of Moore's writing. Clearly Moore understood her own temperament, for her reviews, which were to appear in *The Dial* before long, were definitely more meditative than any daily journal could appreciate. In this same letter, Moore takes a dig at William Rose Benét's poem in the October issue of *Yale Review*, which had only recently rejected her "Dock Rats." Increasingly in the 1930's, she was to see her work as restricted in terms of a possible audience; it was an attitude that she was never entirely to lay aside.

In the meantime, Warner was completing his overseas tour and taking up residence in a house in Berkeley, California. Constance's father had settled $2500 per annum on her; indirectly this helped Moore and her mother, for Warner could now send them money more frequently to supplement the estate. Warner occupied himself by reading Rauschenbusch's *Social Principles of Jesus*; he continued to see his religion in large measure as a form of social ethics rather than a theological mystery. Moore had begun working at the library across the street from her apartment, the Hudson Park branch, for $30 per month. She also told Warner that she was visiting galleries often and was richly repaid for it. Along with many writers, she will be friendly in the coming years with several visual artists, such as Walter Pach, one of the organizers of the Armory Show of 1913; William Zorach, who was to do an oil portrait and a sculpture of Moore, and whose wife, Marguerite, painted Moore and her mother; and Marius de Zayas. Moore was able to tell Warner that she enjoyed the library work much more than her job back at the Indian School in Carlisle, but her mother described her daughter's face as being white, with a monk-like severity that indicated her old merry self-indulgent days were gone, replaced by something she could scarcely identify. The rigors of Moore's self-imposed apprenticeship were not to stop when she left Carlisle; it can be sensed that they continued for many years.

Near the end of October, Moore received from Pound a copy of his latest book of poems, probably *Quia Pauper Amavi*, which contained three Cantos and the "Homage to Sextus Propertius"; earlier she had heard at the Bryn Mawr reunion how he was regarded as a notorious figure. Writing to Warner in November, she half-jokingly suggested one should use a veil for attendance at social events in the city; her sense of modesty was considerably different from that of her peers. That month she and her mother cast their votes for the Republicans and the Prohibitionists, even though they both would be overwhelmed by the forces of Tammany Hall, and thinking such a protest was necessary for their conscience. Though their suffragism had apparently become less an active concern, their views about temperance were still strong. The vote, however, was more than a protest, as Prohibition became law at this time. But the split between her rather conservative views about political and social issues and her artistic tastes was by now quite firmly established.

In the meantime, Warner was still trying to justify his marriage to Constance. Mrs. Moore answered this by reminding Warner how hard his sister and she had worked at Chatham just after he left for the Navy. This was done to reflect glory on his pastorate; it seemed to be mentioned now to induce guilt. But while there may have been strains in the family, there was also good news to report about sundry items. Moore had gotten a new hat, which she described to her brother in detail. There were also invitations to parties to recount: one in Brooklyn given by Kreymborg for *Others*, and yet another at the apartment of Lola Ridge, who was by then an assistant editor at *The Dial*. Mrs. Moore added that Moore wasn't going to the party at Ridge's, but at least the connections with *The Dial* were beginning to take shape.

In the opening days of 1920, Warner proposed that Moore and his mother come to visit him out west. At this time he was still renting a house in Berkeley, but he also had heard rumors that he would be transferred to Bremerton Naval Station, on Puget Sound, beneath the slopes of Mt. Rainier. Constance added her expression of welcome to the two women, and Warner followed with a telegram in the middle of February. The two families were being warm toward one another, in part no doubt to offset the recent strain, and also because Mrs. Moore would have a chance to see her first grandchild. Warner mentions wanting to read his sister's poems in the April issue of *The Dial*. She first appeared in that famous magazine with "England" and "Picking and Choosing." By the end of March, Mrs. Moore had booked passage on the "Mercy," slated to sail through the Panama Canal, only recently opened, to San Francisco. The trip began in late May, and concluded in early August. En route, Moore went ashore in Panama City where she remarked on the local flora and fauna, especially the pelicans and lizards.

By the first of May, Warner had gotten a copy of *The Dial* and read his sister's poems. His reaction to them is very telling, for it reflects attitudes and values that will be repeated over and over among the members of the family. He was impressed with their grasp of life, as he called it, and spoke of their special language, which was not only marvelously handled but also kept any outsiders from understanding the family's special network of feelings and associations. Many critics have pointed out the important role Mrs. Moore had in her daughter's poetry, sometimes even contributing phrases and words. What this letter shows is that Warner, too, felt himself in some sense the special audience, if not in part the author, of his sister's poems. Moore's poetic life and imagination were in an important sense an extension of her family life, even down to her thinking of her effort as possessing a special vocabulary. It is hard to know exactly what Warner is referring to by way of "language"—the two poems are not particularly obscure by Moore's standards—and one might imagine that the poems simply contain individual words that have been the source of puns or other family humor or commentary. Like the early poems in *Bruno's Weekly*, where the nickname "Rat" is used in what amounts to a private pun, many of Moore's poems would contain veiled references to things of special importance to Warner and Mrs. Moore.

After their journey to the west, Moore and her mother received a letter from Warner that expressed the belief that this trip had opened up a new chapter in their lives. Obviously he was still trying to reassure his mother that their family ties were still strong and special, and that his "new" family need not replace his obligations to his mother and sister. Later in the year, however, Mrs. Moore mailed a very sobering letter to Warner expressing her dissatisfaction with Constance and her inability to appreciate the ideas shared by the three Moores. In this letter, dated November 8, 1920, Mrs. Moore also includes another letter, written weeks earlier, in which she complains of the coldness and alienation she felt in Constance's household. Obviously, since the family was together, there is no independent account of the visit, so it is hard to credit one version over another. She had refrained from sending this earlier letter for fear of antagonizing her daughter-in-law, but eventually her feelings overcame her restraint. Constance was understandably wounded by this letter, but appears to have been mollified by Warner's explanations. Around this time Mrs. Moore also suggested that the raising and educating of Warner's daughter be turned over to her and Moore. This plan was never followed through, again apparently owing to resistance from Constance. But it shows the continuing emphasis Mrs. Moore placed on education, especially of an aesthetic and spiritual sort. It also gives yet more proof of how strong the bond was that united the three Moores, and adds special meaning to their sense of Moore's poetry and its use of a special language understood only by the family.

The November 8 letter also mentioned what must be called Mrs. Moore's reconversion experience. During recent years (one assumes since Warner left Chatham), Mrs. Moore had increasingly been drawn to the figure of Christ. She claimed that this new feeling of religious devotion enabled her to deal with people who disliked her. Two days later she writes again to Warner and mentions how his problems in Chatham made it an unhappy place for him; in the same letter she praises her daughter for moving up slowly but surely. Apparently she was still adjusting to the family alignments and displacements. But her correspondence over the next twenty-five years or so displays an increasing piety centered on Christological terminology and sentiments. For example, months after the publication of Moore's first book of poems, Mrs. Moore will urge her to stop worrying about the printer's errors in the book and press on in the high calling of God in Jesus Christ.

Moore, for her part, involved herself yet more deeply in the literary world. In August she paid a visit to Carlisle, but told Warner that the town was stifling and the prettiness not a sufficient compensation. Warner responded with a nostalgic letter about his memories of Carlisle, but Mrs. Moore claimed a few weeks later that one of the great reliefs of absence from Carlisle was their not needing to carry all the burden in conversation. Warner had never felt that characteristic of Carlisle, but it bore down very heavily upon the two women. But there were good things in their current situation to report as well. Moore, for example, often mentioned her work in the library, which she seemed to enjoy thoroughly, especially preparing lectures on contemporary poetry, among other duties.

In August and October, Moore was visited by Robert McAlmon, recently arrived from the Midwest full of literary ambition and social revolt. Though a minister's child, he was aggressively anticlerical. In some ways he was a shallow person, and in his memoir, *Being Geniuses Together*, he could denigrate the stylistic innovations of Stein, Joyce, and Hemingway without ever really clarifying what he meant by genius. He had worked on a garbage scow for a while, and also posed nude for painting classes in the Village. Mrs. Moore told Warner that she had acted too properly at his second visit, no doubt sensing something of McAlmon's less-than-proper character. Perhaps this is where he formed his views of Mrs. Moore that he was later to make a part of his novel, *Post-Adolescence*. In October more visitors arrived: H.D., with her child Perdita, her mother, and Bryher, her intimate friend and benefactress. Mrs. Moore describes the afternoon-long visit to Warner, pointing out that the group, without Mrs. Doolittle, is to spend the winter in California. (Unknown to Mrs. Moore, the two writers were there to pose nude for photographs of themselves as Greek deities). Mrs. Moore also added that H.D.'s mother was a perfect lady.

H.D. warned Moore at this time against becoming a recluse; she may in part have been projecting her own love of solitude on her friend. A week later Mrs. Moore characterized her daughter as beseiged by literary people. This later remark might also reflect upon an episode that rankled Moore. Apparently McAlmon had used her name without her permission in trying to get some of his poems accepted by *The Dial*. Such an incident had occurred once before, with Kreymborg as the guilty party, and Moore fretted about both incidents in a letter to Warner. She went to the effort of hand-delivering her response to McAlmon, suggesting that *he* should clear up the matter with the editors. Yet she was not one to harbor grudges, for later, in September, 1921, Moore could write honestly to McAlmon, saying that religious conviction, art, and animal impulse were the strongest factors in life, and that any one could obliterate the others. This is a very self-revealing statement, for these three topics may indeed be seen as the central concerns of Moore's poetry.

Such pressures on her good will and name were clearly signs of Moore's increasing reputation, especially among the more avant-garde segment of the literary community. Her reputation was to be especially enhanced by a friend of unusual character whom she had met on September 18: Scofield Thayer. Thayer was born in 1890, and graduated from Harvard with the class of 1913. His father was one of the biggest manufacturers of woollen goods in America; his death when Scofield was seventeen years old left the young man with two-thirds of his father's fortune. Scofield met his future co-editor, James Sibley Watson, in Chicago late in 1916, when Watson was on his honeymoon. The two men were probably introduced by Watson's wife, Hildegarde Lasell, whom he had known at Harvard. The men themselves became very close friends. Watson, who was a scientist and inventor as well as an experimental filmmaker, photographed the handsome Scofield, who had a face marked by extremely fine features with the eyes slanted downward, dark hair, and fine clothing to further the effect of an aesthetic temperament. Scofield's own marriage to Elaine Orr was unusual. Despite the birth of a daughter, the two maintained separate residences almost from the beginning. Elaine was to become the mistress of E.E. Cummings, a liaison that was reportedly encouraged by Scofield.

Scofield took an apartment in New York City in November, 1919, after he and Watson acquired ownership of The Dial. The apartment, on the east side of Washington Square in a building called the Benedick, was lavish, with red lacquer painted walls, rare first editions, and Beardsley drawings. But he also maintained quarters atop the floors where The Dial had its editorial offices, at 152 West 13th Street; this top floor was the scene of many dinners which Moore attended, often along with Alyse Gregory and Lola Ridge, both editors at The Dial, and many others. In 1920 the circulation of The Dial was approximately 8000, but its influence and standards made it one of the most important cultural and literary journals in English. Thayer and Watson had taken it over, after the journal had been revivified and housed in Chicago, before moving to New York in 1918, drawing on the name and traditions of the magazine originally associated with the Transcendentalists and edited by Margaret Fuller. At the beginning of 1917, the magazine ran a manifesto that said in part it would "try to meet the challenge of the new time by reflecting and interpreting its spirit—a spirit freely experimental, skeptical of inherited values, ready to examine old dogmas, and to subject afresh its sanctions to the test of experience." That last word was to become especially important for Moore.

Under the two new owners, both of them wealthy, the journal's character changed markedly. First, the magazine's political editor, Randolph Bourne, died, a victim of the great influenza epidemic after the World War. In fact, it was Thayer's friendship with Bourne that first led him to invest in *The Dial.* After Bourne's death, however, *The Dial* began to take on a more completely aesthetic cast; this transformation was accelerated by Thayer, who owned a great collection of modern art, reproductions of which became a regular feature in the pages of the journal. In the late 1910's and early 1920's, the pages of the magazine had been open to such politically and socially concerned writers as Lewis Mumford, John Dewey, Thorstein Veblen, and others, but during the last six or seven years of its existence—the final issue would appear in 1929—its contents were almost exclusively aesthetic.

Thayer was in charge of the magazine on an equal basis with Watson, and they changed it from a fortnightly to a monthly, with a new format designed by Bruce Rogers, a gifted typographer and book designer. Eventually, however, Watson removed himself permanently to Rochester, New York, his hometown. Thayer became increasingly interested in modern psychology; it was through his financial backing that Freud came to America. Thayer himself was analyzed by Freud, but he became increasingly unstable, suffering from paranoia. Freud declared him incurable in 1922, when Thayer was in Vienna, buying art and traveling in Europe. When Thayer died in 1982, having been *non compos mentis* for the last two decades of his life, his art collection, bequeathed to the Metropolitan Museum, was valued at $40 million. Thayer returned to New York City in 1924, visited Europe again in 1925, and eventually settled on Martha's Vineyard, dividing his time between there and Florida until his death.

According to Llewelyn Powys, the husband of Alyse Gregory, the conjunction of the two editors was memorable:

> To see Dr. Watson and Mr. Scofield Thayer together was something to remember. It would have required a Henry James to tabulate and record each interesting tarot card of this astounding association. And yet these two millionaires, in the face of the crass stupidity of the Philistine world, in the face of the sneering hostility of a score of pseudo-literary cliques, have managed to produce in America a journal which, without any doubt, is the most distinguished of its kind to appear in the English language since the publication of the *Yellow Book.* But how quaint it was to see these two working together for the aesthetic enlightenment of the Western world! It was like seeing a proud, self-willed, bull calf-bison, fed

on nothing but golden oats, yoked to the plough with a dainty, fet-
locked, dapple-grey unicorn, who would, an' he could, step delicately
over the traces and scamper to the edge of the prairie, where, under the
protective colouring of a grove of pale wattle trees, he might be lost to
the view of the world.

Apparently, Thayer was the unicorn (perhaps a cruel allusion to his
being cuckolded by Cummings), for Powys goes on to say this:

The taste of Scofield Thayer was the austere aristocratic taste of a Roman
noble, of a Roman connoisseur, who had filled his marble hall with the
work of his Greek slaves; while the Doctor's taste was that of a super-
subtle Nicodemus who had a mania for collecting at night, by proxy,
images of unknown gods, put together by indigent artists whose lack of
rice was never for long out of the mind of this generous young man.

Watson was the scientist and innovator, Thayer the aesthete; Moore
was to admire the former, but to feel something like tenderness and
even pity for the latter. According to Alyse Gregory, in her memoir *The
Day Is Gone*, Thayer's irony was swift, but not necessarily light, and "he
was ice on the surface and molten lava underneath." Among other
things he was a perfectionist when it came to the details of *The Dial*;
after each issue appeared, he would spend hours in a *post mortem* ana-
lyzing every error and tracing it back to the responsible editor or assistant.

From the start of their friendship, Moore felt anxious in the presence
of Thayer. An afternoon tea at his apartment meant attendance by a
butler and an awareness of his recently acquired paintings. During one
such occasion, in the middle of October, Thayer admitted he did not
always understand Moore's poems. This is not surprising, since his own
tended to be much more traditional, even sentimental in a way that
Moore herself would likely have considered old-fashioned. In fact,
Thayer once complained to Alyse Gregory about *The Dial*'s having
published "such matter as the silly cantos of Ezra Pound and as the very
disappointing 'Waste Land'. . ." One of Thayer's own poems, called
"Counsel to a Young Man," begins with these stanzas:

> Clasp not the ankle of the cursive moon
> Nor agitate the stars with your despair:
> They know you not; and singularly soon
> Their beauty shall not be your nightly care.

Impose your will upon the transient earth
And order the divergent ways of man,
Let East Wind know your spirit's mounting worth,
Let cities know which way you will, and can.

Join not with dogs in barking a dead moon,
Increase not mountainous rivers with your grief,
Granite and dumb, outface the raucous noon,
Granite and dumb, hold yourself in fief.

While Moore might have responded to the theme of self-protectiveness, the rather florid vocabulary here is distinctly different from hers. Throughout his poems there is a fairly constant use of traditional stanza and rhyme, with an occasional foray into imagistic free verse, but the poems are so often about loss and alienation that at times they border on the adolescent. Some of them appeared in *The Dial* starting in 1925, when he had less direct control over the magazine, and though a volume of his poetry was announced as forthcoming, it never appeared.

Moore worked with great diligence on her contributions to *The Dial*, often employing her mother to do "collateral" reading if the subject or author under review was not well known to her. Moore notified Warner in November that she'd had another poem taken by *The Dial*, but Thayer had told her that her review need not be long. She and her mother were thus let down gently, but nevertheless a month's work has been rendered virtually useless. As for advancing her reputation, *The Dial* published some of her best poems. "A Grave" and "When I Buy Pictures" appeared in the July, 1921 issue, and "The Labors of Hercules" and "New York" in December. Five others were published in three different issues before she took over as editor in 1925 and declined to publish her own verse. Near the end of the year, Moore kept busy correcting details for a review of a biography of Jacopone da Todi, an Italian mystic poet, written by Evelyn Underhill, which had appeared in the January, 1921 issue. It is Moore's first prose contribution to a journal in which her writing—from major essays to editorial "Comments" to "Brief Mentions," reviews of a paragraph or so—would appear in at least sixty issues over the next eight years. On the same day she attended a church social, and wondered in a letter to Warner when she would be regarded as old enough to be past being identified as a member of the 14-to-20-year-old set.

In addition to her friendship with Thayer, Moore also began to develop strong ties with both H.D. and Bryher. Born Winifred Ellerman, Bryher took her new name from one of the Scilly Islands. She was the daughter of the shipping magnate, Sir John Ellerman, whose obituary in *The Times* claimed he left one of the largest private fortunes in British history. Bryher lived in a very closed environment set up by her protective parents until she was finally able to leave home. Once her independence was established, she spent a great deal of time and money supporting artists, such as H.D. and Moore, several important experimental filmmakers, as well as other worthy causes. She was an important agent in the network that helped people escape the Nazis in the early and mid-1930's. It was her organization that was trying to aid the critic Walter Benjamin until his tragic suicide at the French border with Spain in 1936. Like H.D., Bryher had several sexual relationships with men and women. She and H.D. became lovers, and though their relationship was at times strained, and though later H.D. lived apart from Bryher, Bryher provided H.D. with virtually a lifetime support, both financially and emotionally.

In her memoir, *The Heart to Artemis*, Bryher spoke of her visit to America in the latter part of 1920. She then met Alfred Kreymborg, who seemed to meet everyone, and Amy Lowell, whom H.D. had mentioned to Moore with disfavor. Bryher was also impressed by Marsden Hartley, the painter and critic who was shortly to write one of the early appreciations of Moore's work. The night she met him all the guests were talking about Dada, "the new movement that was sweeping Europe, and wondering whether it was a serious advance or a momentary whim." But what seems to have impressed her most was meeting Moore:

The reward of my first visit was meeting Marianne Moore. H.D. had known her at Bryn Mawr and had helped to get some of her first poems published. She has also told me frequently that if I were interested in modern writing, I must study Marianne's work. I think that "The Fish" was the first poem that I read. It brought the beaches in Scilly vividly into my mind.

Marianne was living with her mother in Greenwich Village at the time and they asked us to tea. "Why, it's a pterodactyl," I thought or rather a resemblance to the heraldic creatures that I imagined them to be, as I watched her come to welcome us with the massive gold that seemed more like a headdress than mortal hair, swaying slightly sideways above a dark green dress. "How could you bear to leave London?" she and her mother said together. "How we wish that we could revisit England."

Most of her contemporaries saw Moore's hair as red, but Bryher's imagination insists on an otherworldly dimension to Moore's features. Bryher was also in this instance the source for a nickname that was applied to Moore, and which she apparently liked: "dactyl," a pun that was short for pterodactyl as well as a traditional unit of verse measure. There followed an exchange about London, Moore and her mother remembering nostalgic details from their earlier trip there, and Bryher countering with the grim wartime facts: muffins were rationed, the blackout increased the feeling of discomfort in the unheated houses. Bryher is evocative but also hardheaded: "It was not my London of shackles and disappointments that Marianne loved but an image built up from books that had been written, in general, a whole century earlier." The contrast between Moore as an exemplar of modern writing and a devotee of English Victorian literature is seldom sharper than in Bryher's first experience of her. Mrs. Moore remarked that "discipline . . . is good for you." Bryher thought to herself how that word had acquired a totally different meaning since 1914.

From California, where Bryher and H.D. visited after they left New York, Bryher wrote back to Moore about her poems.

> I am not sure I have succeeded in discovering the precise meaning of the poems. I have a general impression of a world before the fish age where shells clung to a rock and whether the shell was just a shell knowing its own rock perfectly—the boundary of its own ledge—or whether the shell was the entire world I have neither discovered nor decided.

This is very perceptive on Bryher's part, for the images of Moore's shell-like self-protectiveness can be read either as forms of mere defensiveness or as examples of a whole world, simultaneously criticized and recreated in the poetry's sculpted and scallopine integrity. Such perceptiveness also concludes the part of Bryher's memoir that describes Moore:

> We liked each other from the beginning but we understood our objectives better a few years later on. The repetition of early patterns in later life has always fascinated me and there is an element in both Marianne

and her poetry, a sense of living in an uncrowded land that links her to the mornings when I found ammonites in the chalk pits of the Downs. Her eyes are different from ours, instead of a flashing whole, her mind sees first and they obey its orders in microscopic detail while she seems to lie perched on a rock above a warm and shallow lake, surveying an earlier globe.

Though Bryher is taking evident delight in her descriptive fancy here, her picture of Moore conveys a good deal about the sort of genius of seeing and concentrative energy that makes her poetry distinctive; also accurate is the dual way Moore's sensibility is shown as very modern in its dispassionate control and rather Victorian in its self-possession. It is true that the friendship and understanding developed over time. Furthermore it is through Bryher's, rather than H.D.'s, efforts as a correspondent with Moore that the friendship flourishes.

What Bryher had to say about the relation between mind and eyes in Moore's poetry recalls the poem that H.D. singled out as key to the understanding of modern writing: "The Fish." Bryher obviously responded to the poem's piscine imagery by understanding it as Moore's way of being otherworldly, a continuation of a theme that goes back to "Ennui" and "A Jelly-Fish" from Moore's Bryn Mawr days. But she saw another important element as well, for Moore's poetry was increasingly to concern itself with what might be called the struggles of perdurability. This subject is part of her interest in museums, in the forms of animal life, and in the intersections of nature and culture. What Bryher saw as Moore's living in an uncrowded land and her "survey" of "an earlier globe" are elements in a distinct sense of aesthetic distance that can appreciate the stillness of antediluvian order while it observes the details of an ongoing activity. Here is the second half of "The Fish":

> The water drives a wedge
> of iron through the iron edge
>   of the cliff; whereupon the stars,
>
>   pink
>   rice-grains, ink-
>   bespattered jelly-fish, crabs like green
>   lilies, and submarine
>   toadstools, slide each on the other.

All
external
    marks of abuse are present on this
    defiant edifice—
       all the physical features of

ac-
cident—lack
    of cornice, dynamite grooves, burns, and
    hatchet strokes, these things stand
       out on it; the chasm-side is

dead.
Repeated
    evidence has proved that it can live
    on what can not revive
       its youth. The sea grows old in it.

Here the human activity of building by force (the dynamite groove and hatchet stroke), as well as nature's own human-like activities (driving the iron wedge), comes to naught against the sea's growth, which is a growth of great patience and order made possible by its coming to terms with death and decay. An allegorical reading of the poem, published in 1918, might connect it thematically with Eliot's famous essay, "Tradition and the Individual Talent," which appeared in the same year. Both insist on the mark left by the individual pursuing its destiny even as the larger "defiant edifice" both contains and reorders the significance of such marks. Bryher, for one, was able to read Moore's artistic breakthroughs against a larger background of stable tradition.

The year 1921 was one of the more important ones in Moore's career. This year saw the publication of her first book, *Poems*, brought out by Egoist Press in London, and the appearance of her important early reviews of T.S. Eliot in *The Dial* and William Carlos Williams in *Contact*. There is also a *Dial* review of Bryher's novel. She comes to a reckoning of sorts with George Moore, the late Victorian (or early modernist) novelist and aesthete, for in the following year there appeared her long essay on his work in *Broom*, the new magazine edited by Kreymborg. As for her poetry aside from the volume, she published "A Grave" and "New York," two of her most significant lyrics, and had

"Snakes, Mongooses, Snake Charmers, and the Like" accepted by *Broom*. Laura Benét reviewed her book for a New York newspaper, and Richard Aldington did so for the *Literary Review*. Dr. Sibley Watson discussed her poems in *The Dial*, and Harriet Monroe decided to run a symposium on her work in the January, 1922 issue of *Poetry*. All the while she continued to attend parties and meet more and more authors at a furious pace. In March she complains to her brother that she will die if she meets another person. This wry remark comes in a letter that records that on a single day she saw the actress Yvette Gilbert in a matinée, went to a tea honoring the Benéts, had supper and then went to a reading of Amy Lowell's, having been invited by Amy herself, finishing off with a trip to the studio of Gaston Lachaise, the sculptor. Not a typical day, to be sure, but nevertheless one that was clearly possible in the Village of the 1920's.

In the middle of January she attended a play with Thayer, who asks her to review Eliot's *The Sacred Wood*. She consents, but only after thinking it over, and getting Thayer to agree that she can do so only if he would know ahead of time that she would not speak unfavorably of it. Near the end of the month a letter from Bryher urges her to write a novel, but she tells Warner that she has no such plans. Later on she will undertake such a project, but only one chapter of it will be published during her lifetime. As for Warner, he is still being instructed by Mrs. Moore, specifically about a criticism leveled at his preaching style by his ship's captain. Mrs. Moore again alludes to things said by uncomprehending people in Chatham, and mentions that his marriage has made her think for the first time about establishing some sort of financial legacy for Moore. This implies that Warner and his mother have in some way accepted that Moore will likely not marry.

Moore's relationship with Thayer had become the subject of Village gossip, some of which even mentioned the possibility of a marriage proposal. But in February, Mrs. Moore fills Warner in about Thayer. Apparently many people felt uncomfortable around Scofield, for his views were felt to be puritanical, though Moore says they were often not put forward. Several months later, Mrs. Moore reports Thayer's comment that Moore is the most intellectual person and the most educated woman he knows. At one party, a manipulative Thayer sat Moore next to E.E. Cummings so she might comment on his poems, but she declined to do so, joking to her mother that Cummings guarded against being thought pure and heavenly minded. This same party made Moore so nervous that when she returned home she was unable to finish a full meal. Yet another letter her mother sent to Warner in March reported that Moore was resisting any further affection from Thayer. This letter denies the possibility of platonic friendship, and also says that it isn't fair that Thayer should see Moore so much when he has a wife. Moore's skepticism about platonic relationships suggests that she has absorbed at least some of the modern ethos about sexual relationships, but her concern about propriety regarding Mrs. Thayer, whose relation with her husband was probably understood by Moore, also suggests that marriage is in her eyes still very much a social contract. This tension will be dramatized in her longest poem, "Marriage."

Bryher and H.D. returned to New York from the West in February, and they were invited to tea, along with Thayer and Watson, by the Moores. Mrs. Moore, especially struck by the two women writers, praised them to Warner, mentioning their ladylikeness, elegance, and dignity. The mention of dignity is important, for it suggests that Mrs. Moore may have felt Bryher's wealth and breeding, and more likely the self-possession of H.D. and Bryher in front of the two editors of The Dial. Mrs. Moore also mentioned that it was a long time since she had seen such true ladyhood, perhaps referring to her time in New York City, where women were likely to be much less ladylike than in Carlisle. Some months after this tea party, Mrs. Moore recalls to her daughter that they had not come to New York to entertain low "literati." Bryher clearly had the social graces Mrs. Moore found lacking in Kreymborg and McAlmon, the latter of whom she particularly disliked.

Mrs. Moore may have been shocked, however, when she learned of the wedding of McAlmon and Bryher, at New York's City Hall, on the morning of February 20th. The couple had been introduced to each other only months before, shortly prior to Bryher's trip west. According to the account in his Autobiography, William Carlos Williams had taken McAlmon to see H.D., but it was Bryher who caught his eye. McAlmon was later ready to ship out on a freighter when he got a card from Bryher telling him to wait until she returned from California. He did so, and she proposed to him upon her return. This marriage made a considerable stir in the newspapers and gossip columns, especially considering the divergent economic backgrounds of the people involved. Divorce seemed inevitable; when it occurred, William Carlos Williams quipped that from now on his friend Bob would be known as Robert McAlimony.

A post-wedding reception was held at the Brevoort Hotel, with Williams, Moore, Marsden Hartley, and others. Two days later, Williams received a postcard, signed "D.H.", with a picture of men and women reaching into a pot of money. H.D. denied Williams' accusation that she had sent it. Many years later Moore was to write Williams protesting his treatment of Bryher in his *Autobiography*, and to tell an aggrieved Bryher she had done so, adding that Williams had made many factual mistakes in the book. McAlmon claimed in his memoir that he knew nothing of Bryher's fortune before he married her, a claim that few took seriously. And though he described her father as tyrannical and paranoid, he also blamed Bryher for failing to adjust to her family's special conditions. The entire episode must have struck Moore as utterly unlike anything that might have happened back in Carlisle, yet she seemed to have behaved with aplomb throughout.

Bryher knew it was only a marriage of convenience that allowed her to escape from the control of her family. Moore and her mother were less placid or ironic about the arrangement, for they had both distrusted McAlmon from the start. But it apparently created no strain among the women. Moore knew that Bryher held advanced views; in fact, she had told Moore that *The Dial* was reactionary and hadn't advanced beyond 1912. It was less her advanced views than her mocking irony that would have drawn Moore to Bryher. This irony was evident when Bryher first met Pound. As she retold the story to Moore, Pound rang the buzzer and when Bryher, expecting groceries, answered:

> I thought it was the bread or the potatoes and I was very sorry I had [let him in]. He talked to me an hour about a Saxon king and a Danish chief . . . He said afterward I didn't stand up very well without H.D.

But Bryher was at first protective of McAlmon, and offered his name to Thayer when he asked who the really good writers were. Bryher also told Thayer that Moore shouldn't be "imprisoned," and that she was "one of the most distinguished persons I know." Shortly after leaving America she sent Moore a check for $300 with a note referring to her as "the most sincere artist I know." Other gifts were to follow over the years.

The reputation of *The Dial* was to take some hard knocks over the next few years. Pound became especially critical when his work was rejected there, though he did send Moore a card complimenting her on her review of *The Sacred Wood*. In April she mentioned to Warner a friend's prediction that *Broom* would run circles around *The Dial*. And her review of Williams appeared in *Contact* perhaps because *The Dial* wouldn't be receptive to a review of such an experimental work as *Kora in Hell*, though the magazine eventually awarded Williams *The Dial* Award in 1926, with Moore making the announcement in the editorial "Comment." Little magazines like *Broom* and *Contact*, however, were in some ways direct responses to what people like Pound and Williams considered an insufficient number of outlets for truly experimental work. Moore's allegiance to *The Dial*, where she published many more things than in all the other magazines of the 1920's put together, was a re-flection of the limits on experimentation in her aesthetic sensibility.

Outside of her poems, among the chief aesthetic pronouncements Moore made during this period were her reviews of Eliot and Williams. These reviews show how her modernism was always more measured than the "pure" experimentalism of artists such as Williams, though it is very much to her credit that she could see the virtues in a book such as *Kora in Hell*. However, it was Eliot to whom she had the closest affinity at this time. Earlier, in the April, 1918 issue of *Poetry*, she had written a short review of *Prufrock and Other Observations*, in which she had expressed some reservations about Eliot's "realism," always a source of anxiety for her. She ended the review by saying that "whatever one may feel about sweetness in literature, there is also the word honesty, and this man is a faithful friend of the objects he portrays; altogether unlike the sentimentalist who really stabs them treacherously in the back while pretending affection." She begins her review of his critical essays from *The Sacred Wood* by asserting the relation between creation and criticism: "Criticism naturally deals with creation but it is equally true that criticism inspires creation." This can be read as a formal way of saying that poetry owes as much to books as it does to life, a view that Moore held throughout her life. But she also adds that "too much cannot be said for the necessity in the artist, of exact science," and this countering view provides for the immediacy of exact and rigorous ob-servation as a supplement to literary experience. She had said earlier in her famous poem "Poetry" that "When they [high-sounding interpre-tations] become so derivative as to become / unintelligible, / the same thing may be said for all of us, that we / do not admire what / we cannot understand." Criticism must not become a matter of high-sounding words, but it can and should be an engagement with the literary work as vivid, spontaneous, and exactingly formed as the engagement between the poem and the world. What Moore, as a student at Bryn Mawr, had called "critical poetry" could find something like its mirror image in creative criticism.

One of the key ideas in this review, however, is Moore's sense of the way that the past must be used. This issue is drawn when Moore argues with Eliot about the efficacy of Swinburne's poetry. Here Eliot is arguing with himself about the need to put aside the florid language of his Victorian forerunners, but Moore suggests Eliot is wrong when he claims that it is only words and not things that we find in Swinburne's poems. She may have been recalling her own attachment to Swinburne's aestheticism and the way that it had animated her early stories. Then she agrees wholeheartedly with Eliot's praise of Ben Jonson, quoting his significant claim that for Jonson "the superficies *is* the world." This is especially telling in the light of her concern with the meaning of surfaces as well as depths. But it is near the end of the review that she engages the issue that is perhaps most important for her: the uses of the past. She has the highest praise for Eliot's "opening a door upon the past and indicating what is there." She then concludes by citing a quotation from Swinburne on Victor Hugo: "No form is obsolete, no subject out of date, if the right man be there to rehandle it." Her citing it is simultaneously a slight rebuke to Eliot's censure against Swinburne, a way of indicating her essential affinity with Eliot's sensibility, and a characteristic use of authority to make a point very important to her. Though she does not single out "Tradition and the Individual Talent" for any specific remarks, it is the aesthetic spirit of that essay with which she is most in accord.

It is a very deft review, and one that pleased Eliot, who compared it favorably to others in the *Spectator* and the *Athenaeum*. For shaping a context for Moore's aesthetic views, however, it should be read alongside the review of Williams. Here her reservations are more numerous and more serious. She spoke in a letter to her brother about Williams' "obscenities," and this was to be an issue with her throughout her friendship with the doctor from Rutherford. In the review she is at her most self-protectedly convoluted when she refers to his subject matter as "topics of which the average person never thinks unless inescapably for humanitarian reasons." The principle of modernism that proclaimed that there was no inherently poetic subject matter, an issue debated by Williams and Wallace Stevens, among others, was a principle that never animated Moore, at least not insofar as it entailed the treatment of "low" or obscene material. She also associated such a stance with "realism," an aesthetic attitude she was to condemn for its failure to be a sufficient interpretation of life.

But there was much in Williams' poetry that Moore could praise. She referred to his "concise, energetic disgust, a kind of intellectual hauteur which one usually associates with the French." This is accurate, and often the disgust has not been stressed enough by Williams' critics; it shows, too, that Moore was not squeamish as far as the expression of strong, even negative, emotion was concerned. What most attracts Moore is the seriousness of Williams' undertaking, the sense that he was not merely playing at a new style or trying to shock:

> Despite Dr. Williams' championing of the school of ignorance, or rather of no school but experience, there is in his work the authoritativeness, the wise silence which knows schools and fashions well enough to know that completeness is further down than professional intellectuality and modishness can go.

Here Moore fashions a version of the modernist notion of the sincerity of style, the insistence that good art is the result of a personal commitment to one's own angle of vision, and not something that can be achieved by merely copying fads or duplicating stylistic markers.

After this praise, Moore subtly changes direction by saying that "Dr. Williams' wisdom, however, is not absolute and he is sometimes petulant." What follows is a brief disquisition on manners, not merely in the restrictive sense of social propriety, but in a larger, almost anthropological sense of the relation between nature and culture, or as here expressed, between instinct and convention. Williams has just been quoted as saying that it is folly to accept one's remorse as a form of criticism of one's behavior, and then Moore offers this pronouncement:

> One's manners, good or bad, are conventionalized instincts[,] and conduct as a combination of manners and volition . . . predicates whatever is the result of it, so remorse is automatically a criticism of conduct.

Moore's claims here are the result of serious thought about social experience, and they also suggest the sort of pragmatic sense of things she was slowly developing, in part through her reading of John Dewey. The notion here is that conduct, understood as a dialectical fusion of voli-tion (or individual desire) and manners (or accepted shared forms), entails and must accept its own consequences. This is part of the prag-matic sense of that other combination that Dewey constantly points to, and that both Williams and Moore wrestled with, namely experience and nature. In her Reading Notebook she had copied out, probably in 1917, several passages from Dewey's *Essays in Experimental Logic* (1916), as well as one passage from his *Democracy and Education* (1916). She may also have had in mind a quotation like the following, from *Recon-struction in Philosophy* (1920):

> Society is strong, forceful, stable against accident only when all its mem-bers can function to the limit of their capacity. Such functioning cannot be achieved without allowing a leeway of experimentation beyond the limits of established and sanctioned custom. . . . As the new ideas find adequate expression in social life, they will be absorbed into a moral background, and the ideas and beliefs themselves will be deepened and be unconsciously transmitted and sustained. They will color the imagi-nation and temper the desires and affections. They will not form a set of ideas to be expounded, reasoned out and argumentatively supported, but will be a spontaneous way of envisaging life.

It is not only Williams' axiom "No ideas but in things" that echoes strongly in these lines, but also Moore's concern with the dialectic between tradition and innovation, between the stable form and the individual act.

One of the central subjects of modernism, the status of the artist in a generally uncomprehending, commercially motivated world, was a constant subject of conversation among writers in the Village at this time. In poems such as "Poetry" and "Novices," Moore showed her preoccupation with this issue. In the latter poem she says of novices:

> the little assumptions of the scared ego confusing the issue
> so that they do not know "whether it is the buyer or the seller
>   who gives the money"—
> an abstruse idea plain to none but the artist,
> the only seller who buys, and holds on to the money.

Moore's sense of the artist as one to whom the abstruse is plain is conditioned by her claim that this privileged understanding can be won only after the "little assumptions of the scared ego" are put aside or outgrown. However, she concludes her review of Williams by mentioning as a "preeminent" example of his poetic skill a poem that had recently appeared in *Contact*, namely "Portrait of the Author." In this poem Williams wrestles with his own self-questioning identity as a poet, something that was to be one of his chief subjects from the 1920's to *The Desert Music* and beyond. It is odd at first glance that Moore, known for her objectivity, would single out such an agonized and self-expressive poem for her highest praise, but it shows that she was both emotionally responsive and drawn to such concerns even though she might not treat them in the same fashion.

Moore's prose writings express other questions of self-definition at this time. For example, in the review of Bryher's novel, *Development*, she again mixes praise and blame judiciously, and again takes time to argue questions of value and conduct with the author under review. This time the issue is feminism. Bryher's novel is a veiled autobiographical account of her struggles for autonomy, struggles that have a gender-based dimension. But Moore wonders if this is really the issue:

> . . . possibly in her protest against women's *rôle* as a wearer of skirts—in her envying a boy his freedom and his clothes—her view is somewhat curtailed. . . . If there is any advantage [in dress], it is on the side of woman; . . . women are no longer debarred from professions that are open to men, and if one cares to be femininely lazy, traditions of the past still afford shelter.

Feminists of the time (as well as those of a later period) might complain that Moore is here being too pragmatic, in the vulgar sense, and her willingness to accept "shelter" might appear unsisterly. But Moore could be referring to her own situation, namely living on with one's parent, making do without a full-time job, living, in the loose sense of the term, a non-productive life. What is also at stake is a profound difference of temperament between Moore and Bryher. In the review Moore also praises the heroine by saying that "one feels Nancy's silence under fire is a victory." The poem "Silence," published in *The Dial* in 1924, may be a further comment on this issue, though that poem has been read as possibly ironic in its approval of silence. And the feminism of the 1920's did not have the same attitude toward these issues as does the feminism of the 1980's. While one may well argue with Moore's claim that the professions were open to women in her day, still the question of career opportunities is one of the key issues of feminism in any of its historical stages. What the review shows is that Moore was sympathetic to the main feminist positions, though she was reluctant to pursue some of the questions into areas that were, to her, more symbolic, such as dress.

II. "The force of experience"

These early reviews of her contemporaries show that Moore was quite cogent about her own aesthetics, and many of her attitudes were to remain fairly constant throughout much of her writing career. The reviews also show how skillful she was at balancing praise and blame, and putting each in the context of the other while somehow not allowing the edges between them to blur. This is the result of her skill at quotation and her nimbleness in argument, but it also grows out of her lifelong sense of the importance of choice. To be moral was to be involved in a world of choice, where praise and blame are constants, but also constantly changing and interacting with one another and the surrounding context in demanding ways. This complex sense of intellectual and moral balance and awareness was something that carried over fairly directly into Moore's social experience.

Moore's social identity at this time can be glimpsed from the memoirs of others. One of these is *Troubador*, Alfred Kreymborg's nearly contemporary effort (it was published in 1925). Kreymborg introduces Moore by saying that "no manuscripts required more reading than those of Mina Loy and Marianne Moore." Loy was a poet who became rather notorious because of one line: "Pig Cupid, his rosy snout rooting erotic garbage." Moore's difficulty was obviously of a different cast. Referring to himself and Williams, Kreymborg claims that "both men held the mind of Marianne Moore in absolute admiration. What they lacked in intellectual stability was freely and unconsciously supplied by her. And her familiarity with books on every conceivable theme astonished them." Williams described himself and Kreymborg as "a pair of tongue-tied tyros by comparison." But this admiration doesn't prevent Kreymborg from trying to catch Moore "napping," and he devised a scheme which he describes to Williams in detail:

Never having found her at a loss on any topic whatsoever, I wanted to give myself the pleasure at least once of hearing her stumped about something. Certain that only an experience completely strange to her would be the thing, I invited her to a ball game at the Polo Grounds. This descent into the world of the lowbrow started beautifully. It was a Saturday afternoon and the Cubs and the Giants were scheduled for one of their ancient frays. The "L" was jammed with fans and we had to stand all the way uptown and hang on to straps. Marianne was totally oblivious to the discomfiture anyone else would have felt and, in answer to a question of mine, paraded whole battalions of perfectly marshalled ideas in long columns of balanced periods which no lurching on the part of the train or pushing on the part of the crowd disturbed. Wait till we reach the grounds, I promised myself, and Matty winds up, tosses a perfect fadeaway, the batter misses it, and Marianne goes on talking.

Even allowing for the "color" in Kreymborg's description, Moore's penchant for speaking in perfect sentences and having an encyclopedic range of knowledge was to be remarked on by many people throughout her life. But Kreymborg continues his anecdote with considerable descriptive flair:

Well, I got her safely to her seat and sat down beside her. Without so much as a glance toward the players at practice grabbing grounders and chasing fungos, she went on giving me her impression of the respective technical achievements of Mr. Pound and Mr. Aldington without missing a turn in the rhythm of her speech, until I, a little impatient, touched her arm and, indicating a man in the pitcher's box winding up with the movement Matty's so famous for, interrupted: "But Marianne, wait a moment, the game's about to begin. Don't you want to watch the first ball?" "Yes, indeed," she said, stopped, blushed and leaned forward.

After the first pitch is called a strike, Kreymborg moves in for what he thinks will be the crushing query, but it's he who will miss the object in question:

Delighted, I quickly turned to her with: "Do you happen to know the gentleman who threw that strike?"
    "I've never seen him before," she admitted, "but I take it it must be Mr. Mathewson."
    I could only gasp, "Why?"
    "I've read his instructive book on the art of pitching—"
    "Strike two!" interrupted Bob Emslie [the umpire].
    "And it's a pleasure," she continued imperturbably, "to note how unerringly his execution supports his theories—"

"Strike three, batter's out!" concluded the umpire and, as Shorty Slagle slunk away, glared toward the Chicago bench for the next victim . . .

The whole anecdote skillfully reflects back on Kreymborg's failure to "stump" Moore, and is consistent with the tone of the self-reflexive naif that pervades the memoir. We know Moore had indeed read Christy Mathewson's book, for she had mentioned it in a letter to Warner years earlier, so the anecdote may be grounded in truth. (Of course, for the batter who "slunk away" Kreymborg may well have supplied the alliterative "Shorty Slagle.")

Robert McAlmon has also left a memoir of Moore, though his is more openly fictionalized than Kreymborg's. The novel-memoir is called *Post-Adolescence*, and while it is a typical *bildungsroman* in many respects, the narrator, Peter, seems not fully to have escaped his adolescence by the book's end. What can be read as a somewhat satirical portrait of Moore, renamed Martha Wallus, can also be seen as a moral counterweight to the narrator's rather empty quest. At first Peter's friend Gusta describes Wallus as "rather quaint," but Peter counters by saying that "she thinks anything, disapproves of little, for other people, and is a church-going, cerebralizing moralist who observes sabbath strictly, herself. I can't understand why with a mind like hers agnosticism hasn't eaten into her a little, but it seems not to have, or she conceals it well, for her mother's sake possibly." The two continue to discuss Wallus, saying among other things that "possibly she isn't emotionally developed much, but still there's the force of experience back of her knowledge," and "she needs to be seen apart from the background of her mother to be actual though." These remarks strike home in many ways, and McAlmon could well have drawn upon overheard conversations between H.D. and Bryher. As Peter and Gusta go to call on Wallus they meet a third person, Brander, who joins them. The three arrive at Wallus' apartment, where she invites them in "with formal hospitality that had a whimsical directness." The talk turns to Wallus' work, not her "paid work," but her writing. She describes it in unique terms:

"It is true that I have never expressed so far any of the things that I particularly wish to say. But I shall soon attempt to put down some of my observations; nothing absolute. To put my remarks in verse though, as I have attempted, is like trying to dance the minuet in a bathing suit,

> though I do have some things to say about acacias and seaweeds and
> serpents in plane trees that will have to appear in fragments."

The sartorial disjunction here sounds like McAlmon's invention, but
the subject matter and the general aesthetic is certainly Moore's, and
the tentative attitude toward questions of authoritative form also appears accurately rendered. Martha goes on to discuss her work in the
library, and her mother expresses her disapproval of Irish Americans.
The three visitors induce Martha to accompany them to a Village café
for coffee, where the proprietor is a lusty woman who claims to be an
ex-prostitute. Peter turns introspective, remembering his drunkenness
from the night before and feeling "removed and dumbfounded by all of
life and by any reality." A general conversation on art and life ensues,
until Peter strikes up an "aside" conversation with Martha, who answers his complaint that the atmosphere of indifference in such evenings drives him wild:

> "It's pretty bad I admit, still it's restraining oneself in the midst of
> annoyances to which one is subjected that toughens the muscles. Wild-
> ness in itself is an attractive quality, but it fails to take into account the
> question of attrition and attrition is inevitable," she replied.

Peter tries to understand her temperament, and again the talk turns to
writing, as Martha describes her artistic goals and standards:

> "I am telling you the truth when I say that if I had all the time in the
> world I should not write anything important to myself for some years. In
> order to work as I should have to, I should like to look into certain things
> and make up my mind with regard to the relevance, or irrelevance, of
> certain other things. That may be hard for you to realize but it is quite
> true, and I have, I think, an intuition as to how I am to succeed if I do
> succeed."

Peter wavers "between admiration of, and restlessness about, Martha's
attitude," and his friend Brander observes that she is "one of the few
who comes off into some actuality." Peter concludes his analysis of
Martha by saying that "of course any situation is the best situation if one
knows how to utilize it, but she must want to break away often, and
refuses to admit that she's caged."

Moore's existence as a self-disciplined moralist in the midst of Greenwich Village's revolution in social mores would likely have struck a
writer like McAlmon as more contradictory than paradoxical. His at-

titude toward Moore may well have been exactly like that of Peter's toward Martha, at once respectful of the dedicated strength she exhibited as an artist and yet uncomprehending as to her refusal to insist on more personal freedom. She had written him from Bremerton in October, 1923, for example, that being deliberate in one's art meant running the risk of not producing anything. But his own art does manage to capture some of the tension that is present in Moore's family correspondence, especially in some of the descriptions Mrs. Moore sent to Warner. And though she doesn't use the word "attrition," poems like "The Fish" and "A Grave" are ripe with an intense awareness of decay and the ineluctable entropy in many natural processes. But whether Moore was truly caged or whether she used her armor and self-protectiveness in ways that were assertive and positive is the larger question that in fact runs throughout her life and her poetry. In August, 1921, for example, she wrote Bryher that her experiences at Bryn Mawr made her feel that intellectual wealth can't be superimposed, that it must be appropriated; her experience had given her determination to do just that. The emphasis on experience here is important, in part because of its pragmatic echoes, but also the notion of determination has resonance for Moore's developing sense of her self.

Many people remarked on Moore's social identity as being contradictory. Mrs. Moore, in March, 1921, sent a letter to Warner in which she copied out a portion of Williams' letter to Moore, written over a year earlier, about how he and others perceived her: "I've been writing hasty and lewd letters to many of the rest of the crowd—in which you seem so out of place—so in place, like a red berry still hanging to the jaded rose-bush—that now I feel chastened." Moore's reply was insouciant: "I cannot feel sorry for the red berry when the bush is so full of sap." But in another month Moore was about to come into blossom, for she heard from the Egoist Press asking her if she would allow them to publish her poems in an edition of 300 copies. This is reported to Warner (the offering letter apparently has not survived) and at the same time Mrs. Moore tells her son that Eliot is also urging the publication of a book. Mrs. Moore goes on to say, however, that they had agreed that a little volume was not advisable, since it would only call attention to its own inadequacies. It is hard to separate how much of this reluctance is Moore's own, and how much is induced by her mother. But both women had a firm sense of literary greatness, and some of the reluctance is based on their high standards. Of course, one could see the debate here as barely concealing a desire for large-scale recognition; this struggle between modesty and ambition can be traced back to Moore's childhood mixture of dignity and impatience. What the letter also shows is that Moore cannot have been that surprised when the book appeared, though in later years she created or at least fostered the legend that she had no idea the book was being published and that H.D., Bryher, and McAlmon worked entirely on their own.

This particular letter to Warner also contains a description by Mrs. Moore that in many ways summarizes the social world of Moore while presenting a self-portrait of her mother. Moore has had a number of occasions to complain that she doesn't have enough freedom, though her mother dismissively refuses to give Warner the details. At the same time, Mrs. Moore paints herself as piously grateful for her inheritance, or else she would have been reduced to laboring like a charwoman. Just two days after this letter, incidentally, Mrs. Moore writes to accept Warner and Constance's offer of $1200 per annum to support her and her daughter.

In May, Moore was approached by Pound asking her to "contribute" to *The Little Review,* which was then fighting its legal battles over the publication of Joyce's *Ulysses,* a chapter of which had recently appeared, leading to the confiscation of that issue of the magazine. Moore declined, saying that while she might make an effort for Joyce, she didn't like the editors of the magazine, Margaret Anderson and Jane Heap, and felt their egotism was a genuine failing. Later, as editor of *The Dial,* Moore developed a reputation for being unwelcoming to work she considered obscene, and that may be what is at work here. But one also can hear an undercurrent of resentment for Anderson and Heap, who had caused a stir when they came to New York from Chicago, not least by their obvious lesbianism and their extravagant styles of living. (Moore was only to publish one poem in *The Little Review,* "You Say You Said," in 1918.) For Moore, an artist whose work in many ways relied on the affinity, if not the symbolic equivalence, of artistic style and personal manners, the cause of censorship was never as cut and dried as it was for the usual libertarian ethos of the artistic community. To these observations should be added the fact that Moore wrote her own poems under the eye of her mother. For example, she told Warner in the middle of June that she was determined to finish some poems for

The Dial but her mother felt they were not up to the usual standard, so she had scrapped them. The modernist model of the individualistic author set against all odds and all disapprovals, one of its main Romantic inheritances, does not fit Moore's experience as neatly as it does that of, say, Joyce.

Shortly after the middle of the year, on July 10, Moore wrote Warner that she was very much startled to receive, from Miss Weaver of the Egoist Press, her first book of poems, which had been collected and published by H.D., Bryher, and Mr. McAlmon. She would send along a copy as soon as she made some corrections. She went on to mention that the book was beautifully printed, and had no misprints whatever. (If this were so, then apparently the corrections she was to make before sending it to Warner were those habitual revisions of published texts for which she was later to become so well known. This shows that the habit was not a result of her growing old and revising the work of her youth.) The book was called simply *Poems*, though later Moore said she wished it had been called *Observations*. This was to be the title of her second collection, published in 1924, and obviously alludes not only to the scientific bent in her aesthetic, but to the title of one of Eliot's books, *Prufrock and Other Observations*. In the same letter, she reiterates her sense that it is not to her advantage to publish a book of poems at this time. However, a month later she was telling Warner that she wished the volume had included other poems: "Peter," "A Grave," "To an Intramural Rat," "Molière," and "Ireland," this last being almost certainly what was later retitled "Sojourn in the Whale." She adds that the poems are full of mistakes and irrelevant things that magnify the intricateness of some of them, and that Warner's caring about them was important in reconciling her to having made a public stir.

The book was reviewed by Laura Benét in the *Post*, a review that Warner found amateurish in the extreme. Dr. Watson told Moore that Eliot was set to review it for *The Dial*, and he would have, but he suffered at this time the collapse that was later to provide much of the experience behind *The Waste Land*. However, he did go on to use the pages of *The Dial* to review the second collection, together with *Marriage*, her longest poem, which was published as a chapbook in 1923. This would be a review with considerable consequences for Moore's reputation. Richard Aldington, who had separated from H.D., and—according to an earlier letter of Mrs. Moore—was living with a woman of easy virtue, wrote a long and favorable account of the book in the *Literary Review*, a supplement of the *New York Evening Post*. Aldington had been the first to mention Moore's poetry in print, and in reviewing Eliot's *Sacred Wood* had referred to Moore's review of the same book, so in many ways he was an ideal reviewer.

The review opens with some remarks about the generally dull and uncomprehending nature of London reviewers, especially regarding new poetry. Aldington points out that six years ago he published Moore in *The Egoist*, but ironically quips that "the talent in these poems was too unmistakable to be missed by anyone but a professional reviewer." After quoting several lines from "Roses Only," a poem Moore never collected later, he confesses that he is intimidated by Moore's "air of superiority." Putting this down to his limitations rather than hers, he goes on to praise her and link her name with those of Pound, H.D., Eliot, and Stevens. He calls her a "poet of whom any society might be proud, a poet whose mixture of whimsicality, subtlety, cool intelligence, wit, nimbleness of apprehension and old maidenly priggishness is something quite original." The review ends with a suggestion that someone should write about Moore and H.D. together, showing that H.D.'s weakness is "tenseness" and Moore's is "spiritual pride," but that they "complete each other" and testify to something "peculiarly American." Many of the terms here have stayed a part of Moore criticism, and were clearly influential in shaping the public perception of her style. What Aldington calls "spiritual pride" may also, of course, be read as part of her struggle with her own exalted sense of beauty and excellence, just as her "old maidenly priggishness" can be regarded as the fastidiousness that was to her the inevitable consequence of a concern with conduct as the result and test of a culture. Aldington's own masculine temperament was clearly operating in the formulation of the later phrase.

The book itself contains only twenty-four poems in as many pages. Nearly half of these, eleven all told, were never again to be reprinted in subsequent collections, and so they have not become generally known. Some of these uncollected poems are recycled from Bryn Mawr days, such as "He Made This Screen" and "A Talisman"; while others, such as "Reinforcements," are obscure and largely unsuccessful. But there are also important poems that form part of Moore's canon of later anthology pieces, such as "England," "Poetry," "Picking and Choos-

ing," and "The Fish." The most significant omission from later collections is "Black Earth," about one of Moore's main totemic animals, the
elephant. Though this is differently titled ("Melanchthon") in a heavily
rewritten version to be included in *Observations* and *Selected Poems*
(1935), its absence from later collections is a genuine loss. There are
also distinctive poems whose publication history is part of the biblio-
graphic nightmare awaiting anyone who would attempt a complete
variorum of Moore's poetry. One of these is "Pedantic Literalist," the
volume's opening poem, which appears again in *Observations* and *Selected*, and then again in the *Collected Poems* (1951) and the *Complete
Poems* (1967; 1981). But what would Aldington's professional English
reviewer, or any common reader, make of the poem's first few images:

> Prince Rupert's drop, paper muslin ghost,
>   white torch—"with power to say unkind
> things with kindness, and the most
>   irritating things in the midst of love and
>   tears," you invite destruction.

The opening image refers to a child's gadget-toy of the time, made of
glass and very hard in some conditions and very fragile in others, a
perfect metaphor for the person who mistakes meanings by insisting on
accuracy. Such a person is also insubstantial spiritually and without
grace at the level of manners and self-expression. The controlling tone,
however, in this poem and several others in the book, is generated
chiefly by a rhetoric of indirection: "you invite destruction." Is such
rhetoric a result of a "caged" anger, or is it an "old maidenly priggishness," or is it acutely balanced irony that enacts just the right note of
controlled condescension and active disgust? Clearly it is all of these, or
at least may be read as any one, or any combination, of the three tones.
What chiefly separates it from the typical lyric up to this time is the
note of familiarity combined with the distance of a lexical play that is
both self-delighting and rigorously discriminating. One can't help but
be impressed with the amount of conscious energy that is being expended to achieve the right verbal gesture. As she said of Williams,
Moore herself is aware that she must go below the level of professional
intellectuality and modishness in order to represent the truth of what
she wants to say.

In "Black Earth" Moore asks different questions from the ones concerning conduct and culture. In this poem the issue is the balance between strength and poise, what might be regarded as the source or aim of all culture. "Black Earth" is the utopian antidote to the human failings of "Pedantic Literalist." The poet boldly speaks through the elephant, whom she first shows us under the aspect of nature ("with the naturalness of the hippopotamus or the alligator") and then under the aspect of culture as she says the object in view is a "renaissance." While the poem has several passages of the descriptive power that will characterize many of her later lyrics, the main argument is a moral, even a religious one:

> Black
> but beautiful, my back
>   is full of the history of power. Of power? What
>   is powerful and what is not? My soul shall never
>
> be cut into
> by a wooden spear; through-
>   out childhood to the present time, the unity of
>   life and death has been expressed by the circumference
>
> described by my
> trunk; nevertheless, I
>   perceive feats of strength to be inexplicable after
>   all; and I am on my guard; external poise, it
>
> has its centre
> well nurtured—we know
>   where—in pride, but spiritual poise, it has its centre
>   where?

Echoing the techniques of the fables of Aesop, and anticipating the La Fontaine she is to translate three decades later, and even recalling some of Melville's themes, this poem epitomizes Moore's best animal poetry in its fusion of a self-conscious questioning of values ("What / is powerful and what is not?") and its assertive, almost defiant claims based on experience ("we know / where"). The tension between external and spiritual poise is never fully resolved by the poem, in part because the center of spiritual poise cannot be located, except rhetorically. The poem ends with the question: "Will / depth be depth, thick skin be thick, to one who can see / no beautiful element of unreason under it?" The perception of surface and depth, the very serviceability of an armoring skin, depends on the ability to comprehend, even to comprehend what lies beyond reason. Surface and depth, and especially the relationship between them, will remain important concerns throughout Moore's poetry.

In the summer Moore and her mother visited friends in Carlisle and relatives in Albany. In Albany she went to the gardens with cousin Mary Shoemaker (from the Craig side of her family) and wrote Warner that she was very interested in something called salpiglossis, a kind of lily or petunia in different colors on a tall stem. This flower shows up in the poem called "The Steeple-Jack," that will eventually open her *Complete Poems*. She was constantly collecting such observations, both from her experience and her reading, to recombine them, often at a much later period. Several weeks later she traces out a picture from the *Illustrated News* of an Egyptian glass bottle shaped like a fish, the subject of one of her well-known poems. In September she tells her brother that Carlisle was very pretty, but marked with decrepitudes of various sorts; it would no longer do for her home. She has obviously adjusted to life in the metropolis, or at least been reconciled to leaving the small town behind. In the same month her social life continues to develop; for example, she visited Paul Strand's studio with Bertram Hartman, the painter and critic. Dr. Watson left his gloves at her house and she returned them to the office at *The Dial*, with a poem. Thayer, then in Denmark, sent a postcard showing a church that looked like a "kind of New England house,"perhaps providing Moore with another image for "The Steeple-Jack," with its town full of New England houses and churches. She read Dos Passos' *Three Soldiers*, and gave expression to her lifelong distrust of realism when she told her brother that Dos Passos was too much like a photographic plate, without the harmony and reasoning power of a true thinker. There was also a letter from Bryher who sought to publish the next volume of Moore's poems, or, barring that, a collection of her letters. Her network of literary friends and experiences was already very substantial, just a few years after her arrival in the capital of the literary world.

In the meantime Warner continued to flourish out west; he had recently been impressed by meeting the owner of a sawmill on Puget Sound, a man he identified as having "developed" that part of the country. He also mentions the possibility that he may be assigned back east. Moore, in writing to tell him about the trip to Carlisle and the infirmity of Mrs. Norcross, raised the possibility of another trip out west, though she is skittish about the relation between her mother and Constance. In October, Moore told Warner about a friend of Bertram Hartman who had had his "mother complex" analyzed. She quips that if there was a complex in the Moore family it would be a wilfulness complex. This may have been the period when strains among the three Moores were greatest, and it was a time when the strong will of each was most apparent. In the same letter she expressed her agreement with her mother that Warner should definitely not relocate to Chicago. The family tensions were not far below the surface, and they were often related to questions of geographical location. Eventually a trip to the west coast would be arranged for 1922, and it would prove important for Moore and her poetry, though it did not necessarily lessen any of those tensions.

The year 1921 was not to end, however, without more developments for Moore in the literary world. In October, Moore met Van Wyck Brooks, then one of the leading cultural critics in America. She told him that she had copied passages from one of his books into her reading diary in Carlisle; his attack on the "lowbrow" and the generally stunted nature of America culture might well have struck a note with Moore, who was decidedly Eurocentric in her tastes, if not thoroughly Anglophilic. (By the time Brooks came to reminisce about the period, however, he had considerably altered his views.) He mentions Moore briefly in his memoir of the 1920's, *The Days of the Phoenix*:

> Paul Rosenfeld was the music critic of the *Dial*, and one met in his rooms in Irving Place virtually all the contributors from Zorach to Alfred Kreymborg and William Carlos Williams. There one saw E. E. Cummings, the last of the Yankee come-outers, who came out all the way in his poetry and drawings, and I remember Marianne Moore, on the long sofa by the fire, reading aloud some of her early poems. The mantel and the walls were covered with Marins, Doves, Hartleys and O'Keeffes. One evening Leo Ornstein removed the lid of the piano and smote the keys so violently that he shook these pictures, expressing for Paul, at least, the convulsive activity of the age of steel and the sharp griefs and sharper joys of youth.

The picture of Moore reading her poems amid the new icons of modernist art is especially apt. At this time Moore met Glenway Wescott, who was then a young man of considerable ambition, writing on Pound and Brooks, and many others. Wescott, along with his intimate friend Monroe Wheeler, became a frequent visitor to Moore and her mother. Indeed, both Wheeler and Wescott were great fans of Moore and on their many visits would supply her with considerable literary gossip, often of a suggestive sort. Mrs. Moore was not always amused by the pair, and later Moore herself was to be disaffected, but not overtly. Not long after their first meeting Wescott emigrated to Europe, but not before involving himself in Moore's career. He not only wrote a two-page essay on Moore's work, which was included in the pamphlet *Marriage*, but used a revised version of this to accompany the announcement of Moore's *Dial* Award in the January, 1925 issue of the magazine. Eliot's review of Moore's poem "answers" Wescott's brief essay, and this became a key influence in later attitudes toward Moore's work.

One of Wescott's first efforts was to volunteer to Harriet Monroe that he would review *Poems* in her magazine. Monroe had developed a dislike for Moore's recent work already, perhaps in part because she felt Pound was pushing it too hard. Pound had also begun to attack *Poetry* for printing work he felt was aesthetically reactionary, and his sway over Monroe was clearly fading. In any case, she told Wescott, "Dear boy, I could not trust you to take the right point of view; besides there are two ahead of you." What came of this was something like a review of *Poems* but instead of using a single reviewer, Monroe herself wrote up an article she entitled "A Symposium on Marianne Moore." Wittingly or not, Monroe had begun to treat Moore as someone worth serious consideration and someone whose work was a bellwether for larger aesthetic attitudes.

The "symposium" makes for an illuminating look at the literary politics of the time. Though Monroe had not tried hard to conceal from Wescott her dislike for Moore's work, she claims in the article to judge the poems "without prejudice one way or the other." In apparent pursuit of this ideal of objectivity, she begins by remarking on how this "provocative little pamphlet" has produced such contrary opinions, and proceeds to quote five of them, three for and two against (not counting her own closing remarks, of which more in a moment). The three in favor of Moore are Bryher, H.D., and Yvor Winters, who says, "I am not sure but I think her about the best poet in this country except for Mr. Stevens." Bryher is introduced as a "more moderate admirer" and is quoted at length. She begins by calling Moore a "Marco Polo detained at home." Of most interest is Bryher's concluding suggestion, which is very subjective indeed: "Only, Marco Polo, your sword is ready and your kingdoms wait. May it soon please you to leave the fireside and ride forth." Given Bryher's own flight from home, and her repeated urgings to Moore that she join her and H.D. in Europe, it is no wonder she insists that Moore's "spirit is robust, that of a man with facts and countries to discover and not that of a woman sewing at tapestries."

Then Monroe shifts to the other side of the argument. An associate editor of *Poetry*, Marion Strobel, is cited as saying that "the subject matter of her poems is inevitably dry; the manner of expression pedantic. She shouts at our stupidity: 'Literature is a phase of life' . . . And we yawn back at Miss Moore's omniscience." Pearl Andelson, enlisted by Monroe for the condemnation, argues that "the fact that she wavers between prose and poetry is not disguised by the breath-taking line-formation." The remark about subject matter, of course, is set against the assumption of modernist poetry that no subject is inherently "dry," and the charge of "pedantic expression" misses the tension in the tonal shifts and resonances of Moore's admittedly "educated" vocabulary. The charge that the line between poetry and prose is one that "wavers" is certainly true; it is also a consequence of the modernist questioning of genres and the privileged status of any particular vocabulary or rhetoric. These two critics have not, willingly or otherwise, adapted their styles of reading to the assumptions of the new poetry. But when Monroe herself proceeds to "turn to the book," the outcome is not so clear.

Monroe begins by quoting a long section from "Black Earth," but berates its ending by saying it breaks off "with a quizzical trunk-flourish." She then has a paragraph justifying "meditative self-confession," as she calls it, by reference to traditional and canonic poets. "Unquestionably there is a poet within the hard, deliberately patterned crust" of Moore's soliloquies, she grants. But she immediately objects to Moore's prosy versifying by saying that "no amount of line-patterning can make anything but statement and argument out of the many entries in this book." She points to what she calls the arbitrariness of breaking words at the syllable in order to produce a rhyme, and claims this is part of Moore's reluctance to accept "the limitations of the art's materials." Though she also says there is "little curve of growth or climax" in the poems, there is wit, "wit fundamental and instinctive."

She begins her conclusion by approvingly quoting "That Harp You Play So Well," one of Moore's more traditional poems, published by Monroe seven years earlier in *Poetry*, and not included in the volume. The poem contains the line, singled out by Monroe, "If the heart be brass . . . every royal thing will fail." She asks rhetorically, "Is a deep resistless humor like Miss Moore's the most subtly corrosive destroyer of greatness?"

Since it is hard to know precisely what Monroe meant by "deep resistless humor" the rhetorical question is somewhat ambiguous; it is Monroe's own "quizzical trunk-flourish." But knowing Monroe's private estimate of Moore's work, and knowing how she felt about what she would consider excessive innovation, it can be assumed that the "corrosive destroyer of greatness" is the poet's insistence on her individual talent in the face of traditional demands. The "symposium" seems by its format to strain for fairness and objective judgment, but Monroe's readings of the poems grants them only part of their achievement. Monroe cannot help but see that the poems have not only wit but an argument, but she cannot grant that there is also a more complex sense of form than what she is used to; she says at one point that Moore "gives little heed to the more general laws of shapeliness." This is true in an important way, but with consequences different from those Monroe intends, for modern poetry reacts against just such an idea as "*general* laws of shapeliness." The achievement of the lyrical tones and shapes to be found in *Poems* comes about as an act of defiance, and it is difficult to recover the force of this defiance without realizing the expectations, such as those of Monroe and others, that were thoroughly traditional in 1921. The irony, however, is that for Moore herself these lyrics were also deeply indebted to the literary values of the past.

The year drew to a close for Moore with two other literary issues demanding her attention. The first was the appearance of the collection by Harold Stearns, called *Civilization in the United States*, a compendium of essays by several hands on the general state of the arts and culture in the country. It was largely a pessimistic assessment, much flavored by the views of Van Wyck Brooks, himself a contributor, and Moore followed the reviews of it with interest. One of the most talked about books of the period, the collection included an essay on poetry by Conrad Aiken and one on the literary life by Brooks. Both shed light on Moore's situation at the time, since clearly her own book of poems was a vigorous and even optimistic act based on a complex relation to American culture and its roots in a European past.

The Brooks essay was filled with phrases and claims such as "the creative will in this country is a very weak and sickly plant," our literature is "one long list of spiritual casualties," and one can't avoid the striking fact, when viewing our national literature, of the "singular impotence of its creative spirit." The merchant mentality, with its commercialism and materialism, was all-pervasive from Brooks's point of view. Moore may very well have agreed with much of this, for Brooks's jeremiad often took on a spiritual vocabulary that was close to her sensibility. But what Brooks puts forth as the main concern must have had real force for her. He claimed that the failure was one of leadership: "what constitutes a literature is the spiritual force of the individuals who compose it." All too often the fear of the public produced writers who were willing to hide their true genius or else follow fads and fashions toward commercial success. This calling for an elite leadership, albeit in the ultimate service of democratic values, was one that might have struck Moore with great force. For her at this time, at least two of the potential leaders, Pound and Eliot, were in self-imposed exile. Other possible models of literary greatness, such as George Moore, Yeats, or Hardy, were not interested in the national fortunes of American literature. From remarks in her letters at this time and in subsequent periods, Moore could not have had much faith in the leadership abilities of poets like Kreymborg, Bodenheim, Amy Lowell, or McAlmon. It is true that in the late 1920's and early 1930's she was more sanguine about American poetry, largely because of Stevens and Frost. She could also say, at the end of "England," speaking of a "noted superiority," that "if not stumbled upon in America, / must one imagine that it is not there? / It has never been confined to one locality." But this might more readily be understood as a plea for cultural universalism than a claim of national exceptionalism.

As for the essay on "Poetry," contributed by Conrad Aiken, Moore might have felt most of all her absence from the considerations and the division into several schools or types of American poets. At one point Aiken claims that American poets "hold, less than any other, to any classical tradition; for traditions our poets seldom look back further than the nineteenth century." The types of American poets varied, however, from the "colorists" such as Pound, John Gould Fletcher,

H.D., and Bodenheim, to the poets of "reality," such as Robinson, Frost, and Masters, to the poets of psychological refinement, such as Eliot, Stevens, and Kreymborg. But where would Moore fit here, even allowing for the flexibility of his categories, as Aiken is insistent on doing? Her subject matter and concerns are in an important way psychological, and she is after reality—though not necessarily of a socially grim sort. As for color, she is preeminently a writer of shades and tones of meaning. When Aiken goes on to pronounce that "our poets most need to learn . . . that poetry is not merely a matter of outpouring, of confession. It must be serious: it must be, if simple in appearance, none the less highly wrought," Moore would have agreed vigorously. When the issue came down to a choice between spontaneity and craftsmanship, as it often did in this period of what many liked to call an American resurgence, Moore would likely have stuck with the party of the "highly wrought." But as she said in an earlier poem, though one not collected till 1924, "Ecstasy affords / the occasion and expediency determines the form." Again, something like an aesthetic of pragmatism is operating here, as form and spontaneity are both equally urgent for the transformation into art as experience. This formulation, from "The Past Is the Present," offers Hebrew poetry as one model for the lyric, thus giving the lie, by the way, to Aiken's suggestion that American poets look no further back than the nineteenth century. Moore would later review Aiken and have a pleasant relationship with him, but she might well have had grounds for feeling his essay was deficient, especially in her regard.

The other literary issue of interest to Moore at the end of 1921 was her estimation of George Moore. The essay she published on his work in the January, 1922 issue of *Broom* was very long, her longest prose essay to date and one of the longest she ever published on a single writer. She wrote with relief to Warner on December 11 to tell him she had finished it. She also reviews a critical study of Moore in *The Dial* of December, 1922, and his *Conversations in Ebury Street* in the March, 1925 issue. Based on these pieces, and knowing from her letters how keen she was to review his novel *Heloise and Abelard,* and how disappointed she was when *The Dial* assigned it to someone else, it is safe to assume that George Moore was one of the most important authors for her in the first half of the 1920's.

There are many and varied reasons why this should be so. First, he was Irish and had the same surname she did. Moore's awareness of her ethnic background was never a dominant concern, but it was often present, as the poems "England" and "Ireland" (retitled "Sojourn in the Whale") attest. Immigration was a frequently discussed topic during the 1920's especially in Greenwich Village, located just blocks away from tenement neighborhoods filled with immigrants. Such a topic was also implicitly behind such a book as *Civilization in the United States*. The intellectuals in the Village of the 1920's had much to debate, but the strength of indigenous American culture, and its debt or inferiority in the context of European cultures, was a preeminent subject.

Second, George Moore was at this time a very highly regarded author; his case is indeed something like a classic in the history of revised reputations. He was often ranked with Joyce and Hardy as one of the leading writers in English of his day. Published in multivolume sets, Moore became well known for writing a much-discussed novel about a servant girl, *Esther Waters*, and a rather notorious, somewhat fictionalized memoir, *Confessions of a Young Man*, which served to introduce many people to the Post-impressionist, avant-garde art scene in Paris. His works were eagerly anticipated and he was generally regarded as an important arbiter of taste. But, like the Georgian poets who felt themselves in heated revolt against Victorian ideals, only to be outstripped by imagists and others, George Moore saw himself set against the model of the Victorian sage, but his oppositional role as aesthete was soon to be thoroughly eclipsed.

For Moore herself he must have represented several things: successful author, aesthetic revolutionary, conveyer of sharp "impressions," and a writer wearied of wisdom in the search for experience. Put perhaps too bluntly, he represented for her how she might have seen herself in Greenwich Village from the perspective of Bryn Mawr. For in George Moore's work the issue of maturity and adolescence are always present, though not in those terms. As her essay says of him, "His artificial simplicity—"corrupt simplicity" so called—is the artificial simplicity of every fashion expert and it is not to our discredit that we like it." The part of Moore's temperament that was fascinated by books like *The Psychology of Dress*, an important treatise on fashion that would influence some of her poems, explains a large part of her attraction to a writer like George Moore.

The essay in *Broom* is at some pains to justify her admiration—and it was more than mere fascination—for the man's work. She points out that it is often "the writer rather than the experiencer" who formulates his sentences, but also praises him for careful observation and the avoidance of sentimentality. His descriptions of nature are examples of "fine writing," and they obviously served to influence the sort of poetry for which Moore was to become well known. But by the time she reviews *Conversations in Ebury Street*, her praise has turned to something more like censure. The careful balance between the sensibility of the aesthete and the desire to offer opinions imperiously has broken down. By 1925, Moore has become the author of two books of poetry, and the winner of *The Dial* Award, and she can be more stringent about her past model:

> There are depths of color in these imaginings and there are flaws. As the verbal virtuoso, Mr. Moore is sometimes disappointing, presenting the paradox of a naturalness as oral as Bunyan's; and a naturalness so studied as to annihilate itself. There are inharmonious echoes of the Bible and of the English prayer-book, and an intentional impertinence that on occasion becomes insult; one feels the lack of aesthetic tone in Mr. Moore's displeasure with Hardy.

Much of Moore's feeling is conveyed here by her use of sacred writing to point the negatives, and by her drawing the line between impertinence and insult, such a distinction being central to her sensibility. For her, Hardy is one of the great lyric poets and not someone to be dismissed because of a reader's "displeasure." This willingness to accept certain kinds of displeasure is also one of the key aesthetic assumptions that separates modernism from earlier cultural modes. As she finished the first essay on George Moore, she received two books by her contemporaries, McAlmon and Williams. She rejected McAlmon's stories, from the collection *A Hasty Bunch*, as full of "shallow calfism and sensuality," but of Williams' work in *Sour Grapes* she says it is a "little out of balance but serious as Robert's book is not." It was not experimentalism or sensuality alone that Moore objected to, but the presence or absence of seriousness. Once she detected such an absence in George Moore he ceased to be an active or conscious influence on her writing.

The world of literary reputations and prizes continued to occupy Moore. She began 1922 attending a party for Sherwood Anderson, who had just won *The Dial* Award; he spent some time talking to her, confessing he thought *she* should have won the award, and trying, as she put it, to "enlarge" upon her poems. This was the first of *The Dial* Awards, the one for 1922 going to T. S. Eliot. Anderson is another instance of a highly curtailed reputation, for while his writing about the limitations of small-town life was resonant with much of the literary revolt of the 1920's, his work is now not nearly so highly regarded. Indeed, at the time of the award he stood in for a whole group of writers, known loosely as "social novelists," which included Dos Passos, Howells, Churchill, and others. Their work had little direct relationship to Moore, but clearly Anderson's personal generosity to her was appreciated. On the other hand, she reacted negatively, as would be expected, to the *Poetry* symposium, and Mrs. Moore described it to Warner as several pages of a disturbed mind that needed to rid itself of poison. Moore was in the thick of literary awards, reputations, and personal judgments, and the next seven years were to offer much more of the same.

The problems of personal and family life were of great concern to Moore in 1922. The main event of this year may well have been one that had strong family and artistic repercussions. This was the trip westward, specifically to Bremerton, Washington, where she and her mother visited Warner, who was stationed at the naval base there. In the beginning of the year there were actually plans for Moore and her mother to go to Italy, in part because Warner wouldn't be coming east until at least October. Then, at the end of January, there was suddenly a change of plans, initiated, it seems, by Warner. He began by sending them details of the travel and dates involved, and more important perhaps, letting them know that he is keeping the plans secret from Constance. Constance was living with the children in San Pedro, California, and Warner assumed she would want to come up to the Seattle area when Moore and her mother were there. Warner, clearly acting in accordance with Mrs. Moore's desires, decided that this should not be the case; by the end of February, Warner indicated to his mother that San Pedro was not the right place for the visit, and that Bremerton would be much better. Constance suggested a visit from Mrs. Moore, and Warner put her off, saying that only a visit to San Pedro after a visit to Bremerton would be feasible. By March the situation grew complicated because Constance was planning a trip back east. One of the immediate consequences of the deception on Warner's part may have been that the letters from Moore and her mother, which are missing, may have been destroyed or misplaced in order to keep them from Constance. (Many decades later, there is fairly clear proof that Warner destroyed letters from his sister rather than let his wife see them.) As a result there is little or no information from Moore about herself during the first several months of the year, and then also none from the time she is with Warner, roughly from early July to mid-September. But the letters from Warner that survive do allow us to reconstruct the situation in rough outline, and to see some of the tensions that may have been operating.

When Warner tells his mother of Constance's planned trip back east in a letter of March 4, he also tells how Mole will give Badger a belly-bite. Such reversion to the childlike nicknames was a sign that Warner was still dependent on his mother in important ways, though by now his second daughter had been born and his naval career established. Soon afterwards, in the first week of May, Constance had an allotropic pregnancy and nearly died from a hemorrhage. She was still able to bear children, and recovered well enough that the plans for the trip east were unchanged. But by the end of the month Warner writes to say that his daughter, Mary, will visit the zoo for the first time only in the company of her grandmother and aunt. Warner wanted the children to depend on "Rat" for things only she could give. In the same letter Warner informed his mother that he still hadn't told his wife of the trip west that had been planned, and that he will wait until Constance has been in New York for two or three weeks until he tells her. What eventually happened, it seems, is that Warner himself came east in September and met up with his wife in order to accompany her back to San Pedro. At the same time Moore and her mother were returning home from Seattle, traveling through the Canadian Rockies by train as they had on the way out, accompanied by Warner at least as far as Chicago. In other words, while Moore was in Seattle with her brother, his wife and children were, for part of the time at least, back home in New York with her family. It isn't clear how and when it became known to Constance just what the arrangements were, but she probably felt excluded from the Moore family in an inescapable way. And, perhaps coincidentally, after the trip was completed, Mrs. Moore sold the house on Lacock Street in Pittsburgh, realizing a profit of over $2000, and was to receive a great deal of advice on her investments from Warner in the next several months. Mrs. Moore seems to have strengthened and even reestablished some of the ties with her son.

The trip to Seattle was of great importance for Moore herself, for it was the occasion of one of her longest and most important poems, "An Octopus," which she was writing in earnest in July, 1923, telling her brother she was trying to write a poem on Mt. Rainier but feeling she might not succeed. She had also completed and sent to press what would be her longest poem by the time she began writing "An Octopus"; this, of course, was "Marriage." Both poems were conceived at roughly the same time, and both deal with major concerns, such as the chief values that sustain one's life. Less clear is how "An Octopus" relates to "Marriage." "An Octopus" can be read, in part, as a poem about Warner, and about the choice of Christian over Greek values, and hence a poem about religion as much as cultural values. "Marriage" is concerned about life-choices and self-definition. But the trip and visit with Warner, in which she and her brother spent considerable time with each other, served as the immediate occasion for both poems. They climbed Mt. Rainier together and played in a tennis doubles tournament. Warner's own marriage would most likely have been in some way in Moore's mind as she wrote about a subject that was also the focus of much controversy and discussion among her literary associates in Greenwich Village. As for the choice between Greek and Christian values, though this was a question that no doubt arose as early as Bryn Mawr, it, too, was implicit in many of the literary issues of the day, from Pound's classical interests to the attack on Puritanism mounted by Williams and others, to the praise of Greek love in a preface to an anthology written by Aldington, which Moore had reviewed briefly in The Dial of July, 1921.

The poem, somewhat misleadingly called "An Octopus," spends many lines describing the environment of Mt. Rainier. The issue of a choice between Greek and Christian virtues is posed in the long closing section of the poem:

> The Greeks liked smoothness, distrusting what was back
> of what could not be clearly seen,
> resolving with benevolent conclusiveness,
> "complexities which still will be complexities

as long as the world lasts";
ascribing what we clumsily call happiness,
to "an accident or a quality,
a spiritual substance or the soul itself,
an act, a disposition, or a habit,
or a habit infused, to which the soul has been persuaded,
or something distinct from a habit, a power"—
such power as Adam had and we are still devoid of.

Here the tone is important, and also the question of what we might call "intellectual conduct," for the Greek mind (at least in Moore's version) shuns mystery and will spell out the terms of its understanding even if it has to end in something like a preternatural capability ("or something distinct from a habit, a power. . . . Adam had and we are devoid of"). Meanwhile the Christian formulation does not resolve complexity so conclusively, implicitly because in the Christian view we now suffer from Adam's fall. But in saying that there was once a power that we are now devoid of, the Christian ethos explains things the Greeks cannot. Moore goes on to list charges against the Greeks: "their hearts were hard"; "their wisdom was remote," and though she clearly admires them she boldly offers these charges as real limitations. In her mind the Christian value system relies centrally on what she calls "neatness of finish." At one level this is merely an aesthetic quality, but it has a moral dimension, for it is not achievable without "the love of doing hard things." Aesthetic richness is inextricably linked to an ascetic way of life. Neatness of finish must also be joined with—or at least take cognizance of—another key value, and this is the value that the mountain itself teaches us, namely "Relentless accuracy" with a "capacity for fact." Otherwise, neatness of finish will only produce the weak aestheticism of George Moore, say, whereas accuracy without neatness of finish will give us only the "realism" she had always shunned.

Accuracy of fact and neatness of finish are clearly what Moore herself strove for in her poetry, and so "An Octopus" can be read as one of her many poems on poetry, an *ars poetica*. It must, however, be most fully read as an *ars poetica* with a very strong moral and religious dimension. In fact, it may be the poem where Moore explores most fully the relationship between the aesthetic and the ethical realms. The real poetic strength of "An Octopus" is that its almost relentless cataloguing of facts about the mountain, which Moore drew largely and often verbatim from a Parks Department Handbook about the locale and its flora and fauna, exemplifies the "relentless accuracy of fact." The poetic questions of "An Octopus" are centered on the value of "neatness of finish," a quality Moore introduces through an allusion to Henry James. While the poem is a dazzling display of surfaces, its jointures are not always so seamless, nor is its structure so apparent. If it is a poem about her admiration for her brother, and a celebration of the values he represented over against the values she saw being praised in much of the contemporary writing around her, one might wonder whether its somewhat nervous sense of structure and its oddly inconclusive ending result from her not being able to speak openly about the poem's subject.

Such a nervous hiding of the real subject, or at least her feelings about it, is in part a noticeable feature of "Marriage," as many have observed. Moore herself further hides the subject when she argues, as a note in the *Complete Poems*, that the poem is only a collection of "statements that took my fancy which I tried to arrange plausibly." Yet in an undated letter of 1923, she specifically told Warner that she was hoping to give offense by the poem, especially to those people who too casually assumed that marriage was not a permanent state. But the poem doesn't give offense, largely because it presents so many different attitudes toward marriage. Other letters in 1923 indicate that Moore was increasingly unhappy with the work of many of her contemporaries. Her mother quotes her to Warner as saying that there wasn't anything in *Broom* she couldn't do without, whereas she felt the opposite about the *Spectator* and the magazines she read about natural history. In the same letter Mrs. Moore expressed her and her daughter's view that obscenity was acceptable only if it were subordinate to the worth of the entire work. Moore herself vowed to go to *Broom* with her work only to spite Gorham Munson and Kenneth Burke. This was a dig at Munson's new magazine, *Secession,* which he and Burke were editing, and which Munson polemically presented as better and more advanced than all the other magazines. In fact, Munson included negative appraisals of other journals in early issues, singling out *The Dial,* among others. In the middle of February, Glenway Wescott quoted William Carlos Williams as having said, after Moore left the room, "I am in perfect terror of Marianne," and at the party he had said, when reading his poems, "I have to leave some out, because I could not say such words before Marianne Moore."

It was, somewhat ironically, Wescott for whom Moore was busy at work on "Marriage," as early as April, 1923. Mrs. Moore liked Monroe Wheeler a lot, so much so that she reported to Warner that they agreed to call him "Monroe." Wescott was another matter, however. By the beginning of 1924 Mrs. Moore confessed to Warner that they didn't care for Wescott anymore, but tolerated him for Wheeler's sake. She specifically objected to Wescott's novel then being serialized in *The Dial*, and felt bad that Moore's review of Stevens had to be in the same issue. In May, 1923, Wheeler and Wescott had both told Moore and her mother that they were going to model their lives after the two women and give up literary celebrities. But apparently Wescott's resolution was not to last; among other things, he returned from a trip abroad with news of Pound (he was now sporting a pointed beard), and that Thayer was on the outs with several people for rejecting Mina Loy's essay on Gertrude Stein for *The Dial*.

Nevertheless, in the midst of all this literary jockeying, Moore worked steadily on "Marriage," and was able to show Wescott and Wheeler at least a rough draft by the end of April. By the third week of May, Wescott had prepared a "dummy" to send to the printer in Germany, and he shows it to Moore. The poem was finally printed, as a chapbook, by Wheeler's Manikin Press, appearing late in 1923, in an edition of about 200 copies, mostly for presentation. In several copies there was laid in the two-page essay on Moore's poetry written by Wescott and later used, in a revised form, in *The Dial*. Wescott and Wheeler both took delight in telling Moore that Thayer, when he saw the book, "went white," apparently with surprise. So the poem that Moore hoped would give offense to many served at first only as a focus of envious competition.

Still the outstanding irony is that this self-effacing poet who never married wrote her longest poem on a subject that was controversial, timely, and apparently irresolvable. In what is almost a series of musical riffs or movements, the poem is built largely on quotations, though no more so than "An Octopus." It is a classic example of the modernist poem as an exercise in perspectivalism, shifting its tone, its vocabulary, and its point of view frequently and often without notice. The poetic sequence, so often resorted to by modernist poets, might have been a more "comfortable" format for what Moore wanted to say, but for whatever the reasons and the consequences, the poem proceeds—at least typograpically—in one uninterrupted flow. The opening, with its self-conscious correction:

> This institution,
> perhaps one should say enterprise
> out of respect for which
> one says one need not change one's mind
> about a thing one has believed in,
> requiring public promises
> of one's intention
> to fulfil a private obligation. . . .

has enough of a mix of an apparent attempt at honesty ("perhaps one should say") and a still evasive tone ("one says one . . .") to indicate that the lyric impulse will be folding back on itself in complex ways. The poem does have moments of celebration and anguish, even of humor and biting satire, but if it were expected to deliver a final answer, or even a definitive but subjective opinion, about the worth or desirability of the married state, such a definitive formulation is itself clearly called into question:

> Psychology which explains everything
> explains nothing,
> and we are still in doubt.

Not only do we hear Adam on Eve, and Eve on Adam, but any number of authorities are cited, in such profusion that one could imagine that Moore was gently satirizing authority itself, as Chaucer did with his Wife of Bath, also an expert manipulator of cited wisdom on the subject of the relations between the sexes.

Many readers of the poem, almost in despair, one feels, have turned to its ending to try to see if there are any final formulations. Again, a typical Moore image, this one drawn from high culture, both embodies and seems to dissolve the many dilemmas the poem has strung together:

> "I have encountered it [love]
> among those unpretentious
> protégés of wisdom,

> where seeming to parade
> as the debater and the Roman,
> the statesmanship
> of an archaic Daniel Webster
> persists to their simplicity of temper
> as the essence of the matter:
>
> 'Liberty and union
> now and forever';
>
> the Book on the writing-table;
> the hand in the breast-pocket."

Here the essence of the matter seems to be spelled out, and in terms of the normal understanding of Christian values, it is. Marriage is a union designed to last forever, but mysteriously to provide people with liberty as well. For many latter-day readers, however, Moore's answer is more generally read in a heavily ironic context. People have suggested that the hand in the breast pocket, with the whole pose of statesmanship, is self-defeatingly pompous, especially in the light of the skepticism elsewhere in the poem. And yet it is not so much Webster himself who is the embodiment of the poem's closing value, as it is his "unpretentious protégés," who are more trusting, one assumes, more willing to believe in ideals of love, freedom, and self-sacrifice. The syntax of the poem's closing argument locates love in the protégés, but it directs the reader's gaze at Webster's pose, thus combining a trusting view of a mystery with a potentially ironic undercutting of its high claims. Knowing Moore's concern with making fine distinctions between emotional and social gestures and values, the fact she calls the protégés "unpretentious" means she offers them high praise. In October, 1923, Mrs. Moore wrote to Bryher from Bremerton that the latter part of the poem was her daughter's argument in favor of the indivisibility of the married pair, and that the image of Webster came to her while they were skating on a pond in Central Park and saw the statesman's statue there. Mrs. Moore remarked that the motto on the base of the statue was as true of the family as of the state.

Moore herself might have shared Mrs. Moore's rather unequivocal views on the subject. But she just as likely would have had a more complex view. For example, she could have remembered that she wrote

H.D. back on March 27,1921, in connection with Bryher's marriage to
McAlmon, observing at the time that no marriage is prudent but it must
be treated as a crusade, with the awareness it always has an element of
tragedy in it. She went on in the same letter to say that she could only
smile ironically at the news of McAlmon fitting in with Bryher's family,
and then added later that perhaps she had exaggerated the momentous-
ness of marriage.

Moore may also have discussed with Alyse Gregory an article Gregory was writing for *The New Republic* in which she discussed D.H.
Lawrence's views on marriage. The piece appeared in the issue of July
4, 1923, and was called "The Dilemma of Marriage." It is a searching
examination of the institution, which is indeed treated as an enterprise
in some ways:

> Women are still, to a large extent, secretive, proprietary, jealous, hyp-
> ocritical in the sex relation, because they have developed these qualities
> in their economic struggles for shelter and a mate, just as men have
> developed the same qualities and legitimized them into institutions and
> codes of honor in their competitive struggles for power in the business,
> political and professional worlds.

Gregory goes on to argue that men and women do become dependent
on one another, but this often involves some instances where pity
"rivets" them to one another. And "pity . . . makes slaves of the strong
and tyrants of the weak." Near the end she boldly declares, "It is hardly
an exaggeration to say that most monogamous marriages are compro-
mises based upon mutual illusion, and maintained by fear." Some of
Gregory's anti-illusionary attitudes in the review were obviously her
own, but some may have come from her husband, the English novelist
Llewelyn Powys, who rather prided himself on having a modern attitude toward relations between men and women. Moore's poem obviously shares some of the anti-illusory quality that is the main ingredient
in Gregory's essay on the matter. In any case, Moore apparently had in
mind at least three quite distinct marriages as she approached her poem:
her brother Warner's to Constance, Bryher's to McAlmon, and Gregory's to Llewelyn Powys. This alone would account for the multiple
perspectives that form the poem's structure.

It might have occurred to Moore that her distinction between marriage as an institution or as an enterprise might present problems if
applied to the literary life. For in 1923, and afterwards, the enterprising

efforts of various literary friends and associates to advance themselves
and their views might well have seemed all-consuming. She herself was
caught up in such efforts. For example, Mrs. Moore wrote Warner in
May that Moore was avoiding William Benét and his fiancée at the
time, Elinor Wylie. Wylie is a literary type they chose to shun: she had
come from a prominent social family, but Benét was her third husband
and she had been ostracized by the highest levels of society. She was
generally considered a better poet than Benét, but their marriage was
under strain from the beginning, and she was thought to be susceptible
to hysterical reactions. Many people in the literary world remarked on
her penchant to discuss openly her abortions and miscarriages. But her
poetry had become better over the years, and she stressed the relationship between personal freedom and artistic creativity. Moore also mentions to her brother a new young poet named Hart Crane, whom she
sees as too dependent on Monroe Wheeler. Being a literary type to be
shunned might well mean being too modern, in the sense of being too
outspoken or obvious about one's private psychology.

Moore was occupied as well, near the beginning of the year, with all
her friends' negative reaction to Louis Untermeyer, who was bringing
out the series of anthologies of contemporary American poetry that
would shape the tastes of several generations. In November she completed her review of Wallace Stevens' first book, *Harmonium*, for *The
Dial*. Entitled "Well Moused, Lion," this is one of the early important
reviews of the man who became a major modern poet. Moore's review
was an important defense against the charges of obscurity and dandified
language then, and later, so frequently made against Stevens. In the
spring she had gone with Williams to visit the ailing Charles Demuth
in a sanatorium in Morristown, New Jersey, where he was being treated
for diabetes. Many years later she recalled to Williams the flowers in the
room and other details of the visit, especially Demuth's remarkable
good cheer. Near the end of the year she visits the Wildenstein Gallery
and there sees Demuth talking to Alfred Steiglitz and Georgia O'Keeffe.
Demuth reported to her that T. S. Eliot had been saying some nice
things about her.

Demuth's remark almost certainly referred to Eliot's review of *Marriage* and *Poems*, a review Eliot had planned to do earlier, but which
eventually appeared in *The Dial* for December, 1923. On November 30,
1923, Moore told her brother that Thayer brought over the Eliot review

for her to see. She observed that if bolstering by the profession can do one any good, she would certainly be helped by such a review. On December 9 she could also tell Warner that William Carlos Williams had come over with a "beautifully written" review of her poems, which he planned to send to Eliot for publication in *The Criterion*. (The piece finally appeared in the May, 1925 issue of *The Dial*.) The positive review of her new book by two of the most important American poets of the century is high praise, indeed. In the middle of December, she confessed to Warner that she had already felt that T. S. Eliot overpraised her work. A few days later Wescott boldly suggested she might win *The Dial* Award and she demurred. According to Mrs. Moore, "Rat" has rightfully lived in retirement and it would be excessive to bring her into embarrassing prominence. It is impossible to ascertain how much this reaction was a *pro forma* expression of humility, especially for Warner's sake, and how much was an evasion of her own ambition. Incidentally, the 1924 award went to Van Wyck Brooks, a writer Moore liked personally though she disagreed with his views. The following year Moore herself received the award.

Warner for his part was delighted with his sister's literary success. He reacted to the Eliot review, for example, by requoting some lines of Moore that Eliot had cited, commenting that nothing else he had ever read struck him as so religious. Describing his experience reading about his sister's poetry as being on a shore, he uses the most sublime and religious images to convey his reaction. Warner saw his sister's poetry in these exalted terms throughout his life, and it seems at least in part to be his way of elevating her devotion to poetry to a level commensurate with his calling as a minister. On the other hand, such a reading and reaction might have been induced by his sister's own talks with him about her poetry, for we know that she did see her work as a truly spiritual, though not an ecclesiastical, undertaking. Yet another force behind such a way of speaking was, of course, Mrs. Moore's presence, for both son and daughter were bound to her and her ways of thinking and feeling. Whatever the outside world might think about her ambiguous meanings, Moore's immediate family thought her poetry was indubitably a spiritual achievement.

The Moores were together out west in 1923, for Moore and her mother made a second trip to Bremerton in the summer months. Again, Constance was not there, having stayed in San Pedro. In the summer she had given birth to her third child, another daughter. Moore obviously found her trips to see her brother very emotional, even though Constance complained bitterly about the arrangements. Warner sent his sister a straw hat in March, 1923, and Moore compared it to the Aleut Indian baskets they had seen in a shop in Seattle. In November she tells of polishing an oil dish Warner had given her, this probably on the second trip. Such talismans were precious to her for their aesthetic and emotional aspects. In March, 1923, Mrs. Moore wrote to her son to say that objects were surely no more than the dust of the earth: they could be balls of iron, but also alabaster containers of ointment. This remark was immediately occasioned by a handbag that Moore had recently purchased, but such a view would apply generally in Moore's sense of the world of physical things.

III. *Observations*

If 1921 was an important year for Moore, so, too, was 1924. Eliot's review in the December, 1923 *Dial* started the year auspiciously; the publication of *Observations* continued it splendidly, and the granting of *The Dial* Award, with its cash gift of $2000, capped it bountifully. The Award, given for a writer's overall contribution, was announced in the January issue of each year between 1922 and 1929. Moore's award was announced in January, 1925, though of course she had been informed several weeks earlier. She was the grantee between Van Wyck Brooks and William Carlos Williams, and she had at the time a rather small body of work, but a great deal of respect from many of her peers. Much of this respect was built on her agile conversation, her intelligence, and her bracingly high standards. The latter were most in evidence in 1924 in the reviews she published in *The Dial*, especially those of Wallace Stevens, Vachel Lindsay, and Maxwell Bodenheim.

Stevens came in for much praise. When describing his artistry, Moore quoted one of the principles that guided her important technical standards. This principle was borrowed from her early critical writing, an essay called "The Accented Syllable," published in *The Egoist* in 1916.

The central claim of that essay was repeated in the Stevens review when she said, "The better the artist . . . the more determined he will be to set down words in such a way as to admit of no interpretation of the accent but the one intended. . . ." Of course, strictly speaking such an achievement is impossible, since different readers, even competent and highly trained ones, will read a given line or sentence with some variations. Yet the impulse behind this sweeping claim is understandable. In some ways it resembles Williams' theory of the "variable foot"; while no foot as a fixed measure can be intelligently variable, Williams needed this apparent contradiction to master the demands for a new measure, one responsive to the pressures of modern reality. It was his way of struggling against fixity without succumbing to formlessness. Moore shared in many parts of that struggle. In other ways Moore's theory of the accented syllable resembles Frost's formulation about "sentence sounds," namely that the underlying cadence of a syntactical structure conveys some crucial meaning about a sentence's tonal and semantic thrust. In all three cases the poets are looking for some alternative to the canons of accentual meter, some way of giving their verse a discipline that will be earned and yet not simply applied because of traditional requirements. Eliot's claim that no verse is ever free for the person who would do it right is also back of this need to liberate the poem from meters that the poets felt were exhausted, but still to avoid the too easy slide into the indulgences of something like John Gould Fletcher and Amy Lowell's "polyphonic prose."

Moore's praise for Stevens was not restricted, however, to his technique. She praised the range and complexity of his feeling, for example, when she formulated the paradoxical insight that "one's humor is based upon the most serious part of one's nature." For her, Stevens' "poised uninterrupted harmony" was due in large measure to the fact that he was "[i]nfinitely conscious in his purposes." Conscious purpose and poised harmony were cognate with the accuracy and finish she had joined together in "An Octopus."

Even when voicing negative criticism in the reviews, she remained consistent. She attacked Maxwell Bodenheim's lack of accuracy and also pointed to a possible confusion about his conscious purpose: "one is forced in certain instances to conclude that he is self-deceived or willingly a charlatan." What she faulted most stringently were his views of Christ and his views of women. On the latter point she was at her most droll in answering Bodenheim's swagger with the following riposte: "There is zest in bagging a woman who is one's equal in wits; the possibility of bagging a superior in wits not being allowed to confuse the issue." Considering Bodenheim's notoriety as a philanderer—several years later, he and his female companion were murdered by a psychotic they had met in a bar—it can be argued that he was the most infamous of all the Greenwich Village figures. Moore's strictures, however, were based on his work, and she quotes often to prove her points. In another review, this one of Edwin Arlington Robinson's *The Man Who Died Twice*, she says of the literary scene that it is a "day of much shallowness, muddy technique, and self-deluded mystery." In this review she is also very outspoken about those critics who have missed Robinson's strength; she was more and more confident in her ability to make pronouncements about what she felt was necessary to achieve literary greatness. An essay on Francis Bacon, the seventeenth-century philosopher and essayist whose aphoristic style was a major influence on Moore, admitted he was demanding and distant, yet Moore insisted that "expressions of deep conviction, in all ages, weather coldness." She buttressed this point in her first paragraph by allusions to Burke on the sublime, Ruskin, and Santayana, thus using eighteenth-, nineteenth-, and twentieth-century aesthetic authorities to make her point.

She was not able at all times to appeal to such respected authorities, however. It turns out that her dislike for Wescott was not only personal, for she was compelled to tell him that his novel, *The Grandmothers*, was "wrong," and had earlier told her mother that it was infected, but was prevailed upon by Mrs. Moore to soften that opinion to Wescott. She was also negative about the story he published in *The Dial* of February, 1924. Further, she didn't enjoy the concerts that Wheeler and Wescott took her to, because her taste in music tended to the classical rather than the modern. Moore also did not care much for Llewelyn Powys, perhaps because of his attitudes toward sex, about which he tended to be outspoken in his memoirs. His wife Alyse Gregory continued as a good friend, however, as did Lola Ridge. The essay she wrote on Bacon had been promised to Gorham Munson, for his new journal *Secession*, but he apparently made a remark about *Contact* taking her and Williams "off the hands" of Munson, and this angered her, and she offered it to Thayer, who accepted it for *The Dial*. She was always very proud about her work, and rather particular about who published it. In May, for example, she told Warner that Williams wanted her to let Contact Editions bring out a volume of her poems, but she declined, saying that she didn't like McAlmon's taste. But she had continued to develop a friendship with Williams, despite her growing aesthetic reservations about his work.

In the spring Mrs. Moore had a severe illness that prevented her from speaking; Moore informed Warner it was pharyngitis and laryngitis. This is one of the early episodes of the affliction that would eventually make her bedridden in the 1940's; and a throat cancer is to be one of the main causes of her death. Warner at this time was discussing a possible move to Brooklyn, to be stationed at the large Navy Yard there, but the move would not take place for a few years. Moore tells him that no amount of money could repay the toil she'd expended on the review of Bodenheim and the other hack work she'd done, apparently referring to the brief reviews for *The Dial*. In January, Thayer took her to dinner and offered her an office job at *The Dial* but at that time she declined. Her mother remarked that "they've" resisted Thayer in the past, the plural pronoun here being especially suggestive.

On January 8 she had written Warner that Moore had gotten the literary career she so deeply craved in large part through the pages of *The Dial*, and that while her work didn't partake of the modern atmosphere of the journal with its nudes and frank discussion of sex, at least the glimmer of her poems hadn't been dulled by those pages either. All the same, Mrs. Moore and her daughter wished her work could appear in the pages of *The Atlantic Monthly*. One possible implication here is that Moore was split in her own mind about the sort of public forum and appearance she wished to be associated with, and the actual sort of writing style that she adopted. She sometimes sounds like a reluctant modernist, especially in her future dealings with other writers when she is editing *The Dial*. Some of the tension between the two styles, the traditionalism of *The Atlantic* and the liberality of *The Dial*, may have been more a result of Mrs. Moore's perception and wishes than her daughter's immediate experience.

In May, Wescott told Moore that he had gathered all of the pieces she'd written for *The Dial* to give to Herbert Gorman, the literary editor of *The New York Times*. Gorman will be one of the several reviewers of *Observations*, and his "research" into Moore's other writings shows that he had considerable respect for her reputation. In the same month she attended a lecture by Bertrand Russell; afterwards Mrs. Moore quoted her as having said she could have told Russell a lot, but found him charming nonetheless. The dinners at *The Dial* were now almost a weekly affair for her; Moore mentions dining there with Padraic Colum and his wife Mary, whom she did not particularly like; Paul Rosenfeld, soon to publish a book, *Men Seen*, that would praise Moore; Stewart Mitchell, a poet; Alyse Gregory, and others. In May, Thayer suggested that she become his secretary and she toyed with the idea but rejected it. Mrs. Moore lamented the social pressure "they" felt from Thayer and how relieved they are when he vacations for a time in Bermuda. Thayer is also described by Moore as "bursting with inequity," his negative views of much contemporary writing being quite strong even in Moore's eyes.

The central fact for Moore as a writer in 1924 was the publication of *Observations*, but she says little about it in her letters to Warner. However, Warner was transferred back east in the fall, soon to be assigned to the USS Detroit, stationed in Boston. He set up residence on Long Island, though, so there is relatively little family correspondence in the second half of 1924 and for all of 1925. Letters about *Observations* might have been lost by Warner during his various moves. In September, Mrs. Moore told her cousin Mary Shoemaker in Albany that Warner looked ten years older than he was. This may have been only a mother's concern, but it may also reflect the toll of his naval duties and the growth of his family, as well as his wife's illnesses. But in January, 1925, he was promoted to Commander, and in July reassured his mother that the next chapter in their lives would be a great one. This clearly anticipates the Moores' family reunion on the east coast in some more or less permanent way. Though it will be a few more years, during which Warner's assignment is shuffled around, the move to Brooklyn in 1929 is to be a major event in their next "chapter."

Moore was soon to become the editor of *The Dial*, to win its Award, and to publish her *Observations*. The volume was definitely an artistic advance over the *Poems* of three years earlier, and it was received more positively. The second volume dropped only three short poems from the first book, and it added thirty-two more, for a total of fifty-three poems. This more than doubled the number of the twenty-four poems in the first book; in addition, it came in hardcover, where the first had only paper wrappers. Just after the table of contents of *Observations* there was the following announcement: "With additions, this book is a reprint of "poems," published in London in 1921 by The Egoist Press, that collection being made and arranged by H.D. and Mr. and Mrs. Robert McAlmon." Though technically accurate, this announcement was misleading, since the phrase "with additions" seemed so bland. Not only were the additions greater than the original volume, their quality was considerable. Included in the new poems were not only the important long poems "An Octopus" and "Marriage," but "Critics and Connoisseurs," "New York," "A Grave," "Silence," and "An Egyptian Pulled Glass Bottle in the Shape of a Fish," to name only the ones that have become popular anthology selections. In fact, only nine poems were to be added to these fifty-three to make up the 1935 *Selected Poems*, the volume, with T. S. Eliot's introduction, by which Moore's reputation was to be solidified. So *Observations* is, if nothing else, the culmination of Moore's "early" work as a poet and altogether a most impressive volume.

The reviews in America were by and large quite favorable, even respectful in some instances, for despite many comments about the obscurity and elitism of the poems, readers seemed to realize that not only did Moore have the respect of important fellow poets but that her poems were genuinely intelligent. The reputation of poets, either lagging behind or gaining latter-day strength, is seldom in step with their creative power. But with Moore the volume she published in 1924 coincided with a widespread critical sense that was largely positive, discriminating, and in tune with her art. One could say that the book was noticed only by people who made it their business to notice everything new, so they were disposed favorably to someone of Moore's inventiveness and orginality. But these were not the only attributes that attracted attention. Several reviews remarked as well on Moore's gender, as if both puzzled and pleased that a woman had produced such poetry. One recalls the famous remark attributed to Alfred Stieglitz on first seeing drawings by Georgia O'Keeffe: "Finally a woman on paper." Indeed there were at least broad convergences between Moore's career and O'Keeffe's, both born on exactly the same day in the same year, both arriving in New York a year apart, O'Keeffe's first one-person show in 1923, Moore's *Observations* in 1924, and a period of withdrawal from the public in the 1930's. But O'Keeffe was never satisfied with the reviews of her work, even when she induced Mabel Dodge Luhan to do one. Moore, on the other hand, was pleased with Eliot's, Williams', and Wescott's, as noted, and there must have been things in the others as well that gave pleasure.

In *The Nation* on March 18, 1925, Edwin Seaver went to the heart of several issues when he said that:

> Miss Moore hews to an ideology that is aristocratic and severe and pure. Against the commonplace and the easy her subtlety of sarcasm is devastating. Herself a modernist by all the earmarks discernible, she is yet austerely conservative, gifted with an instinctive taste and the wit to prove its supremacy.

Seaver had read well, though one regrets the limitation of space didn't allow him to explore just how the modernism and the conservative feeling are joined, and to examine how the wit "proves" its supremacy, presumably by using its devastating "subtlety of sarcasm." Later he remarks that Moore's mentality is simple and sophisticated at the same time, and yet is "aware of that element of the ridiculous in both approaches to experience." One is reminded of Eliot's formulation of the wit in Andrew Marvell, which is based on an awareness at all times that there is more than one emotional reaction possible to any experience. Moore was so pleased with this review that she wrote Seaver to thank him for it, and for finding something to praise in her Puritan proclivities.

In the *New York Post Literary Review* on August 8, Margaret Widdemer was much more cautious than Seaver. She begins by remarking on how hard it is to review a prize-winning book. Though granting Moore's poetry is the quintessence of what *The Dial* stands for, Widdemer seems rather beside the point when she claims that "[t]here are not the magnificent depths of piercing irony one hoped for as her justification." She also says, "You have to work too hard to find out what she means, as over a difficult translation, to have time to feel." This is the same reaction of the two readers in the *Poetry* symposium who had refused to accept the modernist attachment to difficulty, the belief that what one truly feels is only to be comprehended by and with difficult "translation." As for Moore's technique of breaking a word to accentuate a rhyme, for Widdemer this is "not a great new effect of style; it is merely bad workmanship." The reviewer perhaps inadvertently reveals her limitations when she signs off with the pronouncement that "epigram, no matter how gorgeous, will never be poetry."

If Widdemer was not sophisticated enough to appreciate Moore's art, the anonymous writer of the column called "The New Euphues," in *The New York Times* of February 8, was perhaps not alert enough to Moore's simplicities. This columnist begins by citing *The Dial* Award and the accompanying commentary (the review of the volume itself had just appeared in the *Times*), and the passage where Moore is compared to Francis Bacon in terms of analytic power. It calls this passage a "solemn frolic of fancy" that leads the reader to think the commentary is worthy of the poetry. Then there follows the sarcastic conclusion:

> O GONGORA! O EUPHUES! O EZRA POUND! O GERTRUDE
> STEIN! O admirable elbows admirably crooked at the gold bar of heaven!
> In the presence of this altogether concinnity impeccable, high rears and
> higher bolts in the memory that Pegasus which Commissioner of Public
> Works J. ROLLIN M. SQUIRE rode in the City Hall Park until he was
> thrown; from 1885 arise the quite soul-dissolving overtones of his thren-
> ody on General GRANT:

> > No faltering marked the Titan's task,
> > No shrinking from the trial;
> > He faced the foe e'er Freedom's hand
> > Fell shattered from Time's Dial.

To set beside Moore's poetry this sort of doggerel in the service of public virtue would be funnier if the attack on *The Dial*'s commentary succeeded in revealing its excessively convoluted, or euphuistic, prose. But surely *The Dial* announcement, composed by Wescott, is itself being deliberately and playfully theatrical, even ironically baroque, when it speaks of Moore's analyses as having "admirable elbows admirably ad hoc, [and] high rearings and higher boltings, their altogether porcupinity impeccable—these are just Miss Moore's private ways of delivering Miss Moore's esthetic fact." As for Moore's work itself, as opposed to *The Dial*'s announcement, it is not euphuistic because it doesn't take delight in ornamentation for its own sake, nor does it engage in excessive patterning of simple thoughts.

In its review of *Observations*, the *Times* did a much more sober job of getting at Moore's qualities. Herbert Gorman begins by remarking on how the slight body of work Moore had so far produced would not lead one to expect for her an award like *The Dial*'s. But from the start, Gorman assures the reader, as if anticipating the anonymous column in his own paper a week later, "there is no pose, no dependence on unusual subterfuges, no wilful attempts to astonish." Without acknowledging that he is borrowing his scheme from Wescott's earlier review of Moore, included in the pamphlet *Marriage*, Gorman says that contemporary art is split in two directions: "an attempted return to primitive values," and a movement "along more formalized ways [that] is emphasized by those ritualistic adornments that become the elaborate adumbrations of difficult connotations." Moore, he suggests, is emerging along the latter path. Her emotion "is an emotion of the mind," and she is "the direct opposite of sentimentality." He also discusses her "color," referring to her "more selective equipment of subtler pigments," and speculates on the meaning of "observations" as both pictorial representations and intellectual comment. As for her technique, it "is a dogmatic one, a conscious bit of mathematics, but it seems to suit her, and after one has read her poems a few times and gotten memories of Alfred Lord Tennyson out of one's mind, the reader will discover a quaint pleasure in this new form." The review mentions several poems, and quotes from three, including all of "To Be Liked by You Would Be a Calamity" and "Those Various Scalpels." Considering this is a response to Moore's first book-length collection published in America, such a review in the nation's most reputable newspaper could only be considered thoroughly comprehending and helpful. While Moore was often to have her detractors, and the sort of complaints registered against her work in the "Euphues" column and the *Poetry* "Symposium," she did not always meet the level of hostility usually conjured up in discussions of the reception of modernism.

The review of *Observations* in *Poetry* appeared in its April, 1925 issue; it was written by Yvor Winters, a relatively unbridled theoretician of lyric poetry. Fully the first third of the piece is taken up with a theory in which three forms of progress from image to image are offered: logical, psychological, and mixed. We are told that "that poem will be most intense which most fully exhausts the possibilities of the medium," a version of the formalism that lies behind much of the criticism of modernist art. What follows praises Moore's "imagic sound-values," and her general structure. We are told that the poem "Black Earth" is "packed with thought as with sound," but almost no thought or idea is mentioned, let alone analyzed. The review ends with the claim that "it is a privilege to be able to write of one of whose genius one feels so sure." Winters was later to become known for his negative assessments of Hart Crane and Wallace Stevens, but this praising review certainly added to Moore's standing among her contemporaries.

It was Glenway Wescott, in effect, who reviewed *Observations* for *The Dial,* as he wrote the essay announcing the Award in the January, 1925 issue. He, too, was a formalist in many of his concerns, praising how "each word conveys an emotion as clearly as if it were a color." In the earlier version, which he included in the pamphlet *Marriage,* he had made a distinction between proletarian art, which worked on sentimentality, and artistocratic art, which employed ritual. This distinction was not alluded to in *The Dial* version, though he did begin by saying that Moore's poetry widens our knowledge of life and heightens our familiar experiences by "penetration into one's surroundings." He also directly invoked John Dewey, quoting him as saying, "definiteness, depth, and variety of meaning attach to the objects of an experience just in the degree in which they have previously been thought about." By thus calling on a term such as "experience," and by raising the issue of Moore's dealing with what has been thought about, Wescott made it clear that Moore's poems are rich in subject matter and thematic development. He points out several of her claims, for example that "the happiness we associate with Greece [is] effete and a compromise," and "that nature has an intelligence." When it comes to characterizing the form of the poems he says they are "essences of conversation" and their "discrepant dictions are blended in an energetic, harmonious rhetoric." Near the end he says Moore's art is baroque, and mentions the "florid and surcharged" styles of Proust and Joyce, though he also claims she is indebted to neither man. He admits that "the novelty and complexity of her work may cause it to be neglected," but closes, as did Gorman, by quoting the end of one of Moore's central aesthetic statements, her poem "In the Days of Prismatic Color":

> Truth is no Apollo
> Belvedere, no formal thing. The wave may go over it if it likes.
> Know that it will be there when it says,
> "I shall be there when the wave has gone by."

Many generations, including Moore's saw the statue of the Apollo Belvedere as the highest epitome of classical aesthetic standards. These lines slightly echo the structure of the end of Keats' "Ode on a Grecian

Urn," but they have the surprising, almost playful twist, of rejecting "the" classical artwork. Of course, a similar rejection is part of the point of "An Octopus." For Wescott, Moore's real virtues seem centered in her ability to conduct "the exploration of fresh types of material [which] inevitably culminates in an apparent revelry of expression." It is just this freshness and revelry that the anonymous writer of the "Euphues" column for the *Times* had failed to appreciate.

Just as Moore began the decade by setting out her views on Williams and Eliot, so her work was first most fully discussed by these two poets. Eliot's review, which appeared in *The Dial* of December, 1923, was on *Poems* and *Marriage*, not on *Observations*, but it goes to the main issues of Moore's art. Williams' piece was more essay than review, and it appeared in the same journal eighteen months later. Between them, the two poets were exceptionally perceptive and appreciative. But there were also evasions: Eliot, for example, had nothing at all to say about the subject matter of "Marriage," not so surprising given the state of his own marital situation at the time. And Williams touches on the ethical content of the poems, but only briefly and toward the end, as he is much more concerned to have Moore's experimentalist features on display. While both men praise aspects of Moore that are clearly germane to their own efforts in poetry at the time, they do manage to enter into the spirit of her work.

Eliot begins by rejecting Wescott's distinction, made in the essay he included in his edition of *Marriage*, between proletarian and aristocratic art as "artificial and unimportant . . . with dangerous consequences." All real art is aristocratic for Eliot, but not like the "Baltenland aristocracy of foreign race." Fine art is the "refinement," not the antithesis of popular art. For Eliot, Moore's art is aristocratic in three ways: its new rhythm ("the most valuable thing"); its peculiar and brilliant use of "the curious jargon produced in America by universal university education"; and a "primitive simplicity of phrase." As for the third element, Eliot had already meant it as high praise for his contemporary Wyndham Lewis when he said he combined the thought of the modern with that of the primitive caveman. So, here he echoes Wescott's depiction of the aristocratic artist whose use of ritual hankers after some primitive quality. Eliot and Wescott may have in mind something of Moore's axiomatic drive, her tendency to summarize the thematic point so bluntly that it looks primitive, as in the ending quoted above: "I shall be there when the wave has gone by." There is also the end of "Critics and Connoisseurs," where she asks, "What is there / . . . in proving that one has had the experience / of carrying a stick?" Another way to characterize this quality is to call it epigrammatic, precisely that feature that Widdemer had found "unpoetic."

But it is Eliot's second point, about the sources of Moore's language, that is perhaps most telling. Though he does not develop the point at great length, he says later that this language shows up in a "speech which characterizes the American language, that pleasantry, uneasy, solemn, or self-conscious, which inspires both the jargon of the laboratory and the slang of the comic strip." Though Moore's lexical range is quite broad it can be identified as largely Latinate, and related to the "universal university education" which so affected her at Bryn Mawr. She had shown signs of using such language before Bryn Mawr, however; indeed, it seems to be the language that is heard in Mrs. Moore's family correspondence, the language of an educated person who is struggling to have that education maintain her spiritual and social character. The language is "elevated," but it also allows for puns and pet animal names and various kinds of wordplay that can be both sophisticated and simple without relying exclusively on either dimension. It is also a language that can unselfconsciously mimic that of the comic strip. Eliot says Moore is able to work "this uneasy language—as of a whole people playing at clenches and clevelandisms—with impeccable skill into her pattern." What he doesn't quite say, though it is implicit here and in the later version of Eliot's review that serves as the "Introduction" to her *Selected Poems*, is that this language is the perfect vehicle for Moore's themes. What he does say is that all aristocratic art springs from ritual and it is to ritual that it must return for nourishment. But we must know that this is true for Moore not because it suggests the rituals of organized religion or politics, but rather the "smaller" rituals of daily intercourse in "polite" society.

Eliot closes the review on a cryptic note:

> And there is one final, and "magnificent" compliment: Miss Moore's poetry is as "feminine" as Christina Rossetti's, one never forgets that it is written by a woman; but with both one never thinks of this particularity as anything but a positive virtue.

The quotation marks around both "magnificent" and "feminine" suggest that Eliot was aware his remarks might be misconstrued, and that while he detected some special quality in Moore he couldn't very well put it down "simply" to gender, especially as he had earlier argued that good art had no real class distinctions. His formalism led him, in other words, to reject any class or gender quality in what was supposed to be a universal human activity. But the question of gender was not so simple. In *The Dial* for August, 1921, Eliot had published a "London Letter" that argued that Virginia Woolf's writing had a feminine quality:

> that makes it art by feeling, and by contemplating the feeling rather than the object which has excited it, or into which the feeling might be made . . . [she] gives you the minutest datum, and leads you on to explore, quite consciously, the images and feelings which float away from it.

Eliot may have meant to separate Moore's poetry from this quality, for her work is generally keener in contemplating the object than the feeling it has been excited by. Or, as in his own theory of the "objective correlative," Eliot may have been suggesting that Moore makes the feeling into an "object" rather than let it float away. Or he may have needed to state, and yet be evasive about, the quality in Moore's work that would be distinctly and unqualifiedly feminine, for if hers was feminine, then another term would be needed for Woolf's. All told, this is another example of how Eliot's critical vocabulary at this time was far from being consistently thought out.

Eliot also had to face the contradiction about national characteristics in art. His appeal, in characterizing Moore's work, to a special American language was a remark largely about the poems' language, a remark at least potentially offset by his attention to how Moore wove this language into "her pattern." There is a tension in the logic here, but a tension endemic to formalism because it claims that the language is at the same time "merely" the material of the poet, something objective and employed for certain patterns and thus not determined by gender, nation, or class. Yet it also claims the language is the fullest register of everything the poet represents, the deepest expression of his or her identity. Eliot might well have been praising in Moore what he himself was striving for, a feeling of impersonal suspension by the artist above his or her material, a suspension that would be best reflected in an ability to control "popular" material with "aristocratic" means.

At one point, Eliot suggests that Moore's future growth will depend on whether she has the "ability to *shatter* this formation [of elements in her poems up to this time] and painfully reconstruct." (Eliot's emphasis.) To Williams—speaking almost in answer to Eliot, whose *Waste Land* he felt was a betrayal of experimentalism to the classroom of academicism—Moore was already a preeminent agent of shattering and reconstruction. His essay about her work is complex and suggestive, and it begins with several paragraphs praising the work of those who are engaged in "blasting aside" the old forms of art. Williams then uses three images to characterize and compliment Moore's genius: her poetry is a multiplication of impulses that, "crossing at all eccentric angles, might enlighten"; it possesses a "rapidity of movement," a "swiftness that passes without repugnance from thing to thing"; and, lastly, it resembles a compact and accurate "garden of porcelain." Williams is forcibly struck by her lack of connectives, and her handling of materials that is "intensely, intentionally selective."

All of this may well refer to Moore's habit of building the poem through metonymy, by a swift succession of associated thoughts, rather than metaphor, in which thoughts and images are articulated through and because of their common or analogous relation to a main idea. Williams boldly speculates that "a poem such as 'Marriage' is an anthology of transit." Williams was keen at this time to develop a poetry of process, some form of expression that would allow him to register the extremely challenging and complex sense of change, in everyday life as well as in the larger cultural forces, that he saw around him. He was probably praising Moore for her ability, in a poem like "Marriage," to maintain points of contact with many different areas of experience and valuation without becoming rigidly attached to any one of them in particular. There are several different ways Moore has of getting from point to point in her structure, and therefore several different structural principles at work, almost as happens in a Cubist painting, though Williams does not draw this comparison.

Later in the essay, Williams insists that for Moore "an apple remains an apple whether it be in Eden or the fruit bowl where it curls." Here the "garden of porcelain" idea clarifies that the "direct object" seems unaffected, that one doesn't feel "that as an apple it has anything particularly to do with poetry or that as such it needs special treatment." Here he may well have in mind the "objectivism" of Moore's poetry and its formulations in "poetry" about "business documents and

school books." He would have also appreciated her avoidance of anything like a clichéd use of traditional symbols. Williams also praises her
rhythm as that of an animal moving freely, not a "Swinburne stumbling
to music." Reverting to the distinction between proletarian and aristocratic art, he alludes as Eliot did to Wescott's distinction, saying that
even if there is a proletarian taste, and one organizes it, then there is
art. He grants that poetry has a component of ritual, but he is at pains
to say that in Moore's case this is the ritual of one who leads, not one
who follows along afterwards in an already established, pleasureless
pattern. The essay draws to a close with a description of Moore's language:

> With Miss Moore a word is a word most when it is separated out by
> silence, treated with acid to remove the smudges, washed, dried and
> placed right side up on a clean surface. Now one may say that this is a
> word. Now it may be used, and how?

Again we hear the echoes of Dewey's philosophy, which went by the
name of instrumentalism as well as pragmatism, for it saw thought and
language as instruments of understanding, but also insisted on having
them stand as any tool should stand, clean and recognizably ready for
use. Williams also remarks on Moore's moral sense, noticeable because
"there is surely a choice evident in all her work, a very definite quality
of choice . . . but a very welcome and no little surprising absence of
moral tone." Moore's poetry was, like Williams', prepared to be moral
but determined not to sound moralistic. At the close of the essay
Williams exults, "This is new! The quality is not new, but the freedom
is new, the unbridled leap." Not until Kenneth Burke writes his piece
called "Motives and Motifs in the Poetry of Marianne Moore," in 1942,
does her poetry receive such a deep and convincing reading.

Just six months after the publication of *Observations* and *The Dial*
Award, Moore took over as associate editor, and shortly thereafter as
acting editor, of the journal that had given her the literary opportunity
she had so deeply craved.

Chapter 5

152 WEST 13TH STREET:
THE DIAL YEARS

I. "A love of letters knows no frontiers"

In many ways, Moore epitomized *The Dial*, at least in its last five years of publication, for she represented at once several of its qualities and its contradictions. A number of years after her time there, Moore was to refer to the "compacted pleasantness" of the offices at *The Dial* (she always insisted on the article as part of the title), a "three-story brick building with carpeted stairs, fireplace and white-mantlepiece rooms." And later still she said in an interview that *The Dial* was "self-propulsive," and it excelled because of its lack of fear. She expounded:

> I think that individuality was the great thing. We were not conforming to anything. We certainly didn't have a policy, except I remember hearing the word "intensity" very often. A thing must have an "intensity." That seemed to be the criterion.

Many of those who have tried to explain the demise of the magazine felt the absence of a policy was the main cause. But obviously for Moore the aesthetic perfectionism of Thayer and the bold wisdom of Watson were sufficiently individualizing forces to create the sort of intensity that was desired. The journal was capable of printing work by George Saintsbury and Ezra Pound in the same issue, thereby yoking together, with some violence, the last Victorian man of letters and the modernist *enfant terrible*. There is also the example of a "Comment" column in the May, 1921 issue (probably written by Watson) that makes sport of William

Carlos Williams' blustering claim that the best thing that could be done for American poetry was for someone to give Alfred Kreymborg $100,000 to start another magazine; Kreymborg would not inspire Watson with his critical acumen. And yet, in the June issue immediately following, there are poems by Alfred Kreymborg. It is no wonder that Gorham Munson, writing critically in his own magazine *Secession*, could claim that he felt *The Dial* coming apart in his hands.

Because of the lack of any enunciated policy or aesthetic theory, *The Dial* was subject to negative charges from both ends of the spectrum. In the late 1920's it was attacked not only by Munson's *Secession* but by Eliot's *Criterion*. Even before Moore became an editor there, she had heard the magazine criticized by Ezra Pound and others; nevertheless, she was clearly drawn to its openness to established European writers as well as some of its more experimental voices. It had some of the fashionableness of *Vanity Fair* minus the false glitter; some of the acerbity of Mencken's *Smart Set* minus the vitriol. But Moore felt at home there, to the extent she did, because the magazine stood for the values of liberality and intelligence that she always associated with the literary life as a worthy vocation.

There were also the personal ties with Thayer and with Watson. Thayer's aestheticism could very well have reminded her of her commitment at Bryn Mawr—recorded in her early stories—to an aesthetic sensibility that marked her first emergence as a writer. Watson, on the other hand, was a scientist: his interest in filmmaking and radiology bespeaks an interest in the visible and the invisible, both realms being of continuing interest to Moore. As she put it in her memoir of the magazine, "Above all, for an inflexible morality against 'the nearly good'; for a non-exploiting helpfulness to art and the artist, for living the doctrine that 'a love of letters knows no frontiers,' Scofield Thayer and Dr. Watson are the indestructible symbol." Moore's own best work would combine the positive attributes of the sensibilities of both men, and she felt a deep personal affection for both of them as well.

An article by Watson might have had the most influence on her commitment to *The Dial*: an essay he published as an "American Letter" in the May, 1921 issue. By this time she had published only two poems in the magazine, but Watson saw fit to link her name with others he valued most highly. The "American Letter" was only one of two such pieces Watson published—the other was on film—using the pseudonym

of W. C. Blum. Some have suggested the pseudonym indicated Watson's allegiance to the poetry of Williams. In any case, the essay was an
argument about what was to be perhaps the most debated literary question of the 1920's in America: was there an indigenous national spirit
that was being, or should be, manifested in American poetry?

Watson began by arguing that the group that was most vocally ad-
vocating this national spirit was too sure of itself and was thus likely to
miss certain important writers. He referred to these advocates as the
"Seven Arts Group," after a short-lived magazine edited by Randolph
Bourne and others. Watson started out with a strong warning:

> . . . the Seven Arts Group was too ready to disregard and despise as
> un-American very admirable and very American poets like Ezra Pound,
> Marianne Moore, and William Carlos Williams for one to have much
> faith in their affection for art. . . . The Ordeal of Mark Twain and Our
> America remain to show how admirably an idea can be run into the
> ground by a patient and an impatient mind.

The Ordeal of Mark Twain and Our America were written by Van Wyck
Brooks and Waldo Frank, respectively, to advance the idea that the
cultural spirit of America was lost unless its artists actively opposed the
predominant materialistic ethos of America, an ethos still enmeshed in
its Puritan past. Watson counterargued that Brooks, Frank, and others
preferred psychology to aesthetics and were interested in the "mind" of
the author and his or her attitudes toward life rather than in strictly
aesthetic qualities. On the other side of the argument Watson ranged
not only Pound, Moore, and Williams, but the spirit represented by the
imagists, The Egoist, and The Little Review. The tension here is between
people who value a purely artistic set of qualities and those, such as
Bourne, with a more "leftist" or radical political stance. The aesthetic
positions of these latter people are actively related to their politics. To
those with a more aesthetic point of view, politically radical voices
become, artistically speaking, backward-looking or even reactionary.
This is, of course, one of the major arguments inside modernism in all
its manifestations, and Watson's formulation is clear and pointed.

Watson praised those modern writers who had chosen to return to
what he called "clear, energetic, and pure sensations which lie immediately under the skin. . . . By producing such vigorous elements, a
work of art is produced which is quite subtle enough (the subtlety is in
the arrangement) and which is less likely to lead the spectator astray

from the primary aesthetic intention." But Watson wasn't simply publicizing work he admired. Though he praised Williams, for example, he also expressed doubt about his theories, and he questioned whether anyone could "say whether a given piece of writing shows contact with the writer's environment." He then answered his own question by saying "certainly Robert McAlmon can't." Moore would have been impressed with Watson for not allowing his allegiance to Williams to prevent him from rejecting McAlmon. After some praise for Cummings' work, and as if saving the best for last, Watson turned to Moore.

> When Marianne Moore rhymes she reminds us that the eighteenth century, too, desired lucidity. . . . Separate lines of hers often read like the classical prose to which we are supposed to have become accustomed in school. She borrows or invents long quotations . . . which she works into her poems without the slightest inappropriateness. Like Rimbaud she uses the most matter-of-fact constructions, critical rather than poetic phrases, so that extraordinary expansions of mood are uncovered without warning. . . . These penetrating or sensible remarks, spoken so distinctly and as though with the back turned, following one another with such shattering politeness and efficiency, have a broken rhythm—pile up and resolve.
> There is no end of other tricks besides.

Watson concluded his piece with this somewhat cryptic claim. Not only was Moore listed with writers she admired, and not only was her work said to be in some ways more pure and disinterested, which would have appealed to her greatly, but the references to Rimbaud and the eighteenth century captured almost too nicely the mixture of experimental and traditional elements in her poetry. She had been in New York City barely three years, and had published no book with an American publisher when this essay appeared. Always an admirer of Watson's intelligence and seriousness, she must have felt a true sense of gratitude for such a generous benediction by one of the guiding spirits of *The Dial*. Because of the publication's variety, it is difficult to say that any one writer epitomized *The Dial*'s aesthetic. Still, some have suggested Moore might fit that description because of Watson's piece, the Award in 1924, and her later editorship.

Besides being welcomed into the pages of *The Dial* as a poet, Moore was also respected by the editors as a critical intelligence. In the October, 1921 issue, for example, a "Comment" column (listed by one author index as written by Thayer, but more likely by Watson) praised Moore's review of Williams' *Kora in Hell*. The column, without naming Moore, said that the review, which appeared in *Contact*, was "infinitely the finest of the three or four . . . notices of these vigorously imagined improvisations." The claim was given extra force because its author said he had written one of them himself. Two unsigned columns about Moore's poetry also ran as "Comment" pieces after her *Observations* had appeared; obviously by Thayer, these praised Moore's habit of using quotations in her poems.

All in all, Moore had various social and artistic ties to the magazine— ties that had become strong and manifold by 1925. In addition to Thayer and his personal fondness for Moore, there was Lincoln MacVeagh, the publisher of Dial Press, located in the same building but not directly connected to the magazine. MacVeagh was married to Margaret Lewis, a Bryn Mawr alumna from the class of 1908. One of Moore's first reviews for the magazine had been of a book of poems by Stewart Mitchell, who served for a while on the editorial board. For her to be assigned this review meant she had the solid confidence of Watson and Thayer.

The balance between intensity and dissolution, however, was to characterize almost all of the time Moore spent in an editorial capacity at *The Dial*. It was in April, 1925 that Thayer first offered Moore the job of associate editor. This offer was brought about by several changes at the magazine, chiefly the departure of Sophia Wittenburg, the wife of Lewis Mumford, as one of the two people, along with Alyse Gregory, who handled the daily affairs of the magazine. More important was the departure a little while later of Alyse Gregory as the acting editor. Her husband Llewelyn Powys had developed tuberculosis and needed care; at first this was accomplished by the couple's moving to upstate New York. From there, Alyse had served as acting editor, commuting to the offices at 152 West 13th Street. But eventually, in 1926, they decided to return to England, creating the vacancy that Moore filled as editor. Coincidentally, Thayer was spending a good deal of his time in Europe, and when he returned to the States, he often went to Martha's Vineyard instead of staying in New York. Watson, in the meantime, had completed his medical studies at New York University and moved back to Rochester, there to become involved in experimental cinema and to develop significant advances in radiology. The continuity of the magazine was to be preserved by the continued efforts of the critics who wrote the regular columns: Paul Rosenfeld on music, Henry McBride on art, and Gilbert Seldes on theater. Eventually this community was to give way to various replacements and substitutions: for a while Kenneth Burke did the music column, Edmund Wilson did the theater piece for two issues, and so forth. There was also a booklet drawn up by Alyse Gregory, of rules covering editorial and managerial operations. But the fact remained that circulation and advertising revenue were not increasing while costs continued high, and Thayer and Watson were both developing other interests.

Thayer was concerned that the magazine survive, however. Years later, Van Wyck Brooks revealed that Thayer had offered him the editorship at this time, but Brooks was just recovering from a mental breakdown and didn't accept. Moore told Warner in 1926 that Thayer was considering endowing *The Dial* in the event of his death and making Moore the permanent editor. Her fastidiousness as an editor surely appealed to Thayer. He was to suffer a severe illness in 1926, which Moore doesn't name; this was probably related to his mental condition, which was becoming slowly more unstable. His hospitalization and near dying caused her considerable concern. She was always worried about Thayer; he told Alyse Gregory in a letter that Moore tried to dissuade him from expatriation over lunch at the Brevoort Hotel before he left for Europe in 1925. Several entries in her date book make it clear that there had been a number of meetings, and surely the final one before Thayer's departure was a tense one for Moore. He wrote to Gregory that Moore had at first felt he was not spiritually an expatriate, but after their talk she was no longer sure. Thayer's sensitivity was often an issue. In December, 1926, Moore asked Powys to remove references to syphilis and madness from a review. Powys and Alyse had recently paid a visit to Thayer in Vienna, where he was undergoing analysis with Freud. Such editorial watchfulness would become a byword for Moore in the last three years of the magazine's existence.

During the 1920's and after, many rumors would be circulating about Thayer and Moore. William Carlos Williams, for example, recounts that Thayer proposed marriage to her, and there is a reference in the family correspondence that would tend to support this at least as a possibility. But in their written correspondence the two maintained a formal attitude that is perfectly in keeping with their public image. In the unlikely event that they were ever intimate, there is no record of it—indeed, virtually no hint of it—in their letters. But their letters do show that Moore and Thayer developed a relationship that both prized very much. Thayer's earliest letter, dated September 12, 1920, mentions not finding Moore at home when calling on her; he also asks her to dinner, and to consider submitting some prose to *The Dial*. She wrote back immediately to accept both offers, and to explain that she was at the time unproductive, though she wanted more than anything to write. A few months later she interceded for her friends H.D. and Bryher, recommending work by both for *The Dial*. Thayer at this time called attention to a remark by Williams in a recent issue of *Contact* which Thayer resents, for, as he puts it, he does not consider himself either "derivative or dependent." Moore may very well have sympathized with this particular line of self defense, though she was also often willing to admit to her influence and models. Over the next few years the letters that pass between Moore and Thayer concern submissions and acceptances, usually of commissioned reviews. Thayer at one point mentions her review of Eliot's *The Sacred Wood* and says, "Now and then something comes to us which really makes us happy. This is such a thing."

Thayer also admired Moore's poetry, praising, among others, "Sea Unicorns and Land Unicorns," and the way Moore ironically uncovered other meanings in the material she quoted. At the end of 1924, Moore wrote Thayer to thank him for conferring on her *The Dial* Award. In her programmatic modesty, she called it a bit of foolishness to give her the award, saying it amazed everyone. But she also said it would help turn aside any of the audience's resistance to her work, and this reflected her common sense. A month later she wrote to Thayer again, this time addressing the letter to Watson and Alyse Gregory as well. In it, she mentioned her appreciation of Wescott's essay on her work that accompanied the announcement of the award, adding that the short reviews in the January, 1925 issue were a memorable gift known only to Thayer and her. It is hard to say positively what this refers to, but the short reviews include two unsigned pieces that would have been of special interest to Moore: notices of *Literary Studies and Reviews* by Richard Aldington, and *The Sleeping Beauty* by Edith Sitwell. Both of these are written by Moore and are reprinted in her *Complete Prose*, but the reason for her gratefulness is probably that she asked to review both books. The Aldington would be especially important to her, for he had been the first person publicly to mention her poetry. If this speculation is correct, it would indicate that as early as 1924 she had already begun exercising her influence editorially at the magazine. She also added in this letter a reference to the symposium in *Poetry* that had treated her work less favorably, noting that though *Poetry* had called her a painful acrobat, *The Dial* more than compensated for this by comparing her to Emily Dickinson.

The *Dial* Award was one of those positive events that shape a writer's career in ways that are hard to overestimate, and Moore seemed to appreciate this from the beginning. In the *Bryn Mawr Alumnae Bulletin* for April, 1925, there is a letter from Moore describing herself, obviously in response to a request from the editors of the *Bulletin*. The letter creates an interesting self-image of the author at one of the high points in the first part of her career. She begins modestly by saying fifty words rather than five hundred would suffice to tell of her accomplishments (though in fact the letter is much closer in count to the latter figure). She lists those things that had helped her succeed: reading, then specific authors, such as Chaucer, Spenser, Johnson, Hardy, Yeats. She then singles out Carey Thomas's "formal addresses and extempore speaking," which led her "to analyze the relation between method and effect in literary composition." And it was especially the conversational quality of Thomas's writing that most impressed Moore.

Another paragraph lists a wide variety of printed matter that had influenced her: *The English Review* of 1907–11, *Punch* and the *Spectator*, books and illustrations of Gordon Craig. There were also technical books, McGraw's and Mathewson's books on baseball, Tilden's on tennis, and a manual on dogs published by the *National Geographic*. Moore ends by saying that she has submitted critical work to places such as *The Dial*, but that such work "has never in any case . . . achieved what entirely satisfied" her. What is striking about this self-description are its modesty, its generosity in acknowledging influence, and its consistency with many of the later such lists and accounts Moore gave of the background of her style. Moore's response to publicity and the curiosity seekers who trailed in the wake of awards and prestige remained remarkably consistent; she spoke openly and fully, and this created a rather eccentric picture. But her deep and eclectic reading was itself a result of curiosity, and her speaking of it openly reflected her direct approach to factual information. Later her readers would turn these traits into a somewhat different portrait.

By the end of 1925, Thayer had already left the journal and gone to Europe. But he continued to write to Moore frequently. On December 6, he says that he has heard that she is working late on her editorial duties, and he feels responsible for this; his concern for details plagues him, but it shouldn't plague her, he argues. He also mentions that her salary cannot be reduced, obviously countering her request to do so. In the middle of the month there is a letter referring to the conditions under which Thayer left, apparently some unpleasant incident or misunderstanding that created bad feelings. These feelings lingered, and Moore did her best to dissipate them. Thayer doesn't describe exactly what occurred, since Moore was apparently familiar with the events, but he does at one point mention that someone openly insulted him to his face. He suggests that some people be dismissed from the journal, and that he doesn't feel comfortable submitting work to the journal with the current staff in place; he had planned to send in a "Berlin Letter." Over the next few months, Moore sent several letters that tried to reassure Thayer that he had the respect of everyone at The Dial, and that an unexplained dismissal of a large part of the staff would only focus more bad feeling on him.

There is some circumstantial evidence that the offending party in this episode was Sophia Wittenburg. At one point, Thayer writes "Miss S. I know knows her part in this," adding a reference to "those she serves." Sophia Wittenburg was at the time married to Lewis Mumford. Mumford had written most of his contributions for the issues of The Dial before Thayer's editorship, when the magazine had a clear political position. Mumford and Waldo Frank had earlier been involved with a short-lived journal called The American Caravan and another called The Seven Arts, both of which had addressed cultural questions in a framework of social and political issues. There is, then, some reason to believe that they would have liked to see The Dial resume its political identity and might have seen Thayer's departure as a chance for that to happen. On the other hand, Thayer did suffer from a paranoid complex, and he may very well have imagined that insults were intended when they were not. Moore's reassurances to him sound genuine, but her temperament probably would have kept her from accusing anyone even if she knew they bore some animus against Thayer.

Moore was to work very diligently at her editorial duties. She was in a somewhat precarious position, because while Watson and Thayer obviously trusted her editorial judgment, she doubted herself. At least she felt that she had continuously to consult the two men on major decisions, such as those concerning major authors who were past contributors to the magazine. The daily running of the magazine was also burdensome; many of her letters to authors concern deadlines for returning corrected proofs and planning for the next several issues. *The Dial* archive in the Berg collection of the New York Public Library contains an example of her care. She wrote Watson a letter in February, 1928 that included a draft version of the table of contents for the next issue. Beside each author's name there is a numeral indicating the number of pages that his or her contribution will occupy. This listing is followed by a supplementary list of another six or seven names who can provide substitutes for articles or reviews included in the projected contents. Watson was thus free to alter the makeup of the issue at the last moment. This was two years after Moore had had her title changed from "Acting Editor" to "Editor." Her respect for Watson's opinion and taste obviously made such an arrangement workable, though many editors would find such a review process cumbersome, to say the least.

The Berg archive shows that her editorial letters to would-be contributors contained a range of tones. In some instances she had to be deliberately discouraging. In many others, obviously not preserved, she simply included a preprinted card. Occasionally, authors would get a written response for one rejection, and then later a printed card. If they asked about this apparent discrepancy, Moore would calmly and politely explain that their second submission simply inspired no comment. Other letters encouraged the writer to submit work in the future. Somewhat less frequently, she would be moved to offer advice. Since the submissions are not available, it is hard to know how apt such advice was, but it was almost invariably expressed in an abstract way. Often Moore would encourage more technical rigor, reminding the writer that *The Dial* was interested in the purely aesthetic (as opposed to the political or instructional), and, somewhat contradictorily, that literature should reflect an elevated concept of life. These letters are consistent with Moore's taste, which was more aesthetic than political in its orientation, and which steered away from realism and naturalism, especially of a sort that contained "low" subject matter and a more or less deterministic view of the world. Such advice was written against a background of understanding that *The Dial* had what Moore called a special "field" or area in which it operated.

There are also letters she wrote to various journals and reference magazines in which she set out the sort of magazine *The Dial* was aiming to be. In these letters, Moore most directly emphasized technical rigor and aesthetic purity. The journal did not accept detective stories, for example, nor would it publish work that had appeared elsewhere, nor, except in special circumstances, would it accept unsolicited translations. More than once, she had to instruct someone seeking information, or a disgruntled writer, that the best method of appreciating the journal's aesthetic stand would be to consult past issues and see in them its exemplification. She once or twice could not contain an edge of frustration, suggesting it would be considerably better if writers would spend as much time and effort reading as they did composing.

A few of her letters to previous contributors addressed slightly different problems. She was compelled to explain to the poet Robert Hillyer, for example, that unlike Thayer and Watson, she would urge changes on a piece of writing rather than reject it outright. To Charles Sears Baldwin she had to write rejecting a manuscript of his, but she found a way to soften the blow by asking him in the same letter to review a book for an upcoming issue. She had to reassure Paul Valéry that his essay on Leonardo da Vinci had been well translated, and that the translation had been checked by Ellen Thayer and Dr. Watson himself. A poet named George Le Soir submitted a poem that he had dedicated to her, and she decided this was not acceptable since it would seem like self praise for her to publish it. She also turned back a story by Mary Butts, and mention the journal's somewhat austerely English taste. To Ezra Pound she wrote that Watson had decided to take only one of two cantos submitted, namely Canto XXVII, but that they would consider another of like character.

Moore was often encouraging to young writers, making a point of telling one that any journal would be proud to be the source of a good writer's first publication. Moore suggested that young writers might especially try to make their work affirmative in some way, noting that writing about life as it is can be done with talent, but writing about life as it might or should be was even more demanding and rewarding. One young aspirant, Martha Gellhorn, caught Moore's attention. Even though Moore had to reject her work, she made a point of extending her every courtesy, including an invitation to visit *The Dial*'s office. Martha Gellhorn was later to become a well-known journalist and the wife of Ernest Hemingway. What may have caught Moore's attention, besides the probable high quality of the writing submitted, was Gellhorn's address: Pembroke East, Bryn Mawr College.

There were constant complications, of course, and Moore had often to exercise a level of tact that even she might have found taxing. At the end of 1926, she had to hold out repeatedly, as she put it in a letter to Warner, against the pleadings of Coomaraswamy to publish his wife's offerings; she was able to resist his arguments, and the wife's writings never appeared. Less than a month later, she was busy consoling Kreymborg for the negative piece that Williams published about his poems. At one point in 1927 she had to reject a piece Alyse Gregory had written for a "Comment" column, and write one herself in its place. In March, 1927 there occurred one of the most distressing episodes of all. Because of faulty communication between Moore and Watson, a misunderstanding developed about an excerpt from Joyce's *Finnegan's Wake*, specifically the Anna Livia Plurabelle chapter. Moore was against publishing it because it was an excerpt and because she felt it to be too obscure. However, she wrote to consult Watson, knowing of his commitment to Joyce. Thayer's opinion, apparently, was not sought in this instance. Eventually, Watson wrote an ambiguous reply; it was not so much his liking for the story that suggested acceptance, but the very principle of supporting new work, although he added that his principles were never that strong. Moore was given the leeway to decide for herself, and she rejected the piece, sending a special-delivery letter to Joyce's agent, Lewis Galantieri. Many years later, in October, 1958, Moore described the incident to Richard Ellman, Joyce's biographer, sending a carbon copy to Watson. For her, the main problem was that an extensive serialization would have disrupted the attention and commitment of the magazine's readers. According to Moore, Watson had been quite prepared to publish all of the book. Unfortunately, no compromise could be reached.

A somewhat similar story concerns the publication of a poem by Hart Crane. Here the story is ringed with contradictions and revisions. What seems certain is that the poem, "The Wine Menagerie," had been submitted by Crane in the spring of 1926, and that Moore had suggested some substantial changes and a new title. Crane accepted. Later he was to protest that he did so only for the money involved. Moore, for her part, realized the booklet of editorial rules drawn up by Gregory included an admonition not to change work but to accept or reject it as it stood when submitted. She protested that she bent the rules in this case because she felt Crane to be a good poet, even a friend, and that the poem could be improved.

Matthew Josephson, according to his memoir *Life Among the Surrealists*, played a part in what followed. Crane had dinner with him one night and began to cry in speaking of his humiliation at the editorial cuts to his poem. Josephson took it upon himself to write Moore a long letter of protest, invoking the standard arguments against such procedures and offering to buy back the poem. When Moore received this letter she was furious at what she considered Josephson's meddling, and she called Crane into *The Dial* offices. There she received from him reassurances that he had not encouraged his friend to write the letter, and that he was content with the changes in the poem. Crane later claimed to Josephson that after the altered poem appeared in the May, 1926 issue, all of his subsequent submissions were accepted without any changes. (However, in September, 1928, Mrs. Moore wrote Warner that Watson had rejected a Crane poem submitted through Kenneth Burke, and that if he had not rejected it, Moore would have. There is also a handwritten draft of a letter by Moore in *The Dial* papers, rejecting two Crane poems, "Harbor Dawn" and "To Emily Dickinson." Her language on this occasion was especially circumspect.) Josephson's memoir goes as far as to suggest that as a result of this much-discussed episode, Moore's editorial alterations were rarer and less drastic. In a later interview Moore archly observed that "[Crane's] gratitude was ardent and later his repudiation of it commensurate—he perhaps being in both instances under a disability with which I was not familiar." This tone may have been prompted by her remembering, if she ever heard it, Crane's comment, referring to her and Margaret Anderson at *The Little Review*, that American poetry was in the hands of two hysterical virgins.

Still, the practice of cutting or editing work from authors was apparently fairly standard at *The Dial* under Moore's editorship. In April, 1928, for example, Moore asked Ezra Pound if she could cut a few pages from his introduction to his translation of Guido Calvacante's "Donna

Mi Prega." She indicated to him the exact cuts by mail, with an opportunity to approve. Since the piece was slated for the July issue, it is safe to assume she thought he would agree with her recommendations. Not long after her arrival at the magazine's editorial offices, Moore suggested to Mabel Dodge Luhan that she would accept her story, "Southwest," but only if some small changes in wording were accepted. Luhan consented, and apparently approved, since she sent Moore a santo from New Mexico as a gift shortly thereafter. Moore would later hang the artifact on one of the doors in her Brooklyn apartment. Given Moore's own penchant for making what sometimes seemed like minuscule changes in versions of her own poems, such fastidiousness shouldn't come as a surprise. Thayer's perfectionism may well have contributed in some ways to Moore's nearly unceasing fiddling with the details of her own work, though it was in many ways consonant with her temperament. Moore once wrote to a contributor that rather than asking for revisions, Watson and Thayer had developed the policy of rejecting material they felt to be slightly flawed. Moore was a bit uneasy in altering this policy; she may in fact have been trying to soften the approach of Thayer's perfectionism.

Many people have observed that Moore published none of her own poetry when she was editing *The Dial*. This doesn't mean that she wasn't, in her own fashion, hard at work on subjects of poetic interest to her. Her interest in natural history, always an important element in her poetic imagination, continued unabated. In the opening weeks of 1927, for example, she was keen to identify the insect on Audubon's drawing of the swan, and she wrote for information to a Mr. Lucas of the Museum of Natural History. But the insect could not be identified. There are several references in the family correspondence to mongooses, even after the appearence of her poem "Snakes, Mongooses, Snake Charmers and the Like," in *Broom* in 1922. She was also pressing Warner for information. On March 4, 1927, she wrote her brother to ask him if he saw a pangolin: "It looks like an artichoke, has a tail about a foot long and lives on ants. (Is in fact, an armored ant-eater.)" Mrs. Moore had heard about them from a friend, and someone else had told Moore they were native to Borneo. Warner was then stationed in Haiti, having earlier been part of the Marine force that invaded Nicaragua. This invasion was led by the Marines, ostensibly to oversee elections which the United States feared would produce too liberal a result. All the parties agreed to the outcome except for the one led by Augusto Sandino, for whom the later Sandinista party was named.

In the middle of March, Warner had to tell his sister that there are certainly no pangolins in Haiti, only in Borneo. Two weeks after Warner's unpromising reply, Moore described her attendance at church as being stationary and like a pangolin. Of course, almost a decade later, this animal would become the focus of one of Moore's most ambitious poems.

In the summer of 1927, Moore and her mother were able to escape for a brief period from the pressures of *The Dial* and enjoy another visit to England, their first there in more than fifteen years. There, they had the pleasure of spending some time with Warner, who was on duty overseas. During this period, Kenneth Burke was to be in charge of *The Dial*, though Moore would take many of her editorial concerns with her. The plans began to take form at the end of March. Shortly thereafter, Mrs. Moore secured reservations at 28 Upper Bedford Place. Moore, busy with preparations, excitedly described herself as a ferocious kivu lizard. In the middle of May she wrote a "Comment" essay on snakes for *The Dial.* In it, she treated snakes in stone and story as "Mice" put it, Mice being Mrs. Moore. As she did on several occasions, Moore used her mother's phrase verbatim in what she published; the section on snakes in the August, 1927 issue issue ends with Mrs. Moore's words, "our mere right to snakes in stone and story." There are also several letters about various animals, about visits to the zoo, and about animal films. One film is especially striking: "Chang," which Moore explains, means elephant in Siamese. In it she sees not only leopards fighting and a baboon picking coconuts, but a pangolin as well. She plans to mention this in her "Comment." By the end of May she is on board ship sailing for England. Though they had pleaded with Warner not to see them off because of their early departure, he came to the dock anyway: Moore describes him standing under the "A" in the large "Bon Voyage" sign.

Because the Moores are together as a family for some of this trip, the correspondence is less frequent than that for the 1911 journey. But there are a number of letters to Warner both before he joins them, and after he leaves them to return to his naval duties. In England, Moore was able to visit a Blake exhibit in Kensington and to meet Bryher's mother. There was a trip to the zoo with Bryher's brother; in 1932, she asks Bryher if the zoo still has its live plumet basilisk, acquired only a year previously. Through her constant reading of the *Illustrated London News*, Moore followed such details in English life rather closely. She also managed to shop at Burberry's and visit Bath. More important on a personal level is a visit to the man who had become very important to her in his role as man of letters: George Saintsbury. In some obvious ways, Saintsbury had begun to fill the role that George Moore once played. She first became acquainted with Saintsbury when she took over her editorial duties at *The Dial*, and he was always to receive special treatment from her. For example, she would recopy his hand-written submissions to the magazine, typing them out laboriously from Saintsbury's nearly illegible hand. His was also the only correspondence from *The Dial* that she took home with her, clearly feeling that their relationship went beyond the professional level.

She also met Raymond Mortimer, an English writer and anthologizer, and secured his services as writer of *The Dial*'s "London Letter." Mortimer had earlier gotten a rather negative postcard from Thayer and was reluctant to approach the subject of writing for the magazine. But this shows how Moore's decisions were crucial at *The Dial*; it was only with Watson that she would occasionally consult. Moore and her mother took a side trip by train to Ripon, and on the train Mrs. Moore admonished a drunken American sailor. Her forcefulness was still apparent to all; only a few weeks earlier Warner had given a sermon on mothers to the crew aboard his ship, and said that "for all this devotion what does a mother ask of us? Only that we succeed in life!" The trip to Ripon occurred after Warner had left for Norway; they had been able to visit together from the end of June until the middle of July. Together they saw several places outside of London, including Windsor, Oxford, Warwick, and the Lake Country. Warner especially liked the silver service at Merton College, York Cathedral, and the echo from Dungeon Ghyll outside of Ambleside. He may have been recalling Wordsworth's poem about this especially picturesque spot. At Cambridge, Moore saw a "connect quadrangle like the library one at Bryn Mawr" and a pair of misereres on the theme of Jonah and the whale, always one of her favorites. Cambridge was rich, declared Mrs. Moore, and yet not as rich and mellow as Oxford. During the last week of July the two women were able to visit Alyse and Llewelyn at their cottage, "The White Nose," in Dorset, where the couple appeared as the embodiment of "poetic scholarly seclusion." Moore also noticed and described to Warner the flowers on the edge of a cliff there; this may well have been part of the inspiration for passages in "The Steeple-Jack," with its lush floral growth and secluded student on a hillside overlooking the town. Later she was also to use a visit to Stinsford to write an especially moving memorial tribute to Hardy for the February, 1928 "Comment": "With yet more immanence, perhaps, the black yews in Stinsford churchyard, the headstones with sculptured angels above members of his family, the peal of bells and the Norman font, are component with what Mr. Hardy has told us. And their important seclusion is his." Warner was on his way to Hamburg by the first week of August, when Moore and her mother arrived back in New York.

The relationship with Saintsbury, which was solidified by Moore's visit with him during her trip to England in 1927, meant a great deal to both parties. It was in June, 1926, that they began corresponding. Saintsbury was then eighty years old, and he had left Oxford in 1867; this was only five years after Mrs. Moore was born. From the beginning this famous critic and arbiter of taste, obviously old enough to be the poet's father, displayed a playful attitude toward Moore that was both patrician and flirtatious. One of his first letters to her, after she had expressed her gratitude for his work, said that it was entirely wrong for a lady to be grateful to a man. Almost right away she began to share with him the details of her life as a writer and editor. In August, 1926, she tells him that Watson had written the July "Comment" for her, and from her vacation in New Harbor, Maine, says that her position at *The Dial* gives her only half power in decision and she often declined to use the whole of that. Saintsbury teases her about being a Salem witch, "so nice and so clever at once." Moore confessed to him that there were certain kinds of modern art of which she was very fond, but some of her friends would say she liked nothing but what is prehistoric. In fact one friend—a certain English lady—referred to Moore as the pterodactyl, though she didn't deserve such an honor nor the one associated with necromancy. Moore's modesty in not naming Bryher matches her teasing response to the charge of witchcraft. By the first of May she tells him of her planned trip to England, and they arrange a meeting.

By the middle of June she has, in the company of Mrs. Moore, already visited Saintsbury in his quarters, and writes him from Bath only days afterwards to tell him she has arranged to have a woodworker build him a new set of bookcases. Months later, back in America, she reminiscences in a January letter about their visit, and she describes the yellow roses that surrounded his doorway. Twice later she refers to these yellow roses, of special significance to her. She kept a painting by Cummings of a yellow rose above her desk throughout several decades, and she has a poem, "Injudicious Gardening," that says, "I could not bear a yellow rose ill will"; the argument of the poem insists that despite authority to the contrary yellow does not betoken infidelity. A month later she writes to apologize that Miss Phillips, an office assistant at *The Dial*, has had the impertinence to reply to him. In this letter she tells him about an incident when, at the age of four, she leaned against a shutter and fell out a second-story window onto an oleander tree. Several months later she is telling him about her grandfather's church in Gettysburg, and how her schoolmates teased her by calling her "Marianna of the Moated Grange," even though her name ended with an "e," for which she was very grateful. She also observes that essays can surely have the beauties of poetry, and the reverse. This was meant to flatter his work as essayist, of course, but it also served as a self-defense of her writing at this time. Indeed, her "Comment" columns and essays for *The Dial* were very much like her poetry, in structure and theme, with their metonymic connections and weaving of quotations.

In the fall of 1928, Moore and her mother visited Warner who was then stationed in Norfolk, Virginia, and took a side trip to Williamsburg. Moore shared details of this trip with Saintsbury, mentioning the many memorials of the English royalty, so abundant that it felt like being in England, and describing the crape myrtles and other gnarled trees. Both of these details were to resurface five years later in another visit to Warner in Norfolk, and to become part of the important poem sequence, "Old Dominion." Near the end of the year she informed Saintsbury she would vote for Hoover over Smith, since she did not like the idea of Tammany Hall politics representing America to the world. She added she was not sure that she could have been called a good American in colonial times, since her sympathy lay with King George and the royal family. Some of this may have been a response to flatter Saintsbury, some may have been a playful exaggeration of her Anglophilia, but it is nevertheless true that the Depression years saw Moore's politics take a sharp conservative turn.

Moore continued to share observations and opinions with Saintsbury, indicating that she was very much at ease with him, and many of these observations were to find their way into later poems. For example, she mentions in the fall of 1930 how Hoover has kept Congress in session, citing the "sin-driven senators" having to endure the one hundred-and-four-degree heat. This detail occurs in "The Steeple-Jack," just as her impressions about a film, "Hunting Tigers in India," end up in "Elephants." She also expressed her concern about her brother who was affected by boils in the late winter of 1930, and even offered an analysis of Saintsbury's handwriting. Saintsbury refers to someone having "fly away brains," and she counters with Francis Bacon's remark about being "bird-witted," a phrase that becomes the title of a poem in the "Old Dominion" sequence. She even offered to be his secretary in August, 1930, shortly before their correspondence ended. He died in 1933, but not before the death of his oldest friend, the Poet Laureate Robert Bridges, and his good friend Lord Balfour, both of whom died a few years earlier. He was every bit a Victorian man of letters, and in 1928 she told him that there were some Victorian things that one could value today.

Moore's literary relationships sometimes flowered into close personal friendships, and these are often reflective of the tensions in her own temperament. In sharp contrast with Saintsbury, for example, stood the figure of Cummings. Moore felt genuine affection for him, even though she had severe reservations about his work, especially its frank sexuality. In May, 1928, Moore wrote her brother that she had told Cummings she did not care for his idea of life and marriage, and for that matter she often thought little of other people's ideas in this regard. This was probably in response to Cummings' having fathered a daughter with Elaine Orr Thayer while she was still married to Scofield. Yet Moore continued as Cummings' friend and correspondent for many years afterwards. For his part, Cummings was one of Moore's staunchest backers from the early days of her career in New York. In an issue of *Secession*, in the contributors' notes, Cummings used the occasion to say that Louis Untermeyer would be remembered as the man who excluded William Carlos Williams and Moore from his anthology; in the next edition of the Untermeyer, both were included, along with Cummings. In 1933, William Benét put together an anthology called *Fifty Poets*, in which he asked each poet to choose his or her poem that would most likely endure. Cummings evaded the question in regard to his own work but added that his favorite poem was Moore's "A Grave," the poem Benét included in the anthology.

Cummings was probably introduced to Moore in the early 1920's through Watson, who was his good and close friend. The two poets shared a keen interest in the visual arts, among other things. Cummings, of course, was already widely known as the author of *The Enormous Room* (1922), one of the classic memoirs to come out of World War I. His poetry, with its typographical innovations, had attracted a lot of attention, and considerable negative criticism as well. He represented one aspect of the bohemianism of the Village as completely as Millay represented another. For all of his radicalism, Cummings was intrigued by social behavior, and was very committed to the idea of a community of like-minded artists who set themselves against the people who "live in furnished souls," as he put it. His worldliness did not altogether block out his innocence and his affection for the straightforward and sincere expression of direct emotion. In some ways, this tension between sophistication and naïveté may have resonated with Moore's own struggles at this time. Additionally, Moore felt an unusual sense of loyalty to her friends, especially those like Pound and Cummings, who championed her work, and this loyalty prevented her from adopting a publicly censorious attitude toward those aspects of their written work that clearly did not agree with her values. In a letter from 1938 she can address Cummings as blasphemous and disreputable. The tone here may be in part teasing, because Cummings obviously enjoyed his role as *enfant terrible,* and no doubt playfully encouraged Moore in her expression of shock. Some of the same kind of relationship existed between Moore and Williams, and for much the same reason.

In *The Dial* for January, 1926, Moore said of Cummings' recently published *XLI Poems* that "if there is not much love in these pages, however, there is glamour." When Moore later wrote of *The Dial* she called Cummings "the really successful avoider of compromise, of scarecrow insincerity, of rubber-stamp hundred-per-cent deadness." She reviewed his *One Times One* , in *The Nation* in 1944, calling it his "book of masterpieces." Years later she would enjoy being photographed by Marion Morehouse, Cummings' third wife, and she would praise his *six non-lectures*, given as the Norton Lectures at Harvard. For many years the two poets exchanged Christmas greetings, and Moore eulogized

Cummings at his death in 1962, in an essay published by the American Academy of Arts and Letters. Moore's "natural reticence" accounts for the way she could avoid becoming disputatious with friends about matters of morals; however, there is also the sense that she could truly identify the positive attributes in her friends and fellow writers, and was disciplined enough to protect those at all costs.

It was around August, 1928, that Moore encountered another difficulty with an editorial decision for The Dial. Mrs. Moore took sharp exception to the photographs of three Maillol nude sculptures that had been scheduled to run in the September issue. In objecting to these photographs, Mrs. Moore wrote to Warner with some touch of self-deprecating humor, and perhaps a measure of sarcasm, that it wouldn't do to create the notion that modern thought was being hemmed in by puritanical standards. She also used her Christological vocabulary in condemning these works of art. Moore reported later that the September issue had been expurgated of the three nudes.

A month later Mrs. Moore observed to her cousin Mary in Albany that the Sabbath had not kept her daughter from her editorial duties; Mrs. Moore may have been subtly criticizing her daughter while at the same time praising her dutifulness. Such disagreements about taste were not, however, always limited to sexual or religious matters. Kenneth Burke took strong exception to Moore's predilection for European writers, and was especially dismayed at her admiration and support for Saintsbury. These disagreements seemed to compound Moore's physical troubles. In the middle of September, 1927, for example, she had an especially bad week. She suffered from headaches and diarrhea, the Saintsbury submission was especially illegible, Watson would not "go after" famous writers, Laurence Gilman had declined to do the music chronicle in place of Rosenfeld, and there was conflict with Ellen Thayer, Scofield's niece, who had been brought in some time earlier to help with running the office. To top it off, Lincoln MacVeagh, the financial director of the magazine, said they could not for the time being afford to buy any new manuscripts. In October, Mrs. Moore told Warner that the manuscript piles from The Dial were so heavy they could hardly be carried home, and she must help her daughter read through them. Between matters of taste and judgment on the one hand, and financial and managerial concerns on the other, Moore was considerably drained by her position.

Her personal life was also marked by several points of tension. Mrs. Norcross was very ill back in Carlisle and Mary had to attend her constantly. Warner, meanwhile, was in Ireland where he visited Merrion Square in Dublin and vividly imagined his grandfather's origins there. He also visited Swift's grave and called it a "life event," obviously inspired by a writer who was also a great preacher. But near the end of September, Mrs. Moore wrote her son a most extraordinary letter. It seems that while the three of them were together in London only months before they had run into the Strongs, a family from Warner's old parish in Chatham, on the steps of the British Museum. Warner greeted a female member of the family most warmly, kissing her on the cheek. Mrs. Moore was enraged by this and confessed her hatred of the event to Warner. Then she confronted him with the charge that he was a separate person, but that she and her daughter are not. Obviously the fears of separation Mrs. Moore felt in terms of Warner's career, his marriage, and his place in the world were never to be fully allayed. On the other hand, her hold over her daughter tended to be emphasized as Warner drew further away. Even though Moore's position as editor of one of the country's leading journals would have appeared to the outside world to insure her independence, this was clearly not the case. If anything, Moore's character was increasingly a reflection of her mother's taste and values; at the same time, paradoxically and with considerable tension, Moore struggled for her own separate identity.

Warner did not immediately respond to his mother's letter. However, he continued to offer her advice on how to counsel Moore on the running of the magazine, and even suggested in October, 1927, that it wouldn't be tragic if *The Dial* were to shut down. Later that month he replied to his mother that he saw nothing wrong with public kissing, and insisted that he was not morally loose. In late October, Mrs. Moore again alluded to the kissing incident in a letter that is both proud and pious, and there the matter seems to have rested, at least on the surface. Moore pointed out to her brother that *The Dial* was her only real sustenance, and though she had considered giving it up, she was committed to it for Watson's sake. Though she had been tired lately she had also come to some important insights and resolutions. On November 26, just after her fortieth birthday, she wrote at some length to Warner. This letter spoke of the need to understand other people's beliefs if you are to criticize them effectively, and of the need for intellectual honesty and bravery when confronting opinions that disturb you, especially if they are held by truly intelligent people. In all this, social tact can be of considerable help, but it alone would not protect you.

The many tensions recorded in this letter are reflected in her poetry, of course. The relations between people and their cultural gestures, and the possible understandings of another person's beliefs and values, as well as a deep mistrust of a crowd mentality and any routinized response, had all been subjects and themes in her poetry prior to this point, and they would continue to be prominent in the major poetry she would write in the 1930's and beyond. But perhaps most noticeable is the lesson that she may very well have learned from her work at *The Dial*: it is not the negative virtue of protectiveness, but rather the ability to know one's own strengths that will save one's individuality. However much she drew upon her mother's character as a source of her own values, she was never in danger of becoming merely a shadow of Mary Warner Moore.

Near the end of 1927, Moore was toying with the idea of totemic animals and was also thinking of designing herself as a letterhead, one that might contain a basilisk, a salamander, or a pangolin. Perhaps she felt such a letterhead would help give her a sense of a distinctly separate identity. There was also near the end of the year a visit from Alyse and Llewelyn, and she told Warner that Alyse looked dreadful, though Moore doesn't make it clear if the strain of her marriage is physical or psychological. The beginning of the new year, 1928, found her having lunch with Frances Browne, her lifelong friend and classmate from Bryn Mawr. About this time, she complained to Warner that her mother's standards were too demanding; she could stand up to her mother, but it was a considerable strain. Through Padraic Colum, she met Æ, the Irish mystic and poet, and they had tea together, where she asked him for a poem for *The Dial*. She produced a praising "Comment" piece on him for the March issue, in which she admits being "[s]usceptible to Irish magic in its various strengths"; she will return to this theme over a decade later, in "Spenser's Ireland." In February she worked on a "Comment" that discussed Cervantes, though the essay didn't appear until the May issue, and she sent T. S. Eliot some books to review. Such possibilities obviously appealed to Moore's sense of literature as a higher calling, since her essay on Cervantes and her admiration for Eliot were based on a reaffirmation of her idealism. Though there is the occasional letter that details confusions and misunderstandings at the magazine, she seems to be somewhat more relaxed about her duties.

But in fact all was not well with Moore and what she felt as her many burdensome duties at *The Dial*. The simple truth is that she was often quite unhappy in her position as editor, for reasons that were both aesthetic and personal. She was at times weary when she wrote to Warner complaining about the workload, but she complained more than once about what she saw as the tendency in contemporary writing to be needlessly obscene. In May, 1926, in urging Thayer not to publish his notice of resignation from the magazine, she reminded him that she had once or twice frankly told him she objected to material that appeared in *The Dial*. In late 1927, Moore had told Warner that he shouldn't pass the magazine around among his naval friends as it would reflect badly on him for anyone not familiar with the literary world. In March, 1928, she referred to the magazine as her dunghill. Part of this attitude was a result of Moore and her mother thinking very little of some of the works that were highly regarded at the time. For example, Moore felt that the Provincetown Players Theatre should have been called "Plague House." There is also an undated letter from 1929, written by Mrs. Moore, that refers to the magazine as a male paradise, and then Alyse Gregory came and the serpent began to appear, but when Moore came there was no more ease, only responsibility. And after a performance of "Bridal Veil," a pantomime by Arthur Schnitzler, Mrs. Moore begged her daughter not to be contemporaneous. On the other hand, Moore wrote an approving account of Gorky's "The Lower Depths" in the "Comment" essay for the September, 1928 issue, so her objections were clearly not to "low" subject matters as such.

On March 14, 1928, Mrs. Moore relayed to Warner a discussion she had had with her daughter, a discussion that focused on the central tension that lay behind much of Moore's dissatisfaction. Mother and daughter had been discussing power, and Mrs. Moore saw it as a spiritual problem, or at least used such metaphors to present the problem, while Moore saw it in aesthetic terms. Mrs. Moore also confessed that she didn't think her daughter's commitment to the magazine was sufficiently ennobling. The letter then mentions that the two women discussed the rhetorical unity of the Lord's Prayer. Mrs. Moore goes on to describe how they had heard of missionary work at church that day, and, when they returned home, Moore said that *The Dial* was pitiable, and asked herself whether she wanted to preach a sermon or run a supercilious magazine. This exchange makes several things clear. First, Mrs. Moore was self-conscious about her desire to conduct the argument in strictly spiritual terms, and she even goes from calling Moore by the pet name "Rat" to the allegorical figure "Christian" from Bunyan's *Pilgrim's Progress*. Her self-consciousness did not eliminate or correct her frame of reference, nor was she able to offer her approval to her daughter. Second, Moore's view of the vocation of literature as spiritual, and her regarding of her "Comment" essays as sermons, was a conscious struggle. The many references by critics to Moore's turn to a "moral" poetry in the 1940's are somewhat off the mark, since her poetry and prose, in her view, had been a moral struggle all along. Third, literature was not something that Moore saw as distinct from spiritual striving or discipline; in an important way, it was continuous with it. It was all a matter of how one chose to use literature. For Moore, with her brother's lifework constantly in view, and her mother's demanding idealizations always at work, literature, to be indulged in at all, must have a spiritual dimension.

II. "The reliquary method of perpetuating magic"

Moore was never to speak openly about her disenchantment with *The Dial*; indeed, as her later public identity was tied up with very flattering views of the magazine, she often presented her days there in a highly revised version. But she was swimming against the tide and she knew it all too well. Stylistically this meant that she often worked by indirection. In her "Comment" columns, for example, she very frequently had recourse to double negatives: "it is not disappointing not to know," "not all of it is without usefulness," "it is not impossible not to be ashamed," "a superiority . . . need not be even to uncommercial eyes, illiterate . . ." and so forth. In some sense this was an outgrowth of a larger strategy of hers that involved constant definition and qualification. For example, in the "Comment" on Dürer she says, "The reliquary method of preserving magic is to be distrusted; nevertheless a living energy seemed still to reside in the wood blocks and engraving tools of Dürer's . . ." Here she refers to earlier columns on magic, where she may have felt she was too accepting of it as a principle of explanation. But the claim for "living energy" residing in tools and any articles of culture is, of course, one of the beliefs on which almost all of her poetry is based. However, before the claim can be made there must be the caveat.

Such stylistic features may very well keep the reader from readily seeing that several of the "Comment" essays are in fact muted criticisms of current values, and together make up a call for a spiritual regeneration. Though Moore published no poems for the seven and a half years between the beginning of 1925 and the middle of 1932, the "Comment" served as her artistic exploration of values and culture. From her first "Comment" in July, 1925, to her final effort, one month before the magazine ceased publication with the July, 1929 issue, she published a total of forty-two columns. Of this total, thirty-two were to appear after her appointment as Editor was announced in the July, 1926 issue. Several are memorial tributes to artists who had recently died, such as Amy Lowell, Thomas Hardy, or Ellen Terry, and make up an important part of Moore's aesthetic formulations. Several are occasioned by the appearance of books, such as a series produced by Virginia Woolf's Hogarth Press or the Society for Pure English. There are also a number that discuss recent exhibitions of visual art, or work by Dürer or a group of American artists associated with Stieglitz: Marin, Demuth, O'Keeffe, Dove, Strand, and others. Still others were centered on those classic off-beat subjects that are important to the tradition of the belletristic essay, recalling Lamb on roast pork or Hazlitt on boxing; for these Moore selected handwriting analysis, or herbal medicine. Each brief essay is fresh because there is usually something "timely" in its subject, but almost all of them quote from literary figures of a previous age, Dr. Johnson and seventeenth-century prose writers being most frequently cited.

In some ways the prose pieces work like one of her poems, built largely by association, by metonymy, rather than by a single metaphoric idea unfolded in all its logical or consecutive implications. Her poems and essays employ a distinctive sort of logic, however, that tends to work by shifting focus to another topic and branching off at a detail in order to establish a connection that otherwise seems remote. In June, 1928, for example, she begins by saying that criticism should preferably be praise rather than condemnation: "in search of pure art we tend to feel betrayed when experts tell us merely where it is not." This sentiment may also be behind her use of the double negative, for she seldom utters a direct and unvarnished negation or condemnation. Then she moves on to cite the "sound advice" of a poet, Arthur Davison Ficke, now little known and then hardly a subject of great excitement, who urges discipline on the younger writer. Rather than explore this at length, she refers to the London booksellers, W. and G. Foyle, who are dedicated to obtaining difficult-to-find titles. The piece concludes with praise of Æ by Padraic Colum and Chagall's paintings by Christian Zervos, both quoted in some detail. In both cases the artists are praised for, among other virtues, their persistence. Were we to reduce the essay's structure to a discursive argument it might go like this: Criticism of art should deal in praise rather than blame; but young writers must not expect too much early or easy praise; they must persevere, as would a good bookseller, to find what's valuable; for example, here are two critics who praise such perseverance.

Beneath the colorful detail and the seemingly casual structure of this essay, there is an urgent argument based on a high sense of the artistic vocation; there is also a self-directed warning to remember that this calling is to be encouraged by praise rather than restricted by blame, though at the same time it must strengthen itself through adversity. And, given her remarks in other places, especially her letters, there seems to be a fairly direct reference to contemporary writers who are railing against standards and critics who fail to appreciate new work. Not all of the essays are this subtle in their arrangement; those on a single figure often don't have the same complexity of structure, nor do those that work by a single point of contrast, such as the one that sets the violence of classical tragedy against that of the contemporary newspaper account. But they all offer some larger lesson.

Take the one just referred to, in the September, 1928 issue, where Moore takes up a subject that was recurrently important to her, namely how to be precisely observant without sinking into what she saw as the excesses of "realism." She begins with a fairly straightforward claim, but the real point is based on the qualifying clause that ends the sentence: "Though tragedy in literature is not literature unless true to life, slayings and sluggings seem counterfeit—as tragedy even felonious—in newspaper reports based on facts, if advertised to provoke the same sensations that provoked the crime." The key idea in the essay lies in the remarks that follow about an anthology of "world tragedies" that is the ostensible occasion for the piece. The selection "strongly supports the conviction that life and death are conceivably more than living and dying. It metamorphoses experience into something beyond epicurean necessities and measures of satisfaction." The essay is trying to show that art must influence us and depict the world, but its main goal should not be the excitation of passion or the satisfaction of voyeuristic impulses.

Moore's tentative tone in a phrase like "conceivably more than living and dying" recurs often in these columns. She will often follow such a tentative sounding formulation with a larger, axiomatic statement. Just as often her Latinate vocabulary and rhetorical turns will continue to generate a contemplative and ironic atmosphere: "It metamorphoses experience into something beyond epicurean necessities and measures of satisfaction." Here the word "experience" pointedly carries its Deweyan overtones, and "epicurean necessities" is informed by the precise meaning of the strict philosophical regimen to which it refers (the necessity to avoid pain and enhance pleasure). The lexical range is as broad and used with as much finesse as we find in her poems. And the dramatic impact can only be realized if the reader is alert to the shifts in tone, which are themselves registers of an artistic insistence on capturing just the right moral and intellectual inflection.

Near the end of *The Dial*'s publication Moore published two "Comment" columns that show her at her best. The penultimate one was in the May, 1929 issue, and it employed a three-part structure. The first part dealt with an exhibit of Russian folk art. Its main point is that sometimes, paradoxically, we can "know better the possibilities of a thing that the unconsciously aesthetic makers know." This repeats the theme of "Critics and Connoisseurs," where it is argued that unconscious art is better than conscious craft, but that it takes a critical self-consciousness to appreciate this. The second section deals with a recent newspaper appearance of a series by Pound on the values and uses of literature. It opens with a highly nuanced context:

> Ezra Pound may proffer too readily Stendhal's remark that it takes eighty years for anything to reach the general public, and he is not afraid of repeating what he has said before; but a discussion by him in *The Herald-Tribune*—"How to Read, or Why"—is a lively, or better say a living, thing, and not undistinctive rhetorically in its dual method of emphasis by over- and by under-statement.

Moore's gentle irony is directed not only at Pound's penchant for bullying, his willingness to repeat what he has said before, but also at his invoking an elite artist as authority even as he himself writes for a mass audience. Her use of a double negative to praise Pound's style, and her pointing out his ability to move his own tonal register both above and below the literal level, are also typical. But none of this keeps Moore from making her central point clearly, namely that Pound is arguing an important claim: "Literature incites humanity to continue living . . . it eases the mind of strain, and feeds it." Pound deserves high praise for his own willingness to exert himself, and for his urging others, in "maintaining the health of thought." Importantly, she credits Pound with a commitment to literature that has a religious, or at least a spiritual, purpose.

The third section describes a visit to the circus. After a detailed description and enumeration of the sights there, Moore develops her main point. Some acts are better to watch than others; for example, a bear riding a bicycle is unpleasant because it looks painful, while there are delightful acrobats who stand with "equipose and fairness." But this discrimination itself leads to a more important observation. The piece alludes to "public taste" and ends with a balanced claim for the virtues of balance:

> Rashness and regality may not teach us anything; animals should not be taken from their proper surroundings, and in staging an act the bad taste of patrons should not be deferred to; but apparently this medicinally mingled feast of sweet and bitter is not poisonous; it is not all aconite.

The reference to aconite is obviously another double negative; aconite is also known as "wolfsbane," an herb known in folklore as a deterrent against wild animals. In modern use, however, the term refers to a sedative. Moore thus says that the circus isn't fundamentally anti-animal, nor is it all placid and reassuring. Taken together the three sections form a meditation, highly instanced, of the relation between folk art and high art, between making distinctions and accepting simple situations simply, and between culture as a form of ease and a form of discipline.

Moore's final "Comment," which appeared in the June, 1929 issue, begins by observing how "bravura as one of the attributes of the 17th century keeps rising into our vision from time to time like the bouquet of a fountain . . ." Moore's affection for the English prose writers of this period, especially Sir Thomas Browne and Sir Francis Bacon, is well known. But her purpose in this case is not to praise traditional writers and virtues so much as it is to examine ideas about death. Some of the minor writers exhibit an "indifference to death," and a sense that "mortality was without personal significance." In a sense the whole column is about death, and it becomes a *memento mori*, a reflection of how "lofty emotion is dealt a blow by expediency," and how death is sometimes best presented in poems that are "more delicately impressed than is easily compatible with the absent-minded pomposity of public poetry." But it is also secondarily a reflection on how to present death artistically, and can be read as another in the series of somewhat covert "sermons" by Moore to her contemporaries and fellow writers. Her closing claim, that "the 17th century bears scrutiny," is not simply a call for greater curiosity, though that is a large part of it, but it also suggests that an awareness of how other periods resolved artistic problems can provide a clue to how we might conduct ourselves, how, as the preceding piece on Pound's earlier series put it, "the reader would 'profit by an orderly arrangement of his perceptions,' and should have 'axes of references by knowing the best of each kind of written thing.' " Read together, and as a series of poetic explorations of themes and preoccupations that Moore had lived with for decades, and was to continue exploring, the "Comment" columns are not only substantial additions to the excellences of *The Dial*; they are also important parts of Moore's total effort as a thoughtful writer. In some ways they are perfect examples of both her bravura and her skepticism.

But even as early as March, 1928, Moore was uncertain how long *The Dial* would continue. Mounting costs and shrinking revenues continued to create a gloomy prospect, though Moore would later insist that the journal did not close for financial reasons. Moore's personal life was also clouded over in some respects. During 1928 she was taking osteopathic and sun treatments; later she was to say that one of the reasons she moved from the poorly ventilated apartment at St. Luke's Place was to have more sun and fresh air. In July, Mrs. Norcross died, but Moore and her mother were unable to attend the funeral because Warner's family was arriving in New York that week. Constance and the children had been living in France for the past few years as Warner completed his overseas tour of duty. Warner himself arrived in Newport, Rhode Island, three weeks later, where he first met his mother and sister, again without telling Constance, before going on to meet his wife at the summer home in Black Lake. Constance apparently offered more money in order to support Moore and her mother, and Moore wrote a sweet note of acceptance and thanks on August 10. Moore also urged Warner to vote against Governor Al Smith in the upcoming election; three weeks later she informed him that Mr. MacVeagh was not thinking of selling *The Dial*. It was also about this time that *The Dial* was sued by a prospective author for losing a manuscript; they settled out of court for $145, but Moore was very distressed by the whole affair, blaming herself in part. Warner planned a trip for Moore and her mother to Norfolk, Virginia. When these plans fell through, he suggested they might meet in Boston later; in the meantime, he took a quick train trip to New York to see them, and this apparently angered Constance. Moore and her mother did visit Norfolk briefly during the first half of October; this is the trip she describes in part to Saintsbury. Near the end of September, a fellow chaplain told Warner that he would try to arrange for him to be stationed at the Brooklyn Navy Yard, which he knows Warner desires. Warner also took time out from his duties to send a long letter to Mary Norcross, advising her on how to deal with "The Mountain," her house at Starrett's Gap, Pennsylvania. At year's end Moore remained occupied with writing the announcement of *The Dial* Award, to be given to Kenneth Burke. The announcement praised Burke's critical intelligence, largely by pointing to his criticism, his translations, and his interest in psychology. Burke was to remain a lifelong friend of Moore, and one of her most perceptive critics.

In the early months of 1929 the closing of *The Dial* became more and more imminent. Increasingly, the rejection letters in late 1928 and early 1929 speak of a backlog of accepted material. Watson told Moore in January, 1929, that the lease for the offices ended in May, and that would be a good time to close up permanently. Moore had told Warner earlier that *The Dial* was never Watson's "baby," that he had always been more interested in his experimental filmmaking. She also explained to her brother that she was paid $2600 a year at the magazine, and her salary at the library had been only $50 a month, so there would be a substantial decrease in her income. In February the news came through that Warner had been assigned to the Brooklyn Navy Yard as he hoped. In March, Moore resumed her part-time work at the library, and told Warner that *The Dial* might last until the end of the year. At the end of the month, she attended a luncheon for people involved in raising funds for women's colleges. She happily accepted some poems by D. H. Lawrence—she was always more fond of his poetry than his fiction, and she talked very positively about his virtues to Saintsbury. But *The Dial* barely lasted through the first half of the year.

On June 15, 1929, Moore wrote a final thank-you letter to Thayer to express her gratitude for the chance of being associated with the nation's leading literary journal. She had had serious misgivings on more than one occasion, and there had been the usual number of bruised egos and misunderstandings associated with any extended stint of editorial services. But on the whole the magazine meant a great deal to her, and her later memoirs of her time there were not simply rose-colored retrospections. In her thank-you letter she said that certain parts of her work at *The Dial* had been the most rewarding of any she had participated in. And then, as if to suggest that her allegiance was as much to the editors and the friendship and praise they offered her as it was to the journal and its contents, she told them she wished she had the power of heaven to give both men gifts to express her gratitude. In a little over a decade she had moved from a small Pennsylvania town where she was only beginning to discover her literary gifts, to the editorship of a widely renowned magazine in a city that was fast becoming the cultural center of the country. It is no wonder her gratitude had to look to the infinite to find proper terms for its expression.

But Moore's life as a resident in Manhattan was also drawing to a close, though she was not able to know this even early in 1929. What had she come to feel about the city that was to become in many ways the capital of modernist art, and where her own modernism flowered with striking results? In many ways, she had mastered the metropolis by rising to a position of prominence at one of its cultural institutions. Yet she remained more than a little uneasy about its mores, and about the way it tended to exaggerate fashionableness as a value in itself. The life she had come to know well in the small town of Carlisle seemed far away, and yet the family bonds that were forged there remained strong. Her own identity as a writer was the source of much of the social attention she received, putting to constant use the lessons she had learned at Bryn Mawr about the nexus of relations between personal and artistic style. But the higher levels of artistic purpose, the sense of "service," continued to elude her in some ways. Such contradictions could easily have been implicated in her imagination with New York itself, locus of much that was glamorous and satisfying, and much that was superficial and distracting.

Some of these feelings are recorded in one of her most striking poems, "New York." While the poem is exceptionally up to date in its feelings and its modernist style, it manages to reach back at least as far as the Elizabethan era, with its reference to "picardels of beaver skin," in order to contain a complex of impressions and reactions. The poem was published in *The Dial* in 1921, just as Moore was becoming identified with that journal. In it Moore may well be answering Carl Sandburg's famous "Chicago" poem that had appeared in *Poetry* magazine in March, 1914. Moore sets herself apart from Sandburg's, Whitmanlike inclusiveness by working with metonymy, since she represents her New York by one industry, actually one "trade," rather than many. But this overriding metonymic structure contains several other rhetorical devices, especially an irony that is often heated to the point of paradox. For her the wilderness is not destroyed, but remains alive in a distance that is both unbridgeable and unignorable. The poem sees the city as "a far cry," but this is a space between cultures and sensibilities as much as space between geographic points. Moore, in her typical "objective" style, lists a series of definitions. (This is the text from *Observations.*)

the savage's romance,
accreted where we need the space for commerce—
the centre of the wholesale fur trade,
starred with tepees of ermine and peopled with foxes,
the long guard-hairs waving two inches beyond the body of the
          pelt;
the ground dotted with deer-skins—white with white spots,
"as satin needlework in a single colour may carry a varied
          pattern,"
and wilting eagles'-down compacted by the wind;
and picardels of beaver-skin; white ones alert with snow.
It is a far cry from the "queen full of jewels"
and the beau with the muff,
from the gilt coach shaped like a perfume-bottle,
to the conjunction of the Monongahela and the Allegheny,
and the scholastic philosophy of the wilderness

to combat which one must stand outside and laugh
since to go in is to be lost.
It is not the dime-novel exterior,
Niagara Falls, the calico horses and the war-canoe;
it is not that "if the fur is not finer than such as one sees others
wear,
one would rather be without it"—
that estimated in raw meat and berries, we could feed the
universe;
it is not the atmosphere of ingenuity,
the otter, the beaver, the puma skins
without shooting-irons or dogs;
it is not the plunder,
it is the "accessibility to experience."

Even in the cryptic opening phrase, "a savage's romance," a definition is implicit. There are also several negative definitions, several "it is not's," and so the poem is a definition by parts, a definition by negation, a definition by series, but throughout all a series of details, each one of which threatens to establish its own center. "New York" is an extraordinarily rich poem, complex in structure and feeling. It furthermore epitomizes the sort of objective style that is the hallmark of Moore's early triumph. Her opening formulation—"the savage's romance"—is an oxymoron, containing the contradiction that energizes the entire poem. The world of romance, with its delayed fulfilments, its idealized sense of beauty and desire, is contradictorily dominated by the qualities usually associated with savagery, namely instant gratification and the full play of instinct. The use of the "wholesale fur trade" to represent the commercial leadership of New York as the national center of wealth and culture has an especially apposite role in this connection. Furs are representative of the savage state of nature and at the same time the symbols of wealth and status, combining nature and culture in a condensed form. Moore plays out the suppositions and consequences of both realms by showing how furs can be seen under the aegis of either silk embroidery or the wilderness.

Moore had read *The Psychology of Dress*, by Frank Alvah Parsons, and recorded passages from it in her notebook. Published in 1920, this book explored the idea that clothes are a key to cultural values. As such, it caught up one of the subjects that Moore was to explore in her personal life as well as her poetry. Besides reflecting her customary interest in the transformation of the realms of nature and culture, Moore's "New York" takes great delight in the furs as objects in their own right, rising yet again to descriptive heights in its first nine lines. Her patterning impulse is also in full bloom as she plays with the figure of the triangle, speaking of the furs and pelts stacked in the form of "tepees" and conjuring up the frontier with a reference to "the conjunction of the Monongahela and Allegheny" rivers. The city of Pittsburgh is located where the rivers meet to form the Ohio, an area sometimes called the "Golden Triangle." Thus, this triangular pattern culminates abstractly in the sense of New York as the apex of the pyramid of commercial transaction that leads from furs in their natural state to the world of sartorial excellence, all driven by the desire to appear wealthy and successful.

Moore wants us to see exactly that the culture and human meaning of the capital is not to be dismissed as either a single "advanced" virtue such as ingenuity, or as a gross manifestation of mere plunder. "Accessibility to experience" is poised on the edge between strong desire and sensible deliberation: New York answers our needs for more of life, but not without framing at least some questions about how best to obtain such enrichment. Moore suggests that America and the material abundance of experience presented in its largest city is there for the asking, but that abundance asks something of us as well. When Moore tells us, negatively, that New York is not to be defined by the fact that "estimated in raw meat and berries, we could feed the universe," the negation serves to remind us of all that the city is in fact. Instead of remaining at the level of raw meat and berries, the goods and supplies of the city have been transformed by its commercial energy into a vast array of other forms of wealth. Such conversion also bears the corollary that we have chosen *not* to feed the universe.

From her first extended visit to New York City as a college student, to her later move there in 1918, Moore could not have helped but have a provincial's view of the cosmopolitan experience. But she was no ordinary provincial, for seldom has anyone arrived in New York from the America west of the Hudson with such a formidably developed sensibility and literary education. When she wittily refers to the "scholastic philosophy of the wilderness," she may well have had in mind something like the rigorous "logic" of Tennyson's nature, "red in tooth and claw." But she may also be referring to the schooling that the frontier of America offered to the national spirit, a schooling that took account of both wealth and rigor. When she playfully refers to the fox furs with their "long guard-hairs waving two inches beyond the body of the pelt," she may well have been thinking of the heightened sensitivity and anxiety of the first-time visitor to the metropolis. "New York" allows Moore to see the city both as a naïf and as a sophisticate as the poem wonderfully combines surface and depth, description and analysis.

Sandburg's "Chicago," with its opening image of the city as "Hog Butcher for the World," describes his great commercial center with a blustering inclusiveness that tries to take the measure of the city's raw power. No doubt Sandburg was thinking of Whitman and the use of catalogues to convey the dazzling variousness of America's wealth. Moore, however, uses a compact version of the catalogue, by listing several varieties of fur, but at the same time she allows the fur trade to stand in for all the many forms of commerce that go to make up New York. She avoids the "boosterism" of Sandburg's approach while losing none of his pungency and detail. By entering her subject at a fairly narrow gate, the fur trade, she is nevertheless free to expand its many facets by metaphorically energizing her details and "tangential" connections. Her craft can be seen as that of the cameo carver or miniaturist, but this would be only part of it. Where Moore has the advantage, and one is tempted to say the *modernist* advantage, over Sandburg is in the way her detailing allows her to move into larger frames of reference, such as the mention of the ability to "feed the universe" without falling into bathos or grandiosity. She, like Sandburg, is not afraid to mention "raw meat and berries," an image that would not sit easily with a genteel reader of poetry at this time. But neither is she, unlike him, reluctant to draw a frame of reference that will include "satin needlework [that] in a single color may carry a varied pattern."

In a notebook she kept in the 1920's, Moore copied out a phrase from Santayana's *The Winds of Doctrine: the Intellectual Temper of the Age:* "nothing absorbs the consciousness so much as what is not given." This emphasis on the not-said was an important part of symbolist poetry, and was thereby important for many modernist poets. Moore put this principle into "New York" in an important way. By leaving something like a negative space in the center of the poem—a gap created by the *implicit* equation between the fur trade and all the forms of metropolitan commerce—she is able to fill her poem with details that become more than mere incidentals. She creates not a more up-to-date or modern poem, but a more modern*ist* one, in which the relation between surface and depth operates differently from Sandburg's personification. Sandburg's vision has to rely on tensions between surface and depth, as is made clear by his poem's central image of the spirit beating beneath the ribs of the personified hero. Such tensions are part of the legacy of Romanticism, just as are his references to the mundane details, which are ultimately redeemed by such values as "spirit" and "destiny." These tensions are hierarchical, since it is clear that the spirit of power and expansiveness is more important that the actual process of butchering, and so the references to such things as hog butchering are finally not much more than picturesque.

But the thoroughly modernist poem, at least for Moore and others, is willing to abandon such a hierarchical scheme to support its references to the mundane. This is less a question of importing "shocking" subject matter into the rarefied spaces of a lyric poem than it is a question of how to represent relations between the world of objects and the world of cultural value. William Carlos Williams said it very well in his 1925 essay on Moore when he claimed that in her poetry an apple is always an apple whether it is "in Eden or the fruit bowl where it curls." In Moore's "New York" the surface detail and the symbolic center have equal weight because both are part of something we might provisionally call a metonymic democracy. In her poem there are references to both embroidery and "raw meat and berries," both of which are surfaces that contain a symbolic resonance. In the same essay Williams speaks of a "porcelain garden" in trying to capture both Moore's precision and her efflorescence. The porcelain garden fuses the orders of nature and culture, just as does the fur trade. Such a fusion of culture and nature is consonant with the leveling of the hierarchy of surface and depth. While Moore extended her experiments with such fusions and levelings throughout her career, her modernist habits of so doing were in an important sense formed in the spaces of the modern city, the place where she spent a crucial decade in becoming an important literary figure.

Eventually several changes coincided to lead her out of Manhattan. The city she moved to in 1918 was a place with sailing ships in the harbor; at the end of the next decade, skyscrapers like the Chrysler Building and the Empire State Building were becoming the city's dominant vertical symbols. Moore decided to quit her library post after April, 1929. This may have been because of Mrs. Moore's illness; in any case, in May she is sick in bed and Moore is busy caring for her. This illness also apparently contributed to Warner's resolve to find a new home for his mother. During this time, and perhaps as a result of her library work, Moore read a number of "inspirational" books, all of which she recommended to Warner for the ship's library: Adler's *Understanding Human Nature*, Sadler's *How to Keep Happy*, and Dr. Austen Fox Rigg's *Intelligent Living*. Moore was still reading about mongooses, having seen a film called "Killing the Killer" about this animal, which she describes to her brother as "careful though courageous." This balance of attributes recalls her other animals, such as the pangolin, who is adventurous but unwarlike, and the elephant, strong but gentle. By June, Constance has selected a house for her family in Bronxville, New York, at 26 Chittenden Drive, and she suggests that Moore and her mother can stay for a while in the next-door house, which is for rent. The two do spend some time there in June, but in July they vacation in Maine. During this period, Constance continued to be open and accepting to both Moore and her mother. In August, for example, she expressed her concern over money they may have lost as a result of buying stock on the advice of Mr. Eustis. But the stock-market crash, only a few weeks away, seems not to have had too dire an effect on the Moores' finances. While Mrs. Moore and her daughter were somewhat restricted in their income for the next few years, Warner's support and the income from the property in the estate sustained them through the worst of the financial crisis.

The important event of 1929 for Moore and her mother is not so much the start of the Depression, but their move to Brooklyn. Warner, it turns out, had spent most of July apartment-hunting while the women were in Maine. On August 13, he found an apartment at 260 Cumberland Street, only ten minutes' walk from the Navy Yard. Moore would leave behind not only *The Dial* and all its importance in the literary world, and for some years would be relatively isolated, and at least physically removed from such friends as Cummings and Williams.

Many changes would affect her daily life and her writing, too, although there will be consistency as well. What she could hardly have guessed at the time is how much of her public identity would eventually be tied up with the borough to which she was moving, and where she would live for the next thirty-seven years.

Chapter 6

260 CUMBERLAND: THE THIRTIES

I. "Decorous and leisurely" Brooklyn

The building at 260 Cumberland, in the Clinton Hill district, was five stories high when the Moores moved there, with a sixth story added later. It is twice as wide as the rowhouses on either side. There are two small bay windows for the front apartments on the second through fourth floors and there is a carved stone lintel over the front door. At first the Moores were to be in the third-floor rear apartment, but they made frequent use of the roof for sunning themselves, and later moved two flights up to the fifth floor. Above the fifth-floor windows there were arched frames that enclosed a bright mosaic decoration. The neighborhood was considerably brighter than what Moore had been used to in the crowded and crooked streets of Greenwich Village. It was also a prosperous middle-class area dominated by families, and it resembled other large American cities much more than it did the borough of Manhattan across the river. Within a year of moving in, she wrote to Saintsbury to say that Brooklyn seemed to her decorous and leisurely, as the outside world did when she was a child. She went on in this nostalgic vein to praise its beautiful churches, and the sense of sunny space. The new environment brought a new sense of her social identity as well, for she told Saintsbury that she had resolved upon living a retired life until her mother was cured of the throat ailment that was so persistent. This letter, written on August 5, 1930, also mentions that Warner is visiting with her, that Constance and the children are away

247

(perhaps at Black Lake). She even mentions their pet bird. Once more she alludes to the yellow roses she saw at Saintsbury's doorway when she had visited him three summers before. The domestic tranquility that Moore always valued was being strongly felt and highly praised.

When she was to celebrate her affection for Brooklyn in an article she published in *Vogue* in 1960, Moore painted this picture:

> Decorum marked life on Clinton Hill in the autumn of 1929 when my mother and I came to Brooklyn to live. An atmosphere of privacy with a touch of diffidence prevailed, as when a neighbor in a furred jacket, veil, and gloves would emerge from a four-story house to shop at grocer's or meat-market. Anonymity, without social or professional duties after a life of pressure in New York, we found congenial.

Here Moore seems to be contrasting not only the pace and texture of the life in the Manhattan she had recently left and the Brooklyn where she has arrived, but also the general change from the artistic bohemianism of the Village to the more sedate, middle-class life she was to settle into for the next three and a half decades. She continues to point up details that convey a sense of reclusion and privacy:

> It was not unusual in those days, towards teatime, to catch a glimpse of a maid with starched cap and apron, adjusting accessories on a silver tray, in a certain particularly correct house of which the parlor windows were screened by a Gauguin-green miscellany of glossy leaves—elephant-ear-sharp and rounder—amid ferns and tiny palms from the sill up, more than ever a grateful sight by contrast with starker windows.

The essay ends with the following sentence: "Brooklyn has given me pleasure, has helped to educate me; has afforded me, in fact, the kind of tame excitement on which I thrive." The oxymoron of "tame excitement" captures reflectively the sort of life Moore was to find for herself outside the "life of pressure" she had left behind at *The Dial*. It may also have offered just the right complement to her temperament of impatient dignity. In moving across the river, Moore was in some ways moving back closer to the time scales and values of her life in Carlisle.

Shortly after the move to Brooklyn, Moore discovered and joined the Brooklyn Institute. It was the Institute, along with the Pratt Free Library, that served as Moore's main source of information and cultural stimulation for the next several decades. The Brooklyn Institute of Arts and Sciences, as it was officially called, sponsored lectures and readings of all kinds, many of which Moore attended, keeping copious notes. She told Pound her mother often joked that she should consider sleeping over, as she sometimes attended events there in the morning, afternoon, and night. Not only did she hear poetry readings there, by Harriet Monroe, Edna St. Vincent Millay, William Butler Yeats, and many others, she herself read there, in December, 1936. Perhaps as important, she heard lectures by a diverse and impressive array of speakers, from Dhan Gopal Mukerji, J. B. S. Haldane, and Edward G. Spaulding to Thornton Wilder, Frank Lloyd Wright, and Edward Alden Jewell, the art critic of The New York Times. She also viewed many illustrated lectures, most of them dealing with natural history and animal lore. She became an even more devoted follower of natural-history films, sending often minutely detailed descriptions of sequences from them to Warner and Bryher, among others. For example, on November 10, 1934, she heard a lecture by Dr. Claude W. Leister, the curator of the Zoological Gardens, on "Photographing Our Native Birds." The notes she took of the lecture indicate that Dr. Leister conveyed much information about the birds' behavior that would make photographing them easier and more effective. Such training in observation obviously contributed to poems such as "Bird-Witted." She also continued to spend a great deal of time at the American Museum of Natural History in Manhattan, taking notes and drawing sketches of various exhibits and specimens.

The Pratt Free Library also played a large part in Moore's writing. Her mother often wrote to Warner that "Marianne" has just either returned from or gone off to the library to check further references for a review or a poem she'd been working on. During one period, while working intensively on a review of a book about Emily Dickinson, Moore had checked out sixteen books from the Library, according to one of her mother's letters. It was to the Library that Moore donated a copy of a Bible after she returned from Norfolk in the summer of 1935, and the Library was very grateful, as their copy of that particular edition had been missing for some time. She remarked on how often the books in the "New Acquisitions" section of the Library were available as soon as advertisements for them had appeared. In some senses, this reading, along with the Institute lectures, became her alternative cultural resource to the manuscripts submitted to The Dial and the literary conversation during the many social gatherings of the 1920's in the Village.

What Eliot had called, in his Introduction to Moore's *Selected Poems,* the "curious jargon produced in America by universal university education," and which he identified as being put to "peculiar and brilliant and rather satirical" uses by Moore, was being further explored, developed, and polished at the Library and the Institute.

Moore's family life also changed, at least at first, since Warner often came to visit at the Brooklyn apartment, though Mrs. Moore remarked to her cousin Mary that he fell asleep as soon as he was left alone. Warner's fatigue must have been serious, for he took a sick leave in the spring of 1930, spending some time in the hospital later that summer. Moore wrote to Mrs. Thayer, Scofield's mother, that her brother was also recovering from a dangerous and nearly fatal carbuncle. He spent the entire summer convalescing with his mother and sister, as Constance was on vacation in Vermont with the children. By October 15, Mrs. Moore could write to Cousin Mary that Warner was healthy and rested and had had lunch with them, a fact that they regarded as precious. There also survive from around this time two small red notebooks of Mrs. Moore, in which she kept notes of various activities and recorded some of her daughter's literary affairs. Sometimes a note of sadness is entered, as when she described in some detail the death of the family's pet bird; she expressed there a sort of sentimentality that she never displayed in public, and which her daughter seldom imitated in her poems.

The time at *The Dial* had been full of hard work but there had been considerable personal commitment as well. In October, 1931, Moore wrote to Dr. Watson to inform him of some news she had heard recently. Apparently there was a rumor afoot that Matthew Josephson and Harold Loeb were planning to start a magazine and call it *The Dial.* Moore commented to William Carlos Williams about this, suggesting that Watson and Thayer would probably sue to prevent it from happening. In fact, Williams had written her in what may have been a part of this scheme, for he asked her to type out an index of all the articles published in *The Dial* during Watson and Thayer's ownership. She put him off, saying there was such an index available in the public library. But she was clearly disturbed by this incident, and remarked to Watson that she disapproved of what she took to be Williams' part in it. She also mentioned in the same letter that she had taken her review of Alyse Gregory's novel to *The New York Times,* and there talked to

Donald T. Adams, the well-known editor of the Book Review. At first she didn't know who he was, discovering his identity only after he closed his office door and she saw the nameplate there. She also wryly remarked that Adams didn't seemed bowled over by meeting her. Making a point of telling Watson that she did not offer work unsolicited since leaving *The Dial*, Moore said that in the case of Gregory she was making an exception. The review eventually appeared in the *New York Herald Tribune*.

About a year previously, in October, 1930, Moore had had another occasion to write to Watson. She told him of having had lunch with Alyse Gregory, who was then residing in Flushing, New York, and recovering from the flu and a high fever. She reported some rather grim news about Thayer. Only a few days earlier, Thayer had telegraphed Gregory to come immediately to see him in Worcester, Massachusetts. There, although Gregory thought he looked well, Thayer was suffering suicidal impulses. He told her he felt "like a leper" and was extremely paranoid about those around him. Gregory went on to tell Moore about her feelings about suicide, as well as those of Llewelyn, which were of a rather dispassionate and secular sort. Moore told Watson she was extremely upset by such talk, but she tried to excuse it, since Gregory's new novel had a suicide in it and Moore felt that part of the argument was a justification for her literary explorations. Much of Moore's moral sense in the next few decades centers on the principle of strength through adversity. No doubt she felt deep sympathy for her friend Thayer, but she could never approve of suicide as a solution to even the most severe difficulties.

Moore was busy writing several things, though her work had not appeared outside the pages of *The Dial* for some time, and though no poems were to appear until 1932, perhaps because of her self-imposed ban on not submitting unsolicited work. She wrote to Alyse Gregory in July, 1930, that a favorable interpretation and history of college life in America should be written, though she had no immediate plans for such a study. She had gotten several requests from people for contributions. Lincoln Kirstein was interested in having some of her poetry for his new magazine, *Hound and Horn;* she was to publish "The Jerboa" there in 1932, a major poem, one on which she worked long and hard. Harriet Monroe at *Poetry* asked for a review of W. W. E. Ross, a poet she admired, and Pound's *A Draft of XXX Cantos*. About the latter Moore wrote one of her most impressive critical pieces, and one of the best early considerations of this famous modernist epic to appear. By July, 1931, she was engaged in what Mrs. Moore called "voluminous reading about Ezra" and saying she would not read the Cantos until just before writing the review. By the end of August, Mrs. Moore explained to Warner that Pound's interest was in poetry written before Dante, so Moore's English tastes had to be adapted to fit the subject. This echoed Moore's own self-description when she first wrote Pound back in January, 1919: "I am Irish by descent, possibly Scotch also, but purely Celtic. . . ."

While Moore gave credit to Harriet Monroe for starting her writing again for magazines after *The Dial* years, and while Eliot was to play a very important role in her reputation with his Introduction for the *Selected Poems* of 1935, the decade also saw her develop an important literary friendship with Pound. She had first heard from Pound back in 1918, when he wrote her in care of William Carlos Williams. She responded by sending him two poems, one of them, "Old Tiger," which he suggested several corrections for, and which he finally published in 1932, along with four other poems, in a magazine called *Profile*. She also sent him a long letter telling about herself, her background, her reading, and her influences. Along the way she praised his energy but pointed out that she "objected to his promptness with the cudgels." He responded to this autobiographical letter by sending her a chauvinistic, spirited, and often hilarious three-page poem-letter. It began with Pound's usual abstract theorizing and continued by unrolling with his nearly clinical paranoia and self-pity, but after several "stanzas" it was bold enough to scramble its own categories:

> The female is a chaos
>
> the male
>
> is a fixed point of stupidity, but only the female
> can content itself with prolonged conversation
> with but one sole other creature of its own sex and
> of its own unavoidable specie
>
> the male
>
> is more expansive
> and demands other and varied contacts

hence its combativeness,
hence its discredit for "taking up cudgels"
hence its utter failure to receive credit
for the ninety and nine unjust times
when it refrained from taking up cudgels
and was done in the eye
by the porcine and uncudgled circumbelliferous;

hence
the debacle of its temper,
hence
its slow recovery and recuperance from the yaller janders
hence also its more widespread insistencies,
hence its exposure to stings and mud-slings of the
ungodly and undecorous
                etc. and ad infinitum

You, my dear correspondent,
are a stabilized female,
I am a male who has attained the chaotic fluidities;
our mutual usefulness
is open to the gravest suspicions of non-existence, but . . .

This sort of preening self display was very much a part of Pound's epistolary style, but his willingness to enter into it with more than usual vigor suggests that he knew Moore had considerable verbal resources of her own. In September, 1935, Edmund Wilson wrote to Moore and described Pound as one who "has the mechanics of a somewhat rare firearm and is no two times alike." Moore would probably have appreciated the explosive and even technological aspects of this metaphor, and she was to be remarkably accepting of the Pound who shot quickly and the Pound who misfired.

During her editorship at The Dial, she had been at pains to solicit work from him, though, judging from her letters (his to her at this period do not survive in great numbers), he was bullying and negative about both Thayer and Watson. But she persisted. Her actions as an editor impressed him, for she was professional and intelligent in a way he was not prepared to believe of many magazine editors. She made several small but good corrections of his translations for the magazine, and was generally respectful about his work, praising not only "How to Read, or Why" but later reading his prose, such as *Jefferson and/or Mussolini*, with care. She was willing to admit her ignorance of economics, and willing also to try and correct it, and this impressed him. She was able to defend many of *The Dial's* decisions and later to stand up to his attacks on fellow writers—such as when he inferred Bryher was Jewish—and at the same time to show him that her own standards regarding their contemporaries was quite high. Often she counseled him to react to bad writing by ignoring it. She also insisted that contributors to magazines could not dictate the contents, and such arrangements as were made about publication and payment were far from perfect but should be accepted. Increasingly his view of a conspiracy among editors and publishers caused him to spend a great deal of time in schemes to advance work he considered important; in the 1930's, Moore seemed weary of her days at *The Dial* and not at all inclined to become involved in such time-consuming activities. Their correspondence is remarkable from the first, however, for she was open and revealing about herself in ways that were not usual for her. Pound, for his part, is bullying, but there are moments of real affection and even gentle instruction. Before his long and disgusting slide into Fascist politics, he is the subject of Moore's admonitions and corrections; later, after the war, she remains a faithful friend without ever condoning even a scintilla of his blind hatreds.

In the 1930's, their correspondence deals most heavily with his plans to have her edit a magazine, and his solicitation of her signature on a manifesto. In both cases she rejects his arguments. She also helps him in his editing, and in 1931 sends him poetry by Elinor Wylie and Thayer, among others, for consideration for his *Profile*, which appeared in 1932, without their work. Pound introduced the anthology, which included five of Moore's poems, and work by Symons, Joyce, Williams, Ford, and others, by saying it was "a collection of poems which have stuck in my memory and which may possibly define their epoch, or at least rectify current ideas in respect of at least one contour." He also at this time evidently urged Eliot to bring out a volume of Moore's with Faber & Faber. She was insistent in recommending Calvin to him as a prose writer, at least his commentaries on the minor prophets. Though she tried to warm up to Louis Zukofsky's work, which Pound recommended enthusiastically, she fell short in this regard. He asked her to contribute something to the *New English Weekly* and to visit him in Rapallo, but she declined both urgings. She mentioned her hearing Yeats at the Brooklyn Institute and how he had two of the most remarkable hands she had ever seen. When she was seriously ill in February, 1932, she had her mother write and thank Pound immediately for the gift of his latest book, on Guido Calvacante. In July of the same year she was sly in suggesting just how her view of him was constructed. She said Yeats was the only person she knew whose failings did not detract from the overall positive impression, and went on to suggest how much better Pound's strengths would be if he could remove certain failings. She was constantly trying to call him to a better version of himself, respectful of his power, but never blind to its inconsistencies and "breaks." She could say bluntly to him in March, 1935, that she thought any impersonal terms of abuse to be an especial affront, but by then Pound was long past correction. He had already begun to sign his letters with the Roman numeral calendar of the Fascist era, in which the year 1921 became year I.

In her review of *A Draft of XXX Cantos,* in the October, 1931 issue of *Poetry,* Moore demonstrates her diligence in reading as a preparation for any serious book review. Though she refers to opinions by Eliot and Williams about Pound's project, she is able to make a remarkably centered and independent estimation of the poetry's purpose and value. She is also focused on the subject matter of the Cantos—"books, arms, men"—and capable of pointing out their weaknesses: "Unprudery is overemphasized and secularity persists." She quotes his passage about Thomas Jefferson seeking a gardener who could play the French horn, and then points out the contradiction in Pound's criticizing America for being too mercenary. Best of all is her summary: "To cite passages is to pull one quill from a porcupine. Mr. Pound took two thousand and more pages to say it in prose, and he sings it in a hundred-forty-two. The book is concerned with beauty. . . . It has a power that is mind and is music; it comes with the impact of centuries and with the impact of yesterday." A witty formulation is used to point out Pound's pancultural synthesizing: "The pale backgrounds are by Leonardo da Vinci; there are faces with the eyes of Picasso; the walls are by Mantegna." She is responsive to Pound's dedication to the cult of Beauty and his belief in the transformative power of literature. She also praises his critical powers as she again quotes the formulation from her earlier *Dial* "Comment" about his urging readers to "establish axes of reference by knowing the best of each kind of written thing." Pound was seldom read so sensitively by any of his contemporaries, nor did Moore very often enter so empathetically but critically into a fellow poet's work.

Mrs. Moore wrote Warner on May 29, 1932, that it was this piece on Pound that induced *Hound and Horn* to ask her to review Conrad Aiken. In the same letter, she told Warner that Moore could never have submitted unsolicited work and so was glad that Harriet Monroe had got her started again. A day later she reported that Moore had given a speech at Bryn Mawr; this exists in a notebook in rough form as "Some Aids to Precision," and later becomes the important essay, "Feeling and Precision." This essay shows how seriously Moore was working at her aesthetic. The appearance at Bryn Mawr, the first of many such invitations, may even be seen as the start of Moore's long-term formulation of a public voice for herself that will enable her to speak as an authority on her art. At first she approaches this task diffidently, but throughout the next two decades she is more and more called upon to lecture and to talk to students and young writers, as well as more general audiences. Such development goes along with her increasing interest in a public poetry, or at least at first a poetry occupied with a public "scene," though her attitudes and views of that scene are to remain for some time rather reclusive.

In 1932, Warner left for a tour of duty in Samoa, a tour that was to last almost three years and was to include his work as the head of public education in this American protectorate in the Pacific Ocean. Moore corresponded with him frequently, of course, still curious about mongooses, among other things. In June she explained to him that the mongoose was the ichneumon; she had in fact been reading up on such things. In the next four years she is to publish at least seven important poems about animals: "Old Tiger," "The Jerboa," "The Plumet Basilisk," "The Frigate Pelican," "The Buffalo," "Pigeons," and the culmination, in some ways, of this mode of allegorizing and covert self-exploration, "The Pangolin." Many of these poems were worked on while she sunned herself on the roof of her building, and they often took a long time to finish. She told Pound at one point that anyone who worked fast would think she hardly worked at all. There were distractions of various sorts, of course. She was also involved, for example, in the rewriting of a manuscript on fly-fishing for a friend, one Dr. Baldwin. But in June, 1932, she was working hardest on "The Jerboa."

Mrs. Moore told Warner on June 5 that his sister was so hard at work on this poem that she wouldn't even come down for breakfast, and she joked that Moore would never finish the poem if she didn't eat some meat. In the same letter she records a five-dollar gift from Bryher and a presentation copy of Pound's latest book, with a card inscribed "Omaggio." Here she mentions Pound's plans to publish several of Moore's poems, including one she had forgot she'd sent him. This is very likely "Old Tiger." She had sent him the other poems in 1918; the ones he eventually published in 1932 (in *Profile*) and 1933 (in *Active Anthology*), with the exception of "Old Tiger," all appeared somewhere else, and so can hardly have been forgotten by her. Although "Old Tiger" existed in some version as early as 1918, it was the first "new" poem to appear after the end of *The Dial* period. It is also never reprinted in book form. It begins elliptically, as do many of the animal poems, and its opening has an air of quiet satisfaction: "You are right about it." The old tiger is not involved in the activity that goes on around him in the zoo, but this does not mean he is not observant: "you / see more than I see but even I / see too much." And this watchfulness is cognate with an attitude toward life. The poem ends, "You know one thing, an inkling of which has not / entered their minds; you / know that it is not necessary to live in order to be / alive." If read in the context of the late 1910's, this poem speaks to the problem of the artist who is shielding herself from the critics, or the paternalistic artist wiser than his peers, and could form part of a series that might include "Reticence and Volubility," "Pedantic Literalist," "To Be Liked by You Would Be a Calamity," "To a Steam Roller," and several others. But read in the context of when it was published and perhaps revised, it may well refer to Pound himself, especially considering a line like "You have read / Dante's Hell // till you are familiar with it." In some ways this poem could be about *both* Saintsbury and Pound, a statement that allegorically connects the Victorian and the modern. But, of course, it could also be a commentary on Moore's own rather reclusive existence in this period.

"The Jerboa," like the uncollected "Old Tiger," allegorically represents more than just one human or artistic type or individual. It includes much more "scientific" detail than many animal poems, especially modernist ones. Its structure is complex, largely trusting that its thematic designs will be eventually discerned. But it is Mrs. Moore who gives a large clue to the poem's possible meaning, for she told Warner that its subject was not an ascetic monarch, but a noble person oppressed by wealth and jewels, who is quite different from his luxury-loving neighbors. It is hard to resist the conclusion that Moore is writing a poem about herself, and specifically about her recent exit from the jeweled setting of Manhattan, where the man-made luxury was in sharp contrast to her new environment. The lines from the poem that are most often quoted:

> By fifths and sevenths,
> in leaps of two lengths,
>   like the uneven notes
> of the Bedouin flute . . .
>
> Its leaps should be set
> to the flageolet;

recall the instrument that Moore used many years previously as a metaphor for her own poetry. By saying the animal should move to the flageolet, she is suggesting that she should act in accordance with the needs and development of her own poetry and not be distracted by any siren calls of ambition or luxury. Mrs. Moore also detailed to Warner how, when Moore was working on this poem, she had received encouragement in the form of letters from William Carlos Williams, as well as Pound's "supervising" and Bryher's monetary support. Near the end of June, Moore could write her brother that "The Jerboa" was her most singular poem. Such enthusiasm suggests the poem had a very deep meaning for Moore. It is also important to note that Mrs. Moore was one of its first and severest editors, for Moore went on to tell her brother that it was very painful to have the poem critiqued by her mother. For Moore, working with the encouragement of her peers, and under the watchful eye of her mother, these animal poems, which were to dominate her poetic output in the 1930's, were genuinely something new, as innovative in their way as the modernist poems of 1915–19.

By the end of June, the poem is finished and sent to *Hound and Horn*, where it appears in the October–December issue of 1932. Almost immediately Moore started composing "The Plumet Basilisk," which

would appear in the same magazine exactly one year later. She told
Warner that she would have preferred to have "The Jerboa" in Eliot's
Criterion, but she had already promised it to Lincoln Kirstein. In July,
Morton Dauwen Zabel asked Moore to review an edition of the letters
of Emily Dickinson. Moore was planning to contribute "No Swan So
Fine" to the twentieth anniversary issue of *Poetry*, in October, 1932,
and so with Zabel's request it was clear that the pages of that magazine
were opening up to her in a regular way. During the next two decades,
in fact, when Zabel takes over as editor of *Poetry* after Monroe's death,
he becomes an important friend of Moore's and one of her chief backers. The swan poem, incidentally, was sparked by reading about the
estate of Lord Balfour being auctioned off, with two swans part of the
sale. Lord Balfour was one of Saintsbury's friends, and this connection
may have been what attracted her to the auction notice. The poem is
an extremely subtle interweaving of the realms of nature and culture, as
the "real" swans are aestheticized by having "gondoliering legs" while
the china swan is energized by perching on "branching foam." The
ending sees the china swan as alive and its original owner as not: the
swan is "—at ease and tall. The king is dead." The two four-syllable
phrases rhyme structurally, suggesting a completely congruent, albeit
ironic, transposition between the orders of art and life.

In late August, she discovered a French art book in the window at
Macy's that showed camelias in full color; this became the occasion for
"Camila Sabina," which she gave to Pound for inclusion in the *Active
Anthology*. And in September she excitedly but deliberately informed
Warner about her early work on "The Plumet Basilisk," and discussed
its planned length with him. This was also the month when Moore
wrote her poem on Herbert Hoover, then the subject of much con-
tumely in the newspapers. The poem, by treating his enemies as
Iscariot-like, implicitly compares Hoover to Christ; this may well be the
result of Mrs. Moore's influence, though Moore's own political views in
this period are strongly conservative. She sent the poem to the *New
York Herald Tribune*, expecting it to be returned, which it was. Later she
sent it to a very pro-Republican newspaper in the midwest, but it, too,
rejected it. It is intriguing to speculate how Moore's poetic career would
have developed differently if this poem had been accepted and she had
followed with others in a similar vein. When the poem was returned
from the second paper, she said that she planned to write a patriotic

poem of more inclusive character, after her political feelings cooled a bit. Later, in the 1950's and beyond, she indulged her penchant for writing "occasional verse" in praise of specifically named public figures. But the people who enjoyed her poems about Yul Brynner, Arthur Mitchell, and the racehorse Tom Fool could hardly have suspected that their prototype may have been a poem on Herbert Hoover.

In October, Mrs. Moore told Warner that she had written Mary Norcross a long careful letter (which apparently does not survive) against socialism, condemning it as "*soviet*-ism" and distinguishing between it and the ethical kind set forth by Ruskin and consistent with Christian principles. This begins a long series of references in the family correspondence to anti-communist sentiments, culminating, in a sense, with Warner's letter to President Lyndon Johnson praising him for the attack on North Vietnam forces in the Gulf of Tonkin in 1968. Almost certainly Mrs. Moore's religious conversion supported her mistrust of Soviet-style communism. Perhaps her mistrust was also fed by a long suppressed dislike of the "liberal" social values of the artistic types she had witnessed with a jaundiced eye in Greenwich Village.

In the middle of November, Moore averred to Warner that Hoover's campaign meant a lot to her; the campaign had put on the record a vocabulary about civic virtues that she valued greatly. But these political concerns did not in the least sway her from her research into poetic and animal subjects. A few weeks later she told Warner about seeing at the Brooklyn Institute a photograph of a tuatera, an animal that she included in the basilisk poem. She also mentions her rejection of Pound's offer to have her edit the journal to be called *Lion & Crown*, which was evidently planning to publish poems in holographic reproduction. This magazine never materialized. Llewelyn Powys meanwhile was enlisting her help in trying to publish a selection from the little-known seventeenth-century English writer, Anthony à Wood. Indulging her predilection for metonymic structure, she proposed writing a poem on the tiger-swallow-tail, the tiger salamander, and the tiger horse; Mrs. Moore rejected the proposal as bizarre. She finished her basilisk poem in the middle of December, but complained to Warner that it didn't have enough spontaneity, and she preferred the jerboa poem, though she thought that what she'd learned would help her in the future. She also met Yeats backstage at his reading at the Brooklyn Institute, where they traded compliments about each other's work.

In 1933 there was a problem with *Poetry*, involving a flap over Moore's review of the Emily Dickinson letters. Moore wanted to include footnotes in the articles and Monroe was reluctant to do so. Zabel threatened to resign if Moore was alienated from the magazine. But other outlets were available to her; in late January, Bryher wrote to ask her to review several films for the magazine she funded: *Close-Up*, devoted to experimental cinema. Moore eventually reviewed several nature films, including R. L. Ditmar's *Strange Animals I Have Known* and Watson's *Lot in Sodom*. Ditmars was the Curator of Mammals and Reptiles at the Bronx Zoo, and became a source of much information for Moore. The end of the month also brought news of the death of Saintsbury, which Mrs. Moore passed on to Warner. In February, Zabel wrote to say he would not have allowed negative references to Hoover in that month's issue of *Poetry* if he'd known they would so offend Moore. Mrs. Moore told Warner that his sister's poems met with little popular approval but that she was working hard to make good work known. Moore was conscious of the fact that only through appearances in places like *Poetry* would her work be requested by others.

Several aspiring writers had, moreover, come to Moore for advice, and she gave it freely, sometimes working for hours on a typed response to a group of poems. At this time she was advising Mary Jones, Catherine Flagg, and Esther Maddox Tennent, the wife of a professor at Bryn Mawr. Though none of these people came to prominence, Moore took such relationships seriously. It was also around this time that Moore was approached by Elizabeth Bishop, then an undergraduate at Vassar, who became a lifelong friend. Moore also went to a few literary parties. One in May was given by Paul Rosenfeld, who had contributed a regular column to *The Dial*, and had written some of the most perceptive early criticism of Moore in his book *Men Seen: Twenty-four Modern Authors*, published in 1925. He was especially perceptive about the structure of her poetry.

> The poems, each with its carefully synthesized vocabulary, recall rambling parenthetical discourses; gradually only does the graphite turn into diamond. Yet finally the whimsical essays are seen substances dense and winged as the elder poetry. There is definitely a form, a surface, a music. . . . It is evident Marianne Moore has dissolved the materials of her art and reformed them about an original principle.

At this party she met Edmund Wilson, known to her at least slightly from *The Dial*, and whom she described as appearing above the battle. He also could be acerbic, however; he told her that Zabel would never be anything but stupid.

During the summer Moore was able to spend some time with Mary Norcross at "The Mountain." She was also able to confess to Warner that she had met T. S. Eliot at a party, but she felt somewhat abashed, since their conversation was trivial and discreditable. She had had plans to meet Eliot and Wilson for dinner, but Wilson called at the last minute to say they couldn't come and would she attend a party with Eliot instead. Mrs. Moore objected to what she called such rudeness, but Moore went anyway, drawn by Eliot's reputation, but finally was unable to say much to him beyond small talk. It was one of the few instances in which Moore went directly against her mother's wishes, and also when her much vaunted ability for conversational inventiveness seems to have let her down. Moore had completed reviews for *Poetry* of Eliot's *Sweeney Agonistes* and two books of poetry by Yeats. There would also be a review of Cummings' *Eimi*, and a piece on Trollope for *The Criterion*. Her output was definitely increasing, though she was still tending to work on one poem at a time, and then with a certain magazine in mind. In later years this custom would be codified, and she would virtually restrict her writing to doing poems by commission for editors or friends.

In May, Warner had written to say he would be back home from his Pacific tour in about six months. Moore wrote to him several times in the next few years about her "story" as she called it. At first this meant her story called "The Farm Show," based in part on an agricultural exhibit she saw during a visit to Mary Norcross in Pennsylvania, but eventually it meant a novel she had begun. She had been approached by a Mr. Jay to do a limited edition of her poems, or a reprint of *Observations*, which had gone out of print. But she put this project aside in favor of the story. On July 9 she told Warner she doubted if it would ever be fluid and natural, but later the same month she said she was desperate about the project and would stay with it exclusively until finished, even if it took a decade. This was an exaggeration, for less than a month later she was writing a poem about peace, which she would eventually submit to a contest; she said she didn't expect to be picked, but she was "just doing my duty." This may have been, in some ways, a more general way of expressing the feeling behind the Hoover poem cast into a more general context.

But the sort of resolve she felt about her novel was quite real, for she worked on it diligently during several periods over the next several years. It was the kind of discipline that was to become evident in the project of translating La Fontaine in the 1940's and 1950's. She may also have gotten interested in fiction as a result of the essay she was to do on Henry James. On October 15, Warner sent a telegram announcing he expected to arrive in Norfolk, Virginia, on February 14, 1934. Moore was ill in November and there is no correspondence from her in this month. Mrs. Moore informed Warner that Mary Norcross had broken a vertebrae in her back, and Mrs. Moore wanted to go to Starrett's Gap to help her. She told Warner how the Pound essay had occupied Moore for weeks, working as she was on criticizing Ezra even as she attacked those who didn't appreciate his worth. As was the case with many of her opinions and actions at *The Dial*, Moore had to conceal or at least trim back some of her negative feelings, in this case out of loyalty to a man who she felt had been one of her chief supporters.

On the first of March, 1934, Moore went with Monroe Wheeler to see a performance of Stein's "Four Saints in Three Acts," which she regarded as a blasphemous but talented work. She also finished her essay on "Henry James as a Characteristic American." In some ways this essay can be read as Moore's answer to those in the 1920's who wanted an indigenous American culture. By calling James, an expatriate and Anglophile, a "characteristic" American, Moore was clearly making a sort of space for herself as well in the American scene. Equally important is how she created a context for James. If her animal poems are important throughout the decade, so is another group of poems on the relations between geography and culture. Beginning with "New York," "People's Surroundings," "England," and others, Moore goes on to write "Spenser's Ireland," "The Steeple-Jack," and, most important, "Virginia Britannia." She may well have begun to formulate her feelings about the themes in these poems when she wrote the opening for the James essay:

> To say that "the superlative American" and the characteristic American are not the same thing perhaps defrauds anticipation, yet one must admit that it is not in the accepted sense that Henry James was "big" and did things in a big way. But he possessed the instinct to amass and reiterate,

and is the rediscerned Small Boy who had from the first seen Europe as a verification of what in its native surroundings his "supersensitive nostril" fitfully detected and liked. Often he is those elements in American life—as locality and as character—which he recurrently studied and to which he never tired of assigning a meaning.

This is a subtle opening on many grounds, not least because it makes a key distinction between superlative and characteristic, while showing that both terms are confusingly substituted, especially in America, to convey largeness or importance. And while it shows James appreciated his European roots and culture, he did so because of habits of thought generated in America, where place and character are meaningful in ways that are different from the ways they are seen in European experience. When she comes to write "Virginia Britannia," with its reflections on place and character as sources of meaning, she may have these reflections on James in mind. The rest of the essay is important, too, for it profiles those aspects of James that overlap with Moore's concerns and themes: idealism, "good nature and reciprocity" as indispensable parts of polite manners, clothes as cultural symbols, and "the rapture of observation." Moore learned much of her modernism from James's irony and self-reflexiveness, and she was also able to reaffirm her sense of the importance of the intersection of artistic and social style and morality from his example.

In the middle of March, Moore had "The Buffalo" accepted by *Poetry* and sent "The Frigate Pelican" off to *The Criterion*. She purchased some books on American art to send to Bryher. A natural history film called "Wild Cargo" attracted her attention and enthusiasm, because it dealt with elephants, always a favorite subject, and showed the ceremony of the "Temple of the Tooth," concerning a myth about Buddha's tooth, which she later incorporated into her poem, "Elephants," published almost a decade later. The film also included shots of a pangolin, with its impressive furtiveness, and a white buffalo. She was especially pleased with the last detail because it allowed her to keep the word "albino" as a rhyme word in her poem about "The Buffalo." She enjoyed a trip to the circus with Elizabeth Bishop, and remarked to Warner that it was almost scary to find a college student with so much sense. In the same month, she mentions a brilliantly carved coach from Sweden that is on display at the Brooklyn Museum; this becomes the subject of another poem published a decade later, "A Carriage from Sweden."

The Reverend John Warner and Jennie Craig Warner, Marianne Moore's maternal grandparents. Jennie Craig Moore was memorialized in Marianne's middle name, Craig, which is how her family members often referred to her.

Mary Warner Moore, with Warner and Marianne, St. Louis, c. 1890.

The Manse, Kirkwood, Missouri. Warner and Marianne are in the foreground with three friends.

Warner and Marianne.

Title page of Mary Warner Moore's edition of her father's sermons. This book's preface contains the first recorded utterance of Marianne.

SERMONS

BY THE

REV. JOHN R. WARNER, D.D.,

WITH

A SKETCH OF HIS LIFE

BY

HIS DAUGHTER,
MARY WARNER MOORE.

PHILADELPHIA:
J. B. LIPPINCOTT COMPANY.
1895.

Marianne Moore
in Carlisle, c. 1910.

The secretarial School in Carlisle, which Moore attended after graduation from Bryn Mawr. Moore is behind the first woman in the right aisle seat.

Suffragist parade, Carlisle, 1916.

Moore and her brother, probably taken in Carlisle.

The front of 343 North Hanover Street, Carlisle, where Moore grew up and lived until 1917.

Above left: Moore on the docks in lower New York City, c. 1920.

Above right: Carolyn Burke, Mina Loy's biographer, has identified this as a pencil sketch by Mina Loy, obviously of Marianne Moore.

Right: A portrait of Moore by Marjori studio, in New York in the 1920s.

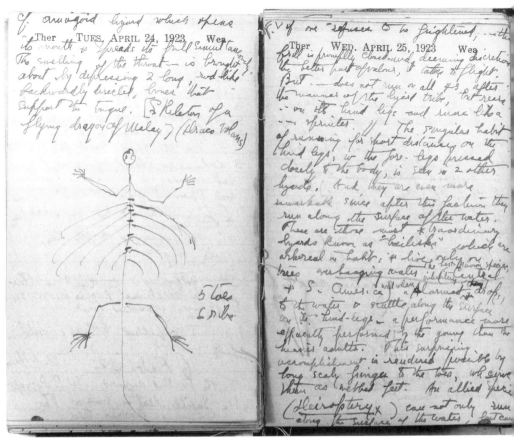

f. armageid lizard which opens
ther TUES, APRIL 24, 1923 Wea
its mouth & spreads its full semicircle
The swelling of the throat — is brought
about by depressing 2 long, rod-like
backwardly directed bones that
support the tongue. [Skeleton of a
flying dragon of Malay] (Draco volans)

5 toes
5 ribs

ther WED. APRIL 25, 1923 Wea
[...] if one "refuses to be frightened," — the
Brill is frequently cloudward deeming discretion
the better part of valour, & takes to flight.
But — does not run or all 4's after
the manner of the lizard tribe, but rears
— on its hind legs and runs like a
— sprinter. // The singular habit
of running for short distances on the
hind legs, w the fore-legs pressed
closely to the body, is seen in 2 other
lizards. And they are even more
remarkable since after this fashion they
run along the surface of the water.
These are those most extraordinary
lizards known as "basilisks" which are
arboreal in habit; & live only on
trees overhanging water inhabiting central
& S. America will when alarmed, drop
to the water & scuttle along the surface
on its hind-legs — a performance more
efficiently performed by the young than the
heavier adults. This surprising
accomplishment is rendered possible by
long scaly fringes to the toes, wh serve
them as webbed feet. An allied species
(Heirophryx) can not only run
along the surface of the water, but can

Moore's notebook, with
drawing of skeleton of
Malay dragon.

Winifred Ellerman,
known as Bryher.

Moore in Fort Greene Park, Brooklyn, just blocks from her home at 260 Cumberland Street.

A letter from Moore in response to a request for a biographical sketch.

260 Cumberland Street
Brooklyn, New York
November 5, 1935

Dear Miss Gray:

I was born in 1887 and was graduated from Bryn Mawr in 1909; but if you have access to WHO'S WHO, a little more information than this is given there. *and to*

The authors I have cared most for are Chaucer, Spenser, Sir Philip Sidney, Sir Thomas Browne, Dr. Johnson, Anthony Trollope, W.H. Hudson, and Thomas Hardy. [See LIVING AUTHORS; The H.W. Wilson Company--in the reference department of most public libraries]. I have been influenced by the Bible and by Bach's* music and point of view I think.   Contemporarily I have been influenced by Ezra Pound, T.S. Eliot, Wallace Stevens, W.C. Williams, and E.E. Cummings; and if the word contemporary could be used in this connection, by Gerard Hopkins.

I have not succeeded in expressing what I feel about life and art, but as verse The Jerboa, The Buffalo, and The Steeple-Jack, please me most.

With regard to technique, I have a liking for the unaccented rhyme, and the movement of the poem musically is more important I feel than the conventional look of the lines on the page. is. Therefore I tend to regard the stanza as the unit of composition rather than the line; and although it is a dangerous principle to follow, because it provokes query and distracts thought from the theme, I sometimes divide a word at the end of a line or end of a stanza; and often use the title of a poem as continuous with the first line of the poem.

My outlook on life appears I think, in a prose article of mine that appeared in THE HOUND & HORN, April-June, 1934: Henry James as a Characteristic American.

I do not see how it is possible for one to live without religious faith, or shall I say without capacity for it. War and the reaction from war are inescapable in their effect on the mind, I admit, and thus enter into the "task" of the writer; but I would say--for myself at any rate--one is not under any circumstances doing anything but trying to express without affectation, the irrepressible conviction that has, in some specific form, taken possession of one. *him.*

Sincerely yours,

Marianne Moore

Marianne Moore

* J.S. Bach

Moore, with her mother on the sofa.

The Moore family: Marianne, Warner, and their mother, Brooklyn, mid-1940s.

T. S. Eliot.

Alexander Calder,
Moore, Marc Chagall,
and Martha Graham.

Moore with Muhammad Ali, then known as Cassius Clay, At Toots Shor.

Moore at the American Academy of Arts and Letters. Seated with her is Muriel Rukeyser; standing behind, left to right, Wallace Stevens, Randall Jarrell, and Allen Tate.

Moore at Belmont Park Racetrack.

Moore receiving an honorary degree at Harvard, 1969. Second from left in rear is Walter Reuther, second from right is David Rockefeller. Immediately to Moore's left is John Lindsay, then mayor of New York City.

Moore, by Cecil Beaton.

Moore, by Cartier-Bresson.

Moore in her Brooklyn apartment. Visible on the ledge behind her is the bust of Moore by Gaston Lachaise, from the 1920s.

Moore at the Gotham Book Mart, with Andreas Brown, Lawrence Durrell, and Frances Steloff.

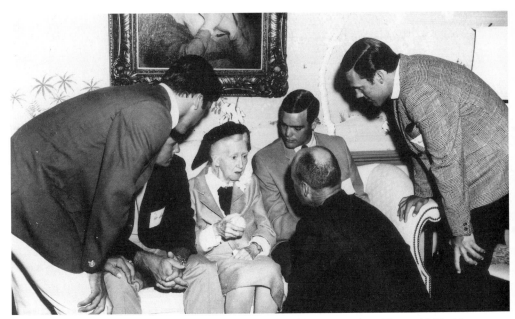

Moore with the University of Texas varsity baseball team, Austin, Texas, 1969. Moore was there discussing the purchase of her archive, which eventually was sold to the Rosenbach Museum and Library, Philadelphia.

Moore with Mrs. Joan Payson, the owner of the New York Mets, and Casey Stengel, the Mets' manager, Shea Stadium, 1965.

Moore throwing out the first
ball on opening day, Yankee
Stadium, 1966. Yankees owner
Bill Burke is seated at her right.

The famous *Esquire* cover, with
Moore and seven other
"unknockables."

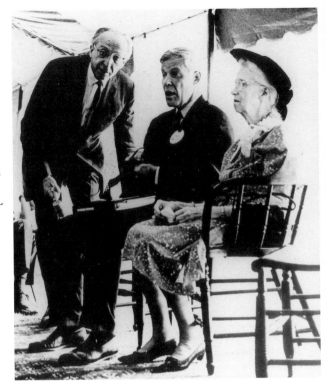

Aaron Copland, Glenway Wescott, and Moore, MacDowell Arts Colony, New Hampshire, where Wescott gave a speech presenting Moore with the MacDowell Medal.

Ezra Pound and Moore, New York Public Library, 1969. This was Pound's last visit to the United States.

Zabel, writing in the June issue of *Poetry*, mentions both her essay on James and a piece on Yeats she had contributed to a journal in Georgia. At the end of June she starts working on "Nine Nectarines," which she finishes in time to place, along with the buffalo poem, in the November issue of *Poetry*.

The summer of 1934 was the occasion for another trip where Moore and her mother were reunited with Warner. Again, the advance details were kept secret from Constance, whom Warner described as very watchful. This trip to Norfolk was made while Constance was at Black Lake. As was the case prior to the earlier visits to the west coast, the three had been separated for some time and they obviously felt the need to reestablish family ties. And as with those earlier trips, this one resulted in several major poems, which will go to make up the collection called *The Pangolin*. Warner's character was clearly an inspiration to Moore, perhaps one of the chief inspirations in all of her poetry. But his presence in her poems is seldom if ever recorded directly. In his sister's mind, his life becomes a model of virtue in action, and she allegorizes him in poems such as "The Pangolin," much as she creates self-portraits of herself. The details of their time together are important for her, and it is tempting to speculate that their conversation also found its way into her poetic views. Just as Mrs. Moore came to play the role of first reader, collaborator, and strictest critic for Moore's poetry, Warner was often the distant, even transcendent audience for much of what she wrote. His response to her work always had an inspirational, even religious cast to it, confirming some of her highest aspirations.

The three Moores took a side trip to Williamsburg, where they visited the Bruton Church they had seen in 1927. Moore detailed this trip to Bryher, among others, and she took back to Brooklyn folders and other literature about the region. Once back home she did a considerable amount of reading for all the poems that would make up "Virginia Britannia" and the other lyrics to be published in the sequence she called "Old Dominion." These poems were approached as all of her poems of this period, as projects that would incorporate the family's experience as well as the historical and scientific facts about their subjects.

The early 1930's were also focused in part by Warner Moore's tour of duty in American Samoa. While there, Warner served as the Director of Education in the school system set up by the American government, and he was responsible for much of the organizational work. Wherever his ship sailed, he was also responsible for educating the sailors on board, not just in Christian doctrine but in general historical, cultural, and geographical information.

Often this information was supplemented by letters from Mrs. Moore, and typed up and reproduced by Warner in the form of newsletters to be made available to the crew before docking in any foreign port. Mrs. Moore was quite conscious of her son and daughter as teachers, as people with a mission to bring enlightenment and culture to others. She would offer advice on his sermons, draft outlines for him, and provide him with a commentary on the homiletic skills of the pastor at Brooklyn's Lafayette Avenue Presbyterian Church. Moore's hunger for information and cultural knowledge was surely deeply ingrained in her own temperament and daily habits, but it is important to realize that it was constantly reinforced not only by her brother's encouragement, but by his example and his own duties. However playful Moore's poems are, they are at the same time didactic. Her didacticism, however, is not of a doctrinal or programmatic kind, but more like the Augustan ideal of art conceived as an activity that seeks to instruct as well as delight, a subordinating of self-expression in order to tell people about the world and how to participate in it fully.

II. Eliot and the *Selected Poems*

The single most important event in 1934 for Moore as a writer was the decision to publish her *Selected Poems*, with an introduction by T. S. Eliot, in both England and America. The idea is first mentioned in a letter of Eliot's in which he offered to write the Introduction; Moore reports this to Warner in a letter of April 23. By the first of June she has received a contract from Faber & Faber. When the signed contract was returned to her in September she was so excited she described the watermark to Warner. She signed this letter "Rat," with the "A" in red, and a note saying "hereinafter called the Author." Later, on June 10, Mr. Latham, from Macmillan, assured her that the American edition would allow her to keep the copyright in her name. It was Eliot's idea to call the book "Selected" despite its drawing on only two previously published volumes, the slim *Poems* of 1921 and the more substantial *Observations* of 1924. While *Observations* contained fifty poems or so, it reprinted most of *Poems,* and so the *Selected* could not even be seen as the gathering of two completely distinct volumes. Eliot reckoned that calling the volume by the adjective "Selected" would create the impression that Moore was an established, well-known poet. She had not written a substantial number of poems, and was herself reluctant to have a new book of poems appear. She had, however, earlier made a point of recovering from the Dial Press the copyright to *Observations.* This apparently contradictory attitude—of wanting her book available and yet in her control, and at the same time feeling she had nothing new to offer the public—was a typical stance Moore took toward the presentation of her work. Clearly concerned all her life about her public impression and force, Moore was persuaded to bring out "Selected" poems largely by the enthusiasm of Eliot. Her reticence and modesty were always in fitful balance with her sense of her own excellence.

Eliot's enthusiasm must have meant a great deal to Moore, for she admired not only his poetry, but his adopted Englishness and his spiritual "weight." Moore had read "The Rock," and shared it with her mother. She had also written reviews of several of his books, and would review his *Collected Poems* in the summer of 1935, though it did not appear until the May 27, 1936 issue of *The Nation.* Eliot had written to her about Pound's *XXX Cantos* and wondered if her planned review of them (which appeared in the April, 1934 *Criterion*) would point out the same strengths and weaknesses he had found in them. The closeness between the poets was to last for decades. Several years later, Moore arranged for Eliot to meet Warner, in Washington, D. C. Eliot wrote to Warner and asked what church he might attend in the capital; Warner must have been aware that few of her sister's literary friends would have needed such information. Not long after Eliot won the Nobel Prize, Moore was concerned about his taking vitamins in the correct dosage. Their correspondence is marked by an easy mixture of personal and literary concerns, and it is apparent that Moore felt great respect and affection for such an important and public man of letters. Very rarely indeed did she cultivate a relationship between one of her literary friends and her mother and Warner.

In narrower literary terms, Eliot's influence was greatly felt in the selection and arrangement of Moore's *Selected Poems.* Not only did he prevail upon her to reprint all of the earlier *Observations*, but it was he who arranged the book so that the poems published after 1924 should open the volume. A small irony is present here: when Moore published one of her earliest reviews, it was of Eliot's *Prufrock and Other Observations*, in the April, 1918 issue of *Poetry*. In it she suggested that Eliot might have helped the reader by arranging his poems so that the sweeter poems came sooner in the volume. Eliot's suggested order, with "The Steeple-Jack" as the first poem, remained unchanged by Moore throughout her lifetime. One effect of this was to give many of Moore's readers in the 1940's and 1950's a distorted sense of her growth as a poet, for not only were many of the poems of 1915–19 not collected later, but the ones that were were placed out of chronological order.

But if Eliot's arrangement of the poems somewhat distorted their origins in a chronological sense, what he had to say about Moore's work prepared the way for her reputation in later years. The Introduction begins with a typical Eliot move, as he raises an important scruple. For Moore, Eliot suggested, the problem was that we cannot truly estimate a contemporary's greatness. Only history and a greater moral and social distance will provide the test of that quality. However, we *can* judge a contemporary writer's genuineness. Such a distinction had considerable force, for it suggested that Eliot was refraining from calling Moore great only out of a sense of confidence that later opinion would arrive at that estimation. In the meantime he could validate her standing "simply" by claiming that in being genuine she had written poems that "form part of the small body of durable poetry written in our time; of that small body of writings, among what passes for poetry, in which an original sensibility and alert intelligence and deep feeling have been engaged in maintaining the life of the English language." This, needless to say, was a large and high-minded claim. What Eliot did to support it was to point to Moore's special vocabulary, which he had singled out in the review in *The Dial* several years previously, and to show the great care she took with sounds and the techniques of structure. What he did not do—for he was, finally, a formalist critic in this instance—was to say what her poems were about. He explicitly said that it "would be difficult to say what is the 'subject-matter' of *The Jerboa*." But he went on to add that "for a mind of such agility . . . the minor subject . . . may be the best release for the major emotions." This approach has dominated much of Moore criticism to this day, for by claiming the subject is minor, while allowing the emotion and the technique to be major and genuine, readers are able to ignore Moore's themes, her arguments about the world and the nature of our experience of it. Remembering Eliot's claim in his *Dial* review about Moore as a feminine writer, this sort of approach may well be the result of a certain sexist or gender-based feeling that women writers express a sensibility, but they rarely make claims about the way things are.

But Moore's poems are not only imbued with a rich sense of how things are, they also argue, elaborately but insistently, for certain values, actions, and truths. Often such arguments are cloaked in a description of a rather rare animal, or an *objet d'art* or social custom. Eliot said, "Moore's poetry, or most of it, might be classified as 'descriptive' rather than 'lyrical' or 'dramatic' "—and it is easy to lose sight of the fact that the argument is the motive of the poem. Moore herself may have contributed to this way of reading her poetry. And one of the chief contributions may have been the "Postscript" she added to *Selected Poems:*

> Dedications imply giving, and we do not care to make a gift of what is insufficient; but in my immediate family there is one "who thinks in a particular way"; and I should like to add that where there is an effect of thought or pith in these pages, the thinking and often the actual phrases are hers.

There is not much surprising here in the modesty and in the revelation about Mrs. Moore's part in the composition of the poems, at least not surprising to those who knew Moore well. But what is somewhat surprising is the phrase "the effect of thought." This suggests either that the poems only appear to be based on ideas, or that the ideas only show through from time to time. Warner was extremely touched by this "Postscript," but what touched him was the reference to his mother, and the humility put him into a very pious frame of mind. He wrote to his sister on April 16, 1935, that the "Postscript" testified to the development of their family's love, and also reflected how a good craftsman had to have a touch of heavenly power; this could be sensed even by those outside the magic circle of the artist's nearest relations. Moore may have read this encomium with as much, or more, satisfaction as she read Eliot's Introduction. Its intensity was in some ways fueled by the family's summer together in Norfolk only a few months previously, and Warner was to respond to *The Pangolin* with the same sort of religious fervor.

Of course the public reception of *Selected Poems* was of a different order. The reviews in the English publications were mixed; all they had in common was their pointing out that Eliot had written an Introduction for the volume. In *Time and Tide*, dated November 5, 1935, D. G. Bridson praised Moore's descriptive powers, and said her "verse might be described as primarily ceramic." But he also said it lacked clear emotion: "Whether or not it is a poetry capable of releasing the 'major emotions' is perhaps open to doubt." He then rather muddied the waters by ending with the claim that "if she is the spiritual daughter of Imagism, she might well be regarded as Imagism's greatest exponent to date." But Moore was as discontent with the limitations of Imagism as was Pound, and she was never its "exponent." Reading Moore's work in the context of Imagism may have contributed to Bridson's inability to see its argumentative and expressive scale.

The Imagist connection was also made by G. W. Stonier, writing in the *New Statesman and Nation* of June 27, 1936: "It is as an imagist, with a vivid fabulous sense of the animal world, that Miss Moore excites our attention." Stonier spent the first half of his review recounting a visit to the zoo, promoted, he claimed, by reading Moore. Such literalism may well have struck Moore as comic, if not pathetic, and it typifies the reaction of those readers who consider that Moore is doing nothing but describing animals. But Stonier was not responsive to Moore's sense of structure, or her mixture of allusion and bald statement: "It has its flavour, its geometrical pattern, which personally I do not always care for." It is a model of the mixed review, with all its adjectives, positive and negative, canceling each other out.

The most positive review was by May Lewis, in the July, 1936 issue of *Forum and Century*. She calls her piece an appreciation, and says it is "a guidepost to those as yet unfamiliar with [Moore's] art." Concentrating on Moore's power of observation, she quotes more than any other English reviewer, and ends with this metaphoric claim:

> Let us admit that this poetry is difficult, but compare it to the repetitious emptiness of an easy, swinging lyric that runs through the hand like water, nothing remaining but a brief sense of refreshment, and then hold fast one of Marianne Moore's prickly products in a fearless grasp and see the kernel of mental and spiritual nourishment that remains in one's possession.

The reference here to "mental nourishment" was quite unusual, especially in the columns of a review. Writing in the London *Sunday Times*,
Desmond MacCarthy seemed to want just that brief refreshment instead
of whatever solid nourishment Moore was offering. He begins with a
lengthy disquisition on the dangers and losses involved when poets
abandon rhyme and regular rhythm. Prose, he insists again and again,
has its virtues, and poets should decide ahead of time if they want to
write verse or prose. What they should never do is mistake the two.
This, of course, was a common insistence on the part of those who
resented modernism's attack on the sharp boundaries between genres.
MacCarthy insists that in Moore the details don't add up, and by
thinking she is using verse instead of prose, she falls into a preciosity
that a normal prose writer would avoid. The review concentrates almost
exclusively on Moore's technique and ends by saying that Moore's work
"renounces incantation without claiming the full rhythmic liberties of
prose." Though he is willing to grant that "there are no doubt psychological and moral causes" behind Moore's technique, he never once
tries to say what they might be. He even reverts to a Sanskrit distinction among prose, verse, and prose mixed with verse, and argues that
Sanskrit authors realize "something incomprehensible," which is the
essential part of poetry, can be attained in prose. He doesn't allow this
transcultural standard to adjust his thinking in any serious way, however.

The most negative review was the anonymous one that appeared in
the *Times Literary Supplement* of January 18, 1936. It begins by quoting
a portion of Eliot's Introduction, and then links Moore with him and
Pound. But the reviewer takes issue with Eliot: "To be candid, he does
not convince us that his admiration of Miss Moore's poetry has been
based on a sufficiently exact apprehension of its principles." These
principles are spelled out, and once again they are exclusively about
Moore's prosody, her versification and syllabic rules. "We should be the
last to wish to discourage experiments in technique," the reviewer
avers, and in fact makes a good exposition of Moore's innovation. But
by failing even to mention what her themes and concerns are, the piece
is bound up by its own prejudices. At the end it can only say that
Moore's "prosody flies full in the face of all the natural music of an
English intonation, and of an American still more," and that her "cul-

tivated refusals and subtle detachment are poison to us." The review epitomizes the approach of an apparently reasoned exposition, which ends with a vicious negative assessment, of the sort that gave anonymous reviewing such a bad name.

On May 29, 1935, Mrs. Moore wrote Warner that Faber & Faber had sent Moore a batch of reviews. Mrs. Moore commented that she had reminded her daughter it was salutary for a writer to see from reviews how much trouble she might give her readers. This is a hint that what contributed to Mrs. Moore's lack of enthusiasm for her daughter's poetry might have been its difficulty and lack of straightforwardness. But the late spring was pleasant for Moore nonetheless, for she went to Bryn Mawr to give a reading, at the invitation of Miss Donnelly, and she attended the circus with Elizabeth Bishop. This may have been the occasion, recalled later by Bishop, when she had to distract the mother elephant momentarily while Moore clipped hairs from the baby—she knew that only baby elephant hairs had the right talismanic properties, securing health and good luck. She had two months earlier gotten a humorous letter from Warner in which he wrote a mocking dialogue between the Oracle and Rat, and described Rat as being surrounded by animals such as the jerboa and the pangolin. In the meantime someone had written her asking about her possible participation in an anthology of writings from The Dial, though this did not materialize. During the later months of the summer there was another trip to Norfolk, and in the fall, more work on her "story."

It would be several decades before Moore would gain the sort of appreciative audience in England that she was gaining in America. Perhaps some reviewers in England were resentful of Eliot's sponsorship of her work; perhaps it was a difference in idiom, for, despite her own considerable Anglophilia, Moore is a distinctly American poet. So it is no surprise that Moore did considerably better with two American reviewers than she had with the English. Her ardent supporter, Morton Zabel, published a long and thoughtful review in the March, 1936 issue of Poetry. He pointed out that the book had added six poems to those in Observation, while also dropping a few from the earlier collection. The most notable advance, according to Zabel, is "a greater luxuriance of detail, austere annotation having given way to a freer imaginative fascination." He characterized very well her use of animals, saying that "only when the physical reality of the creature has become so passionately accepted and comprehended" then its "external appearance, noted with the laconic felicity of science, is indistinguishable from its spirit, and all the banalities of allegory can be discarded." The poems "have avoided using the simplifications of the lyric tradition," and so when "they present a thought, they do so in terms of all the accidents, analogies, and inhibitory influences that went into its formulation." Not since Williams' essay ten years earlier in *The Dial* had attention been called to Moore's use of poetry as an instrument of thought as well as feeling. The limitations in Moore's poetry, which Zabel does not specify, he attributes only to "a contented but passionate humility."

The other American review of substance was written by Wallace Stevens, in the December, 1935 issue of *Life and Letters Today*. Stevens begins by talking about Moore's use of sound patterns, but he then passes on to her subjects and her strategies. In another essay Stevens had called Williams the poet of the unpoetic, a charge, by the way, that upset Williams, because he saw himself as engaged in the obliteration of such categories. But when he comes to characterize Moore, Stevens uses an unexpected term: romantic. In speaking of "The Steeple-Jack," Stevens says, "Out of her whales and the college student and Poole and the danger signs she composes a poem simple, radiant with imagination, contemporaneous, displaying everywhere her sensitive handling. The poem leaves one indubitably convinced that she leans to the romantic." By romantic here Stevens refers to an atmosphere in Moore's work, of spontaneity, sensitivity, and contemporaneity, rather than to any actual adherence to beliefs found in English Romantic poetry. He goes on to say he doesn't mean romantic in the pejorative sense of "obsolescent," but rather just the opposite, "the living and at the same time the imaginative, the youthful, the delicate." Stevens shows his predilection for striking critical formulations when he compares Moore as a romantic to "the most brilliant instance of the romantic" in the sense in which he means it: Eliot. Here he has reference to Eliot's habit of "hybridization," of combining the past and the present in such a way as to create the future. Near the end Stevens, referring to her "wit" and "probity," addresses the question of Moore's "eccentricity" with equal boldness: "Miss Moore's form is not the quirk of a self-conscious writer. She is not a writer. She is a woman who has profound needs." In the summer of 1935, before she could have seen this review, Moore was at work on an essay about Stevens' *Ideas of Order* for *The Criterion*, and she was to praise his work with the same intensity that he devoted to hers.

All in all, with a few exceptions such as the review by Stevens, Moore's *Selected Poems* was not accorded anything like instant recognition as a masterpiece. Though it is the volume that would anchor her reputation, and is one of the milestones of American modernism, few early readers publicly testified to its range and depth of thought and feeling. This was partly due to the surface brilliance of the poems, their descriptive sheen sometimes being understood as the main, even the sole, aesthetic delight. Moore's modernism creates, among other things, a new relationship between surface and depth, largely through its use of a metonymic structure of thought and argument. The part and the whole, the cause and the effect, the outer detail and the inner principle are often exchanged for one another in Moore's poetry. Meanwhile, the simplifications of the lyric traditions, as one critic put it, are avoided in favor of an exuberance of syntax and lexical choice. The poetry has decided to dazzle rather than to lull the reader, and for many people, even professional reviewers, this turns out to be tiring or frustrating. Eventually Moore's poetry will be seen as thoughtful and deeply felt, and then the technical means can assume a more balanced role in the critical estimation.

III. *The Pangolin*

Even before all the reviews of *Selected Poems* had appeared, Moore was at work on another book of poems, called *The Pangolin*. Just as Bryher had joined with H.D. in 1921 in publishing Moore's first volume of poems, she was again instrumental in bringing out one of Moore's books, and again in a limited edition. Moore first mentioned the book in a letter written to her brother on February 2, 1935. The pressure for new poems had grown on several accounts; Eliot wanted something for *The Criterion*, and Mrs. Moore wanted her to give something to *Poetry* (perhaps in return for Zabel's good offices), but most urgent of all was Bryher. She wanted to publish a book of Moore's poems in a fine-press limited edition, to be printed by Maurice Danastière, a famous European artisan. Also of great moment was the desire to have the edition illustrated by George Plank, for whom Moore felt high regard, not least because he had represented the avant-garde to her back in Carlisle.

The writing of the poems in this book occupied Moore for much of 1934 and 1935. Though the book appeared in 1936, in a small run and hence not widely circulated, it marks Moore's first major statement after the appearance of her *Selected Poems*. In it are included what are perhaps two of Moore's best poems, one on an animal and one on a place, "The Pangolin" and "Virginia Britannia." In some sense, it set the pattern for the rest of Moore's publishing of her own poetry. After *The Pangolin* appeared in 1936, she published five more individual volumes, all of them fairly slim, on the average of one volume about every five years. But *The Pangolin* can be read as Moore's masterpiece, the high-water mark of her developing poetic skills and a tightly integrated book in its own right. In this book her modernism reaches new levels of sophistication as Moore gathers together a number of important modernist themes into striking harmony. Bryher's early sense of Moore as occupying another realm, of existing in a different sort of temporality, is more than reaffirmed by the poet's masterpiece. A very good argument could be made that in Moore's special brand of modernism there is no call for masterpieces, at least such as those produced by some of her male contemporaries. It is not only the distinctive, but the distinctively valuable, contribution of her special adaptation of modernist principles that obviates the desire for works of such scale and wilful innovation. Hers is an intimate modernism, almost precious, but redeemed from mere preciosity by great skill and moral balance.

The five poems in the book—the four poems ("Virginia Britannia," "Smooth Gnarled Crape Myrtle," "Bird-Witted," and "Half-Deity") that make up the sequence called "Old Dominion" and the single poem "The Pangolin"—articulate fully Moore's ideas of the peculiar historical and aesthetic pressures faced by the American artist. Taken together as a single work, these poems echo many of the great themes of modernist poetry, and yet no one would ever mistake it for the work of any other poet. But in bringing the poems together into a single book, Moore once again turned for advice to the poet who had helped her only months before in the question of arranging the format of a volume. In a series of letters written while the *Selected Poems* was still freshly published, Moore sought out Eliot's advice on the sequence of poems in *The Pangolin*. In fact she wrote and asked for this advice before she had even finished writing all the poems in the "Old Dominion" sequence, and before she decided to include "The Pangolin" in the volume. This necessitated her writing again to suggest a different order after Eliot had answered by approving her first proposal. He graciously approved the new proposal. It seems from their correspondence that Moore needed Eliot's validation more than any actual advice. Her own sense of how to arrange the poems was clearly a good one, and it is how they appeared: the "Old Dominion" sequence first, opening with "Virginia Britannia," and that sequence followed by "The Pangolin," which would give the volume its title. Moore had earlier requested that Eliot expand his 1923 *Dial* review on her to serve as an introduction to the *Selected Poems,* and many if not all of the reviewers of that volume made a point of mentioning Eliot's introduction. Moore doubtlessly saw Eliot's approval as a public "safeguard" for her poetry as well as a genuine personal testament.

In concert with these larger contexts of identification, Moore used Eliot's poetic practice in a detailed way. In the typescript of the review of his *Collected Poems* she published in *The Nation,* Moore cited the entirety of Eliot's poem "Cape Ann." The lines are redolent with the imagery of "the behavior of birds" and what we might call the "music of geography," both crucially central motifs in the "Old Dominion" sequence.

> O quick quick quick, quick hear the song-sparrow,
> Swamp-sparrow, fox-sparrow, vesper-sparrow
> At dawn and dusk. Follow the dance
> Of the goldfinch at noon. Leave to chance
> The Blackburnian warbler, the shy one. Hail
> With shrill whistle the note of the quail, the bob-white
> Dodging by bay-bush. Follow the feet
> Of the walker, the water-thrush. Follow the flight
> Of the dancing arrow, the purple martin. Greet
> In silence the bullbat. All are delectable. Sweet sweet sweet
> But resign this land at the end, resign it
> To its true owner, the tough one, the sea-gull.
> The palaver is finished.

There are details here that might catch the eye of those interested in sources; for example, Eliot's "bullbat" might become the "bulbul" of Moore's "Smooth Gnarled Crape Myrtle," especially since for her that odd, "broadly generic term" for sparrow is described as singing in "pure Sanskrit," a language Moore may well have associated with Eliot. She would doubtlessly recall his use of Sanskrit sources in *The Waste Land*. But there is also the way the poem ends with a figure of solitary dominance, as "the tough one" could easily apply not only to the John Smith of "Virginia Britannia" but also the featured animal in "The Pangolin." Eliot's poem could have helped justify Moore's interest in lists and details as ways of rendering a justice to the mimetic functions of art, while the sudden "uplift" of the poem's conclusion announces its theme, the need of the solitary figure to dominate space through expressive gesture, a theme that plays an important part in all the poems of *The Pangolin*. Furthermore, Eliot was not the only influence at work during the time Moore was writing the poems that were to make up *The Pangolin*. At least two other major modernists were also much on her mind: Wallace Stevens and Gertrude Stein.

A decade before, Moore had reviewed Stein's *Making of Americans* in the February, 1926 issue of *The Dial*. In addition to having recently seen "Four Saints in Three Acts," she had again recently delved deeply into Stein's published work. While working on a review of *The Geographical History of America*, a review that appeared in the October 24, 1936 issue of *The Nation*, she read all of the author's previously published books, a practice Moore applied to all her reviews, especially those of her contemporaries. In the case of Stein, Moore was influenced not only by the free and experimental use of form but by the content as well. In her review, Moore quoted from the "Introduction" by Thornton Wilder, which spelled out the importance of the relationship between geography and culture. This, of course, was a major subject in the "Old Dominion" sequence, and while Moore had earlier written poems about place, clearly the subject was to be treated in a more intensive way in her poems about Virginia and the colonial roots of American culture. Here is Moore paraphrasing Wilder:

> . . . the emergences of the Human Mind were dependent upon the geographical situations in which the authors lived—flat land conducing to the ability to escape from identity, hilly land conducing to the specific and the insistent.

Perhaps Moore's skeptical mind would question the scientific accuracy of these examples, but the general idea is presented as an important one.

Moore also uses this review to announce two other subjects, both of which have a strong bearing on modernism. The first concerns the relation of the artist to her audience, and the second deals with originality. About the audience, Moore has this point to make:

> When an author writes as if he were alone, without thought of an audience, "for an audience never does prove to you that you are you," it is this which makes a masterpiece.

Here again we might assume that Moore would react with some skepticism about such a bold notion, but certainly she had turned over in her mind during the last ten years the possibility that her work would never be accepted by a large audience. Moreover, ever since her days at Bryn Mawr when she was reading about William James and individualism, she had been concerned with problems of personal identity and integrity. She had written Alyse Gregory in March, 1930, shortly after leaving The Dial, that it wasn't possible for exacting minds to be popular. But she didn't stop with this pessimistic assessment, for she added a claim that has an edge of rebellion in it, insisting that she wasn't going to surrender her vision or her desire to be widely known, but she also wasn't sure just how she would achieve this singular feat. The allegorical treatment of the isolated artist existing as a metaphorical explorer of new territory might have been just the legerdemain that she eventually developed for herself.

As for the second idea, the question of originality, she says that "there can be an effect of originality as one can achieve a kind of Venetian needlepoint by fitting into each other two pieces of a hackneyed pattern of peasant edging." Here the idea of montage serves to generate an original work by linking with delicate, precise craft what William Carlos Williams called those things that have "peasant traditions to give them / character." Significantly, Moore calls the peasant part of the montage "hackneyed" and leaves the resulting Venetian needlepoint unqualified, presumably because she more highly values its cultural worth. But the idea of taking archaic material and turning it into a sophisticated object by skillful cutting and joining obviously stands behind Moore's use of quotations and other "research" material in The Pangolin as well as many of her other poems. In Moore's discussion of Stein there are subjects common in both writers' work at this time: an attempt to use, with solitary rigor, an experimental means of composition to produce an original account of how "emergent" minds are both related to and expressive of the soil that nourishes them.

Moore was always somewhat divided in her response to Stein, never quite sure that the weight of content was equal to the struggle with the older woman's densities of style. The case was different, however, with the other literary figure involved in the background of The Pangolin: Wallace Stevens. Moore worked on a review of Stevens' Ideas of Order during the summer of 1935, and it appeared in Eliot's Criterion in January, 1936. The review is very tightly argued, clearly the result of a deep engagement with the work at hand. Further, Stevens was to be the subject of reviews by Moore throughout her career, and her letters to him have some of the air of respect we can see in the correspondence with Eliot. The Criterion review is a virtual handbook of both thematic and stylistic concerns for Moore, as well as being an insightful appraisal of early Stevens. Moore's working out of her own interests in a review of a contemporary did not obscure or grossly distort the other writer's work; this is what makes her as unique in her criticism as she was in her poetry.

The most important issue in the review is the problem of symbolism, or more exactly, how the poet can create a language that will reveal and contain higher truth while not abandoning accurate observation and mimetic consistency. Moore announces this concern early in the review by stating that "realism need not restrict itself to grossness." We can hear in this somewhat diffident claim the gist of the nineteenth-century battle over subject matter, which began as early as Delacroix and Courbet, and ended with Joyce's Ulysses. Modernism's roots in realism were as often entangled with issues of gross or mundane subject matter as they were with issues of artistic style. Moore was herself sensitive on the issue, as was evident not only in her rejecting pieces for The Dial that she considered indelicate, but also by her consenting to her mother's wish to have photographs of three Maillol nudes canceled from one issue. It would be much too simple to say that Moore felt Stevens had shown the way through this complex of issues, but in important ways he had pointed out the direction.

Put most directly, Moore saw in Stevens a poetry of great inward force in which surface and depth were integrated. Her writing would resemble his in that both could lovingly, even sensuously, linger over the surfaces of description while yet integrating this with a meditative and discursive energy. She saw this integration in his work, as she often sought it in her own poetry, as partaking of an animal grace:

> Poetry is an unintelligible unmistakeable vernacular like the language of the animals—a system of communication whereby a fox with a turkey too heavy to carry, reappears shortly with another fox to share the booty, and Wallace Stevens is a practiced hand at this kind of open cypher.

This witty passage can itself be read allegorically, for we can see Moore as the second fox, come to Stevens' aid in carrying the burden of his poetry. Moore was clearly conscious of poetry as a sort of burden, and this awareness was joined in her mind with the questions of an audience and originality, the same questions she discussed regarding Stein. In praising Stevens she says, "In America where the dearth of rareness is conspicuous, those who recognize it are compelled to acknowledgment." "Those who recognize" rareness may include herself as well as Stevens, but clearly the audience is restricted in number. Moore here takes up the arguments about indigenous American art and its ability to proclaim its own native genius, arguments that raged throughout the 1920's. Since her plans to visit Norfolk, Virginia, to see her brother were already made at this time, and she had begun her preparatory reading for the trip, such questions about the national genius, its depth, and the scope of its audience were likely to be part of her consciousness. But as important to Moore as art's national character was the question of what sort of special kind of activity it was, and it was here that she tried hard to capture Stevens' particular genius. After quoting several passages from his poems, she puts the matter this way, saying that poetry is:

> a classifying, a botanizing, a voracity of contemplation, a pleasure, an indulgence, an infatuation in which the actual is a deft beneficence.

This may well be the best possible short description of Moore's poetics, as well as Stevens'. Though this description is largely based on an outside perspective, it ends with an infatuation and what we might call the blessings of the objective—"the actual is a deft beneficence." It possesses, too, that sense of tension and irony that we associate with modernism, as it uses an oxymoron like "voracity of contemplation" to capture the balance of desire and watchfulness that will become one of the main thematic resolutions in The Pangolin. But by seeing the beneficence of the actual as deft, Moore is again reaffirming that "realism need not restrict itself to grossness." A word like "actual" allows Moore to focus on her infatuation with accuracy without being labeled as "realistic."

But it is not only the blessings of the objective world that Moore sees in Stevens' poetry, for she is also very inventive in formulating his strategies for both disposing and displacing the self inside the poem. Therefore she approaches the questions of inner states of awareness, the subjective world, as well:

> . . . the as if sentimental unsentimentality, the meditativeness not for appraisal, with hints taken from the birds, as in Brahms, they [Stevens' poems] much recall Brahms; his dexterousness, but also his self-relish and technique of evasion as in the incident of the lion huntress who was enquiring for the celebrated Herr Brahms: you will find him yonder, on the other side of the hill; this is his brother.

Moore skillfully integrates the notion of animal language with the concern for artistic solitude and self-regard by turning to the anecdote about Brahms. This anecdote allows her to present artistic evasiveness as something that must be practiced with a witty and graceful manner, and also to suggest that such evasiveness is the direct and unavoidable cost of the special kind of "self-relish" necessary for artistic activity. This mediates between artistic isolation as a desirable necessity and as the unpleasant consequence of unappreciative audiences, such as one might find in America, "where the dearth of rareness is conspicuous." Eventually Moore's attitude about fame and public recognition will change, but in the late 1930's she seemed resigned to solitude.

As for the question of form, Moore turns to musical concepts to convey a complexity that never loses its principle of integration. She had spent a great deal of time listening to classical music on the radio during the early months of 1935, the radio having been left her by Warner when he went off on his tour to Samoa in 1931, when the public transmission of classical music was just beginning. Again, as in all the other passages quoted here, Moore describes an artistic practice that is clearly her own as well as Stevens' when she characterizes his poetic form, a form that employs "the principle of dispersal common to music; that is to say, a building up of the theme piecemeal in such a way that there is no possibility of disappointment at the end." Moore's poetry often proceeds by a series of metonymic connections, in which a figure or term will connect in a non-linear, associative way with the following one. Another way to see this poetic practice is to think of it as a form of dispersal, a "piecemeal" building up of the poem's structure until the conclusion can reassert a metaphoric or thematic consistency. Moore's sense of poetic closure is among the surest of the modernists. Here the development of the shell of the chambered nautilus or the outer integument of the pangolin can serve as illustration, showing that an incremental process of growth is held in tension with a teleological foundation that is not always apparent when the focus is on the details. Finally, for Moore the complexity of Stevens might well involve "a pleasure, an indulgence, an infatuation," but he was at the same time "as serious as the starving-times of the first settlers." In this image can be heard the echoes of the reading in colonial history and Virginia geography that Moore was deeply engaged in during the months prior to her trip south in the summer of 1934. But we can also catch a hint of one of the crucial metaphoric equations that will serve to unify *The Pangolin:* that between the explorer and the artist, both being figures who must confront adversity in the form of fear and solitude in order to further the emergence of the human mind.

In *The Pangolin,* Moore worked out of a very intense sense of place, as she tried both before and after her trip to Norfolk to comprehend a landscape until then unknown to her. In a very real sense it was to be Warner's landscape; indeed she mentions in a later letter how he tended to act too overbearing in his role as guide for her and her mother. But when Moore places a male explorer in the center of "Virginia Britannia" she does so in part to allegorize the struggle of artists like Stevens, Stein, Eliot, and herself, artists whom she saw as extremely sensitive to how their struggle for excellence set them apart from many other people in America. The modernist tension that resulted from a recurrent equation between the aesthetic and the ethical realms caused her to seek mediating figures such as Raleigh, who could abstractly serve to show the way through to a poised and ironic sense of the individual and the culture he or she both expressed and evaded.

In several letters exchanged among them, especially those after the summer visit was completed, all three Moores spoke of their time together in Norfolk with a special feeling reserved for their most deeply cherished memories. Mrs. Moore wrote to Warner after the trip that his having caught a black swallowtail butterfly was the high point of last summer, and she goes on to describe what Moore's poems about that special period embody. In doing so she mentions the mockingbird and its young offspring that were to become the subject of another of the poems in *The Pangolin*. Mrs. Moore also wrote of their time alone, referring to the absence of Constance, and the fact that she and her daughter would spend the days alone while Warner was attending to his duties on the ship. This feeling of specialness is also the reaction Warner had to the finished poems, for he was to write in very fulsome terms to his sister after receiving his copy of the illustrations for *The Pangolin*. The precision and elliptical quality of George Plank's illustrations he compared to Bacon's essays, favorites of Moore as Warner well knew, and their suggestive mysticism he compared to mountain light. Such a letter showed Warner's judgment presumably borrowed from his sister's, and that his sense of her work, and the aptness of the illustrations for it, was informed by many discussions with her.

If Moore saw herself as an artist in the figure of the pangolin, she also saw her brother, as a public man, in the figure of John Smith. His approval was as desirable as his stature was admirable. Happily for Moore, when Warner saw the indirect products of the summer visit, that is, the drawings by George Plank, his rapturous praise and rhetoric of religious exaltation were hardly surprising. Warner had spoken before, and would again, of Moore's poetry in terms that were essentially religious and inspirational rather than merely aesthetic or pleasurable. However diffident and offhanded Moore might have been about her poetry on various public occasions, in her immediate family circle it was seen as something very like the missionary work of a religious figure. Tension existed between the frankly public rhetoric of the poems of this period and the continuing sense that she was writing a special coded language that was especially relevant to Warner, Mrs. Moore, and herself.

That she approached the writing of the poems in *The Pangolin* with seriousness and a sort of awe is apparent from the amount of research she devoted to them. The research was perhaps most extensive for "Virginia Britannia," Moore's major poem about geography and civic virtue. When she wrote an appreciation of William Carlos Williams for *The Dial*, in 1927, she had quoted Henry James in approving of Williams' poetry of place, and went on to say that the poet's "feeling for the *place* lends poetic authority to the illusion of ours, that sustenance may be found here, which is adapted to artists." While centering in its opening stanzas on the figure of John Smith, the early leader and explorer of the newly founded colony, "Virginia Britannia" expands to a meditation on the national character and its engagement with the fallenness of our collective historical existence. Schematically, the poem's structure might be framed like this: Stanzas I–III, John Smith and the historical past; Stanzas IV–VIII, the mockingbird and other animal and floral symbols of the country; Stanzas IX–XII, the collective moral character of the colonists as a present-day legacy. Such a scheme blurs some key details, for example the way animal images occur throughout, but it shows the musical dispersal that Moore spoke of in regard to Stevens, how the poem moves from a strongly historical atmosphere to a modern landscape. The opening stanza, for example, is dominated by reference to "England's Old / Dominion" and a "tomb" that contains the remains of an early settler. The final stanza ends with a current-day sunset and mention of the town's economically preoccupied inhabitants, who are "bothered with wages."

Moore develops the poem's ironic tensions in both the past and current-day contexts. She introduces John Smith only after referring to the tomb of one Sir George Yeardley, and another unnamed parishioner who is memorialized as "a great sinner." Smith is brought to center stage, described as "continuously / exciting," but while "patient with / his inferiors" he was a "pugnacious equal." The egalitarianism of the new colony comes out sounding very ambiguous, indeed, just as earlier Smith had been called "an able / sting-ray-hampered pioneer— / painted as a Turk." These lines refer to an incident where Smith was bitten by a sting-ray, thereby conferring a name on Sting Ray Point in the Chesapeake Bay, and to the habit of painting oneself as imperious in order to impress patrons and supporters. This ambiguous moral portrait of Smith is further delineated by Moore's mention of Smith's odd coat of arms, with an ostrich, gold horseshoe, and Latin motto. The ostrich and the horseshoe symbolize the animal's mythical ability to digest hard metal, a quality Moore celebrated in another poem, "He 'Digesteth Hard Yron.'" The Latin motto, her later note tells us, reads *vincere est vivere*—to conquer is to live. But Smith is both the victim of natural forces and an unstoppable force himself, in other words a leader and a typically representative early settler.

Reading Moore's portrait of Smith might recall not only the Gertrude Stein of the *Making of Americans* but the skeptical positivism of Henry Adams' view of history. Adams, a Northerner, took great delight in debunking the historical myth that had sprung up around Virginia and John Smith. For Adams the forces of history were not likely to be traceable to pure or consistent traits of character locatable in any hero, no matter how much larger than life-size local pride might render him. Smith's career was marked by a self-aggrandizement that was necessary in order to curry favor, but the limits of his form of "advertisements for myself" were very flexible indeed. Moore's attitude resembled Adams' to the extent that the carefully etched portrait she drew allowed more than one of Smith's flaws to show through. The difference in attitude, however, was in the relation between the larger, heroic figures of history and the collective or communitarian traits and destinies of the people they may be described as expressing representatively. Moore, for all the skepticism that lay behind her irony and tension, still believed that the character of heroes was instructive, a key to didactic interpretation, though not necessarily an actual template for everyday behavior. Ironically, more recent historical research has shown that Smith's accounts of his own exploits, while exaggerated, may have more ground in truth than was once thought possible. While Moore's poem is not an exercise in critical historicism, she did read her sources with a characteristically skeptical eye, while at the same time maintaining allegiance to a view of history that honors the force of "representative men." The poem also conveys an underlying suggestion that Moore is questioning America's status as a mythical "redeemer nation."

Moore's echo of Wordsworth in the poem's last image, where the scene is described as being "to the child an intimation of / what glory is," reveals that the subject of fallenness has been central to the poem from the beginning—as is usually the case in poems about gardens and flowers. Moore might also have had Marvell's "The Garden" in mind, especially considering the poem's subtle ironies. If the poem deals with fallenness, then it does so in images of cruelty and domination that are not presented with cruel tones. Moore's central image of fallenness is expressed with an evasive negative, another device she might have borrowed from Wordsworth, as well as from her own "Comment" columns in *The Dial,* and one especially suited to her diffident tensions. She moves from a horticultural form of domineering to a human, historical sort:

> The strangler fig, the dwarf—
> fancying Egyptian, the American,
> the Dutch, the noble
> Roman, in taking what they
> pleased—colonizing as we say—
> were not all intel-
> lect and delicacy.

The wit here is in part located in the euphemistic phrase "colonizing as we say," where one can hear echoed the bitterly satiric passage about colonization in the fourth book of Swift's *Gulliver's Travels*. The moral worth "we" manifest is implicated in the euphemistic words, our attempt to treat objectively a process that is built on a refusal to recognize that "a black savage . . . is not all brawn and animality." At the same time there are trees that "imply amity," and tyranny can rule merely as a kind of "taste" in clothing; in other words our all-too-human failings can be incorporated into the community and their destructive force thereby dissipated by the dailiness of life. We can see and not see, we can conquer and yet be contained. The contradictory nature of Smith and his emblematic bird has been extended to the body politic.

Such a thoroughly ironized picture of a garden can hardly be concluded with a simple upbeat affirmation of civic value. The ending of the poem was, in fact, a passage of great difficulty for Moore. There is one typed version of the poem that has several alternate versions of the final stanza. But if we assume that the poem's conclusion does try to gather up the "piecemeal" presentation of the theme in a way that avoids disappointment, then we should not be surprised to see a formulation steeped in irony and grammatical complexity. What is clear about the concluding stanza as it appeared in *The Pangolin* is that it strives for harmony even while enunciating particulars, and that it ends not with a reality but with an "intimation." Clearly the horizon of the sky above the town is meant to serve as a moral reminder of possible glory, if not as a scourge of actual failings.

> The live oak's rounded
> mass of undulating boughs, the white
> pine, the aged hackberry—handsomest vis-
> itor of all—the
> cedar's etched solidity,

> the cypress, lose identity
> and are one tree, as
>   sunset flames increasingly
>   against their leaf-chis-
> elled blackening ridge of green;
> and the redundantly wind-
> widened clouds expanding to
> earth size above the
>   town's bothered with wages
>   childish sages,
> are to the child an intimation of
>   what glory is.

It is not only as an echo of Wordsworth's integrated visionary power that these lines present the image of unity. The witty play with the motto of "*e pluribus unum*" and the horticultural harmony prefigure the putative social and political harmony that allowed the settlers to transform the historical colony into the current-day nation. The outline of the trees, observed with the sort of modernist clarity Moore so avidly sought, is itself a figure of tension, as the ridge of green, an emblem of hope, is simultaneously seen as "blackening." Moore might have learned this sort of ironic resolution by reading the close of Stevens's "Sunday Morning." In any case, the moral ambiguity of the vision is enmeshed in the visual complexity of the imagery. The playfulness of the "redundantly wind / widened clouds" suggests that the intimated glory may be the sort of spectacle *only* a child can see. After all, the grandeur of the clouds is being excessively expanded to cover, if not occlude, the earth where the species must find its habitation. If the town's "childish sages" are too "bothered with wages" to see nature's glory, for the child, however, it is only a virtual representation of the substantial habits the adult must struggle toward. The child's "view" of the glory is heavily conditioned and contextualized, not only by its own lack of years but also by the weight of historical consciousness. In some sense the theme of the poem might be a version of Eliot's phrase, "After such knowledge, what forgiveness?" But Moore is neither as negative as Eliot at his most lugubrious, nor as affirmative as Wordsworth at his most mystical. And we must remember the glorious light comes from a sunset, not a sunrise.

Moore made extensive revisions to this poem. The version she chose to reprint, and to include in her *Complete Poems,* does not include the mention of sages "bothered with wages." The most obvious point of the revision is that it makes the poem less socially and historically pointed. But to trace the development of Moore's revisions, scholars will need a variorum edition of the poems; this will be an undertaking that requires great skill, because Moore's habit of revising extensively began early and continued late.

"Virginia Britannia" says that nature can provide us with images of civic grandeur, just as animals can emblematize our human qualities, but nature can never eradicate the weight of history with its inconsistencies and its lack of humility. In part, Moore is answering the writers of the 1920's, such as Waldo Frank, who felt America could create a cultural renaissance simply by an act of will. The despair of history is offset by the glory of nature, but nature's glory is conditioned by history's lack of "intellect and delicacy." This theme is fully articulated in the poem, and serves as a backdrop for the other poems in *The Pangolin.* This interplay of historical and natural values parallels the complex intersection of culture and nature that was, throughout her career, Moore's most important subject. Though her modernism was to resemble in many ways the secularism of other artists, such as Joyce and Williams, Moore always had an essentially Christian understanding of guilt and innocence. Her notions of fallenness were never to be treated in the poetry in anything like ecclesiastical terms, however, since she was able to address such matters without frequent resort to biblical or explicitly religious imagery. For her, fallenness was a condition that was best expressed in cultural terms: to be fallen was the ground, the very condition of culture. And yet nowhere was her modernism more in evidence than in her sense that in and through culture we address our fallenness and even combat it, but with no hope of conquering it in merely cultural terms.

In "Bird-Witted" Moore continues to explore the tensions of innocence and fallenness, but in a more playful vein. The subject of innocence has a biographical origin. She described the birds outside her window—and compared herself to them—in great detail in two letters, one to Warner, and another to Bryher. The letters were typical of her daily accounts of things, where she represented natural phenomena in terms of both nature, as when she compared the birds to penguins, and culture, as in the figure of the tone of a broken carriage-spring. The letters also show clearly how the poem had its origin in Moore's family feelings, as the bird nest obviously symbolizes the trio of mother, daughter, and son. At the climactic moment of drama in "Bird-Witted," the parent is seen as "darting down," paradoxically "nerved by what chills / the blood," and the bird is "by hope rewarded—of toil." The syntax is not straightforward here, but the meaning seems to be that hope is rewarded only when there is the attendant toil—surely a sentiment in which Mrs. Moore and both her children would emphatically concur. If the birds' nest is seen as a sort of "flower bed" or garden of innocence, then it requires more than vigilance to protect it.

Moore wrote of "Bird-Witted" in terms that might well support a complex reading of the poem, for she was to claim for it a tightness of form and a level of struggle that are considerable. Along with "The Paper Nautilus" of a few years later, "Bird-Witted" is Moore's reflection on the closeness of maternal love, and also the dynamic tensions it can create in the drama of individuation. In a letter to Warner on November 27, 1934, Mrs. Moore, called "Mouse," is described as having shared the compositional process with her daughter, and the poet saw herself in animal terms, as well as a protective, maternal figure. Being "bird-witted" for Moore may well have involved not only a feeling of belonging to a well-guarded nest but also having the self-protection needed to achieve one's own expressiveness.

Moore's artistry and expressiveness reaches a peak with "The Pangolin," in large part because it shows her ability to merge inner values and outer surfaces with playful ingenuity and yet serious intent. From the poem's opening phrase—"Another armored animal"—we hear that tone of surety that results when an artist has come to know fully her material and to have seen that it fully serves her thematic aims. In some ways "The Pangolin" is the most positive, self-possessed poem of the book that shares its title. Moore has often been discussed as if she had little or no interest in public matters outside of manners and decorum. Her concerns with decorum, however, as well as with perpetual accuracy and artistic responsiveness, have a moral dimension that is fulfilled on a public scale. Too often Moore's concern with armoring and armored animals has been taken to suggest something like hermeticism, as if the armor were equivalent to the monk's walls in his cell. But armor was designed to allow people to go *into* the world, not avoid it.

And so Moore understood that the pangolin is a nocturnal, isolated animal, stealthy and seldom seen, but its solitariness is in the service of genuine virtues: patience, skill, and the wise use of strength.

The witty equation between pangolin and artist gets a playful introduction in the poem's opening stanza:

> This near artichoke
>   with head and legs and grit-equipped giz-
> zard, the night miniature artist-
>   engineer, is   Leonardo's
>   indubitable son? Im-
>   pressive animal
> and toiler, of whom we seldom hear.

The pedigree is a conditioned one, for the pause after "is" indicates not only hesitation but an awareness of the implausible nature of the identification with Leonardo, even if it is only through paternal lineage. The "is" is also highlighted by the comic rhyme with the jutting "giz" two lines before. Moore first locates her metaphoric frame in the world of nature, with the artichoke, before turning to the world of culture with Leonardo. The pangolin is not only a dreamy artist figure, but an "artist-engineer," a creature who masters its environment by purposive activity. This constitutes one connection with the explorer figure of "Virginia Britannia"; while we "seldom hear" of the pangolin, in contrast to John Smith's self-publicizing, the animal has some of the explorer's inconsistency, for it is later described as " 'Fearful yet to be feared.' "

Having begun the identification of animal and artist with her usual tentative touch, Moore is freed to explore the pangolin's habits in a way that can easily be read as an allegory of the moon-struck romantic artist. We enjoy several levels of identification when he:

> endures
>   exhausting solitary
>   trips through unfamiliar ground at night
>   returning before sunrise; stepping
>
>   in the moonlight,   on the moonlight
>   peculiarly, that the out-

> side edges of his
> hands may bear the weight and save the claws
> for digging. Serpentined about
> the tree, he draws
> away from
> danger unpugnaciously,
> with no sound but a harmless hiss; keep-
> ing the fragile grace of the Thomas-
> of Leighton-Buzzard Westminster
> Abbey wrought iron vine, or
> rolls himself into a ball that has
> power to defy all effort
> to unroll it . . .

Again, a pause after the first moonlight suggests Moore is about to lift the level of suspended disbelief needed to tease out the implications of the animal's grace. The economy of the animal/artist is what is perhaps most striking, how he saves his claws for digging, how he allows only a "harmless hiss" to express his fear and disregard, and how, like the durably wrought ironwork of the Abbey's tomb, his fragility is in part illusory. It is no wonder that Moore can end a stanza with a peroration in which the ability to live and even prosper in alternating states can be the distinctive mark of both man and animal. The lines recall one of Moore's favorite authors, Sir Thomas Browne, and his desire to live in "divided and distinguished worlds":

> Sun and moon and day and night and
> man and beast
> each with a splen-
> dor which man
> in all his vileness cannot
> set aside; each with an excellence!

Here Moore echoes not only Hamlet's awareness of man's divided nature but also her own phrase from another poem: "life's faulty excellence." This stanza ending also anticipates the poem's closing lines, where the sun is addressed as an "alternating blaze." Her sense of fallenness, the particular texture of human virtue, its excellencies and its limitations, is richly conveyed in the poem's structure.

It is directly to man's character that Moore turns in the poem's last three stanzas, not altogether abandoning the allegorical framework of animal grace, but emboldened enough to speak directly in a way that is altogether unique in her poetry. Though she draws an industrious picture of where "Beneath sun and moon, man slave[s] / to make his life more sweet," Moore is wry enough to point out that he "leaves half the / flowers worth having." She goes on to emblematize various human traits through the agencies of animal graces, until she presents him as "capsizing in // disheartenment." Drawing back from this near-tragic sense, Moore resorts to some Cummings-like typographical wit (the four "r's" being restored to three in the later editions) in order to leaven the theme's piecemeal presentation before the finale:

> Bedizened or stark
> naked, man, the self, the being
> so-called human, writing-
> master to this world, griffons a dark
> "Like does not like like that is
> obnoxious"; and writes errror with four
> r's. Among animals, one has a
> sense of humor . . .

The slight echo from *King Lear* is clearly ironic, as is the way that last wry sentence does and does not include man among the animals. But it is important to note that now man is the "writing-master," and so literature has a didactic function that links the aesthetic with the ethical. Moore had earlier said, in her array of animal emblems of human traits, that man was "in fighting, mechanicked / like the pangolin." Perhaps she had Leonardo's many militaristic "inventions" in mind. In any case, man is being praised and gently satirized at the same time.

The final stanza is a marvel of structural subtlety, since it refers equally to the pangolin and to man, an equivocation made possible by the closing lines of the penultimate stanza. The equivocation perhaps turns wittiest with the lines "Consistent with the / formula—warm blood, no gills, / two pairs of hands and a few hairs—that / is a mammal; there he sits in his / own habitat." Part of the humor here is the way the Dickinson-like use of riddle is called on to question the "formula" about mammalian identity, a very touchy point in biology. The pangolin, often taken for a reptile, has features that fit the mammalian formula sufficiently, even though they also allow him to be described in a way that applies with almost equal accuracy to humans. (Luckily we have one pair of hands *and* one of feet.) George Plank's drawing at the start of the poem shows a pangolin in a tree under the moon; the drawing at the end of the poem shows a man, clasping his face in his hands under a blazing sun. The identification of the two main subjects of the poem is very much to the point of the poem's argument. As Moore says earlier in the poem, "To explain grace requires / a curious hand." We might even speculate that she was using "curious" here in both its seventeenth-century sense of finely and intricately wrought as well as in the modern sense of desiring knowledge. In either case, the identification of man and pangolin is indeed curious.

Moore's concluding description continues the semantic balancing act of referring equally to man and animal. The irony is heightened as the affirmative salutation is uttered from a very bleak context.

> The prey of fear; he, always
> curtailed, extinguished,
> thwarted by the dusk, work partly done,
> says to the alternating blaze,
> "Again the sun!
> anew each
> day; and new and new and new,
> that comes into and steadies my soul."

Moore suspends the main verb "says" at some distance from the subject "he," and so allows the intervening four appositive clauses to wall in, as it were, the speaking subject. The clauses are semantically involved with forms of limitation and the air of failure, and the address is to a blaze that is far from steady. Yet the moral affirmation of the salutation itself leaps out to the reader from this set of fallen conditions in a way that speaks to the issues raised throughout the book, and throughout Moore's career as well. The sentiment, normally spoken with a cloying piety, is here saved from what might have been its own rhetorical excess by that special mixture of innocence and experience that has served to balance the speaker's authority and winsomeness, in large measure by the self-consciousness of her modes of representation.

In *The Pangolin*, and perhaps most impressively in the title poem, Moore achieved a rare balance between inner conflicts and outer symmetries. In part the achievement comes from a mastery of will, a self-discipline in working out the thematic consequences of her visions without abandoning didactic goals or stinting on artistic delights. In this she made a masterpiece out of her struggles. Her "animal poems" can also allegorically summarize complex poetry that struggles not only against adversity but its own complexity:

> Pangolins are
> not aggressive animals; between
>   dusk and day, they have the not un-
> chainlike, machine-
>   like form and
>   frictionless creep of a thing
>   made graceful by adversities, con-
>
> versities.

Adversities and conversities are complex inner and outer turnings, and like the depth and surfaces of a well-shaped poem, they must answer to the expediencies of form.

Moore received a prize in 1936—actually it was a belated $25 for the Earnest Hartsock prize of 1935 for the "The Frigate Pelican," which had appeared in *The Criterion* in 1934. She also made a gift of a walking stick to Sibley Watson; Watson's wife, Hildegarde, was to be one of Moore's closest friends throughout the second half of her life. This walking stick was to be the subject of a poem Moore published in the November issue of *Poetry* that same year. Another important friend entered Moore's life at this period, for Elizabeth Bishop introduced her to Louise Crane. Crane was the wealthy heiress of the Crane Paper Company fortune, and was an important source of social occasions for Moore. Eventually their friendship was to grow so strong that Moore would name Crane the executor of her estate; this came in part as a result of Crane's monetary support of Moore, and her giving Moore considerable legal help over the years. Moore also spent time in January typing up several pages of her "story," as she continued to call it; she was having trouble naming characters in it, but decided to call one after Oliver Simon, who had designed her *Selected Poems*. Many months in 1936 have no extant family correspondence from Moore and her mother; partly this is because they did spend some time that summer in

Norfolk with Warner, but also perhaps Warner destroyed or lost their letters.

But Moore does tell Warner about a visit George Plank paid her in April. He was very appreciative of what Warner had to say about his drawings. Warner was at this time involved in buying a new sailboat for himself. Several years before he had published, through the journal of the U.S. Naval Institute Proceedings (Volume 56, Number 6), an article on "Small Boat Sailing as a Character Builder in the United States Navy." It was his firm belief that such activity was important for the men who served with him, and he devoted a great deal of effort to organizing sailing races among the crew of his ship. This continued the sporting activities that he had pursued at Yale, and he also reported the results in detail to Moore and his mother. Of course, it would also serve further to link John Smith and Warner in his sister's mind. Moore herself was impressed with this activity of her brother, and she came to treat sailing as an important sport, though she was unable to take part very often. Her poems, of course, are filled with references to the sea, from the tragic threnody of "A Grave" to the optic delights of "The Fish."

In September, Moore's hat had been returned from the cleaners unblocked and she hated it and felt that it misrepresented her. After she and her mother were able to remedy the situation, they rejoiced and remarked more broadly on how pleasant their lives seemed. Later that fall Bryher was to deposit just over $90 in an account for Moore; this was perhaps a royalty payment for the poems in The Pangolin, but it also may have been the start of a fund Bryher had set up to help support Moore. Moore was also busy with writing, her own and that of others. She intervened at Poetry to get one of Bishop's poems accepted. And in October she wrote a tribute on the occasion of Harriet Monroe's death, which appeared in the December Poetry; it included a rather wry turn: "I can but reverently anticipate a continuously increasing expression of praise and gratitude for Miss Monroe from countless ones whose tribute would have astonished her." Miss Monroe's tributes have indeed increased, but surely it is Moore's own tribute that she has in mind when she speaks of one that would have astonished the founding editor of Poetry. There were also several of Moore's reviews to appear shortly, on Stevens, Eliot, Stein, Williams, and an anthology put out by New Directions. She wrote Stevens a personal note about Owl's Clover, in which she mentioned the world would probably overlook his virtues, and the artist had to make his poetry a gift of himself, but also a gift to himself. She also promised Warner that she would do no more reviews until her novel was finished, but it was a promise she didn't keep.

Her notebooks during the 1930's record many interests, and they reflect also how her creative energies seemed to be gaining momentum. She copied out passages about dragons from the *Illustrated London News*, a favorite source, and another from the *Saturday Evening Post* about Helen Wills, the tennis champion, whom Moore went to see play at Forest Hills. Later in the decade she herself began to play half an hour a day, though she was then in her fifties. She also copied out a passage from *Close-Up* on Eisenstein's use of montage and the "dynamization of perception," both ideas that would be incorporated into the technique of her poems. Research led her to a back issue of *National Geographic*, dated May, 1918, and an article on jerboas. A journal called *Landmark*, dated January, 1933, had an article on the grave of Pocahontas by T. E. Elias, which she would have been drawn to while she was working on the "Old Dominion" sequence.

From an unnamed source there are notes on Haile Selassie and his refusal to concede anything to Mussolini; these may have been in her mind when she mentions Selassie in a poem, "Leonardo da Vinci's," published twenty-five years later in *The New Yorker*. This may also have been her way of answering Pound's extravagant praise for the Italian dictator. The use of magazine material sometimes many years later, and the covert personal dimension of her poems, continued to be features of her work. And from Wyndham Lewis' journal called *The Tyro* she wrote out the sentence that said, "The myth that a man makes his transformations according as he sees himself a hero or villain . . ." In her mind at this time may have been not only her poem "The Hero," but her reading about John Smith and the early colonizing of America. For Smith and the "Virginia Britannia" poem, there are mentions of several possible sources: a *History of Hampton and Elizabeth City County, Virginia*, compiled by Lyon Tyler (Hampton, Virginia, 1922); a much older book, William Strachey's *Travaile into Virginia Britannia"*; and the *Travels and Works of Captain J. Smith*, ed. Edward Arber (Edinburgh, 1910). And there was a transcribed passage from an article by Alfred Jay Nock, in the September, 1934 *Atlantic*, on Artemis Ward that might have crystalized her thinking:

A nation is a soul, a spiritual principle evoked by the common possession of a rich legacy of remembrance & by the will to keep improving this hereditary property for the benefit of those who shall receive it hereafter. . . . The great literary artist is one who powerfully impresses a reader with a [sic] attitude of mind, a mood, a temper, a state of being, without describing it. If he describes it, if that is, he injects himself, the effect is lost.

Much of her thinking in the next several years is tied up with a way of being a force for public virtue while not being an exponent of one's own ego. In this effort she was setting herself against Pound in important ways, and relying, too, on the theories of the impersonality of the poet that she'd found in Eliot's criticism. She also records about this time the axiom that "it's better to be indefatigable than to get a thing right by chance the first time."

A number of lectures she heard at the Brooklyn Institute were also recorded in notes, and they almost certainly influenced her thinking during this period and beyond. On January 30, 1935, she heard a lecture by the English biologist and geneticist, J. B. S. Haldane, who spoke on how one could make a geological map of England based on the death rate of quarrymen who worked in the limestone deposits. The lecture based its arguments on the relationship between culture and geography. One month later she heard the Indian philosopher Dhan Gopal Mukerji speak on "Hindu Yoga and American Science." She was told that "a mind like Einstein's or Dante's or Dewey's . . . would be considered a yogi mind in India," for the "mind in abeyance watching humbly finds the secrets of mother nature." The modernist habit of training the mind to stay in "abeyance," combined with Moore's temperamental interest in nature, was here given a new reaffirmation of its purpose. She heard Thornton Wilder speak on motion pictures and literature. And she was told by Professor Edward G. Spaulding of Princeton that "the ethical regarding conduct is more important than the theological." She underlined the word "important" and took very detailed notes on this lecture. And, as if to echo Stevens' review of her work, the art critic for The New York Times, Edward Alden Jewell, on November 11, 1937, said that "at last the triumphant break with nature was achieved in a geometric abstract art. But romance flowed back into art by divers routes."

Warner was to be traveling a lot in 1937, spending the months between August and October up and down the eastern seaboard, having been assigned to the USS Arkansas for two years beginning in May. Moore wrote to him in January to say, among other things, that Bishop was the best of all her friends; her only complaint about the younger poet was that she always arrived late. In the same letter Moore mentioned her college days, recalling the impersonality of the roll call and the atmosphere of academic pride. These observations were directed at Warner's oldest daughter, Mary, who was soon to be of college age. In March, 1938, Moore received a "playbill" from Mary's school showing that she and her sister Sallie had both written plays that were performed by their classmates. Warner also found time to write a letter of thanks to his old Yale classmate William Benét to thank him for recommending that Moore be included in the *Oxford Anthology of American Literature*. Moore took her mother to see the Marx Brothers in "A Day at the Races," which Mrs. Moore objected to, but her daughter found delightful.

One of Moore's lasting desires as a writer was to master the vernacular, as she put it at one point. This meant that she was drawn to fiction, among other things, for the chances it offered a writer to catch the run of spoken language. She had practiced one of the elements of this craft in the recording of actual speech in her "Conversation Notebooks," begun as early as the late 1910's. Much of Moore's writing energies in the late 1930's and early 1940's was to be devoted to her novel. Since the novel has not been published, except for the chapter called "The Farm Show," it is only possible to talk about the work in a fragmentary way. Yet there are many references to it in the letters to Warner over the next few years, and so some sense of the book's development and subject can be glimpsed. She titled one chapter "Job's Protestations of Integrity." In October, 1939, she comments on Lester Littlefield's reaction to a scene in the work, in a chapter called "Standin[g] in the Need of Prayer." Littlefield had found that the English impressions in the narrative lacked a sense of the English population. He also suggested that Moore make one of the characters, called "Eloise," an orphan, advice that Moore apparently followed. Littlefield apparently typed or retyped portions of the story for Moore. He was a Dartmouth graduate, born in 1913, and a bibliographer and early commentator on the works of Pound. Later, in the 1960's, he had plans to do a bibliography of Moore's published work, but the project was never completed. At the time when he was advising Moore about the novel, he gave her a copy of Santayana's *The Last Puritan,* which he presumably saw as having similar aims. Though she told Warner that she realized her story would not shake the world, she complained that Santayana's novel had a certain "baseness." Warner was positive in urging her to keep at work on the story, and to submit it to Macmillan. Later, however, by the beginning of 1940, he suggested to her that it would be rejected, and by the end of January it was. In March, 1940 she wrote to Warner that she hoped to place the book with another publisher, and was trying to cut it with that in mind. Her letters to her brother indicate that the novel contains scenes set in Europe and in Maine, and one of its main characters is guilty of superficiality, disliking both the reverential and disciplined aspects of life.

It is fairly clear from these letters that Moore was putting into the novel in an explicit way her concerns about what she felt were the delinquent morals of the day. This impression is strengthened by a letter Warner sent her on February 27, 1939, where he said that whether the story is accepted or not, nothing would detract from the book as a record of their shared philosophy. There is also an undated letter from Moore to Warner in the same year, and perhaps sent around November, in which she says the work is tedious and needs much correction. Taking into account the stilted quality of the published portion of the novel, and assuming that the major influence was Henry James, it is evident that Moore's concern with social morality and decorum was not something she could translate into a natural sounding fiction.

Moore was also reading intensively a book by Bliss Perry, called *And Gladly Teach.* It was a book that she refers to many times throughout the next decades, and its sense of moral service to society obviously supported the values she had gotten from her mother and the notion of "service" that was prevalent during her Bryn Mawr days. The beginning of 1938 brought some bad news from the net of Bryn Mawr associations, however: Mary Norcross died in the middle of February. Moore and her mother wrote to tell Warner about it, but neither of them went to Carlisle for the funeral. This may have been because Mary was the last of the Norcross family to whom they were close, her parents having died some time earlier, and they were not particularly involved with any other residents of Carlisle. They may also have been prevented from going because of an unnamed illness of Moore's, which Warner's daughters alluded to in letters in March. Later, at the end of May, Mrs. Moore mentioned to Warner that a piece on Mary, written by Moore, was to be published in the *Bryn Mawr Alumnae Bulletin.* In the June, 1938 issue it reads as follows:

> In Carlisle, Pennsylvania, February 14th of this year, after a short illness terminated by pneumonia, Mary Jackson Norcross died—not a person of many words but of shining personality.
>
> Subsequent to graduation she assisted for some years in the Bryn Mawr College Bursar's office, then returned to Carlisle, where her father, Dr. George Norcross, was pastor of the Second Presbyterian Church. The local and state campaigns for women suffrage at this time received no small aid from her; but her natural trend, like that of William Morris, was toward art as embodied in individually shared experience of creative effort, and she became interested in hand weaving, in which she did very beautiful work. There was in her, too, an evident kinship with Blake, in the associating of the poetic with the supernatural, and in her capacity for variety.
>
> Some time after her father's death, she and her mother removed to Sterrett's Gap in the North Mountain, nine miles from Carlisle. It had been her long-cherished hope to establish for the native mountain people a school center of education and recreation. There was, however, the prior condition of livelihood to be earned, and a fund to be accumulated; nor did Mrs. Norcross, from whose affectionate presence she derived strength, live long.
>
> Though she thought of herself never as a mentor but as a listener, Mary Jackson Norcross was in the community to which she made her life a gift, unconsciously a college and unconsciously a Christ. In repeated instances, the lone and destitute were cared for—to whom but one door, that of the poorhouse, had been open—not even a needy animal ever being driven away. Her exalted, unproud, selfless use of the self, was life's strongest denial of death. Might it be, someone has asked, that Heaven enriched by its saints, will yet accomplish through their spirits, those ends which in their lifetime, as it is called, they lacked the years to complete?

This touching tribute combines Mrs. Moore's Christological concerns with Moore's aesthetic sensibility, as well as her sense of Bryn Mawr College as a reservoir of responsibility and social "service." The phrase "never as a mentor but as a listener" may also suggest Moore's special sense of Mary's reticence, yet another trait that Moore may have emulated. By speaking of art as an "individually shared experience of creative effort," Moore expressed both her feeling about the importance of individual expression and her recognition of the need to have a receptive audience, even if limited in size. And the allusion to Blake, of course, marks how very precious Mary's friendship was to Moore.

In June, Moore was visited by Elizabeth Bishop and Louise Crane, who had bought a house in Key West, Florida, and were back in the city. Bishop was to reside in Key West, while Crane lived in New York, but the two saw each other often, and together visited Moore frequently. Throughout May, Moore was in the care of a doctor, apparently still bothered by that illness that is never specified in the family correspondence, though at one point Mrs. Moore tells Cousin Mary in Albany that the doctor has said it is a condition not well understood medically. Mrs. Moore herself had been ill throughout much of the winter of 1936, and again in 1938, hampered by shingles, and also later by a tic in a facial nerve. Her throat also continued to inflame periodically. The worst part of the episode with shingles was that it affected her eyesight and made reading and writing letters difficult.

Warner was cruising throughout the Caribbean in 1939, still receiving installments of his sister's novel. When Mrs. Moore wrote him in April her handwriting was shaky, a result of the cumulative illnesses of the past few years. In May, Moore was able to visit with Pound, though her mother was still ailing. This was the famous trip where Pound felt he could prevent the war if only he could talk to Roosevelt. He failed to see the President, and a ten-minute visit with the Secretary of Agriculture, Henry Wallace, apparently did little good. Moore took Pound to lunch in Brooklyn; it was the first time they met, though their correspondence had begun twenty years earlier. By the fall Warner was back in the States, now at the New London, Connecticut, submarine base. It is in Connecticut that Warner will live after the war, though for the war years he was stationed for a while in Washington, D. C. There are few family letters from this period, as obviously they were able to use the phone to communicate, and Warner would make occasional visits to Brooklyn.

In the middle of November, Moore wrote Warner, quoting their mother as having said that all of us are intolerant. This gloomy assessment was a response to her reading, along with her daughter, a piece on Hitler by Reinhold Niebuhr. The shadows of the war in Europe were becoming less and less ignorable, and Moore was to feel a deep sense of futility in the coming years. The war tested her moral resolve; it coincided with the increasing illness of her mother, and something of a decline in her writing, after a period of considerable productivity in the late 1930's. She published only one poem in 1942, for example, as she struggled without being able to complete her novel. The moral conservatism of the Depression and post-Depression days seemed to have become an ingrained part of her outlook, at least for the first part of the 1940's. She was to spend a lot of time reading Niebuhr, a very influential thinker and commentator on social and ethical issues; Niebuhr was himself to become increasingly conservative in his outlook after the war years.

On November 17, 1939, she mentioned to Warner that she had had a visit from W. H. Auden—a most important encounter. Auden's friendship, advice, and influence were to be among the most powerful of all the sources of new thought and reflection for Moore in the coming years. In some sense she may well have seen Auden in the context of her earlier affection for George Moore, and then Saintsbury, and, though at a distance, Eliot. Auden was an established, intelligent Englishman whose literary authority was considerable. He was very kind to her, he was socially well placed (she was to take great delight in attending parties and the opera with him), and he wrote about moral issues, being, among other things, close to Niebuhr for several years after his immigration to America.

One of the poems she was working on as the decade drew to an end—the one Auden called "a low, dishonest decade"—was "Spenser's Ireland." But far from being a picture of a distant land and a distant time, Moore used the poem as a way of speaking of herself in direct terms that were most unusual for her. But such directness may be seen as a measure of the disequilibrium that was the result of the war and the cause of her next stage of growth. As the poem draws to a close Moore focuses on emblematic Irish animals, the "guillemot / so neat and the hen / of the heath and the / linnet spinet-sweet," all of whom "bespeak relentlessness." In response to their situation, these animals disappear from sight, much like the earlier plumet basilisk; this offers Moore a chance to complete her identifications and end the poem with these lines:

> The Irish say your trouble is their
> trouble and your
> joy their joy? I wish
> I could believe it;
> I am troubled, I'm dissatisfied, I'm Irish.

Moore's dissatisfactions were to increase in the next decade, and they would offer a considerable challenge to her sense of her own identity.

Chapter 7

260 CUMBERLAND:
THE FORTIES

I. "Refusing to be less than individual"

Moore was to enter upon several different areas of concern in the 1940's, areas that were extensions of her earlier work, but also in some ways new territory. The World War that marked the start of the decade was increasingly to turn Moore's poetry away from modernist experiments and more toward a poetry of public values. Her largest single project was the translation of La Fontaine's *Fables*, which was to take a considerable amount of her creative energy for almost ten years. The *Fables* continued her interest in the dynamic relationship between nature and culture, but it took her away from the innovative lyrics of her first two books. On March 20, 1940, for example, she wrote to Warner that technical virtuosity was not what she considered essential nourishment at this time. Despite her great virtuosity, Moore had always prized a naturalness in speech and language, and throughout the rest of her life she would act more and more on this valuation. The presence in Europe during this time of many of her friends and fellow writers, such as Eliot, Bryher, and H.D., kept her constantly aware of the war and its manifold threats. There was also Warner himself to consider, who spent some of the war years in the Pacific Ocean, and his safety was obviously of great moment to her. On May 27, 1940, he wrote to tell her that Germany would lose the war before the year was out. This certainly was faulty judgment, but it may have been an attempt to put his sister at ease.

However, her literary efforts did not stop, though they did change directions. In January, 1940, she received a letter from Mr. Latham at Macmillan rejecting her novel. This rejection may have led her to consider setting the work aside. Once, when she was at *The Dial,* Saintsbury had told her that he never re-submitted work that had been rejected. If one editor judged it not worthy of publication, he would have felt he was insulting any other editor to whom he might send it. Moore was not quite this fastidious, but she may have remembered the incident. In adjusting to the rejection she told Warner that T. S. Eliot's "Idea of a Christian Society" suffered from the same trouble as her novel. But public interest in Eliot's pronouncements kept him from deferring the work, as he might have. Presumably she felt Eliot's effort was too directly moralistic, a problem she was to wrestle with in her own work. Just how insistent or explicit could a writer be in offering her moral values? How could she inculcate a moral reawakening on a social plane without undercutting her firm belief in individual responsibility?

One of the lyrics she worked on at the beginning of the new decade was the one she called her reindeer poem. This was published as "Rigorists," in the September, 1940 issue of *Life and Letters Today,* an English journal that had been purchased by Bryher and edited by Robert Herring, one of her friends. The poem celebrates moral and cultural renewal but does so through a rather unusual example. A relative of the Norcrosses, Sheldon Jackson, was responsible for introducing reindeer into Alaska as a way of supplementing the diet of the Eskimos. For Moore, these animals are "rigorists," in part because they adapt so well to an adverse environment, and for her Sheldon Jackson is a source of virtue, who combines quiet determination and visionary insight. The reindeer themselves are seen under the aegis of culture, as they become resplendent ornaments, but their place is in a nature that is nearly barren:

> this candelabrum-headed ornament
> for a place where ornaments are scarce, sent
>
> to Alaska
> was a gift preventing the extinction
> of the Eskimo. The battle was won

> by a quiet man,
> Sheldon Jackson, evangel to that race
> whose reprieve he read in the reindeer's face.

Jackson's ability to see what others missed combines with his quiet persistence in winning out against bureaucracy and public indifference to make him the ideal model for Moore. The language of "evangel" and "reprieve" contains echoes of the Christian morality to which Moore was increasingly drawn in this period. The poem also marks a willingness by Moore to use occasions for her poetry, events and details that occur in a personal context. Paradoxically, as her poetry increasingly occupies itself with public morality, it also includes more frequent forays into occasional poetry. Indeed, one of the tensions that serves as the center of the poetry throughout the rest of her life is the way an individual must subsume her personality into larger issues of discipline and decorum. Such tension, however, is frequently concealed by surface details in the lyrics.

Moore remained active in several ways despite having to spend more and more time caring for her mother. In one week in February, 1940, for example, she tells Warner of her attendance at a fund-raising event for the MacDowell Colony, another such event for a Bryn Mawr scholarship fund, and delivering a talk to students at Brooklyn College. Three weeks later, she acted as a judge for a high school poetry reading contest in Newark, New Jersey. Warner was offering her advice on how to keep her name in the public eye, though he had also suggested in March that she put aside her novel for a while. Her poem "What Are Years?" which came to be one of her best known, was rejected by The Atlantic Monthly in March. This magazine was one she had always valued highly, and such a rejection may have embittered her. In May she wrote Warner that she was busy reading the story of Job in the Bible; this was long an important work for her, and she turned to it now, perhaps because of the many pressures of the war and her mother's growing infirmity. She spoke fervently of Job's hunger for belief and his ability to survive chastisement, stressing how it was an inner action that the story portrayed. One of the words that occurs often in her correspondence is "embitterment," and she uses it in several contexts, but she tends to use it most frequently by mentioning it as a threat to herself.

Despite the frequent illnesses both she and her mother suffered, and despite the many hours spent in their apartment, Moore continued to live a very literary life. In April, Hildegarde Watson sent some of Moore's poems to Cummings, and he sent her a letter that she found wonderful. Moore had more than once objected to Cummings' liberal attitudes, but she maintained a long and friendly correspondence with him and his wife, Marion Morehouse. Mrs. Moore mentioned to Warner later that month that Williams was doing a lot to publicize Moore's poetry. So the old friends were being helpful, and Moore was genuinely appreciative. It wasn't that long ago that she felt her audience was severely restricted in number. She gave a talk at Sarah Lawrence College, at the invitation of Horace Gregory, and also a lecture and reading at the "Y" that spring. When describing the latter she told Warner that her old Bryn Mawr talk would suffice, with some recent revisions. She recycled these lectures often throughout the next few decades, adding quotations from her reading, and sometimes restructuring the talks. Such restructuring was done by outlining passages on certain themes in colored pencil and then going back through various versions to take out material on certain topics. Moore sometimes used colored pencils in reworking her poems as well; this may have been a legacy of the draftsmanship she learned in biology lab. Taking the lectures seriously, Moore worked hard on them and sometimes complained to Warner that she felt the sponsoring institution was draining her. But she continued to accept at least as many invitations as she declined.

In May she was hard at work on her "ostrich" poem, and had to go to the library to get an article from the January 14 *New York Times* to help her. This poem is published as "He 'Digesteth Harde Yron' " in the *Partisan Review* of July–August, 1941. Moore had at one time considered calling the poem "The One Remaining Rebel," but her mother dissuaded her. The moral center of the poem is in these lines:

> The power of the visible
> is the invisible; as even where
> no tree of freedom grows,
> so-called brute courage knows.

The ostrich is a symbol of justice for Moore, as she has learned from many ancient authorities in natural history, and she depicts the bird as put upon by greedy and thoughtless men. "Heroism is exhausting," she says, stressing that virtue is always the result of hard work and self-discipline. Though the axiom about the power of the visible was first spoken by Mrs. Moore, the moral thought of the poem is indebted to Moore's reading in Reinhold Niebuhr and Bliss Perry, among others. There was still an existential cast to her morality, as she sensed that faith and spiritual strength were not to be had except in a context of purposeful action. She wrote in a notebook at this period a line from Emerson: "Asseveration does not constitute belief." She also wrote just above this entry a veiled critique of her friends Lester Littlefield, Glenway Wescott, and Monroe Wheeler, saying they acted as if they were always right. For Moore, being right and being heroic were not likely to be attributes one could claim openly or without considerable struggle. If merit proclaimed itself, it was automatically to be mistrusted.

In June, Moore received a check from the *Kenyon Review* for three poems: "Four Quartz Crystal Clocks," "The Paper Nautilus" (originally published as "A Glass Ribbed Nest"), and "What Are Years?" The latter would become the title poem of the book she published in 1941. For some unexplained reason, Moore said she wanted the title of the book to appear without a question mark, but the title of the poem to have one. And this was the way they were printed in the first edition. Moore told Bryher that since she had won the Shelley Memorial Award in 1940, Macmillan felt it would be appropriate to bring out a book of her poems. No poems had appeared at all in the years 1937–39, so this collection was a gathering of work that went back almost ten years. The volume included these three poems, all of the poems from *The Pangolin* (except "Half-deity"), her "ostrich" poem, and "Rigorists," "Spenser's Ireland," "Light Is Speech," and "The Student," this last being from the three-part poem she had published in *Poetry* in 1932 as "Part of a Novel, Part of a Poem, Part of a Play." "Spenser's Ireland" had appeared in a new journal called *Furioso,* which was published at Yale and described to Warner by Moore as a not very savory undergraduate magazine, which Moore subscribed to only so she could stay in touch with new work.

What Are Years, dedicated to John Warner Moore, is a volume marked by strong moral and social awareness, perhaps nowhere more so than in "The Student." The closing lines of the poem seem to be describing Moore's own character, perhaps partly apologetically, partly assertively:

> With knowledge as
> with wolves' surliness,
> the student studies
> voluntarily, refusing to be less
>
> than individual. He
> "gives his opinion and then rests upon it";
> he renders service when there is
> no reward, and is too reclusive for
> some things to seem to touch
> him; not because he
> has no feeling but because he has so much.

With echoes of "service" from her Bryn Mawr years, to the playful disjointedness of nature and culture in the wolves' surliness and the student's wilfulness, the poem leads to a conclusion that is apt for Moore's poetic strategies. It is perhaps especially in the 1940's that Moore will equate a "too reclusive" attitude with a sensibility that is afflicted with too much feeling. Her notebook at this time recorded many such formulations as "they who enslave are the slaves," and "the storm within {oneself/myself." She wrote down a thought from her friend the Reverend Dr. Alvin Magary, pastor of the Lafayette Avenue Presbyterian church, in a sermon he called "The Disillusioned Christian," where he said that it is hard to find the mirage an illusion, but it was much worse to find reality and call it an illusion. It is also significant that "The Student" is republished next to the poems from *The Pangolin*, harmonizing as it does with their subjects of heroic self-discipline and the "dangers" and "patience" of discovery, and that the volume which contained them all was dedicated to Warner.

In November, Moore received two singing telegrams for her fifty-third birthday, one from Elizabeth Bishop, another from Louise Crane. But all the news was not for celebrating. Just after her birthday she heard from James Laughlin, the founder of New Directions, that Macmillan had remaindered her *Selected Poems*. This involved selling the 496 remaining copies to the Gotham Book Mart for thirty cents each. In relaying this news to Warner she tried to put a brave face on it and described it as just housekeeping. The next day she heard that Elizabeth Bishop was chronically depressed and Louise Crane had taken her to a psychiatrist. To Warner this was presented as a case of sensitive people being harder to help.

In the middle of December, Moore had occasion to talk to Frances Steloff, who owned the Gotham, and heard of Steloff's attempt to get a visa for Sylvia Beach, so that she might escape from Paris. But rumor had it that Beach had already fled to London. Steloff was also able to tell Moore that it was she who had initiated the offer to buy the copies of *Selected Poems* from Macmillan, and that the book was selling well. Still, Moore may have felt that her career of the 1920's was already becoming a remote memory. She was to tell H.D. that, prior to 1941, her *Selected Poems* had only sold twenty-eight copies, and most of those she'd bought herself. The isolation she had felt in the 1930's was not wholly imaginary.

Moore was to spend a good deal of time in 1941 trying to come to terms with her views about war and peace. An undated letter from this year plaintively says that people should fight the large-scale reliance on military force as though it were a private emergency. But by the middle 1940's she can confidently say that she is not a pacifist. Back in the years during World War I a few of her poems reflected a largely, but not exclusively, antiwar attitude. Her brother was not a jingoist, but he certainly believed in the moral right, even the righteousness, of the Allied effort. There is another undated letter from 1941 in which Warner says he has refused to attend a Methodist service because Senator Wheeler, an isolationist, was to appear. Early in 1941 Moore tells Warner she wants her poems to be clearer, and that she will try to reflect the spirit of Pétain in what she writes. Of course, this allusion to the French general refers back to his record of heroism in World War I, and not to the collaborationist government that he headed in the 1940's. Referring to the Shelley Award, which she says has activated her, she tells Warner that writing can have a moral force. In February, Warner told his sister how he felt George Washington was our greatest idealist and the epitome of our civic religion. The idealizing that justified the vocation of the writer was becoming more and more prominent, and its connection with a sense of civic responsibility was also becoming more obvious.

There was also personal loss, though somewhat at a distance, which touched Moore near the beginning of the year. Laura Benét's mother died, and Moore's acquaintance from childhood was distraught. Laura had thought of Moore in January, 1941, when she copied out by hand and sent her a copy of the memorial service for the poet Lola Ridge, Moore's friend from the Village days, who had died several months earlier. In March, 1943, Moore had written to console Laura on the death of her brother, Stephen, and said that she admired the "patient laboriousness" of his work. All about there were tales of personal grief and the need for some sort of consolation. Moore observed to her brother that she had always admired Frost, in part because his son's suicide and his wife's death had given him a depth of experience that other poets lacked. She also mentioned reading Vera Britain's book, *England's Hour*, about the need to forgive one's enemies.

But such serious reflections did not halt all the details, mundane and otherwise, of the literary business. Moore complained about a "publicity stooge" from Macmillan whom she had to deal with at tea. And Mrs. Moore told Warner that Moore had defended James Laughlin when he was being castigated by William Carlos Williams, this despite her having recently sent back to Laughlin a book she felt so negative about that she could not write a blurb for it. And in June there was a party at Paul Rosenfeld's which was attended by André Breton, the leader of the French surrealists. Williams arrived in time to "help" Breton, and they spoke volubly together in French. Williams at one point in the evening attacked Eliot as his "bête noire" and claimed that Pound was totally ignorant of music. Again Moore was called on to defend people to whom she felt indebted. She was also sent an article about *The Dial* that she had to correct; the article suggested that the magazine's influence was due chiefly to its being backed by millionaires, and Moore felt this was irrelevant. Her own reminiscence of *The Dial*, in every way favorable, had appeared in *Life and Letters Today*, in December, 1940.

During both 1942 and 1943, Warner was stationed at the Navy Yard in New London, Connecticut, where he served as chaplain, so there are few letters between Moore and him. They must have talked together on the phone often, of course, and Warner had occasions to visit when naval business took him to Brooklyn. For the most part the early years of the war saw him busy with preaching and conducting marriage services for the sailors. In May, 1941, Warner had given the commencement address at the Coast Guard Academy in New London. In 1942 his sister had several speaking engagements of her own: at Brooklyn College, Bryn Mawr, the Commonwealth Fund, and the Poetry Society. She also taught a class during the summer at the Cummington School in Massachusetts, something she would do for a number of summers in the coming years. In 1943, Warner was sent to the Pacific Ocean, and was stationed in Honolulu by September of that year. Letters to him from Moore during this period are apparently lost. Later that year, Mrs. Moore tells her cousin Mary that Moore was hard at work on translation, having already begun her work on La Fontaine's *Fables*. This would mean, given the publication date of the book in 1954, that Moore worked for over a decade on this project. There are some reviews by Moore in *The Nation*, which Mrs. Moore tells her cousin is not the family's favorite magazine, apparently because of the journal's liberal political stands. But Moore formed a friendship with the literary editor there, a writer named Margaret Marshall. Moore dealt with several books, such as the poems of Jose García Villa, a biography of John Steuart Curry, the Kansas painter, and Cummings' *One Times One*, among others.

One of the more important reviews was of Louise Bogan's *Poems and New Poems*, which appeared in the issue of November 15, 1941. Bogan was an important poet and critic of the time. The review was serious and favorable, and posed a question, "For mortal rage and immortal injury, are there or are there not medicines?" before it closed with this somewhat dour paragraph:

> Those who have seemed to know most about eternity feel that this side of eternity is a small part of life. We are told, if we do wrong that grace may abound, it does not abound. We need not be told that life is never going to be free from trouble and that there are no substitutes for the dead; but it is a fact as well as a mystery that weakness is power, that handicap is proficiency, that the scar is a credential, that indignation is no adversary for gratitude, or heroism for joy. There are medicines.

There is clearly being conducted here a struggle of moral claims, of assertions and questionings, challenges and submission, and this struggle is one of the main subjects in Moore's poetry written during the war. Much of the tension in this passage also harks back to the struggle over her religious feelings that Moore had had in the later 1920's. While her mother was alive, Moore never expressed her commitment to religion in a fervent way.

In January, 1944, Moore received word from Macmillan that they

intended to publish her next book of poems, entitled *Nevertheless.*
Moore described this to Warner as "my six poems." It was her shortest
book to be brought out by a commercial press, and included, in addition
to the title poem, "Elephants," "The Wood-Weasel," "A Carriage from
Sweden," "The Mind Is an Enchanting Thing," and "In Distrust of
Merits." The latter was to become one of her best known poems,
though its most famous line, "There never was a war that was / not
inward," has served as a focus for those who object to a quality of
sentimentalism that they feel creeps into Moore's explicit moraliza-
tions. But the poem projects a genuine sense of struggle, and its controlled self-dramatization keeps it from being merely preachy. The sense
of morality is existential rather than absolutist, for the poem finds its
energy in its self-doubt and self-definition. The allusion in the closing
lines to an "Iscariot-like crime" indicates the Christian background, but
the more fully explored context is that of a humanist ethics: "I must /
fight till I have conquered in myself what / causes war, but I would not
believe it."

It is an ironic sense of humanism that animates "Elephants," with its
picture of the strong serving the purposeful, even if the purpose is
occasionally lost in the dullness of routine and complacency. The religious ritual at the center of the poem—a procession in which the relic
known as Buddha's Tooth is carried by an elephant dyed white—turns
the animals themselves into "toothed temples blessing the street."
Eventually, however, the elephants become models of an important
philosophical truth. Moore alludes to Socrates for this, to show that she
is not only dealing in the exotica of a "foreign" culture but is talking
about Western philosophy as well: "the wisest is he who's not sure that
he knows." The poem can also be read as part of a dialogue about the
contrast between and among Christian, Greek, and Eastern values,
begun at least as far back as "An Octopus."

Moore collected sculpted elephants all her life, and the mantel in her
Brooklyn apartment was virtually covered with them. From as far back
as "Black Earth," the poem she wrote in 1917, later renamed "Melanchthon," but never reprinted after 1925, she had given pride of place in
her personal zodiac to this strong but gentle creature. She recorded in
her notebook in 1943 that Cicero had aroused the feeling that the
elephant was somehow allied to man; this was taken from a book she
had read, called *Animals for Show and Pleasure in Ancient Rome.* It was

this classical reference that may have suggested her allusion to Socrates. In that earlier poem she spoke through the elephant; in the later poem the elephant is given a very complex social and cultural framework, as if to suggest that it is more than a mouthpiece for subjective fear, indeed it is an emblem of our deepest cultural transformations. "Elephants" ends with a motto: "Who rides on a tiger can never dismount; / asleep on an elephant, that is repose." It is a very typical lexical move in which Moore shows us the human difference between false energy and real power by making a distinction between sleep and repose.

Two of the poems in the book are playful. "The Wood-Weasel" is a sixteen-line poem that contains an anagram for Hildegarde Watson. The first letter of each line, read in reverse order, spells out her name. We can assume that she had as one of the chief parts of her character the same quality that Moore assigns the animal, namely determination. We also catch a glimpse of Moore herself near the poem's end: "Well, / this . . . weasel's playful and his weasel / associates are too. Only / Wood-weasels shall associate with me." The other poem in the book also plays with orthography: "A Carriage from Sweden" claims that "S" stands not only for Sweden, but stalwartness, skill, and surface. The poem continues the interlocking of depth and surface that marked "An Egyptian Pulled Glass Bottle . . ." as well as many other Moore poems about poetic principles. Stalwartness and surface pleasures, playfulness and determination, are combined in both poems as the principle of structural tension that both holds the verse together and drives it along.

Perhaps the most challenging poem in *Nevertheless* from an aesthetic point of view is "The Mind Is an Enchanting Thing." The poem opens with a teasing restatement of an old philosophical paradox, for by changing object into subject, the "enchanting" mind of the title becomes the "enchanted" mind of the first line, showing us how our consciousness can be both an objective of our knowledge and the subjective principle of our identity. This poem can be read as looking back to the modernist poetics of the 1920's, for it embodies a very complex model of the mind, a model that is aestheticized in a way that many modernists would recognize. By artfully combining the physical imagery with a spiritual or mental tenor, Moore is able to show the complexity of thought even as she explores a sort of pragmatic directness: the mind "walks along with its eyes on the ground," always in touch with a material world, even as it is "trued by regnant certainty," the crucial principle of self-adjusting rationality so important to pragmatism. The poem's final lines, however, and one of its chief notions, namely the "conscientious inconsistency" of mental operations, were suggested to Moore, as a notebook entry makes clear, from a lecture Reinhold Niebuhr delivered at the Brooklyn Institute, in which he praised "that admirable virtue, inconsistency." So the poem looks ahead as well to Moore's sense of moral struggle as something that must take place by submitting "its confusion to proof." The mind must never become blind and unable to change, like an oath of Herod; such would be bad epistemology, but it would produce bad morality as well.

February, 1944, brought news that Moore had won a prize of $50 from the Baltimore magazine *Contemporary Poetry*, for her poem "Nevertheless." The central image of this poem was based on an observation by her mother about how the sap has gone through the resisting plant in order to make the cherry red. The lines, "The weak overcomes its / menace, the strong over / comes itself," are consonant with Moore's sense of paradox and dialectical tension, which she had often displayed before. The following line, however, "What is there / like fortitude!" sounds more like Mrs. Moore in her homiletic vein, and is a measure of how far Moore had come from the strict modernist irony of the late 1910's and the 1920's. The judge was Allen Tate, someone she chose not to be very close to, as she told Warner.

Later in the month she completed her poem on Sweden, despite some strict censures from Mrs. Moore. She also attended a lecture by Jacques Maritain on immortality, and in March was offered the position of Consultant in Poetry at the Library of Congress. Informing Archibald MacLeish of her decision to reject the offer, she tells him she couldn't live in Washington; she tells Warner that she didn't fancy the idea of doing reference work for senators. (She would suggest to her brother in October that MacLeish was currying favor with her because he wanted to meet Eliot and Pound. She was never an innocent in the world of literary politics.) During the spring she was hard at work on an article on the dancer Anna Pavlova, for *Dance Index*. When it appeared in the March, 1944 issue, it showered praise on the ballerina, and ended with the sentence, "That which is able to change the heart proves itself." Even in this sharply observed piece about a performing artist, Moore was concerned with the question of emotional rightness, and the ability of strong feelings to give shape to our experience.

Many forms of acceptance were to present themselves during the year. Harry Duncan, the master printer who worked for many years at Cummington, where Moore taught for a few summers, offered to publish Moore's essays in the spring of 1944. She declined, saying that Macmillan wanted to see them, though they were not to appear in book form for another seven years. In August, Mr. Putnam made the specious argument that he felt the publication of her essays might distract attention from her poetry. In March she told Warner she had selected her clothes for an appearance at Bryn Mawr. W. H. Auden accompanied her on this trip to her alma mater. At the 30th Street Station in Philadelphia, where they were changing trains, Auden rushed ahead and held the Bryn Mawr local for her. This chivalric incident greatly impressed Moore, and she mentioned it to several of her correspondents. She was also greatly impressed with this trip to Bryn Mawr, relating many details to Warner; it was as if she had been accepted in a way that was different from earlier visits. In May she was told by Tate and Louise Bogan that she had been chosen to receive the Harriet Monroe Memorial Award from *Poetry.* Tate quoted Edmund Wilson as saying that Moore was the most intellectual woman he had ever met, and he asked her if he could come and visit her. But no visit seems to have taken place. However, the artist Joseph Cornell paid a visit to Cumberland Street in July, and Moore was lavish in her praise of his manners. This surrealist painter and sculptor, whose boxes of arcane objects and collages in some ways resemble Moore's lyric poems, was at the time a relative recluse. He may have come to know Moore through Monroe Wheeler, who had started working at the Museum of Modern Art, supervising the publications department. Moore's literary world was beginning to regain some of the scope and sparkle it had not had since the end of *The Dial.*

In the Autumn, 1944 issue of *Sewanee Review,* Moore published an important essay, "Feeling and Precision." This was her most significant direct prose statement of her aesthetic since "The Unaccented Syllable," which had appeared in *The Egoist* almost thirty years earlier. The essay was a distillation of thoughts and lectures she had given over the previous ten years or so. As mentioned earlier, Moore would take the typescripts of her lectures and mark in colored pencil certain passages that she would later recombine into other lectures. These lectures were an important way for her to clarify things for herself, as they usually involved weaving together quotations, axioms, and other pithy sayings from her reading with examples of poetry that had especially moved her. This shows yet another similarity between her prose and her poetry, both being like Cornell boxes, locales of passionate preference and dispassionate analysis. By constantly recirculating the material, Moore was able to test and retest her aesthetic principles, and also to show where the principles often did not quite explain—at least did not explain away—the force of the examples. The logic of these lectures is often associative and metonymic, proceeding by lateral connections and pivotal points of expansion, obviously like the structure in her "Comment" columns from *The Dial*, as well as in many of her poems.

"Precision and Feeling" begins by restating some of the principles of Pound's Imagism. For her first two points, Moore urges conversational rhythm as a way to clarify complex thought, and she insists that it is overexplanation that spoils natural movement—"the leap of the lion," as she calls it. These points closely resemble Pound's emphasis on composition that uses the rhythm of the phrase rather than the metronome, and his strong emphasis on condensation. But with her third point, Moore begins to separate herself from Imagist principles. She urges us to accept the need to "be as clear as our natural reticence allows us to be." Later she seems to revert to this principle, or at least one of its elements, when she says that we "must have the courage of our peculiarities." Moore is here struggling with the impulse she mentioned to Warner in 1941, when she said she wanted to make her poems clearer, and that technical virtuosity was not necessary in a time of war and strife. In a lecture she gave at Vassar in 1941, she appeared to be asking for a new clarity when she said that "Imagism did this simplifying but we seem to need a restatement of Imagism." It is also in this lecture that she proclaimed her distrust of the desire to be original, claiming that "novelty is always a by-product," an un-looked-for result of genuinely individual feeling. Though many readers felt that Moore's poetry was baroque, she strove to convey an effect of naturalness. She often said she disliked poetry, not only in the famous lines from "Poetry" but also in a talk at the Harvard Summer School in 1950, where she said that "we are estranged from [poetry] by much that passes for virtuosity —that is affectation or exhibitionism." By this she meant that she disliked the poeticized effect whether it results from trying to be original or trying to sound like others. These critical clarifications of her practice and predilections were to become the basis of her rather severe modifications of the "purer" modernist poetics of the 1920's.

It is perhaps too simple to say that the aggressively modernist poetry Moore wrote and published between 1915 and 1925 was based on a precision of visual observation and lexical acuity, whereas the poetry she wrote from 1940 onward was based on a precision of moral sentiment. But something like a long evolving shift in this direction is behind the poetic principles in "Feeling and Precision." In a lecture prepared for delivery at Bryn Mawr in 1936, a lecture illness prevented her from giving, Moore spoke of the word "intimation" at the end of "Virginia Britannia" and how it had made her uncomfortable because of its clear echo of Wordsworth. But she accepted the word and went on to argue in the lecture that "depth of utterance is better than a pinnacle of self-sufficiency." Later, at a 1948 talk at Harvard sponsored by the Morris Gray Foundation, she said, "I am inclined more and more to feel that MORALS [her emphasis] in the old-fashioned Sunday-school sense of the word have a bearing on technique." And as far back as 1937, in a talk she gave at Columbia University and at the Philolexian Society in New York, she quoted from Thomas Mann, who said that "religious faith is not to be overthrown by a reversion to a lower moral level than that to which it raised mankind." For her, "depth of utterance" came more and more to mean a way of speaking with moral seriousness, while at the same time she remained committed to the principle of tolerance in strictly religious matters.

In the middle of the "Feeling and Precision" essay, Moore talked about the need to keep vocabulary precise, to avoid the "semi-academic" use of adverbs such as "awfully," "terribly," and so forth. She added that "we have ruined the word 'fearful' as meaning full of fear," and lamented the weakness of the common meaning of "very," where the etymological force of *veritas*, or truth, has been drained away. Again, all of these examples would be applauded by someone like Pound, whose modernist style owed a great deal to the rejection of flaccid rhetoric and an empty lexicon. There is also a brief excursus on the notion of "antithesis" as an especially useful tool to achieve precision. The supporting examples do not themselves employ double negatives, but there is a sense that Moore's use of this device is a form of antithesis. Her motto-like ending to "Elephants," "Who rides on a tiger

can never dismount; / asleep on an elephant, that is repose," is, however, clearly an example of what she means by antithesis.

Near the end of the essay Moore introduces two ideas that would give
Pound pause. The first of these points may even be directed specifically
at him. What she aims at in this instance is the ability to see that a
literary effect may be profoundly double-sided. On the surface, the
example she uses says that what looks distanced and controled may be
just the opposite. Clearly she is echoing the sentiment from "The
Student," who is reclusive, "not because he / has no feeling but because
he has so much." But by quoting Pound she is also citing what is to her
an important literary authority while at the same time showing the
limitations of his position:

> . . . although Henry James was probably so susceptible to emotion as to
> be obliged to seem unemotional, it is a kind of painter's accuracy for Ezra
> Pound to say of him as a writer, "Emotions to Henry James were more or
> less things that other people had, that one didn't go into."

The "kind of painter's accuracy" Moore has in mind is likely the one
that acknowledges that a painter constructs a version of the truth, his
or her own special and individual angle of vision in the portrait, while
we all know that there is more to any complex individual than a
single portrait can convey. It is apparently contradictory but true—for
Moore—that James as an author is both too emotional and yet without
emotion of his own.

The courage of one's peculiarities is relevant here, for the truly
distinctive individual will always be seen somewhat differently by other
individuals. Because James is a complex author he can be seen accurately both in her terms and in Pound's. Such complexity of interrelationship was always a part of Moore's imagination. Moore always fought
fiercely for her independence: from the earliest days, when she was
concerned about social identity and preserving one's own integrity, as
reflected in the stories she wrote at Bryn Mawr, to her early published
poems instructing the "critic" how to regard her, and on to the struggle
with her contemporaries during the 1920's in the Village. This fight is
what made the relationship with her mother so complex, for the motive
power behind the struggle, as well as one of its chief objects, was clearly
the strong will of Mary Warner Moore. Being "as clear as our natural
reticence allows" means keeping a part of one's self in reserve, guardian

of one's own personality, even to the point of peculiarity. But not making a fetish out of originality, being willing to sacrifice the "pinnacle of self-sufficiency" in order to gain a true depth of expression, runs counter to this call for personal integrity. The tense balance between individual feeling and a willingness to imagine self-sacrifice would require the use of antithesis, double negatives, and all the integrated grace of animal movement in order to be fully expressed. But this fruitful tension becomes the source of much of Moore's best poetry in the coming decades. For her, it was a time of "expressionary need."

The second point that Moore makes as she closes "Feeling and Precision" refers back to the lecture on immortality that she had heard Jacques Maritain give some months before. This short paragraph condensed much of Moore's feeling about the overwhelming destruction of the war. Along with her review of a book-length poem called "Behold the Jew," published in the October 16, 1944 *New Republic,* this was one of her few direct observations about the holocaust. In the review she says of our relationship to the victims, "If we yet rescue them—those who are alive to be rescued—we are still in debt and need to ask ourselves who would have rescued whom." What is important in the closing paragraph of "Feeling and Precision" is how technique is subordinated to feeling:

> Professor Maritain, when lecturing on scholasticism and immortality, spoke of those suffering in concentration camps, "unseen by any star, unheard by any ear," and the almost terrifying solicitude with which he spoke made one know that belief is stronger even than the struggle to survive. And what he said so unconsciously was poetry. So art is but an expression of our needs; is feeling, modified by the writer's moral and technical insights.

Moore's use of just the sort of word she was warning against—"terrifying"—seems designed to show the difference between appropriate and inappropriate applications of strong feeling. Art as an expression of our needs may, for Moore, mean a willingness to sacrifice originality and even virtuosity.

In the summer of 1944, Warner began to angle for the job of Head of Navy Chaplains, so that he might stay in Washington, D. C. His sister felt that a Catholic "bloc" might prevent Warner from achieving his desire, and his mother was not particularly fond of his staying there. As for Moore herself, she wrote to her brother that she planned a less public life for herself, probably meaning that she planned to do fewer lectures and readings, but she seems not to have kept her resolution. It was also at this time that Moore began eating "health foods," and recommending them to her friends. She may have experimented with new dietary ideas because of her mother's difficulty in swallowing, or because Bryher's talk of rationing in England made her conscious of such matters. But it was a practice that took on more importance for her. In September, concerning her poems, she told Warner that she hadn't had to struggle with them as she did many years previously. But three days later she tells him that the poem is progressing slowly, and she can't seem to get it just right; the poem is "Keeping Their World Large," published in *Contemporary Poetry* in the Autumn, 1944 issue. In the meantime Warner had been ghost-writing speeches for Admiral Nimitz.

Glenway Wescott took her to a party at the end of September, where she met Janet Flanner, who asked her to write on vegetable juice for *The New Yorker* (a piece that apparently never materialized), and Somerset Maugham and others, all of whom treated her grandly. The fall also saw the publication and reviews of *Nevertheless*. The book was treated favorably by Babette Deutsch, and also by Auden in *The New York Times Book Review*. The Auden review especially meant a lot to her, and she quoted from it to her brother, saying that it was "consummately ingenious and protecting." The last word was a signal that Auden was playing a role that Eliot and Pound had played earlier. A few days later she wrote Warner that Auden's review had caused a stir, and she repeated the story of his holding the train for her in Philadelphia. Auden sent a letter in the middle of October asking Moore if the rumor were true that she had had a book rejected (this probably referred to Macmillan's decision to put off publishing her prose); if so, Auden said, he would personally go on the rampage for her. Moore mentioned to her brother the possibility of nevertheless being reviewed by Mary Colum, the wife of Padraic, the Irish writer whom Moore knew from the years at *The Dial*. She told him she could tolerate it, obviously expecting a bad review, though Colum seems not to have written on the book. Apparently there was ill will between the two women; Colum rather pointedly does not mention Moore in her memoir of the period. Moore described the book to her brother as neat and businesslike, and that she was more interested in it than in her other books. She also told Warner that she had received nice letters about the book from Alfred Barr and Wallace Stevens.

As 1945 arrived, so did a letter from Eliot offering to publish for Moore a "Collected" poems after the war. Moore relayed the favor, so to speak, when she wrote a letter of recommendation for Elizabeth Bishop to receive the Houghton Mifflin Award. The amount was $1000, and carried with it publication of a book, in this case Bishop's *North and South*, her first volume of poems. Moore was also at this time solicited for a poem by *The New Yorker*, where she was to appear frequently in the last two decades of her life, starting with "Tom Fool at Jamaica" in 1952. And in the first few months of 1945 she began thinking seriously about the La Fontaine project. Auden had mentioned the project to Reynal & Hitchcock, the American publishers, who wrote to her in February to see if she had plans for publication. Auden had been working on an anthology of poetry in translation, and had asked Moore for suggestions. In their discussions it developed that Auden felt she should translate all of the *Fables*. Moore prepared a poem and sent it to Mr. Walter Pistole at Reynal, who telegraphed back that he was tremendously excited by the sample. It was Pistole who sent the early samples to Harry Levin at Harvard. Levin found at least one of them a masterpiece, and from then on was a tremendous help to Moore, who was anxious for him to prevent her from misunderstanding the meaning of the French.

Other news and offers were also arriving; there was a letter from Professor R. S. Crane at the University of Chicago, seeking her help in selecting speakers for a program, and a request, which she rejected, to judge a poetry contest at Mount Holyoke. A translation that she had assisted Elizabeth Mayer with, of *Rock Crystal*, a fable by the German author Adalbert Stifter, was nearing completion, though she later complained to Bryher that she was not sent proofs to correct. Marianne Moore, Warner's second daughter, was now a student at Wellesley, where she had Vladimir Nabokov as one of her instructors. She asked the Russian émigré novelist to autograph a copy of *Three Russian Poets* for her aunt. Later, Moore was to be very impressed with Nabokov's memoir, *Speak Memory*, and mentioned it often in her public lectures. In May, 1945, Moore was given a Guggenheim Award, largely through the recommendations of Zabel and Louise Bogan. This provided genuine financial relief, and enabled Moore to concentrate more energy on her *Fables*. She told Bryher at this time that she was planning to do a page a day, but as it turned out she was lucky to complete a page in four days. As her life became increasingly busy in the next few years, her progress was often much slower than she projected.

As the war finally wound down in the middle of the decade, Moore found herself increasingly occupied with the care of her mother. But she was able to maintain and even develop some important friendships, one of the most important of which was with Bryher. It was on a trip to America in 1947 that Bryher had her first meeting with Moore after the war. Bryher was divorcing Kenneth Macphearson, her second husband, whom she had married in 1927, and who had recently taken up with Peggy Guggenheim, the patroness of modern art. *Beowulf*, Bryher's novel about the war years in London, had just been published in England, and she had finished a historical novel, *The Fourteenth of October*, the first of several that would occupy her throughout the rest of her career as a writer. She would also visit H.D.'s child, Perdita, who was now living in the United States and taking out American citizenship; and H.D.'s brother, Harold, a successful businessman, who surprised Bryher by informing her that H.D. was a wealthy woman in her own right as a result of family investments. The visit with Moore also held some revelations for Bryher, as she wrote to H.D.:

> She terrified me, she was so very queer about her mother. The mother was thought to be dying of cancer and in such agony Marianne wanted the Dr. to do something, as the mother could neither eat nor speak, and could eat nothing, because she could not eat if Mother could not eat, and thus got rashes and kidney trouble and pains. Now she will only eat her mother's diet—raw vegetable juice. Really I was frightened about Marianne.

Surely Bryher knew how close Moore and her mother were, for Mrs. Moore's correspondence with Bryher during the war was fairly detailed and it continued for several years. Many of Mrs. Moore's letters to her are written in an extremely shaky hand. And even when the women had first met twenty years previously, Bryher had observed the closeness of their relationship. But the physical presence of Moore obviously struck Bryher in ways that the letters had not prepared her for.

Bryher, Moore felt, had done heroic work during the war, helping refugees escape and keeping her own spirits high. Moore had been especially observant about the differences in their daily lives, often

remarking in their correspondence on how Bryher, and H.D. and others as well, had had to get along on rationed food and under the terror
of the bombing raids. Moore did everything she could to make life easier
for Bryher, and her letters are filled with the sort of praise that Moore
seldom used except for those to whom she felt closest. From as far back
as the publication of *The Pangolin,* and even earlier, their friendship had
been marked by frequent exchanges of gifts. Now Moore could send
along food and books as well. She had also taken to reading Bryher's
magazine, *Life and Letters Today,* and commenting on the contents of
every issue. Bryher had been lucky enough to buy up a sufficient stock
of paper to allow her to publish the magazine right throughout the war.
Moore even went so far as to propose that a collection of Bryher's prose
writings be published, though nothing came of this. Moore's letters
almost always included a report on her own and her mother's health,
and questions about H.D. and Perdita. When Perdita moved to America and married John Schaffner, Moore became very friendly with both
of them. And when Moore's niece, Sallie, went to spend some time in
Switzerland in April, 1947, Moore arranged for her to meet Bryher.

Moore told Bryher in May, 1940, that her poem on the reindeer had
begun when Bryher, having recently visited Lapland, had said casually
in a letter that "we see reindeer browsing." When she wrote to tell
Bryher that Robert Herring had accepted the poem for *Life and Letters
Today,* she mentioned hearing a lecture on the work of W. H. Auden,
in which the lecturer said that only poets can say "let's change the
world." For Moore, Bryher was clearly someone who had the sensibility
of a poet, one who had a vision of a changed and better world, but also
one who was a "rigorist." This was not simply because of Bryher's
financial generosity and her unobtrusive way of dispensing it. For some
time Moore had been receiving dividends from a fund that Bryher had
set up for her in a Pittsburgh bank; originally the money had been given
to Moore in 1922 so that she might bring out another volume of her
poems. Moore always reported on the receipt of these dividends, carefully noting to Bryher the amount of each check when it arrived. It was
also during the war that Moore served as a sort of business agent for
H.D., making sure that royalties from her books were sent to her
brother, Harold Doolittle, and an accounting sent to Moore, who relayed the details to H. D. Moore also took up the struggle to see that
the reprinting of H.D.'s poems was done in a way that removed the

misprints. Boni & Liveright, which had published H.D.'s *Collected Poems* in 1925, went bankrupt, and a new edition was brought out by the successor company in 1940.

The correspondence was more frequent between Bryher and Moore than between H.D. and Moore, but Moore herself at times served as a liaison between the two women, on occasion telling H.D. in London about Bryher's situation in Switzerland during the early days of the war. Eventually Bryher was to escape through Portugal and make her way to England, where she rejoined H.D. in their apartment at Lowndes Square. And the three women discussed more than financial and health matters. Moore, for example, mentioned to H.D. in December, 1940, a book by Hans Kohn, *Not By Force Alone,* which argued that nationalism was on the decrease. Though clearly over-optimistic, such a thesis would have appealed to H.D., who became increasingly committed to world peace in the last decades of her life. And in August, 1942, Moore told H.D. that as she opened a gift from her of a book by Edith Sitwell, she saw the embossed rose on the cover, which reminded her of the little rose in Sitwell's *Street Songs,* and she knew an air of romance was guaranteed.

They all shared many enthusiasms, despite their marked differences in temperament. As far back as September, 1938, Moore had told Bryher that anything by Charles Sheeler interested her, and that Constance Rourke's book, *Charles Sheeler and the American Tradition,* was a source of special pleasure. In 1937, Bryher had read a chapter on England from Moore's novel-in-progress, and approved of it, urging her to continue with the work. Moore had arranged a meeting between Elizabeth Bishop and Bryher near the end of 1936, and she recommended Bishop's work to *Life and Letters Today.* In the early 1940's, Moore wrote several pages of detailed suggestions about Bryher's novel, *Beowulf.* In May, 1947, Moore heard T. S. Eliot lecture on Milton at the Frick Museum in Manhattan, and told Bryher about it, though Bryher was not particularly favorably disposed toward Eliot's poetry. Eliot's *Criterion* had published a negative assessment of *Life and Letters Today,* but Bryher still sent Moore a copy of Eliot's *Four Quartets* at the end of 1944. In November, 1948, Moore had dinner with Lincoln Kirstein and Auden, and both Osbert and Edith Sitwell were there, too. The Sitwells were especial favorites of Bryher, and they became good social friends with Moore, partly as a result of this. Moore genuinely admired

Edith's poetry, and felt Osbert was especially gallant and brave about his illnesses.

Every year Bryher was to send Moore a birthday gift, usually a silk handkerchief. In 1921, shortly after meeting them, Bryher gave Moore and her mother a camera, which they used with delight, often sending copies of their snapshots to her. In December, 1935, Moore described how she was seated before a new table in her apartment, wearing a Macphearson plaid while Mrs. Moore wore two especially beautiful shawls, all given them by Bryher. The decade culminated in a special token of appreciation, with Moore receiving a $2500 award from the Bryher Foundation, established to help artists and writers. Moore, in a characteristic act, offered $500 from this check to Bryher to fly to America for a visit in September, 1950. When Moore said in a letter of September 13, 1950, that she might not be realistic about the cost of coming over, one might imagine she was being falsely naïve about Bryher's enormous wealth. She pursued the point, discovered what a return air fare cost, and mailed a check for that amount to Rene Wormser, Bryher's secretary. Such gift-giving was clearly an important part of the relationship. Mrs. Moore and her daughter never allowed their relatively limited means to prevent them from engaging in the sort of codified social behavior practiced by their far wealthier friends. It was, among other things, a way they had of asserting their individual tastes and values.

II. "Efforts of affection": Elizabeth Bishop

From her days at Bryn Mawr, Moore had learned the values of friendship. She had learned the further and deeper uses of friendship when she entered the literary world, in considerable measure through the help of Bryher and H.D. Indeed, having a friend who was both a female and an artist was a special pleasure that Moore had discovered as early as her close relationship with Mary Norcross. Elizabeth Bishop was also to be an important friend for Moore, for among other things she was the most talented poet younger than Moore to be directly influenced by her. This meant that Moore had a confidante of sorts, and that, in a way, the scope of her own poetry would be extended. As circumstance had it, however, Bishop met Moore as Moore's own poetry was moving away from the experimentalism of the 1920's and toward the more directly moral poetry of the 1940's. This change was reflected in many ways, large and small.

Moore talked with Bishop about religion, and even urged her in the late 1930's and early 1940's to treat more serious subject matters in her poetry. In 1938, Moore was very enthusiastically recommending Niebuhr's *Beyond Tragedy,* and later she pressed Kierkegaard's *Journals* on Bishop as well, along with a book called *The Psychology of Christian Personality.* Bishop, however, was resolutely secular for the most part. In fact, in 1953, when mentioning that she didn't particularly like the young women at Bryn Mawr that she had met on a recent visit there, she explained that it might have been due to her Communist streak. This may have been to shock or tease Moore, but Bishop always professed left-wing political views. But there was also the "smaller" technical question of rhyme. Moore claimed to Bishop that she didn't approve of rhyme, but she complimented Bishop for rhyming "antennae" with "many," and would frequently ask Bishop to supply rhymes for one of the *Fables* she was working on. And once she retyped a poem of Bishop's that had come to her with triple rhymes and tight stanzas; in recasting the poem Moore made it much looser, as if replaying the move in her own poetry in the 1920's from formal stanzas and rhyme to free verse. Yet the two women were united by an admiration for intensely accurate description, and a penchant to be retiring and even reclusively objective in their poems, despite very different political views. While their tastes in other writers were quite similar, Bishop needed to be sharper in her judgments, so as to clear a way for her own work, while Moore tended to be discreet and reserved even about writers of whom she strongly disapproved.

It was as an undergraduate at Vassar, where she was the classmate of Mary McCarthy, among others, that Bishop had first heard of Moore's poetry. The woman who arranged an introduction between her and Moore was Fanny Borden, a librarian at Vassar who had known the Moore family back in Carlisle. The two poets met at the New York Public Library, and Bishop was struck by Moore's punctuality and her volubility: "her talk, like her poetry, was quite different from anyone else's in the world," as she put it in her memoir, *Efforts of Affection,* written about thirty-five years after their 1934 meeting. They went to the circus together, and saw nature films, and Bishop later sent Moore her college paper on Gerard Manley Hopkins; Moore especially liked the parts about mathematics and music. Bishop was studying the harp-sichord at the time, having bought an instrument from the famous craftsman Arnold Dolmetsch. She was shy, but Moore put her at ease. Moore was earning considerable repute for herself, and Bishop teased her about the *Selected Poems* being sold out at Macy's, thereby portend-ing a large fortune for Moore. Bishop also liked the stylish George Platt Lynes portrait of Moore that appeared in the *Times* to accompany the review of the book. Moore helped Bishop in her first book appearance, as she wrote an introduction for a selection of Bishop's poems that were published along with those of other poets in a volume called *Trial Balances,* edited by Ann Winslow in 1935. Moore was clearly the "se-nior" of the two, in age and prestige, but both women were meeting as writers and this formed the center of their friendship.

After college, Bishop went on a tour of Europe with Louise Crane and Margaret Miller. The three women were involved in a car accident, in which Bishop apparently was the driver, and Miller, a painter, lost her arm at the elbow as a result. Moore was comforting to Bishop during this ordeal, in 1937, and also offered advice on other matters as well. For example, Moore had arranged for Bishop to meet Bryher in Europe, who wanted Bishop to be psychoanalyzed in order to relieve severe asthma that afflicted her. Moore mistrusted psychoanalysis, and this partially confirmed Bishop's resistance. Bishop told Moore at this time that Freud did not see that the artist had a social role to play, and she, Bishop, felt herself to be a radical. She quoted Christopher Caudwell's *Illusion and Reality,* an important early study of Marxist aesthetics, to prove her point. Such evidence would hardly have swayed Moore, however, who never hid her political conservatism from Bishop. Many years later Moore remarked about the danger of Brazil, where Bishop had gone to live, slipping toward Communism. In fact, Bishop was living with a woman at the time, Lota Soarez, who was close to the leadership of the progressive government in Brazil and working on various social-reform programs. But these apparently fundamental dis-agreements did not prevent the women from sharing with one another their views and their artistic opinions and advice.

When Bishop received her copy of Moore's *Pangolin,* the gift itself testimony to the closeness of their relationship, she remarked on how she had not realized what a unity the poems made until she was able to see them all together. It was also about this time, in the fall of 1936, that Moore counseled Bishop about her vocation, suggesting that she was a good enough poet so that giving up the study of medicine would not be a loss. Bishop was trying to expand her own poetry; she told Moore of her attempt to write a small dramatic piece after seeing a short play by Auden, *The Dog Beneath the Skin*. The women often shared a great deal of news about their respective careers. And they had some compositional habits in common, as well. For example, Bishop was as capable as Moore of letting a poem incubate for years and years; in August, 1946, Bishop told Moore in a letter about the incident that was decades later to become the basis for one of Bishop's most famous poems, "The Moose." Moore was being sent many of Bishop's poems in progress, but Bishop was beginning to develop her own sense of things so that she could sometimes resist Moore's suggestions. In 1938, Bishop submitted a story to *Partisan Review* without telling Moore, who was a bit miffed, or at least pretended to be. After the story was accepted, Moore sent several pages of detailed suggestions about it. Bishop almost always praised Moore's work very highly, and she even claimed that the first stanza of "What Are Years?", which had been rejected by *The New Yorker*, said all that Auden had been trying for years to say. In late 1939, Bishop's manuscript was rejected by Viking and she was considering submission to Knopf and Simon & Schuster. By this time she had had her poems accepted by *The New Yorker*, *Poetry*, and several other good magazines. In fact, Moore suggested that it was Bishop who had arranged for *The New Yorker* to request a poem from Moore, but Bishop denied it. In 1940 the situation reversed itself, as Bishop suspected that a letter from Harcourt, Brace, asking to see a book-length manuscript of her poems had been instigated by Moore. This was not the case, however, and indeed Harcourt rejected the poems.

Bishop, as mentioned earlier, also expanded Moore's social life by introducing her to Louise Crane, who had been Bishop's classmate at Vassar. Crane was active in the formation of the Museum of Modern Art, and was also the sponsor of many concerts. It was through one of these concerts that Moore came to hear Zooty Singleton, the jazz musician, and Billie Holiday, among others. Crane and Bishop traveled together from time to time, and owned a house together in Florida, so the three women were closely in touch throughout the 1940's and later. Crane also sponsored a journal, *Iberica,* which was published to support the Republican cause in Spain, and she appointed Victoria Kent, a friend of hers, to edit it. The support went both ways, as Moore tried to arrange an exhibit of drawings by Jose Bartoli, who did several line drawings for *Iberica.* Mrs. Crane, Louise's mother, owned a rare parchment edition of the *Fables* of La Fontaine, which Moore borrowed for a time. Perhaps the most intriguing social contact was one that didn't occur. As it turned out, Bishop's home in Florida was close to that of John Dewey's, and they became friendly. Crane gave a reception in December, 1940, which was attended by both Moore and Dewey, but Dewey arrived too late to meet Moore. According to Bishop, he was very disappointed, since he had admired Moore's work for "years and years."

Bishop had built a considerable reputation for herself by the poems she published in journals, and she waited a decade after her early appearances, which occurred while she was still in college, to bring out her first book. This patience, by her own account, was one of the things that she had learned from Moore. When *North and South* appeared in 1946, many reviewers noticed the similarity with Moore's work. Louise Bogan, in *The New Yorker,* wrote gently of Bishop's "slight addition to the poetic methods of Marianne Moore." Bogan suggested that Bishop could proceed in her descriptions, as Moore did, by using two distinct methods, either "through canvassing all sides of a central idea," or bringing "into imaginative relation with one central theme a variety of subjects." The first of these is metaphoric, the second metonymic, the latter of which was used by Moore much more frequently. But some reviewers also remarked on important differences. Robert Lowell, writing in the Summer, 1947 issue of the *Sewanee Review,* was perhaps most accurate when he said this about Bishop's relation to Moore:

> Her dependence should not be defined as imitation. . . . Although Bishop would be unimaginable without Moore, her poems add something to the original, and are quite as genuine. Both poets use an elaborate descriptive technique, love exotic objects, are moral, genteel, witty, and withdrawn. . . . But the differences in method and personality are great. Bishop is usually present in her poems; they happen to her, she speaks,

and often centers them on herself. . . . Compared with Miss Moore, she
is softer, dreamier, more human and more personal; she is less idiosyncratic, and less magnificent.

Lowell is here calling attention, without using the exact term, to the
narrative quality of many of Bishop's poems ("they happen to her"),
which often work by her teasing the events into the shape of a parable.
Moore usually works more indirectly in one sense, because she has no
straightforward "plot" to organize the description. But in another sense
Moore is much more direct than Bishop, less "dreamier," because she
does not rely on inward reflection or reverie, instead staying very close
to surface and factual detail.

When Moore herself reviewed the volume, she began by praising
Bishop's accuracy and modesty, and waited until the end to take up
Bishop's ideas and themes. The final long paragraph of the review seems
to be itself a bit of a homily to the younger poet, even as the mechanics
of the homiletic are being discussed. Moore suggests that one of Bishop's themes is the recognition that forgiveness is essential to happiness.
She then alludes to Reinhold Niebuhr's recent claim in *The Nation* that
international diplomacy required contrition, adding that we cannot be
selectively contrite about only some of our wrongs. Moore goes on to
suggest that Bishop has speculated about religious faith in her "book of
beautifully formulated aesthetic-moral mathematics," only to end with
irony and tentativeness. She herself concludes with these reflections:

> With poetry as with homiletics, tentativeness can be more positive than
> positiveness; and in *North and South,* a much instructed persuasiveness is
> emphasized by uninsistence. At last we have a prize book that has no
> creditable mannerisms. At last we have someone who knows, who is not
> didactic.

Throughout their correspondence, Moore and Bishop were to discuss
the relationship between religious conviction and secularism, with
Bishop often resisting any ecclesiastic or organized form of belief. But
Moore continued to send her the titles of books on the spiritual life, and
she probably made it clear enough in their conversations that people
like Niebuhr were of great importance to her. This review is in many
ways a subtle argument, a tentative homily, in favor of moving unin-
sistently toward such subjects. Moore rhetorically asked near the end of

the review: "is not anything that is adamant, self-ironized?" Whatever religious certainty Moore struggled toward in later life, she had been an important modernist poet, and a chief practitioner of irony, for too long not to realize that adamancy was the enemy of truth.

Bishop, of course, had some occasions of her own to comment on Moore's work. In letters written shortly after publication, she mentioned how *What Are Years* had a "wonderful alone quality . . . like the piano alone in the middle of the concerto," and of *Nevertheless*, she singled out for praise the "balancing, suspended-in-air quality" of "The Mind Is an Enchanting Thing." She also felt that in the special issue of the *Quarterly Review of Literature* devoted to Moore, and published in 1948, she liked best the piece by John Crowe Ransom. This was somewhat ironic, because Moore had written negatively of Ransom's poems back in *The Dial*. Bishop had her own contribution to the *QRL* issue, an essay called "As We Like It." Calling Moore "The World's Greatest Observer," Bishop focused almost exclusively on her descriptive powers. Her only reservation, buried rather deeply, was that "perhaps the sense of duty shows through a little plainly," obviously referring to Moore's concern with questions of morality and propriety. But Bishop also praised Moore for her "uncondescending" attitude toward animals, and her prosodic inventiveness and ease, even suggesting that sometimes Moore was so talented that she made verse patterns hard for herself just to keep matters fair. Finally, Bishop was extremely acute about Moore, both as artist and as a person, in her memoir, *Efforts of Affection*. Near the close of this sharply observed piece, Bishop turns to one of her important literary forebears, Gerard Manley Hopkins, and quotes a letter he sent to his friend Robert Bridges, in order to set up the terms of what was for Moore a great struggle:

> . . . gentlemen do not pander to lust or other basenesses nor . . . give themselves airs and affectations. . . . If an artist or thinker feels that were he to become in those ways ever so great, he would still be essentially lower than a gentleman that was no artist and no thinker. And yet to be a gentleman is but on the brim of morals and rather a thing of manners than morals properly. Then how much more must art and philosophy and manners and breeding and everything else in the world be below the least degree of true virtue.

The ascending order of values here, from the artistic to the mannerly to the truly virtuous, has a Victorian ring to it, and is indeed the sort of order that in many ways modernism was intent on challenging. But for Moore, at least since the days at Bryn Mawr when personal manner and artistic style were nearly equivalent, it was an order that was complexly involved in her poetry. Bishop ends her piece by murmuring, "Manners and morals; manners *as* morals? Or is it morals *as* manners?" In many ways for Moore it is a false question, for manners and morals were utterly intertwined, as Bishop surely knew. But in her dealings with Moore, Bishop must sometimes have felt that the two orders of human experience were often capable of being frustratingly confused as well as illuminatingly identified.

In December, 1948, Moore was introduced for a lecture at the Grolier Club in Manhattan by her old friend Monroe Wheeler, who called her "internationally the most famous poetess of our nation." She read her essay, "Humility, Concentration, and Gusto," which was published in the club's *Gazette* in May, 1949. Lincoln Kirstein, who had written recently to say how true *Nevertheless* was to his experience of the war, offered to cast in bronze Gaston Lachaise's bust of her. The issue of *QRL*, guest-edited by Jose García Villa, itself additionally testified to Moore's continuing reputation, for it had contributions from a list of notable writers: in addition to Bishop and Ransom, there were Williams, Stevens, Bogan, and Vivienne Koch. It included two poems by Moore, "Voracities and Verities Sometimes Are Interacting" and "By Disposition of Angels." The first claims that "unobtrusiveness is dazzling, / upon occasion," and the latter meditates on the theme of virtue revealed by adversity: "One has seen, in such steadiness never deflected, / how by darkness a star is perfected." This poem, Moore told Bishop in a letter of September 19, 1948, was based on a passage in the New Testament, Acts 7:53, "We have received the law by disposition of angels and have not kept it." These poems obviously continue the themes of the poems of the early 1940's, typified by "In Distrust of Merits" and "What Are Years?" The issue also included a poem by Bishop, "For M.M.," later published as "Invitation to Miss Marianne Moore." This lyric, definitely written *con brio*, has the refrain, "please come flying," as the younger poet bids her friend to come "over the Brooklyn Bridge," so they can together sit and weep, or shop, or "bravely deplore" (though she discreetly doesn't say what or whom they will deplore), all with "a priceless set of vocabularies." The poem echoes, at least faintly, some of Whitman's "Crossing Brooklyn Ferry," in describing the harbor between Brooklyn and Manhattan. This may be an inside joke, for years later, in her memoir, Bishop tells of how Moore reacted to a mention of the good gray poet by saying, "Elizabeth, don't speak to me about that man!" Bishop described Moore's tone on this occasion as "mock-ferocious," but she also never again mentioned Whitman to her. Whitman clearly presented a point upon which the propriety of Moore and the more liberal sentiments of Bishop could not be mediated.

III. "One face photographed by recollection . . ."

By the late 1940's Moore and her mother were often referring to Warner by the nickname "Bible." This referred, of course, to the constant commentary generated by both Warner and his mother on the biblical quotations used in his sermons. Warner's presence in the lives of the two women was still considerable. For example, in the fall of 1946, he sent his sister a three-page typed letter outlining how she should use domestic help in running the apartment in Brooklyn, and giving advice and instructions for the hiring of nurses and others to look after Mrs. Moore. By this time, Moore had the benefit of the services of Mrs. Gladys Berry, the woman who would remain her housekeeper and good friend for the next twenty-five years. As the end of 1946 saw Warner's letters get more and more prayerful about his mother's health, his sister reported that she would often take down the family Bible and she and her mother would read from it and pray together. Warner, still in Washington, at the Potomac River Naval Yard, had a visit from T. S. Eliot in July, 1946, and he happily reported to Moore that everything had gone well. He also was able to tell her that nothing had come up that evening about Pound, but he would make sure Eliot was given the $10 gift that Moore intended him to deliver to Ezra the next day at St. Elizabeth's Hospital.

Mrs. Moore's health was failing rather badly by the beginning of 1947. There are few letters between Moore and Warner for this period, as they probably communicated by phone as one emergency after another arose. Mrs. Moore, however, was a remarkably durable woman, and there are letters from her to her cousin Mary in Hagerstown,

Maryland, in March, April, and May of 1947. Though her hand was incredibly unsteady, and the letters are nearly illegible, her mind seems to have remained clear and strong. She was even able to dress and go out for small errands as late as April, as Moore told Bryher. But early in July she was admitted to a hospital in Brooklyn, and Warner came up from Washington to be with her. On the ninth of July, early in the morning, at the age of eighty-five, Mary Warner Moore died. For the preceding several years, Moore had been her constant attendant and nursemaid, seeing to a formidable array of medicines and treatments. She had suffered from throat trouble for years, and Moore told Louise Crane that the autopsy revealed that her thyroid gland had been so distended that it went "far down" into her chest. In 1946, Moore told Bryher there had been a fall in which Mrs. Moore had injured her throat, and doubtlessly this contributed to the final debilitation.

Moore described the funeral service to Bryher as being very plain, since there were no flowers and no singing voices, only music supplied by a young organist. Mrs. Moore was buried beside her parents in Gettysburg. Moore went from the funeral to Hagerstown to visit Cousin Mary, and then on to stay for a few days with Louise Crane in Windsor, Massachusetts. But the recovery of her spirits seemed to have begun during her stay with Marcia Chamberlain and Kathrine Jones at their home in Ellsworth, Maine, where she was also to summer in 1950. The comfort given by these women to Moore was of great benefit to her, and they seemed perfectly tuned to her needs. By the middle of 1949, Marcia Chamberlain was referring to Moore as "Baby Moore," and herself as "Mama" Chamberlain. Later in the year, Warner wrote her a letter in which he suggested she get a photograph of their mother and make an enlargement of it to help keep her memory in mind. When Moore wrote to her closest friends, such as Bryher, Bishop, and Crane, to tell them the news of her mother's death, she did so with a quiet resolve and a muted sense of self-comforting. She used a religious vocabulary for this, for the most part, but she was far from pious. Surely the death was no surprise to her, yet just as surely she could hardly have been prepared for it. Much of her surface life would readily reassert its cohesion, yet there were bound to be deep changes as well. Writing to Bishop in August, for example, she could still take time to praise Bishop's magnificent poem, "At the Fishhouses," which had just appeared in The New Yorker. But two months later she asked Bishop for support, and even averred that she would not imitate her younger friend's poetry and begin to see writing as a source of moral strength. This was almost certainly said as a way of enforcing humility on herself. In her notebook for November 3, 1947, Moore recorded the notion that the nerves of our souls fail to obey us. Three weeks later there are notes for the beginning of a poem that doesn't seem to have gotten very far: "People grow old they can't smile they cant see But not she." Stunned as she was, she turned to her writing, especially the *Fables*, to give herself a focus for the immediate future.

Moore's first publication after her mother's death was a limited edition of a single poem, "A Face." This was produced by Harry Duncan, the famous printer, from the Cummington Press, in an edition that supplemented the poem's appearance in the journal devoted to fine printing, *The New Colophon*. The poem is rather cryptic, but the reference to a face "photographed by recollection" may suggest that the poem is about Mary Warner Moore, or more precisely, about her daughter's morally felt obligation to remember her mother.

> "I am not treacherous, callous, jealous, superstitious,
>   supercilious, venomous, or absolutely hideous":
>   studying and studying its expression,
>   exasperated desperation
>   though at no real impasse,
>   would gladly break the mirror;
>
> when love of order, ardor, uncircuitous simplicity
> with an expression of inquiry, are all one needs to be!
>   Certain faces, a few, one or two—or one
>   face photographed by recollection—
>   to my mind, to my sight,
>   must remain a delight.

The first stanza can be read as a complaint against self-consciousness, the tangle of disabling awareness that results when we try to see into our own character with certainty and end up with only frustration. The second stanza offers the "answer," a different set of dispositions, presided over nevertheless by a saving curiosity. It is tempting to see the first stanza as Moore's self-accusatory self-portrait which is then put aside in favor of her memories of her mother's straightforward and uncomplicated character.

There can be little doubt that her mother was the most important person in Moore's life, followed closely by Warner, of course. But even Warner was loved in some way as a reflection of his mother's character. Mary Warner Moore was an exceptionally resolute person, recalling her daughter's remark about the wilfulness "complex" in the family. Warner was able to establish his own family in the face of his mother's disapproval, if not opposition. But he also constantly felt the need to maintain and, when necessary, re-establish his ties to his mother and sister. The arduous time immediately after the Reverend Warner's death, breaking as it did the charmed circle of the manse at Kirkwood, bonded the three Moores through the twin forces of adversity and aspiration. Moore and her mother may well have formed a different bond, or developed slowly a different sort of bond, during the time at 260 Cumberland. The themes in Moore's poetry throughout the late 1930's and the 1940's were often built on the subjects of strength in adversity and the overcoming of self-doubt through discipline. These clearly owe something to Mrs. Moore's character, especially her ability to use a language that is largely spiritual—such as the lines about "the power of the visible is the invisible"—while at the same time having that axiomatic force that characterizes Moore's later poetry.

But "I May, I Might, I Must," published in book form in 1959 and yet written during her years at Bryn Mawr, tells us that resolution, even of a potentially threatening sort, was part of Moore's character from the first. Her "dignity and impatience" she may have learned or inherited from her mother, and she often had to face the fact that she would turn such forcefulness on her mother as well. Moore's loyalty to figures with whom she strongly disagreed, or with whom she had deep temperamental or artistic differences, such as Pound, Williams, Cummings, Bishop, and Monroe, came from more than simply "strategic" considerations. Such loyalty was possible because Moore had learned that the people who give you aid and comfort could be the same people who frustrate you with their views and their self-assertions.

After her mother's death, Moore experienced some troubled days. She mentioned to Bryher in January, 1948, that she had recently spent fifteen days in bed, and that she felt an attack of pneumonia a year or two previous had made her very susceptible to temperature. Though the time spent with friends, especially in Maine, was restorative, Moore wrote to her brother about her feelings of grief and weakness. In January, 1948, for example she had him tell *Vogue* magazine that she was still too frail to be photographed, and would he ask them to use a previous portrait of her. Warner was continuing to preach, still enunciating his own brand of the civil religion, saying in November of that year that espionage between Russia and America was at an all-time high level, and that the greatest living example of applied Christianity today was the Quaker, ex-President Herbert Hoover. An earlier letter to his sister, on March 24, 1948, had compared his mother to Hoover, praising her for having no sympathy with those who wanted "peace-at-any-price." Such sentiments probably strengthened Moore, but she may have needed a different sort of solace as well.

On the back of a letter dated October 19, 1948, she wrote to Warner that she was contemplating seeing a psychiatrist. She had developed the habit of misplacing things and being reluctant to do things when the time came, though she had been enthusiastic about them earlier. But she also recalled Thayer's psychoanalytic experience with Freud, who apparently told him that he saw clearly into himself, and what he needed was self-discipline. In a sense this is the cure that Mrs. Moore would have recommended, and it had been internalized by her daughter. But slowly Moore returned to her social world, and her literary efforts, too. The completion of the translation of the *Fables* may in part be understood as the one definitive answer to the problem of the reluctance to follow through with projects undertaken heartily. But even here the going was not to be smooth.

Reynal & Hitchcock were the publishers to whom Moore had sent samples when she first began translating the whole of the *Fables*. But she found out in February, 1948, that the editor whom she knew at that firm had left, so that she now had to find another publisher. She thought of Macmillan, and of Mr. Latham, who had been supportive in the past. But in May of the same year, Macmillan rejected the manuscript. Only the year before, Moore had been elected to the National Institute of Arts and Letters, and she was faced here like a beginning writer with a letter of rejection. Clearly this was a blow for Moore, and Warner tried hard to comfort her, speaking of how the rejection had knocked the pencil out of her hands. He also sent her another letter in July, 1949, advising her how to answer Latham about the question of whether she was the right person to translate La Fontaine. Obviously the rejection was something that took several months to adjust to, since she had experienced nothing like it since the rejection of her novel-in-progress. But though that was a work that was to remain unfinished, the translation of the *Fables* was a project that had a built-in closure. By the first part of 1949, Viking Press had become interested, eventually bringing out the work in 1954.

Moore gradually resumed her social and literary activities. There was a talk she was able to give at Harvard in December, 1948, where she was hosted by Harry Levin and met F. O. Mathiessen, the famous scholar of American literature. She wrote him a thank-you note for the tickets she and Marcia Chamberlain were given to a performance of "Troilus and Cressida" that he had arranged for his students. A month earlier she had had dinner with Auden, the Sitwells, and Lincoln Kirstein. There were still several forms of support available from the literary world. In March, 1949, she was given a Bollingen Award. In July, 1949, when she was discussing an exhibit of her work at Yale and a planned bibliography of all her writings to date with Norman Holmes Pearson, he delivered to her a check for $2500 for the Bryher Award. She wrote to Warner asking if she had the strength to complete her *Fables,* and she answered herself positively, referring to her brother as her beloved and valiant argonaut.

In the meantime, Warner was having difficulties of his own. In March, 1948, as he and Constance prepared to visit 260 Cumberland, he wrote to Moore that Constance never understood Mary Warner Moore, and he felt she shouldn't sleep in her bed at the apartment. By the fall of that year, things had become even more recriminatory. Warner wrote to say that Constance was jealous of not only Moore, but anyone that Warner was close to, and that she needed to be cured of this just as if she were an alcoholic. They were campaigning to save their marriage, he wrote in the same letter. Warner felt the break had become inevitable and he told his sister that he was very eager to join her. At the end of September, he reported to Moore that Constance had lectured him on the proper relationship of husband, wife, and sister, and that the children had rallied round their mother. Among other things, Constance insisted on reading all the correspondence between her husband and her sister-in-law. Some of Warner's strong emotions may have been fueled by grief and even guilt at his mother's death, a feeling that he had in fact disappointed her with his marriage. Constance, however, had grounds for her feelings, as she must have felt

excluded from the Moore family circle as it was built around Mrs.
Moore. And, at least as far as the correspondence of all parties is
concerned, Constance was always attempting to be kind and accepting
to her in-laws.

Within a matter of a few months, however, calm was being slowly
restored, and Warner planned a move away from Washington. He told
his sister that he had never liked his home in the capital, recalling that
his mother had visited there only once, and also that his sister had not
been well treated there. His thoughts turned back to Connecticut,
where he had lived during the years before the war, and where he could
visit his sister more easily. He made the move in December, 1948. At
first he talked of studying farming at the University of Connecticut, this
perhaps a throwback to his days as a young man working summer jobs,
perhaps as a balance to all those years at sea. But by April, 1949, he was
appointed chaplain at the Gunnery School, a boy's prep school in
Washington, Connecticut. Moore saved the clipping from *The New
York Times* announcing the event. That summer Moore herself was
celebrated with an honorary degree from Wilson College, one of her
sixteen such awards. After receiving the degree she visited with her
cousin Mary, and they went to see the Warner gravesite in Gettysburg.
While there she saw the carved headstone for her mother, which was
still in its crate. She signed her letter to Warner at this time by calling
her brother a dragon-slayer and referring to herself as Rat, the animal
nickname that seemed to have the greatest staying power.

The last poem Moore published in the 1940's was "Efforts of Affection." The poem is dense in meaning and symmetrical in format. A
rhyming couplet is followed by a seven-line stanza with only one clear
rhyme, between the fourth and fifth lines, and this is followed by yet
another rhyming couplet. Then the whole eleven-line ensemble is repeated to create a twenty-two-line poem. In the two long stanzas, each
seventh line is in fact a half line; respectively, these are the phrases,
"how welcome" and "Thus wholeness." In each instance this half-line
phrase serves to introduce the "concluding" rhyming couplet. Each of
these two "concluding" couplets contains the word "integration," and
it thus becomes the main subject of the poem. By integration Moore
seems to mean something like a concerted gathering of emotion, an
integrated effort of affection, that by its very wholeness is proof against
harm. It is, of course, the subject of strength through adversity, or at

least strength in the face of adversity, but it has a special turn as the second half of the poem begins to reach its climax. The poem appears to refer playfully to a plant, of a common household variety, that might be used to conceal one's motives or failings. This especially incongruous image gives way immediately to the high sententious "truth" of the poem, and then the "moral" is enunciated.

> Unsheared sprays of elephant-ears
> do not make a selfish end look like a noble one.
> Truly as the sun
> can rot or mend, love can make one
> bestial or make a beast a man.
>   Thus wholeness—
>
> wholesomeness? say efforts of affection—
> attain integration too tough for infraction.

The simple texture of the lines about love are becoming familiar in Moore's later poetry, as is the use of the sun, so prominent at the end of "The Pangolin" and in several poems thereafter. The device of using a choice—between words closely or casually related—"wholeness" and "wholesomeness"—to make a key point in the poem's aesthetic tuning, is something Moore employed from very early in her career. The rhyming of Latinate words, especially those ending in "-ion," was a sound effect she discussed with Bishop as especially appealing. While all these devices were developed and integrated in a number of the poems Moore wrote in the last three decades of her life, the reference to elephant-ears remains hard to puzzle out. Frequently in the later poems she will use such a domestic or mundane object in an unusual way. Here, knowing her affection for the elephant, she might even be engaging in a sort of private pun, playing the elephant as a symbol of loyalty and strength off against the house plant's overly large leaves as an interior decorator's way of concealing empty space: true nobility and a false cover. Might she have had Twain's pun in mind, where he said that the difference between the best word and a nearly right word was like the difference between lightning and a lightning bug? This is indeed fanciful, but just prior to the lines quoted there is an image of another plant, the rubber fern commonly known as the "bleeding heart." This plant and its metaphoric name also seem to be used punningly.

Moore always struggled with the artistic balance between her much vaunted sense of self-discipline and a genuine desire to seem natural and spontaneous. These oddly incongruous figures based on mundane objects give her poetry a decidedly spontaneous cast, as if she had found her illustrative metaphor in the course of her daily activities. But they also can be read as elaborately coded references, private jokes that work by playing with almost secret metonymic connections. They keep her later poetry feeling fresh and give it something like a harmonious tie to the experimental verse of the 1920's. But they also generate the feeling that many of her later poems are in the tradition of "occasional" verse—some obviously and successfully so—and they have done much to foster the image of her as "an eccentric genius," as the phrase on the paperback edition of her *Complete Poems* puts it. But reading a poem by Moore requires the assumption that deep thought may well lie behind it, and that a theme is being worked out with a real emotional struggle.

Mundane images can also be seen in the context of Moore's ongoing adjustment, if that is the word, to the modernizing world at which she was alternately amazed and somewhat shocked. In poems like "Four Quartz Crystal Clocks," first published in 1940, she uses a poetic perspective to view a technological wonder, even directly quoting the language the Bell Telephone Company used to convey its new achievement. She employed puns in this poem, such as the line she took from Bishop, "the bell-boy with the buoy-ball," and references to Greek and Roman mythology. She did this because she always liked to work against any notion of a lexical purity. And she was to speak later about her fascination with the language of advertising, something that can be traced back in part to her early years and the amusement she shared with Warner at corny jokes and "bad" riddles. In "Armor's Undermining Modesty," published in 1950 but begun and almost certainly completed in the previous year, we find these lines, that begin by rejecting whatever is ostentatious:

> No wonder we hate poetry,
> and stars and harps and the new moon. If tributes cannot
> be implicit,
>
> give me diatribes and the fragrance of iodine,
> the cork oak acorn grown in Spain;
> the pale-ale-eyed impersonal look

which the sales-placard gives the bock beer buck.
What is more precise than precision? Illusion.

This passage begins by rejecting one sort of art, the kind that immodestly practices an explicit form of making claims, and ends by putting in its place the illusion-making art of the everyday. But to call the final flourish of images the everyday is to be too general. They include the sort of everyday image under discussion ("the fragrance of iodine"), but they also offer the advertising image, the ordinary but remote object (the Spanish acorn), and the excessive expression of emotion (the diatribe). The list perhaps seems organized only by its expression of miscellaneousness, but it is also a sort of homage to the individuality of taste, and by extension to individualism itself. At the same time it paradoxically calls for a principle higher than mere self-expression.

"Armor's Undermining Modesty" is a very complex poem. Moore's great subject of culture and nature is being worked out thematically, and in personal terms, as the struggle between a need for self-protectiveness and the desire for spontaneity. This struggle is behind many of her poems, especially all those concerned with aspects of style. But after Mary Warner Moore's death, Moore may well have turned reflectively back to her own struggles with her mother, struggles that required at times an attitude that was perhaps "excessive in being preventive." This phrase is from the poem, where it is applied to Mars, the god of war and, according to some legends, the first to wear armor. Moore is paradoxically both very guarded and very open in this poem, as suggested by the list of mundane images quoted above. In it, she tries to explore the tense relation between an attitude—modesty—that can be at once a virtue and yet in some ways subversive and undermining. The question the poem implicitly plays with, and to which it gives only ambiguous answers, is one that would have a summary force at this point in Moore's life, namely, what exactly does armor undermine by its modesty?

A notebook page dealing with early drafts of this poem has two entries that are relevant: "Letter perfect is not perfect" and "Sensibility / It is responsible for suffering." (The first of these may eventually have been changed into the line, "What is more precise than precision? Illusion.") In "Efforts of Affection" she had praised an "integration too tough for infraction," but that was not the complete picture, for in its idealized wish it had left out much of the struggle. "Armor's Undermining Modesty" seems an exercise in self-discipline, as if Moore were trying, among other things, to correct her own strict self-protectiveness, especially when it becomes the cause of pain in others. In another entry, this one dated July 11, 1949 (approximately two years after her mother's death, an anniversary Warner had observed by sending Moore a telegram), there is the line, "I have a horror of coercion." The poem goes on to praise armor-wearing soldiers who "did not let self bar / their usefulness to others who were / different." Again, Moore is trying to show us that armor is not only for protection or reclusiveness, but it allows one to enter the world prepared to meet the other psyches in life. The poem ends with two thoughtful stanzas that show the complex symbolism of armor for the psychological type who needs it. Containing an antithesis between attitudes, in this case an undermining modesty and an innocent depravity, the poem's conclusion reads like this:

> I should, I confess,
> like to have a talk with one of them about excess,
> and armor's undermining modesty
> instead of innocent depravity.
> A mirror-of-steel uninsistence should countenance
> continence,
>
> objectified and not by chance,
> there in its frame of circumstance
> of innocence and altitude
> in an unhackneyed solitude.
> There is the tarnish; and there, the imperishable wish.

It is often hard to distinguish between the excesses of self-regard and a genuine love of "unhackneyed" solitude; this is a problem that Moore faced as early as the short stories she wrote at Bryn Mawr. Innocent depravity can result if we use armor to blind ourself to other people's needs and differences, and to this Moore prefers the modest strength of a self-discipline that would undermine false bravado. But such strength, like self-knowledge, is a rare thing, and the closing image of the poem shows how circumstantial—in several meanings of the word—such uninsistent strength can be. In the suit of armor, much like the personal photograph in a frame on one's desk, there is a tarnish surrounding something permanent. A simple reading of the last line might suggest that the armor is tarnished by contact with the world, while the desire to remain pure is imperishable. But in reality fixity of armor and the mutability of our selves have changed places. The armor that meets and attempts to overcome circumstances might represent a changing desire to hold back loss; on the other hand, it is the person inside the frame who endures.

Moore read this poem in public at Brooklyn College on May 1, 1950. At the time she commented that "a man's life is fundamentally selfish or unselfish." She also said that she was especially impressed by virtues of liberality and chivalry, and that she associated such values with the memory of her mother.

Chapter 8

260 CUMBERLAND:
THE FIFTIES

I. "Be infallible at your peril"

On the eleventh of July, 1950, approximately the third anniversary of her mother's death, Moore recorded in a notebook the phrase, "the neuralgia of nostalgia." She was sixty-two years old at the time. Obviously some of her reflections were focused on the earlier periods of her own life, but she was also unwilling to settle for living in the past. In fact, in the next two decades she was to enter something like a second life, one based on public recognition and a social status comparable to that of a national celebrity. Such celebrity status was in some ways thrust upon her, but there is also a sense in which she cultivated certain aspects of it, and it is quite clear that she enjoyed much of it. At first the main source of this new status was a flood of academic honors. But then, especially after the appearance of her *Collected Poems* in 1951, and the several awards bestowed on it, the horizons of her life enlarged, in the sense that she became the focus of journalists and other arbiters of taste in the media. This attention was of a different source, different in quality and purpose, from the admiration of her fellow writers and close friends. This difference made a difference, in her life and in her poetry.

The publicity network in which Moore was caught up developed in America almost exponentially in the postwar era. This was due in large measure to the new medium of television, and the ways in which this medium caused others—such as weekly newmagazines—to adapt themselves to a new system of circulating images and information. There was not much indication that Moore looked upon these developments analytically, or that she saw them as having a possibly negative effect on either civic discourse or poetic language. Another element in this system seemed to escape analysis, at least at first, and that was a demand to typify or categorize individuals felt to be in some ways especially gifted (the debasement of the word "genius" is a mark of this), and to turn this typification into something like an icon: luminous and otherworldly, but also fixed and two-dimensional. For Moore, this took the form of presenting her as a sort of saintly grandmother figure, an especially fastidious and well-dressed eccentric who was known to write poetry that was full of charm and obscurity. This system of publicity had little room to convey how Moore's early poetry had been built out of rigorous mental discriminations, or how her later work was equally rigorous in its pondering of the interplay between personal style and public morality.

The movement in Moore's work toward a more explicitly moral and public poetry had been going on since at least the beginning of the war years, and was implicit from at least the period of "Virginia Britannia." The death of Mrs. Moore may have increased the force of such a movement, as Moore in some ways began to express those values that she had internalized from her mother's example and statements. Now she had less need to take a position of reticence when it came to openly spiritual questions; indeed, she may have felt the need to speak out about such issues as a way of vindicating and prolonging the presence of her mother in her life. One occasion that demonstrates this is her brief response to a *Partisan Review* symposium, actually a questionnaire, on the issue of "Religion and the Intellectuals," which appeared in its February, 1950 issue. She expresses her belief that the "breakdown" in the individual is responsible for ills on both the social and individual planes. She also suggests that "reverence for science and reverence for the soul can interact." This is her effort to maintain a sense of the Enlightenment's trust in rational thought while not abandoning the realm of religious belief; she goes on to suggest that "culture, so far, has not existed without religion and I doubt that it could." Leaving open the question of cultural pluralism by asserting that Christianity "partakes of varied cultural elements," she also argues that "imposed piety" results in disbelief. She makes her boldest claim when she avers that "one could almost say that each striking literary work is some phase of the desire to resist or affirm 'religion.' " By saying "resist or affirm," Moore is probably thinking of religion as the very background of any possibility of transcendent truth; in this sense, she is still making an argument against what she called, in the last days of *The Dial*, "realism," or the acceptance of life simply as it is, with no effort at discrimination between its sordid and elevated aspects. But by leaving open the possibility of a drama of resistance against false or misleading transcendence, Moore restated one of her central modernist positions.

These responses to the questionnaire are a balanced blend of religious affirmation, though of a non-ecclesiastical sort, with an enlightened tolerance, but one that stops well short of secular skepticism. They show that Moore's modernism always rested on a sense of self-discipline, a sense heavily indebted to her own religious background, but not simply a restatement of religious "truths." "Religion that does not first of all result in self-discipline will never result in 'social discipline,' " she argues. In some ways, her religion might be equated with self-discipline, for while she became increasingly active as a member of the Lafayette Avenue Presbyterian Church in the 1940's and 1950's, she always eschewed anything like proselytizing. The period of religious doubt in the 1920's, and its attendant guilt, may not have been completely eradicated from her memory, and so she might have been not only cautious but uneasy about any attempt at "imposed piety." Where the response is strongest is at its conclusion: "But this is certain, any attempted substituting of self for deity is a forlorn hope." Such a belief may well be a corollary, or a precondition, of a growing mistrust in the larger, Romantic claims for lyric poetry, and a turning toward the public, almost Horatian poems of Moore's later years.

The publication of her poetry continued more or less as before, though its style and subjects changed. Her poems continued to appear in the essential rhythm that had marked them in the books of the 1940's. Individual poems appeared only at the rate of three or four a year, and often in magazines that had requested them. Then, every four or five years, she would gather the dozen or so poems that had previously appeared in magazines since the last volume and publish them in the traditional cloth-bound volume. After the appearance of the *Collected Poems*, Moore was to publish four such individual volumes of poetry. Admittedly these were slim volumes, but each was larger than

Nevertheless and roughly equal in size to *What Are Years*. There was also the appearance of her prose in the volume she called *Predilections* (1955), and the appearance of the complete *Fables* (1954). Add to this the compilation of her poetry, prose, and translations in *A Marianne Moore Reader* (1961), and there are seven substantial volumes published after 1951. When we realize that there are only seven books (not counting *Marriage* as a separate volume) up to and including the *Collected Poems*, then we might say that in 1951 Moore still had half of her career ahead of her. Whatever the later years showed in terms of a lessening frequency of publication, as compared to the high water marks of the decade between 1915 and 1925, Moore continued to write at a consistent pace. She told Joe Garagiola in a 1967 television interview on the National Broadcasting Company's "Today" show that she went to her desk each morning after breakfast, working out of the clippings and phrases she had stored up in an inexpensive notebook, one that bore the heading "School Assignments." Whatever else had changed, Moore had adopted a decidedly non-Romantic approach to her work habits.

In June, 1949, Moore traveled to Chambersburg, Pennsylvania, to receive an honorary degree, from Wilson College. This was the first of several such degrees awarded to Moore in this period. By 1955 she had received five more of them: from Mount Holyoke (1950), the University of Rochester (1951), Long Island University (1953), and two schools, Smith College and Douglass College of Rutgers University, in 1955. These public awards were, of course, always mentioned to Warner and his family, who increasingly took delight in the growing fame and recognition of their relative. Warner was now serving on the faculty at the Gunnery School in Washington, Connecticut. Mary Markwick, his oldest daughter, married John Reeves in 1951, and his son, John Jr., was soon to be engaged to Virginia Smith, from Park Ridge, Illinois. Family life for Warner was to be somewhat less tense in the coming years, as the crisis with Constance seems to have passed. Warner was to remain a major source of emotional support for his sister, and one of the many major appreciators of the fame that would come her way.

Because of Warner's proximity to Brooklyn, he visited his sister often, as did her nieces, especially Sarah Moore, who would eventually live in Greenwich Village. This meant that there were relatively few letters between Moore and Warner; there was also the unusual situation where Warner destroyed many of the letters he received from his sister. This was almost certainly done in order not to disturb Constance. Such secrecy was a result, of course, of the many years of tension with Constance, and the strong bonding that existed between Moore and her brother. But there are several surviving letters from Warner to Moore, which of course did not need to be destroyed, that allude to this situation. In one, it is clear that Warner has read his sister's letter at the mailbox outside his home in Connecticut and destroyed it before he walks back into the house.

In 1951, Moore's *Collected Poems* appeared. This volume further assured her reputation as a major modernist poet. The English poet Roy Fuller, reviewing the book for a publication in London, expressed concern that she not become sentimental with age. Moore wrote to Bryher of her wish that Mr. Fuller might have the experience of many sentimentalities. Though in some ways she was making light of a review, she was also indicating that she knew her poetry was growing more directly expressive of its network of affections and sympathies. The *Collected* reprinted most of the poems from the *Selected* volume of 1935, maintaining the order of appearance as set by Eliot, and virtually all of the poems from the subsequent volumes. The few that were dropped included "Half-Deity" from *The Pangolin*, "The Student" from *What Are Years*, and "Walking Sticks" from *Nevertheless*. ("The Student" was to be restored in the *Collected Poems* of 1967; however, that volume omitted "Melanchthon," a poem praised by many.) Besides the poems from the various volumes there were also included nine previously uncollected poems, including "A Face," "Efforts of Affection," and "Armor's Undermining Modesty."

Of the several reviews of the *Collected Poems*, perhaps the one that stands out most is that by Randall Jarrell, in the November–December, 1952 issue of *Partisan Review*. The tone of the review is chatty, which is important, since part of its argument is that Moore's poetry is not nearly as difficult as many make it out to be. Also, the review touches on many of the themes and questions raised by previous criticism of Moore's poetry, and so it becomes a sort of "mid-career" stock-taking. One other feature of the review, perhaps having some negative consequences, is that it tended to set the context for Moore's readers, especially on subjects such as her use of armor, her occasional self-parody, and so forth. But this excerpt will give the flavor of Jarrell's criticism, both at its best and when it is setting up persistent categories as well:

> She wished to trust, as absolutely as she could, in flat laconic matter-of-factness, in the minimal statement, understatement: these earlier poems of hers approach as a limit, a kind of ideal minimal statement, a truth thought of as underlying, prior to, all exaggeration and error; the poet has tried to strip or boil everything down to this point of hard, objective, absolute precision. But the most extreme precision leads inevitably to quotation; and quotation is armor and ambiguity and irony all at once—turtles are great quoters. Miss Moore leaves the stones she picks up carefully uncut, but places them in an unimaginably complicated and difficult setting, to sparkle under the Northern Lights of her continual irony.

Much of this is accurate and telling, but some of it is exaggerated or partial as well. Some of Moore's poems, even some early ones, take a delight in exaggeration and play. And her use of quotation is not simply a result of her armoring; it is often a kind of homage, or a way of representing a plentitude of viewpoints, a fullness of consciousness, as in "An Octopus" or "Marriage." Obviously, Jarrell is reflecting the taste of his era, subsequent to Moore's and indebted to it in many ways, in which New Criticism held out for especial praise a well-made poem that exhibited "exactness, concision, irony," to quote Jarrell just prior to the above passage. But Moore's modernism had features that were, by New Critical standards, extravagant and even occasionally baroque. Also, Jarrell's image of the "Northern Lights of her continual irony" suggests a distance and a cold removal on the part of the poet from her subjects and themes, whereas Moore was often writing out of an agonized and self-dramatizing context. Recall her lines from "Marriage" about "the strange experience of beauty," where she says "its existence is too much; / it tears one to pieces." Jarrell is able to register some of this feeling, but the effect of such a passage as the one quoted above is to make many readers see only one side of the issue. Later in the review Jarrell argues that in Moore's poems "morality is usually simplified into self-abnegation." This sort of remark is also one-sided, or can all too readily produce a one-sided reading, ignoring as it does how for Moore morality is always a social matter and a question of balanced self-awareness as well. In some ways, this one-sided version of Moore contributes to the public image of her as somewhat eccentric, matronly, and restrained. However, Jarrell does quote at some length, especially from important poems such as "Armor's Undermining Modesty" and "The Pangolin," and lists the titles of the best among her poems, choices that are hard to dispute.

The possibility that Moore might extend her reputation beyond that of exclusively literary reviewers and readers was foreshadowed, as it were, by the review of *Collected Poems* in the December 24, 1951 issue of *Newsweek.* The unsigned review was entitled "Best Living Poet," and it occupied one whole page of the magazine and included two photographs. One of the photographs was of Jim Thorpe, erroneously identified as being one of Moore's own pupils at the Indian School in Carlisle; in fact, he was never in her class. The review began by citing Eliot's high praise for Moore, something that had by this time become a reflex reaction of many commentators. Then the reviewer sets out to correct what he calls a "double error in poetic public relations," by denying the poems are "extremely difficult" and that Moore is a Dickinson-type recluse. The use of the phrase "public relations" becomes a telling sign of what is developing around Moore and her "image." Roughly half of what follows is biographical background, and then only two poems are quoted, a couplet from "Marriage" and a longer passage from "Propriety." Some literary gossip is reported, as the reader is told that some of Moore's latest poems are so clear that "ominous mutterings about 'sentimentality' are starting to be heard."

It is possible to see this single review as the harbinger of the main themes of the "public relations" that began to cluster around Moore from this point on. By describing her poems as "essentially . . . definitions," and as "encyclopedia articles set to music," the writer not only fails to offer any sense of what values the poems set out to engage or what sort of arguments they make, but he also makes their curious surfaces their main attribute. Moore herself is described as being "outspoken in a quiet way," and this adds to the overall effect that the poet is primarily engaged in creating "delightful" effects. Overall, the air of eccentricity and even quaintness dominates, and the struggle of the early breakthroughs in modernist style is obviated by the focus on surface features. Also especially telling is the use of the quotation from Eliot, by this time a figure of international fame, to validate Moore's talent.

The *Newsweek* review closed by citing the words of Louise Bogan.

Bogan had by this time become the poetry critic for *The New Yorker*, and she, too, reviewed the *Collected Poems*, in the August 2, 1952 issue of that magazine, where Bogan could report on the national awards the volume had garnered. Bogan is able to insist, with the use of italics, that Moore's "poems are beautifully *about* something," but she doesn't take enough space to say just what that is. Bogan is accurate in calling Moore "a naturalist without pedantry and a moralist without harshness," but here the final effect is that she is simply confirming a majority opinion about Moore, or at least the opinion of a majority of those "who read American poetry with any attention." In many cases Bogan was a perceptive reviewer, but here she may have unwittingly contributed to the reinforcement of a received opinion. After the *Collected Poems*, Moore's poetry is frequently subjected to matching pieties, of a professional and a popular sort. Such piety has, among other undesirable consequences, a way of obscuring the poems that are most challenging. As she herself had told Alyse Gregory two decades earlier, it was hard to see how an exacting mind could be popular. The reverse of this rule would have more and more consequences for the reception of Moore's poetry.

Two of the "Previously Uncollected" poems—"Voracities and Verities Sometimes Are Interacting" and "Propriety"—are in many ways typical of the sorts of poems Moore would write in the next two decades. In some ways, these two types of lyrics had their origin in the longer and more complex poems of the period of 1915 through 1925, when Moore was able to proceed with surface details and moral analysis in a more integrated way. But even there the mixture was volatile, and occasionally it would produce something like "Pigeons," which was never reprinted, where the listing of surface details drained the energy from the poem's argument. The two types were really there all along: the poetry of personal temperament and the poetry of moral definition. Though the two kinds of poem sometimes cross-fertilized and lent features each to the other, there is a discernible difference between the two. The first sort is capable of becoming merely an occasional poem, the sort of "signature" statement of the well-known personality that celebrates both individuality and the intrigue of celebrity. In Moore's hands it often has a great deal of redeeming wit, but at its weakest it can also devolve into something like name-dropping or even an expression of personal pique or sentimentality.

The beginning stanza of "Voracities" sets the tone, with its brio and the slight hint of exasperation in the last line:

> I don't like diamonds;
> the emerald's "grass-lamp glow" is better;
> and unobtrusiveness is dazzling,
> upon occasion.
> Some kinds of gratitude are trying.

Knowing the earlier complex ironies of Moore's poetry, and knowing of her struggle to adjust self-expression and self-discipline, the qualification of the fourth line can be extremely resonant. By leaving open the importance of the individual occasion, the affective weight of particularity and circumstance is stressed, but only at the level of an abstraction. As if aware of this tension, Moore turns, in the second stanza, to a very particular instance, though she makes it so particular that she must add a clarifying note to say the book is Man-Eaters of Kumaon, by Major James Corbett. (The book was a gift from Louise Crane, and there is a letter to Elizabeth Bishop where Moore praises emeralds; the poem's theme of gift-giving and the obligations of friendship is one that had engaged Moore for many years.) After the second stanza, the poem concludes with a couplet that echoes a passage from St. Paul's epistle to the Ephesians; the couplet's tone also combines an air of shared knowingness and self-acceptance that encapsulates the style of this sort of "occasional" poem.

> Poet's, don't make a fuss;
> the elephant's "crooked trumpet" "doth write";
> and to a tiger-book I am reading—
> I think you know the one—
> I am under obligation.
>
> One may be pardoned, yes I know
> one may, for love undying.

There are many other overtones in this poem, of course. For example, in the line "Poets, don't make a fuss," there is the theme of the Renaissance poet, exemplified by George Herbert (a favorite of Bishop's as well as Moore's), that says "Look in your heart and write." Another way to read this poem is to see it as the opposite of those early poems of

Moore in which she castigated critics and other uncomprehending readers. Whereas she once began her poetry with addresses to those who lacked half-wit, she is able to speak in her sixties to friends who know her allusions and her emotional code. Normally a modernist poet would not allow such a phrase as "love undying," recorded in one of Moore's notebooks as having come from St. Paul's Epistle to the Ephesians, to be used without irony, but Moore is no longer writing as the isolated modernist who must develop her audience selectively as she goes.

The second sort of poetry that occupied much of Moore's energy is represented by "Propriety." This poem can be seen as a prototype of such later lyrics as "Like a Bulwark," "Blessed Is the Man," "Style," "Charity Overcoming Envy," to name the more obvious examples. These poems often use one of Moore's distinctive stanzaic forms or rhyme schemes, though sometimes, as in "Propriety," the rhymes are erratic. They can be read as the legacy of Moore's attempt to write a public poetry during the war years, though they are seldom as directly moral in their arguments as, say, "What Are Years?" The metaphoric equations between the observed nature in these poems and the human concern with ethical and social values is more pronounced. Here are the first two stanzas (out of a total of five) from "Propriety," where the title is also the first word of the poem:

> is some such word
>   as the chord
>   Brahms had heard
>   from a bird,
> sung down near the root of the throat;
> it's the little downy woodpecker
>   spiraling a tree—
>   up up up like mercury;
>
>   a not long
>   sparrow-song
>   of hayseed
>   magnitude—
>   a tuned reticence with rigor
> from strength at the source. Propriety is
>   Bach's Solfegietto
>   harmonica and basso.

Moore's lifelong concern with the dialectic between the orders of nature and culture is clearly on display here, as is her way of seeing aesthetic and moral issues as intertwined. The "strength at the source" has begun deep in the throat of the bird, in a purely naturalistic context, but is converted through Brahms' aesthetic sensitivity into something that is clearly a human virtue. After the long ordeal of caring for her mother through her extended illness, Moore was seldom able to forget about strength as the key to all values, the very source of moral worth.

Moore was to continue with her preoccupation with an ideal of self-sacrifice. Near the end of 1950, she wrote to Bryher to tell her of how Warner's feeling that he should be of service led him to consider developing a theology course for veterans. She also told Bryher that Warner was sometimes so solicitous of her that if things were not going well, he would not confide in her. On her sixty-fifth birthday, however, he continued to equate her spiritual work and her writing, for he wrote to tell her that her many impressive honors were an offering to their mother. Up until July, 1952, when Kathrine Jones died, Moore would spend time visiting her and trying to comfort her friend, Marcia Chamberlain; both of these women had been of great support to Moore, who constantly praised them to her other friends and correspondents. Often they would speak of expanding their circle. Through Marcia Chamberlain, Moore came to hear of another woman, Ena Molesworth, a good friend of both Chamberlain and Bryher. Moore never met Molesworth, but she joked that her name "makes me expect a great deal," probably referring to the fact that Mrs. Molesworth was an English writer of well-known children's books that Bryher had perhaps mentioned to Moore. She may also have been punning on her nickname for her mother, "Mole," taken as it was from a children's book. Sometime later, in the fall of 1953, Marcia Chamberlain was in a hospital in Brooklyn, suffering from a stroke. Moore again was called on to be of service, and aided her friend until July, 1955, when Chamberlain died.

A flood of public recognition came to Moore in the first six months of 1952. What came to her in this period was unprecedented for an American poet to receive in such a short period of time. It was this recognition that would alter her identity not only in the academic community but throughout the larger public as well. It began with the Bollingen Award, announced in *The New York Times* on January 12,

1952. This award had been given to Pound in 1948 for his *Pisan Cantos*, and had touched off a furor unmatched in American literature. Those who felt Pound was guilty of either treason or anti-Semitism (or both) were aggrieved that an important national honor should go to a man with such despicable character and opinions, which he was not at all willing to keep out of his writings. Others defended him by saying that excellence in art and attitudes in politics were, and should be, separate issues. The theories of the New Criticism, which argued that poems were to be judged solely on grounds of aesthetic principles, were the orthodoxy of the day. But the Award survived this scandal, and when it was given to Moore, she was able to take full satisfaction in it. And there were more to come.

The National Book Awards were announced at the end of January, and Moore's *Collected Poems* won in the poetry category. At the ceremony where the awards were distributed, Moore said that "I don't know why my work should be called poetry except that there is no other category in which to put it. Anyone could do what I do." This self-denigration was to become a key element in her public image. Many would hear in it echoes of the famous first line of "Poetry": "I, too, dislike it." And the formulation that her lyrics were not poems, but uncategorizable otherwise, would be repeated often, by Moore and by her commentators. Such a statement stressed her humility in one sense, but it also stressed her eccentricity. The tension between these two meanings, one negative and self-effacing, the other positive and self-aggrandizing, would both preserve and yet accommodate the public's idea of the poet that had developed in the modernist era. Most costly, however, was the way the label of eccentricity tended to conceal how the hard-won victories of poetic form were a testament of Moore's intelligence.

In the same talk, Moore went on to formulate a version of a saying by Confucius: "If there is a knife in your heart there is no precision in your mind." She may well have meant this to be directed at Pound, or at least to serve as a signal to those who would know of Pound's appropriation of Confucian ethics in the early *Cantos*. Such a moral apothegm wove together Christian sentiment and aesthetic discipline in a way that was thoroughly in keeping with Moore's practice. But such an axiom also helped the public accept the writer as someone who was essentially affirmative and charitable before she was artistically demanding. Regardless of the sincerity and naïveté with which Moore made her remarks, the public that was to begin paying her more and more attention had to assimilate her to their understanding of what it was to be a writer. The Bollingen Prize of 1948 might have been given to Pound, who struck some as a pariah, but in 1952 the winner was clearly acceptable to all.

On May 6, 1952, *The New York Times* announced that Moore's *Collected Poems* had been given the Pulitzer Prize. This completed the "sweep" of the three major prizes for poetry given annually in America. It should be pointed out that each was given as a result of a vote by a panel of distinguished writers. As such, these three awards represented for Moore an acknowledgment by her peers that she was an important writer. But the fact that she was given all three in the same year, and for what was still by many measures a limited body of work—the *Collected Poems* ran to only 150 pages of poetry—meant that the public was invited, if that is not too weak a word, to use her as a standard by which to define the very notion of a poet. Less than a year later, in April, 1953, Moore was given the Gold Medal for poetry by the National Institute of Arts and Letters, the nation's most prestigious cultural organization. This was not an annual award, but was given for a lifetime's achievement. Moore had been named a member of the Institute in 1947, the year her mother died, and she was only the fifth woman to be honored with the Gold Medal. It is fair to say that at this point there were few other honors left to give her that would match the ones of 1952–53.

The many honors and awards that came to Moore did not overwhelm her completely, though she would still occasionally talk to her friends in the early 1950's as if she were a recluse who seldom left the house. But Moore was able to continue with a round of literary and social events. In February, 1951, for example, she heard Stevens read, though she missed the award presentation for him at the Poetry Society of America. There was also a United Nations Conference at Hunter College, where she read some of her *Fables*. In December, 1952, her old friends Glenway Wescott and Monroe Wheeler sponsored a tea for Osbert and Edith Sitwell. A few months later she began teaching a course at Bryn Mawr one day a week, at the invitation of an English professor there, Laurence Stapleton. She promised herself that she would finish the *Fables* before the course began, a promise which she apparently almost kept. Later, she reported to Bryher that the task was finally completed in June, 1953. The course she taught at Bryn Mawr had a reading list that included poetry by Eliot, Pound, and Sitwell, but also Paul Valéry's "A Letter from Madame Teste" (an exercise in self-consciousness that had long fascinated Moore); a Borges story, "The Zahir" (a disorienting fable about obsession with an object or image); Nabokov's memoir, *Circumstantial Evidence* (which would have appealed to Moore's nostalgia); a story by Elizabeth Bishop; and James Thurber's *Thirteen Clocks*.

In June, 1953, she received what must have been one of her more cherished honors, the M. Carey Thomas Award of Bryn Mawr College. Though she modestly told Bryher that there were others who deserved it before she did, the choice nevertheless was a very popular one. In March of the same year she discussed the upcoming visit to the college with Professor Stapleton, and offered to read, among other things, her new poem about a race horse, "Tom Fool at Jamaica." She told Stapleton that she had very little that was not already collected in a book. But she was eager to please her host and the students, and afterwards wrote an apology that she was not able to attend the varsity basketball game. The invitation for the award ceremony gave the date of May 15, 1953, at 8:30 P.M., in Goodhart Hall. Three earlier recipients of the Award were Ms. Thomas herself; Jane Addams in 1931; and Eleanor Roosevelt in 1948.

The visit for the medal ceremony also led to a series of notes afterwards, as Moore and her brother tried to arrange for Stapleton to buy a gift in their name for Katharine McBride, then the president of the college. At first they had wanted a special plant, but when this proved impossible to obtain, a piece of silver was selected. The care and attention given to this was typical of Moore's sense of propriety, as well as that of her brother. To both of them, such an award was more than an occasion for mere ego gratification. As with her habit of treating her wealthy friends in an evenhanded manner when it came to money, Moore also went to great lengths to reward, as it were, those who had chosen to honor her. The circulation of gifts, tokens, and well-chosen words, all seen as both personal testament and cultural ritual, had always been a key part of her personal ethic, and in her later years this dedication never wavered. If anything, her attention to it increased.

In the typescript of the remarks she made that night, Moore singled out some of the concerns and challenges of President Thomas that she felt were especially important. Chief among these was one that turned on Thomas's penchant for differentiations: "How does the Good differ from the Preferable?" Such differentiations form a crucial part of Moore's poetry, of course, and it is hard to tell if she made them a part of her sensibility before or after she saw this concern in Thomas. Moore also praised Thomas by saying that "she did not minister to one's vanity," a theme Moore herself treated often in the 1950's. In her acceptance speech, she went on to say that Bryn Mawr was "an intellectual hearth and home," and that Dalton Lecture Hall was like a miniature Greek theater and the "pleasantest lecture room I know." Recalling Pembroke dining hall, she praised it as being "as genuinely Jacobean as ever," and she fondly referred to the mottoes carved on the walls of various buildings and rooms, especially the "Veritatem Dilexi" of the dining hall. The culminating remark of the evening was one that could summarize much of Moore's lifelong aesthetic and personal concerns, for she said that "the test of culture is the ability to pay voluntary attention." Paying attention and making differentiations both lie at the center of Moore's best poetry, and her poetry often explores the relationship between these two activities. Exploring such a relationship goes beyond the common sense that sees considerable overlap between these two human faculties, and instead pursues how one demands the other, both as its necessary precondition and its aesthetic completion.

Of course, not all the awards for poetry in the decade were given to Moore, and the beginning of 1954 brought her the news that W. H. Auden had been given the Bollingen Award; this pleased her very much. Auden had endeared himself to Moore several years earlier when he ran ahead and held the train for her at Philadelphia's 30th Street Station as they were transferring to the local line that would carry them to Bryn Mawr. She mentioned this incident repeatedly to many of her friends, each time casting it in a chivalric context. Even prior to that, as early as November, 1939, he had visited Moore and her mother for dinner at the Brooklyn apartment. In a thank-you letter, he told her that American writers "more than most" had to accept isolation as a blessing; the dinner conversation may well have lingered on this subject, since it is a part of Moore's poetry throughout the 1930's. He also told her that she was like Rilke, in that she was capable of true praise in her poetry. This element of praise is one that would also bind them in the next three decades, as it became an important part of their poems.

Moore responded by saying that she was much in the dark about her own work, but that she admired Auden's poetry, and quoted several lines and phrases from *Another Time*, such as "show an affirming flame." In the same letter she could point out, however, that his tendency to use vulgar language was something she could tolerate but not approve; she told him that he must know she felt he should be scolded for many things. A year and a half later, he wrote her from Ann Arbor to thank her for her review of *The Double Man*, and to ask for a reference for a Guggenheim grant, which she gave him. In her letter to the panel of judges she referred to Auden as an "indispensable" poet. In 1944 they served together as judges for a student poetry contest at Swarthmore, and Auden told her that her "In Distrust of Merits" was "the only war poem so far that made any sense." In 1944 he also reviewed *Nevertheless* for *The New York Times Book Review*, a review that made very public Auden's continuing private admiration for Moore. It also came at a time when Moore was slowly turning toward more public and social concerns. Though caring for her mother would obviously take up much of her energy in the middle 1940's, by the end of the decade she was to be on the brink of great public recognition. Auden's review, then, came at an important time for her. But more than its timing, its argument helped to gain greater acceptance and understanding for Moore's poetry. In some ways, meeting and befriending Auden was one of the most important developments for Moore as a writer in between the time she left *The Dial* and when she won the major awards in the early 1950's.

The review was a masterly stroke of disarming criticism. At this time Auden was himself moving more and more toward a directly moral poetry, having dropped much of the obscure experimentalism of his earlier work. Under the influence of the war, Augustinian theology, and Kierkegaard's existentialism, he was to become a poet especially suited to "The Age of Anxiety," to use one of his more popular terms. So when he began the review by saying that he had at first had difficulty understanding Moore's poetry, many readers must surely have felt reassured. When he followed this admission, however, with the statement that he agreed with Eliot that Moore's poems "form part of the small body of durable poetry written in our time," he left no doubt as to his estimation of her stature. He went on to compare Moore to Rilke, whose "new objectivity" was ostensibly concerned with describing animals and objects. Then he suggested that the influences on her work were in fact hard to specify; he named three possible sources: Mallarmé, Horace, and Emerson. The very startling triangulation of such figures would impress many readers, and Auden was becoming better known as an arbiter of taste and a reliable and penetrating critic. His own work would owe more and more to Horatian attitudes toward poetry, and he was at the same time enough of an exemplar of modernism to speak with authority on Moore's unique combination of models. Moore wrote to him to thank him for the review, and she pointed out that indeed he was right about the question of influences. Continuing her thoughts about the willingness to be unoriginal, a position she was drawn to in the 1940's, she commented that it was a help, at times, to be helplessly in debt to one's sources. She also mentioned to Auden how much Mrs. Moore liked his work, praising especially his heightened and ironic awareness.

It was around this time that Auden reacted in a very energized way about a rumor that one of Moore's books had been rejected; he was willing to mount a public campaign of embarrassment against the publishers if Moore thought it would do any good. Moore wrote to clarify the situation, and to defuse any outcry; the Cummington Press had suggested some plans to publish a selection of her prose, and then Macmillan asked to see the manuscript, only to decide against it. Auden would in turn enlist Moore's aid in one of his projects. He had started in 1945 to compile an anthology of poetry in translation. At first, he wrote to Moore to ask her if she recalled any usable instances from *The Dial,* or from her own reading. She consulted the index for *The Dial,* and marked what might interest him. To this list she added Ezra Pound, and Mallarmé as rendered into English by Fry. She also singled out Nabokov's edition of three Russian poets in translation. Auden had earlier suggested to his editor, Mr. Pistole, that Moore might be induced to translate La Fontaine. She approached Pistole with a sample, and he was very encouraging. She wrote to tell Auden of this and he responded delightedly, saying that the most readily available translation, by Edward Marsh, an Englishman, sounded too much like *Punch,* the satirical English magazine known for its combination of the arch and the supercilious. At the beginning, Moore was thus supplied with at least a negative model.

Though there are not a great many letters between Auden and Moore, since they often conversed on the telephone, there are nevertheless several signs that their friendship had grown stronger. In March, 1951, Moore wrote to congratulate Auden on his anthology of the works of Edgar Allan Poe, and remarked that his analysis of the American writer was chivalrous, a term Poe himself would have appreciated. In February, Moore wrote to Auden excitedly about the production of "The Beggar's Opera," the libretto he had written with his friend Chester Kallman. Earlier, in 1950, Auden had sent Moore two playful postcards of photographs of his cats. These were addressed to "Aunt Marianne." A year or so later, when one of the cats, named "Lucinda," died, Auden sent a notice to Moore that read: "In Memoriam LK-A 1950–1952," the initials presumably standing for Lucinda Kallman-Auden. In 1963 there is a postcard from Auden that is co-signed by Moore's niece Mary Markwick Reeves and her husband, John, who were visiting Auden in Illinois. This indicates that Auden felt comfortable with Moore's playfulness toward animals, and with close members of her family as well. In 1957, Auden commented on the entries in a poetry contest he was judging, lamenting that many were of low quality. He chose Ted Hughes, however, and asked Moore what she thought of the choice. She admitted that he was clearly a good poet, though perhaps too strident. In the same letter she mentioned going to see a play with Reinhold Niebuhr and his wife, friends with whom she shared an important interest in Auden.

In some ways, Auden and Kallman played a role in Moore's life similar to that played by Monroe Wheeler and Glenway Wescott in the 1920's. They were highly aesthetic writers, very involved with the gossip and goings-on of the literary scene. The homosexual style and aesthetic sensibility of these men did not discernibly make Moore uncomfortable. In fact, there were among her good friends and acquaintances several homosexuals or bachelors, many of whom were also bibliophiles, and they treated Moore with great deference while at the same time being playful and artistically very knowing. This combination of knowingness, which at times approached pedantry, and a playful teasing was, of course, evident in Moore's poetry. From her earliest days as a poet, her sensibility allowed for a great deal of artifice even as it praised what are generally regarded as the more serious values. Because Moore chose to remain single all her life, she was perhaps disposed to be more than tolerant of those who had not started a family of their own. This would include many of her female friends, such as Elizabeth Bishop and Louise Crane, as well. But in many if not all such instances, Moore was able to give her friends, as they gave her, a very intense and complex emotional support. Her own experience as a member of a family was, of course, in one way that of the traditional nuclear model, formed by a very close bonding between parent and child. But without the benefit of a father, Moore in some ways obviously felt that friendships could have something like an extraterritorial dimension, formed on the basis of a commitment to artistic and cultural values that went beyond those one learned from one's parents and siblings. In addition, there was the possibility that her relationship with her friends could be imagined as a kind of family relationship. In June, 1949, for example, Marcia Chamberlain, after helping Moore through the period of mourning for Mrs. Moore, wrote her a letter in which she referred to her as "Baby Moore," and herself as "Mama Chamberlain." As long as her friends observed the social proprieties, Moore was quite willing to accept them as kindred spirits.

Several times in the late 1950's Auden gave parties for his literary friends, to which he invited Moore. These were gala events, for Auden was a gregarious person who had a wide circle of friends drawn from the artistic and publishing worlds, as well as from fellow poets. On at least two occasions, Auden invited Moore to such evenings with an engraved invitation. These invitations included a note at the bottom that read "Carriages at One A.M." Referring to the car that was arranged to take Moore back to Brooklyn, this sort of note is just the touch of "chivalry" at which Auden was adept. Moore would have appreciated not only the practical consequences of such an arrangement, and the thought behind it, but she almost certainly would have liked the touch of playfulness in the expression as well. Though she often protested against people inconveniencing themselves over her, and thanked them profusely for their efforts, friends such as Auden, who indulged her with great concern, were a regular part of her social world.

One of the greatest compliments that Moore paid to Auden was her including him in her series of commentaries on contemporary poets, delivered at Bryn Mawr in 1952. The other poets chosen were Stevens, Pound, and Eliot. Obviously Moore thought very highly of Auden to put him in such company, and she devoted more space to the commentary on him than on the other three, quoting him extensively. Each poet was approached with a different emphasis, though each was quoted often; the commentaries were much like her book reviews in that they relied on the compilation of examples rather than on detailed analysis. With Stevens, she treated his sensibility; with Eliot, by concentrating on his criticism, she dealt with his intelligence; with Pound, she considered his literary technique and the influence of his standards and judgment. When she came to Auden, Moore concentrated on his ideas and beliefs. She began by praising his "capacity for drawing general conclusions," something Auden had praised in de Tocqueville. She also singled out his concern with praise, something her own poetry would increasingly turn to, and with virtue. For her, Auden was clearly a Horatian poet—if not a Christian one—treating of moral behavior by urging repentance and the correction of the will. Occasionally, details of technique are mentioned, but Moore returns again and again to the ethical content of Auden's vision. She concludes with these claims:

> Even a tinge of "greed" makes him "very ill indeed." His studies of Henry James and of Poe show to what heights of liberality he can rise. As a champion of justice, he will always have a champion in the pages he has penned; and as the Orpheus of our mountains, lakes, and plains, will always have his animals.

By saying that Auden's studies of James and Poe demonstrate his liberality, rather than, say, his sensitivity, Moore shows how moral is the context in which she places her fellow poet. The last reference is the only one that does not mention an explicit virtue, but by calling him an Orpheus, Moore links Auden with the animals she herself wrote about, and with the themes of praise and pastoral purity that the Greek poet symbolized.

Several talks she gave throughout the 1950's reflect what might be called an Audenesque approach for its habit of "drawing general conclusions," often in a language that combines aesthetic and moral concerns. As she put it in a talk at City College in New York, on October 31, 1955, "A technical triumph is usually, in some degree, a moral triumph." Less than a week later, at Barnard College, she alluded to Niebuhr's *The Self and the Dramas of History*, when she said that "the self does not realize itself most fully when self-realization is its conscious aim." And she adds to this her own formulation, that "egomania is not a duty," as she put it in the poem, "Blessed Is the Man" (1956). On April 8, 1956, in a letter to Elizabeth Bishop after attending Auden's lectures on Shakespeare at the YMHA, Moore could say that he was not only the very best teacher in the world, but was always exciting technically.

In 1961, at the College Woman's Club of Montclair, New Jersey, she quoted Niebuhr directly as saying that "creativeness must transcend aesthetics or it is a perversion of the love of life into the love of self." Such transcendent sentiments, often grounded in Christian humility, appear in her poems from this period, too, not only "Blessed Is the Man," but also "Logic and 'The Magic Flute' " ("one need not shoulder, need not shove"). But Auden would have recognized this way of formulating his concerns, and he may also have introduced Moore to the work of artists she might otherwise not have known, such as the German, Georg Grosz, who claimed that for an artist the key is "observation, research, and a great amount of joy in the thing." Since Grosz's visual style would seem to have little in common with Moore's sensibility, she may have chosen this formula from his writing through Auden's having shown it to her. She quoted this often, however, and also more than once she mentioned Auden's injunction that "a poem should praise all it can." In these talks, Moore continued her habit of quoting various examples from a range of writers to make her technical points, but the talks are generally more concerned with the interrelation between aesthetic and moral questions than they are with the problems of verse technique, as were many of the talks in the late 1930's. Moore's role as teacher, one she adopted somewhat gingerly in the early 1930's, but one that had blossomed by the late 1950's, was something that she learned to be comfortable with in large measure from the example of Auden.

Moore was not content to praise Auden as a great teacher in a letter to Elizabeth Bishop; she also wrote a poem about him that made the same point, adding to it her sense of his chivalrous nature. The poem, called "Unprosaic Mosaic," was never published, but it exists in a typescript version that has the words "Dear Wysten" [sic] in Moore's hand in the upper right corner of the page. Added in the same place are the typed words "Praeceptor [a]nd guardian." The poem has an "occasional" feel about it, as if it were written for a time when Auden might

have introduced Moore at a reading, or it might even have served as her
introduction for him. The poem reads:

> I bow (catching my wide brimmed hat
> as gravity would take charge of it
>
> An an an anomaly, this:
> as the monastery lion was made to transport wood—
> A gift of words has been enacted of you.
>
> GOD BLESS YOU, SIR.
>
> With portcullis guarded by you,
> Enchanter in the world's sometimes prosaic garden,
> Need I stir? No.
> Since you are our master,
> Could I rhyme er with Sir?
>
> Yes yes our prime enchanter
> much more than prime "amuser."

The last lines of the poem may be Moore's reassuring Auden that his
work, while containing playful and even irreverent elements, is still a
source of artistic power; it is quite possible that he often would reassure
her in similar terms.

Moore enjoyed other friendships that resembled the one with Auden
in that they combined a love of books with an access to a social world
where she could be comfortably respected. One of these was with
Frances Steloff. Moore had first made the acquaintance of Steloff in the
1940's, when the Gotham Book Mart offered to stock the remaindered
copies of *Selected Poems*. The friendship between the two women grew
for the next two decades. Steloff was a Russian immigrant who had
slowly and tenaciously turned her love of literature and culture into a
successful business. In this tenacity she resembled other supporters of
modernist culture, such as James Laughlin, whose avocation and taste
were to serve as mainstays to many writers and artists who needed
friendly recognition. Steloff used her store to stock works of mainly
modern literature, and it became a center for readings and publication
parties, too. In some ways it had a role like that of Sylvia Beach's
"Shakespeare & Co." in Paris. Steloff was especially generous with

Moore, and efficient as well. Throughout their friendship Moore relied on Steloff, and her assistants at the store on West 47th street, to supply her with the latest books and journals. Many times Moore would send along to the store important issues of small magazines that she had acquired, and she offered these for sale to offset her many purchases. Steloff also would go out of her way to fill Moore's requests, sometimes even going to other booksellers or pursuing secondhand dealers in order to obtain a rare or elusive title. Moore would send pertinent information about the title of a desired book, often along with the name of a friend or relative to whom she wanted it shipped. Quickly and accurately, Steloff would see that the books went out.

But the relation extended beyond buying and selling. It was Steloff who introduced Moore to so-called health foods, and encouraged her to use a variety of new items in her diet. As a result, wheat germ and various honeys, as well as brewer's yeast, figs, and protein supplements, were to become part of Moore's regular meals. Steloff was especially adept at finding honey from many sources, and invariably Moore's thank-you notes were effusive. The notes were equally expressive when it came to the books that Steloff took care of as well. One of the titles was especially interesting: Jim Corbett's *Man-Eaters of Kumaon.* As early as 1946, Moore arranged for this to be sent to her niece, Sally, then serving in the Navy in Bethesda, Maryland. A year later, she had it sent to Warner. All of this was another response to the book that had been given to Moore as a gift by Louise Crane, and which was the occasion for the poem, "Voracities and Verities Sometimes Are Interacting." It was typical of Moore to convert a gift given her into gifts for others. Moore was also especially grateful for Steloff's efforts in obtaining *The Lincoln Reader,* edited by Paul Angle, for Mrs. Moore, just months before her death. Not only does this show how Mrs. Moore remained mentally active, but the gesture seemed to cement the relationship between Moore and Steloff. Steloff's letter of condolence to Moore when her mother died was especially touching and especially appreciated. In the letter, Steloff remembered with fondness a visit that Moore and her mother had paid to the shop in 1945.

Moore arranged for a list of books, chiefly on biblical commentary and spiritual guidance, to be shipped to Warner for use at the Gunnery School in Connecticut, and there were items sent to Mrs. Crane and others. Moore also shared with Steloff details of her social and literary life. One of these events is especially striking. In January, 1951, Moore wrote about attending a reading by Wallace Stevens. She later told Elizabeth Bishop about Stevens' reading style, which involved reading very deliberately with dramatic pauses, and never looking at the audience and never moving his feet. Afterwards, a driver hired by Mrs. Church, the widow of one of Stevens' friends, took Stevens to the Drake Hotel, dropped Marcel Duchamp at 14th Street, and then proceeded to drive Moore back to 260 Cumberland. Duchamp, who was supported for many years by the Churches, was doubtlessly a fascinating figure for both Moore and Stevens, though they probably also had a lot to speak of just between them. In any event, it was a distinctive ride. In her memoir of Stevens, published in *The New York Review of Books* on June 25, 1964, Moore recalled having lunch with Mrs. Church, Stevens, Duchamp, and Dubuffet. This was some years after the death of Mr. Church, and may have been around 1951. She remembered that Stevens resolutely refused to repeat an anecdote he had told about goats. Later, she added that after a reception given by Mrs. Church, perhaps the one in 1951, Stevens stopped her and inquired after Warner, whom he described as "an ornament to civilization." If Stevens had meant to flatter Moore, he could not have chosen a better way.

In March, 1951, Moore, working with a crowded schedule, left a dinner for the Sitwells in order to attend a reading by Laura Benét held at the Gotham Book Mart. She wrote Steloff a note expressing her enjoyment, but there were also many invitations to readings at the shop that she had to decline. Once, Steloff gave Moore a statue of an elephant, knowing that Moore collected these representations of one of her favorite animals; she joked that the "herd" had grown to a considerable number, thirty-six in all, counting the one from Steloff. In 1951, Moore published some of her drawings in the inaugural issue of a magazine, *Tiger's Eye*, and asked Steloff to secure a number of copies of the issue. In 1952 she arranged for a copy of the special Dante issue of *Kenyon Review* to be sent to Reinhold Niebuhr. In 1955, Moore had an operation on an "overgrown" bone in her foot, and excused herself from several invitations that Steloff sent; these were usually for readings or autograph parties for writers Moore knew or admired. Steloff also sent Moore a book in 1957, *Practicing the Presence of God*, by Joseph Goldsmith, which Moore found especially comforting; she referred to it in later letters, and such works of piety also contributed to the friendship between the two women. In 1961 she arranged for Steloff to send some books to her while she was recuperating from another illness: she wanted the anthology called *The World of Zen* and a new translation of the Odyssey. In 1967, when Moore published her brief essay "Crossing Brooklyn Bridge at Twilight," in *The New York Times*, she mentioned the Gotham Book Mart and its famous sign that carries the slogan, "Wise Men Fish Here." She commended the store's "new compactness" and made it plain how it contributed to her feeling that she could say, "But of any cities I have seen, I like New York best."

Though the early years of the decade were marked by her work on the *Fables*, there were other projects around this time where Moore entered into the work of another author. Maria Edgeworth's novel, *The Absentee*, had originally been written as a play and then converted to a novel. Moore published a version of this work as a play in four acts. *The Absentee* appeared in 1962, in a limited edition of 300 signed copies, but she had finished a complete draft of it as early as 1954. In February of that year she gave a copy of the manuscript to Martin Browne to take back to London for possible consideration. Browne was a theatrical director who was in New York at the time to direct Eliot's play, *The Confidential Clerk*. From the first its chances of success as a play were small, evidently because there were too many parts for Irish actors, a rare breed in the London theater world at that time. Robert Giroux, Eliot's publisher, interceded for Moore and asked if Browne would take the manuscript under consideration, but obviously nothing came of this. Giroux was probably influenced in his efforts by Eliot himself; in May, 1955, he took Eliot and Moore to dinner, along with Marion Kauffer, the widow of McKnight Kauffer. Moore particularly enjoyed this evening, which took place at Voisin's, a very exclusive restaurant, and she wrote to Warner about it in the most glowing terms.

Moore may well have come to the idea of writing a play because of her observation of Eliot's successes in this realm. Of course, she had always admired Shaw and was very enthusiastic about her experiences as a playgoer from as far back as her college days. But why would she turn to an early nineteenth-century work for her material? Maria Edgeworth's novel concerns the controversial subject of land ownership and management by the Anglo-Irish of their estates in Ireland. But the dramatic version as rendered by Moore is focused on questions of manners and the destiny of love. In her introduction, Moore cites the remark by John Ruskin that he felt he could learn more about Irish politics from *The Absentee* than from a thousand Blue Books. But in Moore's treatment, the political situation is implicit and doesn't really come under analytic scrutiny. At the end of the introduction, Moore asks, somewhat rhetorically, "Does it hold the attention? Does any of it apply?" Many readers may well answer with a reluctant "no," for the play's topicality and local detail may well keep it from ever being performed. The narrative also relies heavily on certain outdated novelistic conventions, especially the theme of the abandoned orphan made happy by the recovery of a "lost" fortune.

Moore may well have been attracted to the play because of its Irish themes and setting, but she probably found one of its central characters especially appealing. Grace is the niece and ward of Lord and Lady Clonbrony; in the first act of the play she speaks of regarding Ireland as a friend. Later in the play she remarks that "of course at times it [poetry] does express things better than you can express them yourself." This young lady thus echoes one of Moore's poems, "Spenser's Ireland," and her early Bryn Mawr story, "Pym." Indeed, Moore's reworking of the Edgeworth novel resembles in many ways her early stories written at college. As in the Bryn Mawr stories, with their concern for tokens given "in earnest," *The Absentee* features a spoon warmer given to Grace as a wedding present. This gift is inscribed with the motto, "Deo ducente nil nocet" (a rough translation is: "If God is leading, no harm will occur"). The wedding itself is made possible because it is discovered that Grace is not the niece of Lord Clonbrony, and so is both an heiress and free to marry Kilcullen, Clonbrony's son. The discovery scene reveals that a marriage certificate, drawn up on a battlefield by a dying man, would prove Grace's parentage, but it was never properly delivered. When Grace hears the news that untangles her fate, she faints in the best tradition of novelistic heroines. But of course the play ends happily with the wedding of Grace and Kilcullen.

In the 1950's, Moore formed a friendship with another woman who, like Frances Steloff, had been very active in the innovations of modernist art, the sculptress Malvina Hoffman. Hoffman was born in 1887, the same year as Moore, and died of a heart attack in 1966, having achieved considerable fame through her sculpture, an art she had studied with Rodin in Paris in the early 1920's. Her memoir, *Yesterday Is Tomorrow*, was published in 1965, and it was polished and edited by

Moore. The most famous of Hoffman's sculptures is perhaps the series called the "Races of Man," cast in bronze in a heroic scale, which is now exhibited at the Chicago Natural History Museum. But she also did busts of prominent artists, such as Paderewski and Pavlova, and most notably one of Henry Frick, which now stands at the entrance to the Frick museum in New York. An alabaster bust of Rita de Acosta Lydig is in the Rosenbach Museum and Library in Philadelphia. The Rosenbach also has an "imaginary" death mask of Keats; Hoffman said that she had a vision of the dead poet one day, and cast this sculpture to record it. She also executed a commission dedicated to commemorating the American soldiers who died in World War II; this was for a site at Epinal, in France, and was completed in the early 1950's. She sent Moore a photograph of an angel that was part of this commission, and this may have interested Moore because of her recently published poem, "By Disposition of Angels." Hoffman also sent Moore a transcription of the engraved mottoes from the Palais de Chaillot, which were lines composed for that site by Paul Valéry, a figure whose work Moore increasingly admired. The two women met through their common membership in the Academy of Arts and Letters, and they spent time together in New York as well as two summers in Maine, where Hoffman had rented a house that was formerly owned by F. O. Matthiessen.

Hoffman lived a life very devoted to beauty and the claims of artistic inspiration that she learned at an early age from her father, a concert pianist. She wrote in her memoir about her first contact with modernism at the Armory Show in New York in 1913. "The violence of the rejections and cheers disturbed me, and I couldn't make up my mind how I felt," she recalled later. She admired the Brancusi, especially for its daring elimination of unnecessary details, but she also felt she herself would never be unstintingly committed to experimentalism. "Classic work has endured, and there must be a reason," she argued. She appreciated the need for mastery of technique, and realized certain discoveries "remain deep in the mind," but she struggled to be watchful for what Rodin had cautioned her to respect: "the accidental." In these struggles she found a kindred spirit in Moore, who shared an early enthusiasm for the experimental but who now was more and more concerned with the enduring elements and with the individuality of impressions and subjects.

In her memoir, Hoffman speaks of meeting and befriending Moore, and since Moore helped her polish the manuscript of the book, we must assume that the recollections are accurate. In August, 1954, Moore told Warner that the memoir possessed moral force and novelty. The tone of the book is one of respect and a certain touch of awe. More important, perhaps, is the light the memoir sheds on Moore's attitude toward her own poetry, especially her habit of nearly constant revision that had struck so many of her critics. Of course, one of the obvious reasons for such revisions should be mentioned: Moore was a perfectionist, a person who believed that the details and surfaces were significant. In Moore's own copy of Hoffman's memoir there is a clipping about the pianist Paderewski where he is quoted as feeling "a constant sense of dissatisfaction with my work." It was clearly a sentiment the two women shared and discussed with one another. There is also the fact that Moore spoke against poetry's intellectual vanity; this is part of what is serious behind the famous opening line, "I, too, dislike it." But what comes out in Hoffman's memoir is a different sort of attitude:

> I confess that I found her poetry hard to understand, so I would ask her to read one of her poems aloud to me. Then I would say, "I really don't know what that's all about, because of my own ignorance, I'm sure, but just possibly you might explain it to me." She would start explaining it, and then she'd say, "You know, I don't really understand much of it myself," and she'd laugh and say, "Of course, I was convinced I understood it when I wrote it. I'll have to work some more on it," and then there would be jottings in the margin, and revision. She didn't mind my saying what I did—she liked the truth, a mending kind of adhesive to stick over any possible misunderstanding.

Here, Moore is very much in the tradition that treats the poem as a process rather than an object, as is obvious in poems such as "The Mind Is an Enchanting Thing." For all of her love of objects, and the objective style in description, and the respect for the exacting methods of the physical sciences, the concern Moore felt for "natural" expression was crucial.

This concern also animated her other engagement with Hoffman as friendly critic and consultant. Moore never spoke French fluently, as Hoffman did, so she would call on the phone while translating the *Fables* and ask Hoffman to "do an unrehearsed, direct translation" of a certain fable. Then she would read her translated version. Hoffman would ask, "Is that the same fable?" for Moore's version would be "full of adjuncts and additions and curious new angles." But then "without replying," Moore would "ring off and go back to her work," intent on rendering the French in a way that was both accurate and natural. Moore was fastidious about the accuracy of her versions, and she relied on Harry Levin, among others, to make sure that she had not misconstrued the original meaning. Indeed, her habit of frequent revision may have been reinforced by her work on the *Fables,* as she came more and more to see each poetic statement as a translation or approximation of a truth that could only be gathered in the doing or thinking of the moment. As she said at the end of one of her poems, "Ecstasy / affords / the occasion and expediency determines the form."

Hoffman also paid Moore a considerable compliment in her memoir. This had to do with Moore's ability as a visual artist. From her early childhood, on through the biology labs at Bryn Mawr, and well into her later years, Moore spent time on her drawing skills and her interest in watercolors. Vacations were a time when this interest could be indulged, and Hoffman remembers one particular incident in which Moore was able to demonstrate her craft in another medium besides words.

> When she wasn't so occupied [reading books from the cottage's library], we would go off together to do watercolors. This was typical of our several summers together (one at Penobscot Bay): we would spend a sympathetic couple of hours in the afternoon that way, perfectly independent of each other. We would go to a granite quarry, for example, that to me was a very exciting place as a whole—all pinks and grays, beautiful colors of stone. I'd be trying to get all of it in at once, as usual, the three floors of ladders going down to the water below, the derricks, the men working. But Marianne would select just one thing, a piece of chain on a pulley, and paint that. And she painted it very well. She did excellent miniature watercolors, perfectly evocative and imaginative.

What is interesting here is not just the approval from an established, professional artist, but the contrast in the two women's sense of scale. Moore's choice of a small area to focus on may, of course, have simply been a result of her limited skill, but there was probably also a reflection of her general aesthetic and her sense of humility. Many of the several dozen pencil sketches and watercolors of Moore that survive are of scenes, frequently of extensive views, that are located in Maine—some showing the place, Kittery, and the date, often the summers of 1953 and 1954. The drawings of animals, some done at the Museum of Natural History in New York City, and others done in various rural locations, are skillful though not especially detailed. The most enjoyable of the works are marked by a delightful sense of color, quite well handled in the watercolor medium. (The painting of the pulley, if it survives, is not at the Rosenbach. Perhaps Moore gave it to Hoffman.) The note of mutual independence is also telling, because Moore doubtlessly respected Hoffman's artistic vocation and the concomitant need for solitude.

The memoir Hoffman published includes a reproduction of a portrait that she drew of Moore. The medium is apparently pencil, and the drawing is neither dated nor discussed by Hoffman in the book. In this portrait Moore's pose and clothing, specifically the tricorn hat and black cape, are strikingly similar to that of the famous photograph taken by George Platt Lynes and used on the paperback edition of the *Complete Poems*. But the face is different. In Hoffman's version the cheeks are much thinner, and the eyes are fuller and darker. A strong sense of melancholy and suffering are added by these changes. Indeed, the famous public image is given here a somewhat haunted and personal dimension that is, if accurate, based on an intimate knowledge of the subject. It was while Moore and Hoffman were together in Maine that the news of the death of Wallace Stevens came to Moore. And since Hoffman began to know Moore shortly after the death of Mrs. Moore, she probably shared Moore's sense of loss on several occasions. Moore may very well have needed someone to take over, in part at least, Mrs. Moore's role as the poet's chief critic and "first reader." Hoffman, as well as Hildegarde Watson, may well have been of considerable comfort to Moore in this context.

In later years, Moore was to write about Hoffman on three occasions: she contributed a short sketch on her life and work to the *Texas Quarterly* in 1964; she reviewed the memoir in *The New York Times* in November, 1965; and, only a few months later, she had the task of composing an obituary for the *National Sculpture Review* after Hoffman's death in 1966. In each case, Moore stressed her friend's dedication to her art, as well as her personal generosity. In each case she also mentioned the incident where Hoffman set up a fund to provide artificial limbs to a boy who had lost his legs when he fell under a trolley. There was also a fund set up for artists who suffered financial need; it was called the "trouble fund," and Moore remarked on the direct nature of such a name. Each article also mentioned the Chicago Hall of Man commission, and Hoffman's insistence that it be executed in bronze or stone, instead of the plaster that was originally specified. Each article also mentioned Hoffman's tools and her technical proficiency, giving as one instance the books of instruction she published for students. In the obituary notice, Moore called one of these books, *Sculpture Inside and Out,* a "kind of monument which had become, for me, her own self-portrait." In the first article she also mentioned Hoffman's studio, and, in a sort of reprise of her poem, "People's Surroundings," spoke of how Hoffman's "arrangements symbolize an instinct for performance; and 'usefulness.'" Hoffman in many ways epitomized an aesthetic close to the spirit of Dewey and his philosophy of instrumentalism.

II. La Fontaine's *Fables, Predilections,* and *O to Be a Dragon*

One of the most important of Moore's accomplishments in the 1950's was also one of the more satisfying of her career, if the completion of a sustained project offered to her, as it does to others, a special pleasure. This was the publication of her translation of La Fontaine's *Fables.* To this large and even daunting task, Moore called on a great many of her literary gifts and expended a considerable amount of artistic and physical energy. In some ways, the effort was a culmination of many tendencies that had begun to manifest themselves in her poetry; in other ways, the project shaped her career during this period and even beyond. The affinity that drew her to this particular poet, and the temperament that led her to translate the entire body of over 250 separate poems, clearly went beyond superficial features. Yet there are also important superficial resemblances that have a particular resonance. Translation done at this level and with thoroughness always involves a complex act of cultural interpenetration, as it just as often involves some complex personal discoveries.

La Fontaine himself, paradoxically, was very far removed from Moore, by nationality, gender, and history. Yet, he "answered" her concerns and interests in surprising ways. La Fontaine lived under the reign of Louis XIV, whose artifact Moore had written about in "No Swan So Fine." The contemporary and friend of such writers as Boileau, Racine, and Molière, La Fontaine was part of the age of French neo-classicism in writing, but his major work hardly represented such an austere and restrained style. Still, the conditions of his life as a writer were very much a part of the social milieu that these other writers shared, especially the system of patronage. La Fontaine was born the son of a royal keeper of the forest in the small town of Château-Thierry, along the banks of the Marne, about fifty miles east of Paris. His early writing career was marked by the publication of his *Contes*, which began appearing in 1665, a set of rather ribald stories modeled on Boccaccio's *Decameron*, and drawing on the traditions of the *fabliaux* that reached back to Chaucer and before. This work was dedicated to a patron, but Louis XIV objected to them, and when they continued to appear even after this royal disapproval, La Fontaine's standing at court was threatened. Near the end of his life, he disavowed this work. Another composition was undertaken with the patronage of Fouquet, whose extravagance in building and designing his estate also earned the king's disfavor; this, too, harmed La Fontaine's chances of royal sup-port. Eventually, he was to work very hard at the business of using not only patrons but printers and engravers to see that his work was well received. Legend has it that the twelfth book of *Fables* was presented by La Fontaine himself to the king. One version says that the poet, always known to be incorrigibly forgetful, failed to bring the copy with him to the ceremony.

When he published the first book of his *Fables*, in 1668, La Fontaine dedicated them to the Dauphin, Louis XIV's son. Later he was to dedicate Book XII to the Duke of Burgundy, also in line for the throne. The Dauphin was a boy of seven when the dedication appeared, and the Duke of Burgundy was twelve years old when Book XII was published, so La Fontaine could help justify his dedications by using the polite fiction of the *Fables* being a work for educating children. It is as a work for children that the *Fables* earned, in part, their reputation and became a classic of French literature; for many generations, school children throughout France were made to memorize various of the tales. But, of course, the *Fables* are very much an adult work, closer in spirit to the astringent wit of La Rochefoucauld (to whom one of the fables is dedicated) than to the child-like simplicity of the fairy tales authored by Perrault (who was one of La Fontaine's early appreciators). Perrault's characterization of La Fontaine's style as paradoxically embodying "an ingenious sympathy and a witty naïveté" is still perhaps the best summary. The critic Hippolyte Taine called La Fontaine the "French Homer," and Addison began what would become a growing chorus when he praised the poet in the *Spectator* in 1711. Moore herself composed a brief life of La Fontaine, which she published in the *American People's Encyclopedia* in 1965. It ended with this judgment:

> Deploring controversy as interfering with serenity, he called himself lazy and a daydreamer; whereas in fact his decorum in complicatedly intricate stanzas that could have been attained only by assiduous perseverance, his gifts of narration and satire even at his own expense, make him one of the best loved persons in literature.

Moore felt warmly toward what she depicts as a gentle paradox in the man, and the combination of self-deprecation and perseverance has an obvious note of self-portraiture on her part.

In strictly literary terms, however, the *Fables* are quite daring. In the neoclassical age, literary works needed to belong to a recognized class or genre, and they had to maintain a stylistic consistency inside the terms of the genre to which they belonged. La Fontaine not only varied the style within the *Fables*, moving from homely to satiric to mock epic, but there was no recognized generic category to which such a work might be assigned in the first place. They were certainly not epic, though there were twelve books of them; they were not lyric poems, though each tended to be between twelve and thirty lines long, in rhyming stanzas; they were not dramatic, though they often used narrative structure and dialogue between clearly shaped "characters." The subject matter was not consistently pastoral, or elegiac, or mythical, or religious. They combined what were "low" materials, especially when they used animals in speaking roles, but their motive was to instruct the reader, ostensibly in commonplace morals, but actually, through subtle allegorical extension, in the mores of the court and polite society.

La Fontaine's friend, the writer Patrus, was quoted as saying of the animal fables that *"leur principal ornement est de n'en avoir aucun"*— their principle ornament is that they don't have any ornamentation. But La Fontaine was to counter this literary definition by using a great deal of stylistic polish, mainly in the form of witty metaphor and subtly ironic transitions, to produce a work that delighted the most fastidious French courtier. It was in this subtle undermining of the rules of genre and style that La Fontaine exhibited the radical innovation that is often the important ingredient of what becomes a traditional, even a canonical work. The paradox of a writer who treats ethical questions in a context of an apparently well-accepted moral order, while undermining their stability through stylistic subtlety and ironic qualifications, is a picture that fits both La Fontaine and Moore.

In an Arts Club lecture given in October, 1953, Moore told of speaking with Pound about the *Fables*. Here was someone she considered a literary authority whose reputation, positive and negative, rested in considerable measure on his work as a translator. Indeed, his encouragement of her in this project was equaled by no one, with the possible exception of Auden. She had been trying to keep to the word order in the French originals, and found herself entangled like a kitten in a snarl of expensive silk. Pound suggested that she remember the traditional English syntactical order of "subject-verb-object," and this proved to be crucial advice, as she went back and redid the entire work with this in mind. Though this might be seen as submitting totally to traditional literary methods, it was actually innovative, since most translations of La Fontaine up till that time used inverted word order and archaic diction in order to try and give some sense of the French style. Moore's dedication to what she called a "naturalistic" style, by which she meant an easy, almost colloquial manner, had been reaffirmed earlier by Pound's dictum that the poet should not write anything that he or she could not imagine someone actually saying. This principle was something Moore relearned at this time, and from the same instructor.

Pound, perhaps remembering his own tendentious approach to the Chinese and Provençal traditions, also suggested that she lighten her load by translating only the best. She decided she would be dowdy and do them all. "Well," Pound said, "if at your mature age, you feel that you must mold character, I suppose you must." Translating La Fontaine was in some ways Moore's vindication of herself as a "professional" writer, someone who doesn't abandon inspiration or the love of doing something well, but who subordinates such feelings to the virtues of thoroughness and consistency. Whatever other forces led Moore to this task, and there were several important ones, she approached and completed it with an attitude that was close to the one that marked her work at *The Dial*. Her attitude to her own poetry was in contrast to this, for she tended to accept the quota of a few poems a year, and to speak of them with self-deprecation. The attitude toward the La Fontaine was in some measure the attitude inside La Fontaine: skeptical, more than a touch wry, but always eventually accepting of limits and trusting of an order larger than the personal.

In some sense La Fontaine was himself a translator. The sources for his *Fables* are numerous, but chief among them is an edition of fables ranging from Aesop, the Greek who invented the form, to Abstemius, an Italian humanist of the fifteenth century. This edition was published in France in 1610, and reprinted in 1660, under the title *Mythologia aesopia*, edited by Nevelet. In the later fables, commonly called Part Two, and consisting of Books VII–XII, La Fontaine drew on an Indian author, Pilpay, whose fables and folktales were translated into French in 1644. There were also the versified fables of Phaedrus, who used Aesop's prose for his material; these verses were used in the French schools to teach Latin. What La Fontaine was able to fashion out of this medley of sources was what he himself called an *"ample comédie a cent actes divers / Et dont la scène est Univers"*—which Moore translated as an "all-embracing theater, / With scenes of every character" (VII, 1, 27–28). Her lines stress the diversity of the material, including as it does stories of animals, men, and supernatural spirits, whereas La Fontaine's original suggests the medieval roots of the metaphor of the world as a stage in which universal laws are revealed. Out of all his diversity, La Fontaine could not help but trust in something like a neoclassical sense of essential truths. Moore's encyclopedia article mentioned that "to La Fontaine animals are vehicles for his philosophy, not studies in natural history." His philosophy, moreover, was borrowed in large part from Gassendi, an opponent of Descartes, who argued that animals were not machines, but had souls of a sort that shared attributes with human souls.

The fable from which the lines above are drawn is in fact an *ars poetica*, which relies very heavily on the use of antithesis, one of Moore's favorite devices. La Fontaine uses other stylistic devices that would have resonance for Moore. One of these is a precise observation that contains a witty twist through metaphor or some sort of parallel association with another context. In the fable Moore calls "The Hag and Her Two Servants" (V,6), for example, we hear something like an epic invocation in the line, "Daybreak! with the sea ablaze where the sun had rested." The incongruity of this with the actual scene, of the hag who "fumbled on petticoats which grease made unwearable," typifies La Fontaine's irony, which is often partly satiric, partly wry, but never bitter or corrosive. A similar effect is in Book VI, number 18, which opens with the French line, *"Le phaeton d'une voiture à foin."* Moore renders this as "Poor phaethon with hay heaped on his wain," using the alliteration to convey a sense of abundance and yet keeping the ironic contrast of the mythical name and the mundane activity.

Moore obviously worked hard on the literal sense of her translation, using Professor Harry Levin of Harvard to check for errors. But she also tried to make the whole project uniform, and this meant casting about for some prosodic and lexical rules of her own. In one lecture she explained that this was in part achieved by paying close attention to the sound patterns of the French without seeking to duplicate exactly the sense of the rhymes. In fact, La Fontaine was an erratic rhymer, and he also often resorted to variations within a stanza form, especially by using short lines for effect. Moore's versification before the 1940's already had some affinities with such an approach, and after she began her translation effort she used such devices even more. She told an audience at Vassar just before the translation appeared that a rhyme in the French between "rone" and "profonde" (VII,3) was modulated in the next rhyme to one between "siens" and "biens." She tried to capture this effect by rhyming "want" with "haunt," and then following with a rhyme between "saint" and "faint." Then "want" and "saint" were brought together in a concluding line and a half: "God provides for the wants / Of those who profess to be his saints."

One way to see Moore's success, however, is by looking at a passage from a single poem and comparing it to a previous translation. Here is a version of one of the more famous of the fables, "The Oak and the Rush" (I,22), as rendered by Reverend W. Lucas Collins, from the late nineteenth century:

> The Oak said to the Rush (when Oaks could talk),
> "Nature has dealt but hardly with you, friend;

The wren's light weight sits heavy on your stalk;
   The lightest breeze that for a moment's space
      Ruffles the water's face
        will make you bend."

     Then the Rush spoke—
"Your pity shows a generous heart, 'tis true;
   But pray be not uneasy for my sake:
Storms are less dangerous to me than you—
      I bend, but do not break."

Collins has purchased his simplicity by leaving out the ornament; it is as if he reverted to the claim of Patrus and ignored what La Fontaine did to play off a series of regal touches against the homeliness of the vegetable world. He also uses some quaint filler for the sake of his rhyme: there is no justification in the French for the phrase "when Oaks could talk." Also, the poeticism of "a moment's space" probably also results from a need for a rhyme word.

Here is Moore's version, which contains much more of La Fontaine's ingenious style without losing all the simplicity:

   The oak said to the reed, "You grow
Too unprotectedly. Nature has been unfair;
A tiny wren alights, and you are bending low;
   If a fitful breath of air
   Should freshen till ripples show,
   You heed her and lower your head;
Whereas my parasol makes welcome shade each day
And like the Caucasus need never sway,
   However it is buffeted.
Would that you'd been born beneath this towering tent I've
                      made,
   Which could afford you ample shade;
   Your hazards would not be severe:

   "I'd shield you when the lightning played;
   But grow you will, time and again,
On the misty fringe of the wind's domain.
I perceive that you are grievously oppressed."
The rush said, "Bless you for fearing that I might be distressed;

It is you alone whom the winds should alarm.
I bend and do not break. . . ."

The dialogue is clearly operating on at least two levels, one that deals with the sharp observation of natural processes, such as the blowing air that "freshens till ripples show," and the other that treats the problems of power and self-image, as the oak uses a political and imperious vocabulary ("Caucasus," "towering," "oppressed"). Nature and culture are thus seen as both illustrative of each other's processes, even as each becomes an ironic context for viewing the other.

The reception of the *Fables* was generally positive, though the tone struck by reviewers was more often one of respectful admiration for the size of the project, rather than enthusiastic praise for the details. Wallace Fowlie, in *The New York Times Book Review*, referred to Moore as "the predestined translator of this particular poet." Some of the professional critics, however, were not nearly so appreciative of Moore's efforts. John Ciardi, for example, writing in *The Nation*, had some harsh assessments. So, too, did Howard Nemerov, in the *Sewanee Review* in October, 1954, where he singled out several lines that he found marked by Moore's "making complexities out of simplicities." But he didn't stop with particulars:

> Even when things are going well so far as the translation is concerned, the tone and the texture of the language remain very uncertain; just when we think we begin to hear in English the modesty and humorous dignity of the fabulist, along comes some monstrous circumlocution or complicated syntactical maneuver to ensure the fall of the rime. And meanwhile the meter is, to say the least of it, very strange. . . . The difficulties of the matter seem to have been faced up to, but rather added to than overcome by the translator's own predilections and powers.

By referring to "the fabulist," Nemerov might here give the impression that he is measuring Moore's work against some generic idea of fable writing, rather than the particular textures of La Fontaine. But Nemerov quotes enough of the French to show that he has La Fontaine himself in mind. However, part of the assumptions that animate the negative assessment are tied in with a distrust of modernist innovation, for he goes on to point out that "the famous revolution in modern poetry, accompanied by a special uprising [sic] in the translation business, destroyed at least the security of that idea of English verse," namely "a very simple idea." This simple idea Nemerov illustrates by a sample quatrain from a translation by Elizur Wright, a translation that reads a great deal like that of Reverend Collins. But of course, La Fontaine destroyed the idea of simple French verse. For that matter, Moore's occasional circumlocutions can be seen as part of her effort to register the different tonalities of the French writer, for she apparently felt that his ingenuity was at least as important as his simplicity.

If the critic viewed the translation in the context of Moore's work, rather than by some objective standard of correctness, the result would likely favor Moore. This was the case with the review in *Poetry* in September, 1954, where Hugh Kenner praises Moore's translation for just the features that led Nemerov, however reluctantly, to criticize it. Kenner hearkens to La Fontaine's "curiously *pastoral* urbanity (not the least like Pope's)" (original emphasis). By so doing, he puts the urbanity in the position of the substance and the pastoral in the position of qualifier, just the opposite of Nemerov. And so he can find in Moore's version a praiseworthy

> artlessness [that] isn't at all like La Fontaine's transparency; it resembles the "unconscious fastidiousness" which she once illustrated by adducing "childish . . . determination to make a pup eat his meat from his plate." Her air of plunging without premeditation into tortuousness which she subdues *ambulando* is sometimes annoying, but it confers virtue, too, complicating the plain sense enough to fend off *simplesse*.

Kenner gives several illustrations that further clarify his point that Moore is working the way she is because she perceives that "French neatness would make for empty English." Where Nemerov saw the faults as a result of Moore's modernity, Kenner views the project in the light of Moore's own style and achievement, without losing sight of the original French text. Though admitting that sometimes her "oddness of expression (for the sake of tone) complicates the sense beyond easy decipherment," Kenner insists that Moore's translation has an excellence that is "surprisingly sustained," something that is clearly "the work of a deliberate and indefatigable intelligence."

Obviously, and in crucial ways, Moore's translation of La Fontaine was a part of the development in her poetry toward a more openly moral poetry and one that was focused on publicly defined values. She found in the French poet someone who had arrived at an ingenious solution to the problem of combining artifice and naturalness, sophistication and simplicity, traditional understanding and innovative style. In the talk given at Vassar on March 24, 1954, Moore was bold enough to sum up the moral message of La Fontaine.

1. sobriety is attractive; it is not synonymous with gloom

2. . . . the aside and the afterthought have a special grace . . . the light touch is the strong touch

3. if you are moralizing, better not compromise, state your convictions con brio.

When the *Fables* appeared, Warner sent his sister a letter, filled with a high spiritual vocabulary that resembled his response to *The Pangolin*. He mingled the worlds of art and religion in a way that the family had often done, and he referred to the family's bond when he wrote that the *Fables* were a jewel that would commemorate the lives the three Moores lived together. Such religious feeling is not particularly consonant with the morality and style of La Fontaine, and yet Moore worked so hard on her *Fables* that it is easy to see why Warner would have this reaction, especially considering his own character and the loss of their mother. The hard work extended over a period of nearly ten years, and Moore said that she had completely redone the entire project four times. She called on virtually all of her friends for one kind of assistance or another, and mentioned the progress of her work to many of her correspondents. The project was also effective in helping her ground her literary efforts in the period of uncertainty after her mother's death.

Not long after the *Fables* appeared, Moore was interviewed by Mary Seth for *Presbyterian Life*, a national publication sponsored by the church. The interviewer was typical of those who wrote on Moore for national publications in the last two decades of her life. Part of what makes such an article typical, of course, is the format itself, which tries to create the air of discovery as the interviewer is led into the private world of the celebrity. Seth does this by telling the reader about her commuter train trip from Philadelphia, and how she has spent weeks reading Moore's *Collected Poems*, one poem a day for weeks prior to visiting the poet in Brooklyn. The visit itself features many details about Moore's appearance and environment: the graying hair still tied in braids around the top of her head, "her remarkable eyes that seem perfectly round and manage to look darker than blue usually looks," the tool rack in the kitchen, the surprising lack of pets, the friendly walk through the neighborhood where well-wishers call out greetings. Seth also adds some biography, and mentions Warner's status as a chaplain and Moore's attendance at the Lafayette Avenue church's Bible class, taught by the Reverend Alvin Magary. Eliot's line about the "small body of durable poetry" is cited in the penultimate paragraph, but there is very little about the poetry itself, at least the way it makes its arguments or its innovative sense of structure, and so forth. In short, the article is what magazine editors would call "the celebrity treatment." The cover for the April 16, 1955 issue that includes the feature has a George Platt Lynes photograph of Moore on the cover. There, under the woman in tricorne and cape, is the identifying caption: "Marianne Moore—Poet and Presbyterian." Such display and appropriation of her public image would become a constant part of Moore's life during the rest of her life.

In the year after the *Fables* appeared, Moore published a collection of her prose, under the title *Predilections*. This collection was drawn from thirty years of essays and reviews, and featured such important pieces as "Henry James as a Characteristic American," "Feeling and Precision," and "Humility, Concentration, and Gusto." The volume was published by Viking, her new publisher since the *Fables* had been rejected by Macmillan. *Predilections* did not receive much attention, perhaps because people almost invariably considered Moore a poet, and because she had never staked much of her authority on her prose. Now that the *Complete Prose* (1987) has appeared, this view will almost certainly change, especially among scholars. But the earlier collection of prose was truly a miscellany; without any apparent organizing principle, such as, say, Pound used in *The Spirit of Romance*, the average reader was left with a very indefinite context.

The reception of *Predilections* was somewhat limited, since a poet's essays are not usually accorded the attention the poetry receives, but the tone of the reviews was respectful, as with the *Fables*. Charles Poore, in the daily *New York Times*, said that "quoting other writers is Miss Moore's favorite occupational therapy," suggesting that her reviews and essays are secondary activities. Randall Jarrell, in *The New York Times Book Review*, referred to the book as "particular appreciation, not general criticism." This reflects the dominance of the so-called New Criticism of the time, which tended to lengthy analysis of

individual works or general academic arguments about the work's background of ideas; anything else tended to be dismissed as "appreciation."
Though Jarrell says that the "criticism of a poet is itself a poem," by
suggesting that the book's "faults seem individual and endearing," he
subtly dismisses the work as mere opinion. In a way, this is in keeping
with the public image of Moore as someone whose opinions are likely
to be eccentric or quaint, and whose poetry is certainly remarkable, but
whose ideas or serious thoughts do not weigh that heavily in the larger
scheme of things.

Something similar happens in a review by Irving Howe, in the *New
Republic* for May 23, 1955. Though Howe pays a certain amount of
respect to Moore's stature as a poet, arguing that "the blandness of
formidable lady poets . . . [is] never more formidable than when most
fragile," he fails to give the prose very high marks as literary criticism.
He calls attention to her "slender elegant prose, too much given to
ellipsis and a kind of imagist particularity." But he saves his bluntest
dismissal for the fact that Moore's criticism is "excessively literary," and
that "everything seems to come from books or clippings, and the total
impression is one of claustrophobic solipsism." For Howe, Moore fails
to approach the "deepest possibilities of literary criticism," except from
her peculiar distance, and so he calls such criticism "the greenest land
she's almost seen," a twist on one of her lines in "Spenser's Ireland."
This is said "with no malice and no little admiration." It's hard to tell
if this final qualification stems from Howe's respect for Moore as a poet,
or because he glimpses some other role for criticism than that of the
then prevailing orthodox academic style, a role that Moore herself may
not fully realize.

Moore's literary criticism is, of course, distinctive, both as to its style
and its content. She more or less accepted the idea, which has roots as
far back as Kant's aesthetic, that literary values were autonomous, and
the "purely literary" was a realm that one could enter and move about
in without having to subordinate the experience to other values. This
view was somewhat modified as her poetry became more directly moral,
but it was a view she never completely abandoned. The style of her
prose developed from this view, as its intention is to reflect the center
of the intention of the work under scrutiny, rather than to measure the
work by some explicit criteria. Moore did not believe such reflection
could take place transparently; she valued the flavor and the point of

388 _____ MARIANNE MOORE

view of the critical intelligence at work. But she saw in literary criticism a special activity that was adjunct to reading, and reading was a process that involved being conscious of previous texts in a special way. The term "intertextuality," used to convey the belief that all literary texts take their origin, and hence their meaning, from their relationship to other, previous texts, could well have a working precedent in Moore's criticism. The cause and effect of Moore's "intertextual" criticism is her habit of representing her subject indirectly and metonymically—what Howe called her "ellipsis and a kind of imagist particularity." Howe is also right to say that in her critical prose "everything comes from books or clippings," but for Moore that is not a limitation but a form of enhancement.

Shortly after *Predilections* was published, Moore entered into another sort of language game, one that was not exactly prose or poetry. On October 19, 1955, an executive from the Ford Motor Company in Dearborn, Michigan, wrote to Moore to ask her help in naming what he referred to as "a rather important new series of cars." Moore accepted the challenge, and the ensuing correspondence was published in *The New Yorker* three years later. This particular incident did a lot to increase Moore's standing as a celebrity, especially among those who follow cultural news and current events with an eye for wit and diversion. Witty and diverting the correspondence certainly is, and in the pages of a glossy magazine it read almost like a sort of whimsical invention. The whimsy dominates in the actual names suggested by Moore, but there is also the comic irony of her reluctance to accept payment prior to concluding the task, and the Ford executive's need to have a signed contract beforehand. All in all, the incident reads like a fable about genius misunderstood but appreciated.

Though it wouldn't do to drain the humor, and even the whimsy, from the letters, it is possible to read them in at least two other contexts: the mechanics of celebrity, and Moore's particular sense of language. The Ford executive, Robert Young, began by telling Moore that the company's own suggested names were, so far, "characterized by an embarrassing pedestrianism." In light of the eventual selection of "Edsel" as the car's name, the wish to avoid the pedestrian is especially ironic. But Moore takes a cue from this, and says she will consult her brother, who "would bring ardor and imagination to bear on the quest." By aestheticizing the selection process into a quest, Moore is able to transmute what is essentially a commercial endeavor—the executive asked for "a name, in short, that flashes a dramatically desirable picture in people's minds"—into an exercise in imagination. This took place before the sort of manipulative advertising techniques analyzed in *The Hidden Persuaders*—were exposed, so Moore proceeds without any sense of irony. Moore had always enjoyed the language of advertisement, delighting in its inventiveness and ebullience, and even relating it to the poetics of praise. In "The Arctic Ox (or Goat)" (1958), after discussing the qualities and usefulness of the animal's fur, she could say: "If you fear that you are / reading an advertisement, / you are." Several years after the Ford correspondence, she was asked in an interview by Donald Hall if she didn't feel that her efforts in this matter might have contributed to the further separation between expression and meaning, a separation deplored by modern poets such as Pound. Moore responded that she didn't think so, and in fact she had even studied "motors and turbines and recessed wheels," and that because she enjoyed mechanics, she enjoyed the "assignment."

But the terms Moore suggested as names did not reflect the world of mechanics; indeed, at the end she says that "I regret that I concentrated on physical phenomena." But physical here means the appearance in a visual or formal sense, because most of her proposals stress something like the metaphoric suggestiveness of the car's outline or, to use an advertising term, its "image." Halfway through the correspondence, Mr. Young manages to send Moore some sketches of the new model, though they both recognize the need for secrecy in such matters, so exact drawings were not made available. She suggests some terms that seem close to the then current lexicon of automotive models, such as "Anticipator," "Thunder Crester" (obviously suggested by the same company's successful "Thunderbird"), and "Silver Sword." But the last of these Moore discovered in a book of flowers: it is the name of a floral species that grows in Tibet. The other names, in fact, are closer to the exotic resonance of a Tibetan flower: "Regna Racer," "Magigravue," and "Turcotingo" (after a South American finch). Then there are names that are exotic to the point of being bizarre, as Moore indulged her sense of whimsy: "Pastelogram," "Mongoose Civique," and "Utopian Turtletop." The last suggestion prompted the company to send Moore a floral tribute of two dozen roses with white pine and spiral eucalyptus.

Moore's lexicon in this matter was based in some measure on the techniques of advertising, but it also reflected a curious sense of nature, or more specifically, a feeling for taxonomy in a system that is a blend of nature and culture. Two examples show this fairly clearly: "The Intelligent Whale" and "The Resilient Bullet." These terms straddle the two realms, the first humanizing an animal and the second giving a living quality to an unyielding, manufactured object. Animals and plants figure in virtually all of Moore's suggestions. An exception would be "andante con moto," which she suggests is a good description of a motor; here the cultural realm is invoked. Such systems of taxonomy as Moore knew well from natural history and science are, of course, processes by which the realm of nature is preserved in some sense as "natural" or objective, while nature, through language, is brought under the aegis of culture. The more strained of her suggestions, such as "Mongoose Civique," combine the realms in a disjunctive way since their disjunction is what strikes us. In short, Moore's suggestions for the car's name are like her poems, but they show the limits of a poetry without expressiveness. Despite her admiration for the mechanical, Moore never seems to be describing the automobile or her reaction to it.

While much of Moore's time in the 1950's was occupied with finishing the *Fables*, attending award ceremonies, and deepening her friendships with people like Steloff and Hoffman, she found time to do some traveling as well. There was a trip to California in 1956 to inaugurate the Ewing Lectures at the University of California, Los Angeles. (The Ewing Lectures were published in 1958 as "Idiosyncrasy and Technique.") There was also another westcoast trip two years later, as well as a vacation to Bermuda in the early spring of 1956, with her longtime friends, Frances Browne and her sister, Norvelle. In Bermuda, she was able to execute some watercolors. These trips were often physically exhausting, for Moore was now well into her sixties and not always in the best of health. But the honor of the Ewing Lectures must have appealed to her, and the second westcoast trip, with its chance to revisit Seattle, must have had an emotional appeal as well. In every instance, she was treated with great courtesy and respect, and was often able to meet with old friends, too, as when she visited the Kenneth Burkes and revitalized an important association. She reviewed Burke's *Book of Moments: Poems 1915–1954* in 1956, and was rereading his *Grammar of*

Motives in preparation for this; she wrote to Warner that Burke's "views and his subject matter are cosmic and I am nothing if not local."

In 1956, Moore published *Like a Bulwark*, her first book of her own poetry to appear after the *Fables*, and the first to appear with Viking. This volume contained only eleven poems, and the title poem had appeared almost a decade earlier, shortly after her mother's death. But the other ten poems had been published within the space of just four years. One poem, "The Staff of Aesculapius," was written on commission, and published in the newsletter of Abbott Laboratories; another, "Tom Fool at Jamaica," was initiated by Moore's reading about a race-horse in the newspaper, and was requested by Katherine White, wife of the editor at *The New Yorker*. "The Sycamore" was about an albino giraffe that Moore saw only in a magazine photograph, and "Logic and 'The Magic Flute' " was written to commemorate, in a sense, the first color telecast of Mozart's opera, which Moore attended at the NBC studio in Rockefeller Center. The studio was located near the corporate skyscraper that houses the magazines published by the Luce enterprises, which she describes as:

> Near Life and Time
> in their peculiar catacomb,
> abalonean gloom
> and an intrusive hum
> pervaded the mammoth cast's
> small audience-room

Such details give many of Moore's later poems their "occasional" feel. But these details also show how her poetry grew out of both her reading—always noticeable—and her interest in current affairs, especially technical scientific discoveries and development. Her last three individual volumes were *Like a Bulwark*, *O to Be a Dragon*, and *Tell Me, Tell Me*. Two of her later poems, "Apparition of Splendor," about the porcupine, and "Then the Ermine:", about rarely seen animals, treat of the virtue of resistance. The first of these two says that its subject "is not a waverer," while the second uses a motto that is translated as, "I don't change, am not craven." Since these two poems open the volume, this virtue dominates the book, coming up, for example, in "The Staff of Aesculapius." Here, the line that claims "A 'going on'; yes, *anastasis* is the word" serves as the key to scientific discovery. Even in "Style,"

where she celebrates ice skaters, racquet champions, and Spanish danc-
ers, the poem opens with an image of the "constant of the plumbline."
Much of the delight of the book comes from this celebration of steadfastness, partly as spiritual virtue, partly as aesthetic grace, played off
against the occasional nature of the exemplifications.

In the fall of 1956, Moore also added to her celebrity with an unusual
publication. On October 3, Warner sent a telegram to his sister, care of
Professor Ewing at UCLA, congratulating her on the publication of her
poem "Hometown Piece for Messrs. Alston and Reese," on the front
page of the *Herald-Tribune*, on the first day of the World Series. It was
obviously a coup from a publicity point of view, for overnight Moore's
name would almost certainly be known by more people than had read
her work up to this point. What this new expanded audience didn't
know, and perhaps would not appreciate the irony of, is that the poem
had been rejected by several publications prior to its acceptance by a
major metropolitan newspaper. But now she was definitely local, since
from this point on, if not before, she would always be linked with the
borough of Brooklyn, as well as increasingly universal, since her name
was becoming more and more recognized.

The poem, written in rhyming couplets, is not Moore at her best,
even her comic best, and it may be close to doggerel at times. One
passage on the first baseman Gil Hodges contains several qualities, from
a striking description of a first baseman's move to a predictable rhyme
that ends a rather limping sentence:

> As for Gil Hodges, in custody of first—
> "He'll do it by himself." Now a specialist—versed
>
> in an extension reach far into the box seats—
> he lengthens up, leans and gloves the ball. He defeats
>
> expectation by a whisker. The modest star
> irked by one misplay, is no hero by a hair;
>
> in a strikeout slaughter when what could matter more,
> he lines a homer to the signboard and has changed the score.

Many decades earlier, when Moore reported on baseball slang to
Warner, copying out phrases like "old gum glove," she showed that
her lexical curiosity was virtually endless. This poem reflects that, as

she mixes standard baseball slang like "round-tripper" and "really fire
the ball" with the names of all the Brooklyn players. The poem's
structure, however, doesn't utilize a narrative frame; instead, the feeling is of a sort of super fan conversing with other people at the park,
whooping and urging on her team. Sometimes later Moore would tell
a friend that she was distantly related to the man who wrote "Casey
at the Bat," the most famous of America's poems on sports. Whether
true or not, such a claim shows how Moore would have liked to be
associated with baseball at the level of its standing as the "national
pastime," an activity where great skill and popular enthusiasm met in
a utopian medley of gestures that are both practiced and spontaneous.
A few years later, in "Baseball and Writing," Moore would write a
poem that made the connections more directly, and would end with
an image of apotheosis, but there she used more of the style that had
first made her a recognized poet, so the later poem is less well-known.
In 1964, three years after "Baseball and Writing" appeared in *The
New Yorker*, she said in an interview in *Harper's* that it was the display of "dexterity—with a logic of memory that makes strategy possible" that made baseball especially appealing to her. It was the sort
of succinct and flexible formulation, applicable to all sports, really,
that made her the sinecure of interviewers.

Another piece, of a sort different from the Dodger poem, brought
Moore further considerable notice in the winter of 1957. This was a
profile by Winthrop Sargeant, published in *The New Yorker* on February
16, under the title "Humility, Concentration, and Gusto." The piece
was very respectful and accurate, and its very context put Moore in a
pantheon, since this was the format that had earlier featured such
"Profiles" as Lillian Ross's on Hemingway. But even if the format didn't
make the implicit point strongly enough, Sargeant spelled it out in the
opening paragraph:

> Among people who like to feel that they know just how things stand,
> Marianne Craig Moore is regarded, variously, as America's greatest liv-
> ing woman poet, or as one of America's greatest living poets, or even as
> America's greatest living poet—three views that combine to establish
> her squarely as a literary monument, handily labelled for ready reference.

The interviewer added that for a public that had never "opened any of
the books responsible for her fame" she was "a quaint and rather stylish

spinster who, at the age of sixty-nine, lives in a cluttered apartment in Brooklyn and writes poems about animals." The profile relates many interesting things about Moore, both as a person and an author, such as the story about how she went to the race track and even bet on Tom Fool, who finished second, and that cured her of gambling. The opening of the piece, however, complete with a citation of Eliot's claim that "her poems form part of the small body of durable poetry written in our time," gives the essence of the public identity that Moore had achieved at the time.

The profile filled in the public outlines with private details by examining the interior of Moore's apartment, remarking on her books, her bric-a-brac, and the bowl of subway tokens she kept near the door for use by her visitors on their return home. At one point, Sargeant quotes Moore as complaining about friends who give her gifts: "People present you with things they think may suggest an idea for a poem, but there simply aren't enough alcoves and embrasures to put them all in." And by quoting some of Moore's conversation, "remarkable for its diversity," Sargeant gave some idea about the ways the poems are built up through her sense of associative logic, which progresses in a way that is sometimes sequential and sometimes parallel. Here is the latter half of a long passage in which Moore is speaking:

> I like Goethe. My favorite language is German. I like the periodic structure of the sentences. "And Shakespeare inspires me too. He has so many good quotations. And Dante. He has a few, too." That's from Ruth Draper. At Monroe Wheeler's once, we played a game called "Who would you rather be except Shakespeare?" I wouldn't mind being La Fontaine, or Voltaire. Or Montaigne? No. I wouldn't be Montaigne— too somber. I have always loved the vernacular. It spites me that I can't write fiction. And that book of essays I wrote. I let myself loose to do my utmost, and now they make me uneasy. The critics didn't care a great deal for them, but their reviews weren't really vipish. Those readings of my verse I made for the phonograph—well, they're here forever, like the wheat in the pyramids. I'm fond of Bach and Pachelbel and Stravinsky. I'm also fond of drums and trumpets—snare drums. If I find a man plays the trumpet I am immediately interested. . . .

Of course, one can make sense of the connections here easily enough when the remarks are transcribed to print, as Moore said later in the profile, "It isn't jumping around. It's all connected." One can also appreciate that a *vive voce* delivery could be confusing. But the first remark about Goethe is "explained" by his writing in German, which in turn is explained by its sentence structure. Shakespeare is then introduced as being someone else's favorite writer, and the reasons are given for that opinion. These reasons parallel Moore's to some extent, even as they suggest by their whimsicality the futility of the whole enterprise of playing a game like "name your favorite writer." Then an actual game is introduced, at which point Moore "seriously" plays her version of it. She then contrasts somberness and casualness, in the form of the vernacular, thus continuing the contrast she has playfully intro-duced between "great" writers and "silly" games. This leads to a lament about her self-judged failure to capture the casual vernacular in fiction, and also in her essays. The same issue—how to capture one's natural run of speech or ideas in a fixed form—reminds her of her phonograph recordings, and these remind her of music, and she returns to the "game" of naming her favorite composers. And of course the whole passage can be read ironically, as being both a genteel performance in the role of the celebrity being interviewed, and a puckish parody of the notion that such opinion-mongering is anything worth recording for posterity—the wheat in the pyramid survived, but only because the pyramid was a true monument.

At the end of his essay, Sargeant tries to capture Moore's paradoxical character with a pointed contrast. He points out that Moore bears "no ill will toward the world of business, finance, and technological progress," though he does not suggest that this attitude might come from Warner (whom Sargeant describes in some detail as a "person of a wholly different outlook" from Moore the artist). But while Moore doesn't have the standard attitude of a modern artist who deplores the business world, she is nonetheless otherworldly. For at the very end of the profile, Moore is seen as a trapeze artist who floats above the mundane:

> Among her friends is one who likens her to a daring performer on a flying trapeze, hugely enjoying her own acrobatics but reassuring herself every now and then by glancing down at a safety net that is sturdily supported by Gibbon, Julius Caesar, Xenophon, the Presbyterian Church, and a handful of male contemporaries, military and scientific, who are accus-tomed to think—as she conspicuously does not— in what she approv-

ingly calls "a straight line." In this view, Miss Moore, soaring and pirouetting above the world of reality, assumes the role of a charmingly quixotic intellectual flirt, seeming, both as a poet and a personality, to tease those who put their faith in humdrum logic but at the same time to regard them with admiration and a certain coquettish timidity. Any attempt to discern in this spectacle so much as a trace of a consistent philosophy can lead only to bafflement, but few philosophers, after all, have been good poets.

Sargeant succeeds in making his contrast quite sharp, but at a cost of some elaborately figurative language. What his figures of speech contain is a portrait that is somewhat like the one feminist critics have drawn: Moore is capable of subverting the patriarchal order by teasing "those who put their faith in humdrum logic." But obviously a feminist critic would look askance, to say the least, at the imagery of quixotic flirtation and timid coquetry. Then there is the picture of a support guard of male authorities, themselves protected by the instruments of army and church. We are now more alert to such gender stereotyping than were readers in the late 1950's, but here it seems so obvious that one can only wonder if it passed unnoticed then. Also, whatever else Moore may express or represent for her audience and friends, the furthest thing from her work is any sense (there is not "so much as a trace") of a consistently thoughtful picture of the world that might possibly be shared in an instructive manner with others. The poet is placed in the most unpragmatic situation, hanging above where men conduct the affairs of the world.

In March, 1956, just after Sargeant had finished the profile and shown it to Moore, who let her brother see it, Warner wrote to caution his sister. He felt he may have been indiscreet in the interview, and that Moore must be very cautious about describing their father's "nervous breakdown." Warner was also anxious about telling Sargeant that Moore had made many trips to Washington, D.C.; this may have been because of Pound's presence there and the negative reputation that he had with people in Warner's circles. So concerned was he that he wrote another letter the same day, March 5, asking his sister to be sure to keep Warner's family out of the limelight. This concern was either effective or misplaced, for Sargeant says little about their father that Warner and Moore had not themselves previously revealed; the entire account is a model of tact. Moore had long lived with the polarity of a public

identity and a private life, and from at least as far back as the years at
The Dial there were tensions between the two. By the late 1950's such
tensions had been fully mediated, in large part by Moore's extensive
circle of friends, many of whom were themselves well-known public
figures. In her later years, she would have been interviewed or solicited
for answers to some symposium or another, in many magazines: *Partisan
Review, The New York Times Magazine, Harper's, Harper's Bazaar, Esquire, Ladies' Home Journal,* and *McCall's.* Part of her public image,
however, and a part she worked hard to maintain, was that she had a
private life that could only be glimpsed, never fully explored. So she
became something like a famous grandmother, quaintly authoritative
and benignly indomitable. Just as her private life was mediated by a
public identity, so was her public identity forced to be consistent with
some approved cultural role. One of the consequences of this was that
her opinions would always be regarded, in part at least, as eccentric and
impractical.

As the 1950's came to a close, Moore published a volume of poems
called *O to Be a Dragon* (1959). This book, published just three years
after *Like a Bulwark,* has a miscellaneous air, and resembles the previous volume in that respect. The sense that the poems are miscellaneous in their subjects, idiosyncratic in their structure, and
occasional in their inspiration, is heightened if read against the background of Moore's celebrity. They seem to be the casual sayings of the
wise old poet. But the volume does have a thematic consistency, despite this casual air. It reprints poems that had appeared or been written five decades earlier ("I May, I Might, I Must," from *Tipyn O'Bob,*
and "A Jelly-Fish," composed at Bryn Mawr), as well as poems written on commission ("Enough: Jamestown, 1607–1957") and for special occasions ("In the Public Garden"). It also contains "Values in
Use," which was inspired by remarks made by Philip Rahv, the then
editor of *Partisan Review,* at a 1956 Harvard Summer School Conference on Little Magazines that Moore attended. The poem is partly a
school reminiscence, partly a wry comment on the pragmatism that
had been part of Moore's intellectual framework from the beginning
of her career. The student in the poem recalls the similar figure from
"The Student" of 1932, and the plot, such as it is, glancingly recalls
the poem "He Wrote the History Book," in which the young boy
"identifies" his father. In this case the similarity comes from the wis-

dom imparted by an offhand remark, as the "anonymous friend" becomes something like an interior voice or a depersonalized expression of a wisdom that must be systemic if it is to be effective. Like the Dodger poem, this is written in rhyming couplets, but with a tighter sense of rhythm:

> I attended school and I liked the place—
> grass and little locust-leaf shadows like lace.
>
> Writing was discussed. They said, "We create
> values in the process of living, daren't await
>
> their historic progress." Be abstract
> and you'll wish you'd been specific; it's a fact.
>
> What was I studying? Values in use,
> "judged on their own ground." Am I still abstruse?
>
> Walking along, a student said offhand,
> " 'relevant' and 'plausible' were words I understand."
>
> A pleasing statement, anonymous friend.
> Certainly the means must not defeat the end.

This poem reaches back to the idea of "service," that ideal of a liberal arts higher education, and adjusts the idea to that of Deweyan instrumentalism. The common misunderstanding of instrumentalism, or pragmatism as it came to be known, was that it argued that the end justified the means; as long as any method or value system produced results it was acceptable. In fact, Moore's last line gets it right, for what was put forth by Dewey, James, and others was that if a system of knowledge or social organization ignored or misconstructed its own instruments of application, it was a failure. Only by seeing to it that the ideas it advanced were indeed "relevant" to the problems it sought to cure, and "plausibly" adapted to the circumstances, would a society be completely responsible for its own visions and values. This poem also had the added advantage of being in part an interior dialogue in which Moore questions whether she can make herself clear ("Am I still abstruse?"), as she allegedly was unable to in college. But now she has a lifetime of effort to set in the balance against such charges, and she can be reassured—"certainly"—that she has understood the problem.

Moore ended her poem about Jamestown by alluding to a principle that would seem to be an important supplement to pragmatism, namely that "it is enough / if present faith mend partial proof." Here she was indirectly quoting a minister who argued that all spiritual commitments involved trusting in one's project in order to look beyond short-term failure or incompletion. But "partial proof" is usually the most that anyone can have, circled by contingency as we are. "Nothing's certain," as she said in "Then the Ermine:". A good pragmatist realizes this, and is far from abjuring all "belief" in favor of some phantom of "factuality." Increasingly for Moore, from "Like a Bulwark," published twenty years previously, to poems from O to Be a Dragon such as "Melchior Vulpius," the language of Christian strength and the contexts of American pragmatism become intertwined. The moral struggle, in a sense, becomes defined as the difficulty faced in trying to distinguish between a deadening persistence and a redemptive perseverance.

Another way to state this struggle is to see it as the problem of applying general wisdom and the rules of knowledge in a way that is genuinely useful to one's own situation. Otherwise one is faced with an increasing separation between fact and value, between knowledge and the ability to apply it in human contexts and for human ends. Art remained for Moore one key instance of such a successfully mediated struggle, just as it does for Dewey. "In the Public Garden," composed on the occasion of an Arts Festival held in Boston in 1958, praises the possibility of poetry and intellect being joined. The lyric ends by making the point that a mediation between general and particular, mind and feeling can be achieved in poetry, a point that reached back to the poetic theory of the 1920's, with its emphasis on the importance of accurate particulars:

> . . .still one need not fail
>
>> to wish poetry well
>> where intellect is habitual—
>> glad that the Muses have a home and swans—
>> that legend can be factual;
>>> happy that Art, admired in general,
>>> is always actually personal.

The swans, of course, refer to the swan boats on the Charles River that flows through Cambridge into Boston's bay, but they also recall the "little locust-leaf shadows like lace" from "Values in Use." Both images, in addition to being local particulars, convey the aesthetic touch that nature provides as culture mediates it into the human dimension.

The title poem of *O to Be a Dragon* raises a different sort of issue, for while the poem ostensibly treats of the magnificence of fabled creatures, it can also be read as a self-portrait that suggests a different range of tensions and mediations. The poem is only six lines long, but its lack of a symmetrical stanzaic structure suggests an imbalance, a suggestion increased by the use of ellipsis, as well as the subjunctive and exclamatory moods:

> If I, like Solomon, . . .
> could have my wish—
>
> my wish . . . O to be a dragon,
> a symbol of the power of Heaven—of silkworm
> size or immense; at times invisible.
> Felicitous phenomenon!

There is more than an echo here of the child-like fantasy, familiar from *Alice in Wonderland,* of changing the size of one's body, and this fantasy mingles with the connotation of wisdom and power evoked by the allusion to Solomon. But the phrase "at times invisible" may also suggest that Moore wishes some of her publicity could be controlled, even curtailed. One of the traditional functions of the dragon, to be sure, is to repel intruders. Moore spoke of this poem being occasioned by a remark she heard at a party; while her dragon is heavenly, its power could well be a compensatory fantasy, both for years of self-imposed humility and for an externally generated public role that was increasingly defined and unchangeable. The poem, however, seems to mediate its own invoked power, and Moore's objective poetics, based as it is on a certain mistrust of subjective indulgence or emotional aggrandizement, tries to make a beast that is at once small and immense. The habit of proceeding with self-conscious correctives, what Mrs. Moore had praised in Auden's irony as "the dilemma of awareness," persists even when it appears the poet is trying to wish it away, in favor of a true excess.

One of the notes to "O to Be a Dragon" tells us that Solomon's wish was to have an understanding heart. Since the poem opens with this allusion, but then proceeds instead to a desire for power and splendor, Moore may be using a favorite device of antithesis. In this case, the desirability of power and splendor have a somewhat illicit air to them, chosen as they are over against the possibility of choosing wisdom. Teasing out the implications of this, one could suggest that Moore is also writing about her mother. The dragon, in this interpretation, would be a figure of great power who was at once present and yet invisible, much as Moore's mother was in her daughter's life as a writer. Moore's desire to be the mother is a desire to call her back from the realm of the absent, the invisible, and yet at the same time to take on the mother's power for herself. The poem is both innocent and ambiguous, and by being so it invites an autobiographical reading. The volume for which it is the title poem reaches back to two of Moore's earliest poems and reprints them as if they were recent. In an autobiographical reading, this would indicate a persistence of selfhood, as if Moore were saying, I am as I have always been.

Indeed, the theme of "I May, I Might, I Must" can be taken as the definition of the self by the conquering of the other. On the other hand, the subject of "A Jelly-Fish," which opens with the words "Visible, invisible," is the instability of the intentional world, subject as it is to "a fluctuating charm." It should be recalled that it was Moore's mother who formulated the line, "The power of the visible is the invisible," from "He 'Digesteth Harde Yron.'" The poem that appears between the two early college poems is "To a Chameleon," a poem that Moore first published in The Egoist in 1916, collected in her first two books, and then did not reprint for another thirty-five years or so. Its theme, of course, is about the adaptable nature of the animal it describes, one that is able to "snap the spectrum up for food." By printing these four poems together in the opening pages of the book, Moore is suggesting a complex understanding of the self, a cultural construct that is at once persistent and ephemeral, given to us only by our interplay with others, but that for which we alone are responsible.

The final poem of the volume can be read as another self-portrait, though of an admittedly idealized sort. "Leonardo da Vinci's," with its five eight-line stanzas making it one of the longer poems in the book, combines a number of motifs that are typical of Moore. Leonardo, of course, was alluded to in "The Pangolin," and his sketch of St. Jerome and the lion forms the focus of the poem and adds an allusion to the

Bible, translated by Jerome into the so-called Latin Vulgate. There is also the use of domesticated animals, as the lion is converted into a bearer of wood after Jerome, according to legend, removed a thorn from its paw. All these motifs make the poem virtually a compendium of Moore's typical sources, especially if we add that Haile Selassie is also present because Moore saw his picture in *Life* magazine, with lions being used as both his personal symbol and as guard animals for his palace. The composite portrait in the poem, then, uses elements of saintly devotion, a monastic quiet, a love of animals, and a sense of personal control over one's environment, all tied together by Leonardo's artistic skill into a blazing picture:

> And here, though hardly a summary, astronomy
> or pale paint makes the golden pair
> in Leonardo da Vinci's sketch—seem
> sun-dyed. Blaze on, picture,
> saint, beast; and Lion Haile Selassie, with household
> lions as symbol of sovereignty.

The closing imagery is illuminated by the sun, much like the closing lines of "The Pangolin," and the lines help us see—bearing in mind other poems such as "Keeping Their World Large," "Blessed Is the Man," and "Sun," the final lyric of Moore's final volume—that the sun is, along with the sea, one of the constant fixities in her poetic universe. As the sea is often the destructive sublime, as in "A Grave," the sun is frequently the redemptive sublime, a source of both intellectual strength and spiritual steadfastness.

Around Christmas, 1958, Moore damaged a blood vessel in her throat and was ordered by her doctor to rest for several months. She was to receive no visitors, make no trips, attend no parties. The fact that a throat illness is what afflicted her mother so severely at the end of her life may well have frightened Moore. An unnamed friend in the Sargeant profile is quoted as saying that Moore often suffered from a psychosomatic flu. It is true that many of her letters in the last two or three decades of her life speak of exhaustion after trips or public appearances. And she would often speak of how she might like to escape such responsibilities, but also of how diligent she had to be in executing them. Many of her acquaintances would end their letters to her by insisting their communication deserved no answer, that her busy schedule shouldn't be further hampered by taking time out for even such a small matter as a postcard reply. These acquaintances included people who admired her poems, or wanted a book autographed, or were inquiring about some fact of her life or work. Just as often, Moore would reply with some rather extravagant compliment on the person's thoughtfulness, and ask them not to trouble with a reply. Indeed, if she had a query about some detail of business or the time of a meeting, she would include a self-addressed postcard that the correspondent could use for the answer. Such civilities were a part of her temperament and her training, but beneath their facade one can hear the murmur of anxiety as her volume of daily correspondence increased.

But there were always the lasting pleasures of hearing from those closest to her. In the late 1950's and beyond, Moore would receive every year a child-like valentine from Warner, as well as other occasional cards from him. Near the end of the decade, on October 8, 1958, Warner sent her a letter steeped in reminiscence. In it, he tells her there are two scraps of paper in his wallet that he carries with him at all times. One of them is a note from Moore about a pair of slippers he gave her as a birthday present in 1941. On the other is a quotation that Moore had copied out for him, one that expresses a sentiment that can be found at the heart of "In Distrust of Merits," as well as many of the poems she wrote in the 1950's. It is from *Two Gentlemen of Verona*: "True love cannot speak; for truth hath better deeds than words to grace it." Moore had sent this quotation to her brother on the occasion of what would have been their mother's ninetieth birthday.

Chapter 9

35 WEST 9TH STREET:
THE FINAL YEARS

I. "Profit is a dead weight"

Moore began the last full decade of her life with the award of the Gold Medal of the Poetry Society of America, in January, 1960. It was the Society's fiftieth anniversary year, and the ceremony featured Robert Graves and Robert Frost as guests of honor along with Moore. In terms of her publication, the decade began for Moore with three pieces that comprised something like a timely self-portrait of the poet who had become famous as a woman of letters. These pieces were an essay on Abraham Lincoln, which showed Moore expressing herself directly in ethical terms; a review of a new anthology of poetry that demonstrated her ability to comment on innovations in verse technique; and the introduction to the *Marianne Moore Reader* (1961), itself a testament to her stature in the world of literature. The first of these, a celebration of a mythic national leader, also served as an occasion for Moore to enshrine sentiments that she had shared with her mother. Shortly before her death, Mrs. Moore had taken to reading Lincoln, and Moore had given her a copy of a selection of his writings as a gift. Appropriately, in May, 1959, she read the essay to an audience at the Gunnery School, where Warner taught, before publishing it in a collection of pieces by various hands, called *Lincoln for the Ages.* Perhaps the most important aspect of Lincoln for the Moores was his ability, as they saw it, to express a heroic set of values, centered in perseverance, in a language that was dignified but unstilted.

Lincoln's "use of words became a perfect instrument," Moore argued, and the "largeness of the life entered into the writing." Filling her essay with quotations, she shows that the statesman was a constant user of "antithesis, reiteration, satire, metaphor; above all *the meaning,* clear and unadorned." But in addition to his genius for words, Lincoln applied himself with diligence to master them. This is the pivotal virtue, as it were, since it is diligence and perseverance that also lay behind his "indomitable ideal—that what the framers of the Constitution embodied in it be preserved." The ability to maintain one's ideal, to persevere in adversity, and to be able to continue to express the ideals in a way that is effective: these were Lincoln's achievements, as they were, in Moore's eyes, those of her mother as well. Equally important for Moore was Lincoln's emotional tact, his ability to use satire when it would work and to offer consolation when it was needed. At the end of the essay, Moore refers to Lincoln's "proposition" as "a Euclid of the heart." By this figure of speech, she suggests not only that Lincoln understood the forces of emotion and value, but he knew their proportions as well and was able to balance, combine, or divide his affections as the situation demanded.

In her review of the Donald Allen anthology, *The New American Poetry: 1945–1960,* Moore moved to very different ground from that of the Lincoln essay. This anthology was to become very influential, and was one of the main causes of the so-called anthology wars of the 1960's that tried to sort out the leading schools and figure in contemporary poetry. The Allen anthology, as it is popularly known, made a fair bid to establish the importance of three groups of poets: the New York School (comprised of Frank O'Hara, John Ashbery, and others); the San Francisco Renaissance (including Allen Ginsberg, Gary Snyder, Robert Duncan, and others); and the Black Mountain or projectivist poets (headed by Charles Olson, but including chiefly Robert Creeley and Edward Dorn). Moore's review shows no concern for this grouping, nor for the larger issues of acceptance that the anthology raised. In a small observation at the end of the review, Moore suggests others who might have been included, such as Daniel Hoffman and George Starbuck, but this very suggestion indicates she wasn't aware of the polemic thrust of Allen's selection process. Of course, it had been over four decades earlier when Moore was in the center of the questions that circulate when an innovative poetic style is trying to gain acceptance.

Clearly she had little interest in entering such a debate again, at least with anything like the determination she had shown earlier.

What is remarkable about her review, however, is how shrewd her judgments are. She singles out several poems that have since been widely accepted as representative of their authors, such as "Instruction Manual," by John Ashbery. She also says that Jack Kerouac "is not for prudish persons," and leaves it at that. She does offer some qualifications to Olson's notion of "projective verse," which Olson advanced as a way of breaking out of the stultified forms in the academic poetry that dominated much of the 1950's. For Moore, "projective" verse was nothing other than art that fought against its (often self-imposed) formal difficulties. And she concludes her discussion of this part of the review by reverting to what was virtually the first aesthetic principle she had uttered in print, over forty years earlier, in "The Accented Syllable." Agreeing with Olson that "anemia and incompetence" were to be avoided, she said that this was accomplished when "the writer is able to compel the reader to put the accent where the writer wishes it put." The tenacity of mind that would enable Moore to reiterate this principle four decades later is, of course, the same quality that shapes much of her poetry, as she borrows motifs and republishes poems from earlier decades. It is the aesthetic equivalent, in certain ways, of the ethical perseverance she prized. In strictly artistic terms, we might see it as a desire for strong-willed control by the artist over her material, even though Moore is, among modernist poets, relatively "invisible" in terms of artistic will. Perhaps it is fair to say that this principle is her way of insisting on the importance of artistic will but without the encumbrance of artistic ego. The principle of the accented syllable could be compared, not only to Frost's notion of "sentence sounds," but also to Pound's notion of sincerity, the need of the artist to stand behind his or her word. It could also be seen as her version of what Wallace Stevens had called the pressure from within that would counter the pressure from without. In any case, her bringing it up in a review of new poets shows not only that she felt it was still valid, but that it had something to offer each successive group of innovative stylists.

The third part of Moore's self-portrait in prose in the beginning of the decade was her "Foreword" to the *Marianne Moore Reader*. This volume was an attempt to represent Moore's accomplishments as essayist and translator as well as poet. The book also included an interview

that she had given to Donald Hall, and the letters to the Ford Motor
Company about the naming of what became the Edsel. Such selections
suggest that the *Reader* was designed at least partially to take advantage
of Moore's celebrity status. The book reprinted a selection of poems
from the *Collected* volume of 1951, all of *Like a Bulwark* and *O to Be a
Dragon*, as well as a few new poems, twenty-five pages of La Fontaine
translations, four essays from *Predilections*, and recent essays and reviews, including the pieces on Lincoln and the Allen anthology. All in
all, it was a very "generous" selection, as publishers are wont to say, and
it accurately represented Moore as a writer of wide interests and a long
career. But by slighting the poems from the early years (only about a
half-dozen lyrics were taken from before 1935), the selection also clearly
represented the Moore who had become a public figure. Almost completely obscured was the poetic innovator, the editor of *The Dial*, and
the contemporary of H.D., Lola Ridge, and William Carlos Williams.
Moore would dismiss the book by apologizing to her friends for presum-
ing to ask them to buy work that had already been available. But the
rationale for the book, and the image it created of Moore as a public
figure whose artistic work began just prior to World War II, were to
reflect the way many people perceived her for the remainder of her life.
By turning her into a grandmotherly figure, although one trailing clouds
of past glory, the sense of struggle and growth were removed from her
work, which was supplied with a virtually genderless author.

However, if the principles behind the book were those of "marketing" and packaging a major author for an audience who needed an
overall picture of the writer's career, the "Foreword" itself proceeded
with principles quite opposite to these. Again, Moore struck a dominant note of humility and self-effacement. But there were also the usual
paradoxes as well. The opening sentences create a complex stance:

> Published: it is enough. The magazine was discontinued. The edition was
> small. One paragraph needs restating. Newspaper cuts on the fold or
> disintegrates. When was it published, and where? "The title was 'Words
> and . . .' something else. Could you say what it was?" I have forgotten.
> Happened upon years later, it seems to have been "Words and Modes of
> Expression." What became of "Tedium and Integrity," the unfinished
> manuscript of which there is no duplicate? A housekeeper is needed to
> assort the untidiness. For whom? A curioso or just for the author? In that
> case "as safe at the publisher's as if chained to the shelves of Bodley,"
> Lamb said, smiling.

As with many another self-portrait in old age, here we are allowed to see the artist looking back over her accomplishments. But the past work has taken on at least two simultaneous aspects: cherished fragments of an order now lost but once striven for, and mere impedimenta and curiosities that hardly seem worth the effort of preserving. In fact, the artist can no longer distinguish for whom she makes the effort, herself or some curiosity seeker. It should be enough, she feels, to have published the material once, but the fragile orders of publication and distribution—like *memento mori*, perhaps—cannot sustain themselves. Yet the paragraph ends on a positive note, complete with a trademark quotation, and the author's smile is restored by an awareness that there are agencies that give an author life beyond the first breath of publication.

The next paragraph immediately turns to Moore's criteria of selection, though she doesn't explicitly name them as such. The criteria come in the form of questions: "Does it hold the attention? 'Has it human value?' Or seem as if one had ever heard of 'lucidity, force, and ease' or had any help from past thinkers?" The triplet of "lucidity, force, and ease" recalls another of Moore's triangulated criteria, "Humility, Concentration, and Gusto." But humility itself keeps her from quoting one of her own essay titles as if she had uncovered a universal formulation. She also invokes the sense of tradition, the "past thinkers" serving as a benchmark and a support. What follow in the next four pages of the Foreword are brief accounts of the occasion of some of the pieces, occasions usually given in the form of limitations or self-chastisements. She mentions her habit of quoting others, and says that her poems are "a kind of collection of flies in amber." And she also mentions the Buddhist philosophy she had recently been reading, pointing out its emphasis on egotism as a form of ignorance. She tries yet again to characterize what she called, in a different context, "straight writing," and to show that the accent should be unmistakable, with the rhythm generating "something built-in as in music."

Turning to questions of subject matter, she asks rhetorically why she is interested in animals and athletes. She says they are subjects but also exemplars of art, and praises their self-possession; but then she adds the qualification, "Perhaps I really don't know." She quotes Charles Ives: "The fabric of existence weaves itself whole." Moore was to remain committed to the principle of art as based on organic unity, one of the many legacies of romanticism that found its way into her modern approach. Then, in discussing her views, she defends Eisenhower's farm policies as utilitarian, and his foreign policy as based on self-discipline. She shifts the context by quoting an interview she herself gave to an anonymous "inquirer" who proposed to call the poet a "moralist." Moore quickly agrees, but then demurs somewhat to say that she does not "thrust promises and deeds of mercy right and left to write a lyric— if what I write ever is one—." Near the end, she makes a distinction between prosody, a "tool," and poetry, "a maze, a trap, a web," she calls it, quoting I. A. Richards.

She then names The Book of Job her favorite poem, and closes by citing William James: "Man's chief difference from the brutes lies in the exuberant excess of his subjective propensities. Prune his extravagance, sober him, and you undo him." By citing the spokesman for pragmatism in one of his more romantic moments, Moore is able to capture her own paradoxical combination of sobriety and extravagance. In turn, this paradox animates her throughout the "Foreword," as she must mediate for herself between the roles of artistic sage and self-effacing moralist. This mediation becomes visible in the "Foreword" by Moore's use of questions posed to her as well as by her, and to the use of quotations from other authors. The self is elusive in Moore's view of authorship, and in her own self-image, too. At one point, after quoting I. A. Richards' definition of poetry, and before quoting some lines of his poetry, she says that "the quarry is trapped in his own lines." This pun, even if made unintentionally, reflects the dilemma of the artist who searches for a way to trap or contain her experience, only to find herself trapped by the quest itself. The mind is both enchanting and enchanted.

There were other honors and publications at the start of the 1960s. Bryn Mawr gave Moore a certificate of honor, along with seventy-four other alumnae, as part of a celebration of its seventy-fifth anniversary, and Goucher College gave her an honorary degree, both in the spring of 1960. Moore also published her memoir of her home borough, "Brooklyn from Clinton Hill," in Vogue, even though the conditions of her neighborhood would soon begin to deteriorate to a point where she would have to move. There were also reviews, one of George Plimpton's book on baseball, Out of My League, and of a memoir of a Viennese writer. Her life was to become increasingly occupied by her association with such public figures as Plimpton. Near the end of 1959, Moore wrote to Barbara Church that she had had an unusual dream. In it Charles de Gaulle had come to see her, though he was in fact looking for someone else. She got out her plate with the map of Paris on it and put some Euphrates crackers on it; then a neighbor came and asked for ginger ale, in case anyone would happen to drop in. Moore then replied to the neighbor, "No one ever does." The dream can be read as a revelation about Moore's insecurity in the face of other celebrities, and about her missing the world of casual neighborly contact. The aesthetic paradox that combined self-effacement with the role of sagacious artist may have been harder to apply to everyday life.

Domestic and artistic concerns continued to occupy Moore, of course, and continuing involvement with friends. The husband of Gladys Berry, her housekeeper, suffered a fall at a construction site and was hospitalized for an extended period. Moore relied very much on Berry, who was to remain with Moore for over thirty years. The poet herself was afflicted with throat trouble in 1960, and the recurring "psychosomatic flu." Her voice, which always had a Midwestern flatness to it, became thinner and a bit hoarse. Along with such daily concerns were inquiries and requests from friends. Early in 1960, Lester Littlefield wrote to Moore to express his opinion that her recent poetry was too detailed about ephemera, and suggested that her work on the *Fables* was the cause of this. But he again invited her to Europe, and suggested that she write a long poem. A year later, he was planning to do a full bibliography of Moore's work, despite his failing eyesight, afflicted as he was with cataracts. He stepped aside from this project in 1963, in deference to Donald Gallup, but Gallup never completed it. Moore listened patiently to people like Littlefield, especially if their relationship, as was the case here, went back many years. Littlefield even suggested, in the fall of 1961, that Moore was surrounded by "courtiers" who would not tell the Empress she was wearing no clothes—this, again, in reference to what he saw as the weakness of her "occasional" poetry. Near the end of 1962, he wrote to insist, "know it or not, like it or not," that Whitman was her grandfather. She herself must have felt something like parental protectiveness toward Littlefield. He encouraged such a relationship, for at one point he had had two blowouts on a trip from Maine to Florida, and resolved to make out his will, leaving everything to Moore.

Singling out her poem about Yul Brynner, Littlefield said that she was guilty of self-parody. This poem, which she reprinted in what would be her last single volume of poetry, *Tell Me, Tell Me* (1966), took up a variation on the theme of perseverance: the rescuing of threatened people or cultural symbols. (In *Tell Me, Tell Me*, the poem appears right before her lyric about the rescue of Carnegie Hall from "the cannibal of real estate.") Brynner, though well-known as an actor from Broadway and Hollywood, was in fact active in relief services for refugee children. Moore's poetic strategy is to picture herself as incompetent—"a pygmy citizen"—as she makes Brynner into a "magic bird with multiple tongue," referring to his mastery of five languages. Introducing one of her favorite subjects, the curtailment of egotism, she also praises him for declining the honor and increased recognition that goes with the role of public leader: "Instead of feathering himself, he exemplified / the rule that, self-applied, omits the gold." There are references to his stage abilities, and in conclusion Moore puns on his name, turning him into a Yule log. The poem relies on conceits such as puns and golden-bird imagery to avoid the heavy tread of the moralistic tone. Though Littlefield's judgment may have some validity, what it does not seem to address is how hard it is to write the poetry of praise in an age of anxiety. Moore's approach relies on many of the traditional devices of epideictic poetry, such as witty but specific references to the person being praised, but they are often the very devices that would leave her open to Littlefield's complaints.

In May, 1960, Moore visited the Women's House of Detention in lower Manhattan, and there met with and read her poetry to the inmates. There were also many visits to schools and colleges for readings and lectures. In 1960, for instance, she made "local" appearances at St. John's University in Queens, the First Unitarian Church in Brooklyn, and William Gaynor High School, also in her home borough. She made trips to Pennsylvania State University in September and Wesleyan University in Connecticut in October. At Wesleyan she quoted Nathan Pusey, the president of Harvard, as saying that methodical thinking alone cannot produce creativity, and at the Unitarian Church she quoted Alfred Kazin, from a June, 1960 issue of *Time*, who had said that "if the theater is a mirror of our society then the only revolutionary act in American life is to be a thinker." She was aware of the difficulty of trying to develop values contrary to those of the mainstream, but she also saw part of society's problem as its failure to act on the accepted values with sufficient diligence and "exuberant excess." As early as 1919 she had recorded in one of her notebooks the observation that to call anything popular in America was to destroy it in the eyes of serious artists.

In October, 1961, at a lecture she gave at the YM-YWHA, she remarked that "you don't intentionally maintain a reputation." This was in response to what she identified only as a "friend's warning." This friend may have been Littlefield, or any of the several other acquaintances and friends who tended to take her literary reputation as both an object of awe and a subject of watchfulness. A number of acquaintances gave her material that they hoped she would turn into a poem: Brendan Gill, editor at *The New Yorker*, sent Moore a picture postcard that became the occasion for "Old Amusement Park." Chester Page gave her a mechanical crow. Page, who had a career as a concert pianist, served as secretary for Louise Crane. He had first written to Moore in 1955, sending along a copy of her *Poems* (1921) for an autograph, and mentioning that he had never met a poet before. Near the end of the decade he told her that she was "as varied in inventiveness as Mozart," and praised *O to Be a Dragon* as one of her "most beautiful" books. Page proved to be a temporary embarrassment to Moore when he wrote to Bryher in July, 1960, and introduced himself as Moore's friend. When Bryher told Moore of this, she immediately wrote to Page and told him that Bryher demanded privacy, and Moore went so far as to say that even she didn't write to her.

The mechanical crow, however, became the subject of the poem "To Victor Hugo of My Crow Pluto," and indirectly for the prose essay, "My Crow, Pluto—A Fantasy," which appeared in *Harper's Bazaar* in October, 1961. These two pieces are unlike anything else Moore ever wrote. They can be appreciated as something like acts of pure playfulness. But they can also be read as works that only an accomplished author would dare to publish, for at the same time they mock the very seriousness of the social role of the artist. The poem is written in a sort of tourist Italian, mixed with what Moore calls "pseudo/Esperanto." Ostensibly no more than a fond description of a pet crow, the poem nevertheless invokes the literary augustness of Victor Hugo to defend its subject against false understanding. As with the animal subject in Elizabeth Bishop's famous poem "The Fish," the poet ends by releasing the symbol-bearing beast back to something like a natural state. But before the *jeu d'esprit* is over there is, for the attentive reader, a very serious motto to be uncovered, one shared by the crow and the poet: "lucro / è peso morto." Moore translates this in her notes to the poem as "profit is a dead weight." In a later essay, titled after this phrase, Moore says she found the expression in her Italian dictionary, but was struck by it because she considered greed "the vice of our century." This goes back to her objections to materialism in the 1930's. In the essay she was able to express seriously the social concerns she chose to hide under an Italian phrase. The need for accurate naming is transferred to the need for charitable surrender: "And so / dear crow— // gioièllo / mio— // I have to / let you go." If the crow is not to be misunderstood, and not mis-symbolized, one must be prepared to release it, in the literal sense, from human constraints. But even as Moore says "addio" to the crow, she playfully calls it by its "other" name, Plato. As she said in the "Foreword" to her *Reader,* animals "do not make us self-conscious; look their best when caring least."

The prose version of the crow Pluto is even more playful, and can also be read as more serious. It is truly a "fantasy," developing as it does the conceit that a "real" crow, befriended by Moore in Fort Greene Park not far from her apartment, accompanies her on errands and even fetches her books, such as a vest-pocket dictionary. The prose essay repeats several key motifs from the poem: the crow is defended against its bad reputation, and it is released at the end of the narrative. Moore also manages to score several witty points against her own self-image. For example, the crow is attracted to her because of the crow feathers on one of her hats, always a key part of her public image. He also likes her diet of health food, a topic of some good-natured gossip about Moore among her friends and acquaintances. And she manages to mention slyly that she has endorsed one of the dictionaries that is a competitor with the vest-pocket version that Pluto fetches for her.

Being a part of a Moore poem, Pluto turns out to be a very literary crow, for it perches on a bust and recites the word "Nevermore." The bust, by the way, is cast by Gaston Lachaise, and is a gift of Lincoln Kirstein, the director of the New York City Ballet. What Moore doesn't say is that this bust is of her; she thus manages to mix some adroit name-dropping with a bit of self-effacement. With a self-reflexive turn at the end of the piece, Moore says:

Losing him was not simple but the spirit of adventure finally got the best of him. If what you have been reading savors of mythology, could I make it up? and if I could, would I impose it on you? Remember, life is stranger than fiction.

As with the boxes of Joseph Cornell, whose resemblance to her poems she appreciated, Moore here deliberately points to the fantasy element in her piece, its "made upness," as well as its fragility and otherworldliness. Both crow pieces could be taken as Moore's insistence on the play element in all cultural imaginings; they are her way of saying that proper naming is inextricably bound up with correct valuation, but that the imagination can name heavenly and earthly things unthought of in the philosophy of common sense. The rhetorical questions at the end of the prose version suggest that Moore is addressing an audience that she finds, at least in some respects, too skeptical, too close-minded. She may also be suggesting, in her roundabout way, that some of her readers don't always take her seriously enough.

But if her fame allowed Moore to make playful adjustments in her relationship with her audience, it did not exempt her from the duty of most writers who live six decades or more: memorializing their contemporaries. The sixties meant much memorializing for a number of Moore's friends and peers. Malvina Hoffman died in 1966, H.D., in 1961, E. E. Cummings, in 1962, and Morton Dauwen Zabel, in 1964.

In 1960, H.D. had been able to visit America for what would be the last time. Luckily, Moore had a chance to talk with her, on the evening she was given the Gold Medal of the American Academy of Arts and Letters. Moore wrote to Bryher about the meeting, but supplied no details about the conversation. However, a few weeks earlier Moore had traveled to the exhibit of H.D. material at the Academy with Harry Levin, looking at the cases of manuscripts, books, and memorabilia. Moore quoted to Bryher a remark by Levin to the effect that one could tell it was H.D.'s work just by seeing the shapes on the pages. The Award ceremony was a delight for the reclusive H.D., now quite frail with a weakened heart. She met younger poets such as Denise Levertov and Robert Duncan, who was to write a long study of her work. Staying at the Stanhope Hotel in New York, she could walk across the street to the Metropolitan Museum and see the Greek antiquities that were central to her imagination. It must have been especially touching for Moore to see her old friend and classmate, different as they were in style, yet closely tied by their commitment to verbal accuracy and emotional honesty. H.D., who died at the Red Cross Hospital in Zurich, was remembered in the pages of the Bryn Mawr Alumnae Bulletin, as Moore quoted Pound's early exclamation—"straight talk, straight as the Greeks!"—and May Sinclair's encomium. Moore also recalled H.D.'s repeating Norman Douglas's description of her: "You are like the Italians, you eat with your eyes." The two women shared a love of the visual, seeing in its erotic stringency an escape from the imprecisions of subjectivity. H.D. had seemed to enjoy thoroughly the fame that had been accorded her by the Academy, even though it came late in life. But she immediately returned to her retreat in Switzerland, whereas Moore continued to enjoy the rewards of public acclaim on almost a daily basis.

Cummings' tribute was given at the American Academy of Arts and Letters, and published in its Proceedings. Moore avoided altogether any mention of her old friend's sometimes indelicate subject matter, and instead praised his paintings as well as his poems. She recalled how the art critic from The Dial, Henry McBride, whose taste and insights she always valued, spoke of Cummings' paintings as having "the purities of mushrooms blooming in darkness." She herself quoted part of two of her favorite poems of Cummings', one about Gravenstein apples, whose musical structure pleased her, and one on the singing bird that, "if earth and sky should break in two / he'd make them one (his song's so true)." The latter may have reminded her of the bird in her own "What Are Years?" She also mentioned his "art of economy," citing the example of when "instead of saying that the prison cell was six feet long and four feet wide, he says it was six feet short and four feet narrow." It was a good illustration of one of her devices, using a new perspective in the pursuit of a greater, more accurate naturalism.

Morton Dauwen Zabel was instrumental in bringing Moore's name back into prominence after her years at The Dial and the fallow period that followed. As Assistant Editor and then Editor at Poetry, he was able to open the pages of the magazine to Moore when Harriet Monroe had been unreceptive to her work. Her memoir of him stressed his standing as a critic, and also listed his many literary friends. She ended by remarking on his high chivalry, a word she had used chiefly in connection with Auden, and called him "a very great gentleman." Zabel had first written Moore in 1931 to congratulate her on her review of Ezra Pound. A year later he had visited Moore and her mother in their Brooklyn apartment, a sign that he was courteous enough to be pleasing to Mrs. Moore, and he sent back snapshots of the two women from the University of Chicago, where he taught while also working on *Poetry*. In the 1930's Moore shared her literary opinions with Zabel, saying that she wouldn't sign one of Pound's manifestos, but would sign a protest "against corrupt and influenced criticism," and that while she liked Louis Zukofsky well enough, she felt the term "objectivism" was forced. This, of course, was consistent with her reluctance to be a part of any movement, such as imagism, but to speak up for certain principles and for those whose work she valued. In 1936, Zabel took over as editor at *Poetry*, and immediately asked Moore for contributions. In October, 1936, she urged Zabel to print all of the Pound material he could get, even if he had to put it in a supplement, which she would bear the cost of printing. But when Zabel sent her the three Cantos Pound had submitted, she advised him to print two but reject the third. And in 1936, Zabel solicited her advice for the Harriet Monroe Prize; she listed Stevens, Bogan, Cummings, and Williams, in order of preference. She added that she would also have chosen Auden and Eliot, but for the stipulation that the recipient had to be an American. In a letter sent in November, 1938, she spoke of herself as still hoping to give the world some of her work, and further hoping it would be appreciated by those who knew *Poetry* and *The Dial* from the old days. Zabel was able to play the role of confidant and patron, mentor and pupil, and so Moore was able to confide in him and even display her literary ambition, which she did not let others see very often.

Throughout the 1940's Moore shared with Zabel her enthusiasm about Niebuhr and Auden. In 1944, Zabel saw to it that she received the Harriet Monroe Prize, and in accepting the news of it she disclaimed the honor of any prize and lamented her mother's recent ill health. She also said that she supported the Bollingen Prize being given to Pound in 1948, and that it was good to separate one's literary achievements from one's "behavior and political affiliation." In the 1950's he again drew on her services in several ways, as she reviewed a number of books for *Poetry*. She wrote very enthusiastically about her dinner with Eliot, Marion Dorn (Mrs. McKnight Kauffer), and Robert Giroux at Voisin's, a very luxurious Manhattan restaurant, in December, 1950. She was quite impressed by this event, and mentioned it to several correspondents more than once; she also was pleased to report that Eliot was looking more relaxed than he had for some time. He had just returned to New York from giving the William Vaughn Moody lecture at the University of Chicago, at Zabel's invitation. Zabel's letters about this visit, stressing how impressed he was with Eliot, further strengthened Moore's admiration for both men.

Zabel invited her to deliver the Moody Lecture in 1951, but she declined because of work on the *Fables* and a case of pleurisy. But she did manage to give the lecture, and a reading of her poems, in 1953, and Zabel wrote a glowing introduction for her. She returned the favor by nominating him for the Institute of Arts and Letters, going so far as to say in the recommendation letter that "if there is not room, I feel that he should have my place." She also nominated several visual artists who were also old friends, such as McKnight Kauffer, Loren McIver, and Bruce Rodgers, as well as her advisors on the *Fables*, Harry Levin and Wallace Fowlie. In 1957 she again gave a poetry reading at the university, on her way back from the Ewing Lecture at the University of California, Los Angeles. Zabel suggested that she read the poem on the Brooklyn Dodgers as an "encore" piece, and it brought down the house. She told Zabel in October of that year that the craftsmanship and artistic style of the Wiener Werkstatte was her "veneration" in the 1920's, but also that she hoped she had developed her taste since then, and that this was a most important statement to be able to make. She also corrected some details in the *Encyclopedia Britannica* article he wrote about her work in 1958, pointing out that all her poems had rhymes, though she often concealed them, so to say her first book was a slender volume of "free verse" was inaccurate; then she added in the margins of the letter that she could "bear" such a description. There were also details about her *Poems* of 1921 that she wanted to clarify, such as Bryher's having initiated the project, paid for it, and chosen the cover, only then to give the credit to others. She also asked Zabel to drop the word "wholly" in the phrase "wholly committed to poetry," adding that she objected to an interviewer who quoted her as having praised a poet's "sensitivity," this being a word she never used.

Her last letter to him expressed regret that he had again narrowly missed election to the Institute. So their relationship concluded on a note of literary professionalism, which had been one of the main elements that drew them together. Zabel was a gossip, and often his literary politics could irritate Moore and her mother as well. But Moore had learned from Zabel something that went beyond even what she had absorbed at *The Dial.* He exemplified for her, at a time when she was not very self-assured about her public role, the skill and energy it took to maintain one's place in the literary world, with its changing tastes, hierarchies, and fortunes. With their shared friendship with world-famous figures such as Eliot, and their seemingly constant preoccupation with awards and membership in cultural institutions, Moore and Zabel negotiated the maze of literary affiliations with considerable skill. In her memoir of him she praised his tact and his contemporaneity: "Devotion, patience, and unflagging kindness marked his attitude to contributors [to *Poetry*]. 'No resentments, grievances, arguments.' His Notes in fine print which concluded issues of *Poetry*, summarizing items of current interest, constitute an index to poetry of that period." If Auden was in many ways an artistic guide and teacher for Moore, Zabel served as an instructor and even protector in the area of professional matters. While the accepted picture of Moore's career displays a rather sudden entrance into the public eye after the major awards of the early 1950's, the truer account would show finer lines of influence. These lines of influence, epitomized by a person like Zabel, helped prepare Moore for the wider public recognition about which she had been divided in the late 1930's. It is tempting to see Zabel as a reduced version of Saintsbury and Auden, men of letters whose social bearing and literary intelligence were considerable, and quite ready to be put at the disposal of someone such as Moore. And if there were people such as Zabel who were reduced versions of more important figures, there were also people who were reduced versions of Zabel.

During the last decades of her life, and especially from the 1960's onward, Moore was more or less constantly approached by people who wanted to meet a famous poet, who needed a book autographed for a present or for their own collection, or who wanted some information about a particular poem to satisfy an academic need or personal curiosity. She remarked in a late interview that on some mornings it took her an hour and a half just to open her mail. She even copied Edmund Wilson's device of having cards printed up saying that she did not give interviews, did not sign petitions, and so forth. But she was always outwardly good-natured about the irritations that she must have felt, knowing they were the more or less inevitable consequences of renown.

Occasionally people would send her material that they hoped would inspire a poem, and perhaps earn them a place in one of her famous "Notes." And the particular use of detailed information in her poems, especially that drawn from a cultural context, at least indirectly encouraged such hopes.

Moore had several audiences near the end of her life, as any established and complex artist does. Hers included a large group of people who admired her moral sense and saw her as a spokesperson for humane values, and many of the talks she gave at places like the YM-YWHA and high schools spoke to this audience. A second audience would be the academic critics who saw in her work an important part of the cultural legacy of modernism, and who taught her poetry in the classroom. For them, her work was further proof that the range of styles contained within modernism was broad, and that intelligence and beauty could be marshaled to help heal the breach of alienation that was widespread in a world that had separated facts and values. There were also those socially prominent people who saw her as highly sophisticated, a true "ornament" of the artistic world, people like Louise Crane and Lincoln Kirstein, themselves prominent and influential in artistic and social circles. Finally, there was the audience of established and would-be writers and students of the arts and literature who enjoyed establishing a personal relationship with a great poet. Sometimes these were people who had genuine talent of their own, such as Chester Page and Brendan Gill, and who enjoyed recognition and friendship from an established figure. Moore especially enjoyed visual artists who approached her in this context. In 1959, Monroe Wheeler had suggested that a friend of his, Robert Andrew Parker, illustrate an edition of Moore's poems to be published by the Museum of Modern Art. Parker admired Moore's handwriting, and suggested the book included facsimiles of Moore's handwritten fair copies of the poems. This was arranged, and the limited edition, entitled *Eight Poems*, finally appeared in 1963. Dudley Huppler, another visual artist who befriended Moore, also was interested for a time in illustrating one of her books. He had first written Moore from his home in Madison, Wisconsin, where he taught English literature. He described Moore as the "most perfect poet," and as a gift sent her some of his drawings, which he had reproduced in sets of small cards. The drawings were mainly of animals, rendered with some precision, though slightly sentimentalized. Eager not to have to teach for a living, he wanted to establish himself as an artist. Moore helped him by sending his work around and recommending it to her friends. Huppler was especially glad to have it shown to Auden, for example, and sent Auden a note about his favorite writer, Ronald Firbank, about whom Auden had written. Huppler felt that Moore was like Firbank, a writer who valued preciocity and who even served for a while as the epitome of the camp sensibility, with its highly droll irony and theatrical gestures. In the early 1950's Huppler and Moore discussed the possibility of using his drawings to illustrate Moore's translation of the *Fables*. But Huppler decided that his drawings were not in the right mode to be using in this way, admitting that they were too "chic." Their correspondence was never highly personal; the last surviving letter is a request from Huppler in 1965 for a recommendation to Yaddo, the writers' colony, and an expression of thanks for an earlier recommendation Moore had written for him for a Wurlitzer Fund Grant.

Moore was also sought after by many who valued her poetry and her personality; her audience included bibliophiles as well as visual artists, for they knew that she valued the art of the printed word. One bibliophile who came to know Moore well in the 1960's was Robert Wilson, of the Phoenix Book Shop in Greenwich Village. The Phoenix specialized in poetry and first editions, and Wilson sent Moore a copy of his catalogue in early 1964. He mentioned that the catalogue also went to many people she knew, and he listed, among others, Chester Page and William Kienbusch, an artist about whom Moore had written a brief essay for a catalogue of his exhibition in 1963. A year or so later, Wilson published a small book of poems by Jeffrey Kindley and Moore contributed a "blurb" to the volume. Wilson would occasionally leave packets of books for Moore to autograph, usually for his personal library. In 1967 he published a limited edition of her poem, "Tipoo's Tiger," about a mechanical tiger that emitted low groans while swallowing a man. The same year Wilson set up an elaborate window display at his shop featuring Moore's latest volume, the *Complete Poems*. For her eightieth birthday, he sent her a "nonsense" verse that wove together the titles of her various books.

Laurence Scott was yet another visual artist who befriended Moore and supplied her with information for her poetry. He began writing Moore in April, 1960, when he realized, along with Guy Davenport, the critic and short-story writer who wrote an essay on Moore, that she had incorporated the initials of Hildegarde Watson in her poem, "The Wood Weasel." Scott worked for a while in the art department at *The New Yorker*. After the first letter, Scott continued to send Moore many sorts of visual images, often in the form of reproductions. He sent her his own drawing of a pangolin, as well as information about the animal from a book called *Living Mammals of the World*. When there was a *Festschrift* published for Moore on her seventy-seventh birthday, Scott contributed drawings of animals from several of her poems. A postcard reproduction of a fifteenth-century tapestry from the Glasgow Art Gallery and Museum became a source of the poem "Charity Overcoming Envy," which appeared in *The New Yorker* in 1963. Other items of interest followed, such as information about Dalgrén, an engineer whose work was mentioned in "A Carriage from Sweden." On August 25, 1966, he wrote to tell her he had a drawing of an aardvark in that week's *New Yorker*. It was Scott who suggested the title for the poem "Occasionem Cognosce," which was printed as a keepsake by Lowell House at Harvard University in 1963. The printing was arranged and designed with the help of Scott and friends of his at Harvard. This poem appears in the *Complete Poems* with the title "Avec Ardeur," and after about two dozen very brief couplets complaining about imprecise usage, ends with the claim, "Nothing mundane is divine; / Nothing divine is mundane." In some ways the poem can be read as an attack of just the sort of special and overly dramatized vocabulary that is frequently a hallmark of the camp sensibility. Yet at the same time its tone is one of fastidiousness that borders on the fussy: "am, I / say, by // the word / (bore) bored." Moore even admits to still being "trapped // by these / word diseases." Her lexical range, always striking in its depth and breadth, was no guarantee that she could always find a fresh formulation in a time of "expressionary need." The nets of personality and temperament, as well as the strictures of social pressures, confine the range of even the most inventive poet.

Moore's health grew fitfully worse in the late 1960's, and there were troublesome episodes before then as well. She suffered what she referred to as a stroke sometime in the first year of the decade. Writing to Mrs. Henry Ware Eliot, the sister-in-law of the Nobel laureate, in September, 1960, Moore said, "Am better—surely am, but can't rush as I did—lest I suffer another near attack or 'stroke.'" Five months later she wrote again that she might be deprived forever of being able to do what she was accustomed to do. In January, 1960, she had told Bishop that last year an unspecified illness nearly carried her away. Then she added the word "stroke" to clarify the sentence. Earlier, in March, 1959, she had written to Mrs. Barbara Savage, an acquaintance and classmate from Bryn Mawr, declining an invitation with the excuse that for a long time she had been hampered by the effects of a near stroke. In an interview, Ethel Taylor, a registered nurse who served Moore in the last four years of her life, spoke of Moore's having suffered a slight stroke as early as 1947. This, of course, was the year her mother died. Moore may have been referring to a series of "near" strokes that occurred before Taylor entered her employ, and the possibility exists that Moore dated the onset by reference to her mother's death. According to Taylor, however, this was part of Moore's medical history, and Moore was afflicted with recurrent symptoms for the next two decades. These included sudden fevers from time to time, especially in stressful situations, and a slurring of speech when such attacks developed. This could have been the condition that one of her friends referred to as Moore's "psychosomatic flu." But aside from Taylor's interview, there is only circumstantial evidence, and such remarks as those cited above, to show that this was a chronic condition.

In 1955, Moore began using the services of Dr. Nagla Loofy, a female physician recommended to her by Bishop. Loofy used hypnosis on Moore and administered vitamin shots to her. Thanks to Frances Steloff, Moore had also become a steady user of "health" food, such as carrot juice and brewer's yeast. And in the late 1950's she began to drink bottled water on a regular basis, supplied to her as a gift from Hildegarde Watson. She continued these regimens, relatively unorthodox for their day, for many years; the diet was to remain a part of Moore's habits, and eventually her image among her friends, until the end of her life. Moore always spoke positively about such a diet, insisting, for example, that eating half an avocado a day kept her hair lustrous. In the 1960's Moore began to consult regularly with Dr. Annie Baumann, whom Louise Crane had referred her to during a particular illness. Dr. Baumann was a stern figure who had many famous patients, including Elizabeth Bishop and Alfred Kazin. She was extremely conservative in her manner of treatment, and Moore was quite content to go along with a physician who did not often prescribe drugs. It was

Baumann who engaged the services of Ethel Taylor after an incident in 1968 when Moore tripped over a rocking chair and injured her ribs. This was probably the occasion when Hildegarde Watson talked to Moore on the phone and became worried about the way she sounded. After a call by Watson to Louise Crane, matters were taken into hand, and Crane arranged for the nurse, as recommended by Dr. Baumann. Crane also at this time took Moore's finances into account, and after arranging for a financial advisor, managed to double the value of Moore's investments.

Generally Moore remained in good health, considering her age, for long periods throughout the early 1960's. Many who met her in this period remarked on her vitality and alertness. Though she would tire easily, and would be weak after the fever that would accompany one of her "attacks," this did not prevent her from making many public appearances, and even from taking two trips overseas during the decade. The first of these was one that must have given her special delight, for she prepared for it with the same thoroughness that she had shown when she went to England for the first time fifty years earlier. In May, 1962, Moore wrote to tell Bryher of a "secret" trip she had planned to Greece with Frances Browne and her sister, Norvelle. This trip, according to a letter Warner wrote to Hildegarde Watson, was made necessary by the overwhelming crush of publicity and requests for readings and appearances, all of which had tired Moore considerably. Watson had urged Moore to put "an ocean between you and New York," for she knew from her daily correspondence with her how heavy were the demands of Moore's public. Actually, the plans began to take shape somewhat earlier, for Moore wrote Pound in the summer of 1961 to tell him she was going to visit Venice, and to ask if he'd be there. She was on board ship by the middle of August the next year. She was able to visit Italy and saw Michelangelo's tomb of the princes. Two Botticellis at the Uffizi, the "Birth of Venus," and the "Primavera" were judged to be "sublime," though the crush of tourists presented a problem. There was also some time spent in Lisbon, and a visit to Chopin's villa at Valledemo. The tour through Greece included several islands, and a trip up Mt. Olympus. There was a very brief meeting with Pound, though she mentioned this to few people. (Lester Littlefield was to send Moore a copy of a letter he had received from Olga Rudge, Pound's mistress, who mentioned the visit.)

A year or so later, on the occasion of her seventy-fifth birthday, she was given a dinner in her honor by the American Academy of Arts and Letters. She made some brief remarks, which included a reading of her new poem, "Charity Overcoming Envy." The remarks concentrated on two virtues, the need for leisure, and the uses of hospitality. On the latter topic, she recounted instances from her recent trip:

> Hospitality—say generosity—as I discern it, is giving what you could profitably use yourself; golden examples of which abounded in the parts of Italy and Greece in which I was last summer; exemplified by ship companies, inns, and even very poor persons: the white rose and spray of lemon verbena spontaneously given by a museum guard who had it on his table; five pomegranates glowing scarlet in the afternoon sun, like apples of the Hesperides, given five itinerants by a large family with food scarce; a little heap of pins for the use of clerks, in a shop in Athens, presented in a glazed white gold-edged box "with the compliments of the shop" when a patron proposed buying ten or so.

Moore continued well into her seventh decade to lavish attention on details, and to try to connect her most important principles to the events of everyday life. "Charity Overcoming Envy" ends with a cryptic motto, "The Gordian knot need not be cut." One interpretation of this may be that Moore is suggesting that the larger mysteries of the world need not be solved before we practice the simple virtues.

Two summers later she returned overseas, this time to England and Ireland. She was able to pay a call on her fellow poet Edith Sitwell, who died shortly afterwards. At the National Gallery, Moore especially enjoyed Botticelli's "Nativity," noticing for the first time the figure of the old man on the right of the picture; she told Hildegarde Watson that his hands were beautiful. There was also a very pleasant visit with Eliot, who by then had become even more content than when she had dined with him at Voisin's in 1950, and again in 1956. Peter du Sautoy, an editor at Faber & Faber, was with them when they dined out, and he quoted Eliot's remark that Wensleydale was the Mozart of cheeses, but added that this didn't mean that Mozart was the Wensleydale of composers. Most touching of all, perhaps, was the call she paid to her old friend and associate, Alyse Gregory. It was October before she reached Gregory, living alone in a small cottage in Morebath, Devon. Her husband Llewelyn had died years earlier, and Gregory was now ailing physically, but her mind remained very bright. Well into the 1960's she would be reading widely and perceptively in much of the new literature, advising Hildegarde Watson about her memoirs, and staying quite informed about the matters of the world. In 1967 she wrote Moore to reflect on some news she had gotten about Thayer; evidently he was still writing in both French and German, though he was often incoherent. Gregory wondered what it must have been like for him all those years since *The Dial.* Her life had diverged greatly from that of Moore, but the two women were possessed of impressive literary intelligence, and they never stopped learning and inquiring about an enormous range of knowledge and experience. Back in London, Moore listened to a broadcast on the BBC that included her reading "Rigorists," and on August 30 the London *Times* ran an interview with her, conducted by John Horder.

The other highlight of the 1964 trip was Moore's first visit to Ireland. She recalled how many years earlier Warner had gone there and seen Merrion Square, where he identified the house their grandfather had been born in, referring to the visit as a "life experience." It was also very moving for Moore. She had written about Ireland more than once, and had rather stridently defined herself as Irish in "Spenser's Ireland," having earlier told Pound that she was "purely Celtic." The trip would very likely have sparked many memorable associations, going back to the first trip to England in 1911, the meeting with Saintsbury in 1927, and the visit to Gregory and Powys while she was working on a *Dial* "Comment" on Thomas Hardy. England had always been a special place to her, and she never failed to include the "standard" English authors, such as Chaucer, Bacon, and Dr. Johnson, in her lists of favorites. And in the 1940's she and her mother had been serious followers of the fortunes of the royal family. Gregory had written her early in the decade to tell her that her reputation in England was very high. There were also the Faber & Faber editions of several of her books to certify her citizenship in a republic that extended beyond America.

Back home in Brooklyn, however, things had taken a negative turn in Moore's neighborhood. As early as March, 1960, there was a mugging in the subway near Moore's apartment that concerned her friends. Mrs. Crane, Louise's mother, arranged for her to have a car service at her disposal. In March, 1962, Moore wrote to Bishop that break-ins were becoming rather frequent in the neighborhood. A new security lock was installed in the apartment, but the general tone of the area was beginning to decline. In a later interview it was mentioned that there were sometimes people sleeping on the stoop of her apartment building. By the winter of 1965, she admitted to Bishop that she had grown scared in the neighborhood, but many of her references to the general conditions played down the severity of her fears. However, it was decided by her family and friends that she was no longer safe living in Brooklyn, so an apartment was found for her in Manhattan. This was located at 35 West 9th Street. Here her niece, Sarah, who also lived in the Village, could look in on her. The new location also made it easier for her to attend the various parties and literary and cultural events to which she was frequently invited, held as they often were in Manhattan.

The move was an event newsworthy enough for coverage by *The New York Times*, which devoted a column to it on January 20, 1966. The reporter, Michael Stern, relayed the anonymous remark that with Moore's move Brooklyn had lost its last gem. But much of the article was devoted to describing the new apartment. Her nieces had helped her move, and in order to facilitate matters had worked out a filing system. It had gone tolerably well, though at least one carton was missing, and Moore hadn't yet settled in enough to begin working. But she admired the view from her kitchen, comprised of the lights of all the tall buildings downtown. Moore exclaimed that it was quite magical at Christmas. She also called the reporter's attention to the sofa, which had been her mother's, and the pillows covered with Fortuny velvet, a gift from a friend. In an article called "A Great American Poetess Remembers the Village," which ran in the *Village Voice* in February, 1957, Moore had reminisced about the 1920's, recalling how Lola Ridge, Genevieve Taggard, and Elinor Wylie had used the branch library where she worked. She also recalled Maxwell Bodenheim, who put out his cigar when asked to do so by Mrs. Moore, and remembered that Edna St. Vincent Millay "was in a rather glamorous stratum of Village society." The Village had thoroughly changed by the middle of the 1960's, its artistic bohemians now caught up in such styles as Pop Art and the expanding subculture of drugs and anti-Vietnam protests. Moore disapproved of the subculture, but she nevertheless took great delight in her strolls through the area where she once found "the literary opening [she] so deeply craved."

II. "Our crowning curio"

But if Moore would become a Manhattanite for the last six and a half years of her life, the public often still identified her as the poet from Brooklyn, and the poet who wrote about baseball. *Look* magazine had run a feature entitled "Marianne Moore's Brooklyn" in its May 7, 1963 issue, complete with photographs by Esther Bubley. Moore herself encouraged these identifications, even after the move to Manhattan, when she published "The Camperdown Elm" and attended the World Series, where she threw out the first ball on opening day at Yankee Stadium in 1968. The Camperdown Elm was a tree in Brooklyn's Prospect Park that had attracted the concern of local people who saw that it was in poor condition. Contributions to a fund to help save the tree were solicited by a committee; this committee asked Moore to help them in their efforts. She responded by writing a poem about the tree. But she also contributed an introduction to the *Prospect Park Handbook* (1967) in which she mentioned the Durand engraving that opened the poem, and she mentioned the tree itself in a prose piece called "Crossing Brooklyn Bridge at Twilight," published by *The New York Times* in the same year. The engraving, entitled "Kindred Spirits," depicted a scene, painted by Asher Durand, in which the American painter Thomas Cole and the poet William Cullen Bryant stand beneath a spreading tree and look out over a stream. The poem uses this engraving to invoke the theme of leisure as the basis of culture, an idea that Moore had mentioned in her seventy-fifth birthday address to the American Academy.

"The Camperdown Elm" is in many ways a perfect "occasional" poem. By starting with a parallel to a historically important scene, in which American cultural figures are seen in a natural American setting, Moore begins by enlarging her own subject. The second stanza of the poem then reviews several other trees, using the rhetorical device of amplification, but suggests that all these trees are less important than the rapture Bryant and Cole would have felt at seeing the Camperdown elm. This elaborate antithesis—not those other admittedly important trees, but this tree of ours—builds on to the conceit of conjoining the nineteenth-century artists enjoying the shade of a twentieth-century tree. But the conceit, though imaginatively "strained," is nevertheless apt, since the tree was planted in the nineteenth century (so it is not impossible that Cole and Bryant could have seen it) and yet the poem pleads for its continuance into the twentieth century and beyond. The poem turns from this conceit to the world of pressing actuality:

> . . . but imagine
> their rapture, had they come on the Camperdown elm's
> massiveness and "the intricate pattern of its branches,"
> arching high, curving low, in its mist of fine twigs.
> The Bartlett tree-cavity specialist saw it
> and thrust his arm the whole length of the hollowness
> of its torso and there were six small cavities also.
>
> Props are needed and tree-food. It is still leafing;
> still there. *Mortal* though. We must save it. It is
> our crowning curio.

Moore plays delightfully with the echolike rhymes of "torso," "also," "mortal though," and "curio." Also delightful and more important, botanically speaking, is the parallel between the tree's exterior combination of the massive and the small (she even seems to make the tree self-watering with its "mist of fine twigs") and its interior combination of a large cavity with several smaller ones. The cavities threaten the tree, of course, just as its combination of exterior features makes it such a "crown" to the landscape of the park. Moore played with such parallels and antitheses in earlier poems such as "An Egyptian Pulled Glass Bottle in the Shape of a Fish." Her use of them here shows that her poetic abilities were undimmed by age. The civic pride of Brooklyn could hardly have been better served than by such a deft act of description, praise, and exhortation.

As for baseball, Moore's association with it had grown steadily since the publication of "Home Town Piece for Messrs. Alston and Reese" in 1956. Moore's last published prose essay was a brief contribution to *The New York Times*, entitled "One Poet's Pitch for the Cardinals to Win the World Series," just before the 1968 series began. As it turned out, she was quite accurate in her prediction, when the pitcher Bob Gibson—whom she said "could be expected to win two games"—won three for the Cardinals. There were other items in her favor, too. She

had a stuffed alligator that she referred to as her "pet," and named it
Elston Howard. The boys in her neighborhood would often ring her
doorbell and ask to see it. Then there developed a relationship that
increased Moore's identification as the poet who wrote about baseball.
In April, 1961, she published a review of *Out of My League*, by George
Plimpton, an account of his attempt to play professional baseball.
Moore reviewed the book positively, astutely pointing out Plimpton's
skills, which were comprised of the fomulation of wry similes and accurate sounding dialogue. Plimpton appreciated the review, wrote to
tell Moore this, and they struck up a friendship. From this friendship
came not only several pieces connected to baseball, but also Moore's
attendance at a prize fight between Floyd Patterson and George Chu-
valo, and a meeting with Muhammed Ali.

It was in September, 1963, that Plimpton first proposed he and
Moore attend a World Series game, and to use the occasion to write an
article about it for a national magazine, *Sports Illustrated*. That year the
Los Angeles Dodgers swept the New York Yankees in four games;
Plimpton, Moore, and Robert Lowell attended the second game, held
at Yankee Stadium. But the account of the game did not appear until
the following fall, and in *Harper's* rather than *Sports Illustrated*. The
account, written in the form of a letter to a friend, begins with Plimpton
fetching Moore in a limousine, having lunch with Robert Lowell, and
then proceeding to the game. It is filled with humorous touches and
quaint descriptions, such as Lowell's walking out to find a ticket scalper
so he could see the game, only to discover eventually that there were
still tickets left for purchase in the bleachers. Plimpton enlivens the
description of Moore by having two fans recognize her, while another,
a fat man with a pork-pie hat, sitting in the seat in front of her, is
definitely bemused and slightly irritated by her responses to the experience. There is also the limousine driver, who is impressed by Moore's
account of smelling a musk-ox, and who claims she's the most interesting of all the clients he's ever had, not excluding Richard Nixon. As
an account of a baseball game, the piece is rather fey; as feature journalism, it is very good; as a portrait of Moore, it generally reproduces
the image of her that had already been solidified by the media. Her
main feature is that she is talkative, and often apparently randomly so,
to the point of distraction, though clearly "lively" and possessed of
outré bits of abstruse information. The only lines of poetry quoted are

the first three from "Hometown Piece," misprinted as if they were a triplet.

In a subsequent issue of *Harper's*, Moore published her responses to ten questions sent her by Plimpton. The answers were amusingly formulated, though they contain little new biographical information. Moore repeats the story of James (Jim) Thorpe offering to hold an umbrella for her one day, and has some intriguing things to say about style in athletics. There is also a question about style and animals, so that this side of Moore's interest is exposed, but not especially in relation to her writing. The piece ends with a listing of the sculpted animals in Moore's collection, heightening the connection between her tastes and the world of bric-a-brac. All told, the questionnaire and the essay by Plimpton that preceded it create a coy air that fosters the identification of Moore as an "eccentric genius," as the jacket blurb on the paperback edition of her *Complete Poems* has it. But the piece also supplied those people who seldom if ever read poetry with a picture that coincided with the "common sense" notion of a poet as otherworldly, while at the same time reassuring them that poets were "safe." This picture was reinforced by the sensation, true or not, that Plimpton himself had never read Moore's poetry or certainly had never read it with any depth of comprehension. Apparently he didn't know about Kreymborg's account of his visit to the ballpark with Moore several decades earlier. He called Moore, in the opening paragraph, "a great American poet," but considering there is no further reference to her career as a writer, it seemed a reflex description, a repetition of a press notice. One writer has defined celebrity status as being well-known for your well-knownness. Moore's presentation by Plimpton often relied on this sort of special status. Such a presentation served to create the impression that Moore had no part to play in the modernism of the 1920's.

Plimpton was not satisfied to publish his account of a visit to a single game, however. In February, 1964, he sent Moore a draft of the article that would appear eight months later, and also included a proposal that they turn the "project" into a book. Lowell was to be included in this plan, and some contribution from him would be added to the essay and the questionnaire. This letter reveals that the addressee of the "letter" used as the format of the essay was Jean Seberg, the actress. Plimpton pursued this project over the next several months, and had lunch with Cass Canfield, an editor at Harper & Row whom he reported as being enthusiastic. It was also at this time that Plimpton proposed Moore meet Cassius Clay, as Muhammed Ali was still called. A year later Plimpton tried to arrange through friends a nighttime visit by him and Moore to the Bronx Zoo.

The following winter Plimpton arranged a "pre-fight" dinner for Moore and afterwards they joined Norman Mailer's table at Toots Shor's restaurant. Moore was especially entertained by Norman Mailer on this occasion. She excitedly wrote to Warner that it was snowing heavily and she had on her best tricorne, but the car was close by to prevent her from getting soaked. Plimpton also wrote her afterwards to identify for her the man who had sat on his right (it was Philip Roth), and to urge her to write an account of the evening's main event, the Patterson-Chuvalo fight, and about her nighttime visit to the zoo, which, as things turned out, never occurred. Mailer, of course, had become a fairly notorious figure, a constant guest on talk shows, and, a few years later, one of the main figures in the march on the Pentagon during the antiwar protests of the late 1960's. Roth, by now one of America's best-known novelists, was famous then for his first book of stories, *Goodbye, Columbus*. It seemed that Moore had strayed into a world of authors and celebrities quite different from her days in the Village, not to mention the quiet decades when she first lived in Brooklyn. And this sort of world was epitomized by a cover of *Esquire* magazine that appeared in June, 1966, with the caption "The Unknockables," featuring Moore and the ex-heavyweight champion, Joe Lewis, among others.

Moore was sought after in the 1960's, it would appear, for her eccentricity and even her incongruous dignity; in turn, she made her observations about this new world with a bemused interest developed during her many visits to the circus and the zoo. The new mix of celebrities from politics, entertainment, sports, and culture originated in large measure from the demands and mechanics of the visual media, especially television. Moore's sense of the importance of the visual, as a measure of accuracy, sincerity, even moral probity, was now to be located—if not totally misappropriated—in an altogether different context. Her sense of the visual had, of course, been extended to her own person, through her interest in fashion. So the "trademark" tricorn hat and cape, fastened at her neck with a silver dollar, was sometimes read as a "parody" of the founding fathers, George Washington in particular. Moore had an impish sense of humor and a satirical streak. However, she bought her first tricorne while still in college at Bryn Mawr, so it is unlikely she first conceived of her image as a parody of the father of her country. What does seem likely is that her self-image had several elements in it: self-protectiveness, a genuine love for formal fashion, a sense of play, a desire to have a public role, and even some personal vanity. The young woman in Carlisle had widened her knowledge considerably through reading constantly in all manner of publications. But by the 1960's, the conditions of literacy had changed considerably, as the printed word was by and large made subservient to the visual image.

In contrast to the Plimpton material, there was, however, a very informative and intelligent piece about Moore and baseball that had earlier appeared in *Sports Illustrated*, in February, 1960. Written by Robert Cantwell, it features not only some interesting photographs of Moore, but also fills in a lot of detail about her experience at the Indian School in Carlisle. Cantwell pursues an interesting double thesis. He argues that the Indians at the school were creating a new myth about themselves by forging a group identity through sports. But he also suggests that Moore, despite her self-deprecation, was a sort of poet in action with the students she had circumstantially found herself teaching. The piece reprints the entire text of "Hometown Piece" and mentions Eliot's praise for Moore's poetry. But after these somewhat predictable opening moves, it provides the background on the history of the Indian School, even down to details about its founder, General Pratt, and his eventual dismissal for being too outspoken about the Indian Bureau's shortcomings in dealing with the students. This helps explain the overly cautious attitude Warner took to Moore's relationships with her superior there, though of course some of this was due to Warner's temperament.

Cantwell also sketches in the activity of other athletes at the school besides Jim Thorpe, and he gives a good sense of the social history of the time and how it influenced the fate of the school. He gives a brief biographical account of Moore's life at the time and quotes "I May, I Might, I Must" to give the flavor of her character. He readily admits that "the poetry that made her famous had nothing of the Indians in it," and reports her as saying that she "felt . . . an imposter there . . . it wasn't really my work." At the same time, he also records her remark about the appearance of the Indians: "There was something Grecian about them." She says that the whole town of Carlisle was proud of them and followed their athletic exploits with genuine interest. Cantwell manages to present this chapter in Moore's life in such a way that its genuine interest is highlighted, and the background and its unusual human figure are given equally their due. The essay is one of the better biographical sketches to appear about Moore during her lifetime, and perhaps because of its limited focus, it avoids the clichéd picture of her as an eccentric.

It was baseball, though, that remains linked with her public persona. Somewhat contrary to popular opinion, it was not only the Dodgers that Moore championed. The then owner of the Yankees, Michael Burke, extended an invitation for Moore to join him on opening day in 1967, along with Mayor John Lindsay; he also supplied Warner with two seats as well. Warner made a special point of sending both Burke and Lindsay thank-you letters that combined gratitude for the respect shown his sister and a fan's genuine delight in being able to see a game from such a special vantage point. Burke increased the honor next year when he asked Moore to throw out the first ball at the season's opener in 1968. On the back of an envelope dated February 20, 1964, Moore sketched out some lines for a poem she wanted to write about Casey Stengel and the New York Mets. The Mets had recently been organized as a so-called expansion team, and Stengel, who had become famous as a manager of the Yankees, achieved something like legendary status as the skipper of the new club. Moore's poem was going to stress how Stengel was expert in his patience and wisdom in dealing with young ballplayers. The owner of the team, Mrs. Joan Payson, had entertained Moore as a guest, and was photographed with Moore and Stengel. Virtually every newspaper article and interview with Moore printed after the publication of "Hometown Piece" mentioned the poet's interest in baseball. These two elements—Brooklyn and baseball—would be linked with her name every time her audience extended beyond those who read her primarily as a modernist poet.

III. "Celebrity costs privacy"

Moore was the guest of honor or an invitee at a number of formal, even extravagant parties in the 1960's, as well as the subject of several features in the print media. In February, 1967, *Life* magazine ran a photograph of her standing in her Manhattan apartment in front of her pegboard loaded with tools. There was also the famous *Esquire* "Unknockable" cover, mentioned earlier. Some of the parties, such as the one arranged by Plimpton at Toots Shor's, were done with publicity in mind, while others were in a more discreet key. The Academy of Arts and Letters gave a reception to open an exhibit of her books and other memorabilia in 1962, to mark her seventy-fifth birthday. One of the more formal parties was one given in honor of Moore, again for her seventy-fifth birthday, by Arthur Goldberg, then serving as the United States representative to the United Nations. On her eightieth birthday, in 1967, she spent the evening quietly at dinner with her old friends Wheeler and Wescott, joined by Warner and Constance. Her eighty-third birthday was the occasion of a much more elaborate celebration. This was a party given by Louise Crane at her Fifth Avenue town house. It featured eighty-three vases located throughout the house with a single white carnation in each, a set of candelabra totaling eighty-three candles, and a "serenade" by Arthur Thompson, a singer at the Metropolitan Opera. Thompson was the nephew of Ethel Taylor; he sang songs by Ives, at Moore's request, and knelt in front of the sofa so he could be at her eye level as she sat and listened. Though Moore fussed about such events, said Taylor, and always modestly turned away compliments, she thoroughly enjoyed celebrations in her honor.

On November 28, 1966, Moore attended a party that would serve better than any other to measure her status as a celebrity in the cultural world. This was the so-called Black and White ball given by Truman Capote at the Plaza Hotel in New York. Capote's own celebrity status had recently increased with the publication of *In Cold Blood*, a partially documentary account of a gruesome murder in Kansas. With this book, Capote tried to launch what he called a new genre, the non-fiction novel. He set out deliberately to stage the biggest literary party of the century, inviting hundreds of people from the worlds of fashion, culture, politics, and entertainment. He insisted his guests wear only black and white, so as not to clash with one another or the decor, and to wear masks until midnight. He made Katherine Graham, the publisher of the *Washington Post*, his guest of honor. This, plus a guest list that was long but restricted to only the most well-known celebrities of the day, ensured ample press coverage. Capote is said to have paired his guests in order to stress the incongruities of the world of celebrity and fashion. Moore was paired with Mariana Agnelli, heiress to the large fortune of the Fiat company in Italy. He also arranged for the guests to have separate dinners before the party, in small groups. Moore was a member of the group "chaired" by Glenway Wescott, which included Katherine Anne Porter, among others.

The party was, even by Capote's standards, an overwhelming success. People were reportedly desperate to be invited, and stories circulated about the machinations involved in getting an invitation for those not on the list. Capote stood at the door to police all those who entered, since he had made no secret of his delight in having snubbed many people by excluding them from this grand event. Someone suggested that the party might best have been called "In Cold Spite." Diana Trilling, turned sociologist for the moment, remarked that it represented "a very complicated social moment in this country's life." But the things that were complicated about it, outside of the seating arrangements, were the overlapping and merger of the worlds of politics, entertainment, and culture, a phenomenon that had been building in America since the Kennedy Administration at least. Moore was photographed dressed for the party, but she apparently never recorded her impressions of the event.

Whatever opinion Moore formed of the world of celebrities, and whatever the pleasures she took in it, she did write a number of pieces about fashion in the 1960's. Two of these appeared in *Harper's Bazaar*: "Worth of Rue de la Paix" in 1962, and "Of Beasts and Jewels" in 1963. Two other pieces followed, "Dress and Kindred Subjects" in *Women's Wear Daily* in 1965, and "In Fashion Yesterday, Today and Tomorrow" in *The New York Times* two years later. The first two pieces are interesting as aesthetic formulations about fashion; the two later ones are curious attempts to relate standards in fashion to standards in behavior and morals. The four together almost add up to a comprehensive examination of the cultural significance of clothes and fashion, or what might be called the ethology of clothing. But this is to claim too much for them, since they are disparate in their approach and focus. Even though Moore may have thought about fashion for most of her life, and was clearly influenced by a book such as Frank Parsons' *The Psychology of Dress*, she never set down her own philosophy of clothing in so many words. These four pieces do say something significant about her attitude on the subject, as well as her general sense of the aesthetic.

The first piece is a sort of review of the designer Charles Frederick Worth. It begins with a paragraph that evokes the values of artisanship and also echoes Moore's sense of the mind walking "with its eyes on the ground," though here instead of a mind with eyes, we have an imagination with fingers:

> In this day of jets, blenders, and a page of print grasped at a glance, the perfected workmanship—inside and out—of a dress by Worth seems as unaccountable as the flawless replica—wrong side like right—of antennae, wing-spots, eyes and moth fur, of Chinese embroidery on imperial satin: an abnormal calligraphy of the imagination-by-finger (finger in gold thimble, as one pictures it), faintly etched.

This passage, with its picture of a natural organism like the moth "written" into culture calligraphically on Chinese silk, echoes other poems as well, such as "Critics and Connoisseurs" and "Nine Nectarines." Moore is playing with the notion that all fashion begins in the imaginative "beautification" of nature, a process that is motivated by a desire for precision and permanence ("flawless" and "faintly etched") and something that finds cultural expression even though it is rooted in a realm prior to culture ("unaccountable"). Some of her sense of play is evident in the humor in the piece, as when she says, after describing Worth's impressive construction of a "high armhole and narrow sleeve," that "you could put your hat on but could scarcely breathe." The piece ends by mentioning that Worth's daughter married the jeweler Cartier, and adds "the picture was all of a piece." Fashion tends toward the lapidary as one of its extreme manifestations, but the jewel-like elements in fashion, while stunning, lack the ease and natural flexibility that Moore also valued in dress.

This naturalness is evoked in the opening sentence in "Of Beasts and Jewels": "Which of us has not been stunned by the beauty of an animal's skin or its flexibility in motion?" Again, Moore playfully introduces another aspect of fashion when she says further on that we can learn from certain animals how to dress. "Having afforded us counsel, snakes—perhaps a lizard—could have an influence on what we wear." The allusion to snakes and counsel, of course, conjures up the story of the Garden of Eden and so suggests that the reptilian influence may be a legacy of our "fallen" nature. This essay says more about jewels than about fashion proper, but it reminds the reader of how both jewelry and clothing not only deal in "replicas" of the natural world, but also have "contributed much confusion." By this confusion, Moore means not only jewels and clothes, but art, which has spent much of its energy "combining the recognizable with the incompatible, quadrupeds with men's faces, and herbivorous tails with carnivorous bodies." She ends by arguing that "only imagination that towers can reproduce evanescence and render rigidity flexible." The human urge to replicate the world is twined with the need to express something more than its surfaces and the solidity of its materials.

The two later pieces on fashion move more directly into and beyond the subject of dress itself. By adding on a discussion of "Kindred Subjects" Moore means to prove that "dress is an adjunct and should conform with behavior." She introduces this other subject by expanding on certain topics, such as makeup, which she declares "is strictly for the stage." But then instead of discussing behavior as a direct reflection of clothing styles, she wanders into other related subjects, such as possessions. Here she lists a number of curios, such as her mechanical crow and "a fly of amber with gold legs and a real fly in the amber of the big one—both given me by Miss Louise Crane." There are also paragraphs on recreation and diet, and even a passage that begins with the question, "What makes a good life, a balanced life?" She quotes Confucius' saying, which she both borrowed from and set against Pound, "If there be a knife of resentment in the heart, the mind fails to act with precision." But the essay is miscellaneous in structure, and it lacks even the sort of associative, metonymic coherence that animates her best poems and the "Comment" pieces from *The Dial*.

The final piece on fashion has some of the same miscellaneous structure, concealed in part by the brevity of the effort. It is in part a plea for tolerance and a respect for cultural difference, as Moore mentions how fashions and customs in Siam can be "unfreakishly right," and adds some "modifying words" to offset the appearance of her "dogmatism."

Yet there are places where fashion and propriety become entangled. For example, she describes a tintype of well-dressed ladies in Philadelphia in 1880, adding at the end of the description the curt observation that they did not "slouch." She insists ballplayers' uniforms should not be so loose as to look like "babies' sleepers or snowsuits," and that men are better dressed if they wear hats. Near the end of the piece she suddenly mentions "inexplicable epidemics of violence," and a general sense of social disorder. This is, in her view, best counteracted by self-discipline and Confucian "sympathy." The internal logic of the essay is strained, since in one sense fashion always has "dictates," more or less inflexible rules of appropriateness, though Moore wants at the same time to preserve the liberality of culture that good dress is meant to exemplify. At the same time, standards of fashion must signify the level of social order (or, at the very least, attention to fashion would become a totally trivial subject). Yet social disorder is too serious a topic to introduce by talking about men's headwear.

The last two essays on fashion show that Moore could not always turn a paradoxical tension to her advantage; sometimes the opposing points of view simply did not cohere. Indeed, in these two pieces, it is possible to read some of the tensions that run throughout Moore's later career, with results that are not always integrated into an aesthetic order. Her strong feeling that humility and self-sacrifice were essential to ethical probity conflicted with her desire to enunciate rules that would have weight and application for a general public. Her early years as a modernist, working against the too-easy moral dicta of the late Victorians and the sentimentality they fostered, would not allow her to speak about matters such as social decorum with an unequivocal direct-ness. Yet the sense she had developed in the 1930's and later that there was a general lowering of ethical standards in society, and the concom-itant belief that poetry requires direct expression of important values, drew her to the role of sage and teacher. What is striking, and quite puzzling, is the way the role of teacher was at odds with the picture of the "eccentric genius" fostered by people, such as Plimpton and others in the media, who saw Moore as a certified but "safe" artist.

What happened with Moore and fashion was similar in many ways to what occurred with her and baseball. The connections in each case are quite clearly the result of Moore's desire to extend the aesthetic realm into areas of everyday life. The attempt rests on a firm metaphoric base. In baseball and verse the link exists between efficiency of movement and the expressivity of self-control; in fashion, the linked functions between workmanship and imaginative development of natural motifs suggest a strong connection to poetry. Yet in both these areas, especially considering the nexus of publicity and marketing that accompany professional sport and fashion in America, an essentially innocent or naive self-delight can too readily be misappropriated. The aesthetic realm in Western European culture has been largely, though not exclusively, the place where a counterview to the dominant values of society could be preserved and tested. Moore must have respected, even if she could not always maintain, the delicate balance between poetry's opposition to everyday life, especially its too-ready acceptance of a common sense that can be degrading to people's best impulses, and its celebration of the ordinariness that binds societies together. In "Baseball and Writing," published in 1961, she seemed to be talking about herself when she said "Drat it! / Celebrity costs privacy!" But she was also speaking about the poet when in the same poem she praised those who were "all business . . . and modesty."

Moore's commitment to the ability of poetry to record ordinary reality, as well as the imagination's ability to "reproduce evanescence," had been an important source of her innovation from the beginning. The ability of poetry to include "business documents and school-books," as she put it in a long version of "Poetry," could lead it into a triviality every bit as limiting as the clichéd sentimentality of late Victorianism. Combined with the threat, if that is the right word, of an unredeemable subject matter, there was also the possibility that an attitude that mistrusted "inspiration" as a version of poetry's method, would also undermine a writer's success. One example of this was Moore's contribution to "Pencil Week." In 1967 the Pencil Manufacturer's Association decided to commission a poem from Moore to celebrate National Pencil Week. As they put it in the one-page handout on which the poem was reproduced, they had "forsaken the usual leggy and bosomy 'queen' in favor" of Moore. Such a phrase indicates a certain amount of good humor, even a self-consciousness about the several incongruities involved. But the poem, which praises the pencil called "Velvet Mat," does rather little to forward any festive spirit:

> Velvet mat
> is my cat.
>
> Beaver fur
> makes my hat.
>
> Our best pencils
> write like that.

Moore, long a fan of the language of advertising, had praised its exuberance and inventiveness, even saying in "The Arctic Ox (or Goat)," "If you fear that you are / reading an advertisement, / you are." But the exuberance is lacking from the pencil poem, perhaps because of Moore's age, perhaps because she relied on a commission instead of any inspiration.

A similar poem was produced even nearer the end of Moore's life, after she was physically infirm. After Ethel Taylor became Moore's nurse, they would take frequent walks in the Village; Moore especially enjoyed sketching some elephants carved into a doorway on East 11th Street. However, she would tire readily, and when Taylor mentioned this to Dr. Baumann, a wheelchair was prescribed. At first Taylor and Baumann were worried that Moore's vanity would not allow her to accept the chair, so they broached the subject gingerly. "How would you like to be driven around the Village?" Baumann asked. Moore said, "But who would drive me?" Taylor said, "Oh, I will be your driver," and the issue was resolved. Shortly after this arrangement was made, according to Taylor, *The New York Times* called the apartment and asked Taylor if they could have a poem from Moore for a Christmas feature. Taylor said she would ask Moore as soon as was convenient. Later that day, when Taylor relayed the request, Moore said she had just the thing. She took out a pencil and wrote a poem on the spot, and then told Taylor to call the *Times* back and read it to them. The untitled poem appeared in the newspaper on December 21, 1969:

> Santa Claus,
> How would it be
> if you gave it to me
> all at once for Christmas

> Three dark sapphires
> all the same size, Love

Marianne Moore

The editors of Moore's *Complete Poems* decided not to include this effort in the 1981 edition. However, the poem draws on one of Moore's most important themes, that of the importance of the gift, just as the pencil poem recalls her interest in the quality of materials. But of course the importance of the subject has never saved a weak poem.

Many intellectuals and academics, as well as other serious readers, feel embarrassed by such poems, as they feel embarrassed by Moore's absorption into the world of celebrities. But why did Moore allow such poems to be published? Two answers, putting aside Moore's physical state, suggest themselves. To be serious is not necessarily to be grim or lugubrious, but it does entail a willingness to distinguish between frivolity and emptiness. An artist need not be serious in the grim sense, but he or she should guard against lacking seriousness if it results in producing work that is empty. And Moore, a poet whose work explores the nature of distinctions, should have been alert to this one, but in this case simply was not. The second answer says that distinctions between serious and trivial really don't apply, except as a way of making class or group distinctions. Moore might be defended on these grounds by arguing that she didn't care to observe such distinctions, because she never identified herself as an intellectual or academic.

Part of this problem can be glossed by a reading of Moore's poem "Dream," published in 1965, where she imagines academics confronting artists-in-residence. Here artists are, by intellectual or academic standards, almost foolishly prolific in their inventiveness. To illustrate this, the dream features an image of Bach at Northwestern University, where his success is so phenomenal that it induces Haydn to ask his patron, Count Esterhazy, "to lend him to Yale." Moore labels her dream vision "dazzling nonsense," but the phrase could apply as well to the output of the composers. Art's fecundity always outstrips criticism's balance. It does this in part because art remains essentially self-delighting. In her dream Moore sees the composer's coat-of-arms, and it reads like a parody of an advertising slogan: "BACH PLAYS BACH!" The poet, despite the nearly anonymous persona in some of her early experimental poems, never completely abandoned the Romantic idea of the artist as autonomous, and the artist who is most artistic is the one who plays best at being herself.

But of course not all of Moore's time and public identity in the 1960's were involved with celebrity parties and occasional verse. In 1966 she published *Tell Me, Tell Me,* her last single volume of poetry, and then in 1967, to mark her eightieth birthday, Macmillan and Viking cooperated in the publication of her *Complete Poems.* This latter book, dedicated to Louise Crane, was reissued in 1981 with minor changes, and remains the version in print today. *Tell Me, Tell Me* received an excellent review by Muriel Rukeyser in *Saturday Review* on October 1, 1966, which also ran a color portrait of Moore on the cover of the same issue. The *Complete Poems* were reviewed by John Ashbery in *The New York Times.* Rukeyser was a generation younger than Moore; in fact, she was briefly a classmate of Bishop and Mary McCarthy at Vassar. Ashbery was a generation younger still, and he was to become the most heralded poet of his generation, even as his review of Moore appeared. Rukeyser was a poet of ethical concerns; Ashbery's work featured a highly refined and self-conscious aesthetic sensibility. The two reviews together show that Moore's impact on other writers was broad and not limited to a single generation. Praise from two highly admired and quite different poets such as Rukeyser and Ashbery was in some ways the highest compliment Moore's poetry could have received.

Rukeyser's review included references to a visit she paid to Moore's apartment, so it echoed some of the themes of celebrityhood by attending to the personal habits and environment of the great artist. But the overall tone was not at all slavish, and Rukeyser was able to capture some important aspects of Moore's poetry. She proceeded by talking about the entirety of Moore's career, claiming for it a unity of spirit and tone. With a closer look, the review suggested, "objects appear to face each other" in the poems, and what "had seemed crystals . . . take on a further growth." The poems claim their form by their use of "clarity," and, glossing "the mind, intractable thing," Rukeyser refers back to "The Mind Is an Enchanting Thing." She argues that the new poem adds "praise and harsh, confessing grace" to those qualities long associated with Moore, such as probity, "vital diffidence," and "exotic dailiness." Rukeyser presses on and asks how are we to picture Moore, as a "wry, odd zoo-keeper?" Or a poet interested in the edges of things, "bringing them together to offer them to us as juxtaposed as joints of crystal . . . ?" Novelty is one of Moore's great benefits, but at the same time she owes a great deal to her sources. For Rukeyser this is the chief paradox, and it is held together and guided by Moore's humility. But this humility is not to be confused with passivity or self-protectiveness. Rukeyser ends by quoting from Stevens, who said "the humble are they who move about the world with the love of the real in their hearts." This intelligent and sensitive review must have pleased Moore, most of all, perhaps, in its use of Stevens, long a favorite of hers, to focus the climactic note of praise.

John Ashbery's review of the *Complete Poems* was, if anything, even more insightful than Rukeyser's and probably pleased Moore greatly. As was befitting for a lifetime's work, the *Complete* volume was introduced with a long vista:

> It is more than 30 years since Marianne Moore published her "Selected Poems"; 15 years ago she gave us her "Collected Poems," and now, in the month of her 80th birthday, "Complete Poems" appears. If this sounds inexorable, one should note that Miss Moore shows no sign of abandoning poetry; the new book has new poems and new versions of old ones (notably a reworking of "The Steeple-Jack" which not only restores the drastic cuts made in the "Collected Poems" version, but actually adds to and improves on the seemingly unbeatable 1935 text of this master-piece). There seems no reason not to look forward to "More Complete Poems"; as long as we can ask, like the student in her poem of that title, "When will your experiment be finished?" we may expect the reply, "Science is never finished."

This combines nicely a pragmatic sense of poetry's project with a play-fully mythical image of Moore as a preternatural spirit of boundless vitality. Ashbery anticipates the worst case against Moore, namely, that she is an American La Fontaine, a "tiresome moralist." But he then insists that, though we usually assume there can be no poetry without mysticism, Moore is a poet of "caution, healthy disrespect, restraint." He strengthens the case for her greatness by characterizing her as "not a moralist or an antiquarian, but a poet writing on many levels at once to produce work of an irreducible symphonic texture." This, of course, also describes Ashbery's poetry, but here the self-reflection is accurate and appropriate. Ashbery's work is one of the places where Moore's influence is most alive in American poetry today. The uses of language "appropriated" from a wide range of contexts, and the variety of prose rhythms, as well as a very musically complex sense of form, are part of what Ashbery has taken from Moore.

Ashbery quotes what had become the almost obligatory remarks by Eliot about the "small body of durable poetry," and he even confesses to not always being able to follow Moore's logic in a poem. But he neatly captures Moore's mental distinctiveness when he says her mind always "moves in a straight line, [but it] does so over a terrain that is far from level." This sense of a paradoxical form recalls the excellent description offered by Paul Rosenfeld forty years earlier when he said of the form and texture of Moore's poems that "never have exquisite perceptions been so loosely set." Ashbery was an ideal reader for Moore because he saw that her moral qualities were important to her, and that her intelligence was equally valuable, and most of all that she was able to combine her "symphonic" tensions in a paradoxical but pleasing order. He ends by quoting her lines from the end of "The Past Is the Present": "Ecstasy affords / the occasion and expediency determines the form." In many ways, this enunciates the perfect pragmatic formula for poetry.

For Moore the late 1960's were marked by many appearances and interviews; two of these were especially revealing, one to Donald Hall, and the other to Grace Schulman. The Hall interview was the second she had given him; the first appeared in the *Paris Review* series of interviews with famous writers, and Moore said that Hall had adroitly put it together out of what she felt was a very rambling and diffuse session. It has often been reprinted and cited by critics. But the 1965 interview, which appeared in *McCall's*, shows the more personal side of Moore. It contains remarks about how she answered her milkman when he asked her about marriage ("It's the proper thing for everyone—but me"), about her church's minister, Reverend George Litch Knight (he "can stabilize the fabric of this neighborhood if anyone can"), and her seeing Eliot shortly before his death ("an ideal visit"). She also reminisced about Mrs. E. P. Howard, from Kirkwood, a classmate of her mother's at the Mary Institute:

> . . . [she] would take us out in a brougham with two horses with cropped tails, and we used to see swan boats on the lake in the park, like the ones there are in Boston. Well, she sent to us at Carlisle Christmas boxes that were almost like a party—a piece of jewelry for each, something to wear, pralines and fruitcake.

From childhood Moore's standards for gift-giving were set quite high.

The other revealing interview appeared in the *Quarterly Review of Literature* in 1969, though it was conducted two years earlier. Grace Schulman, the daughter of a good friend of McKnight Kauffer, had known Moore and her work for some time. She was writing a doctoral thesis on Moore's poetry and went to interview her concerning certain ideas she had about the dialectical structure of her verse. The review contains some detailed discussion about technique, especially in regard to certain poems such as "To Victor Hugo of My Crow Pluto." But near the end of the published version, Schulman turns the focus onto the war in Vietnam, and the morality of armed conflict in general. Here the difficulties and contradictions in Moore's stand in favor of the war became evident. The war had already become the most divisive issue in the country by this time, and protests and demonstrations were common in many places. Moore herself had been present at the New York University commencement ceremonies on June 13, 1967. There she was given an honorary doctorate, while the main speaker, Hedley Donovan, editor-in-chief at Time, Inc., warned students not to let their antiwar attitudes become rigid. Himself a supporter of the war, he acknowledged on the other hand that the nation's leaders might have to admit they were wrong if the war was not successfully prosecuted. Nathan Pusey, president of Harvard, and someone Moore had quoted previously, gave a speech on the same day affirming the values of civilization against the charges of those protesters who saw the war as symbolic of a systemic crisis. But throughout the nation many artists and writers were united against the war. Moore's old friend Kenneth Burke asked her in May, 1967, if she would speak out against the war in Vietnam. But she declined, and when pressed on more than one occasion, she defended the use of military force by the United States.

In the interview, Schulman proceeds tentatively; she begins by asking Moore how she feels "about war—now." Moore answers by insisting that she doesn't even like to kill the smallest animals; "automatic announcements" about death tolls in war make her regard such human loss as "absolutely unpermissible." Then she goes on, in answer to another Schulman question, to equate World War II with Vietnam. At the same time she admits to not understanding the rationale for Vietnam: "I can't reason it out, except that Commander Westmoreland was so honest. He's been there. He's been in it, and thinks we are getting our way out of the thicket to clear it up." Moore says that she doesn't "dare face it," when confronted with the possibility that the war might not end soon. Warner had told her two and a half decades earlier that the war in Europe would be over shortly; he repeated a similar prediction about Vietnam. He had also written to both Presidents Johnson and Nixon to express strong support for their policies. Here Moore was in an untenable situation, torn between a nearly instinctive aversion to killing, and a belief in the authority of men who had steeled themselves to it. She felt patriotism was a virtue allied to perseverance, something in which she had staked a great deal of ethical trust, while the value of living human beings was nearly an absolute. And so to persevere in killing out of patriotic duty was only tolerable if the end was in sight, a practical qualification. Such views are not that far removed from the argument theologians use in defining a just war.

Schulman challenges Moore's apparent contradictions by referring to "In Distrust of Merits." But before Schulman can cite the poem, Moore says, "I don't consider that a poem. It's just a burst of feeling. It's emotion recorded." This is the crux of the interview, for Moore invokes a formalist criterion of disinterestedness for poetry in order to disqualify what had become one of her best-known poems. It is not exactly that she disqualifies the poem, but she considers it inadmissible as evidence against her position; the tensions of the poem, which Schulman points out and Moore acknowledges, are not to be set against the real life contradictions of a pacifist caught in the necessity of justifying bloodshed. (She even extends the inadmissibility claim to "Marriage," which she describes near the end of the interview as containing "statements that I believe with all my heart, but I think a poem should have a form, a sound, like a symphony. And that piece is prose.") The world of prose, with its contingencies, its shapelessness, is finally set apart from the world of poetry, and vice versa. Just as the "practical" considerations of the war's duration being short enough to tolerate outweigh the seemingly insistent demands of a higher sensitivity to the loss of life, so poetry tells a truth that does not change—or even really address—the force of prose's claims.

Of course, Moore was no more successful than many writers, especially those in her generation, at bringing the formalist sense of a poem, based on the belief that art deals with a truth of its own not to be measured or mediated by other forms of knowledge, out of its autonomous, self-protective realm. She had not felt, for example, that the evil ideas in Pound's *Pisan Cantos* should obliterate the book's standing as poetry. Little wonder, then, that she wouldn't be able to follow the logic of a poem, even her own, to a conclusion about matters of life and death. She quoted Confucius, one of those Pound claimed as a master, in her interview with Schulman: "If there is a knife of resentment in the heart, the mind fails to attain precision." Moore did not seem to realize how this axiom, if applied, would seriously undermine the worth of Pound's poetry, and might also cast a shadow across hers as well. But applying cultural statements explicitly to didactic and moral questions, not to mention questions of public policy, presented for Moore and her contemporaries a challenge to the belief in art for art's sake that was unresolvable. She had, more than most, taken up the burden of writing a fully public, fully moral poetry, but she, too, eventually experienced her limitations.

In June, 1969, Ezra Pound made a short visit to America, where he was entertained by his publisher, James Laughlin. He attended an evening at the American Academy of Arts and Letters, and was able to meet and speak briefly with a number of old friends. Moore, too, met with him, and they were photographed together in the lobby of the Public Library on 42nd Street, both looking quite frail but animated. Ethel Taylor, who had accompanied Moore on this occasion, said their conversation was brief and touching, "Oh, Ezra," Moore said, and Pound responded, "Oh, Marianne," and they held hands and faced each other for the last time. For Moore it could well have been an exclamation that mixed gratitude, exasperation, and sorrow. She had never accepted his anti-Semitism and from the first had accused him of using his "cudgels" too freely. For his part, he had needed to discover her, even though she had published at first without his help or even his knowledge. He praised the "arid clarity" of her poetry, which he described as "a distinctly national product." Unable to fully comprehend her "mind cry," he labeled it with his term, logopoeia, and tried to supply her with an influence, the French poet LaForgue, a master of irony and detachment, whom she had never read. Yet Pound saw from the first that she was "interesting and readable"—though he was compelled to add "(by me, that is)."

Near the end of his life Pound talked about the unity of the *Cantos*, and how he had "botched" the project. He had wanted at one time to use the biology of Louis Agassiz as the organizing principle of his epic poem, but it did not "cohere." Moore would have sympathized with this interest in Agassiz, one of America's great scientists and the teacher of William James and scores of others. The commitment of modernist poets such as Pound and Moore to natural science comes from complex sources, and in many cases it was an extensive and long-lived commitment. Moore herself was reading Lamarck, Cuvier, Humbolt, and Darwin as late as 1969. Darwin's early work, *The Expression of Emotions in Men and Animals*, was a book she took note of as early as 1919. This interest in science combined with an interest in technology, too, as she had become in the late 1960's a devoted watcher of programs on the history of invention and technology on television's "Sunrise Semester." Unlike Pound, however, Moore never contemplated the use of these disciplined bodies of knowledge as a framework for a long poem. But her faith in the ability to know the world had some of the Enlightenment's trust in principled inquiry. As she put it in "Enough: 1969," one of the last poems she published, "Am I a fanatic? The opposite." She concluded the poem with a quotation from a prose work by Ben Jonson, the seventeenth-century English poet: "In 'Discoveries' he then said, / 'Stand for truth. It's enough.' "

The awards and honors never seemed to stop for Moore. The *Festschrift for Marianne Moore's Seventy-seventh Birthday* (1965) was edited by Tambimuttu, an Indian scholar who had never met the poet. It contained essays, poems, and recollections by many of the country's leading writers and scholars, such as Conrad Aiken, Harry Levin, May Swenson, Robert Penn Warren, and Allen Ginsberg. The same year saw the appearance of Jean Garrigue's pamphlet of forty pages, called simply *Marianne Moore*. It was one of the earliest studies of her entire body of poetry, and is still one of the best critical introductions to her imagination and style. Moore and Garrigue had a correspondence that was largely professional in nature, but it reveals the unique strengths of both writers. In 1967, Moore was given the MacDowell Medal by the writers' colony in Peterborough, New Hampshire, where her old friend Glenway Wescott gave the address. The Poetry Society of America honored her once more when it gave her its Gold Medal for Distinguished Achievement in April, 1967. Lowell, Spender, Tate, and Eberhart read tributes in her honor. A year later she was awarded the National Medal for Literature, and an honorary degree from Princeton.

Nearing her eightieth year, Moore was at work on her memoir. It is referred to several times in her correspondence, and word of it had gotten around to other writers. For example, Laura Benét wrote to her in June, 1969, after a visit to Carlisle, where she had looked for the Moores' house on Hanover Street, and at first couldn't find it because it was painted a different color. But Laura mentioned she had heard that Moore was "writing her life." Moore also mentioned the memoir to Hildegarde Watson in the late 1960's, saying that Viking was anxious to have her complete it. This memoir is now in private hands, and has never been published or seen by many people. Along with Moore's unfinished novel, it remains the most important of the unpublished works, except for the seventy or so poems that are available in only two copies. These copies were produced for copyright reasons: one copy is at the Library of Congress and the other in the Rosenbach archive.

Another event that forms part of the machinery of literary immortality was the sale of Moore's letters and notebooks to a library. At first Moore had wanted to give her material to Bryn Mawr. But she realized that she could sell the bulk of her literary estate for a sum considerably greater than her alma mater could afford. She had been approached by several institutions and in May, 1968, a trip to Austin, Texas, was arranged by Andreas Brown, who worked at the Gotham Book Mart. Moore and Frances Steloff were to visit the University of Texas to see if Moore would be willing to have her papers lodge there after her death. The trip was pleasant enough, Moore told her friend Hildegarde Watson; the varsity baseball team was even brought in to meet and be photographed with her. But Moore decided to sell her work to the Rosenbach Museum and Library instead. The Museum even arranged to reproduce in exacting detail the living room from Moore's apartment. One could argue that this sort of memorial contributed to the sense of Moore as living in a world of bric-a-brac; in any case, it celebrates a poet who was herself often an energetic celebrant of cultural curios. She had always had good memories of Philadelphia, from her days traveling through there on her way to Bryn Mawr; it was, after all, the place where she had bought her first black tricorne hat. The scale of the Rosenbach appealed to her, too, being much smaller than an archive such as the one in Texas. The contract was signed in June, 1970, and the payments were to be staggered for tax reasons. Only two of the payments were made before Moore's death.

Moore's health began to deteriorate in the late 1960's. She told Hildegarde Watson in December, 1967, that she asked her doctor if she were "mentally defective." She had begun leaving off the final letter of words when she typed. The doctor asked her if she were aware she was leaving them off, and when she said she was, he assured her that she was not losing her mental capacities. She told a visitor that year, according to the *Times*, that she was "good-natured but hideous as an old hop toad." Describing how hard it was to keep her hair looking neat, she went on: "My physiognomy isn't classic at all, it's like a banana-nosed monkey. Well, I do seem at least to be awake, don't I?" But her physical condition grew weaker, even though she still managed to make visits and occasionally attend parties. In May, 1967, she attended a reception at Gracie Mansion in New York for the Russian poet, Andrei Voznesensky, and astonished the guests by reciting some of his poetry in translation. In the summer of that year she was still strong enough to travel to St. Louis, to give a reading at Washington University. And in February, 1968, she was a guest on the Tonight Show on NBC, hosted by Harry Belafonte in the absence of Johnny Carson. Since this show did not have Carson as host, NBC decided not to keep a tape of it. In March, 1969, the BBC sent a film crew to her apartment to record an interview with her, conducted by George Macbeth. Evidently they tore up her apartment rather badly, according to Ethel Taylor. When she requested damages, they gave her less than $40, as if it were another price privacy had to pay to celebrity. The feature was never shown.

During the summer of 1969, Moore suffered a stroke that left her quite weakened. She was admitted in early July to Lenox Hill Hospital and had to spend more than a month there. From this time on she wrote very little. Letters to such old friends as Hildegarde Watson stopped altogether, and her handwriting grew more spidery and illegible. Even her most essential correspondence had to be entrusted to Ethel Taylor and Gladys Berry as her amanuenses. According to Ethel Taylor, Moore suffered very little as she weakened. She died peacefully in her sleep on February 5, 1972.

The New York Times ran a full-page obituary four days later. It included a sampler of her poems ("To a Prize Bird," "Hometown Piece," and "What Are Years?"), and a critical evaluation by Thomas Lask, who wrote that a "good claim can be made that . . . Moore was the most original and singular" of twentieth-century poets writing in English. The notice also said, in what has to count as a considerable understatement, that "Miss Moore, the personality, was more extensively known than Miss Moore, the poet." But it conveyed an accurate sense of her place in the literary world even as it gave many details about her public identity. The London *Times* ran a long obituary full of praise. Though anonymous, it apparently expressed the views of someone very favorably disposed to Moore, and familiar with her work from the beginning. At one point it offered a capsule description of her poetry's main themes, and came as close as anyone has to a strikingly accurate summary:

> Her poetry concerns the dangers to that unity [of Nature] and to the developed life within it, how to maintain a measure of heroic dignity by being, as she and her poems were, alert, discriminating, pliant, and surprising, enjoying the particular person or thing or scene for its specialness, and taking it with joy. . . .

Even the author of many of the "Comment" columns in *The Dial* could scarcely have put it better.

The last fully achieved poem Moore published was called "The Magician's Retreat," which appeared in *The New Yorker* in 1970. According to her notes, it described a neoclassical building as depicted in a French engraving of the eighteenth century. Moore also alluded in the poem to a painting by Magritte, thus combining the surreal with the neoclassical in a way typical of her aesthetic. The poem begins, again typically of Moore, with a phrase that follows on from the title:

> of moderate height,
> (I have seen it)
> cloudy but bright inside
> like a moonstone,
> while a yellow glow
> from a shutter-crack shone,
> and a blue glow from the lamppost
> close to the front door.
> It left nothing of which to complain,
> nothing more to obtain,
> consummately plain.

> A black tree mass rose at the back
> almost touching the eaves
> with the definiteness of Magritte,
> was above all discreet.

The poem's subject is that promise of happiness that is so vital to all art, though often submerged in the works of the twentieth century. Moore is a modernist poet, and so her happiness must be located in a place, at once real and imaginary, ordinary and numinous. For her such a place could be a version of "The Wren's Nest" in Kirkwood, the "quiet little part" of New York in the 1920's, the "compacted pleasantness" of the offices of The Dial, or even the place she called a "city of trees," Brooklyn. But the idyll here is very democratic, "moderate," "plain," even, though "consummately" so. And just when the structure of cultural perfection seems to fill completely the field of vision, there is nature, a rising mass, that comes dramatically into view. Is it a threat? Or a gesture of communion, "almost touching the eaves"? No, it turns out that nature is like culture in this instance—after all, we are in the world of poetry—because it is both definite and discrete.

On February 8, the Lafayette Avenue Presbyterian Church held two services in Moore's honor; a private chapel service at twelve noon and a public memorial at one o'clock. The memorial tributes were delivered by the pastor, the Reverend George Litch Knight, whom Moore had praised a dozen years earlier for helping to renovate the neighborhood. One of the organ tunes played that day was composed in honor of Reverend Theodore Ledyard Cuyler, founder and first pastor of the Brooklyn church; his fame in the nineteenth century was so considerable that the Reverend John Warner had once expressed a desire to travel from Kirkwood to hear him preach. There was also a tune from a sixteenth-century composer, celebrated in Moore's poem "Melchior Vulpius." "We have to trust this art," Moore had written, and then added in one of her trademark "Notes" a passage from a catalogue about Malvina Hoffman: "And not only is the great artist mysterious to us but is that to himself." The closing prayer was one Moore herself had written, to be recited at the funeral of Mary Warner Moore. It said in part, "We thank Thee for our deepening sense of the mysteries that lie behind our dust, and for the eye of faith which Thou hast opened. . . ."

A Note on the Text and Annotation

Quotations from Moore's poems are from *The Complete Poems of Marianne Moore* (New York: Macmillan/Viking, 1981), unless otherwise noted. Occasionally, especially with the early poems, I have cited the text of the first magazine publication or book appearance. Excerpts from her prose are from *The Complete Prose of Marianne Moore*, edited and with an introduction by Patricia Willis (New York: Viking Penguin, 1986).

The vast majority of Moore's letters are housed at the Rosenbach Museum and Library, Philadelphia, Pennsylvania. There are a few exceptions to this: letters Moore wrote as editor of *The Dial* are in the Berg Collection of the New York Public Library; other letters to Elizabeth Bishop are in the Vassar Library; to H.D. and Bryher and several others are at the Beinecke Library at Yale University; to Lola Ridge, Barbara Savage, and Hildegarde Watson at the Bryn Mawr Library. Professor Eileen Moran generously arranged for me to have a copy of her two-volume edition of Moore's correspondence with Hildegarde Watson.

All quotations from the *Fables* are from *The Fables of La Fontaine*, translated by Marianne Moore (New York: Viking Press, 1954).

The manuscripts of Moore's unpublished novel and a memoir she worked on late in her life will soon be housed in the Rosenbach Museum and Library. They have been in private hands since Moore's death, and I was unable to consult them. The Rosenbach intends eventually to make them available for inspection by scholars.

I have also relied on books and articles about Moore, a selective list of which follows. Other material quoted in the text is listed in the notes for the respective chapters.

Selected Annotated Bibliography of Secondary Works

Abbott, Craig S. *Marianne Moore: A Descriptive Bibiliography*. Pittsburgh: U. of Pittsburgh Press, 1977. Generally reliable listing of all of Moore's publications.

Bishop, Elizabeth. "Efforts of Affection, A Memoir of Marianne Moore." *Vanity Fair*, June 1983, 44–60. Reprinted in Bishop's *Complete Prose*.

Bloom, Harold, ed. *Marianne Moore: Modern Critical Views*. New York and

New Haven: Chelsea House, 1987. Essay by seven critics, including John Slatin, David Bromwich, Marie Borroff, and Pamela Hadas.

Costello, Bonnie. *Marianne Moore: Imaginary Possessions.* Cambridge, Mass. and London: Harvard U. Press, 1981. An important study, thorough and sensitive.

Engel, Bernard F. *Marianne Moore.* New York: Twayne Publishers, 1964.

Garrigue, Jean. *Marianne Moore.* Minneapolis: U. of Minnesota, 1965. One of the best studies of Moore's imagination.

Goodridge, Celeste, ed. "Marianne Moore Special Issue." *Sagetrieb,* 6,3 (Winter, 1987). Another collection by various hands, demonstrating the interest in Moore during her centennial year.

Hall, Donald. *Marianne Moore: The Cage and the Animal.* New York: Pegasus, 1970.

Holley, Margaret. *The Poetry of Marianne Moore: A Study in Voice and Value.* New York and London: Cambridge U. Press, 1988. The first study to give equitable treatment to all the poems, both early and late.

Joost, Nicholas. *Scofield Thayer and* The Dial: *An Illustrated History.* Carbondale, Illinois: Southern Illinois Press, 1964.

Kappel, Andrew, ed. "Marianne Moore Issue." *Twentieth Century Literature,* 30, 2 & 3 (Summer/Fall, 1984). An important collection of articles that helped shape Moore criticism in the last decade. Work by John Slatin, Taffy Martin, Bonnie Costello, and others that first appeared here was eventually incorporated into books on Moore.

"Marianne Moore Issue." *Quarterly Review of Literature,* 4 (1968). An important tribute, with contributions by many poets and critics from the postwar era.

Marianne Moore Newsletter. Volumes I–IV. ed. Patricia Willis. Philadelphia: Rosenbach Museum and Library, 1977–82. Contains a great deal of specific information, most of it in the form of Moore material (letters, notebooks, clippings, etc.) and its relation to specific poems.

Sargeant, Winthrop. "Humility, Concentration, and Gusto." *The New Yorker.* XXXII (Feb. 16, 1957), 38–73.

Slatin, John. *The Savage's Romance: The Poetry of Marianne Moore.* University Park, Pa.: Pennsylvania State U. Press, 1985. Especially good for its treatment of Moore's literary relations with her peers.

Stapleton, Laurence. *Marianne Moore: The Poet's Advance.* Princeton: Princeton U. Press, 1978. The first study of Moore's development as an artist.

Tambimuttu, M. J., ed. *Festschrift for Marianne Moore's Seventy-seventh Birthday.* New York: Tambimuttu & Mass, 1964. Miscellaneous, but some items of interest.

Tomlinson, Charles, ed. *Marianne Moore: A Collection of Critical Essays.* Englewood Cliffs, N.J.: Prentice-Hall, 1969. Contains important early essays by Pound, Williams, Burke, and others.

Wasserstrom, William, *The Time of the Dial.* Syracuse: Syracuse U. Press, 1963.

William Carlos Williams Review. Special issue on Williams and Moore, 14, 1 (Spring, 1988). Includes some feminist studies by Rachel Blau Du Plessis and others.

Willis, Patricia C. *Marianne Moore: Vision into Verse.* The Rosenbach Museum and Library, 1987. A catalogue of an exhibit honoring Moore's centennial; contains much information about the items—clippings, curios, and so forth—that form the occasions of many of Moore's poems.

Willis, Patricia C., ed. *Marianne Moore: Woman and Poet.* Orono, Maine: National Poetry Foundation, forthcoming. A wide variety of essays by two-dozen contributors; some biographical information and an annotated bibliography of articles about Moore.

Notes for Chapter One

Information about the Norcross family was obtained from *The Story of the Thirtieth Anniversary of the Pastorate of George Norcross in the Second Presbyterian Church,* published by the Board of Trustees, Carlisle, 1899, and from a Norcross family scrapbook in the Cumberland County Historical Society Library and Hamilton Library, in Carlisle. The incident of Mrs. Moore's teaching is recorded in the Minutes of the Faculty of the Metzger Institute, a copy of which is in the Cumberland County Historical Society Library. Some reflections on Moore's religious affiliations are in Andrew Kappel, "Notes on the Presbyterian Poetry of Marianne Moore," in Willis, ed., *Marianne Moore: Woman and Poet.* Laura Benét's recollections are contained in her memoir, *When William Rose, Stephen Vincent and I Were Young* (New York: Dodd, Mead, 1976). Information on the trolley line was taken from *The Trolleys of Carlisle,* by Richard Steinmetz, n.p. Traction Press, 1972.

Notes for Chapter Two

The details of Mary Norcross's home in Sterrett's Gap were taken from a letter sent by Louise Norcross Lucas to the then owner of the house, Mrs. Call; this letter was kindly made available to me by Mrs. Cindy Urban, the current owner. The passage from M. Carey Thomas's article is quoted in Barbara Miller Solomon *In The Company of Educated Women* (New Haven and London, Yale U. Press, 1985), 49, where the statistics for college women appear. I also consulted *The Making of A Feminist: Early Journals and Letters of M. Carey Thomas*, ed. Margaret H. Dobkin, Kent State U. Press, 1979. Some details are drawn from "When I Was Sixteen," included in Moore's *Complete Prose*. Additional details on life at Bryn Mawr came from Patricia Willis, "The Owl and the Lantern: Marianne Moore at Bryn Mawr," *Poesis* 6,3/4 (1985), 84–97. I am also indebted to Margaret Holley for a helpful historical tour of the Bryn Mawr campus.

Notes for Chapter Three

The story of Moore's stay at Lake Placid is available in Louise Collins, "Marianne Moore, Melvil Dewey, and Lake Placid," in Willis, ed., *Marianne Moore: Woman and Poet*. Information about the Indian School came from the Cumberland County Historical Society. For information about Bryher and H.D., I consulted Barbara Guest, *Herself Defined: The Poet H.D. and Her World*, New York: Quill, 1984. Peggy Phelan, "Weapons and Scalpels: The Early Poetry of H.D. and Marianne Moore," in Willis, ed., *Marianne Moore: Woman and Poet*, was also helpful. The extent of the literature on the early modernist movement is enormous; for a useful and direct account, there is C. K. Stead, *Pound, Yeats, Eliot, and the Modernist Movement*, New Brunswick, N.J.: Rutgers U. Press, 1986. The pages on Moore in Hugh Kenner, *A Homemade World: The American Modernist Writers*, New York: William Morrow, 1975, show as well as any can how a Moore poem "works" in modernist terms.

Notes for Chapter Four

For Kreymborg, see his memoir, *Troubador*, New York: Boni & Liveright, 1925. Alyse Gregory tells her version in *The Day Is Gone*, New York: E. P. Dutton, 1948, while Llewlyn Powys' memoir of this period is *The Verdict of Bridlegoose*, New York: Harcourt, Brace, 1926. The fictionalized account of an evening with Moore and her mother is part of Robert McAlmon's *Post-Adolescence*, Dijon: Contact Editions, n.d. Two other memoirs supplied incidental details: Richard Aldington, *Life for Life's Sake: A Book of Reminiscences*, New York: Viking, 1941, and Robert McAlmon (with supplementary chapters by Kay Boyle), *Being Geniuses Together*, New York: Doubleday, 1968. Bryher's memories are recorded in *The Heart to Artemis: A Writer's Memoirs*, London: Collins, 1963. Background information is from Frederick Hoffman, *The Twenties*, New York: The Free Press, 1962, and Allen Churchill, *The Improper Bohemians*, New York: E. P. Dutton, 1959. Additional information on the literary scene was taken from Gorham Munson's *The Awakening Twenties*, Baton Rouge: Louisiana State U. Press, 1985. Historical data were taken from Henry Steele Commager, *The American Mind*, New Haven: Yale U. Press, 1950, and from Henry May, *The End of American Innocence: A Study of the First Years of Our Time, 1912–1917*, New York: Alfred Knopf, 1959. Some details about Mina Loy and Lola Ridge came from William Drake, *The First Wave: Women Poets in America, 1915–1945*, New York: Macmillan, 1987.

Information about the Zorachs was drawn from *Marguerite and William Zorach: The Cubist Years, 1915–1918*, by Marilyn Friedman Hoffman, Hanover, N.H.: University Press of New England, 1987. Alfred Stieglitz is the subject of *America and Alfred Stieglitz: A Collective Portrait*, ed. Waldo Frank, et al., New York: Doubleday, Doran: 1934.

Professor Donald Miller, of the History Department at Lafayette College, shared his wide-ranging bibliographical knowledge with me, as well as a typescript of his biography of Lewis Mumford.

Notes for Chapter Five

Most of the information here was drawn directly from *The Dial*, and from the James Watson portion of the archive of the magazine that is now part of the Berg Collection of the New York Public Library. I relied on some biographical details about Scofield Thayer from an oral paper given by Dale Davis, at the U. of Maine, Orono conference on Moore, June, 1987. Sophia Wittenberg also talked with me about her work on *The Dial*.

Notes for Chapter Six

Background on "Virginia Britannia" came from Philip L. Barbour, *The Three Worlds of John Smith*, Chapel Hill: U. of North Carolina Press, 1964, and the information about Henry Adams from William Jordy, *Henry Adams: Scientific Historian*, New Haven: Yale U. Press, 1952. The passages quoted from *The*

Pangolin (1936) differ, sometimes considerably, from the versions of the poems in *Complete Poems*.

Notes for Chapter Seven

The memoir of Moore by Elizabeth Bishop is reprinted in Bishop's *The Collected Prose*, ed. with an introduction by Robert Giroux, New York: Farrar, Straus, and Giroux, 1984. The relations between Bishop and Moore have been explored by Lynn Keller, "Words Worth a Thousand Postcards: The Bishop/Moore Correspondence," in *American Literature* 55, 3 (October, 1983) 405–29, and Bonnie Costello, "Marianne Moore and Elizabeth Bishop: Friendship and Influence," *Twentieth Century Literature* 30, 3 (Summer/Fall, 1984), 130–49. Philip Legler reviewed the *Collected Poems* in *Poetry*, December, 1953, 158–67. Malvina Hoffman's recollections are recorded in her memoir, *Yesterday Is Tomorrow*, New York: Crown, 1965.

Notes for Chapter Eight

The literature on La Fontaine is extensive. I used the following: Raymond Picard, *Two Centuries of French Literature*, London: Weidenfield and Nicholson, 1970; Jean D. Biard, *The Style of La Fontaine's* Fables, Oxford: Blackwell's, 1966; Frank Hamel, *Jean de La Fontaine*, Port Washington, N.Y.: Kennikat, 1970 (a reprint of a 1911 edition); Leo Spitzer, *Essays on Seventeenth Century French Literature*, Cambridge: Cambridge U. Press, 1983; Philip Wadsworth, *Young La Fontaine*, New York: AMS Press, 1970 (a reprint of a 1952 edition published by Northwestern U. Press); and Agnes E. Mackay, *La Fontaine and His Friends*, London: Garnstone Press, 1972.

Notes for Chapter Nine

Details about the "Black and White Party" were taken from *Capote: A Biography* by Gerald Clarke, New York: Simon & Schuster, 1988. Bill Schon shared with me the typescript of interviews he conducted for the NET film he directed on Moore. The story of Moore's dealings with the University of Texas was related to me by Andreas Brown, at the Gotham Book Store, in the fall of 1988. My interview with Ethel Taylor was graciously arranged by Mildred Davidson, and conducted in her house. I am grateful for the kindness shown me by both of them; they made the first months of this project especially exciting.

INDEX